A Guide cum Practice Book for All Subjects

Maths, English, Hindi & EVS

Authors

Maths	English	Hindi	EVS
Parul Tomar	Parneet Kaur	Pawan Gurjesh	Nazma Ansari

Published by

ARIHANT PRAKASHAN

(School Division Series)

Copyright Information

ADMINISTRATIVE & PRODUCTION OFFICES

Regd. Office

'Ramchhaya' 4577/15, Agarwal Road, Darya Ganj, New Delhi -110002
Tele: 011- 47630600, 43518550; Fax: 011- 23280316

Head Office

Kalindi, TP Nagar, Meerut (UP) - 250002, Tel: 0121-7156203, 7156204

SALES & SUPPORT OFFICES

Agra, Ahmedabad, Bengaluru, Bareilly, Chennai, Delhi, Guwahati, Hyderabad, Jaipur, Jhansi, Kolkata, Lucknow, Nagpur & Pune.

PO No. : TXT-59-T068851-1-26

Published By Arihant Publications (India) Ltd.

For further information about the books published by Arihant, log on to www.arihantbooks.com or e-mail at info@arihantbooks.com

Follow us on

PRICE **₹395.00**

PRODUCTION TEAM

Publishing Managers	Project Head	Cover Designer	Inner Designer	Page Layouting
Mahendra Singh Rawat & Keshav Mohan	Ashwani, Manju, Mohit, Shivam	Bilal Hashmi	Ankit Prajapati	Amit Agarwal

EXCLUSIVE FEATURES

1 Quick Summary at the start of each Chapter

2 Solutions/Answers of All NCERT Questions

3 Additional Practice Questions in each Chapter

All in One

Content List

Maths Mela (Maths)

Santoor (English)

वीणा (हिंदी)

Our Wondrous World (EVS)

Maths Mela
(Maths)

WHAT'S IN A NAME

Counting Counting is the process of finding the number of things in a group of things. e.g. We can count the number of apples kept in a basket by touching each apple once.

NCERT Pg 1-2

Q.1 (i) What could Deba and Deep do?

(ii) Did all the cows come back home?

(iii) After a few years, they had many more cows. One day, their wall had this many marks when they left home.

So, they had .... cows.

(iv) Why were Deba and Deep worried?

(v) How many cows had reached home?

(vi) Help Hemant keep track of his cows and sheeps by making marks like Deba and Deep.

Ans. (i) Deba and Deep could make symbol like stick (|) or square (□) for each cow or put a stone in basket for each cow.

** Students can write alternate answer as per their choice.*

(ii) Yes, all the cows came back home.

(iii) 47

(iv) Deba and Deep were worried because they had lost two cows.

(v) 45 cows had reached home.

(vi) Symbol for 1 cow = o and

Symbol for 1 sheep = |

Cows

ooooo ooooo ooooo
ooooo ooooo ooooo

ooooo
o

Sheeps

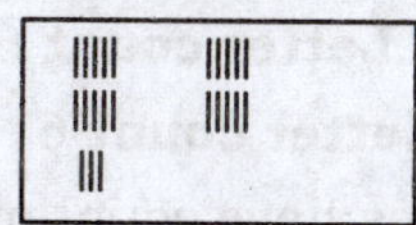

Let Us Do (NCERT Pg 3-5)

Q.2 Some animals and birds got together to play a game. They wanted to make 2 teams. They decided that the captain of the first team will be the one with the longest name i.e. the one with the most letters. The captain of the second team will be the one with the shortest name i.e. the one with the fewest letters.

(i) Find out the captains of these 2 teams.

(ii) Do you know any animal having a longer name than the first team's captain?

Ans. (i) Captains of the 2 teams

First team Elephant, **Letter count** 8

Second team *OX*, **Letter Count** 2

*(ii) Hippopotamus

Letter count 12

Q.3 Who has a longer name? Discuss.

Ans. Mahesh - **Letter count** 6

Kartik - **Letter count** 6

Both names have equal number of letters.

Q.4 Write down the names of some of your friends in the spaces given below and the answer the questions from (i) to (vi).

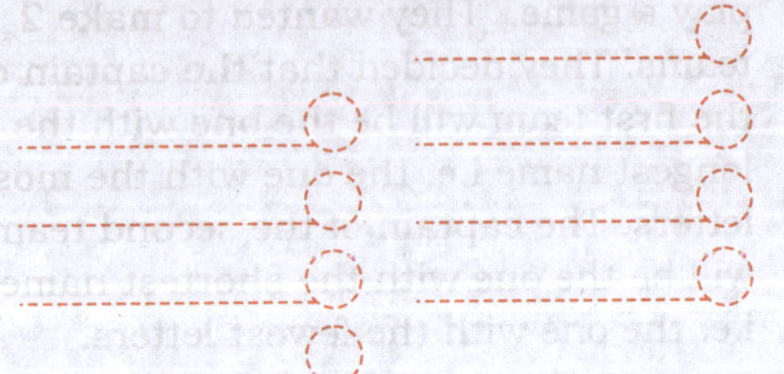

(i) Tick (✓) the longest name(s) and cross (✗) the shortest name(s).

(ii) Write the starting letter of your name.

(iii) Count all the name(s) that have the same starting letter as yours.

(iv) Which starting letter is the most used? Count the names that begin with it.

(v) Count the names with the same ending letter.

(vi) Write the letters that are not the starting letter of any name.

Ans. *

My Name	Rajiv
Deergh	Somya
Anu ✗	Pawan
Rahul	Vanshika ✓
Nirmala	

(i) Longest name — Vanshika

Shortest name — Anu

(ii) R

(iii) 1

(iv) R starting letter is most used in 2 names.

(v) The three names with the same ending letter 'a' are Somya, Vanshika and Nirmala.

(vi) The letters that are not the starting letter of any name are B, C, E, F, G, H, I, J, K, L, M, O, Q, T, U, W, X, Y and Z.

Q.5 Teji and Jojo are making numbers using cards.

One	Two	Three	Four
Five	Six	Seven	Eight
Nine	Ten	Eleven	Twelve
Thirteen	Fourteen	Fifteen	Sixteen
Seventeen	Eighteen	Nineteen	Twenty
Thirty	Forty	Fifty	Sixty
Seventy	Eighty	Ninety	

Teji makes her roll number 43 like this. Its number name has 10 letters.

[Forty three]

Jojo makes his roll number 17 like this. Its number name has ...... letters.

[Seventeen]

(i) Write your roll number using number cards as shown above. Number cards are given at the end of the book.

- My roll number is ....
- Its number name has ...... letters.

(ii) Write some numbers and their number names in your notebook. How many letters does each have?

Ans. Jojo number name-Seventeen has 9 letters.

*(i) My roll number is 54.
Fifty four has 9 letters.

*(ii) Suppose, some numbers are

Number	Number name	Letters in number name
15	Fifteen	7
47	Forty seven	10
32	Thirty two	9
77	Seventy seven	12
58	Fifty eight	10
99	Ninety nine	11

Let us Think (NCERT Pg 5)

Q.6 Teji and Jojo made the number 56 (Fifty six). It has 8 letters. Write other numbers between 1 and 99 that have 8 letters.

Ans. Forty two → 42

Fifty two 52   Fifty one 51

Forty one 41   Forty six 46

Sixty one 61   Sixty two 62

Sixty six 66

Let us do (NCERT Pg 6-8)

Q.7 (i) Write the number(s) between 1 and 99 that have the longest name.

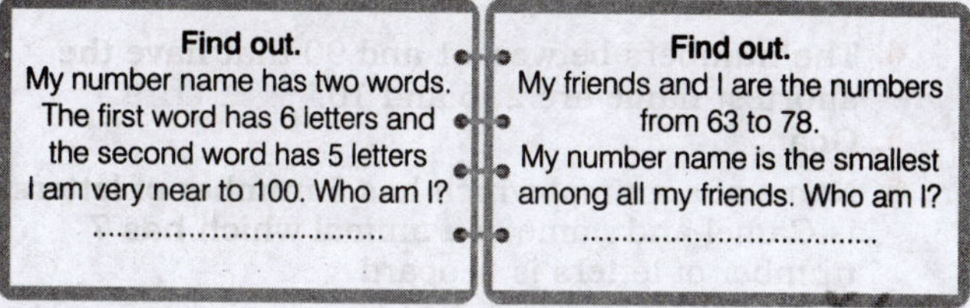

(ii) Make similar puzzles of your own in your notebook and ask your classmates.

Ans. (i) Number that have the longest name 73, 77 and 78.

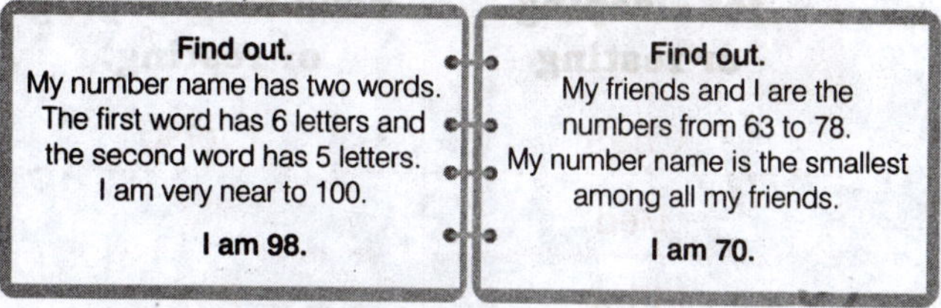

(ii) Do yourself.

Q.8 What is common in each of the groups Jojo has made?

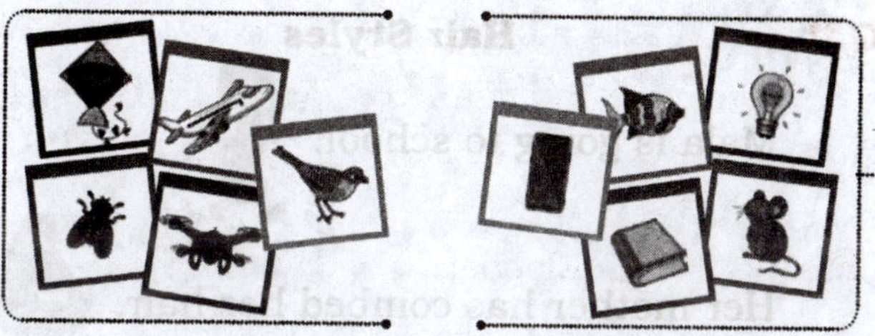

Ans. Jojo has grouped the cards into 'those that can fly' and 'those that cannot fly'.

Q.9 Given below are pictures of some household objects.

Write the names of the above objects in two groups given below.

Ans.

Things that need electricity	Things that do not need electricity
TV	Chair
Fan	Bed
Lamp	Pillow
Clock	Blanket

Q.10 Group the objects given above differently. Write them down in the space below.

Ans.

Things that need for sleeping or resting	Things that don't need for sleeping or resting.
Chair	Clock
Bed	TV
Pillow	Fan.
Blanket	Lamp

Let us Do (NCERT Pg 8)

Q.11 **Hair Styles**

Mala is going to school.

Her mother has combed her hair.

Mala has two ponytails.

Look at the children in your class.

All children comb their hair in different ways. Look and write down.

Hair style						
Number of children						

Ans. Do yourself.

PRACTICE QUESTIONS

1. Multiple choice questions
   (i) The number of letters in sixty two is
   (a) 8 (b) 9 (c) 7 (d) 6
   (ii) Choose the correct option which has 10 letters
   (a) Pillow (b) Picture
   (c) Television (d) Table
   (iii) Choose the correct option which has 8 letters
   (a) Kangaroo (b) Giraffe
   (c) Deer (d) Lion
   (iv) The number of letters in chimpanzee is
   (a) 10 (b) 9 (c) 8 (d) 7
2. Find odd one out
   (a) Four (b) Five (c) Nine (d) Six
3. Which number has the same number of letters as its name?
4. Write the number(s) between 1 and 99 that have the shortest name.
5. Which state has 3 numbers of letters in India?
6. Think and write the name of any two animals which have 5 letters and 7 letters, respectively.

ANSWERS & SOLUTIONS

1. (i) (a) (ii) (c) (iii) (a) (iv) (a)
2. (d) All the number names has four letters except (d).
3. The number has the same number of letters as its name is Four.
4. The numbers between 1 and 90 that have the shortest name are 2, 6 and 10.
5. Goa
6. Name of a animal which has 5 number of letters is Camel and name of a animal which has 7 number of letters is Leopard.

CHAPTER 2 TOY JOY

Cube

A 3-dimensional solid shape with six square faces, eight vertices (corners) and 12 edges is called cube.

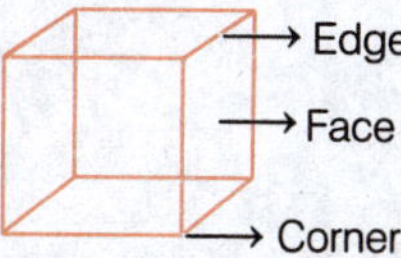

Cylinder

A cylinder is a 3-dimensional solid shape which has two identical circular bases joined by a curved surface.

Edge
Curved surface
Circular surface

Cuboid

A cuboid is a 3-dimensional solid shape with six rectangular faces, 8 vertices and 12 edges.

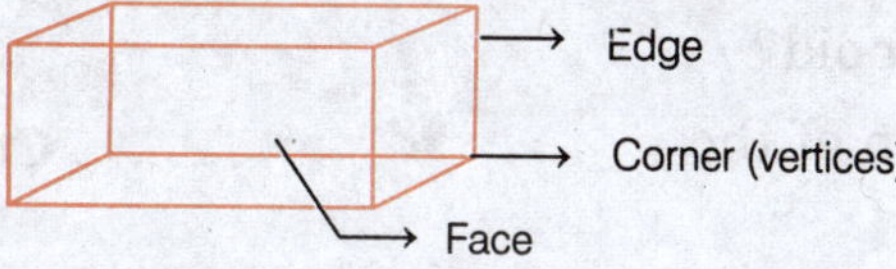

Cone

A cone is a 3-dimensional solid shape that has a circular base and it narrows down to a sharp point called a vertex.

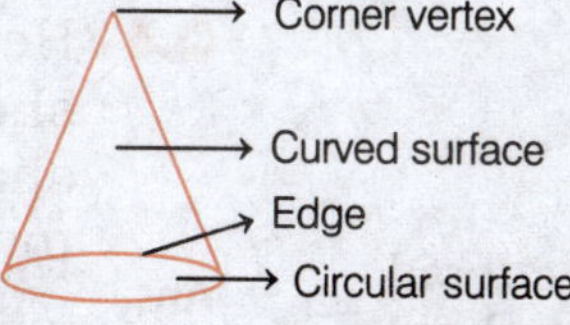

Sphere

A sphere is a 3-dimensional solid object that is round in shape.

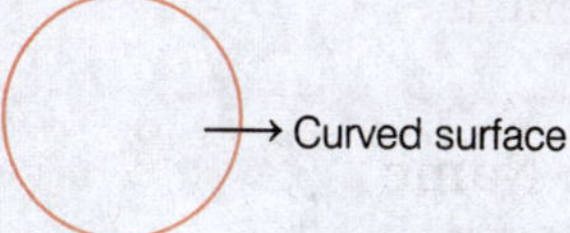

NCERT FOLDER

Let us Do (NCERT Pg 9-10)

Q.1 Use old boxes (cubes and cuboids) and bottles (cylinders) to do craft work. Draw faces on them.

(i) What did you draw on their faces?

(ii) Jaya is building a rocket with her shapes. What shapes has she used?

(iii) How many of each?

Cube ...., Cuboid ....

Cone .... Cylinder ....

(iv) What shape is between the Colour-1 cuboid and Colour-3 cuboid?

(v) What shape is on the top of the Colour-5 cylinder?

(vi) What shape is under the Colour-8 cone?

Ans. (i) Do yourself.

(ii) Jaya has used shapes : cylinder, cuboid, cube and cone.

(iii) Number of each shape used are

Cube → 2 Cuboid → 4

Cone → 1 Cylinder → 1

(iv) The shape between the Colour-1 cuboid and Colour-3 cuboid is Colour-2 cuboid.

(v) The shape on the top of the Colour-5 cylinder is Colour-6 cube.

(vi) The shape under the Colour-8 cone is Colour-7 cube.

Q.2 Collect objects to make a house. Name the shapes and talk about their faces and edges. Which are straight and which are curved? Also, describe how the shapes have been arranged. What part of the shapes can you see from a distance?

Ans. Do yourself.

Q.3 Devika went to a shop and bought a toy engine.

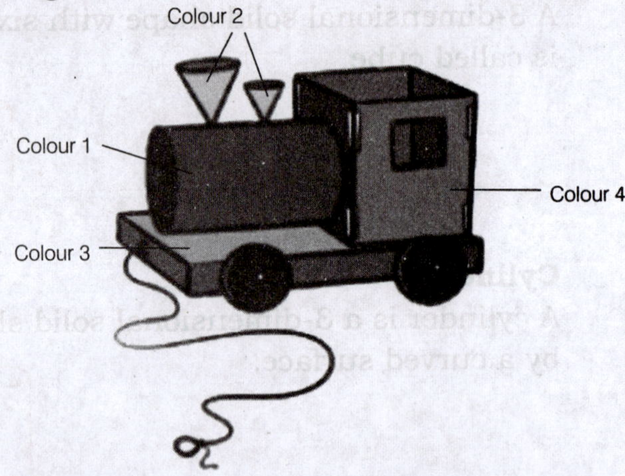

Here is Devika's toy engine. It has many parts. Count and fill.

.... Colour-1 cylinder(s) .... Colour-2 cone(s)

.... Colour-3 cuboid(s) .... Colour-4 cube(s)

Ans. 1 Colour-1 cylinder, 2 Colour-2 cone, 1 Colour-3 cuboid, 1 Colour-4 cube

Let us Discuss (NCERT Pg 10)

Q.4 Here are some more toys from the toy shop. They are made up of different shapes. What shapes are used in these toys?

Ans.

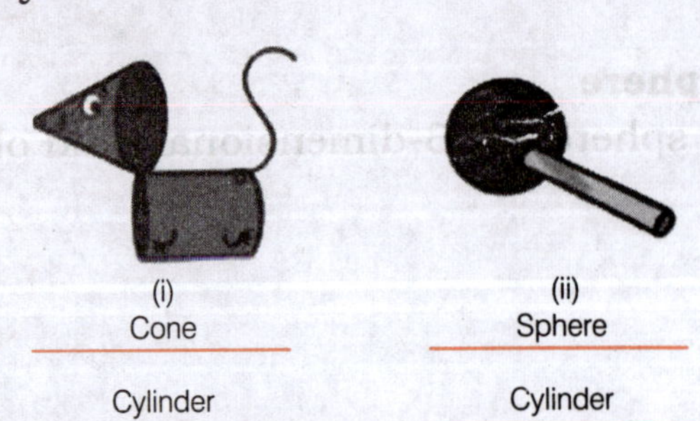

(i) Cone, Cylinder

(ii) Sphere, Cylinder

* *Students can write alternate answer as per their choice.*

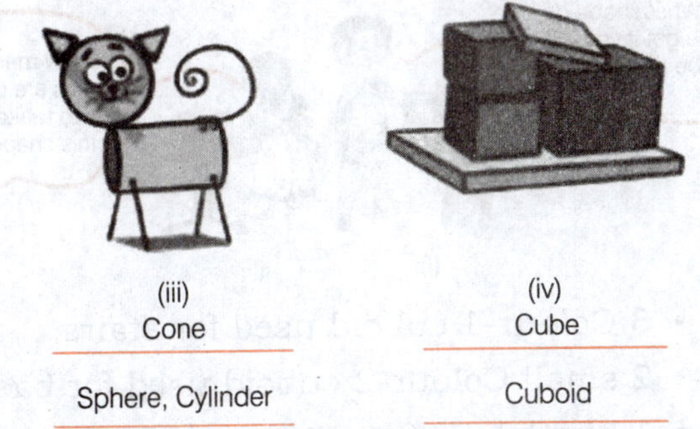

(iii) Cone	(iv) Cube
Sphere, Cylinder	Cuboid

Q.5 Try to build such houses, towers, rockets, etc. using different shapes available around you.

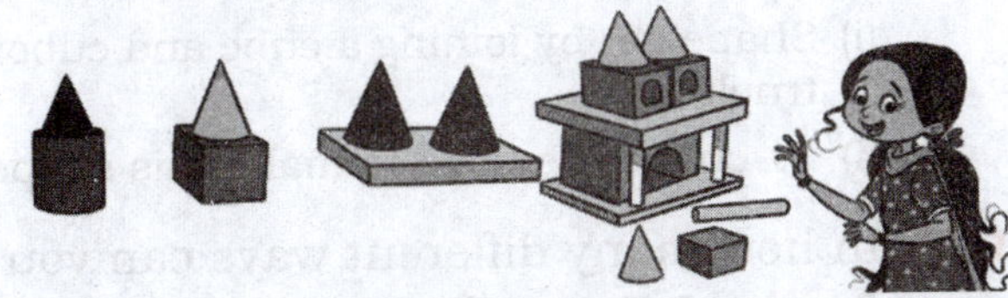

Note that a cube is a special type of cuboid.

Ans. Do yourself.

Let us Do (NCERT Pg 11-15)

Q.6 Can you find these shapes in the classroom? Fill in the table with their names.

Ans. *

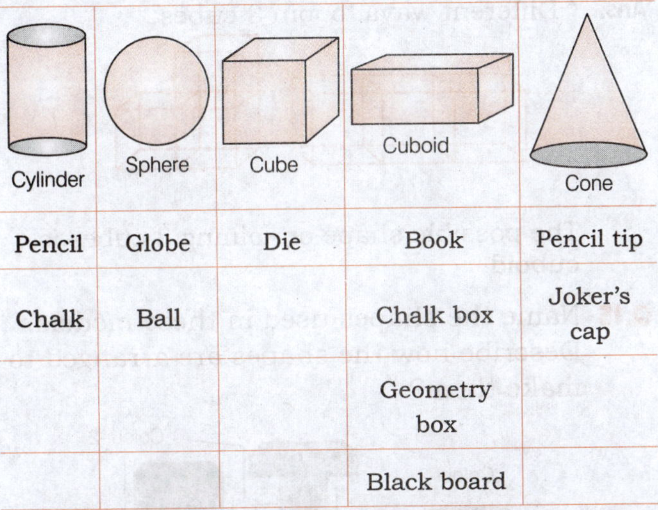

Cylinder	Sphere	Cube	Cuboid	Cone
Pencil	Globe	Die	Book	Pencil tip
Chalk	Ball		Chalk box	Joker's cap
			Geometry box	
			Black board	

(i) Name the shape that you find the most. Cuboid

(ii) Name the shape that you find the least. Cube

(iii) Name the objects that are made up of more than one shape. Chair

Q.7 Look at these shapes and answer the following questions.

- Circle ◯ the cubes.
- Put a tick (✓) against the shapes that are cones.
- Put a cross (×) against the shapes that are cylinders.
- Put a box ☐ around the cuboids.

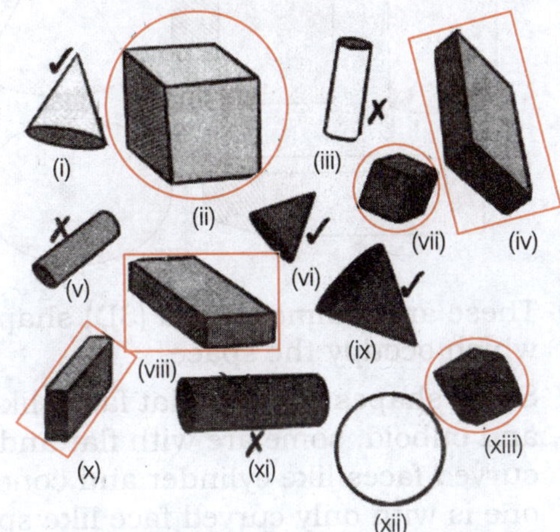

Ans.
- ◯ the cube are (ii), (vii) and (xiii).
- (✓) cone shapes are (i), (vi) and (ix).
- (×) cylinder shapes are (iii), (v) and (xi).
- ☐ cuboid shapes are (iv), (viii) and (x).

Q.8 Name the shapes.

Ans. (i) with no edges. Sphere

(ii) with only flat faces. Cube, Cuboid

(iii) with only curved faces. Sphere

(iv) with both straight and curved edges. None

(v) with both flat and curved faces. Cone, Cylinder

Q.9 Which shapes can you build?

Ans. Do yourself.

Q.10 Try to make these shapes using cube.

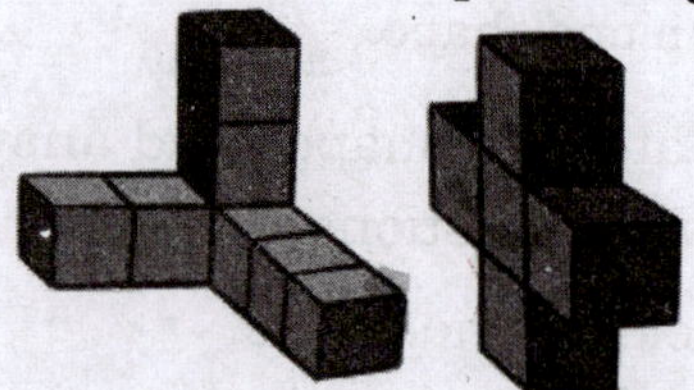

Ans. Do yourself.

Q.11 In what ways are these shapes the same? In what ways are they different?

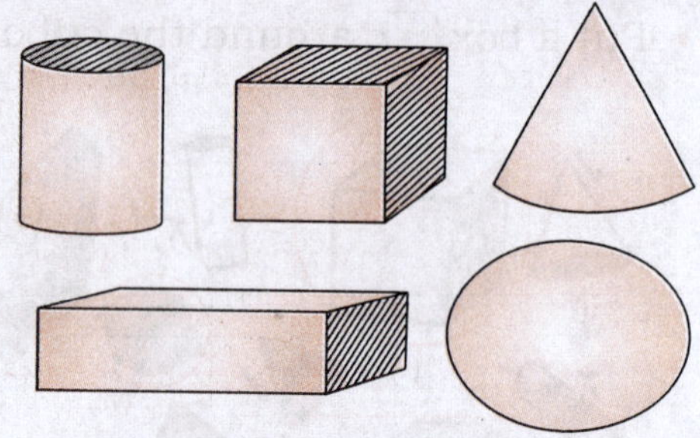

Ans.
- These are 3-dimensional (3D) shapes which occupy the space.
- Some shapes are with flat faces like cube and cuboid, some are with flat and curved faces like cylinder and cone, and one is with only curved face like sphere.

Q.12 Look at a die. The faces have 1 to 6 dots. What number is on

(i) the face opposite number 1? ....

(ii) the face opposite number 2? ....

(iii) the face opposite number 3? ....

(iv) What pattern do you notice? ....

Ans. (i) The face opposite number 1 is 6.

(ii) The face opposite number 2 is 5.

(iii) The face opposite number 3 is 4.

(iv) The sum of opposite faces is always seven.

Q.13 In what order is this model built?

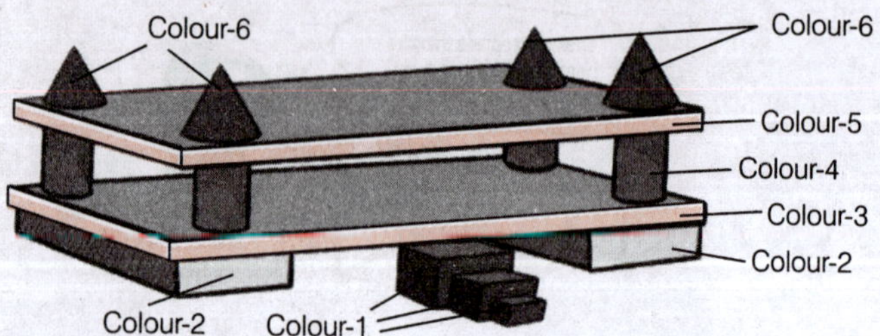

Ans.
- 3 Colour-1 cuboid used for stairs.
- 2 small Colour-2 cuboid used for base.
- 1 big Colour-3 cuboid used for floor and 1 big Colour-5 cuboid used for roof.
- 4 Colour-4 cylinders used for pillars.
- 4 Colour-6 cones used at the top of roof.

(i) Shape get by joining a cube and cuboid is truck.

(ii) 21 cubes are used to make this shape.

Q.14 In how many different ways can you join 3 cubes? Try and see.

Ans. * Different ways to join 3 cubes.

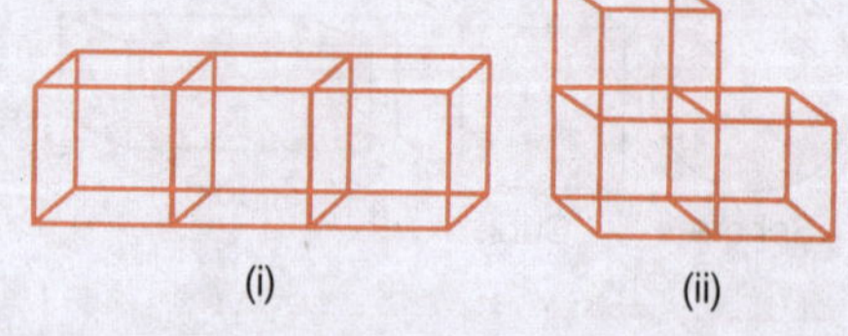

The possible shape on joining 3 cubes is cuboid.

Q.15 Name the shapes used in these models. Describe how the shapes are arranged to make them?

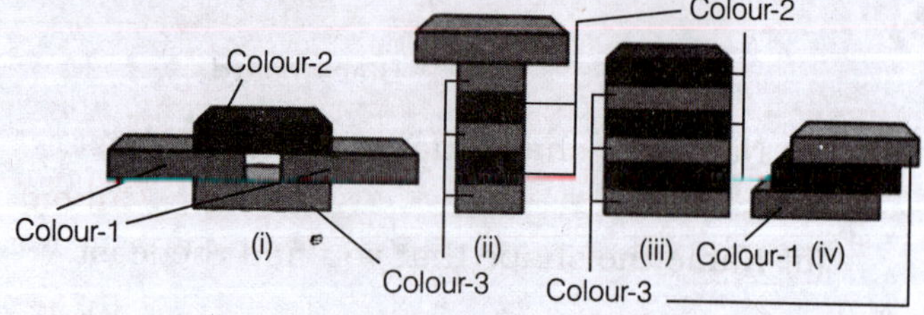

Ans. (i) Uses four cuboids arranged in layers with one Colour-3 cuboid horizontally, two Colour-1 cuboids placed on it horizontally in the middle, and one Colour-2 cuboid at the top of them.

(ii) 5 cuboid of the same size are stacked vertically and then a bigger cuboid is on top of the stalk.

(iii) 6 cuboids of the same size and all of them stacked vertically.

(iv) There cuboids of the same size are stacked vertically with each successive cuboid placed slightly.

Q.16 Use six dice 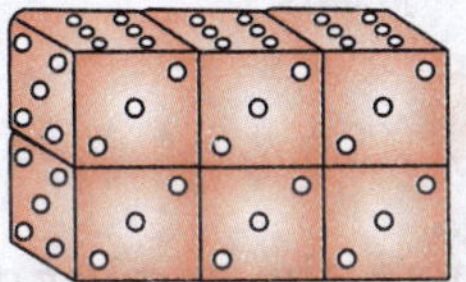 to make the following shapes:

(i) A cuboid (ii) A tower

(iii) Any other shape of your choice

Ans. *(i) A cuboid

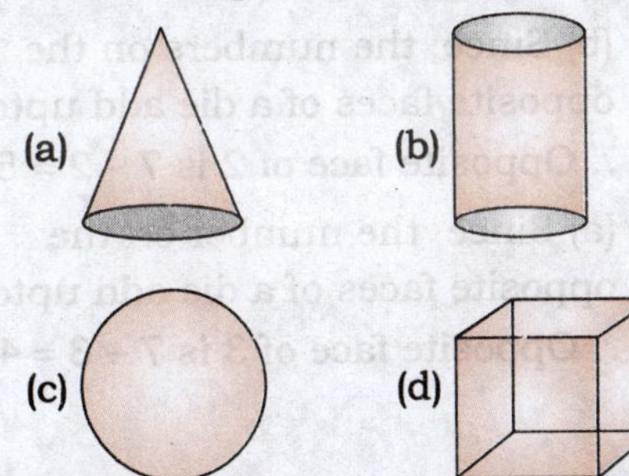

(ii) A tower

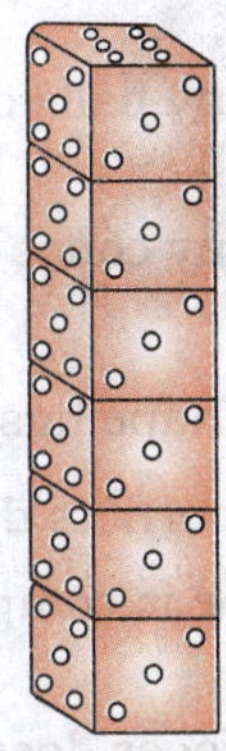

*(iii) Any other shape of your choice

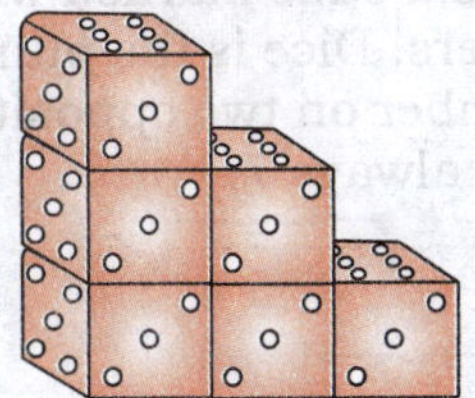

PRACTICE QUESTIONS

1. Multiple Choice Questions.

(i) Which 3D shape has no corner?

(a) Cone (b) Cuboid

(c) Cylinder (d) Cube

(ii) How many corners does a cuboid have?

(a) 6 (b) 8 (c) 12 (d) 4

(iii) Which shape has 3 faces?

(a) (b)

(c) (d)

2. Rahul join 5 cubes and make a tower. Find the number of faces and edges of the tower formed by joining the all five cubes.

3. A shape has 6 faces, 12 edges and 8 corners. It is not a cube. Think and write the name of the shape.

4. Anshika went to market for purchase some things to celebrating her birthday. She buys a matchbox, some candles and a cake which has no corner. Think and write what could the shapes of the items she purchased?

5. A standard die is a cube marked with the numbers 1, 2, 3, 4, 5 and 6. Find the sum of two numbers which are on the faces opposite to 6 and 2, respectively.

6. Picture based questions.

(i) How many cubes do you see in the picture?

(ii) How many balls do you see in the picture?

(iii) How many cones do you see in the picture?

7. Which 3D shape has only one corner?

8. How many corners does a cube have?

9. Which shape is completely round, like a basketball?

10. How many faces does a cylinder have?

11. A die is a cube marked with dots or numbers. Dice is the plural of die. The sum of number on two opposite of a 'standard' dice is always 7.

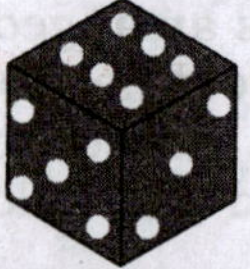

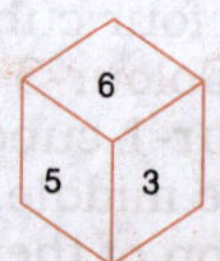

Based on above information, answer the following questions.

(i) Which number is on the face opposite to 6 in dice?
(a) 5 (b) 4
(c) 1 (d) 2

(ii) Which number is on the face opposite to 2 in dice?
(a) 3 (b) 5
(c) 6 (d) 4

(iii) Which number is on the face opposite to 3 in dice?
(a) 4 (b) 5 (c) 6 (d) 1

ANSWERS & SOLUTIONS

1. (i) (c) (ii) (b) (iii) (b)

2. On joining 5 cubes to make a tower, the formed shape will be a cuboid.

   Also, we know that a cuboid has 6 faces and 12 edges.

   Therefore, the formed tower has 6 faces and 12 edges.

3. We know that the shape of cube and cuboid both have 6 faces, 12 edges and 8 corners. But it is given that it is not a cube.

   Therefore, it is clear that the shape is cuboid.

4. Anshika buy a matchbox, some candles and a cake which has zero corner.

   We know that the shape of matchbox is cuboid and the shape of candle is cylindrical.

   Also, we know that the cylinder has no corners, so it is clear that the shape of cake will be cylindrical.

5. We know that the sum of numbers on two opposite faces of a standard die is always 7.

   Therefore, the number opposite to 6 $= 7 - 6$
   $= 1$

   and the number opposite to 2 $= 7 - 2$
   $= 5$

   $\therefore$ Required sum $= 1 + 5 = 6$

6. (i) 7 (ii) 2 (iii) 1

7. Cone

8. 8

9. Sphere

10. 3

11. (i) (c) Since, the numbers on the opposite faces of a die add upto 7.
    $\therefore$ Opposite face of 6 is $7 - 6 = 1$

    (ii) (b) Since, the numbers on the opposite faces of a die add upto 7.
    $\therefore$ Opposite face of 2 is $7 - 2 = 5$

    (iii) (a) Since, the number on the opposite faces of a die add upto 7.
    $\therefore$ Opposite face of 3 is $7 - 3 = 4$

CHAPTER 3 DOUBLE CENTURY

In this chapter, we will learn about counting upto 200 using different objects like snakes and ladders, pot, matchsticks bundles and also represent the numbers on the number line. Tens of thousands of years ago people counting to keep records of their things. They used marks on cave walls and tree barks to record numbers.

Ancient Methods of Counting Thousands of years ago, ancient Indians developed a system using ten symbols : 0, 1, 2, 3, 4, 5, 6, 7, 8, 9.

The Power of Zero The introduction of the zero represented by '0' as a place holder for 'nothing' was a revolutionary concept. It made numerical system efficient and allowed for complex calculations.

Let us Do (NCERT Pg 16)

Q.1 Look at the picture. Estimate and write the number of each of the following objects.

(a) Oranges .... (b) Bangles ....

(c) Laddoos .... (d) Barfi ....

(e) Bindis .... (f) Bananas ....

Ans. *(a) Oranges : 22 *(b) Bangles : 85

*(c) Laddoos : 28 *(d) Barfi : 22

*(e) Bindis : 70 *(f) Bananas : 36

** Students can write alternate answer as per their choice.*

Let us Play (NCERT Pg 17)

Q.2 Fill the missing number on the board.

END		98	97					92	
			84	85					
	79			76	75			72	
61	62		64				68	69	
		58			55	54			51
41	42			45			48	49	
	39		37	36				32	
21	22			25	26		28	29	30
	19	18					13	12	11
1		3				7		9	

Answer the following on the basis of the Snakes and Ladders board:

(i) Which number will you reach if you take the ladder from 13?

(ii) If you are on the snake at number 25, which number will you reach?

(iii) You are standing on 96. Which number on the die will take you to the snake's mouth?

(iv) Show the number written on the tail of the longest snake using bundles and lose sticks.

Ans.

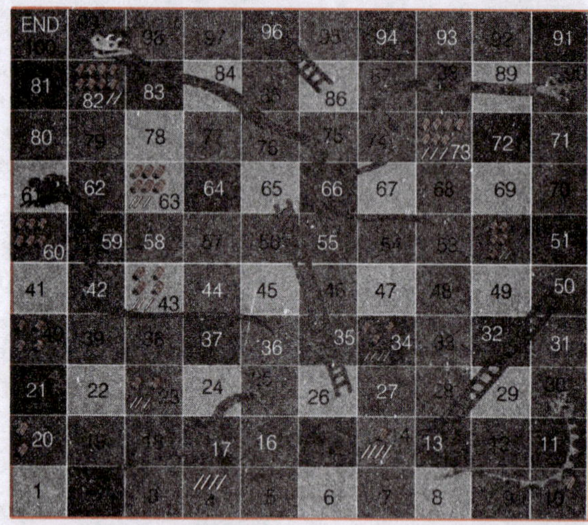

(i) 50

(ii) 2

(iii) 3

(iv) 53,

Let us Think (NCERT Pg 18)

Q.3

Ans.

Let us Do (NCERT Pg 19-20)

Q.4 Fill in the blanks.

Making 100	Number sentence
	70 and 30 makes 100
	__ and __ makes 100
	__ and __ makes 100

Ans.

Making 100	Number sentence
	70 and 30 makes 100
	80 and **20** makes 100
	50 and **50** makes 100

Q.5 Bholu made 100 by jumping on 65 and jumped 35 more.

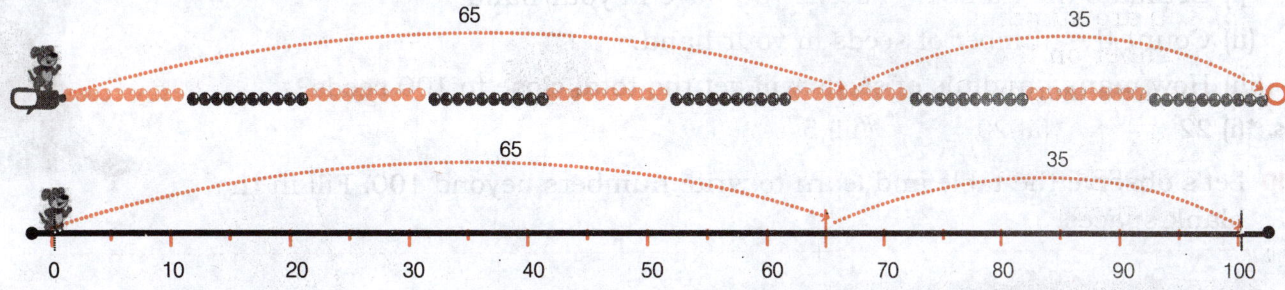

Make 100 by different jumps on this number line.

Ans. Bholu jumping on 35 and then jumped 65 more makes 100.

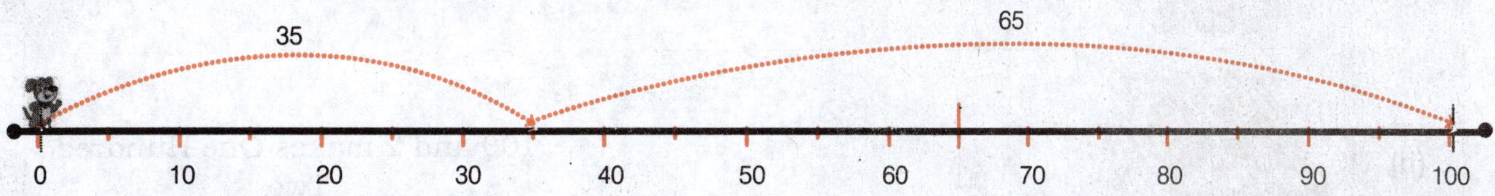

Q.6 Use matchstick bundles and a ginladi to make 100 in different ways. Fill the table below.

60 and 40 makes ...	45 and ... makes 100.
... and 25 makes 100.	... and 85 makes 100.
... and ... makes 100.	... and ... makes 100.

Ans.

60 and 40 makes **100**.	45 and **55** makes 100.
75 and 25 makes 100.	**15** and 85 makes 100.
65 and **35** makes 100.	**30** and **70** makes 100.

Q.7 Write numbers in the blank spaces inside the flower petals so that the numbers in each petal add up to 100.

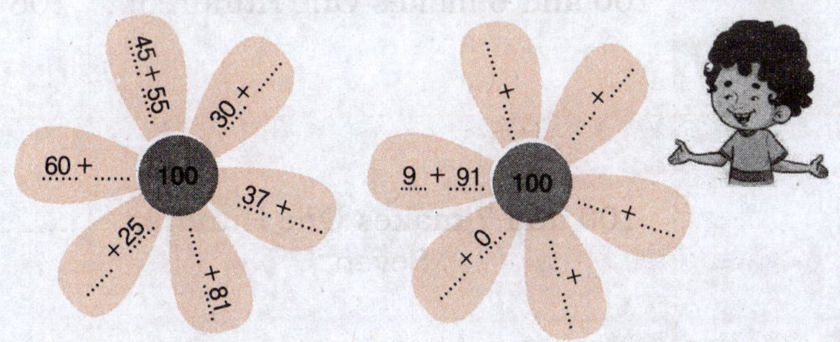

Ans.

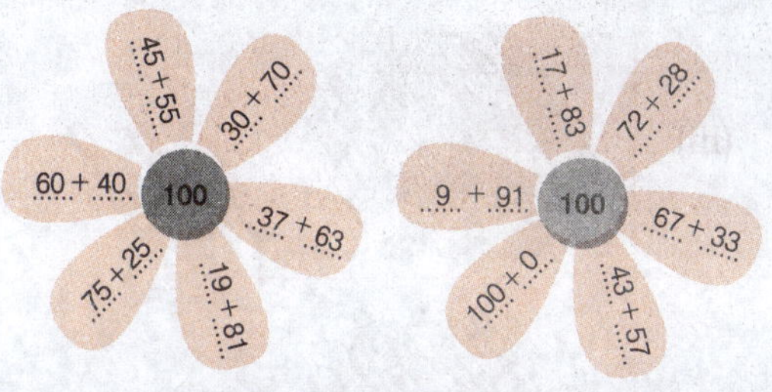

Let us Explore (NCERT Pg 20-21)

How many are 100?

Q.8 Open a full box of matchsticks.

(i) Estimate the number of matchsticks in the box.

(ii) Count the number of matchsticks in the box.

(iii) How close was your estimate?

(iv) How many boxes of matchsticks will get the total close to 100 matchsticks? .... boxes.

Ans. *(i) 45 *(ii) 32

*(iii) 13 less matchsticks than I estimate.

*(iv) 3

Q.9 Take a handful of seeds like kidney beans, chickpeas etc.

(i) Estimate the number of seeds you have in your hand.

(ii) Count the number of seeds in your hand.

(iii) How many handfuls of seeds will get the total close to 100 seeds?

Ans. *(i) 22 *(ii) 20 *(iii) 5

Q.10 Let's observe the table and learn to write numbers beyond 100. Fill in the blank spaces.

(i)		100 and 1 makes One Hundred One	101
(ii)		100 and 2 makes One Hundred Two	102
(iii)		100 and 3 makes One Hundred ...	103
(iv)		100 and 4 makes One Hundred.....	104
(v)		100 and 5 makes One Hundred Five	....
(vi)		100 and 6 makes One Hundred...	106
(vii)		100 and 7 makes One Hundred Seven	....

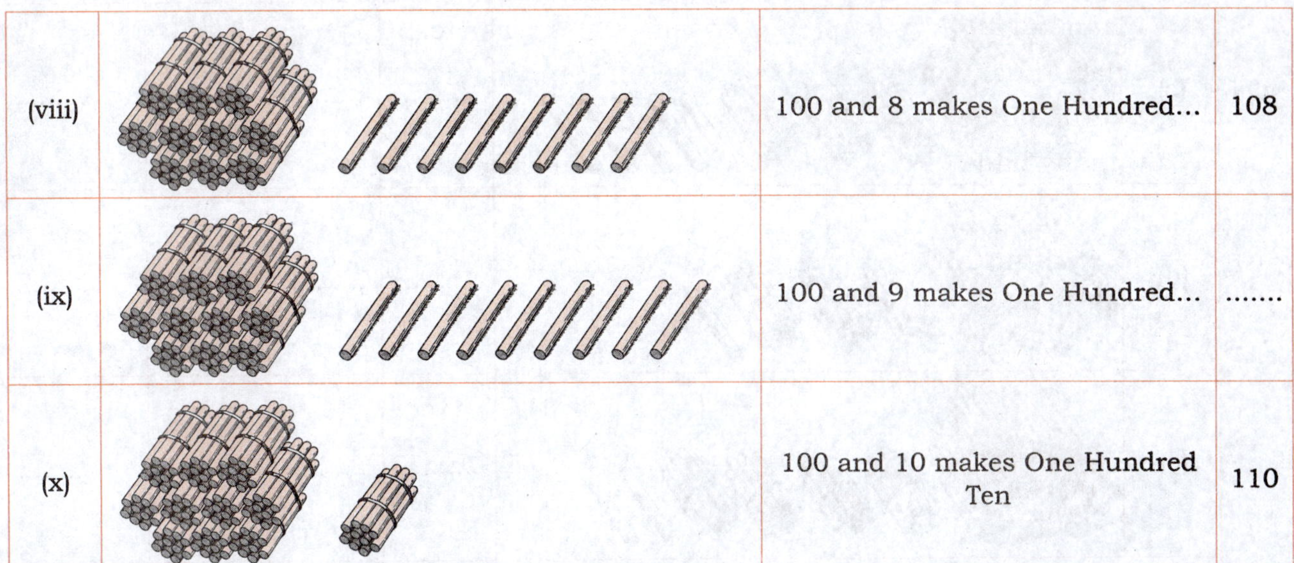

(viii)		100 and 8 makes One Hundred...	108
(ix)		100 and 9 makes One Hundred...	....
(x)		100 and 10 makes One Hundred Ten	110

Fill the blank spaces on the number line given below.

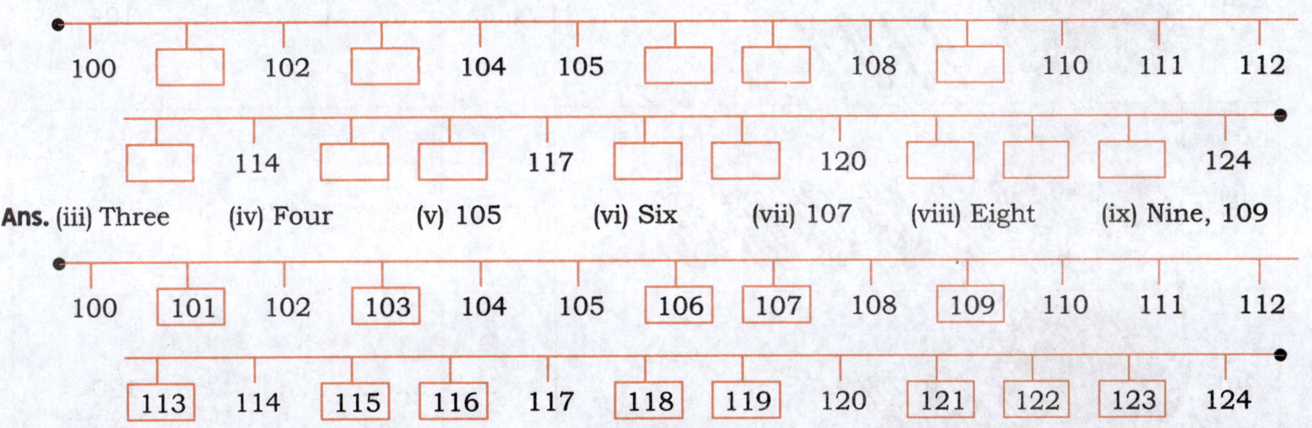

Ans. (iii) Three (iv) Four (v) 105 (vi) Six (vii) 107 (viii) Eight (ix) Nine, 109

100 101 102 103 104 105 106 107 108 109 110 111 112

113 114 115 116 117 118 119 120 121 122 123 124

Let us Do (NCERT Pg 22-23)

Q.11 (i) Let's continue making numbers above 100 using matchstick bundles and loose sticks. In the table given below, identify the bundles and loose sticks and write the corresponding numbers.

Bundles and Matchsticks		Matchstick bundles			Number
		100	10s	1s	
(a)		1	2	3	123
(b)		....	....	....	....

(c)	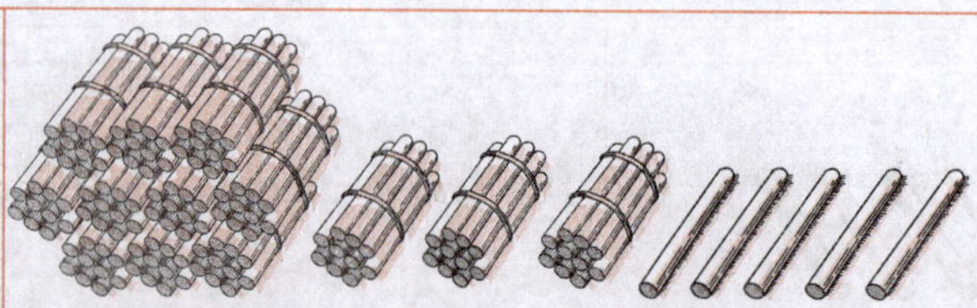	....	....	....	....
(d)	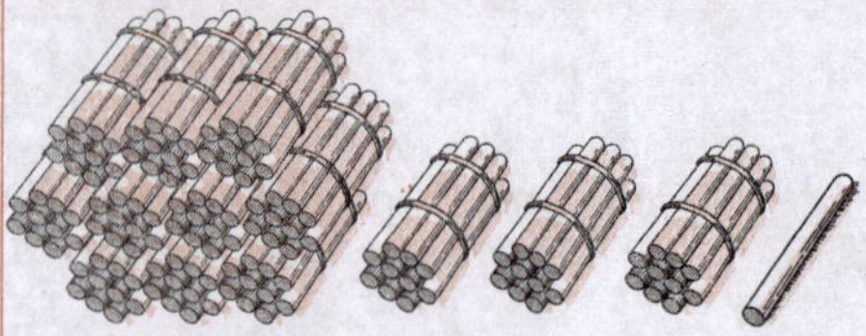	....	....	....	....
(e)	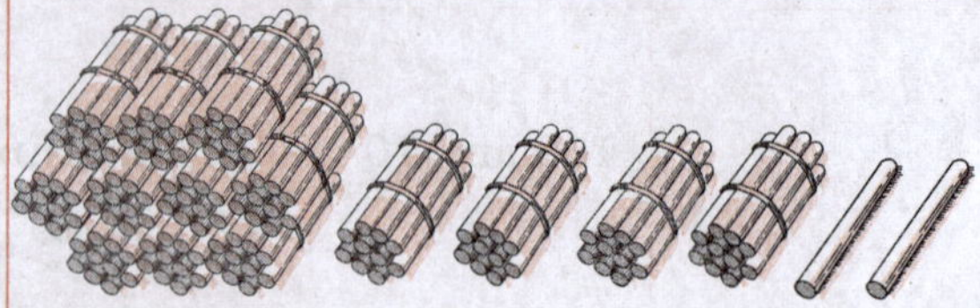	....	....	....	....
(f)	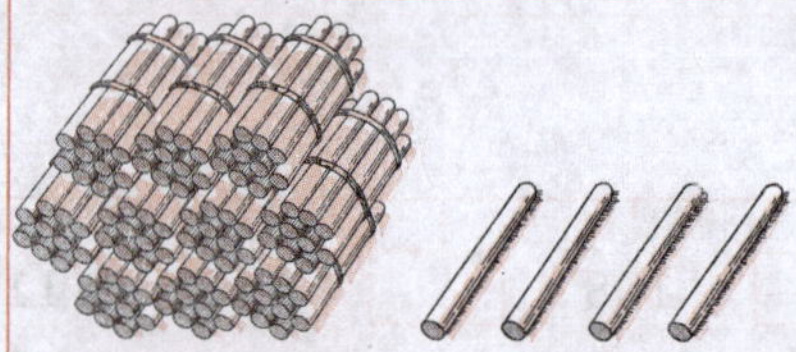	....	....	....	104
(g)	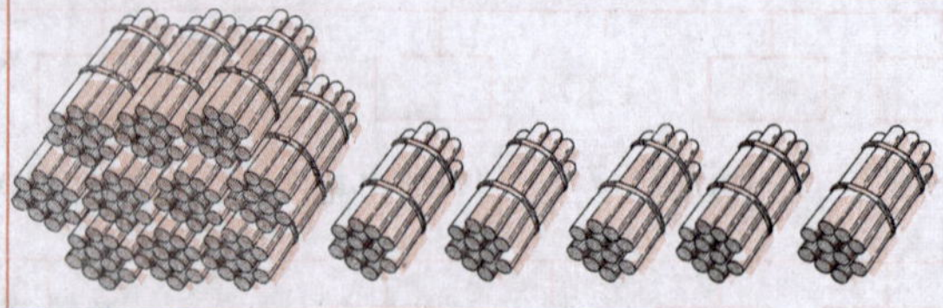	....	....	....	....
(h)	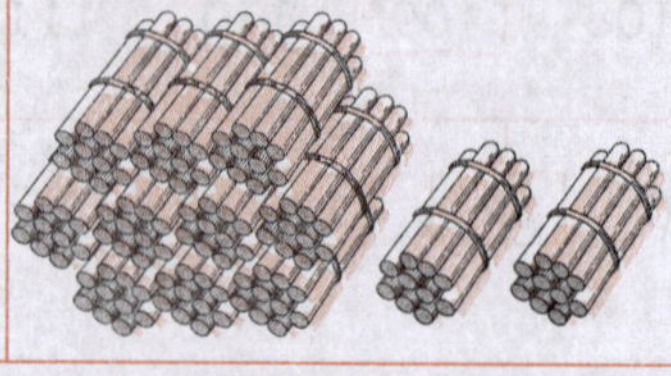	....	....	....	120

(ii) Extend this table in your notebook till 150. Do you observe something common in all the numbers?

Ans. (i) (b) 1, 3, 3, 133 (c) 1, 3, 5, 135 (d) 1, 3, 1, 131 (e) 1, 4, 2, 142
(f) 1, 0, 4, 104 (g) 1, 5, 0, 150 (h) 1, 2, 0, 120

(ii) Do yourself.

Q.12 Match the numbers with the correct bundles and loose sticks.

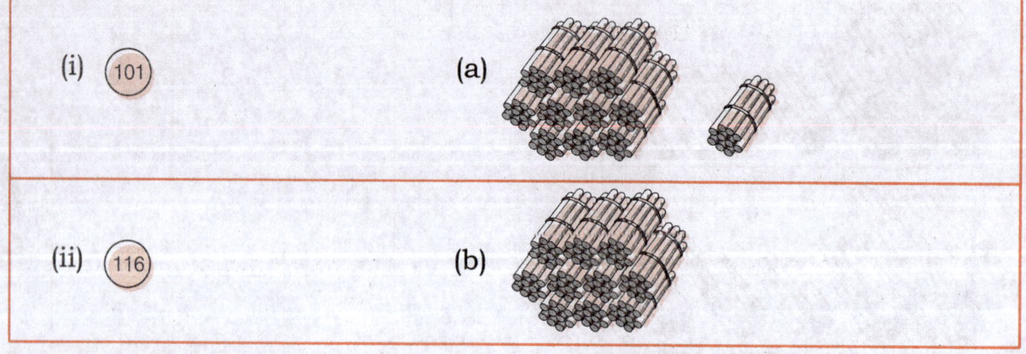

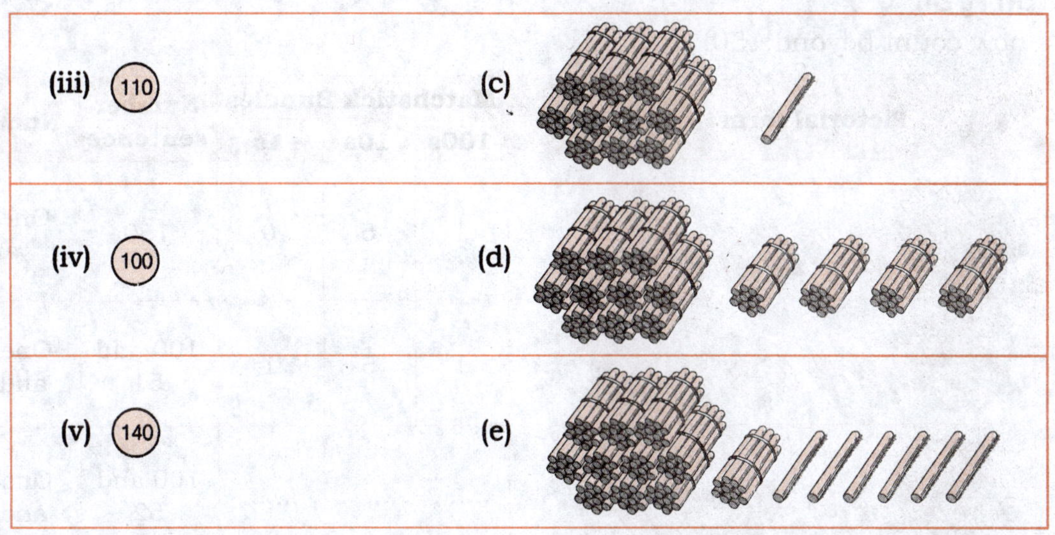

Ans. (i) - (c), (ii) - (e), (iii) - (a), (iv) - (b), (v) - (d)

Q.13 Oh! Talking Pot is back. It will say one more than whatever you say.

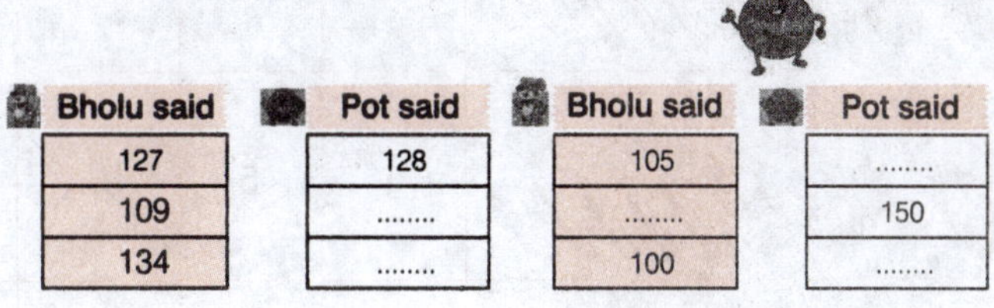

Bholu said	Pot said	Bholu said	Pot said
127	128	105	....
109	....	....	150
134	....	100	....

Ans.

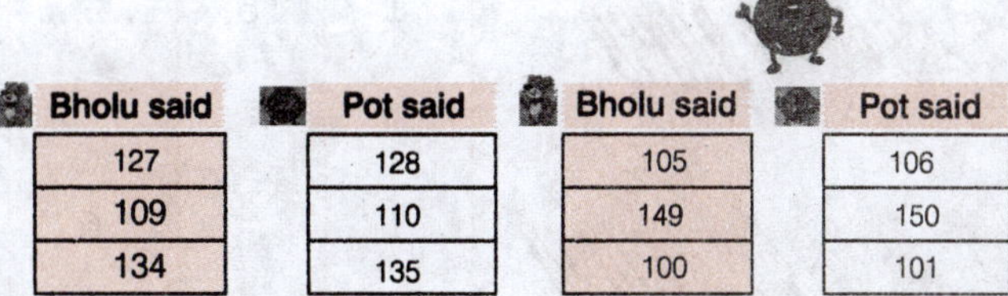

Bholu said	Pot said	Bholu said	Pot said
127	128	105	106
109	110	149	150
134	135	100	101

Q.14 Fill the blank spaces on the number line.

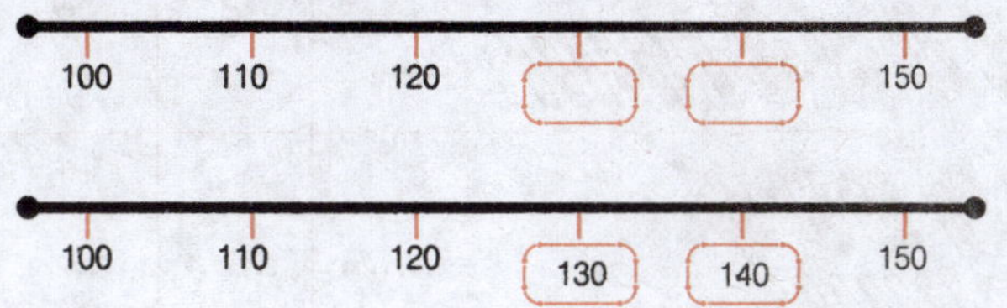

Ans.

Q.15 Show the following numbers on the number line below.

(i) Place an arrow on 125.

(ii) Make a tree on 112.

(iii) Make a smiley on 149.

(iv) Put a cross ⊗ on 137.

100 110 120 125 130 140 150

Ans.

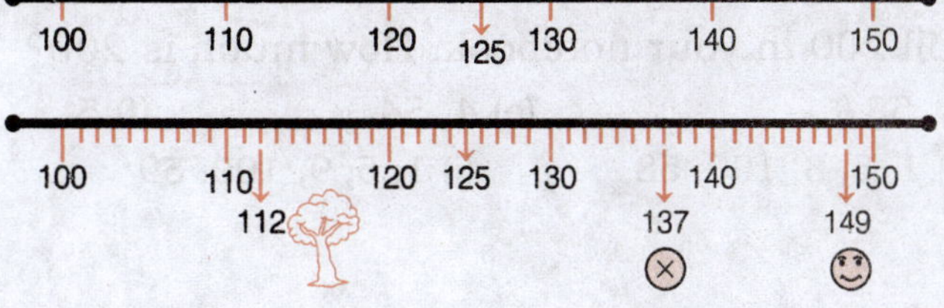

Let us Play (NCERT Pg 24)

Q.16 (i) Let's now count beyond 150.

	Pictorial form	Matchstick Bundles			Number sentence	Number name
		100s	10s	1s		
(a)		1	5	0	150	One hundred and fifty
(b)		1	5	1	100 and 51	One hundred and fifty one
(c)		....	....	....	100 and 52	One hundred and fifty two
(d)		1	....	3	100 and	One hundred and fifty three
(e)		1	5	....	100 and	One hundred and fifty four
(f)		1	5	....	100 and 55	One hundred and fifty five
(g)		1	....	6	.... and 56	One hundred and fifty six
(h)		....	5	7	100 and	One hundred and fifty seven
(i)		....	....	....	...... and	One hundred and fifty eight
(j)		....	....	....	...... and	One hundred and fifty nine

(ii) Extend this table till 200 in your notebook. How much is 200?

Ans. (i) (c) 1, 5, 2 (d) 5, 53 (e) 4, 54 (f) 5 (g) 5, 100
(h) 1, 57 (i) 1, 5, 8, 100, 58 (j) 1, 5, 9, 100, 59

(ii) Do yourself.

Let us Do at Home (NCERT Pg 25)

Q.17 (i) Fill a small container like a small bowl with seeds such as kidney beans, chickpeas, etc.

(ii) Look closely at the container to estimate how many seeds are in it. Your Estimate: .... seeds.

(iii) Now, count and see how close your estimation is to the actual number of seeds. Counted .... seeds.

(iv) Guess how many times you need to fill the container to get close to 200 seeds? Your guess : .... times.

(v) Write the numbers in order on the stones.

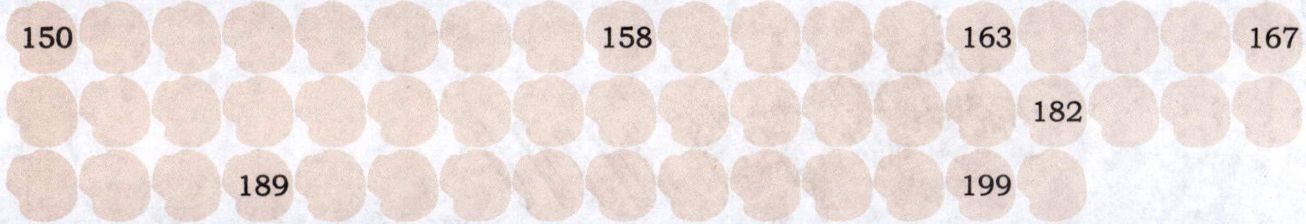

Ans. (i) Do yourself.

(ii) Do yourself.

(iii) Do yourself.

(iv) Do yourself.

(v)

150	151	152	153	154	155	156	157	158	159	160	161	162	163	164	165	166	167
168	169	170	171	172	173	174	175	176	177	178	179	180	181	182	183	184	185
186	187	188	189	190	191	192	193	194	195	196	197	198	199	200			

Let us Do (NCERT Pg 26-28)

Jumping Game

Q.18 (i) Draw jumps of 5 on the number line and write the numbers on the number line in the given spaces.

(ii) Continue jumps of 20 and write the missing numbers on the given number line.

(iii) Fill in the table.

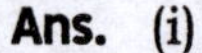

Ans. (i)

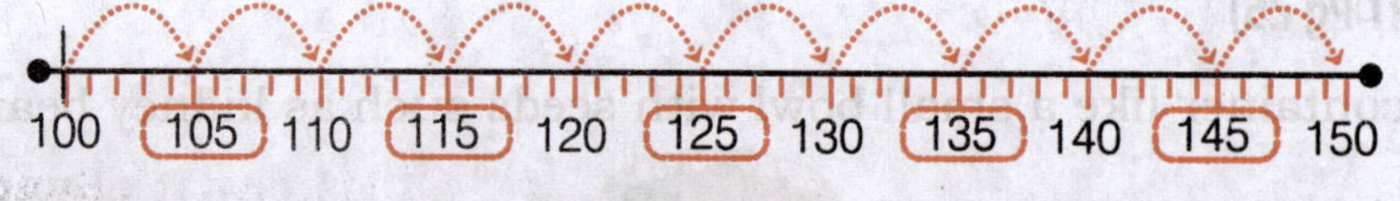

100 105 110 115 120 125 130 135 140 145 150

(ii)

100 120 140 160 180 200

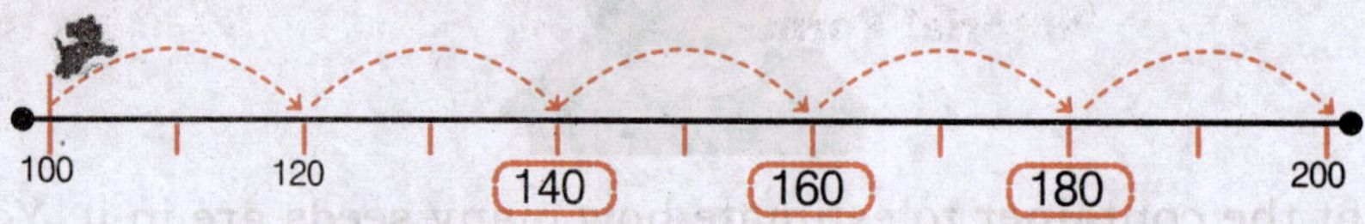

(iii)

1 less	Number	1 more
159	160	161
128	129	130
186	187	188
133	134	135
157	158	159

Q.19 Show atleast two different ways of making the following numbers.

(i) Use matchstick bundles to make 125.

(ii) Make 145 using a ginladi.

(iii) Make 170 on a number line

Ans. *(i)

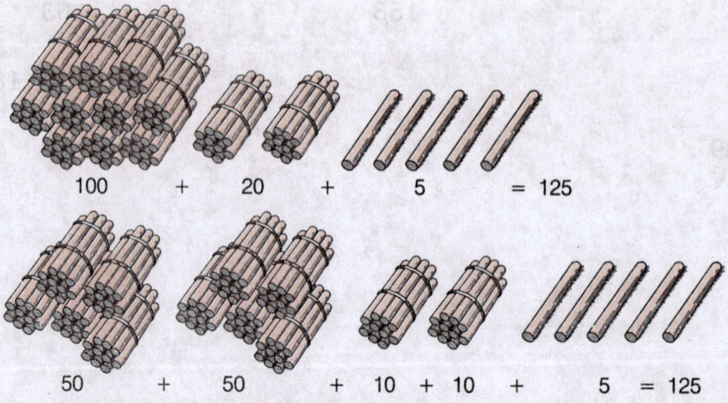

100 + 20 + 5 = 125
50 + 50 + 10 + 10 + 5 = 125

*(ii)

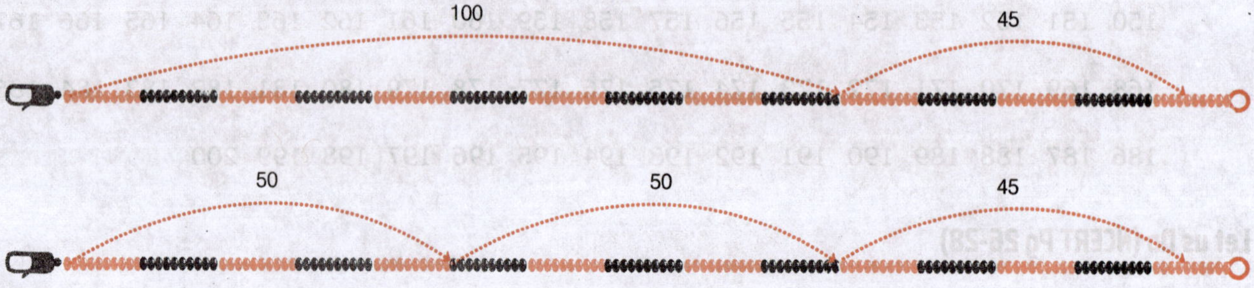

100
45
50
50
45

*(iii)

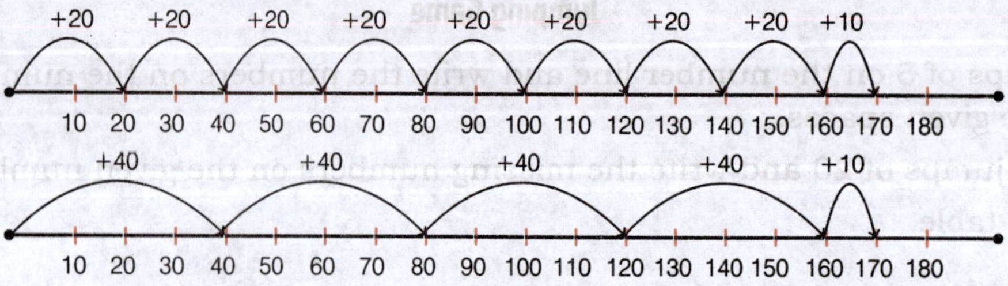

+20 +20 +20 +20 +20 +20 +20 +20 +10
10 20 30 40 50 60 70 80 90 100 110 120 130 140 150 160 170 180
+40 +40 +40 +40 +10
10 20 30 40 50 60 70 80 90 100 110 120 130 140 150 160 170 180

Q.20 Fill in the empty boxes appropriately.

Ans.

Number	Pictorial Form	Matchstick Bundles			Number Sentence
		100	10s	1s	
114		1	1	4	100 and 14 more
132		1	3	2	100 and 32 more
154		1	5	4	100 and 54 more
172		1	7	2	100 and 72 more
108		1	0	8	100 and 8 more
180		1	8	0	30 more than 150
160		1	6	0	100 and 60 more

NCERT Pg 28

Q.21 Mark the following numbers on the number line.

(a) 109, 112, 124, 134, 146

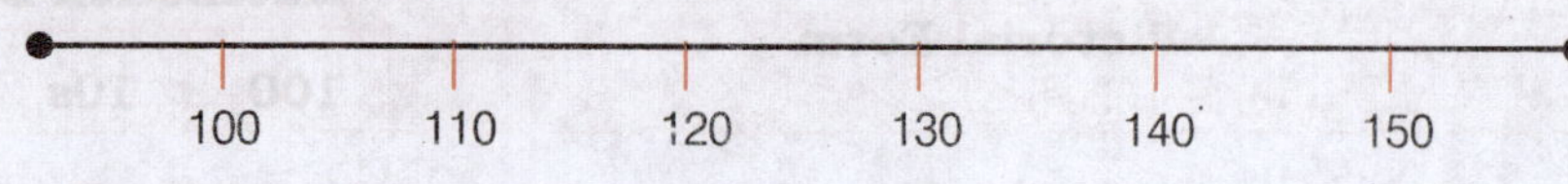

(b) 155, 163, 178, 189, 198

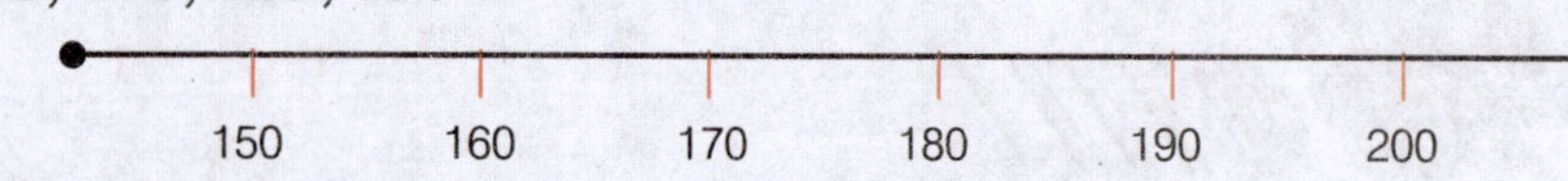

(c) 125, 142, 153, 174, 199

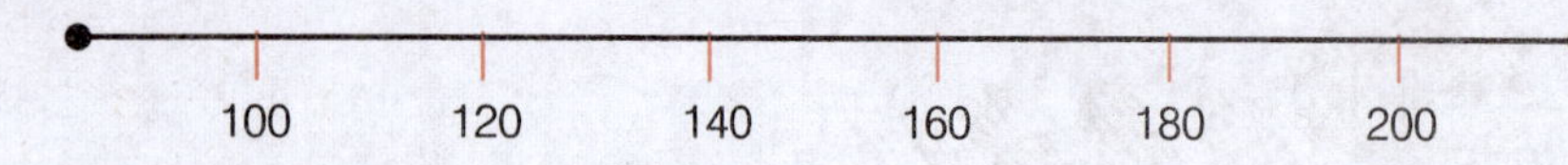

Ans. (a) 109, 112, 124, 134, 146

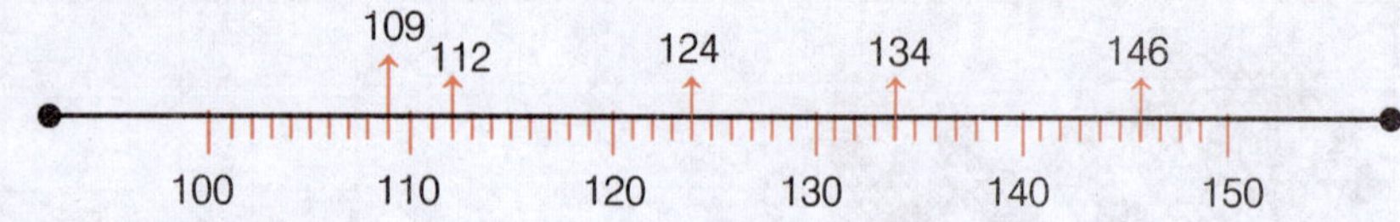

(b) 155, 163, 178, 189, 198

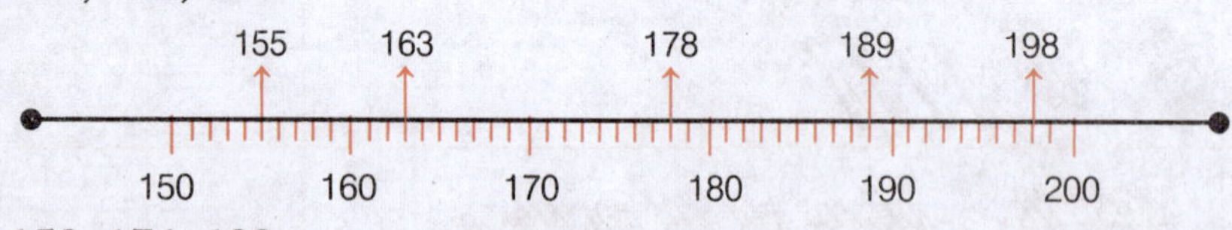

(c) 125, 142, 153, 174, 199

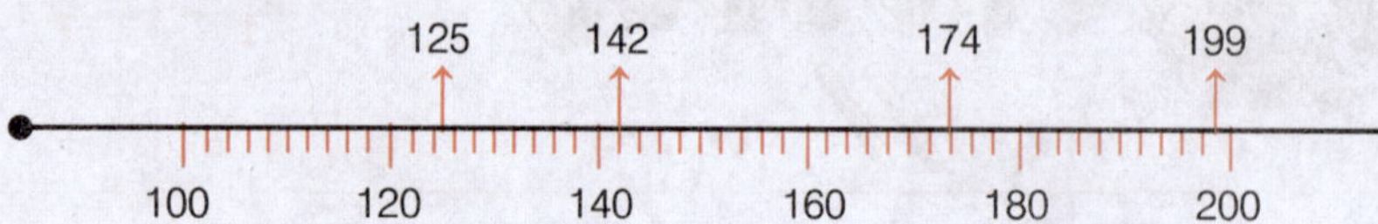

PRACTICE QUESTIONS

1. Fill in the blanks

(i) The symbol for 'nothing' in our number system is ....

(ii) We use .... symbols to write all numbers.

(iii) 10 bundles of 10 sticks, make .... sticks.

(iv) 98, 99 ...., 101, 102, ..., 104, ... , 106.

2. True or False.

(i) The ancient Indians created a method for writing any number using only ten symbols.

(ii) The number 0 is not important in our number system.

(iii) 100 and 7 make one hundred and seven (107).

(iv) 100 and 10 make one hundred and one (101).

3. Multiple choice questions

(i) Which of these numbers is between 67 and 76?

(a) 77 (b) 70

(c) 66 (d) 60

(ii) Seventy nine can be written as

(a) 7 + 9

(b) 7 + 90

(c) 70 + 90

(d) 9 + 70

(iii) The number which comes just after 5 tens is

(a) 16 (b) 49
(c) 51 (d) 60

(iv) If the number 12 is represented as

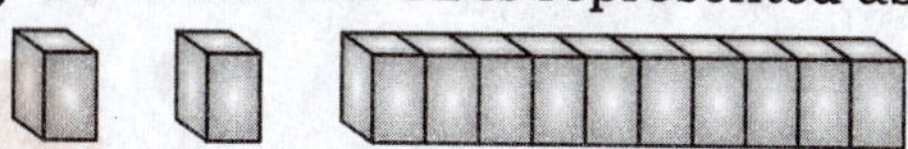

Which number is represented below?

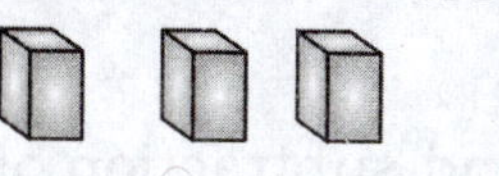
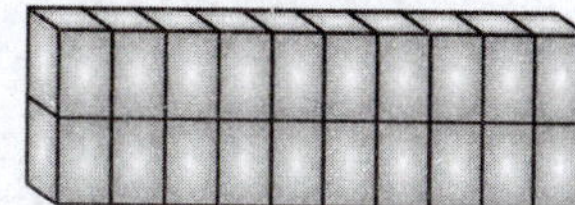

(a) 13 (b) 23
(c) 31 (d) 32

(v) A frog starts from stone 1 and goes to the other side by jumping on every second stone. Which stones will the frog jump on?

(a) Stones 3 and 4 only
(b) Stones 3, 5, 7 and 9
(c) Stones 2, 4, 6 and 8
(d) Stone 5 only

(vi) Jay is writing numbers from 1 to 50 on a number line. Which of these numbers will be nearest to 30 on the line?

(a) 40 (b) 34
(c) 28 (d) 25

(vii) What comes after 189?

(a) 190 (b) 187
(c) 188 (d) 191

(viii) What comes before 199?

(a) 200 (b) 190
(c) 198 (d) 197

(ix) What comes between 187 and 189?

(a) 184 (b) 185
(c) 186 (d) 188

4. Match the following

(i)	One hundred and fifty	(a)	125
(ii)	One hundred and twenty five	(b)	150
(iii)	Two hundred	(c)	187
(iv)	One hundred and eighty seven	(d)	200

5. Circle the largest number

175, 167, 189, 182, 199

6. Solve this puzzle.

I am thinking of a number between 150 and 200.
It has 9 in the tens place.
The sum of its digits is 14.
It is an even number.
What number am I thinking?

ANSWERS & SOLUTIONS

1. (i) 0 (ii) ten
(iii) 100 (iv) 100, 103, 105

2. (i) True (ii) False
(iii) True (iv) False

3. (i) (b) (ii) (d)
(iii) (c) (iv) (b)
(v) (b) (vi) (c)
(vii) (a) (viii) (c)
(ix) (d)

4. (i) → (b) (ii) → (a)
(iii) → (d) (iv) → (c)

5. 175, 167, 189, 182, (199)

6. Since, the number is between 150 and 200, the hundreds digit must be 1.

Also, the tens digit is 9, so the ones digit must be 4 in order for the sum of the digits to be 14.

Hence, the number is 194.

CHAPTER 4 VACATION WITH MY NANI MAA

In this chapter, we will learn about the basics of counting, addition and subtraction of numbers through magic trick. We will learn addition and subtraction through different objects of different methods like seeds, Balushahi, ginladi, number grid, magic sums, matchsticks bundles and number line.

NCERT FOLDER

NCERT Pg 29

Q.1 Nani Maa shows them a 'magic trick'. You hide some marbles with your handkerchief. I shall tell you the number of marbles you have hidden.

Can you tell what the trick is?

Ans. The trick is given below.

Total Seeds = Seeds on the table + Hidden Seeds

Or Hidden Seeds = Total Seeds – Seeds on the table

Let us Do (NCERT Pg 29-31)

Q.2 Perform the trick on your friends. Write the numbers of hidden seeds in the table below.

** Students can write alternate answer as per their choice.*

Ans.

Total seeds	Seeds on the table	Hidden seeds
15	12	3
17	10	7
19	8	11

Total seeds	Seeds on the table	Hidden seeds
20	9	11
23	7	16
27	12	15

Q.3 Nandini had 7 balushahi in her box

and

Chirag had 5 balushahi in his box.

Draw the number of dots.

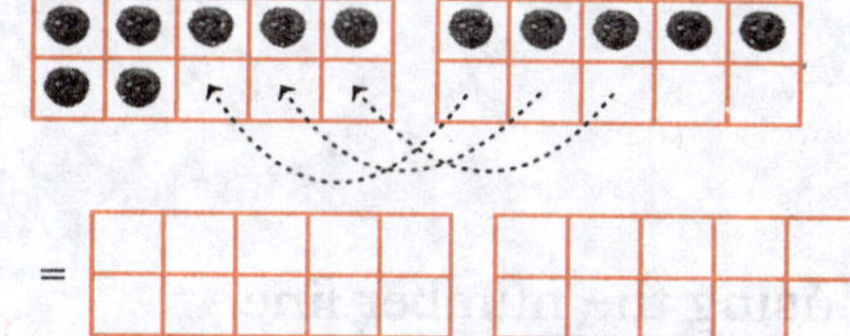

7 Balushahi + 5 Balushahi

= .... Balushahi

(i) How many did he eat? .... balushahi

(ii) 7 Balushahi –5 Balushahi

= .... Balushahi

Ans.

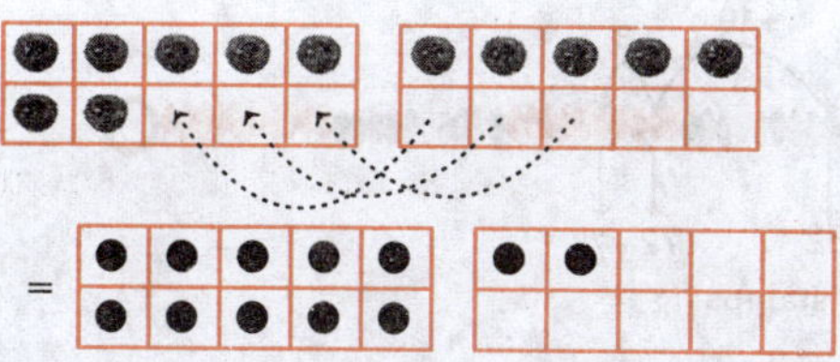

7 Balushahi + 5 Balushahi = **12** Balushahi

(i) He ate 2 balushahi.

(ii) 7 Balushahi –5 Balushahi = **2** Balushahi

Q.4 Chirag got 9 story books for Nani Maa and Nandini got 7 puzzle books for Nani Maa. How many total books did the children get for Nani Maa?

.... Books + ... Books = ... Books

Ans. 9 Books + 7 Books = 16 Books

Let us Do (NCERT Pg 31)

Q.5 Use the tens frame to solve the following.

(i) 6 + 8 = ...

(ii) 5 + 10 = ...

(iii) 9 – 6 = ...

(iv) 18 – 9 = ...

Ans. (i) 6 + 8 = 14

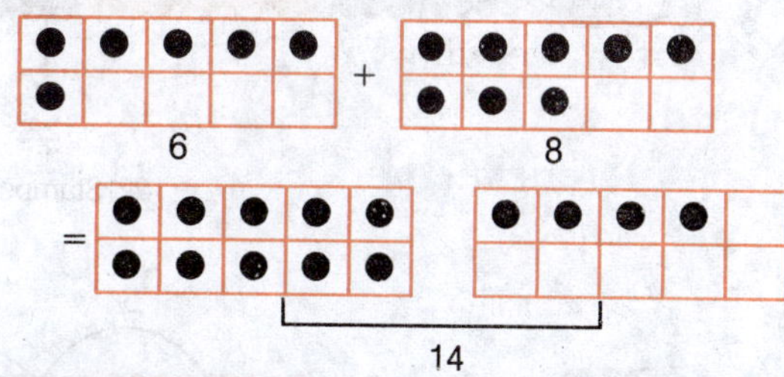

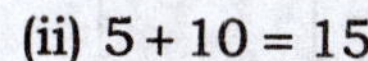

(ii) 5 + 10 = 15

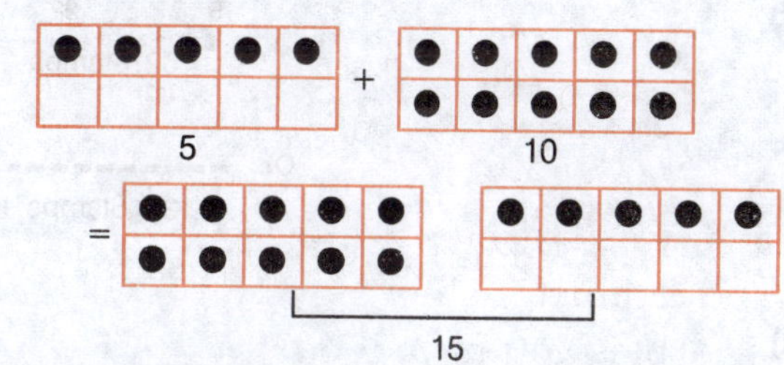

(iii) 9 – 6 = 3

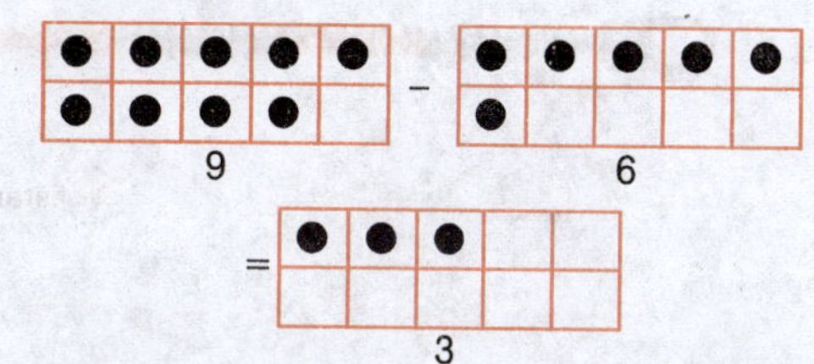

(iv) 18 – 9 = 9

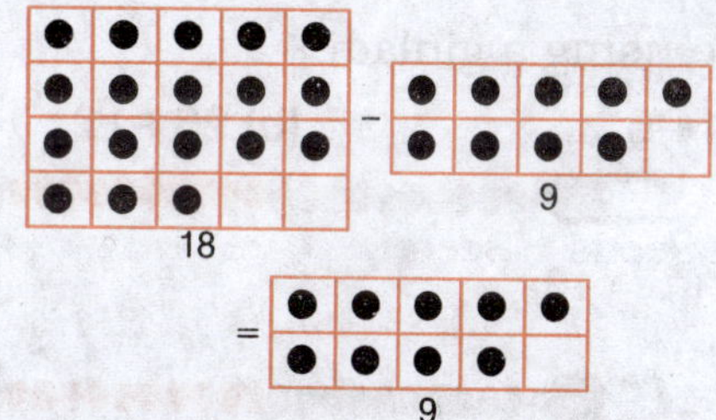

Let us Do (NCERT Pg 32-33)

Q.6 (i) Nandini and Chirag have 22 stamps. Nani Maa's brother gives them his collection of 30 stamps. How many stamps do they have now?

(ii) They have 15 stamps with pictures of monuments. Can you find other ways of doing it?

(iii)

How many more stamps will they need? Figure it out using the number line.

Ans. (i)

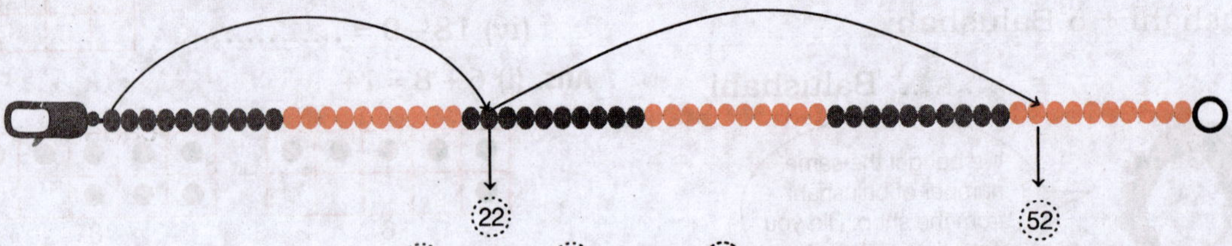

22 52

22 Stamps + 30 Stamps = 52 Stamps

or 22 + 30 = 52

(ii)

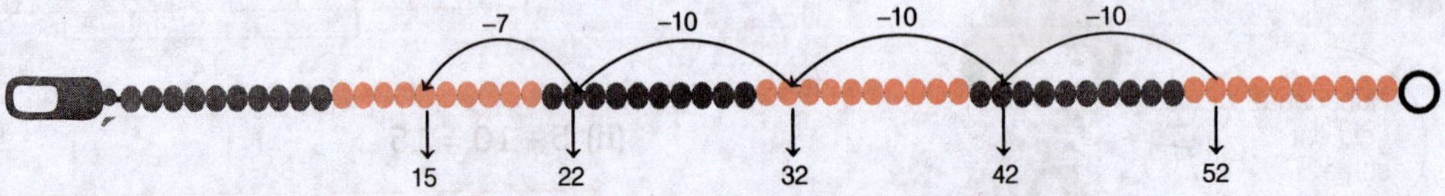

−7 −10 −10 −10

15 22 32 42 52

52 Stamps − 37 Stamps = 15 Stamps

52 − 37 = 15

Or

37 Stamps + 15 Stamps = 52 Stamps

37 + 15 = 52

(iii)

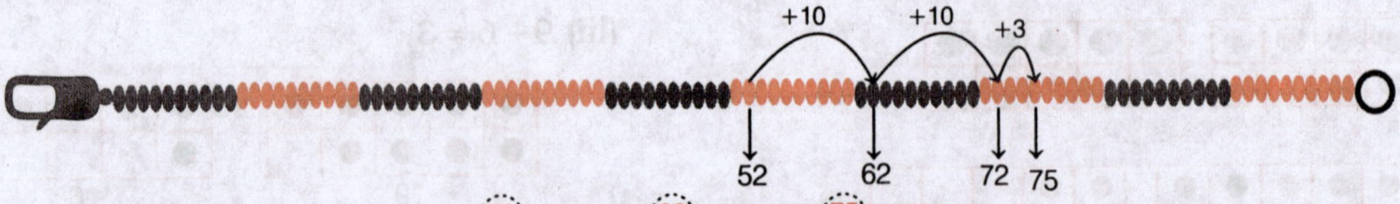

+10 +10 +3

52 62 72 75

52 stamps + 23 stamps = 75 stamps

Or, 52 + 23 = 75

Let us Do (NCERT Pg 34-35)

Q.7 Solve using a ginladi.

(a) 34 + 6 (b) 23 + 12 (c) 33 − 5 (d) 42 − 15

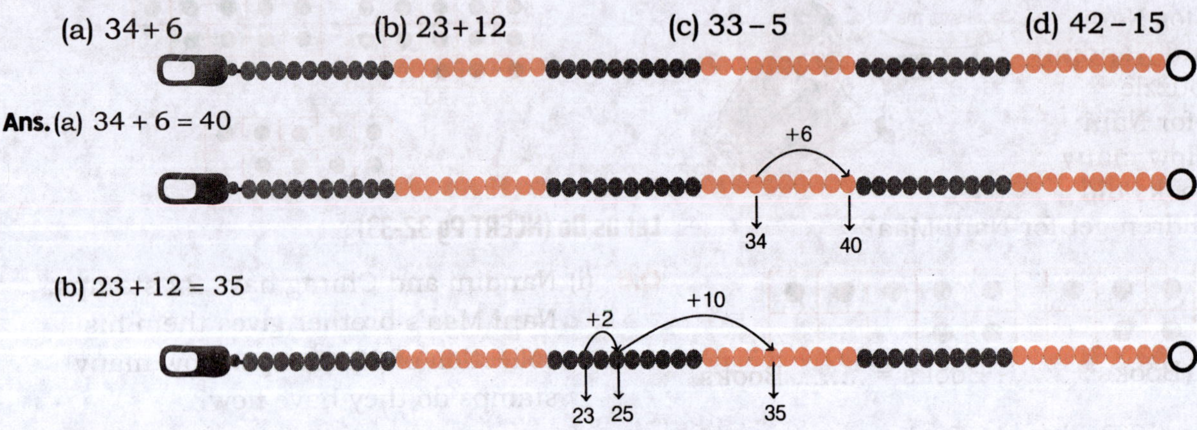

Ans. (a) 34 + 6 = 40

(b) 23 + 12 = 35

(c) 33 – 5 = 28

–5

28 33

(d) 42 – 15 = 27

–3 –12

27 30 42

Q.8 (i) A frog is jumping on the ginladi. He is at 7. He wants to jump 10 beads at a time. Mark the beads that he will jump on and write the numbers.

(ii) The frog again jumps forward by 10 each time. Mark all the places where the frog will land.

Ans. (i) Frog wants to jump 10 beads at a time.

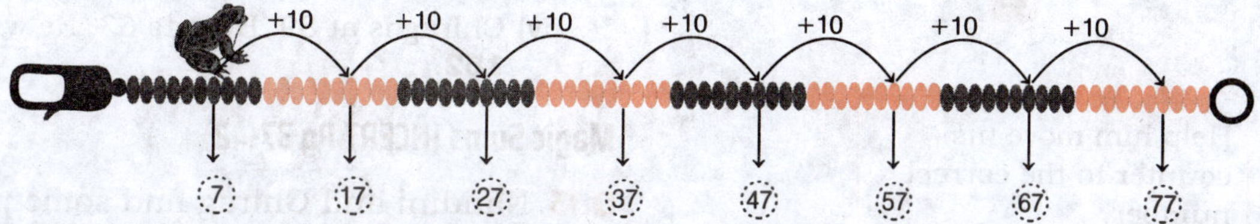

(ii) Frog at 23, jumps forward by 10 each time.

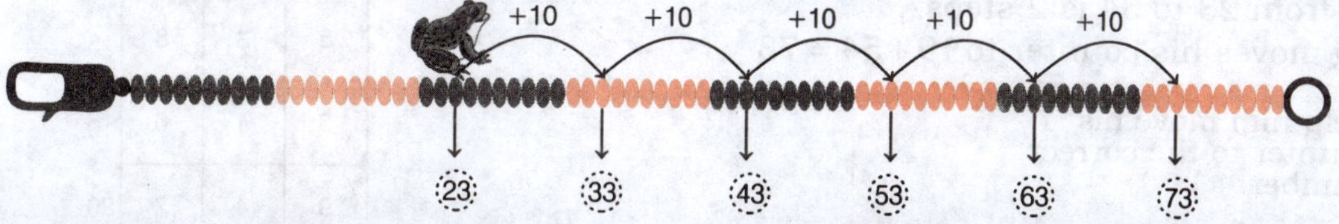

Q.9 The grasshopper jumps backward by 10 each time. Mark all the beads that the grasshopper will jump on and write numbers.

Ans. The grasshopper at 76, jumps backward by 10 each time.

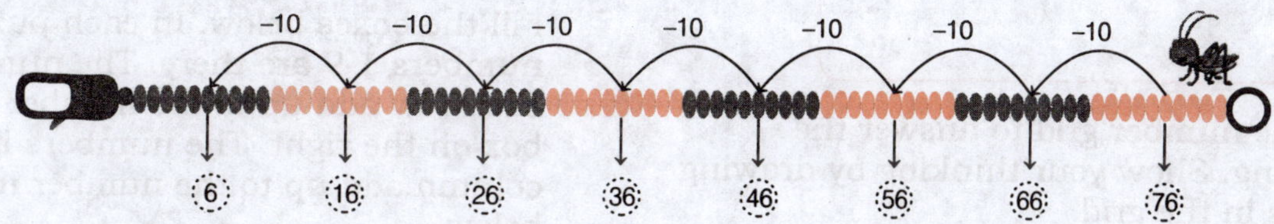

Q.10 Fill in the tables by jumping as instructed.

Ans.

Jump 5

34	56	87
39	61	82
44	66	77
49	71	72

Jump 6

28	59	73
34	65	67
40	71	61
46	77	55

Jump 9

29	12	93
38	21	84
47	30	75
56	39	66

Let us Play (NCERT Pg 35-36)

Q.11

Nandini is at 23. She has got 11 on the dice as the number. She thinks of two ways of moving to 34.

Chirag is at 19. He gets 54 on the dice.

A jump from 23 to 34 is .... steps.

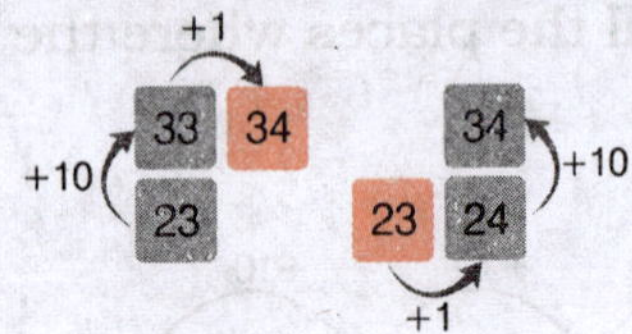

Help him move his counter to the correct number.

Ans. A jump from 23 to 34 is 2 steps.
Chirag moves his counter to 19 + 54 = 73

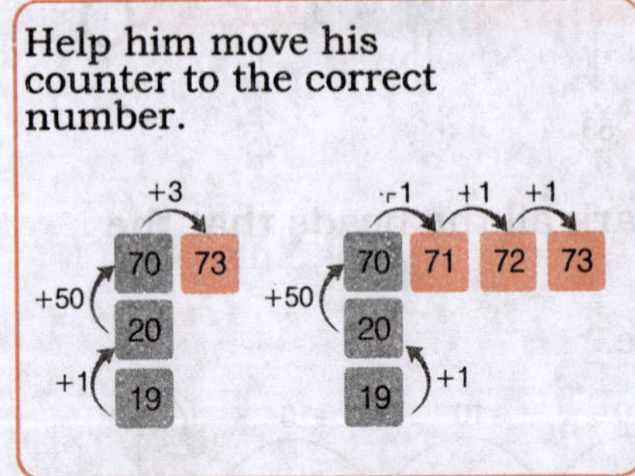

Q.12 Use the number grid to answer the following. Show your thinking by drawing arrows in the grid.

91	92	93	94	95	96	97	98	99	100
81	82	83	84	85	86	87	88	89	90
71	72	73	74	75	76	77	78	79	80
61	62	63	64	65	66	67	68	69	70
51	52	53	54	55	56	57	58	59	60
41	42	43	44	45	46	47	48	49	50
31	32	33	34	35	36	37	38	39	40
21	22	23	24	25	26	27	28	29	30
11	12	13	14	15	16	17	18	19	20
1	2	3	4	5	6	7	8	9	10

(i) Nandini is at 45. She gets 34. She will land on ....

(ii) Chirag is at 75. He gets 56. He will land on ....

(iii) Nandini is at 30. She gets 66. She will land on ....

(iv) Chirag is at 89. He gets 63. He will land on ....

Ans. (i) Nandini is at 45. She gets 34. She will land on **79**.

(ii) Chirag is at 75. He gets 56. He will land on **131**.

(iii) Nandini is at 30. She gets 66. She will land on **96**.

(iv) Chirag is at 89. He gets 63. He will land on **152**.

Magic Sums (NCERT Pg 37-42)

Q.13 Nandini and Chirag find some puzzles that Nani Maa had solved.

5	2	8	15
3	1	6	10
9	4	7	20
17	7	21	

Observe the numbers. What do you notice?

Fill the boxes below. In each puzzle, all numbers 1-9 are there. The numbers in each row add up to the number in the box on the right. The numbers in each column add up to the number in the box below.

	5	8	16
			22
1		4	7
11	16	18	

	3		12
	5		15
	7		18
7	15	23	

		6	10
			19
		9	16
10	12	23	

Ans.

3	5	8	16
7	9	6	22
1	2	4	7
11	16	18	

(a)

1	3	8	12
4	5	6	15
2	7	4	18
7	15	23	

(b)
Not possible

1	3	6	10
7	4	8	19
2	5	9	16
10	12	23	

(c)

The sum of magenta and grey boxes are same 45.

(a) Sum of the numbers in the grey boxes

$= 11 + 16 + 18 = 45$

Sum of the numbers in the magenta boxes

$= 16 + 22 + 7 = 45$

(b) Sum of the number in the grey boxes

$= 7 + 15 + 23 = 45$

Sum of the numbers in the magenta boxes

$= 12 + 15 + 18 = 45$

(c) Sum of the numbers in the grey boxes

$= 10 + 12 + 23 = 45$

Sum of the numbers in the magenta boxes

$= 10 + 19 + 16 = 45$

We find the sum of magenta and grey boxes are same as 45.

Q.14 Fill the blanks to complete the Magic square

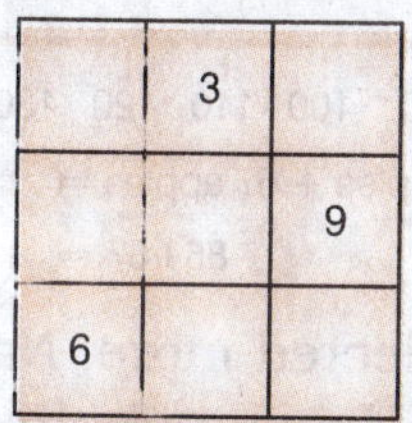

Ans.

8	3	4	15
1	5	9	15
6	7	2	15
15	15	15	45

Q.15 (i) Nani Maa has plucked 25 red radishes and 36 white radishes. How many total radishes has she plucked?

(ii) Nandini starts by drawing the problem on the ground.

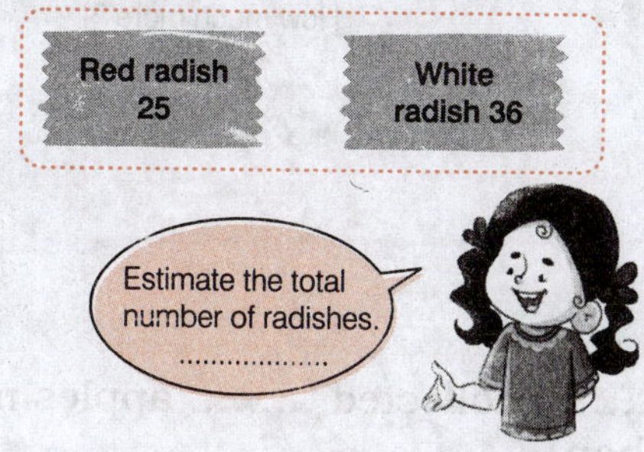

(iii) We need to add 25 and 36 to find the total number of radishes.

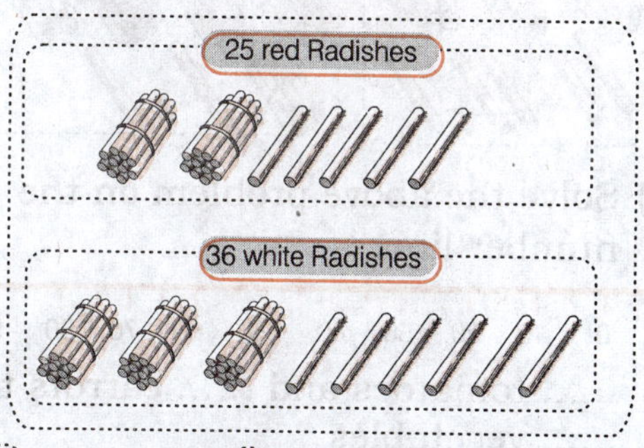

(25) red radishes + (36) white radishes = ( ) radishes

(25) + (36) = ( )

(iv)

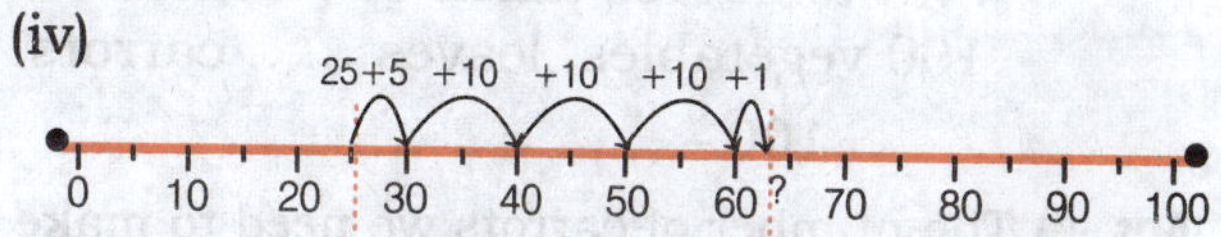

Find other ways of solving the same problem on the number line.

Ans. (i) She plucked total number of radishes is $25 + 36 = 61$.

(ii) The total number of radishes is $25 + 36 = 61$

(iii) (25) red radishes + (36) white radishes = (61) radishes

Or

(25) + (36) = (61)

(iv)

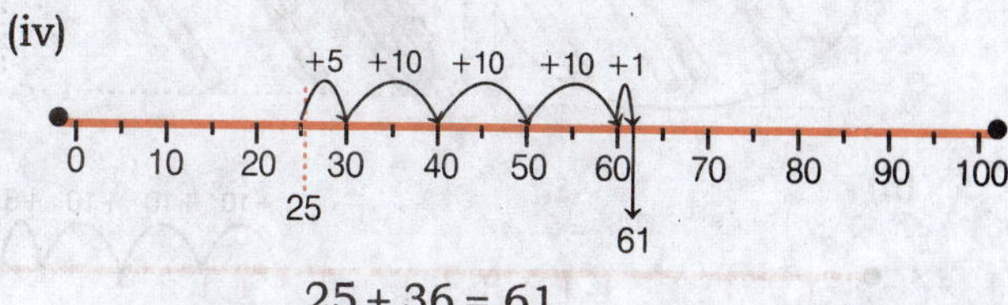

$25 + 36 = 61$

Q.16 (i) Nani Maa puts tomatoes and carrots in a box and writes 100 on it.

Nandini draws the given problem.

Your estimation of carrots ....

Circle the bundle of sticks that shows the correct number of carrots.

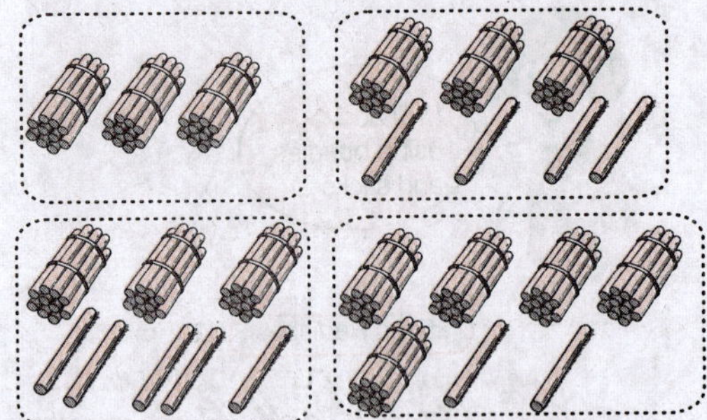

(ii) Solve the above problem on the number line.

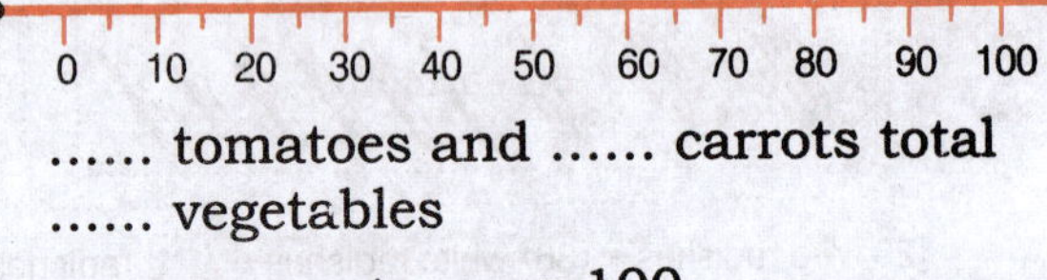

...... tomatoes and ...... carrots total ...... vegetables

...... + ... = 100

...... tomatoes taken out from a box of 100 vegetables, leaves ...... carrots.

100 – ...... = ...

Ans. (i) The number of carrots we need to make 100 vegetables = 100 – 65 = 35

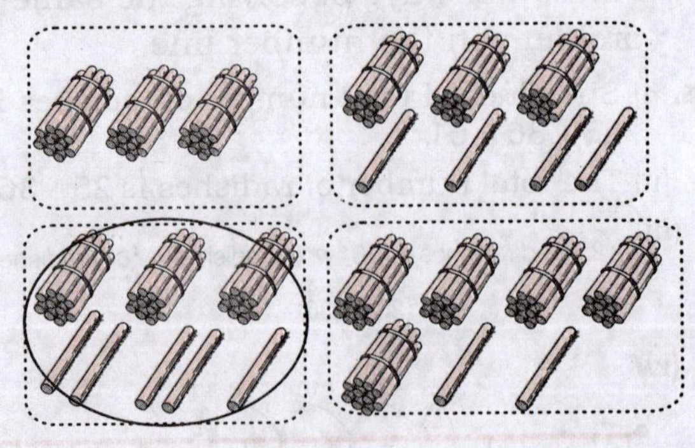

(ii)

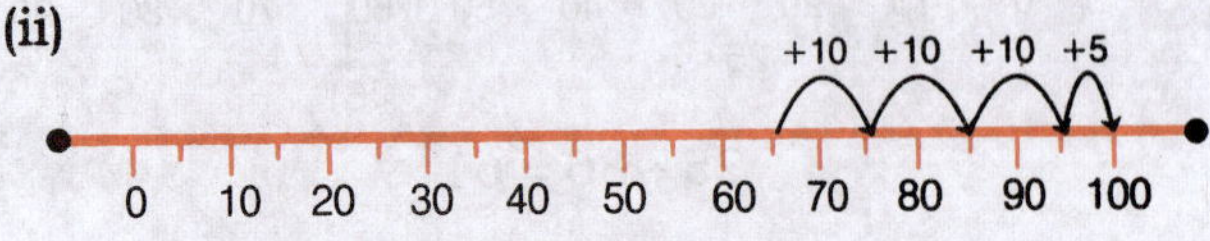

65 tomatoes and 35 carrots

= 100 vegetables

65 + 35 = 100

65 tomatoes taken out from a box of 100 vegetables, leaves 35 carrots.

100 – 65 = 35

Q.17 (i) Nani Maa asks Nandini and Chirag to pluck the ripe apples.

Woho! So many of them.

How many apples in all?

(ii) Try finding out the answer on the number line below.

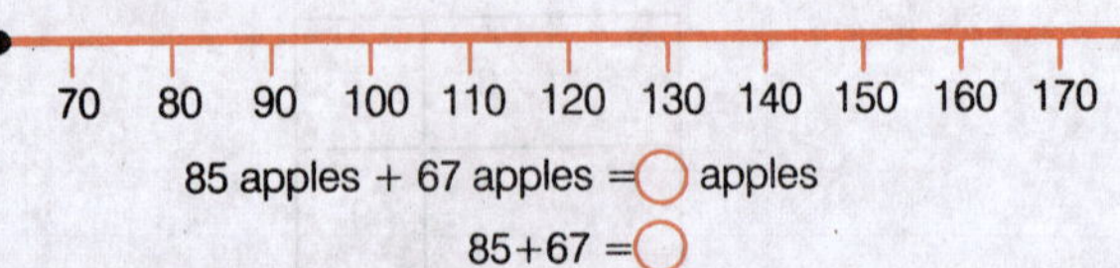

85 apples + 67 apples = ◯ apples

85+67 = ◯

(iii) Who collected more, Nandini or Chirag? How much more?

Chirag draws a box diagram for the problem.

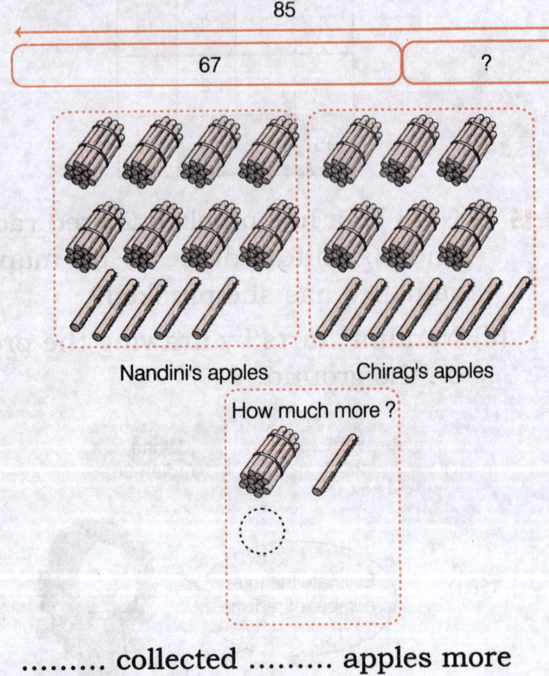

.... collected .... apples more than ....

Ans. (i) Nandini collected 85 apples.

Chirag collected 67 apples.

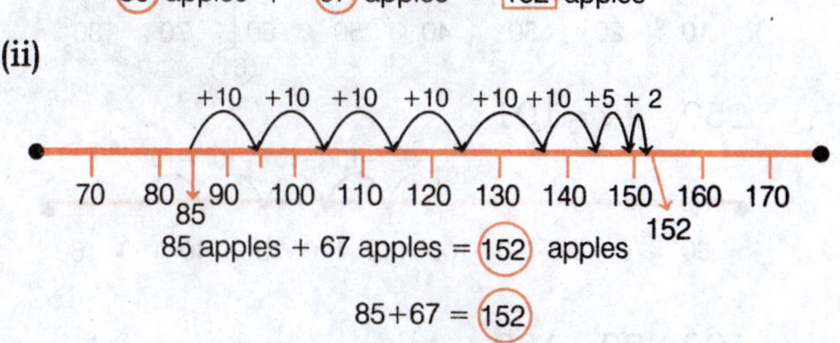

85+67 = 152

(iii)

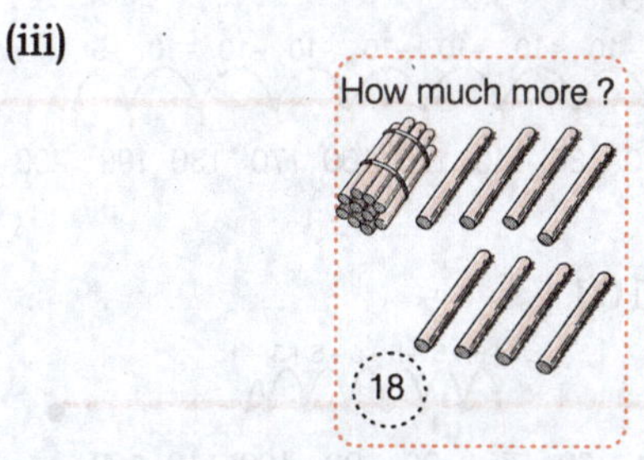

Nandini collected 18 apples more than Chirag.

Q.18 Solve the following problems by first drawing the box diagrams. Use matchstick bundles or a number line to find the answer.

Babli didi sold 34 books on Monday and 45 books on Tuesday. How many books did she sell in the two days? How many more did she sell on Tuesday than on Monday?

Ans. Number of books sold on Monday = 34

Number of books sold on Tuesday = 45

Total number of books sold in the two days

$= 34 + 45 = 79$

Box diagram

← 79 →	
34 books	45 books

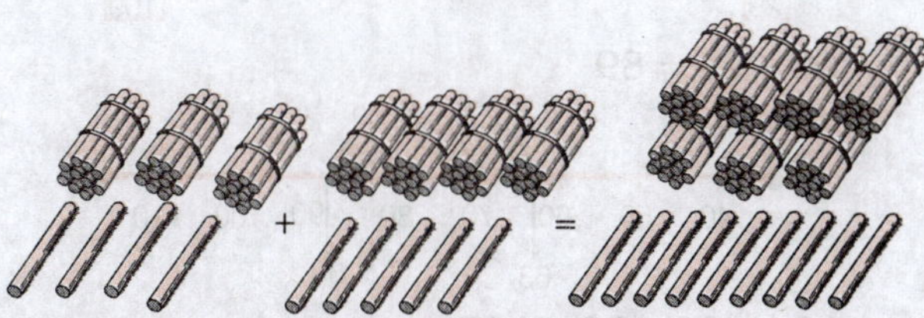

34 books + 45 books = 79 books

Babli didi sold 79 books in the two days.

Number of more books she sold on Tuesday than Monday.

← 45 books →	
34 books	11 books

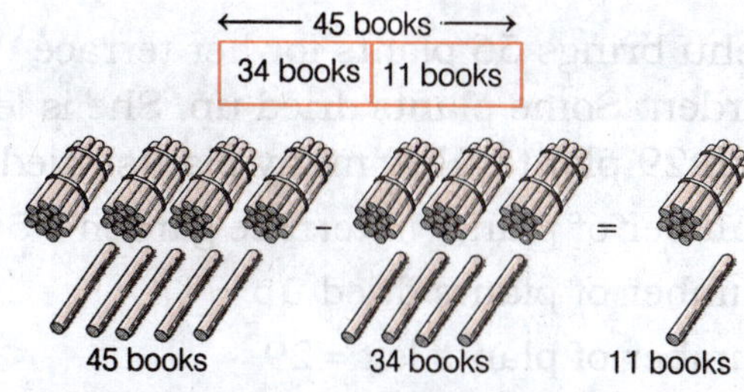

Babli didi sold 11 books more on Tuesday than Monday.

Q.19 In a cricket match at Rosary school, Team Red made 56 runs before lunch and 65 runs after lunch. How many total runs did they make?

Ans. Number of runs made by Team Red before lunch = 56 runs

Number of runs made by Team Red after lunch = 65 runs

Box diagram

← 121 runs →	
56 runs	65 runs

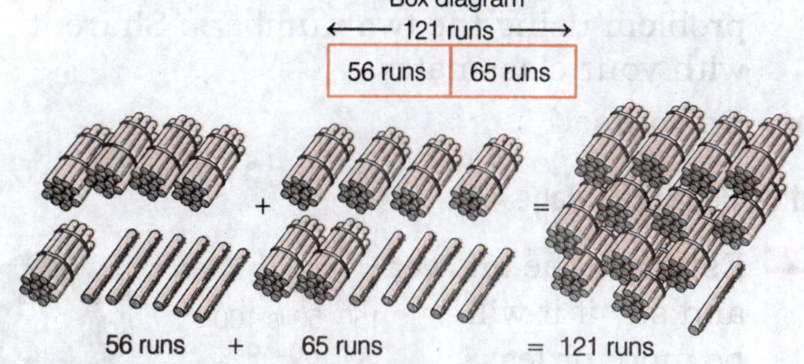

Thus, they make total 121 runs.

Q.20 Rama sells vadas in the school canteen. She has sold 39 Vadas the first day. She sold 12 more the next day. How many vadas did she sell in these two days?

Ans. Number of vadas sold in the school canteen in first day = 39

Number of vadas sold more than first day = 12

Number of vadas sold on the next day

$= 12 + 39 = 51$

Total number of vadas sold by Rama in these two days = $39 + 51 = 90$ Vadas.

39 vadas	51 vadas
90 vadas	

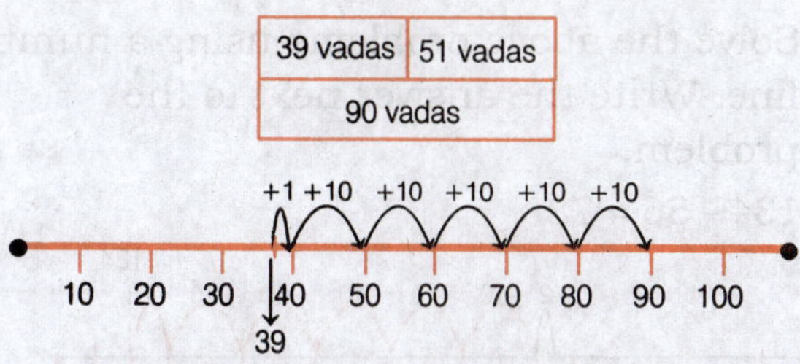

Thus, Rama sold 90 vadas in these two days.

Q.21 Gehu brings 56 plants for her terrace garden. Some plants dried up. She is left with 29 plants. How many plants dried up?

Ans. Number of plants in terrace garden = 56

Number of plants dried up = ☐

Number of plants left = 29

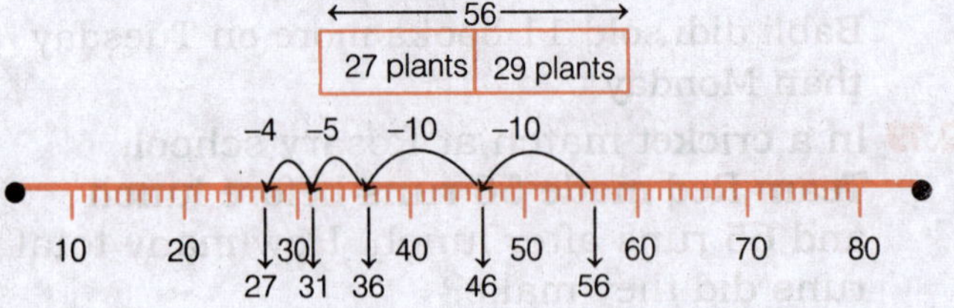

56 plants − 29 plants = 27 plants

Thus, number of plants dried up = 27 plants

Q.22 Choose two numbers. Make a word problem using the two numbers. Share it with your classmates.

Ans. Do yourself.

Lat us Do (NCERT Page 43)

Q.23 Estimate the answer and say if it will be more or less than 100. Match with the correct one.

150–50 is 100. So, 150–49 is more than 100.

Ans.

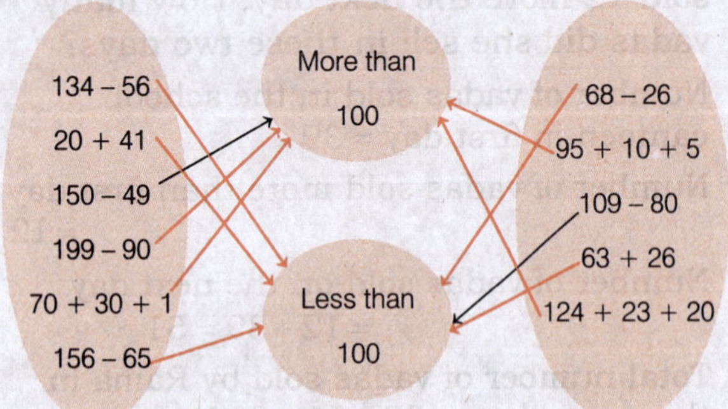

Q.24 Solve the above problems using a number line. Write the answer next to the problem.

Ans. $134 - 56 = 78$

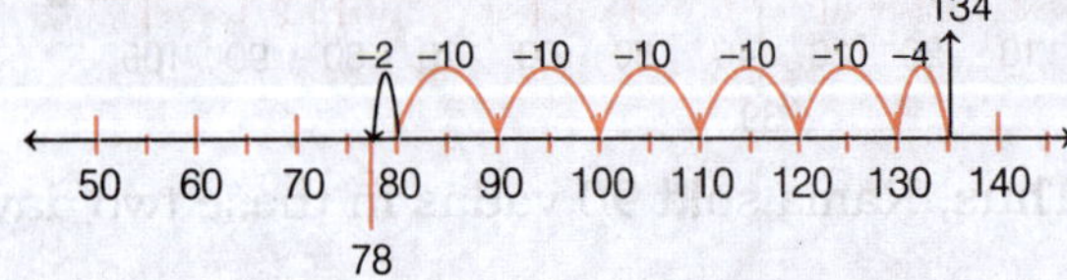

$20 + 41 = 61$

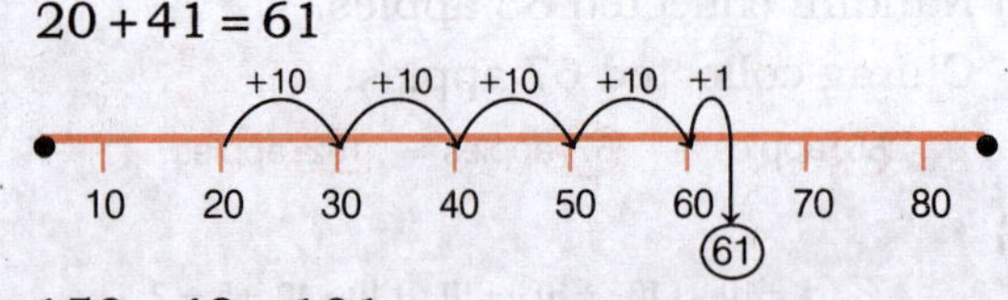

$150 - 49 = 101$

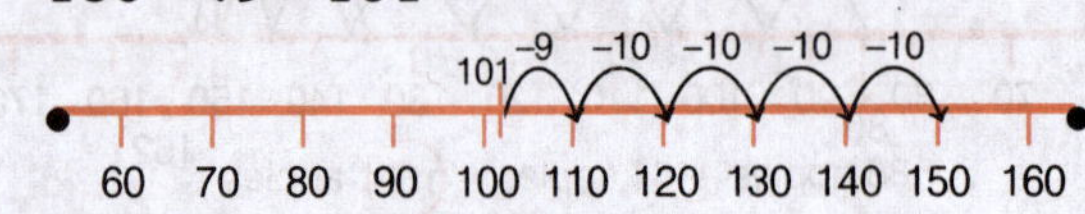

$199 - 90 = 109$

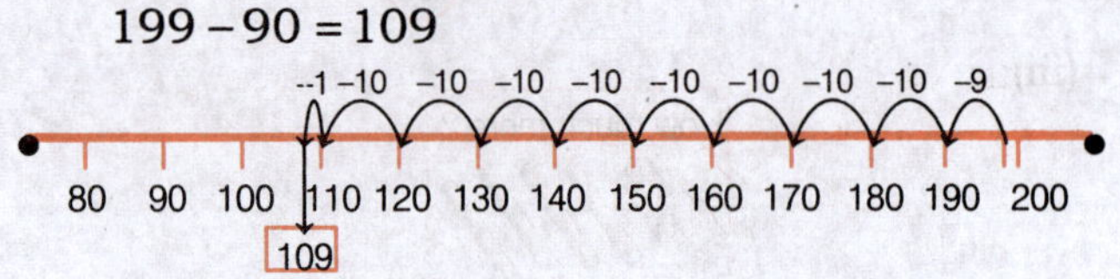

$70 + 30 + 1 = 101$

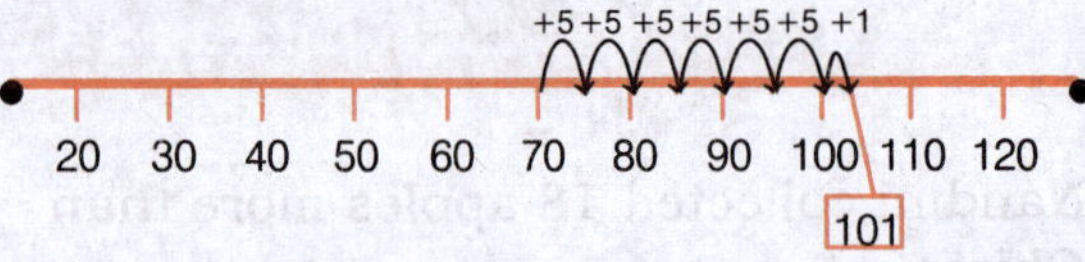

$156 - 65 = 91$

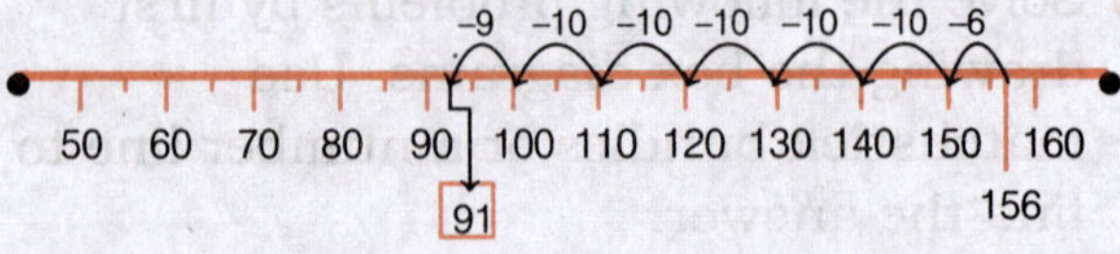

$68 - 26 = 42$

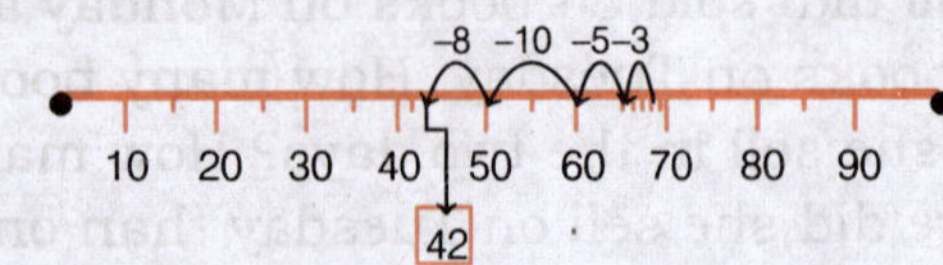

$95 + 10 + 5 = 110$

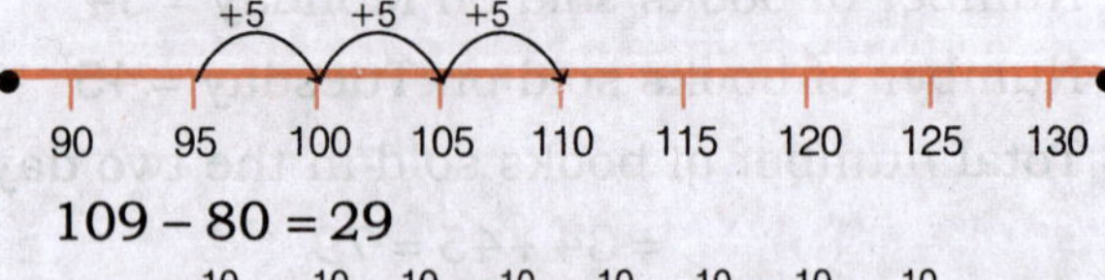

$109 - 80 = 29$

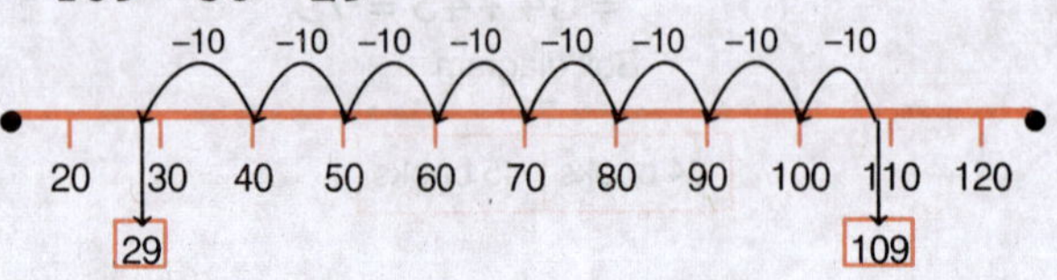

$63 + 26 = 89$

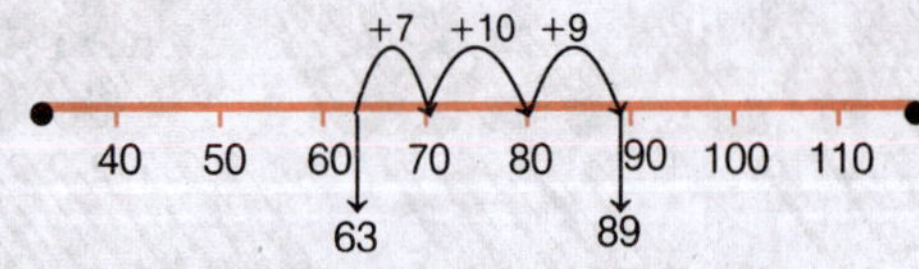

$124 + 23 + 20 = 167$

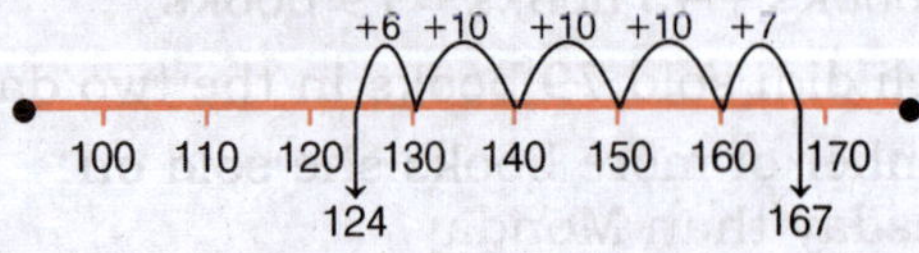

PRACTICE QUESTIONS

1. Multiple choice questions

(i) 21 subtracted from 60 is equal to

(a) 89 (b) 49
(c) 41 (d) 39

(ii) Which of the following is same as $5 + 40 + 2$?

(a) $50 + 4 + 2$ (b) $2 + 50 + 40$
(c) $40 + 7$ (d) $90 + 2$

(iii) $62 - 48$ is equal to

(a) 26 (b) 14
(c) 24 (d) 110

(iv) Which subtraction will give 42 as the answer?

(a) $90 - 52$ (b) $90 - 48$
(c) $90 - 42$ (d) $90 - 28$

(v) Which number will come in the blank circle?

$9 + \bigcirc = 18$

(a) 8 (b) 9
(c) 16 (d) 20

(vi) In which pair of numbers is the second number 20 less than the first number?

(a) 62, 60 (b) 66, 44
(c) 55, 25 (d) 83, 63

(vii) Which number is 18 more than 62?

(a) 80 (b) 70
(c) 56 (d) 44

(viii) Which number will come in the empty place?

$70 - 39 = \bigcirc - 59$

(a) 20
(b) 50
(c) 70
(d) 90

2. Match the following.

(i) $9 - 4$	(a) 10
(ii) $5 + 9$	(b) 8
(iii) $7 + 3$	(c) 5
(iv) $10 - 2$	(d) 14

3. Complete the following number sentences by using number lines.

(i) $35 - 23 = \square$
(ii) $48 - 29 = \square$
(iii) $56 - 17 = \square$
(iv) $50 - 27 = \square$

ANSWERS & SOLUTIONS

1. (i) (d) (ii) (c)
(iii) (b) (iv) (b)
(v) (b) (vi) (d)
(vii) (a) (viii) (d)

2. (i) → (c)
(ii) → (d)
(iii) → (a)
(iv) → (b)

3. (i) $35 - 23 = 12$

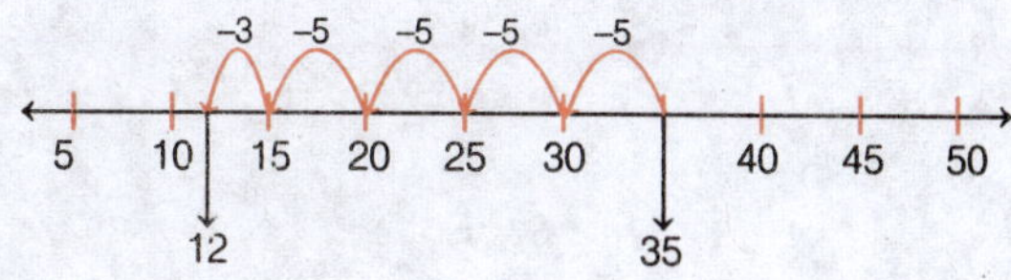

(ii) $48 - 29 = 19$

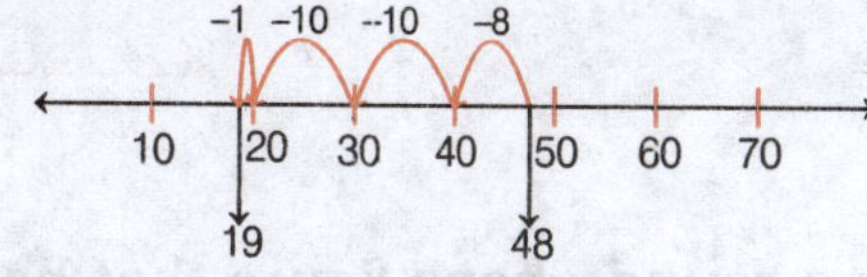

(iii) $56 - 17 = 39$

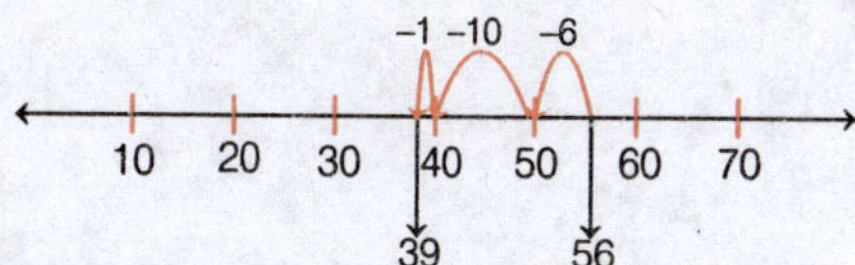

(iv) $50 - 27 = 23$

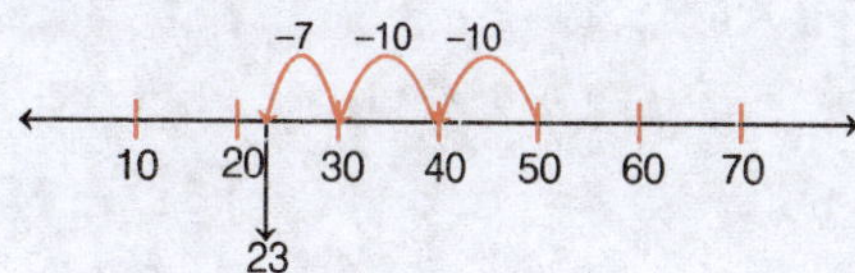

CHAPTER 5 FUN WITH SHAPES

Straight line and curved line

A straight line is a line that connects with two points and extends infinitely in both directions while a curved line is a line that is bent and not straight.

Straight line ________ , Curved line ~~~~~

Square

A square that has four equal sides and four corners.

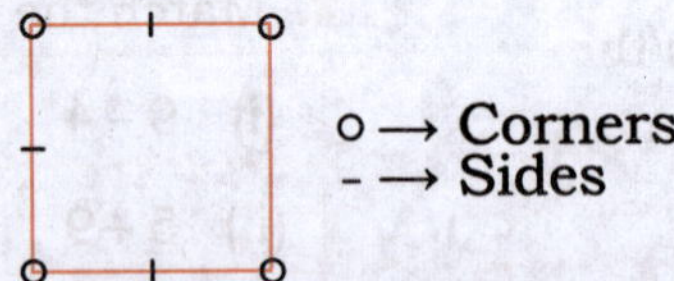

Rectangle

A rectangle is a four-sided shape with four corners and two pairs of opposite sides that are equal in length.

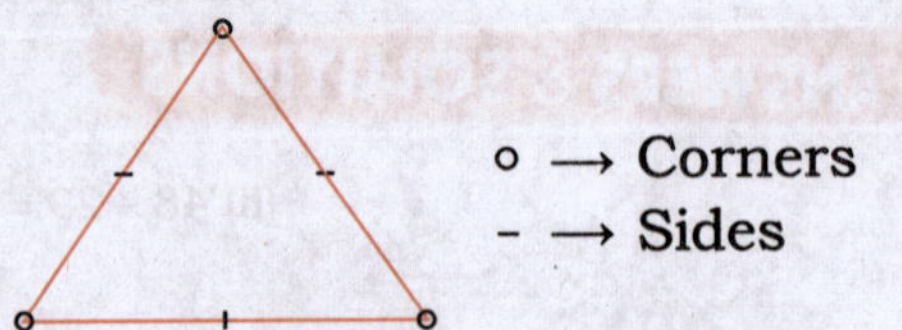

Triangle

A triangle that has three sides and three corners.

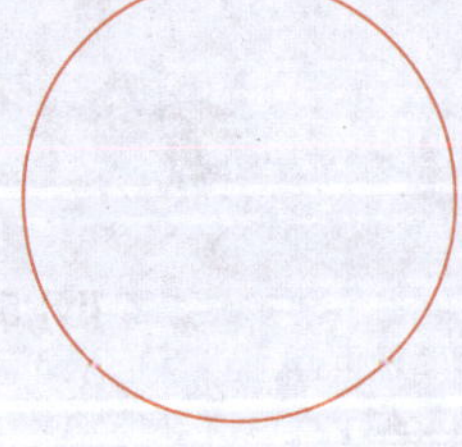

Circle

A circle is a round-shape figure that has no corners.

Let us Do (NCERT Pg 44-45)

Q.1 Make Amma's rangoli on the dots given below.

Ans. *

Q.2 Name the shapes drawn in Amma's rangoli.

Ans. Squares, circles and triangles.

Q.3 How many shapes are made with

(i) curved lines ....

(ii) straight lines ....

Ans. (i) 4 (ii) 10

Q.4 Use cut outs of shapes to make a rangoli design.

Outline the object and colour.

Ans. Do yourself.

Q.5 Try to make the following objects using shape cutouts.

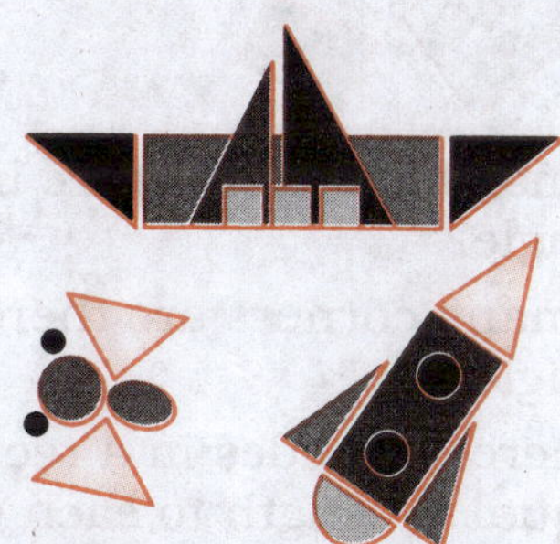

Ans. Do yourself.

Let us Do (NCERT Pg 46)

Q.6 Collect some cardboard boxes and open them up carefully. What shapes do you see in the flattened boxes?

Ans. Do yourself.

Q.7 Make an Envelope. Use a square piece of paper and fold it as shown in the picture.

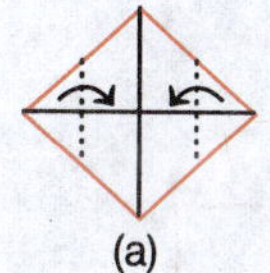
(a)

(b)

(c)

(d)

Ans. Do yourself.

Baking Biscuits (NCERT Pg 47)

Q.8

Why did the two children get different shapes? Discuss.

Ans. Two children get different shapes because wooden box and matchbox are different in shapes.

Q.9 Name any three objects that have rectangular faces.

Ans. * Lunch box, matchbox and pencil box that have rectangular faces.

** Students can write alternate answer as per their choice.*

Let us Do (NCERT Pg 48-50)

Q.10 Trace all the faces of any cuboidal object. (example - sharpener or eraser)

(i) How many different faces did you get?

(ii) What shapes are these faces?

(iii) Did you get a square?

(iv) Can you get six different rectangles by tracing a cuboid?

(v) Can a cuboid have a face like a triangle?

(vi) The faces of a cuboid are .... or .... in shape.

Ans. * Let take a eraser which has cuboidal shape.

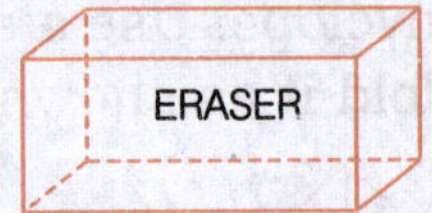

All the faces of this eraser are

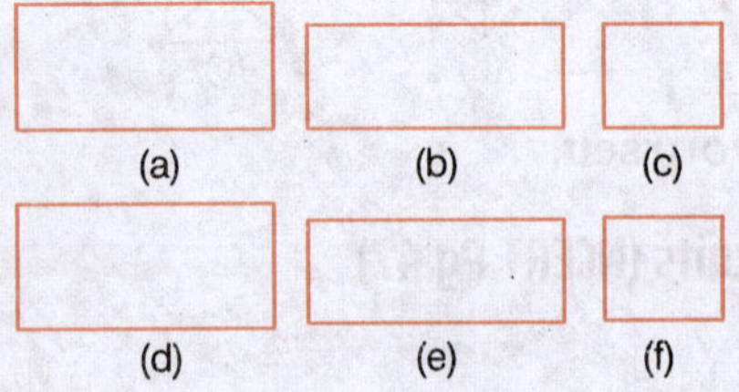

(i) Total number of faces = 6

∵ There are 3 faces are same as other 3 faces. (top and bottom face, front and back face, left side and right side face).

∴ Number of different faces = 3

(ii) Rectangle (iii) No

(iv) No (v) No

(vi) rectangle, square

Q.11 Construct the rectangles using the sides given below.

Ans.

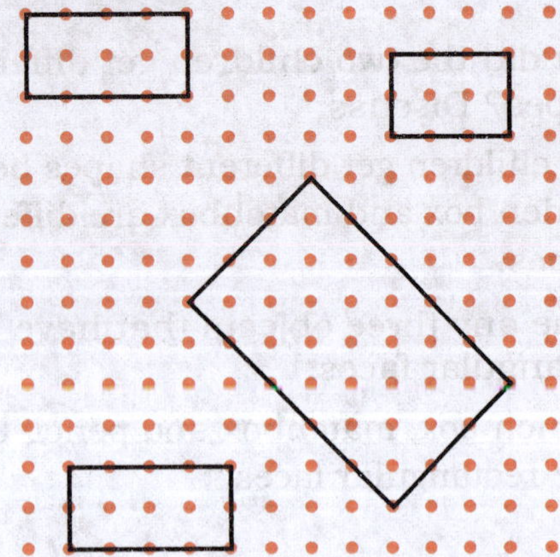

Q.12 Draw 3 bigger rectangles around this small rectangle.

Ans.

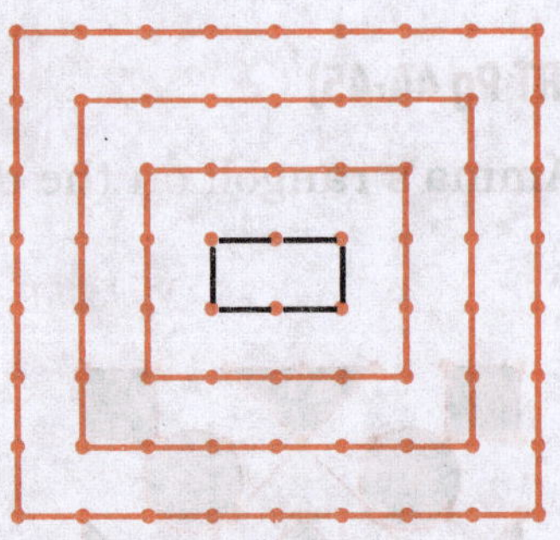

Q.13 Count and write the number of rectangles in the following picture.

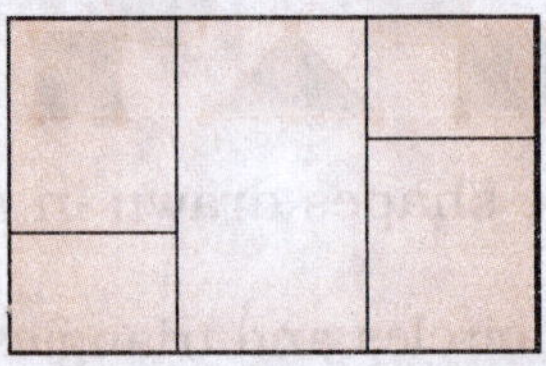

Ans. Total number of rectangles in the given picture is 10.

Q.14 Look at the different rectangles given below and answer the following questions.

(i) How many sides are there in a rectangle?

(ii) How many corners are there in a rectangle?

(iii) Are there any sides in a rectangle that are equal in length to each other?

(iv) What do you notice in a rectangle? Describe it in your own words.

Ans. (i) 4 (ii) 4

(iii) Yes, opposite sides in a rectangle are equal to each other.

(iv) In a rectangle, there are 4 sides and 4 corners. Also, the opposite sides of a rectangle are equal in length.

Same to Same (NCERT Pg 51)

Q.15

(i) Both have .... sides.

(ii) Both have .... corners.

Ans. (i) 4

(ii) 4

Q.16 How many squares do you see in this drawing?

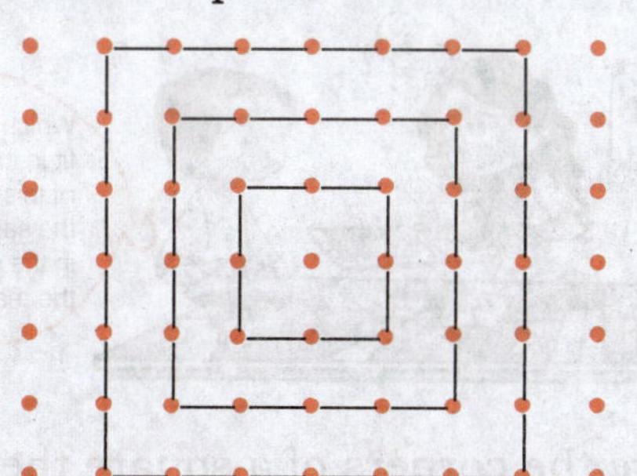

Ans. Total number of squares is 6.

Let us Do (NCERT Pg 52-53)

Q.17 Here is a square. Draw 2 bigger squares around this square.

Ans.

Q.18 Use matchsticks to make a square so that it has squares on all its sides. How many squares did you get?

Ans.

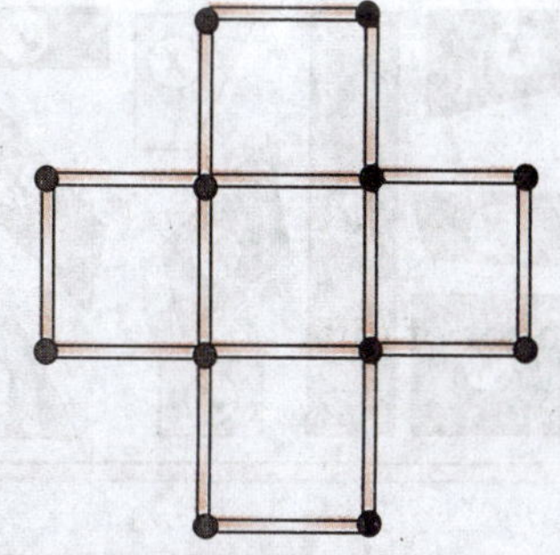

Total squares, we get 5.

Q.19 Complete the squares using the sides given below.

Ans.

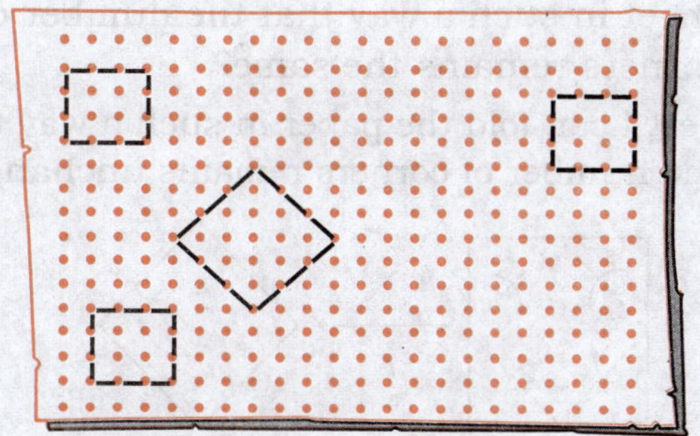

Q.20 Use the square cutouts from the book to do this activity.

How many different shapes can you make by joining

(i) 2 squares (ii) 3 squares (iii) 4 squares

Show them in a dot grid. Some dot grids are provided in the back of the book.

Ans. Do yourself.

Let us Explore (NCERT Pg 53)

Q.21 Tick (✓) the shapes that are rectangles.

Which figures are not rectangles? Explain why.

Ans.

The figures which are not rectangles have been shown by cross (✗) sign. Because opposite sides are not equal.

Q.22 Can you fold all the corners of a square sheet in such a way that the number of corners remains the same?

Ans. Yes, I can fold the paper in such a way that the number of corners remains unchanged.

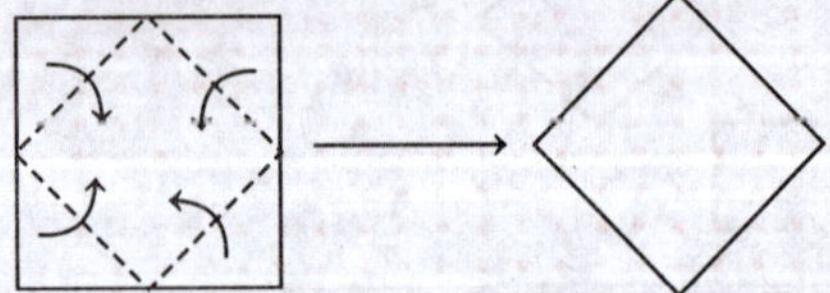

Q.23 (i) Make a square on a cardboard sheet and cut along the dotted lines marked on the square as shown to get 4 triangles. Make as many different shapes as possible by joining three triangles together. How many shapes can you make?

(ii) Now, try with four triangles together.

Ans. *(i)

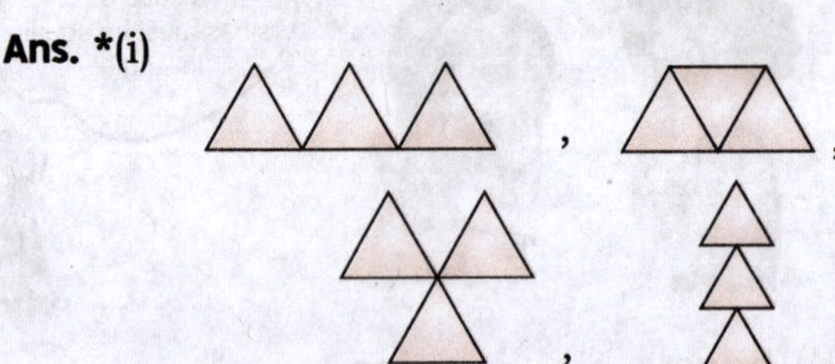

Thus, I make 4 different shapes by joining three triangles together.

*(ii)

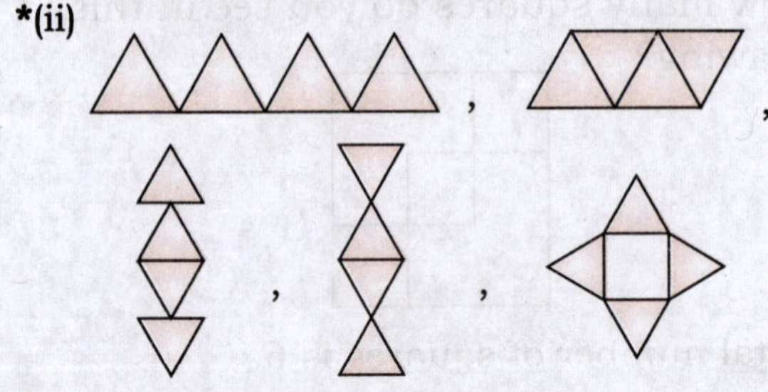

Square Corners (NCERT Pg 54-55)

Q.24

(i) Are the corners of a square the same?

(ii) How do you know?

(iii) Pile up some squares over one another and see.

(iv) Are the corners of a rectangle the same?

(v) How do you know?

(vi) Pile up some rectangles over one another and see.

(vii) Are the corners of the square and a rectangle the same?

(viii) Name some objects in your class that have only square corners.

Ans. (i) Yes, the corners of square are same.

(ii) The corners are perfect L shaped.

(iii) Do yourself.

(iv) Yes, the corners of a rectangle will remain same.

(v) The corners of rectangle are perfect L shaped.

(vi) Do yourself.

(vii) Yes, the corners of the square and a rectangle will remain same.

*(viii) Board, lunch box, window, box etc.

Let us Do (NCERT Pg 55-56)

Q.25 You can join two paper strips to show different corners.

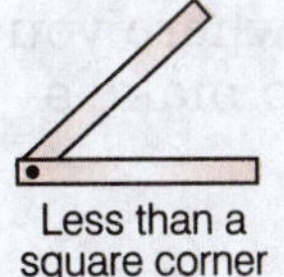

Less than a square corner

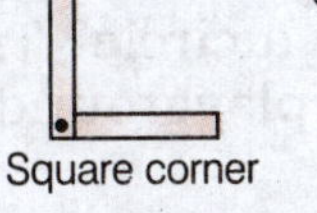

Square corner

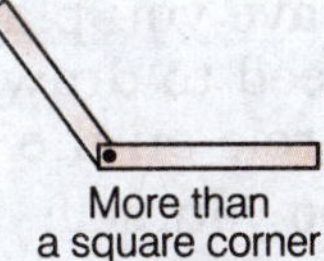

More than a square corner

Use the strips to show a square corner, more than a square corner and less than a square corner.

Can you use the strip to check whether the corner of your table and the board are square corners?

Ans. Do yourself.

Q.26 Mark the square corners in these shapes.

Ans.

Q.27 Connect the dots to make some squares. How many different squares did you get?

Ans.

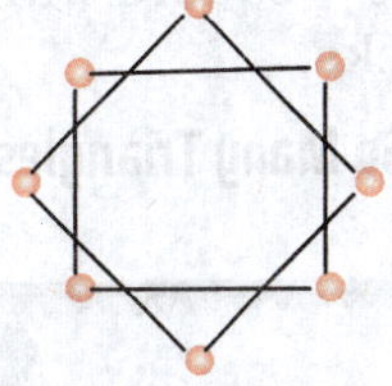

Thus, I get 2 different squares.

Q.28 Look at the picture given below and answer the following.

(i) Count and write the number of corners.

(ii) Circle the square corners.

Ans. (i) Number of corners is 17.

*(ii)

Q.29 Use two matchsticks to make two square corners and then four square corners. Draw and show it in the space given below.

Ans. Do yourself.

Q.30 Murugan made three squares with 10 matchsticks.

How many squares can you make with 12 matchsticks?

Ans. We can make 4 square with 12 matchsticks.

Triangle-Triangle ... So Many Triangles (NCERT Pg 57)

Q.31

Describe a triangle

Triangles have .... sides. They have .... corners.

Ans. Triangle have 3 sides. They have 3 corners.

Let us Do (NCERT Pg 57)

Q.32 Draw and name some triangular objects that you see around you, in your notebook.

Ans. Do yourself.

Q.33 Count the number of triangles in the given rangoli.

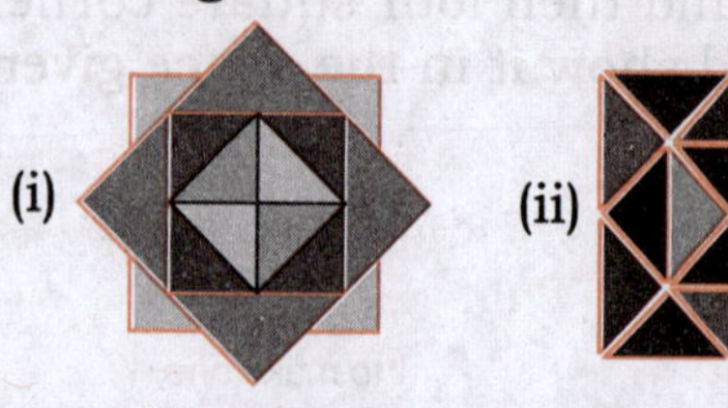

Ans. (i) 20 (ii) 16

Q.34 How many different triangles can be made using the dots on this circle?

Ans. 4

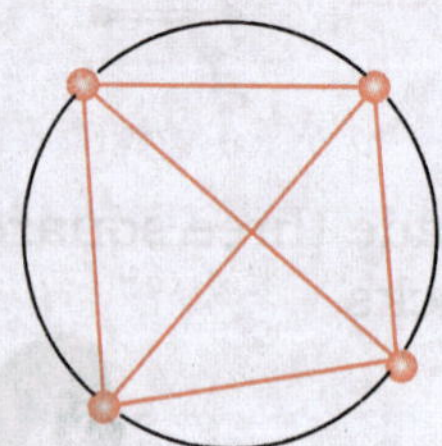

Q.35 Move two matchsticks to turn the one triangle into two triangles.

Ans. *

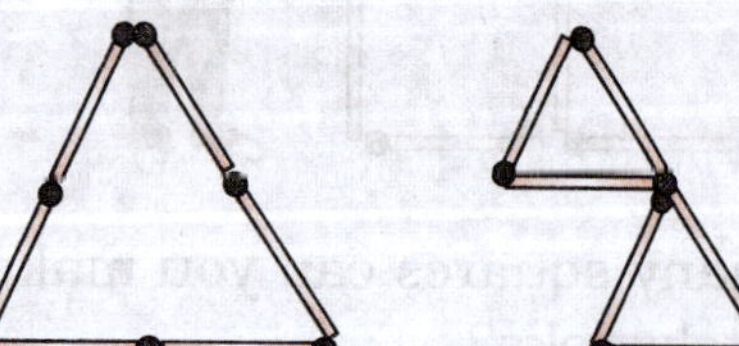

Let us Discuss (NCERT Pg 58)

Q.36 Have you been to a circus?

Ans. Yes.

Q.37 What does a circle look like? How is a circle different from a rectangle?

Ans. A circle is round in shape. A circle has no straight lines and no corners where as a rectangle has two pairs of straight lines and 4 corners.

Let us Do (NCERT Pg 58-60)

Q.38 Name some objects that are like circles.

Ans. *Bangles, ring, coin, wheel etc.

Q.39 Draw colourful circles to complete the circus scene.

Ans. Do yourself.

Q.40 Draw circles by tracing bottle caps, bangles and rings in your notebook.

Ans. Do yourself.

Q.41 Have you played any game where you need to draw a circle? Try to make a circle on the playground.

Ans. Do yourself.

Let us Do (NCERT Pg 60-62)

Q.42 Look at these two shapes and discuss their similarities and differences. Choose the appropriate word.

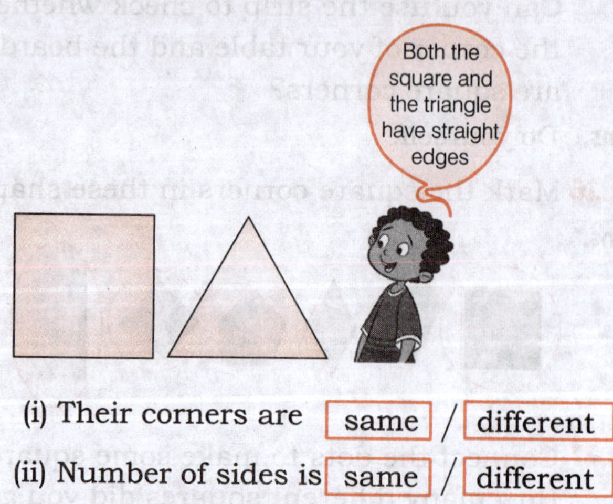

(i) Their corners are same / different

(ii) Number of sides is same / different

Ans. (i) Their corners are different.

(ii) Number of sides are different.

Q.43 Choose any pair of shapes. Share the similarities and differences in these shapes with your friends.

Ans. **Similarities** The edges of each shapes are straight lines.

Differences The number of sides in each shapes are different.

Q.44 Find the largest rectangle in these shapes.

Ans.

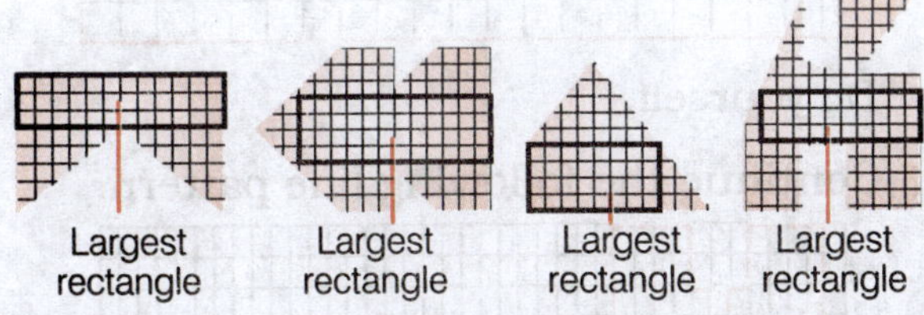

Q.45 (i) I made one triangle. Then, I made another row of triangles. How many triangles are there in the second figure?

(ii) If I make one more row, how many triangles will be there in the third figure?

Ans. (i) 3 triangles are in the second figures.

(ii)

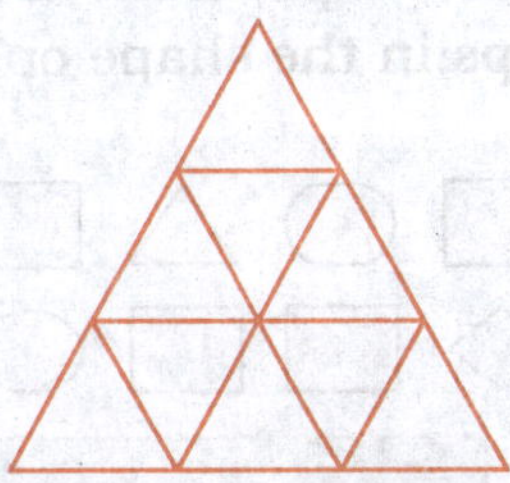

Number of triangles in the third figure = 6

Q.46 Here are some rectangles that are torn. How many square pieces have been torn from each shape?

Ans. Number of square pieces have been torn from each shape.

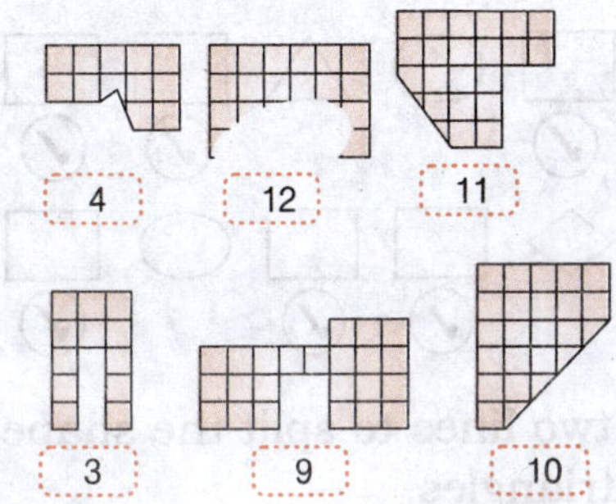

Q.47 Each of these shapes can be the odd one out.

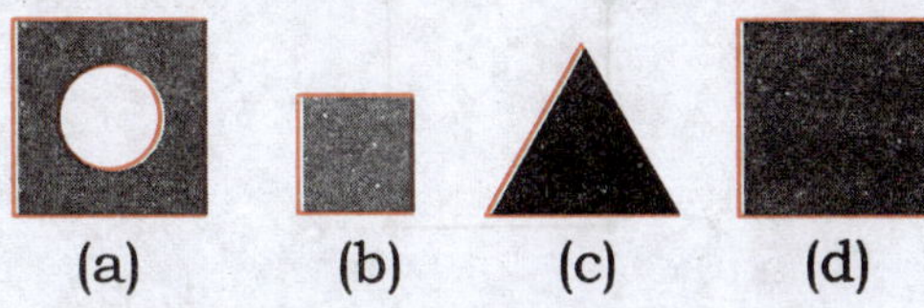

How is each one odd? Discuss.

Ans. * **Figure (a) (Circle within a square)** The shape is unique because it contains both a square and a circle, whereas all other shapes are singular shapes.

Figure (b) It is the shape of a small square.

Figure (c) It is the only shape with three sides and three corners, while the others have four sides.

Figure (d) It is the shape of a square which is large in size.

Q.48 To complete the rectangle, tick (✓) the appropriate shapes from the left side to fill the gaps in the shape on the right side.

Ans.

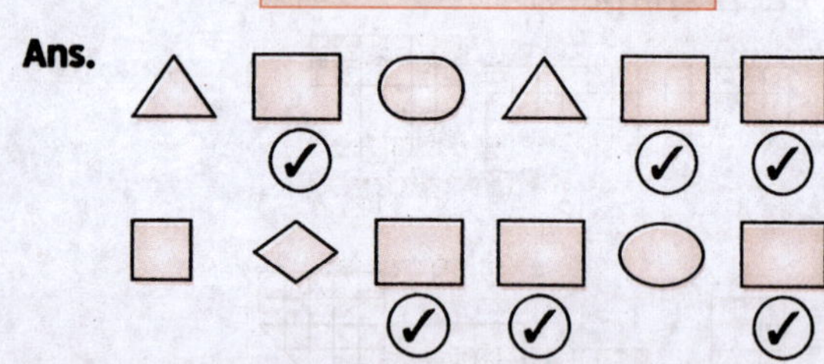

Q.49 Draw two lines to split the shape into three triangles.

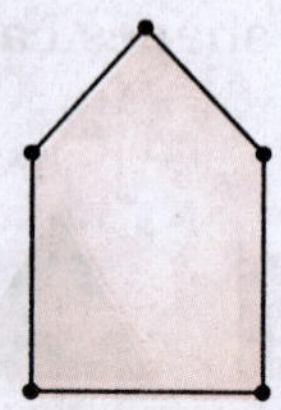

Ans. *

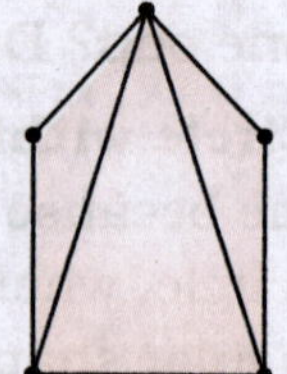

Q.50 Draw one line to split the shape into 3 triangles.

Ans.

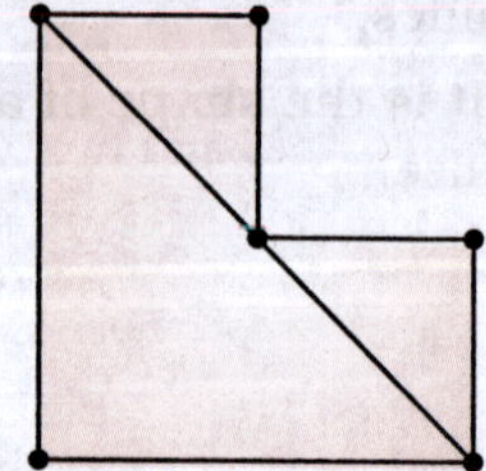

Q.51 Make the following shapes with different sizes and orientations (angular positions) in your notebook.

(i) Triangle (ii) Rectangle

(iii) Circle (iv) Other shape

Ans.

(i) Triangle 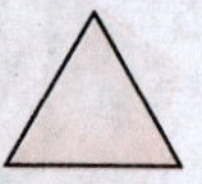

(ii) Rectangle 

(iii) Circle 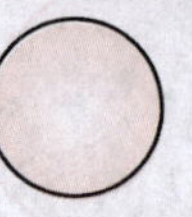

(iv) Other shape 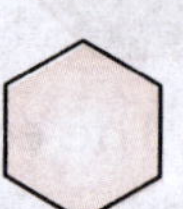

Doors-Dots-Lines (NCERT Pg 63)

Q.52 Try to make your own border designs using both curved and straight lines.

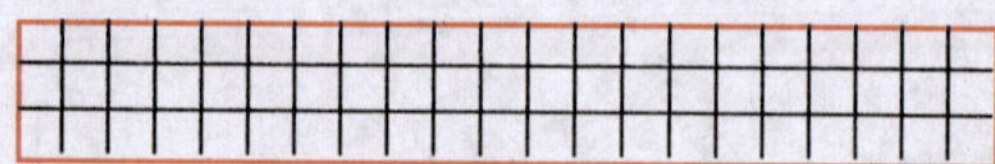

Ans. Do yourself.

Q.53 Continue the following line pattern.

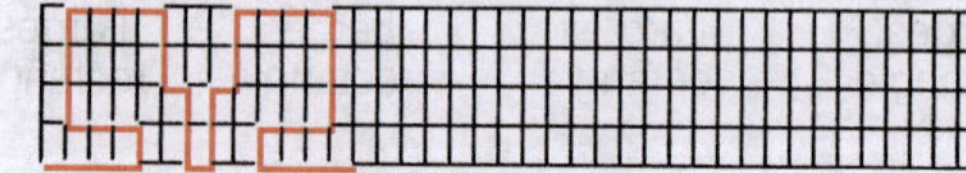

Ans.

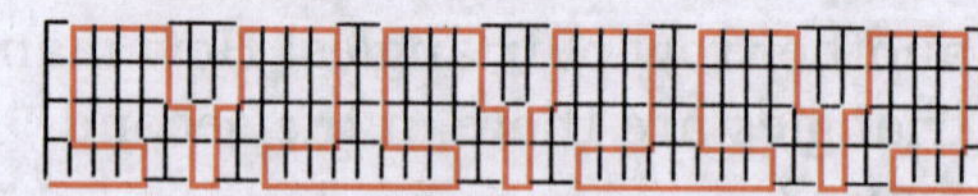

Tangram

Q.54 Use the pieces from the tangram puzzle given in the end of the book. Can you create these shapes using some of the pieces?

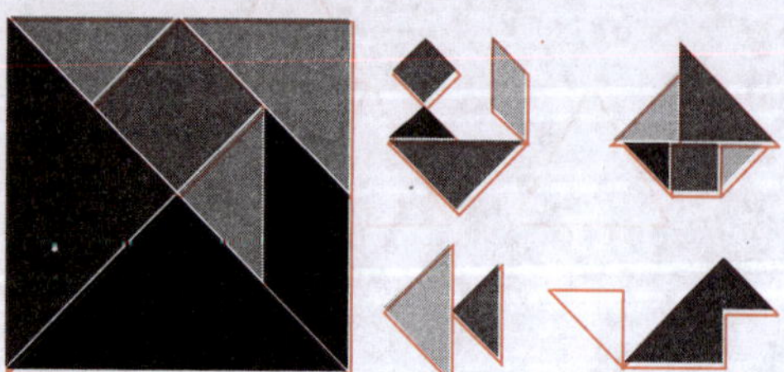

Ans. Do yourself.

PRACTICE QUESTIONS

1. True or False.
   (i) All squares are rectangles.
   (ii) All rectangles are squares.
   (iii) A triangle always has three sides.
   (iv) A circle has one curved line with no corners.

2. Multiple choice questions.
   (i) Which of the following is in the shape of a rectangle?
   (a) a pencil (b) a postcard
   (c) a samosa (d) a cricket ball
   (ii) If a square has 4 corners, how many corners will be there, when two squares are overlapping?
   (a) 8 (b) 6 (c) 4 (d) 10
   (iii) Which box contains three squares?

(a) 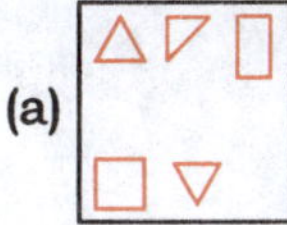

(b) 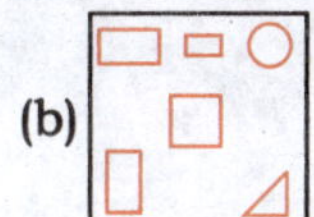

(c) 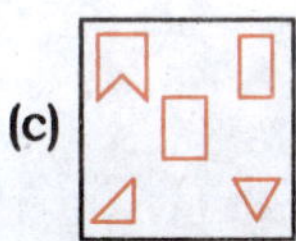

(d) 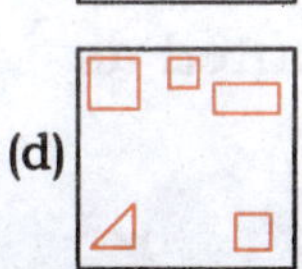

   (iv) The shape has 4 corners.

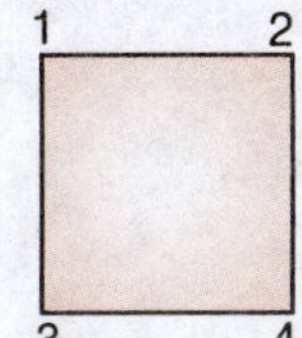

Which shape below has exactly 3 corners?

(a) (b)

(c) (d)

3. Match the following shapes with their properties.

	Column A		Column B
(i)	Square	(a)	has no corners.
(ii)	Rectangle	(b)	has 3 sides.
(iii)	Triangle	(c)	has 2 long and 2 short sides.
(iv)	Circle	(d)	has 4 equal sides.

4. Look at the picture of a house made with shapes.

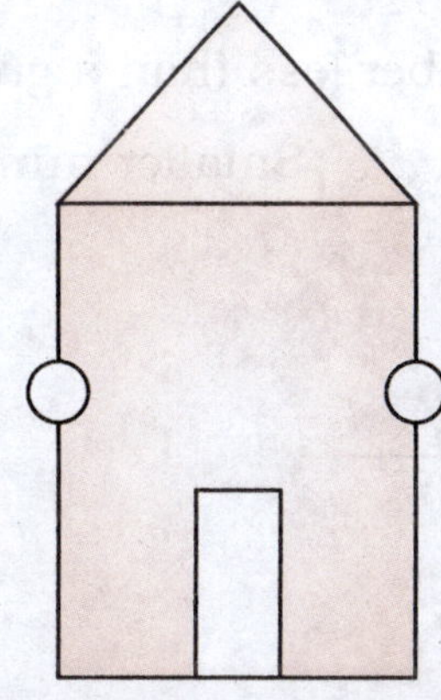

How many different shapes can you identify in the picture? list them.

ANSWERS & SOLUTIONS

1. (i) True (ii) False
   (iii) True (iv) True
2. (i) (b) (ii) (c)
   (iii) (d) (iv) (a)
3. (i) (d) (ii) (c)
   (iii) (b) (iv) (a)
4. In the given picture of the house, we can see following different shape.
   (i) Triangle
   (ii) Rectangle
   (iii) Circle
   In the given picture, there are one triangle shape and two circle shapes and two rectangle shapes in different sizes that is a small rectangle and a large rectangle.

CHAPTER 6 HOUSE OF HUNDREDS-I

In this chapter, we learn to count objects beyond 200 as earlier using the same number names and comparing the numbers.

Comparing and Ordering Numbers

Comparing and ordering numbers is to compare the numbers according to their values and identify the smallest and greatest numbers and order them in smallest to greatest and greatest to smallest.

Use of Less than (<) and Greater than (>)

The less than (<) and greater than (>) symbols are used to compare given two numbers. A greater number greater than a smaller number is represented as

Greater Number > Smaller Number.

e.g. 274 > 143

A smaller number less than a greater number is represented as

Smaller number < Greater number.

e.g. 374 < 474

NCERT FOLDER

NCERT Pg 64

Q.1

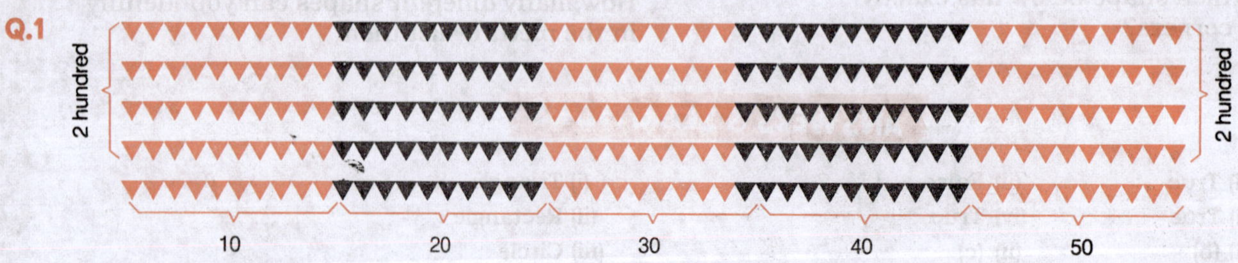

How many triangles are there in a line of triangular toran?

Ans. Number of triangles in a line of triangular toran are 50.

** Students can write alternate answer as per their choice.*

Let us Do (NCERT Pg 66-68)

Q.2 Jojo is jumping on a tiled path inside the mela. Fill in the empty tiles with numbers.

Ans.

Q.3 Fill in the blanks with the correct numbers.

Ans. (i)

291 292 293 294 295 296 297 298 299 300

301 302 303 304 305 306 307 308 309 310

(ii)

(iii)

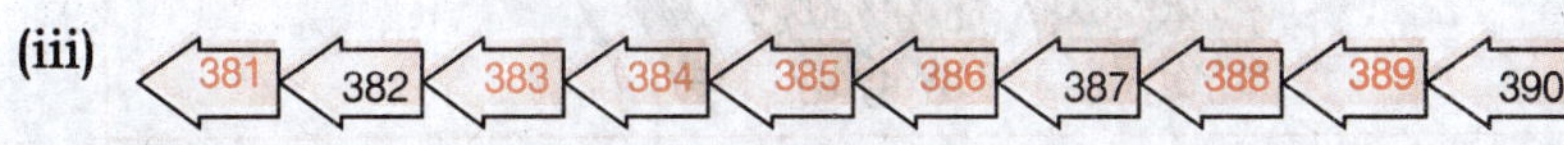

Q.4 Ants have found food on the ground. Guess how many ants there are. Count and check.

Ans. There are 127 ants.

Q.5 Teji and Jojo have learnt to write numbers with the help of matchstick bundles. They can also write number sentences in more than one way. Fill in the blanks appropriately.

Ans.

Matchsticks	Number	Number sentence
	235	200 and 35 more (200 + 35) 15 less than 250 (250 – 15)
	300	300 and 0 more (300 + 0) 50 less than 350 (350 – 50)
	228	200 and 28 more (200 + 28) 22 less than 250 (250 – 22)
	316	300 and 16 more (300 + 16) 34 less than 350 (350 – 34)
	109	100 and 9 more (100 + 9) 41 less than 150 (150 – 41)

Q.6 Place the numbers given above on the number line.

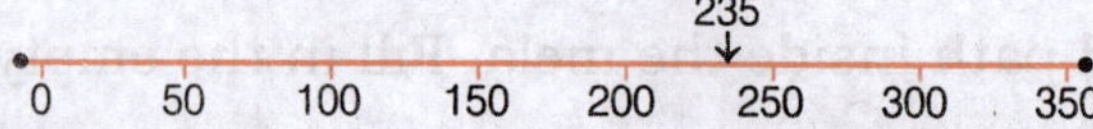

235 lies between 200 and 250.

Ans. Place the numbers given above (300, 228, 316, 109) on number line.

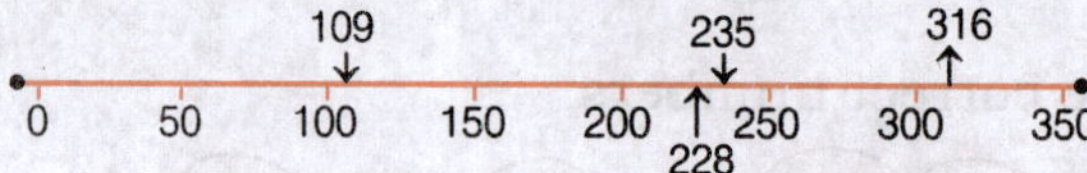

Q.7 Look at the pictures and write the corresponding numbers.

Ans.

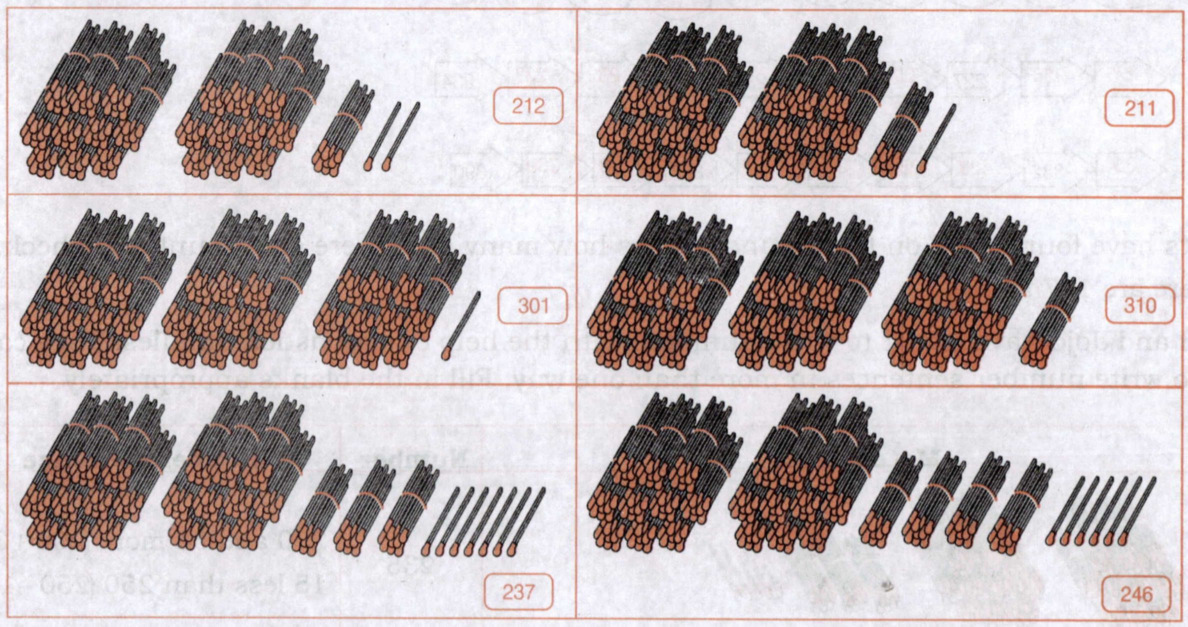

Q.8 Make the number slider as shown in the picture. Increase or decrease the number as given below.

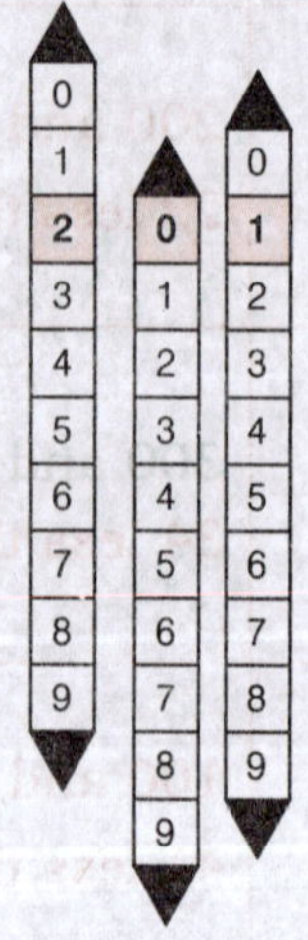

Ans. (i) 285-increase the number by one

286

(ii) 147-increase the number by ten

157

(iii) 367-decrease the number by 2

365

(iv) 289-decrease the number by 10

279

(v) 290-increase the number by 20

310

Magical Count (NCERT Pg 70)

Q.9 Write down any number name. Count the number of letters in that number name and write the name of that new number down. Keep repeating – what happens?

Ans.

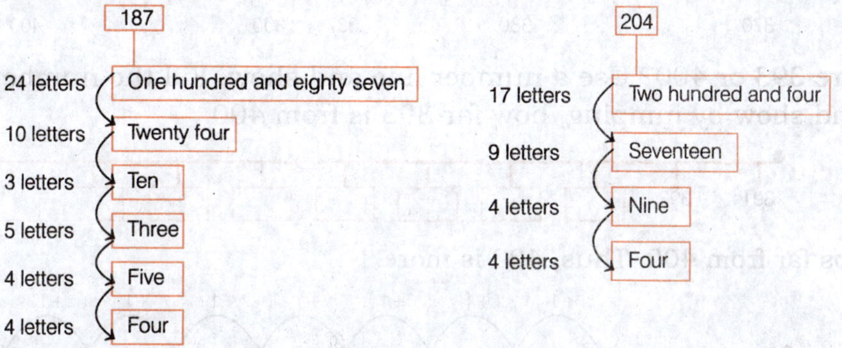

Yes, it always end with four.

Numbers on a Line (NCERT Pg 70)

Q.10 What will be the next hundred number. Write it on the number line below. Can you show the number using matchsticks?

0 100 200 300

Ans. Yes, I can show the number using 4 bundles of 100 matchsticks. So, total number of matchsticks is 400.

0 100 200 300 400

Let us Do (NCERT Pg 71-72)

Q.11 Teji and Jojo are trying to put their numbers on the following number lines. Locate 216, 243, 257 on the number line below.

200 210 220 230 240 250 260

Ans.

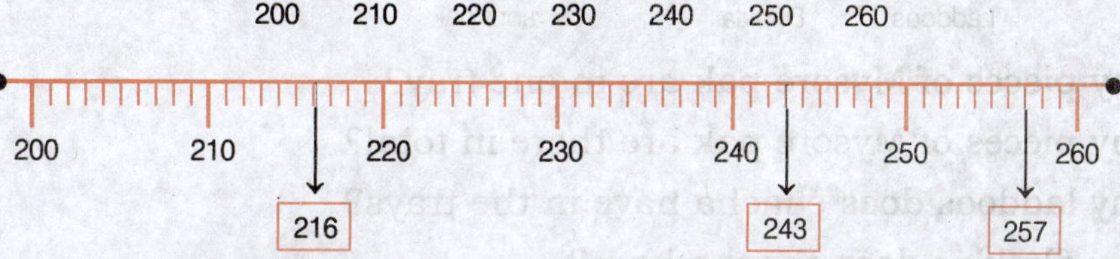

Q.12 Locate 329, 332, 337, 375 and 387 on the number line below.

320 330 370

Ans.

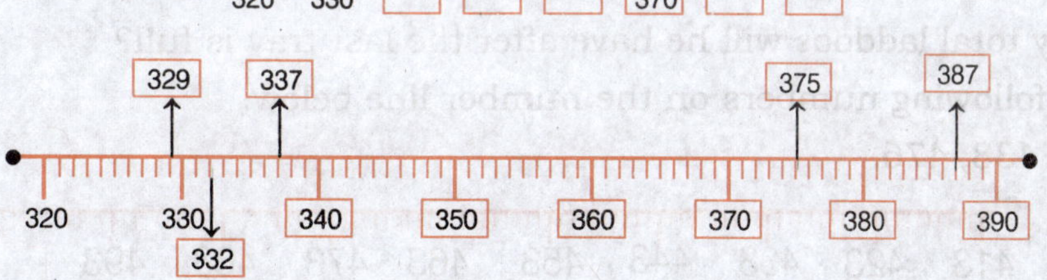

Q.13 Tell how far is 387 from 400.

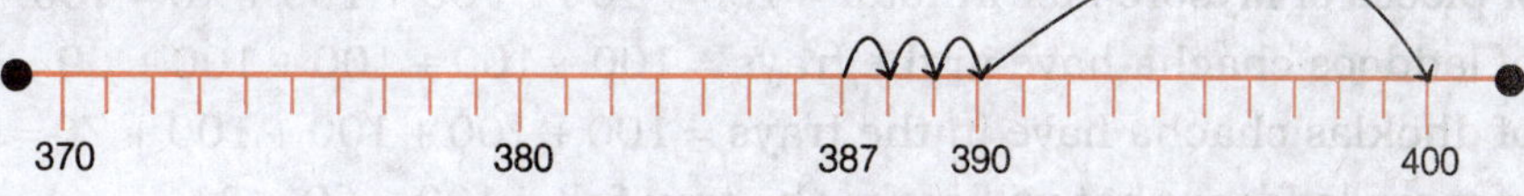

Ans. 387 is 13 steps far from 400.

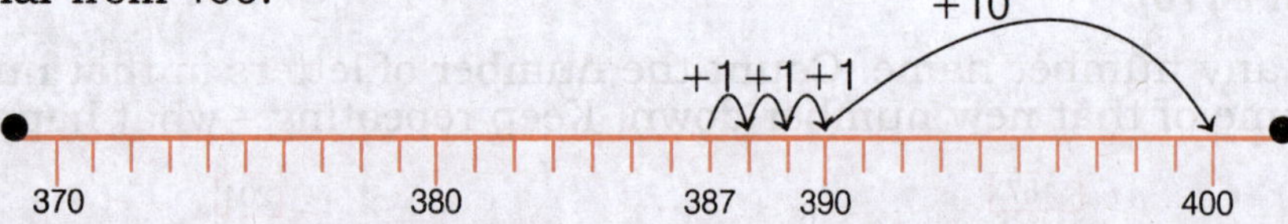

Q.14 Which is more 393 or 400? Use a number line and show. Fill the numbers on the number line below and show by jumping, how far 393 is from 400.

Ans. 393 is 7 steps far from 400. Thus, 400 is more.

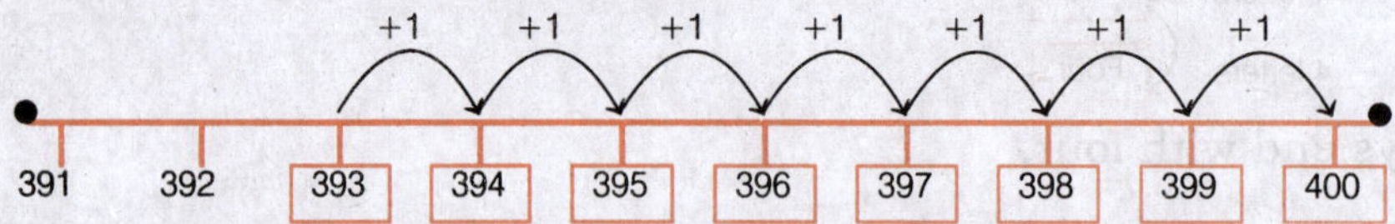

Q.15 Teji and Jojo are hungry after all the running around. They go to Farooq Chacha's sweet shop.

(i) How many pieces of Mysore pak are in one tray?

(ii) How many pieces of Mysore pak are there in total?

(iii) How many laddoos does chacha have in the trays?

(iv) How many dhoklas does chacha have?

(v) Chacha is going to fill the tray with more laddoos. How many more laddoos will make the tray full?

(vi) How many total laddoos will he have after the last tray is full?

(vii) Mark the following numbers on the number line below.
423, 487, 438, 476.

Ans. (i) Number of pieces of Mysore Pak in one tray are 100.

(ii) Number of pieces of Mysore Pak in total = 100 + 100 + 100 + 100 + 45 = 400 + 45 = 445

(iii) Number of laddoos chacha have in the trays = 100 + 100 + 100 + 100 + 69 = 400 + 69 = 469

(iv) Number of dhoklas chacha have in the trays = 100 + 100 + 100 + 100 + 70 = 400 + 70 = 470

(v) Number of more laddoos that will make the tray full = 100 – 69 = 31

(vi) Total laddoos after the last tray full = 469 + 31 = 500

(vii)

Let us Do (NCERT Pg 73-78)

Q.16 Teji and Jojo saw a big apartment.

Ans.

Hop Hundreds Home

Row → ; Column ↓

191	192	193	194	195	196	197	198	199	200
					186		188		
	172		174				178		
	162					167			
		153		155	156				160
		143	144		146				
				135			138		
			124			127			
111	112	113	114	115	116	117	118	119	120
101	102	103	104	105	106	107	108	109	110
						97	98	99	100
	82							89	90
	72	73	74			77	78		
		63	64		66				
					56	57	58	59	60
41	42	43							
						37			
		23	24	25	26	27			
11	12	13	14	15	16	17	18	19	20
01	02	03	04	05	06	07	08	09	10

113 is 10 floors above 13

Q.17 Arvind Dada has to deliver sweets from Farooq Chacha's shop to different houses. Shade the houses to which he has to deliver sweets.

The house numbers are :

209, 228, 242, 258, 267, 276, 290, 315, 346, 367, 389, 395.

Ans. Shade the houses. The house numbers are 209, 228, 242, 258, 267, 276, 290, 315, 346, 367, 389, 395.

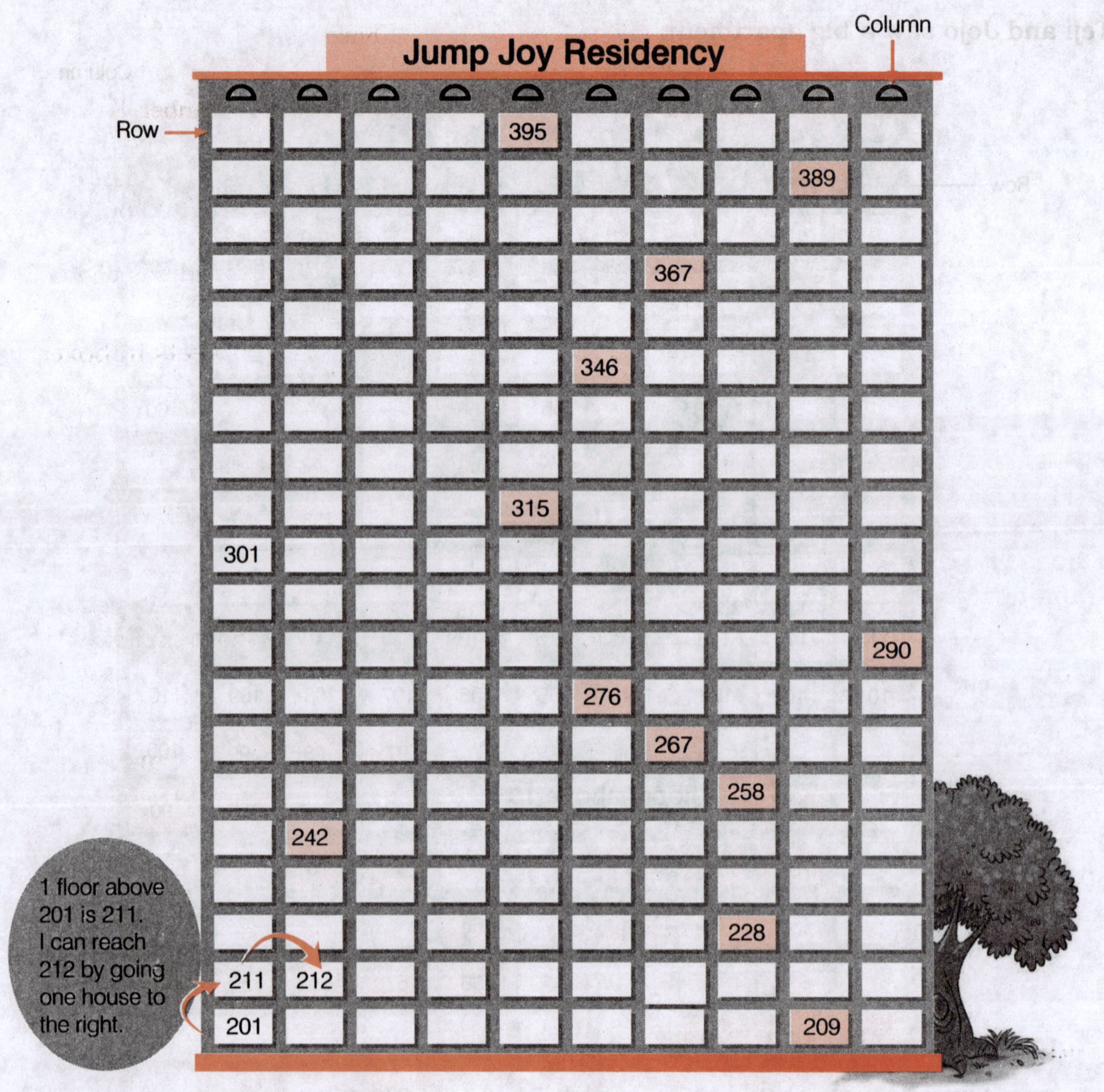

For Q. Nos. 20-21 (See Q. Nos. 18 and 19)

Q.18 Write the floor and column number for each of the following houses.

Ans.

House number	Floor	Column
13	1st	3
67	6th	7
106	10th	6
159	15th	9
192	19th	2
231	23rd	1
245	24th	5
328	32nd	8
380	37th	10
399	39th	9

Q.19 Find the following house numbers from the building and write the appropriate house numbers in the blank spaces. What do you notice? Discuss how the house numbers change when moving up and down and left to right.

Ans.

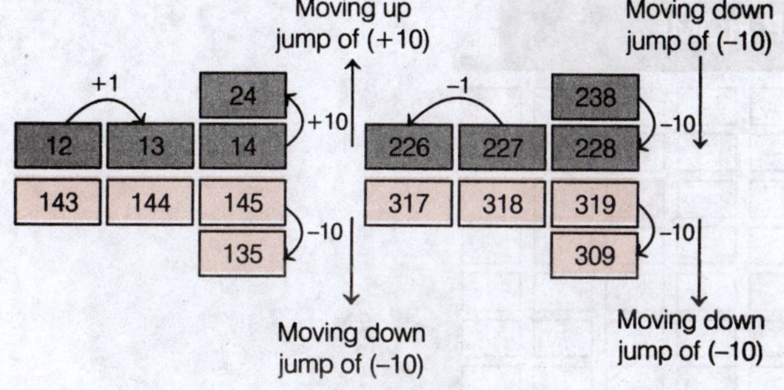

Q.20 Who am I?

(i) I have digits 9, 1 and 5.
I am less than 200.
I have 9 ones.
Which number am I?

(ii) I am a 3-digit number. I have only digits 4 and 0.
Which number am I?

(iii) I am greater than 300 but less than 400.
I have no tens.
My ones and hundreds digits are the same.
Which number am I?

Ans. (i) I have 9, 1 and 5.
I am less than 200.
I have 9 ones.
I am [159].

(ii) I am a 3-digit number.
I have only digits 4 and 0
I am [400] or [404] or [440] .

(iii) I am greater than 300 but less than 400.
I have no tens.
My ones and hundreds digits are the same.
I am [303].

Arvind Dada packs sweets in boxes of 100 (H), 10 (T) and as packets of loose sweets (O). The number of sweets for every house is the same as the house number.

Q.21 Draw sweets for each of the following house numbers.

House numbers	Draw sweet boxes	Types of boxes and packets	Number sentence
211	H□□ T▯ O□	2H + 1 T + 1 O	200 + 10 + 1
309			
275			
423			
365			
343			
458			
562			
606			
800			

Ans.

House numbers	Draw sweet boxes	Types of boxes and packets	Number sentence
211	H □□ T ▯ O ▫	2H + 1 T + 1 O	200 + 10 + 1
309	H □□□ O ▫▫▫▫▫▫▫▫▫	3 H + 9 O	300 + 00 + 9
275	H □□ T ▯▯▯▯▯▯▯ O ▫▫▫▫▫	2 H + 7 T + 5 O	200 + 70 + 5
423	H □□□□ T ▯▯ O ▫▫▫	4 H + 2 T + 3 O	400 + 20 + 3
365	H □□□ T ▯▯▯▯▯▯ O ▫▫▫▫▫	3 H + 6 T + 5 O	300 + 60 + 5
343	H □□□ T ▯▯▯▯ O ▫▫▫	3 H + 4 T + 3 O	300 + 40 + 3
458	H □□□□ T ▯▯▯▯▯ O ▫▫▫▫▫▫▫▫	4 H + 5 T + 8 O	400 + 50 + 8
562	H □□□□□ T ▯▯▯▯▯▯ O ▫▫	5 H + 6 T + 2 O	500 + 60 + 2
606	H □□□□□□ O ▫▫▫▫▫▫	6 H + 6 O	600 + 00 + 6
800	H □□□□□□□□	8 H	800 + 00 + 0

Q.22

(i) Write the house numbers of the grey and coloured houses.

(ii) Write the pattern you see in these numbers.

Ans. (i)

491									500
	482							489	
		473					478		
			464			467			
				455	456				
				445	446				
			434			437			
		423					428		
	412							419	
401									410

Grey 410, 419, 428, 437, 446, 455, 464, 473, 482, 491.

Coloured 401, 412, 423, 434, 445, 456, 467, 478, 489, 500.

(ii) **Grey** The difference between house numbers of two Grey houses is 9.

Coloured The difference between house numbers of two Coloured houses is 11.

Q.23 Arvind dada wants to pack small boxes of 10 in a big box of 100.

(i) How many boxes of 10 can he fit in a box of 100?

(ii) How many boxes of 10 can he fit in two boxes of 100?

(iii) How many boxes of 10 can he fit in four boxes of 100?

(iv) How many boxes of 10 will he find if he opens a box of 100?

Ans. (i) Number of boxes of 10, he can fit in a box of 100, are 10.

(ii) Number of boxes of 10, he can fit in two boxes of 100, are 20.

(iii) Number of boxes of 10, he can fit in four boxes of 100, are 40.

(iv) Number of boxes of 10, he will find if he opens a box of 100, are 10.

Q.24 Number hunt

Write the numbers between 200 and 300 that have 5 as a digit. Is 245 one such number? Write the other numbers.

Ans. The numbers between 200 and 300 that have 5 as a digit are

205, 215, 225, 235, 245, 250, 251, 252, 253, 254, 255, 256, 257, 258, 259, 265, 275, 285, 295.

Yes, 245 is one such number.

Other numbers 201, 202, 203, 204, 206, 207, 208, 209, 210, 211, 212, 213, 214, 216, 217, 218, 219, 220, 221, 222, 223, 224, 226, 227, 228, 229, 230, 231, 232, 233, 234, 236, 237, 238, 239, 240, 241, 242, 243, 244, 246, 247, 248, 249, 260, 261, 262, 263, 264, 266, 267, 268, 269, 270, 271, 272, 273, 274, 276, 277, 278, 279, 280, 281, 282, 283, 284, 286, 287, 288, 289, 290, 291, 292, 293, 294, 296, 297, 298, 299.

Let us Play (NCERT Pg 78)

Q.25 Do you remember this game? Let us play it again. We will record the actions in the table below. One is done for you.

Hundreds	Tens	Ones	Number
Clap, Clap	Snap	Pat	211

Ans. *

Hundreds	Tens	Ones	Number
Clap, Clap	Snap	Pat	211
Clap, Clap	Snap	Pat, Pat	212
Clap	Snap, Snap	Pat, Pat, Pat	123
Clap, Clap, Clap	Snap, Snap	Pat, Pat	322
Clap, Clap, Clap, Clap	Snap, Snap, Snap	Pat, Pat, Pat	433

Let us Do (NCERT Pg 79-80)

Q.26 Compare the following numbers and use the signs >, < appropriately.

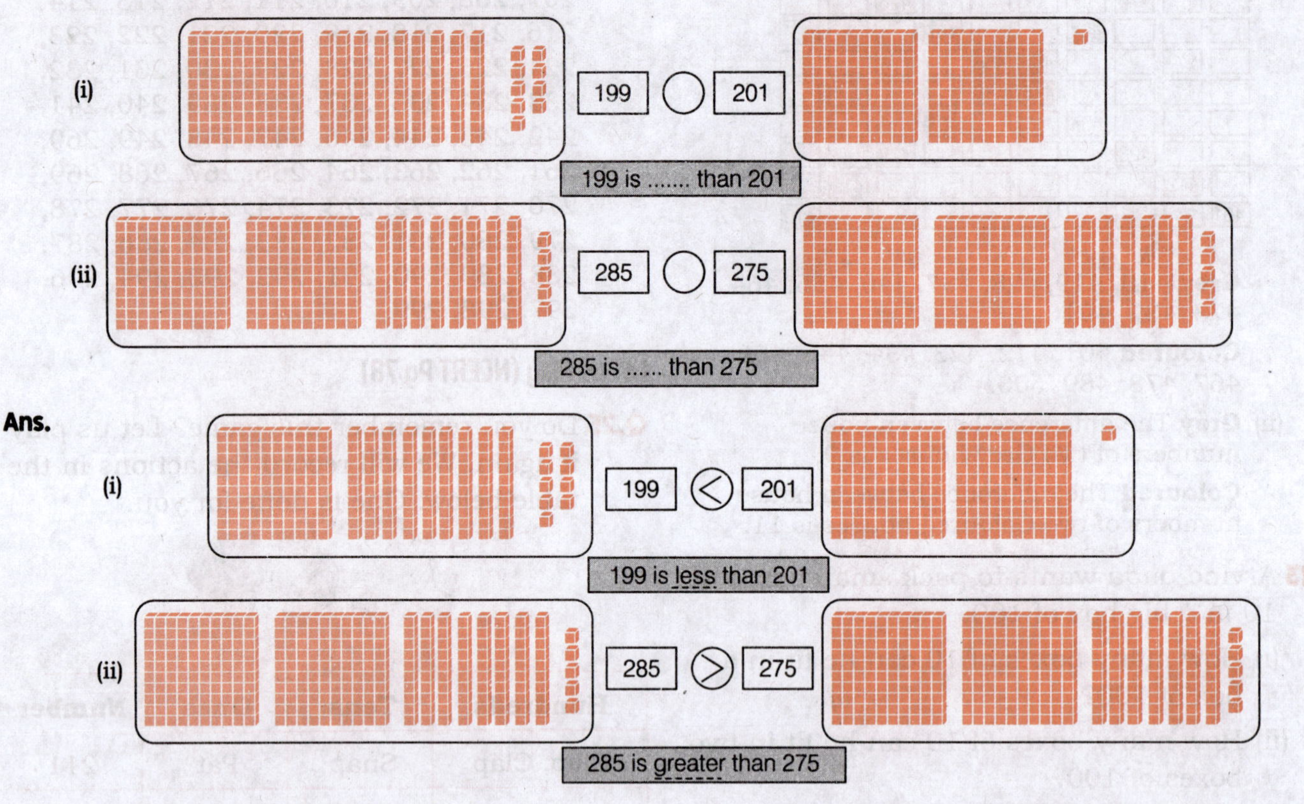

Q.27 Think and match the following.

(i)	325 is more than 235 because	(a)	329 and 392 both have three hundreds. 329 has 2 tens, 392 has 9 tens.
(ii)	235 is less than 523 because	(b)	110 has 1 hundred and 11 has no hundreds (zero hundreds)
(iii)	157 is more than 153 because	(c)	235 has 2 hundreds and 523 has 5 hundreds.
(iv)	432 is more than 423 because	(d)	325 has 3 hundreds and 235 has 2 hundreds.
(v)	329 is less than 392 because	(e)	157 and 153 both have one hundred and 5 tens each. 157 has 7 ones, 153 has 3 ones.
(vi)	110 is more than 11 because	(f)	432 and 423 both have four hundreds. 432 has 3 tens, 423 has 2 tens.

Ans. (i) → (d) (ii) → (c) (iii) → (e) (iv) → (f) (v) → (a) (vi) → (b)

Q.28 Circle the smallest number in each row :
(i) 374, 473, 347, 437
(ii) 239, 123, 321, 456

Ans. (i) 374, 473, (347), 437
(ii) 239, (123), 321, 456

Q.29 Circle the greatest number in each row
(i) 466, 437, 439, 447, 483
(ii) 464, 387, 123, 256, 348

Ans. (i) 466, 437, 439, 447, (483)
(ii) (464), 387, 123, 256, 348

NCERT Pg 81

Q.30 Make 3-digit numbers using 3, 2, and 4 without repeating any digit and circle the greatest number and square the smallest number.

Ans. [234], 243, 324, 342, 423, (432)

Q.31 Now make more 3-digit numbers using 3, 2 and 4 where you may repeat the digits. Circle the greatest number and square the smallest number.

Ans. [222], 223, 224, 244, 232, 233, 242, 243, 322, 323, 332, 333, 334, 343, 344, 422, 424, 433, 434, 442, 443, (444).

Q.32 (i) Arrange the following numbers from smallest to biggest.
456, 389, 207, 99, 110
(ii) Arrange the following numbers from biggest to smallest.
67, 376, 294, 249, 494

Ans. (i) 99, 110, 207, 389, 456
(ii) 494, 376, 294, 249, 67

PRACTICE QUESTIONS

1. Fill in the blanks.
(i) 149, 159, 169, ______, ______ 199.
(179, 189/178, 190)
(ii) 250 is ______ than 347. (less/greater)
(iii) 568 is ______ than 456. (less/greater)
(iv) The number closer to 400 is ______ .
(399/402)
(v) The number 469 has ______ hundreds, ______ tens and ______ ones.
(4, 6, 9/4, 7, 6)

2. True or False.
(i) The number 500 means 5 hundreds, 0 tens and 0 ones.
(ii) 465 is greater than 654.
(iii) 349 < 439.

3. Multiple choice questions.
(i) Which number will come in the box?

(a) 141 (b) 144 (c) 145 (d) 147
(ii) Which of these numbers has more tens?
(a) 579 (b) 489 (c) 769 (d) 398
(iii) 20 ones + 10 tens + 4 hundreds is equal to
(a) 520 (b) 420 (c) 320 (d) 620
(iv) The sum of the largest and the smallest numbers formed from the digits 2, 3, 5 is
(a) 675 (b) 677 (c) 767 (d) 776
(v) The sum of smallest 3-digit number and largest 2-digit number is
(a) 99 (b) 199 (c) 100 (d) 110
(vi) A number is 400 less than 500. The number is
(a) 900 (b) 200 (c) 100 (d) 300
(vii) Find the difference between the greatest number and the smallest number among 309, 416, 445, 567.
(a) 258 (b) 285 (c) 280 (d) 250

ANSWERS & SOLUTIONS

1. (i) 179, 189 (ii) less
(iii) greater (iv) 399
(v) 4, 6, 9

2. (i) True (ii) False (iii) True

3. (i) (b) (ii) (d) (iii) (a) (iv) (c)
(v) (b) (vi) (c) (vii) (a)

RAKSHA BANDHAN

Imagine counting colourful beads or sharing delicious sweets with friends, its so much fun. Get ready for a fantastic day to learning and celebrating as you explore the amazing world of number. Just like solving a puzzle, understanding multiplication, division and counting helps you learn new things.

Multiplication

Multiplication is the process of repeatedly adding the same number.

e.g. $2+2+2 = 3$ times $2 = 3 \times 2 = 6$

That means 3 groups of 2 make 6 in multiplication.

Division

Division is a mathematical operation which involves the sharing of an amount into equal sized groups.

e.g. $30 \div 15 = 2$

That means 30 divided into 15 equal groups and gives 2 in each group in division.

NCERT Pg 82

Q.1 Tomorrow is Gopal's favourite festival. Gopal and Dhara are very excited. Their beloved Atya (father's sister) is visiting them today. They have cleaned and decorated their house. Carefully observe Gopal's house.

(i) What do you find interesting here?

(ii) Find and count the number of each of these objects and write.

Leaves ☐ Glasses ☐

Pomegranate ☐ Flowers ☐

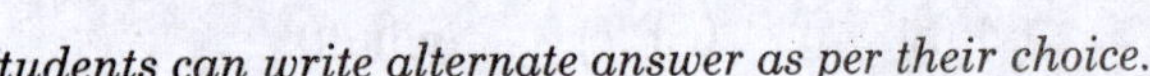

* *Students can write alternate answer as per their choice.*

Ans. (i) We find so many leaves, glasses, flowers and pomegranate here.

(ii) Leaves = 24, Glasses = 30

Pomegranate = 24, Flowers = 20

Celebration Begins! (NCERT Pg 83-84)

Q.2 Let's make Rakhis.

(i)

For each Rakhi we need one flower, ...threads and ....beads.

(ii) How many threads, flowers and beads do they needs?

(iii) For 5 Rakhis, we need .... flowers.

(iv) For 5 Rakhis, we need .... threads.

(v) For 5 Rakhis, we need .... beads.

Ans. (i) For each Rakhi, we need one flower, two threads and four beads.

(ii) They need 10 threads, 5 flowers and 20 beads.

(iii)

1 + 1 + 1 + 1 + 1 = 5

For 5 Rakhis, we need 5 flowers.

(iv)

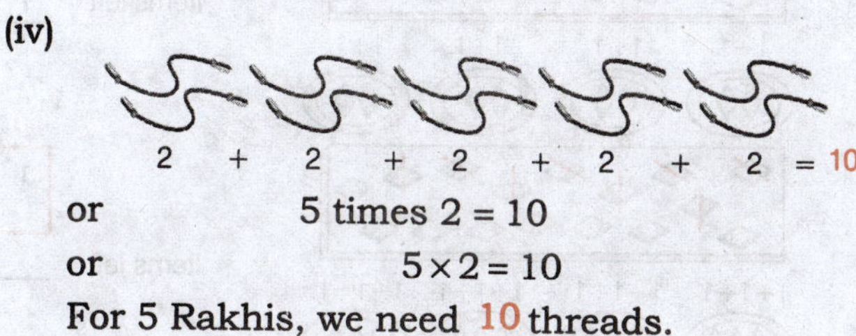

2 + 2 + 2 + 2 + 2 = 10

or 5 times 2 = 10

or $5 \times 2 = 10$

For 5 Rakhis, we need 10 threads.

(v)

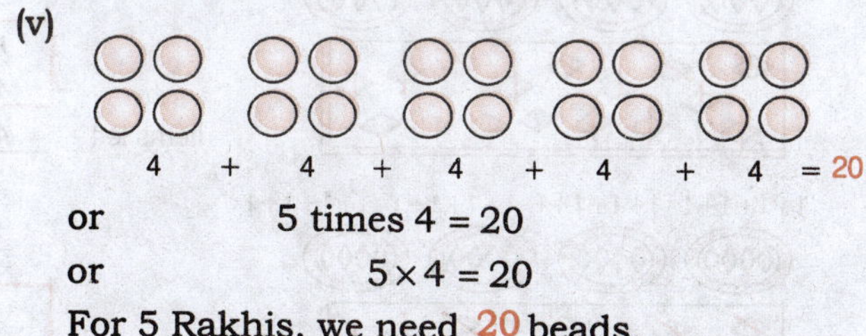

4 + 4 + 4 + 4 + 4 = 20

or 5 times 4 = 20

or $5 \times 4 = 20$

For 5 Rakhis, we need 20 beads.

Try it Out! (NCERT Pg 85)

Q.3 (i) For making 10 such Rakhis, we need ... flowers, ... threads and ... beads.

(ii) There are 30 flowers, 30 threads and 30 beads. How many Rakhis can you make with this material? Use drawings if needed to find out the answer.

Ans. (i) For 10 Rakhis,

1 + 1 + 1 + 1 + 1 + 1 + 1 + 1 + 1 + 1 = 10

or $10 \times 1 = 10$

We need 10 flowers.

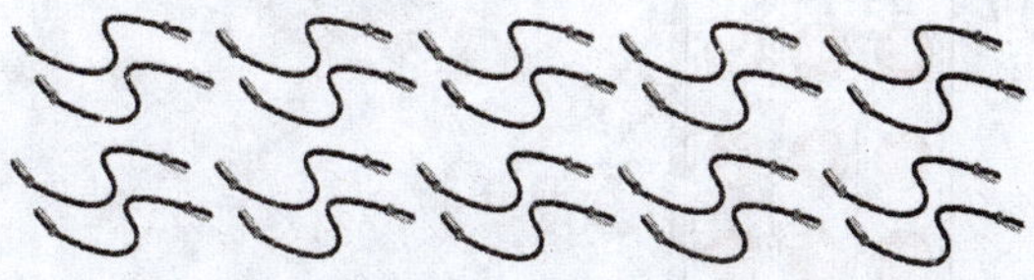

2 + 2 + 2 + 2 + 2 + 2 + 2 + 2 + 2 + 2 = 20

or $10 \times 2 = 20$

We need 20 threads.

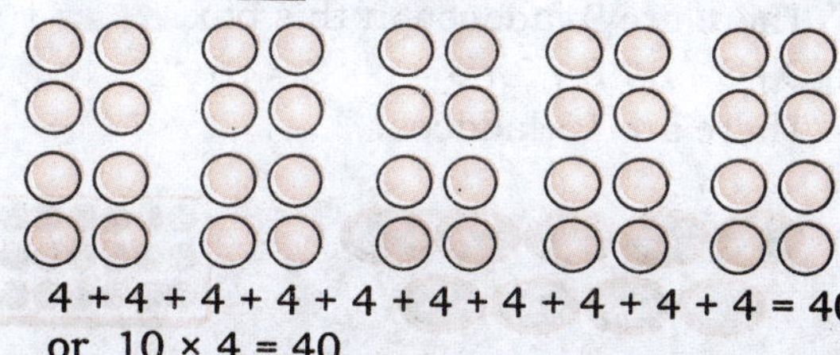

4 + 4 + 4 + 4 + 4 + 4 + 4 + 4 + 4 + 4 = 40

or $10 \times 4 = 40$

We need 40 beads.

(ii) For each Rakhi, we need one flower, two threads and four beads. So, we can make seven Rakhis with the given material.

Fun Activity (NCERT Pg 85)

Q.4 Try making a colourful Rakhi at your home. Show it in the class.

Ans. Do yourself.

Jagannath Sweet Shop (NCERT Pg 86-87)

Q.5 (i) How would we count the laddoos in this box?

3 + 3 + 3 = ...

or three times three equals 9.

or 3×3 = ...

There are ...... laddoos in this box.

(ii)

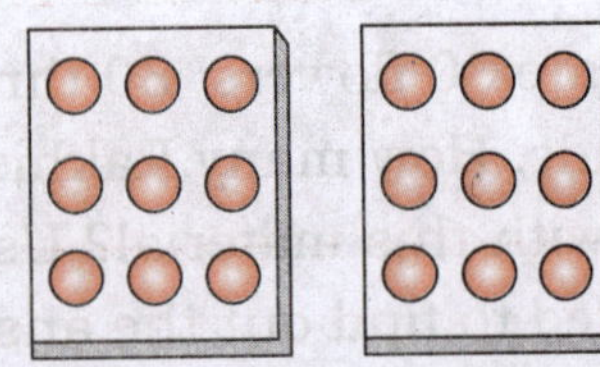

$3+3+3+3+3+3=$ ....

or 6 times 3 equals 18 or $6 \times 3 = 18$

There are 18 laddoos.

(iii) When 18 laddoos are shared equally among nine people, each of them gets .... laddoos.

18 equally shared by 9 is 2 each.

or $18 \div 9 = 2$ laddoos.

Ans. (i)

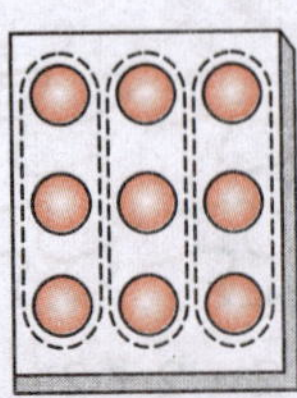

$3+3+3=9$

$3 \times 3 = 9$

There are 9 laddoos in this box.

(ii) $3+3+3+3+3+3 = 6 \times 3 = 18$

There are 18 laddoos.

(iii)

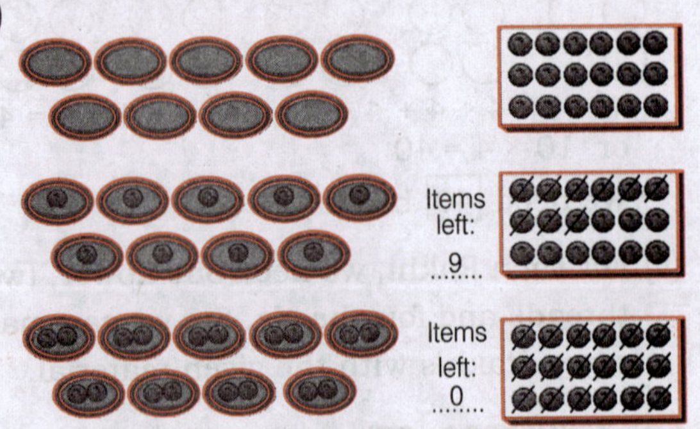

When 18 laddoos are shared equally among nine people, each of them gets 2 laddoos.

18 equally shared by 9 is 2 each.

or $18 \div 9 = 2$ laddoos.

Try it out (NCERT Pg 88)

Q.6 Look at the figure carefully. Estimate the number of kaju katlis.

Count and write the number of kaju katlis.

Total number of kaju katlis = ...

Ans. Total number of kaju katlis = 20

Let us Do (NCERT Pg 90-91)

Q.7 Distribute all the kaju katlis equally among 4 people. How many kaju katlis will each get?

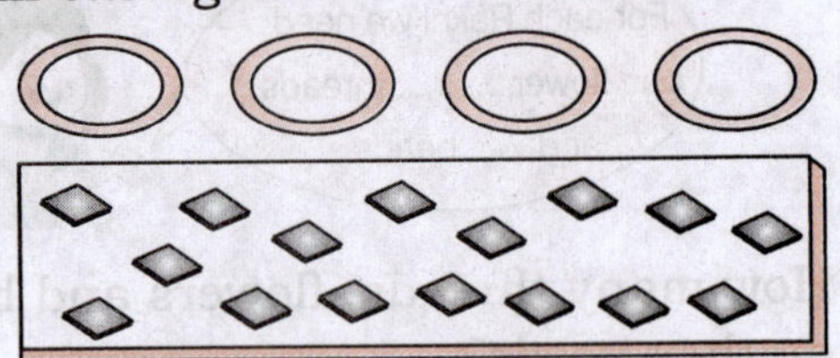

Let us do this in the picture given below. Strike out the kaju katlis from the tray and draw them in the plates. The first step has been done for you.

Each will get .... kaju katlis.

$16 \div 4 =$ ....

Ans.

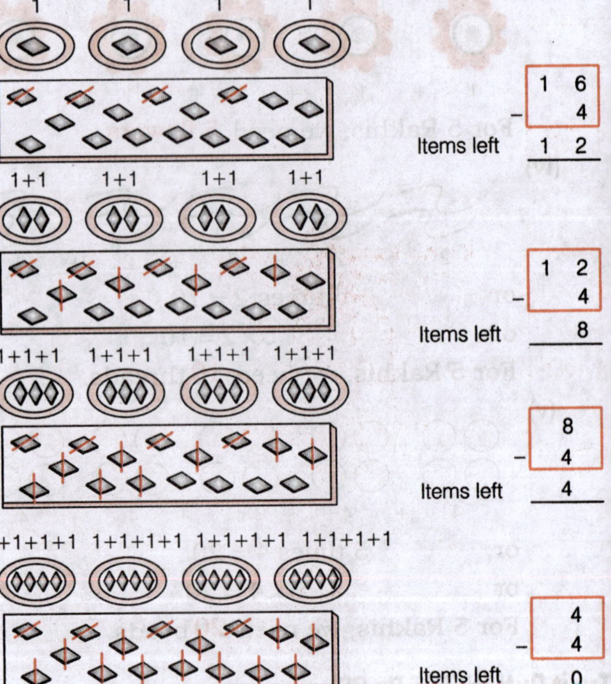

Each will get 4 kaju katlis

$= 16 \div 4 = 4$

Q.8 Distribute all the 15 pedas in plates equally among 5 people. How many pedas will each get?

Ans.

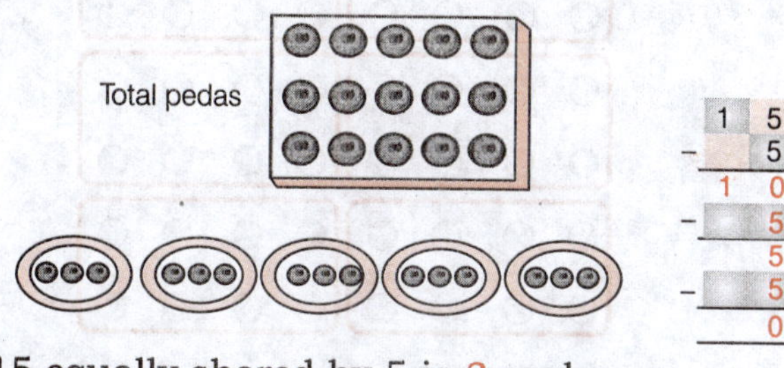

15 equally shared by 5 is 3 each

15 ÷ 5 = 3

Let us Think (NCERT Pg 91-92)

Q.9 Each cycle needs 2 wheels. How many cycles can be fitted with 12 wheels?

12 equally divided by 2 is ....

12 ÷ 2 = ...

Ans. Since, each cycle has 2 wheels.
So, 12 equally divided by 2 is 6.
Thus, 6 cycles can be fitted with 12 wheels.
Hence, 12 equally divided by 2 is 6.

12 ÷ 2 = 6

Q.10 (i) Look at the picture carefully. Count the number of jalebis.

There are ..... jalebis.

(ii) How did you count? Discuss with your friends.

Counting in groups, we see there are six groups of four jalebis each.

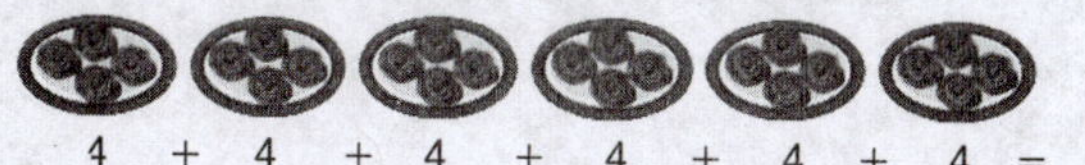

or .... × 4 = ... jalebis.

Ans. (i) There are 24 jalebis.

(ii) 4 + 4 + 4 + 4 + 4 + 4 = 24
or 6 × 4 = 24 jalebis

Q.11

(i) Are there enough jalebis for everyone in Dhara's family to have four each? Share your thoughts in the class.

(ii) How many jalebis should Dhara buy so that everyone can get four each?

Ans. (i) No, 24 jalebis are not enough for everyone in Dhara's family to have four each.
Total member of Dhara's family = 9
So, we need 3 more groups of 4 jalebis.
4 + 4 + 4 + 4 + 4 + 4 + 4 + 4 + 4 = 36
or 9 times 4 = 36 or 9 × 4 = 36

(ii) Dhara should buy 36 jalebis so that everyone gets 4 jalebis each.
4 + 4 + 4 + 4 + 4 + 4 + 4 + 4 + 4 = 36
or 9 times 4 = 36 or 9 × 4 = 36

Plants in the garden (NCERT Pg 93)

Q.12 Dhara and Gopal see a flower bed on their way home.

(i) **Dhara** The number of plants is

6+6+6+6+6+6+6+6 = ...

8 times 6 =

8×6 =

Gopal No, it is 8+8+8+8+8+8

= 6×8

(ii) Who do you think is correct?

(iii) Can you complete this equal grouping and write it as multiplication?

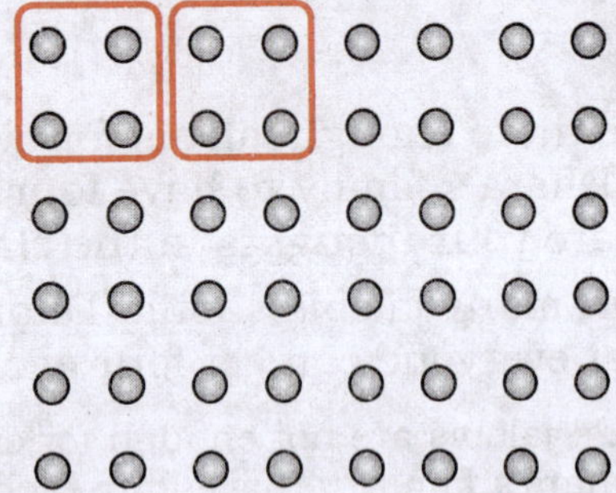

Can you find more equal groups of different sizes? Draw them and write as multiplication.

Ans. (i) **Dhara** The number of plants is

6 + 6 + 6 + 6 + 6 + 6 + 6 + 6 = 48

or 8 times 6 = 48

or 8 × 6 = 48

Gopal No, it is 8 + 8 + 8 + 8 + 8 + 8

= 6 × 8 = 48

(ii) Dhara and Gopal both are correct.

*(iii) Here,

4 + 4 + 4 + 4 + 4 + 4 + 4 + 4 + 4 + 4 + 4 + 4 = 48

or 12 times 4 = 48

or 12 × 4 = 48

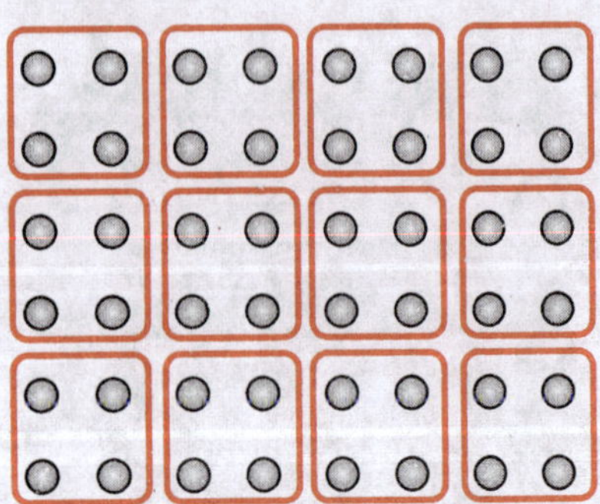

More equal groups of different sizes.

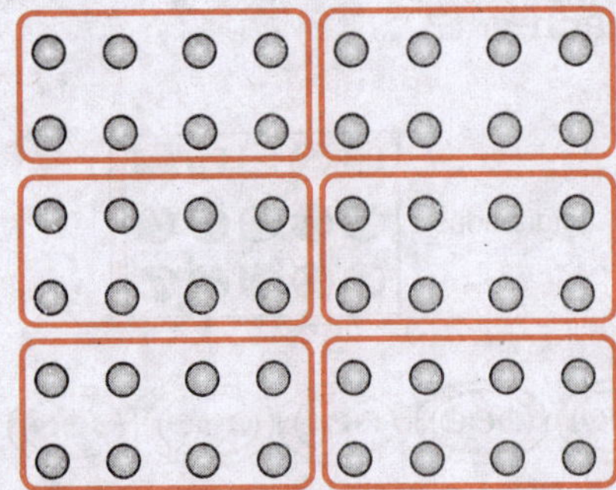

8 + 8 + 8 + 8 + 8 + 8 = 48

or 6 times 8 = 48

or 6 × 8 = 48

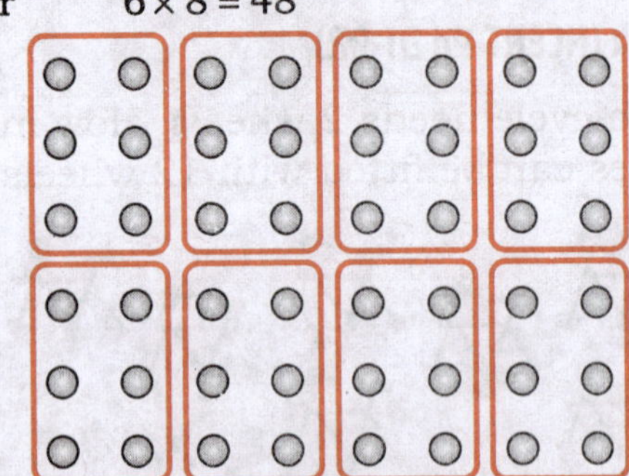

6 + 6 + 6 + 6 + 6 + 6 + 6 + 6 = 48

or 8 times 6 = 48

or 8 × 6 = 48

Visit to a Farm (NCERT Pg 94)

Q.13 The next day the children take their Appa and cousins to the farm. They see a lot of chickens there. Let us count chickens in the farm!

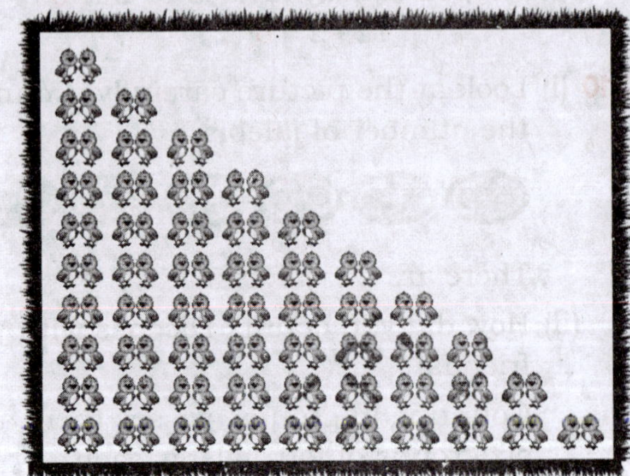

Ans.

1 times 2	is 2	or 1×2	$=2$
2 times 2	is 4	or 2×2	$=4$
3 times 2	is 6	or 3×2	$=6$
4 times 2	is 8	or 4×2	$=8$
5 times 2	is 10	or 5×2	$=10$
6 times 2	is 12	or 6×2	$=12$
7 times 2	is 14	or 7×2	$=14$
8 times 2	is 16	or 8×2	$=16$
9 times 2	is 18	or 9×2	$=18$
10 times 2	is 20	or 10×2	$=20$

Skip Jumping Game (NCERT Pg 95)

Q.14 Starting from 0, Dhara jumps to 3. From 3 she goes to 6. From 6 she goes to 9. Now continue to see how Dhara jumps after 9.

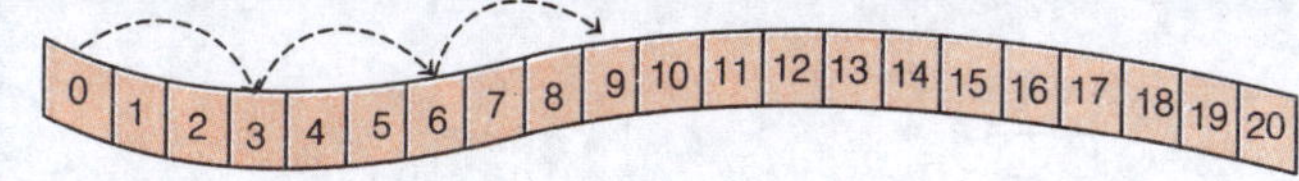

Ans. Dhara is skip jumping by 3

Number of jumps		Number reached
1 jump	→	3
2 jumps	→	$3+3=6=2\times3$
3 jumps	→	$3+3+3=9=3\times3$
4 jumps	→	$3+3+3+3=12=4\times3$
5 jumps	→	$3+3+3+3+3=15=5\times3$
6 jumps	→	$3+3+3+3+3+3=18=6\times3$
7 jumps	→	$3+3+3+3+3+3+3=21=7\times3$
8 jumps	→	$3+3+3+3+3+3+3+3=24=8\times3$
9 jumps	→	$3+3+3+3+3+3+3+3+3=27=9\times3$
10 jumps	→	$3+3+3+3+3+3+3+3+3+3=30=10\times3$

Let us Do (NCERT Pg 96-97)

Q.15 (i) Guess and write the next number she will jump onto.

(ii) Is there a pattern in these numbers: 3, 6, 9, ...?

(iii) How many steps forward is Dhara jumping each time?

(iv) Continue skip jumping by 6 by drawing the jumps on the number track.

(v) Can this skip jumping be used to form times-6 table? Write times-6 table in your notebook.

(vi) Is there repeated addition happening? Make times-4 table using repeated addition in the picture given below.

(vii) Gopal is doing skip jumping of .... steps.
After 27 he will jump on ...... , ...

(viii) What times table can you construct from Gopal's jumps? Make it in your notebook.

(ix) Dhara also skip jumps. Gopal notes down the jumps but he misses the first few numbers.

By what numbers was Dhara skip jumping? Construct the times table of this number in your notebook.

Ans. (i) The next number she will jump onto is 33.

$3+3+3+3+3+3+3+3+3+3+3$
$=11\times3=33$

(ii) Yes, there is a specific pattern. It is a times-3 table or the next number is three more than the previous number.

$1\times3,\ 2\times3,\ 3\times3,$ ...... so on.

(iii) Dhara is jumping 3 steps forward each time.

(iv) Skip jumping by 6

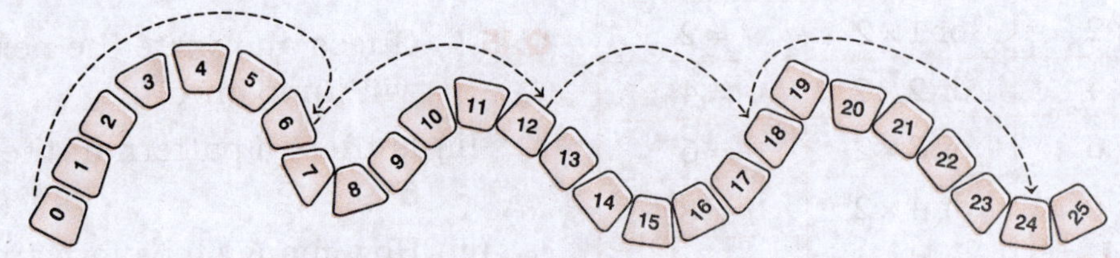

(v) Yes

Number of jumps		Number reached
1 jump	→	$6 = 1 \times 6$
2 jumps	→	$6 + 6 = 12 = 2 \times 6$
3 jumps	→	$6 + 6 + 6 = 18 = 3 \times 6$
4 jumps	→	$6 + 6 + 6 + 6 = 24 = 4 \times 6$
5 jumps	→	$6 + 6 + 6 + 6 + 6 = 30 = 5 \times 6$
6 jumps	→	$6 + 6 + 6 + 6 + 6 + 6 = 36 = 6 \times 6$
7 jumps	→	$6 + 6 + 6 + 6 + 6 + 6 + 6 = 42 = 7 \times 6$
8 jumps	→	$6 + 6 + 6 + 6 + 6 + 6 + 6 + 6 = 48 = 8 \times 6$
9 jumps	→	$6 + 6 + 6 + 6 + 6 + 6 + 6 + 6 + 6 = 54 = 9 \times 6$
10 jumps	→	$6 + 6 + 6 + 6 + 6 + 6 + 6 + 6 + 6 + 6 = 60 = 10 \times 6$

(vi) Yes, there is repeated addition happening.

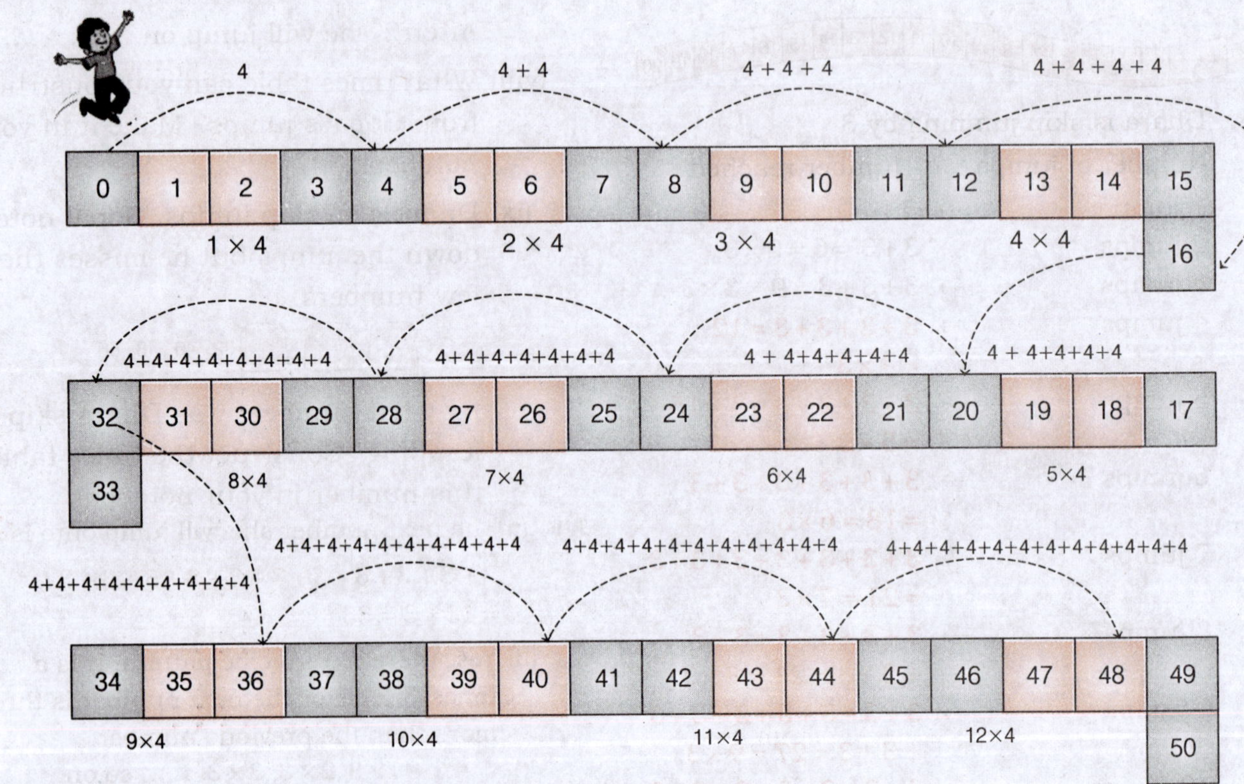

(vii) Gopal is doing skip jumping of 9 steps.

After 27 he will jump on 36, 45.

(viii) We can constructed table of 9 by Gopal's jumps.

Number of jumps		Number reached
1 jump	→	$9 = 1 \times 9$
2 jumps	→	$9 + 9 = 18 = 2 \times 9$
3 jumps	→	$9 + 9 + 9 = 27 = 3 \times 9$
4 jumps	→	$9 + 9 + 9 + 9 = 36 = 4 \times 9$
5 jumps	→	$9 + 9 + 9 + 9 + 9 = 45 = 5 \times 9$
6 jumps	→	$9 + 9 + 9 + 9 + 9 + 9 = 54 = 6 \times 9$
7 jumps	→	$9 + 9 + 9 + 9 + 9 + 9 + 9 = 63 = 7 \times 9$
8 jumps	→	$9 + 9 + 9 + 9 + 9 + 9 + 9 + 9 = 72 = 8 \times 9$
9 jumps	→	$9 + 9 + 9 + 9 + 9 + 9 + 9 + 9 + 9 = 81 = 9 \times 9$
10 jumps	→	$9 + 9 + 9 + 9 + 9 + 9 + 9 + 9 + 9 + 9 = 90 = 10 \times 9$

(ix) Dhara was doing skip jumping of 8 steps.

The first few numbers missed by Gopal are

8, 16, 24, 32, 40, 48, 56

Times-8 table

1 times 8 = $1 \times 8 = 8$

2 times 8 = $2 \times 8 = 16$

3 times 8 = $3 \times 8 = 24$

4 times 8 = $4 \times 8 = 32$

5 times 8 = $5 \times 8 = 40$

6 times 8 = $6 \times 8 = 48$

7 times 8 = $7 \times 8 = 56$

8 times 8 = $8 \times 8 = 64$

9 times 8 = $9 \times 8 = 72$

10 times 8 = $10 \times 8 = 80$

Let us Play (NCERT Pg 97)

Q.16 (i) Atya places a flower on 12. Skip jump with equal steps to reach the flower. No direct jumping to the flower is allowed. The one who reaches the flower in the smallest number of jumps wins. What skip jumping number will you choose?

(ii) Are there numbers that can be reached only through skip jumping by 1? Find 3 such numbers.

Ans. (i) I will choose to skip jumping number 6 to reach the flower in the smallest number of jumps.

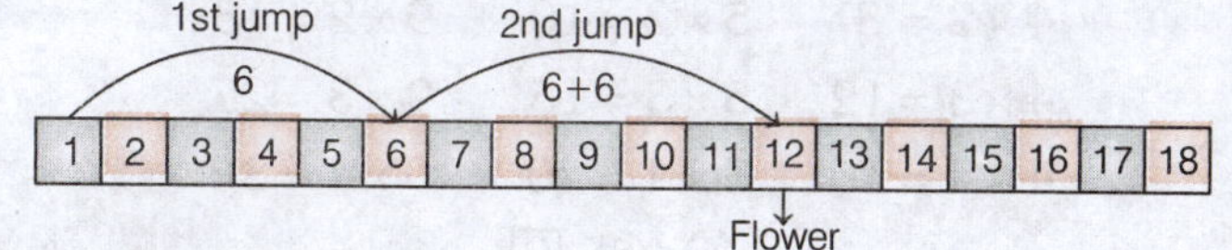

Total number of jumps = 2

(ii) Yes, there are numbers that can be reached only through skip jumping by 1.

e.g. 3, 7, 13 etc.

Fun way of Writing Tables (NCERT Pg 98-100)

Q.17 Let's try making a 5 times table with sticks.

Ans. Complete the times-5 table using sticks

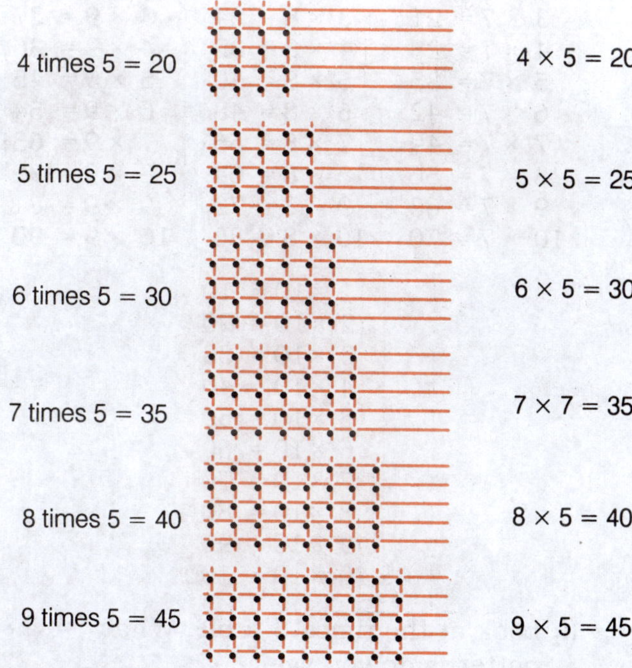

Q.18 Make times-6 to times-10 tables using the sticks method shown above.

Ans. Do yourself.

Seeing Patterns in Multiplication Tables (NCERT Pg 99-100)

Q.19

1 × 1 = 1	1 × 2 = 2	1 × 3 = 3
2 × 1 = 2	2 × 2 = 4	2 × 3 = 6
3 × 1 = 3	3 × 2 = 6	3 × 3 = 9
4 × 1 = 4	4 × 2 = 8	4 × 3 = 12
5 × 1 = 5	5 × 2 = 10	5 × 3 = 15
6 × 1 = 6	6 × 2 = 12	6 × 3 = 18
7 × 1 = 7	7 × 2 = 14	7 × 3 = 21
8 × 1 = 8	8 × 2 = 16	8 × 3 = 24
9 × 1 = 9	9 × 2 = 18	9 × 3 = 27
10 × 1 = 10	10 × 2 = 20	10 × 3 = 30

1 × 4 = 4	1 × 5 = 5	1 × 6 = 6
2 × 4 = 8	2 × 5 = 10	2 × 6 = 12
3 × 4 = 12	3 × 5 = 15	3 × 6 = 18
4 × 4 = 16	4 × 5 = 20	4 × 6 = 24
5 × 4 = 20	5 × 5 = 25	5 × 6 = 30
6 × 4 = 24	6 × 5 = 30	6 × 6 = 36
7 × 4 = 28	7 × 5 = 35	7 × 6 = 42
8 × 4 = 32	8 × 5 = 40	8 × 6 = 48
9 × 4 = 36	9 × 5 = 45	9 × 6 = 54
10 × 4 = 40	10 × 5 = 50	10 × 6 = 60

1 × 7 = 7	1 × 8 = 8	1 × 9 = 9
2 × 7 = 14	2 × 8 = 16	2 × 9 = 18
3 × 7 = 21	3 × 8 = 24	3 × 9 = 27
4 × 7 = 28	4 × 8 = 32	4 × 9 = 36
5 × 7 = 35	5 × 8 = 40	5 × 9 = 45
6 × 7 = 42	6 × 8 = 48	6 × 9 = 54
7 × 7 = 49	7 × 8 = 56	7 × 9 = 63
8 × 7 = 56	8 × 8 = 64	8 × 9 = 72
9 × 7 = 63	9 × 8 = 72	9 × 9 = 81
10 × 7 = 70	10 × 8 = 80	10 × 9 = 90

1 × 10 = 10
2 × 10 = 20
3 × 10 = 30
4 × 10 = 40
5 × 10 = 50
6 × 10 = 60
7 × 10 = 70
8 × 10 = 80
9 × 10 = 90
10 × 10 = 100

(i) Look at the times-5 table. What patterns do you see?

(ii) Guess what will be the last digits of 11×5 and 12×5.

(iii) Give 3 examples of numbers that when taken 5 times gives an answer ending with

(a) 0 ....

(b) 5 ....

(iv) Without finding the answer, can you tell the last digits of

18 × 5, 23 × 5, 32 × 5, 50 × 5.

Ans. (i) In table of 5, I see that the last digit is either 0 or 5.

(ii) The last digits of 11 × 5 is 5 and 12 × 5 is 0.

(iii) (a) 0, 4, 6, 8 (b) 5, 3, 5, 7

(iv) The last digit of

18 × 5 is 0, 23 × 5 is 5, 32 × 5 is 0 and 50 × 5 is 0.

Q.20 Look at the time tables of 2, 3, 5. They have a relation between them. Can you see it?

1 × 2 = ②	1 × 3 = ③	1 × 5 = [5]
2 × 2 = 4	2 × 3 = 6	2 × 5 = 10
3 × 2 = 6	3 × 3 = 9	3 × 5 = 15
4 × 2 = 8	4 × 3 = 12	4 × 5 = 20

Is there a relation between the two circled numbers and the boxed number? Does this happen for the next rows also?

Can you find other examples of two tables adding up to a third table?

Ans. Yes, there is relation between the two circled numbers ②, ③ and the box number [5].

②+③=[5]

It means sum of circled number is boxed number

④+⑥= [10]

⑥+⑨= [15]

⑧+ ⑫ =[20]

Yes, it happens for the next rows also.
Other examples of two tables adding up to a third table.

e.g. Times table of 4, 5 and 9.

4 × 1 = ④	5 × 1 = ⑤	9 × 1 = [9]
4 × 2 = 8	5 × 2 = 10	9 × 2 = 18
4 × 3 = 12	5 × 3 = 15	9 × 3 = 27
4 × 4 = 16	5 × 4 = 20	9 × 4 = 36

④+⑤=[9]

Let us Do (NCERT Pg 100-101)

Q.21 Draw pictures for each of the following problems in your notebook. Use counting, number line jumps or any other method to solve the problems.

(i) There are 5 jars with 4 cookies in each jar. How many cookies are there?

(ii) An idli vessel contains 6 idli plates. In each plate we can make 4 idlis. How many idlis can be cooked in one go?

(iii) 30 cookies are to be distributed among 5 children equally. How many cookies will each child get?

(iv) Roro starts from 0 and takes 6 jumps to reach 18. All his jumps are of the same size. What is the size of Roro's jump?

(v) Toto does not take jumps of the same size and still reaches 18 in 6 jumps. How did Toto jump?

(vi) Suma saves ₹ 8 every day. After how many days will she have ₹ 56?.

(vii) Mary has 63 sea shells. She gives 7 sea shells to each of her 5 friends. How many does she have left?

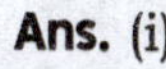

Ans. (i)

4 + 4 + 4 + 4 + 4 = 5 × 4 = 20

There are 20 cookies.

(ii)

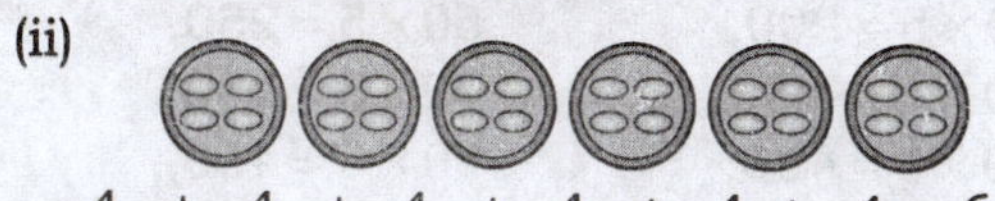

4 + 4 + 4 + 4 + 4 + 4 = 6 × 4 = 24

Number of idlis can be cooked in one go is 24.

(iii)

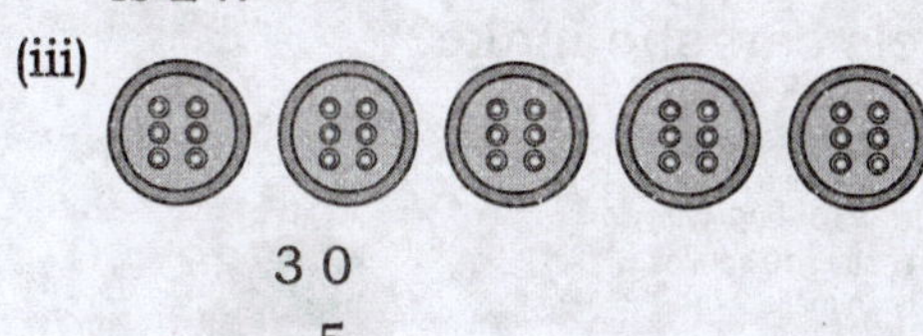

$$\begin{array}{r} 30 \\ -5 \\ \hline 25 \\ -5 \\ \hline 20 \\ -5 \\ \hline 15 \\ -5 \\ \hline 10 \\ -5 \\ \hline 5 \\ -5 \\ \hline 0 \end{array}$$

When 30 cookies are distributed among 5 children equally, each child will get 6 cookies.

30 ÷ 5 = 6

(iv)

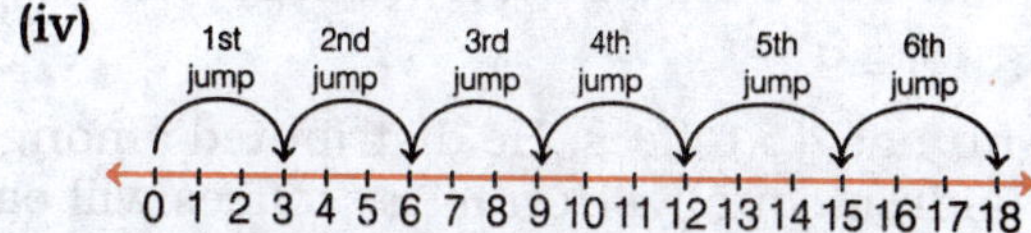

The size of Roro's jump = 18 ÷ 6 = 3

(v) *

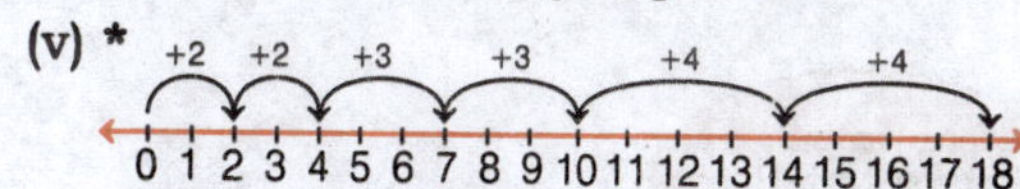

Toto jumped 2 steps in first and second jump, 3 steps in third and fourth jump and 4 steps in fifth and sixth jump and then reached at 18 in 6 jumps.

(vi) Saving of Suma = ₹ 8 per day.

Number of days in which Suma saves ₹ 56 = 56 ÷ 8 = 7

(vii) Mary has 63 sea-shells.

She gave each of her friends = 7 sea-shells

$$\begin{array}{r} 63 \\ -7 \\ \hline 56 \\ -7 \\ \hline 49 \\ -7 \\ \hline 42 \\ -7 \\ \hline 35 \\ -7 \\ \hline 28 \end{array}$$

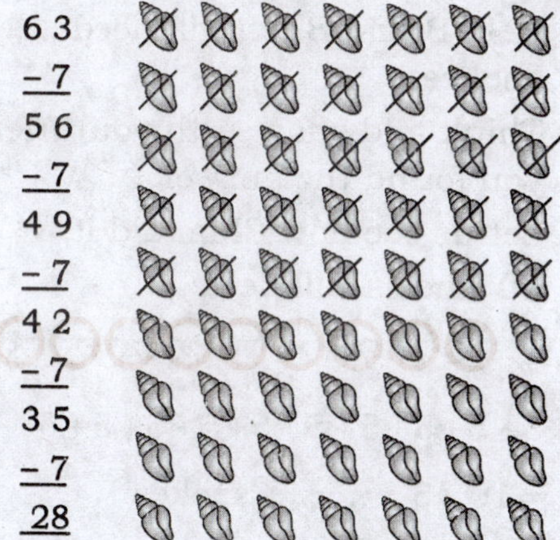

Hence, number of sea-shells left = 63 – 35 = 28

Q.22 Solve the following problems. Try constructing a word problem.

(a) 4×9 (b) $32 \div 8$

(c) 6×7 (d) $45 \div 5$

Ans. (a) $4 \times 9 = 36$

Mary has 4 jars of cookies. Each jar has 9 cookies inside it. How many cookies she have?

(b) $32 \div 8 = 4$

32 sweets are distributed among 8 children equally. How many sweets will each child get?

(c) $6 \times 7 = 42$

Sonu decorated 6 diyas in one row. How many diyas did he decorate in seven row?

(d) $45 \div 5 = 9$

Anu has 45 toffees. He distributed among 5 children equally. How many toffees will each child get?

Q.23

Help Bhim! Bhim will need .... spokes.

Think and share with your friends how you found the answer.

Let us see how Bhim did it.

10 wheels will need:

5+5+5+5+5+5+5+5+5+5

$= 10 \times 5 =$ .... spokes.

Another 10 wheels will need

.........×......... = ... spokes.

So, the total number of spokes needed is

.... + ... = ... spokes.

Ans. 10 wheels will need:

$5+5+5+5+5+5+5+5+5+5 = 10 \times 5$

$= 50$ spokes

Another 10 wheels will need

$10 \times 5 = 50$ spokes.

So, the total number of spokes needed is $50 + 50 = 100$ spokes.

Try These (NCERT Pg 101-102)

Q.24 (i) $30 \times 5 =$ ....

(**Hint** You can find this by counting the spokes in 30 wheels)

First 10 wheels will have ...... spokes

Next 10 wheels will have ...... spokes

Next 10 wheels will have ...... spokes

Total = ... spokes

$30 \times 5 =$ ...... spokes

(ii) Complete the following

$40 \times 5 =$ ......, $50 \times 5 =$ ......,

$60 \times 5 =$ ...... , $70 \times 5 =$ ......,

$80 \times 5 =$ ...... , $90 \times 5 =$ ......,

$100 \times 5 =$ ......

Ans. (i) $30 \times 5 = 150$

First 10 wheels will have 50 spokes.

Next 10 wheels will have 50 spokes.

Next 10 wheels will have 50 spokes.

Total = 50 + 50 + 50 = 150 spokes

$30 \times 5 = 150$ spokes

(ii) $40 \times 5 = 200$, $50 \times 5 = 250$,

$60 \times 5 = 300$, $70 \times 5 = 350$,

$80 \times 5 = 400$, $90 \times 5 = 450$,

$100 \times 5 = 500$

Q.25 (i) Dhara collected 45 spokes, How many wheels can she make?

(ii) Does Dhara have enough spokes to make 10 wheels?

(iii) How many wheels can you make with 60 spokes?

Ans. (i) Dhara used 10 spokes for make 2 wheels. So, she makes 1 wheel with 5 spokes. Number of wheels makes with 45 spokes

$$= \frac{45}{5} = 9$$

Hence, Dhara makes 9 wheels with 45 spokes.

(ii) ∵ Dhara have 45 spokes and 1 wheel required 5 spokes.

∴ Number of spokes required for wheels

$$= 10 \times 5 = 50$$

Dhara does not have enough spokes to make 10 wheels because she needs 50 spokes to make 10 wheels.

(iii) We can make 12 wheels with 60 spokes.

$60 \div 5 = 12$

Let us do (NCERT Pg 102-103)

Q.26 (i) A spider has 8 legs.

(a) 5 spiders will have .... legs.

(b) 10 spiders will have .... legs

(c) 15 spiders will have .... legs.

(ii) How many legs will 23 spiders have?

(iii) A group of spiders have 32 legs. How many spiders are there in the group?

(iv) Here is a 3-wheeled auto rickshaw. How many wheels are there in

(a) 18 auto rickshaws?

(b) 34 auto rickshaws?

(v) Auto rickshaws in a garage have a total of 36 wheels. How many auto rickshaws are there in the garage?

(vi) There is a line of 55 ants (one ant has 6 legs). What is the total number of legs in the line?

(vii) Micky, the mouse, can see 48 legs of cows in the shed. How many cows are there in the shed?

(viii) Karry, the crow, can see 24 horns of cows in the shed. What is the total number of legs in the shed?

Ans. (i) A spider has 8 legs.

(a) 5 spiders will have $\mathbf{5} \times \mathbf{8} = \mathbf{40}$ legs.

(b) 10 spiders will have $\mathbf{10} \times \mathbf{8} = \mathbf{80}$ legs

(c) 15 spiders will have $\mathbf{15} \times \mathbf{8} = \mathbf{120}$ legs.

(ii) 1 spider has 8 legs.

So, 23 spiders have $23 \times 8 = 184$ legs.

(iii) Number of legs in group of spiders = 32

Number of legs in each spider = 8

Number of spiders in group = $32 \div 8$

$= 4$

Thus, 4 spiders have 32 legs.

(iv) (a) Here, 1 auto rickshaw has 3 wheels.

So, 18 auto rickshaws have = 18×3

= 54 wheels.

(b) Here, 1 auto rickshaw has 3 wheels.

So, 34 auto rickshaws have $= 34 \times 3$

$= 102$ wheels.

(v) Since, total number of wheels in garage = 36

Number of wheels in 1 Auto rickshaw = 3

So, $36 \div 3 = 12$

Thus, there are 12 auto rickshaws in the garage.

(vi) Number of ants = 55

Number of legs in 1 ant = 6

So, total number of legs with 55 ants

$= 55 \times 6 = 330$ legs

(vii) Number of legs of cows in the shed = 48

Number of legs in each cow = 4

So, the number of cows in the shed is $48 \div 4 = 12$

Thus, there are 12 cows in the shed.

(viii) Number of horns of cows in the shed = 24

Number of houses in each cow = 2

$\therefore$ Number of cows $= 24 \div 2 = 12$

Since, each cow has 4 legs.

So, number of legs in the shed $= 12 \times 4$

$= 48$

Thus, 48 legs in the shed.

Let us Think (NCERT Pg 103)

Q.27 (i) A frog is at 0. It takes jumps of only 7. What would be the largest number that the frog will reach before crossing 50?

0 1 2 3 4 5 6 7 8 9 10 11 12 13 14 15 16 17 18 19 20 21 22 23 24 25 26 27 28 29 30 31 32 33 34 35 36 37 38 39 40 41 42 43 44 45 46 47 48 49 50

(ii) A frog wants to jump backwards from 50. It continues to take jumps of 7. What is the number after which it is not possible for the frog to make a jump of 7?

0 1 2 3 4 5 6 7 8 9 10 11 12 13 14 15 16 17 18 19 20 21 22 23 24 25 26 27 28 29 30 31 32 33 34 35 36 37 38 39 40 41 42 43 44 45 46 47 48 49 50

(iii) What numbers should the frog start from to reach 0, taking jumps of 7 each time? What do you observe?

0 1 2 3 4 5 6 7 8 9 10 11 12 13 14 15 16 17 18 19 20 21 22 23 24 25 26 27 28 29 30 31 32 33 34 35 36 37 38 39 40 41 42 43 44 45 46 47 48 49 50

Ans. (i)

0 1 2 3 4 5 6 7 8 9 10 11 12 13 14 15 16 17 18 19 20 21 22 23 24 25 26 27 28 29 30 31 32 33 34 35 36 37 38 39 40 41 42 43 44 45 46 47 48 49 50

$7 \times 1 = 7$, $7 \times 2 = 14$, $7 \times 3 = 21$, $7 \times 4 = 28$, $7 \times 5 = 35$, $7 \times 6 = 42$, $7 \times 7 = 49$

Thus, the largest number that the frog will reach before crossing 50 is 49.

(ii)

0 1 2 3 4 5 6 7 8 9 10 11 12 13 14 15 16 17 18 19 20 21 22 23 24 25 26 27 28 29 30 31 32 33 34 35 36 37 38 39 40 41 42 43 44 45 46 47 48 49 50

$50 - 7 = 43$, $43 - 7 = 36$, $36 - 7 = 29$, $29 - 7 = 22$, $22 - 7 = 15$, $15 - 7 = 8$, $8 - 7 = 1$

The number after which is not possible for the frog to make a jump of 7, is 1.

(iii)

0 1 2 3 4 5 6 7 8 9 10 11 12 13 14 15 16 17 18 19 20 21 22 23 24 25 26 27 28 29 30 31 32 33 34 35 36 37 38 39 40 41 42 43 44 45 46 47 48 49 50

$49 - 7 = 42$, $42 - 7 = 35$, $35 - 7 = 28$, $28 - 7 = 21$, $21 - 7 = 14$, $14 - 7 = 7$, $7 - 7 = 0$

Thus, frog starts from 49.

We observe that all jumps are equal and moving backward is subtraction.

Puri Beach (NCERT Pg 104)

Q.28 One wall-hanging costs ₹42. How much do two wall hangings cost?

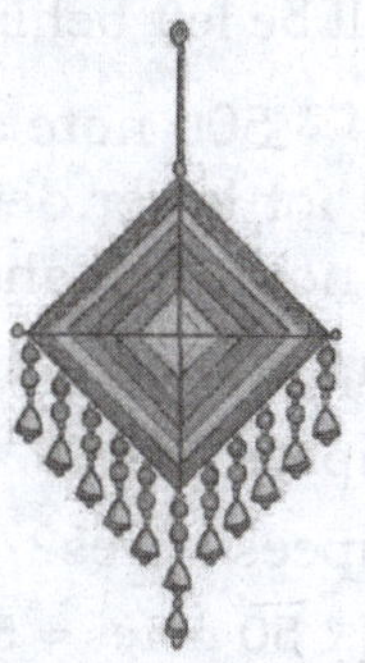

Two wall hangings cost ₹42 + ₹42
= 2 × ₹ 42

The cost of the two wall hangings: ....

Ans. The cost of the two wall hangings = ₹ 84

Q.29 One Rabdi cup costs ₹ 75. Preeti buys 5 cups of Rabdi. She has her mother's purse which has only 100 notes.

How many ₹100 notes should she give the shopkeeper? How much will the shopkeeper then return to Preeti?

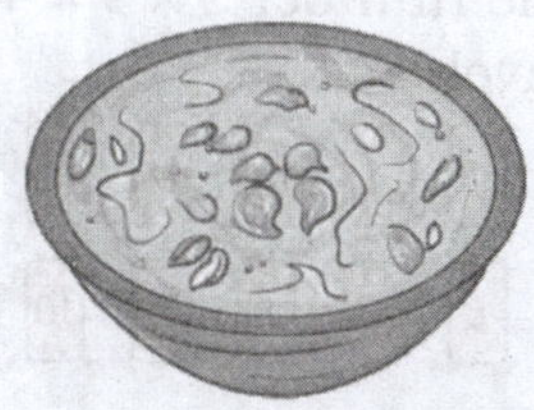

What is the total cost of 5 cups of Rabdi?

Ans. Cost of 1 cup of Rabdi = ₹ 75

Cost of 5 cups of Rabdi = ₹ 75 × 5
= ₹ 375

So, she gives 4 notes of ₹ 100 to the shopkeeper.

Thus, Shopkeeper will return
= ₹ 400 – ₹ 375 = ₹ 25

Sea Shells (NCERT Pg 104-105)

Q.30 Dhruv lives near the sea. He thought of making a necklace for each of friends. He looked for sea-shells the whole day. He collected 112 sea-shells by the evening.

Now, he has many different coloured and shiny shells.

He took 28 shells for one necklace.
112 – 28 = 84

Now, he was left with 84 shells. Again he took 28 more shells for the second necklace.

(i) How many shells are left now?

(ii) Then he took shells for the third necklace. So, he was left with .... shells.

(iii) Are the shells enough for making necklaces for all his friends?

(iv) How many necklaces can Dhruv make from 112 shells?

Ans. (i) Number of shells used in making a necklace = 28

Number of shells remains after making one necklace = 84

So, number of shells remains after making second necklace = 84 – 28 = 56

(ii) After taking shells for third necklace, he was left with 56 – 28 = 28 shells.

So, he was left with 28 shells.

(iii) Yes, the shells are enough for making necklaces for all his friends.

(iv) Number of sea-shells = 112

Number of sea-shells used for making one necklace = 28

So, number of necklaces Dhruv can make from 112 sea-shells = 112 ÷ 28 = 4

Thus, Dhruv can make 4 necklaces from 112 sea-shells.

Try These (NCERT Pg 105)

Q.31 Kannu makes a necklace of 17 sea-shells. How many such necklaces can be made using 100 sea-shells?

Ans. Total number of sea-shells = 100

Number of sea-shells used for making 1 necklace = 17

Number of sea-shells remains after making first necklace = 100 – 17 = 83

Number of sea-shells remains after making second necklace = 83 – 17 = 66

Number of sea-shells remains after making third necklace = 66 – 17 = 49

Number of sea-shells remains after making fourth necklace = 49 – 17 = 32

Number of sea-shells remains after making fifth necklace = 32 – 17 = 15

Thus, 5 necklaces can be made using 100 sea-shells and 15 sea-shells are left.

Q.32 While searching for sea-shells, Dhruv also finds 127 shiny pebbles. He distributes them equally to his 3 friends. How many will each get?

Ans. Total pebbles = 127

Let in first turn Dhruv gives 30 pebbles to each friend.

Number of pebbles given by Dhruv to his 3 friends = $30 \times 3 = 90$

Number of pebbles remains now = 127 – 90
= 37

In second turn, Dhruv gives 10 pebbles to each friend.

Number of pebbles remains now
$= 37 - 3 \times 10$
$= 37 - 30 = 7$

In third turn, Dhruv gives 2 pebbles to each friend.

Number of pebbles remains now = $7 - 2 \times 3$
$= 7 - 6 = 1$

Now, each friend gets

30 + 10 + 2 = 42 pebbles.

Thus, each friend will get 42 pebbles and 1 pebble will be left behind.

Q.33 Preeti has a ₹ 500 note and wants to exchange it for lower denomination notes. How many notes will she get if she wants

(i) All 50 rupees notes?

(ii) All 20 rupees notes?

(iii) All 10 rupees notes?

Ans. (i) Number of ₹ 50 notes = 500 ÷ 50 = 10

(ii) Number of ₹ 20 notes = 500 ÷ 20 = 25

(iii) Number of ₹ 10 notes = 500 ÷ 10 = 50

Let us Explore (NCERT Pg 106)

Q.34 There are ten number cards from 1-10. There are five sealed envelopes. Each has two cards. On the top of each envelope the multiplication of the numbers contained in it is written.

The 5th envelope contains the cards 5 and 9. The number $5 \times 9 = 45$ is written on the envelope.

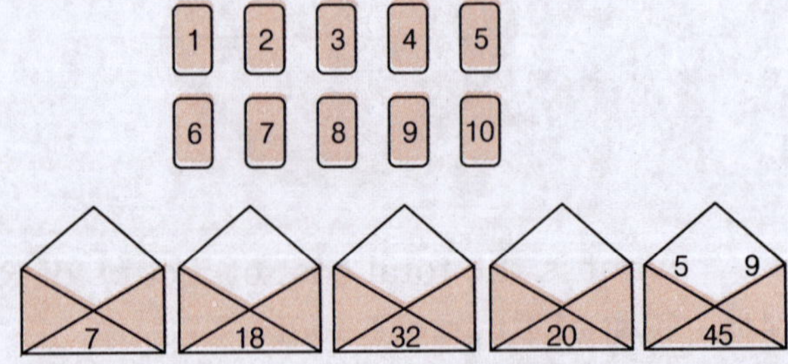

Identify the number cards inside each of the envelopes.

Ans.

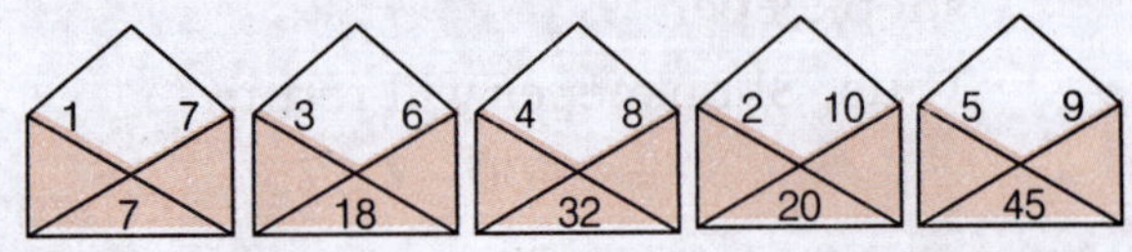

PRACTICE QUESTIONS

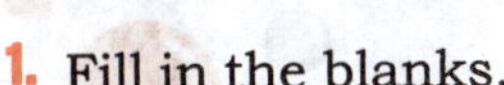

1. Fill in the blanks.

(i) $2+2+2+2=$ .... $=4\times2$

(ii) $3+3+3+$ .... $=12=4\times$ ....

(iii) $4\times65=$ ...... + ... + ... + ...

(iv) .... $\div 7=5$

2. True or False.

(i) $9+9+9+9+9+9+9=7$ times 9.

(ii) One hand has 5 fingers, then 6 hands have 6 times 5 fingers.

(iii) One dog has 4 legs, 3 dogs have 4 times 3 legs.

(iv) Cost of 1 pen ₹ 9. So, cost of 3 pens is 3 times 9 rupees.

(v) $8+8+8+8+8+8+8+8+8$ $=8$ times 9.

(vi) $16\div4=4\div16$

3. Multiple choice questions.

(i) There are seven cars in front of the park. Each car has four wheels. How many total wheels have these cars?

(a) $4+7$ (b) $7+7$
(c) 4×7 (d) $7-4$

(ii) What should be put in the empty box below to make the sentence true?

$5+5+5+5+5=5$ 5

(a) + (b) –
(c) × (d) 3

(iii) What would be put in the empty box to make the sentence true?

2 times $7=7$ 7

(a) 722 (b) +
(c) times (d) 2

(iv) Each box below contains 6 crayons. How many crayons do 5 boxes contains.

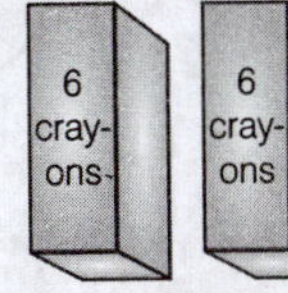

(a) $5+6$ (b) 5×6
(c) 5×5 (d) $6+5$

(v) 4 times 4 is equal to

(a) 8 (b) 16 (c) 40 (d) 44

(vi) If 66 pairs of shoes are arranged equally in 6 rows, how many pairs of shoes are there in each row?

(a) 6 (b) 8 (c) 10 (d) 11

(vii) Rohan distributed 40 toffees among 10 friends equally. How many toffees did each one get?

(a) 5 (b) 4 (c) 3 (d) 2

4. Word Problems.

(i) There are 6 fruits in each basket. If there are 9 baskets filled with fruits, then how many fruits are there in total?

(ii) How many baskets will contain 24 apples if each basket contains 6 apples?

(iii) Renu has 56 strawberries, she wants to distribute all the strawberries among here 8 friends equally. How many strawberries each of her friends will get?

ANSWERS & SOLUTIONS

1. (i) 8 (ii) 3, 3
(iii) $65+65+65+65$ (iv) 35

2. (i) True (ii) True
(iii) False (iv) True
(v) False (vi) False

3. (i) (c) (ii) (c)
(iii) (b) (iv) (b)
(v) (b) (vi) (d)
(vii) (b)

4. (i) Number of fruits in each basket = 6
Number of baskets = 9
Total number of fruits $=6\times9=54$

(ii) Total number of apples = 24
Number of apples in each basket = 6
∴ Number of basket will contain 24 apples $=24\div6=4$

(iii) Total number of strawberries = 56
Total number of friends = 8
Number of strawberries, each friend will get $=56\div8=7$

CHAPTER 8 FAIR AND SHARE

This chapter aims to teach students the concepts of fractions, focusing on halves and quarters. Through interactive activities, students will learn to identify, create and understand fractions by dividing shapes and objects equally, they will explore practical applications of fraction every day life, enhancing their comprehension of equal sharing and partitioning.

Fair and Share

The term 'Fair share' refers to dividing something equally among all participants, ensuring that everyone gets an equal portion.

NCERT FOLDER

Let us Discuss (NCERT Pg 107-108)

Q.1 How do you share object equally?

Ans. We can divide some object by making folds of equal size.

Q.2 Why is Shabnam folding the paratha over itself ?

Ans. For sharing equally.

Q.3 This is a whole paratha.

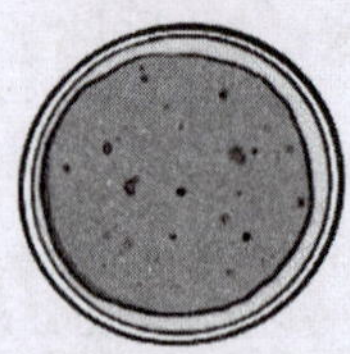

Choose the paratha that has been cut equally.

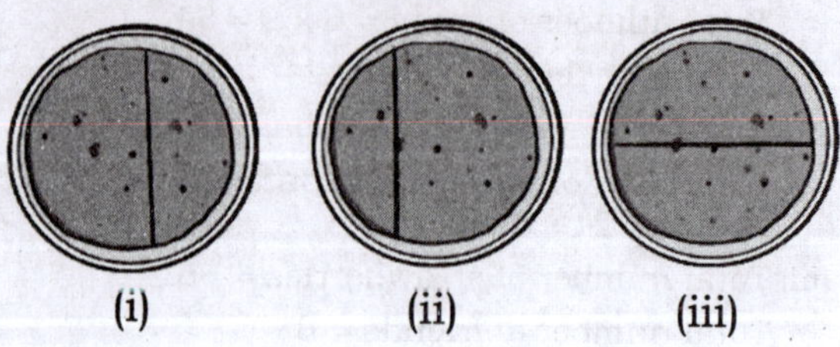

(i) (ii) (iii)

Ans. Paratha (iii) is equally cut.

** Students can write alternate answer as per their choice.*

Q.4 How many halves make one whole?

Ans. When two equal half join together make one whole.

Let us Do (NCERT Pg 108-109)

Q.5 Find the shapes where half of the whole is shaded.

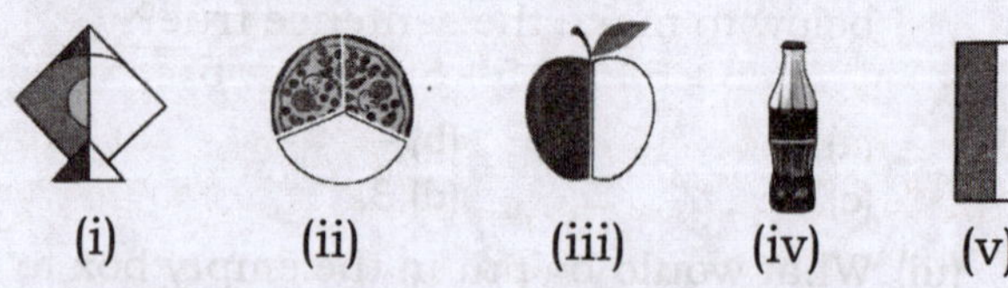

(i) (ii) (iii) (iv) (v)

Ans. (i), (iii) and (v)

Q.6 Draw a line to show one-half of the whole.

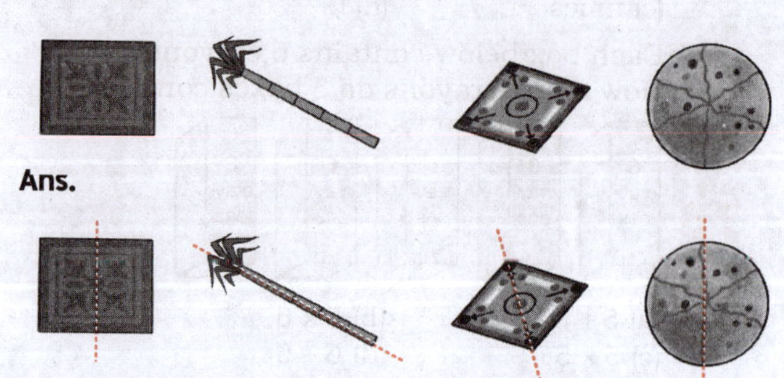

Ans.

Q.7 Shabnam has eaten some chikki from 3 sides.
Find how much chikki is left?

(a) Less than half (b) More than half

(c) Half

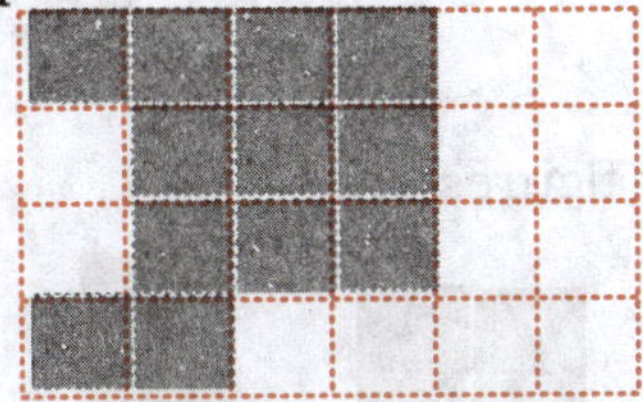

Ans. (c) Half

Q.8 Show by colouring half a chikki that has been eaten from 2 sides.

Ans. *

Q.9 Draw lines to show different ways of making a half.

Ans.

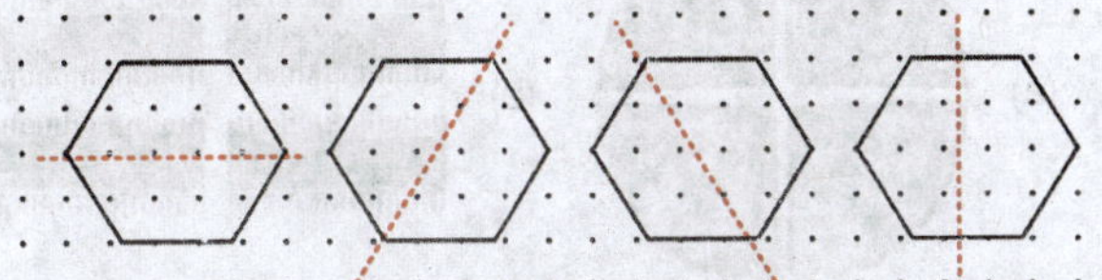

Q.10 Complete the whole picture by drawing the other half.

Ans.

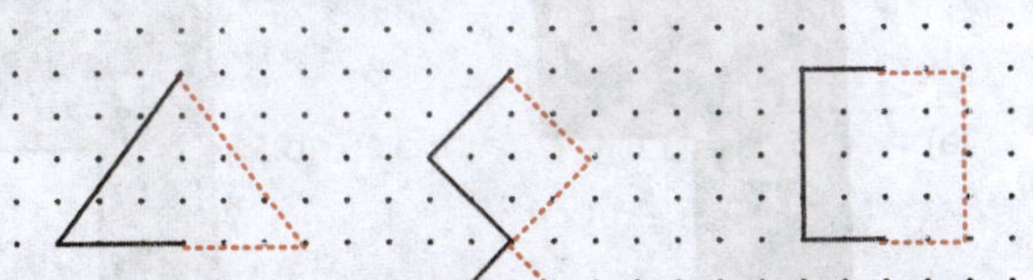

Let us Explore (NCERT Pg 110)

Q.11 Take a rectangular sheet of paper and fold it in half. Find all the different ways to make a half.

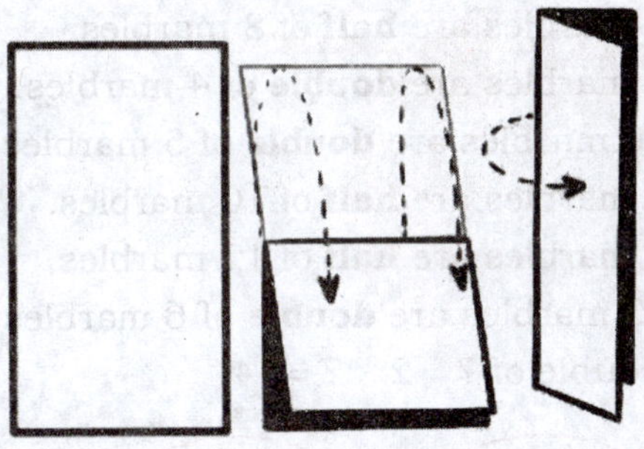

Take a square piece of paper and fold it in half. Find all the different ways to make a half.

Ans. Do yourself.

Let us Do (NCERT Pg 110)

Q.12 Here are some mangoes. Share them equally between the two children.

Ans. Total mangoes = 6

Equally divide between two children

That is $\frac{6}{2} = 3$ mangoes.

Half and Double (NCERT Pg 111)

Q.13 Fill in the following blanks using double or half.

(i) 4 marbles are .... of 8 marbles.

(ii) 8 marbles are .... of 4 marbles.

(iii) 10 marbles are .... of 5 marbles.

(iv) 5 marbles are .... of 10 marbles.

(v) 6 marbles are .... of 12 marbles.

(vi) 12 marbles are .... of 6 marbles.

(vii) On a number line how far is 13 from the double of 7?

(viii) How far is 5 from half of 14?

0 1 2 3 4 5 6 7 8 9 10 11 12 13 14 15 16 17

Ans. (i) 4 marbles are **half** of 8 marbles.
(ii) 8 marbles are **double** of 4 marbles.
(iii) 10 marbles are **double** of 5 marbles.
(iv) 5 marbles are **half** of 10 marbles.
(v) 6 marbles are **half** of 12 marbles.
(vi) 12 marbles are **double** of 6 marbles.
(vii) Double of $7 = 2 \times 7 = 14$.

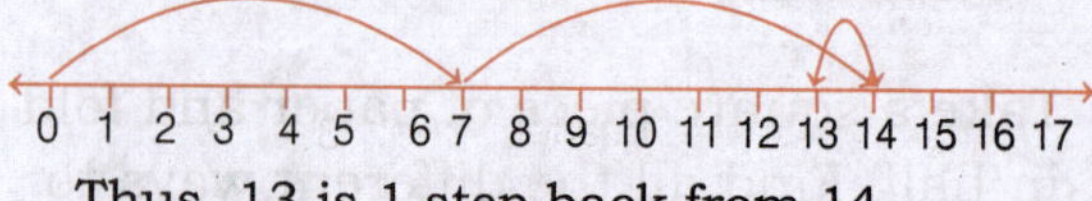

Thus, 13 is 1 step back from 14.

(viii) Half of $14 = 14 \div 2 = 7$.

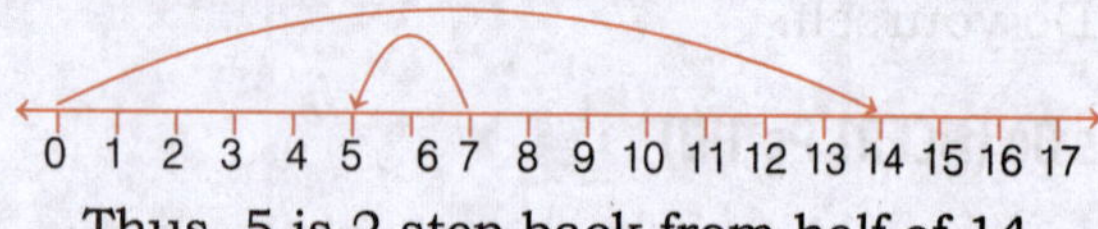

Thus, 5 is 2 step back from half of 14.

Guess who am I? (NCERT Pg 112)

Q.14 Use the clues to find the right fraction. Choose the correct box from the given 3 options.

(i) I have less than double of 3 marbles.
I have more than half of 8 marbles.

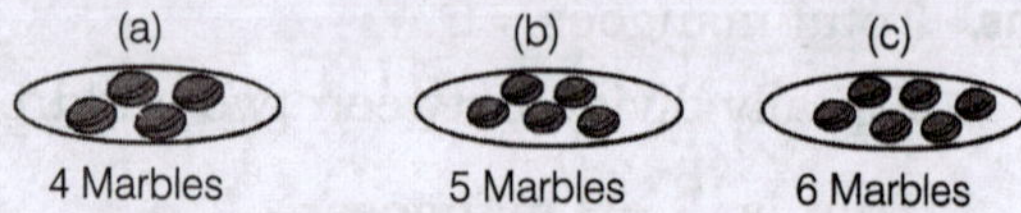

(ii) I have less than double of 4 marbles.
I have more than half of 10 marbles.

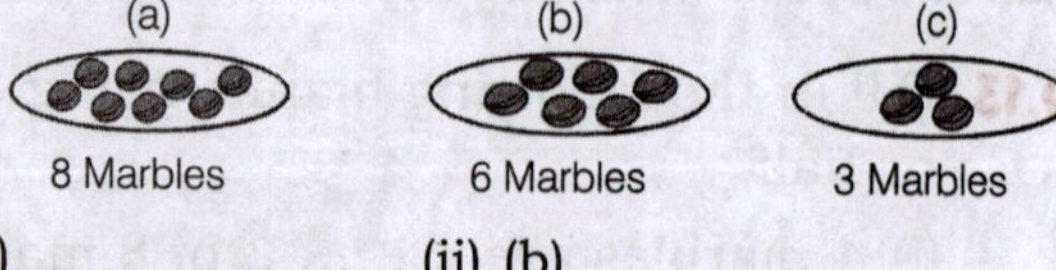

Ans. (i) (b) (ii) (b)

Q.15

(i) What part of the chikki did each get?
(ii) How many quarters in a whole?

Ans. (i) Quarter (ii) 4

Let us Do (NCERT Pg 113)

Q.16 Choose the objects that show quarters.

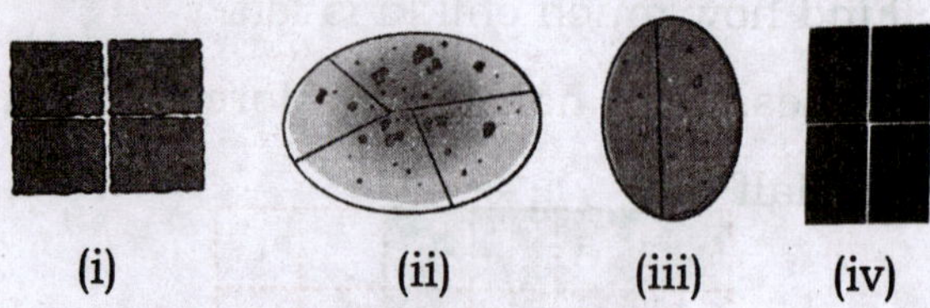

Ans. Quarter figures are

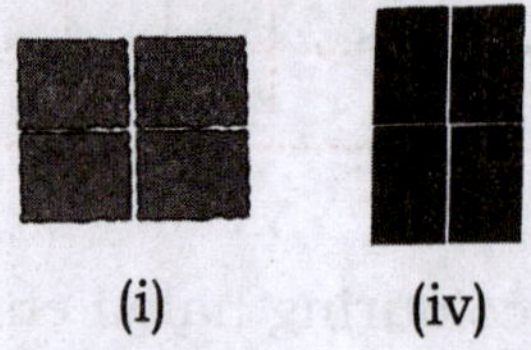

Q.17 Draw lines to make a quarter of the whole.

Ans.

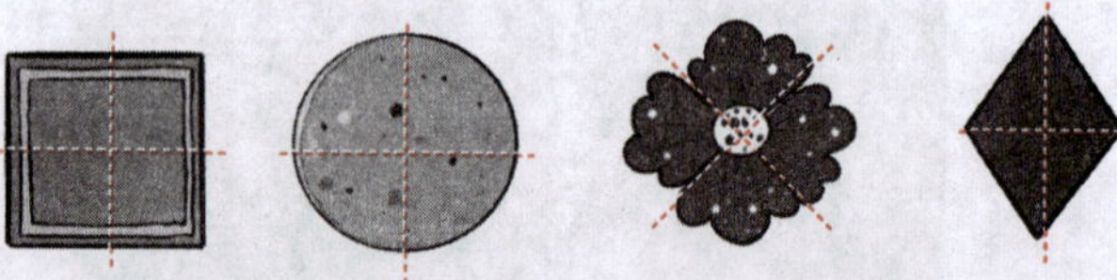

Q.18 Draw the remaining three quarters and complete the whole.

Ans.

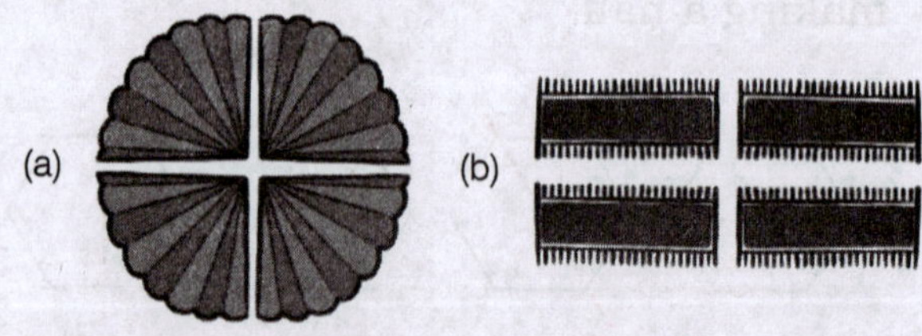

Q.19 Draw the remaining quarters to complete the whole.

Ans.

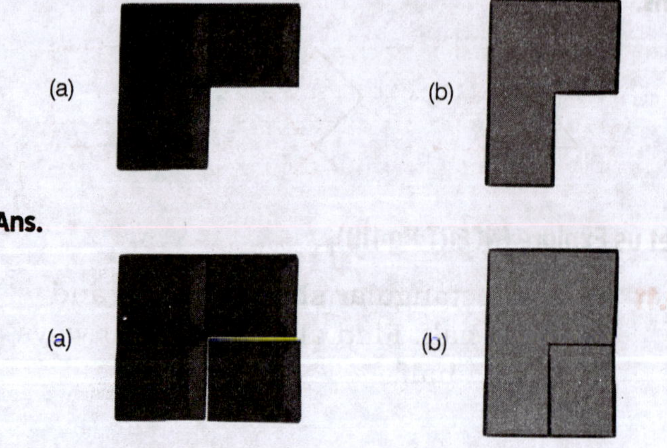

Half or quarter? (NCERT Pg 114)

Q.20 (i) Choose the appropriate word to fill the blank below.

(a) Shabnam has coloured half/ a quarter of the birds.

(b) Mukta has coloured half/ a quarter of the birds.

(c) Shabnam has coloured half/double the number of birds that Mukta has coloured.

(ii) Lakshanya and Peehu have 16 flowers each.

(a) Lakshanya tied half/a quarter of her flowers.

(b) Peehu tied half/a quarter of her flowers.

(c) Lakshanya tied half/double the number of flowers that Peehu tied.

Ans. (i) (a) Half (b) Quarter (c) Double
(ii) (a) Quarter (b) Half (c) Half

Let us Do (NCERT Pg 115-116)

Q.21 Choose the shapes below that show three-quarters.

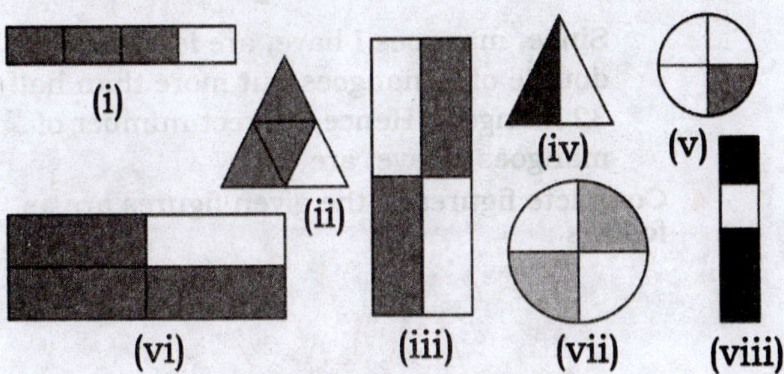

Ans. (i), (ii) (vi) and (viii)

Q.22 Colour the shapes given below to show the fractions as instructed.

Ans.

2 quarters 1 quarter 3 quarters

4 quarters 3 quarters 1 quarter

Q.23 Draw lines and colour the shapes given below to show the fractions as instructed.

Ans.

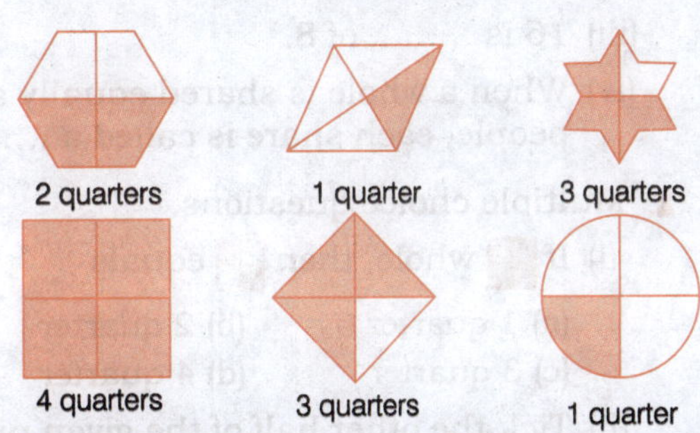

Q.24 Here is a rectangle which shows quarters. Discuss how.

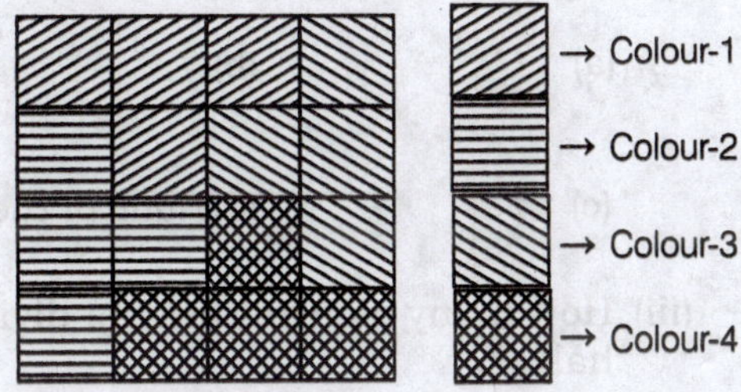

Ans. Total blocks = 16

4 blocks are of Colour-1.

4 blocks are of Colour-2.

4 blocks are of Colour-3.

4 blocks are of Colour-4.

Here, 4 blocks are one quarter of 16 blocks.

So, rectangle is showing quarters.

Q.25 Show quarters and halves in different ways in the grids given below.

Ans. *

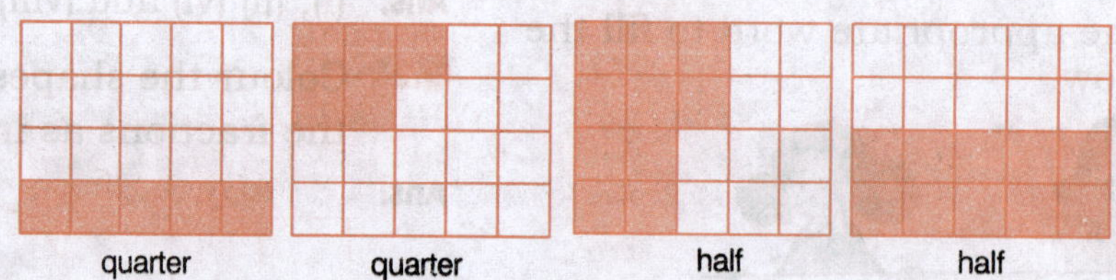

Q.26 Use the fraction cards from your book to form a whole.

Ans. Do yourself.

1. Fill in the blanks.

(i) When 1 whole is shared equally between 2 people, each share is called a ....

(ii) 5 is .... of 10.

(iii) 16 is .... of 8.

(iv) When a whole is shared equally among 4 people, each share is called a ....

2. Multiple choice questions.

(i) If [figure] whole, then [figure] equals

(a) 1 quarter (b) 2 quarter

(c) 3 quarter (d) 4 quarter

(ii) Tick the other half of the given picture.

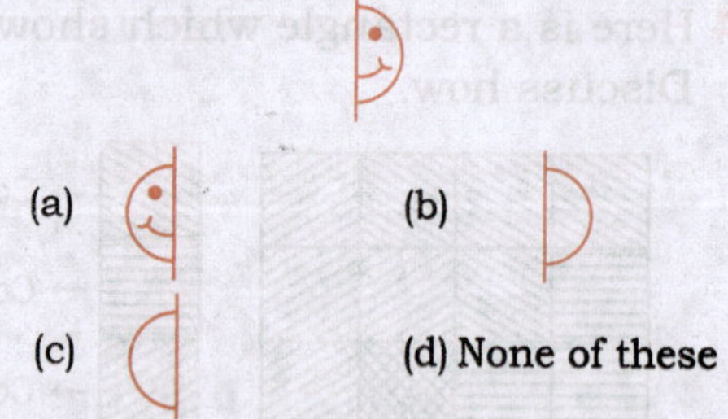

(a) (b)

(c) (d) None of these

(iii) How many pictures are not divided into halves?

(a) 2 (b) 3 (c) 4 (d) 5

(iv) Choose the shape where half of the whole is shaded.

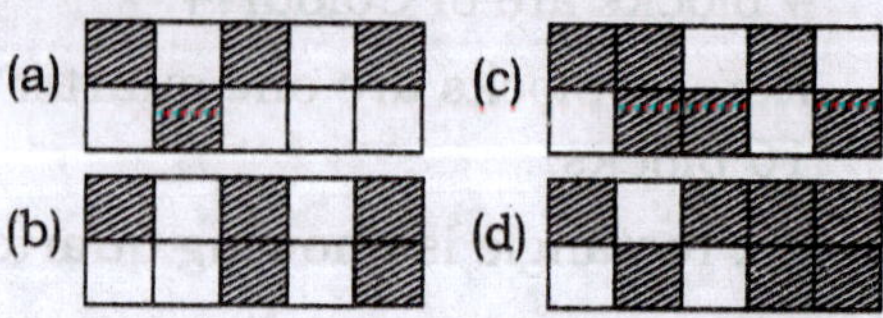

(a) (c)

(b) (d)

3. Puzzles

(i) I have chocolates which are less than double of 5 chocolates but more than half of 16 chocolates. How many chocolates I have?

(ii) I have mangoes which are less than double of 9 mangoes but more than half of 32 mangoes. How many mangoes I have?

4. Complete the following figures which are half drawn.

ANSWERS & SOLUTIONS

1. (i) half (ii) half (iii) Double (iv) quarter

2. (i) (b) (ii) (a) (iii) (c) (iv) (c)

3. (i) Since, number of chocolates is less than double of 5 chocolates but more than half of 16 chocolates. It means number of chocolates is between 10 and 8 because the double of 5 is 10 and half of 16 is 8.

Hence, number of chocolates are 9.

(ii) Double of 9 mangoes = $9 \times 2 = 18$ mangoes

Half of 32 mangoes = $\frac{32}{2} = 16$ mangoes

Since, mangoes I have, are less than double of 9 mangoes but more than half of 32 mangoes. Hence, correct number of mangoes I have, are 17.

4. Complete figures of the given figures are as follows :

CHAPTER 9 HOUSE OF HUNDREDS II

This chapter introduces students to estimate and count large numbers through engaging stories and practical exercises. It helps to understand place value, number sequence and basic mathematical operations. It is also enhancing their numerical reasoning and problem solving skills.

NCERT FOLDER

Let us Do (NCERT Pg 118)

Q.1 (i)

What are you carrying? How many are there?

I am carrying rice. I will show you how many sacks I have using these tiles.

Number of rice sacks [ ]

(ii) Draw tiles like the driver to show the following numbers. You can do it in your notebook.

(a) 832 [ ] (b) 947 [ ]

(c) 726 [ ] (d) 504 [ ]

(e) 620 [ ] (f) 700 [ ]

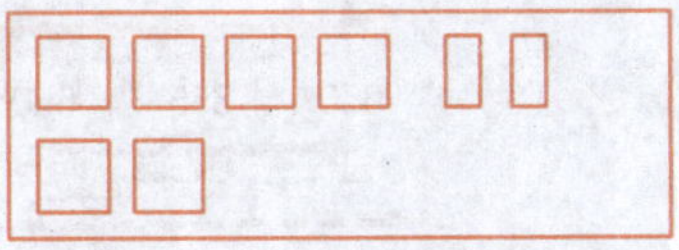

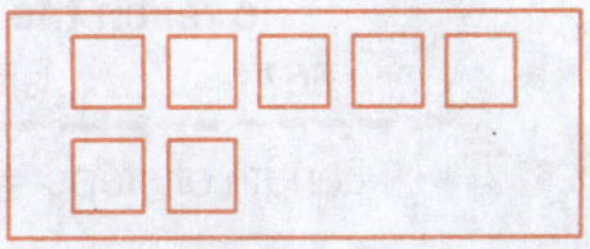

Ans. Here, [big square] → 100, [rectangle] → 10, [small square] → 1

(i) Number of rice sacks = 632

(ii)

(a) 832 = 8 hundreds, 3 tens, 2 ones

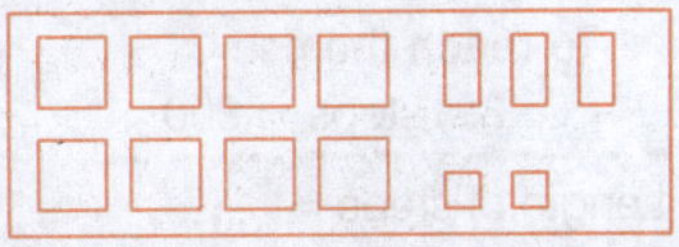

(b) 947 = 9 hundreds, 4 tens, 7 ones

(c) 726 = 7 hundreds, 2 tens, 6 ones

(d) 504 = 5 hundreds, 4 ones

(e) 620 = 6 hundreds, 2 tens

(f) 700 = 7 hundreds

Q.2 Let us locate the following numbers on the number line :

530, 540, 628, 696, 590

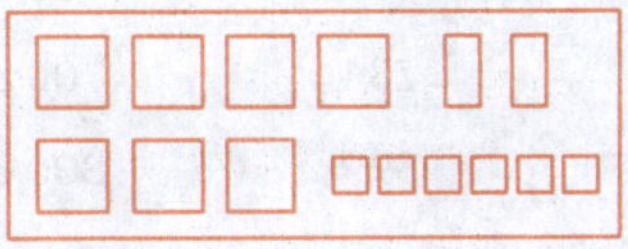

Ans. Number line: 500, 520, 540, 560, 580, 600, 620, 640, 660, 680, 700 — marked: 530, 590, 628, 696 (above); 540, 580, 640 (boxed below)

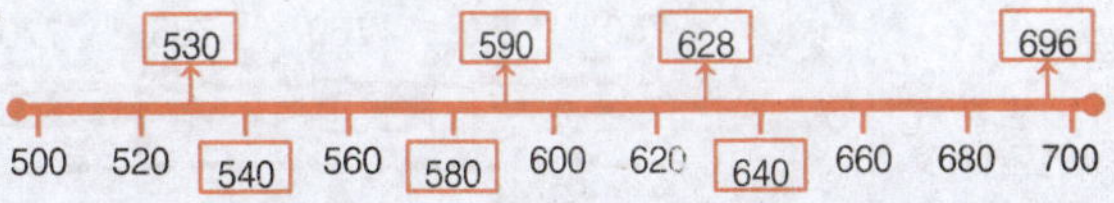

Q.3 Also, locate the following numbers on the number line :

703, 721, 759, 810, 855, 887

Ans. Number line: 695, 715, 735, 755, 775, 795, 815, 835, 855, 875, 895 — marked: 703, 721, 759, 810, 887 (above); 755, 815, 855, 895 (boxed below)

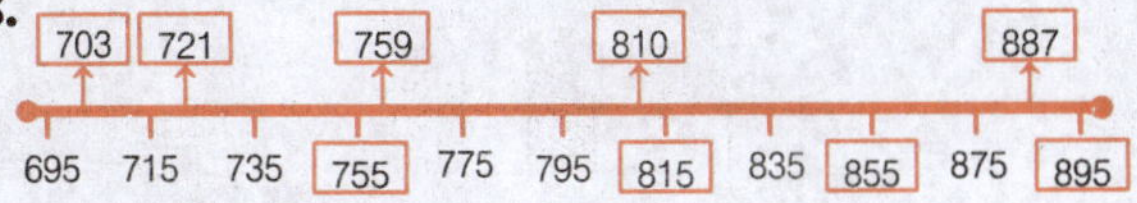

** Students can write alternate answer as per their choice.*

Let us Think (NCERT Pg 119)

Q.4 Write the appropriate numbers between which each of the given numbers lie.

Number	Neighbouring hundreds	Neighbouring fifties	Neighbouring tens
468	400 and 500	450 and 500	460 and 470
183			
345			
693			
734			
899			

Ans.

Number	Neighbouring hundreds	Neighbouring fifties	Neighbouring tens
468	400 and 500	450 and 500	460 and 470
183	100 and 200	150 and 200	180 and 190
345	300 and 400	300 and 350	340 and 350
693	600 and 700	650 and 700	690 and 700
734	700 and 800	700 and 750	730 and 740
899	800 and 900	850 and 900	890 and 900

Q.5 (i) Help crane reach their food using the number line.

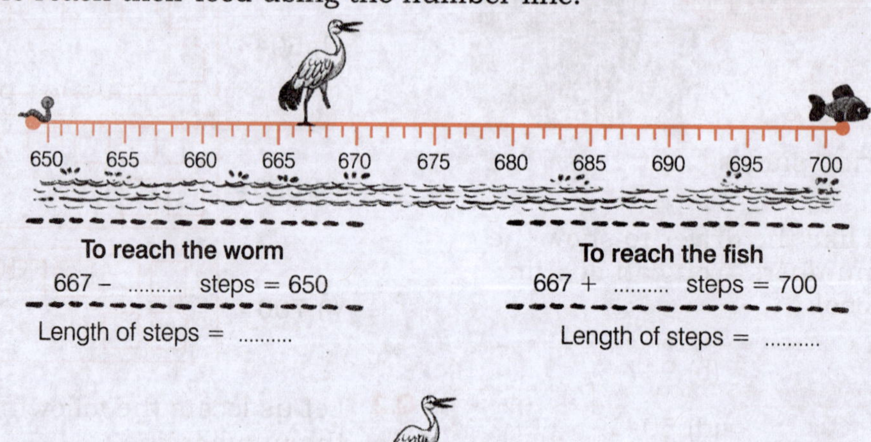

(ii)

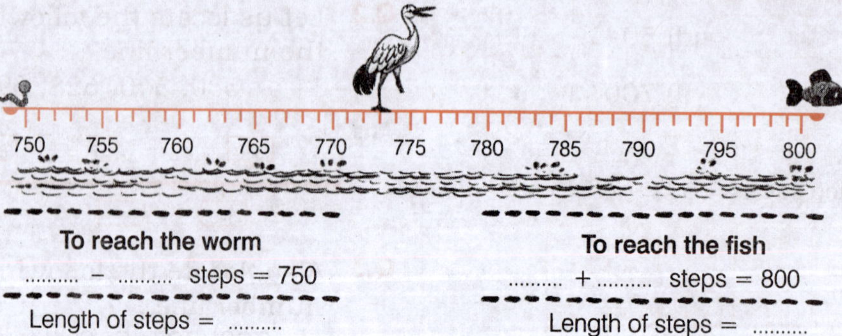

Ans. (i) **To reach the worm**

667 – 17 steps = 650; Length of steps = 17

To reach the fish

667 + 33 steps = 700; Length of steps = 33

(ii) **To reach the worm**

773 – 23 steps = 750, Length of steps = 23

To reach the fish

773 + 27 steps = 800, Length of steps = 27

Tambola (NCERT Pg 120)

Q.6 Fill the grid with numbers between 570 and 630. Strike out all the numbers which match the clues below. You can strike out more than one number. The child who has most numbers cancelled is the winner. One example is given below.

Clues

1. 597
2. A number with 4
3. Numbers between 595 and 605
4. A number with 1 as the tens digit
5. Two more than 610
6. 5 less than 625

572	628	579	599
597	574	581	600
623	573	570	602
609	616	614	626

Ans. Do yourself.

Q.7 Write different ways of making the following numbers. One has been done for you.

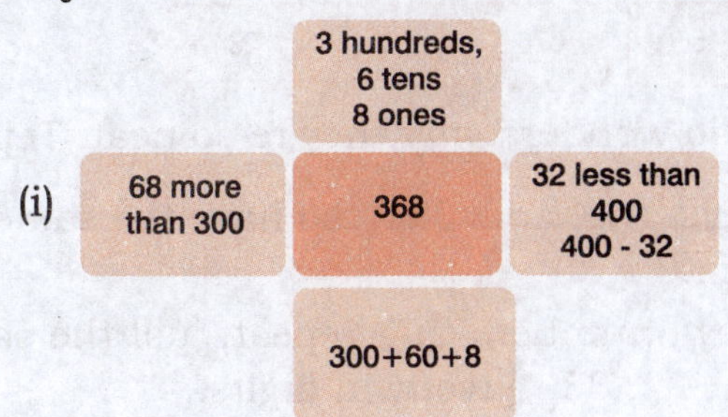

Ans.

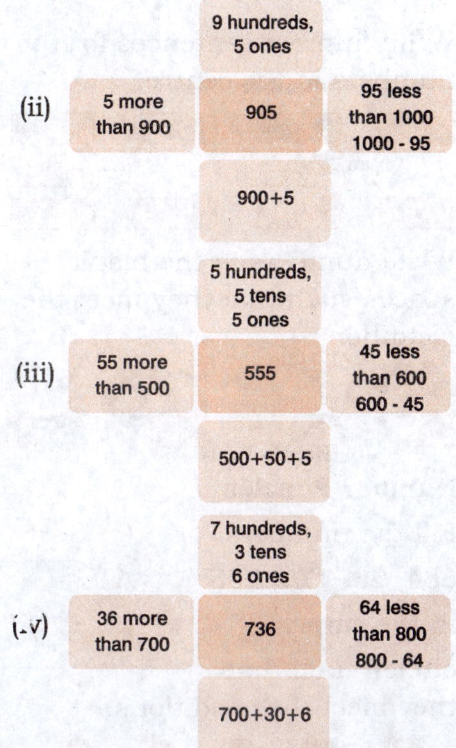

Skip and Solve (NCERT Pg 121)

Q.8 Teji and Jojo are resting. Ajji asks them to complete the number patterns. Let us help them fill in the empty boxes.

Ans.

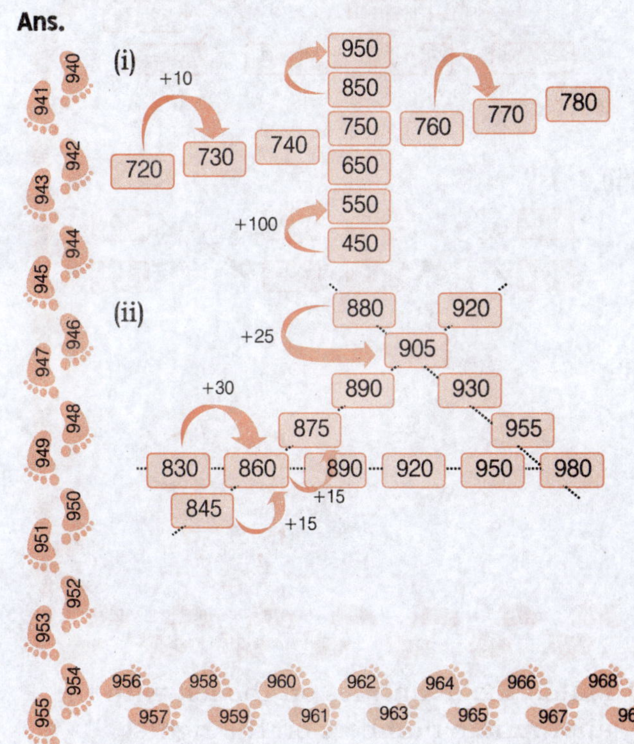

Let us Do (NCERT Pg 122-123)

Q.9 (i) Write number sentences for the numbers in the centre.

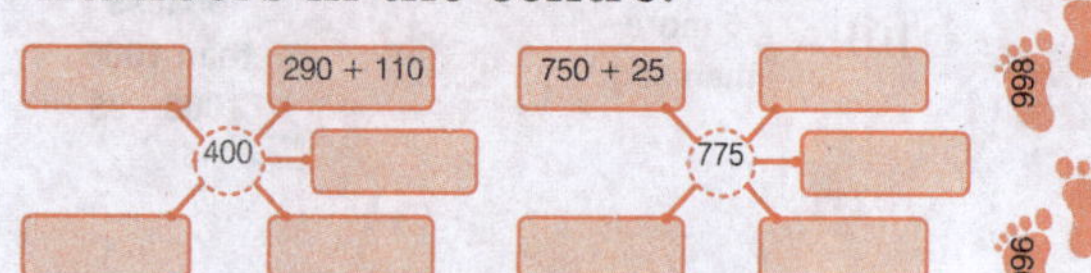

(ii) Write numbers in the blank spaces such that they meet the conditions.

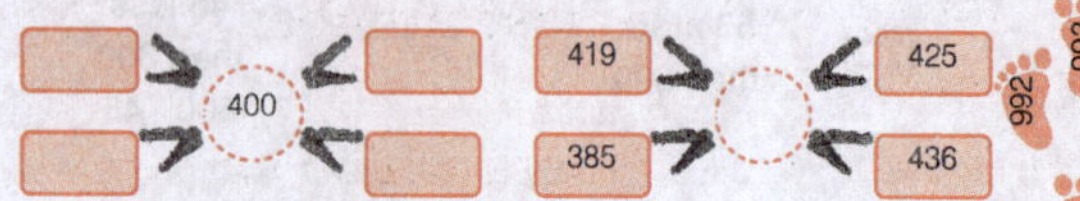

(iii) **Number Puzzles**

Fill the numbers 384, 23, 176, 905 in the empty circles such that they meet the conditions.

Ans. *(i)

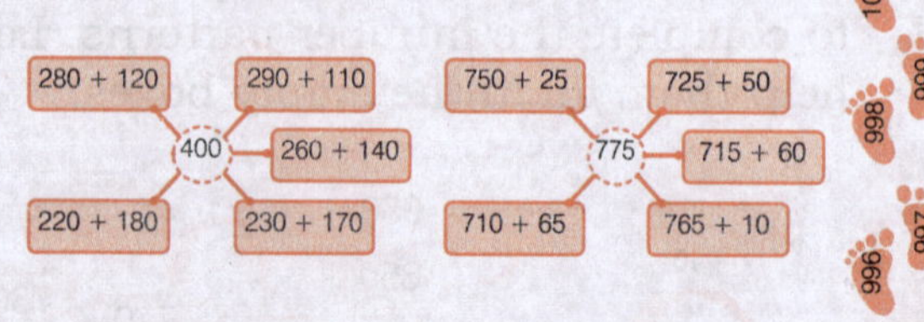

*(ii)

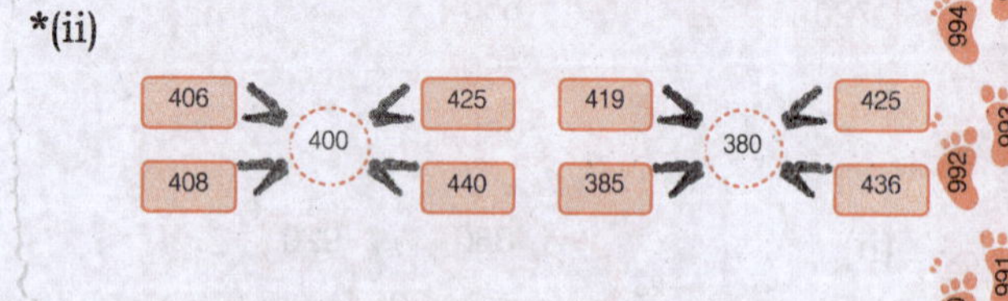

(iii)

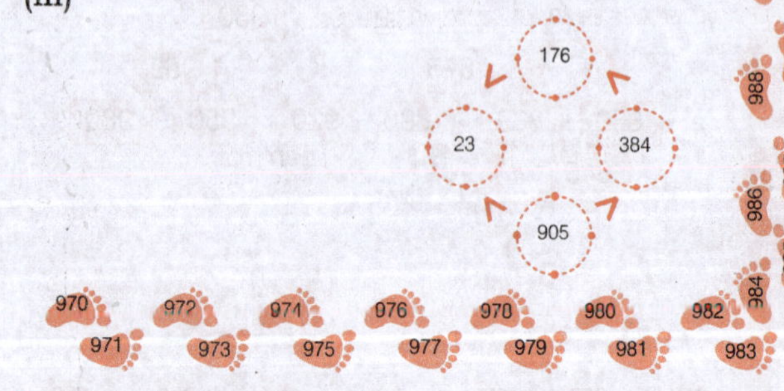

Q.10 Match the quantities on the left with the appropriate numbers on the right.

(i)	Number of children in your school	(a)	0-10
(ii)	Number of books in your classroom	(b)	11-50
(iii)	Number of people in a bus	(c)	51-100
(iv)	Number of pages in your mathematics book	(d)	101-200
(v)	Number of steps you walk in a day	(e)	201-500
(vi)	Number of stars in the sky	(f)	501-1000
(vii)	Number of flowers in a garland	(g)	More than 1000

Ans. * (i) - (e), (ii) - (d), (iii) - (a), (iv) - (c) (v) - (f), (vi) - (g), (vii) - (b)

Q.11 Match the following such that all the conditions are met.

(i)	I have 2 zeroes as digits and am very close to 99	(a)	150
(ii)	I have 3 hundreds, 6 tens and 7 ones	(b)	425
(iii)	I have zero tens and zero ones	(c)	367
(iv)	I am century + half century	(d)	400
(v)	I come between 400 and 450 and I have 5 as a digit	(e)	100

Ans. (i) - (e), (ii) - (c), (iii) - (d), (iv) - (a), (v) - (b)

The Number Detective (NCERT Pg 124)

Q.12 Let us have some fun, with numbers and patterns, everyone!

Look at the hundreds –

Can you find all the hundreds?

Ans.

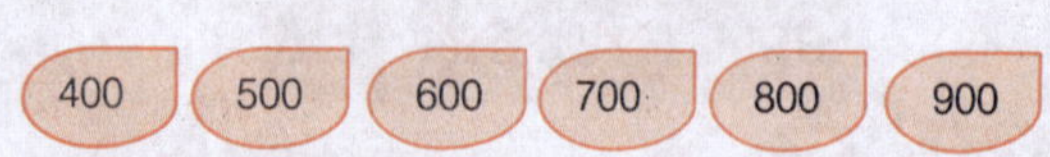

Q.13 Some numbers are special, let's explore, 789 345 and 123, what more?

Ans.

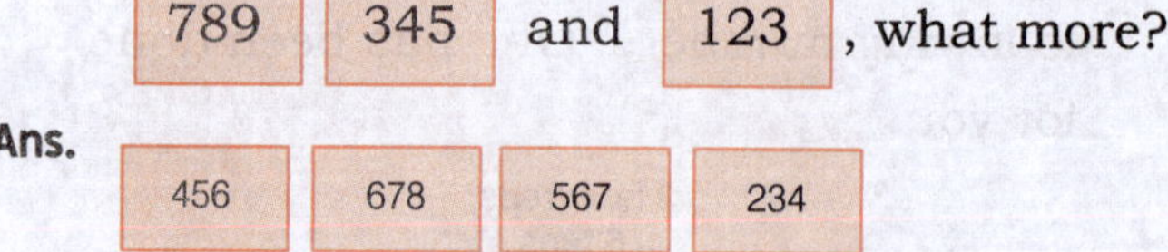

Q.14 Jojo wonders why they're so neat, Teji says 876 and 321 too have the same beat!

Now, numbers that repeat, just the same, 11, 22, 33, have twin digits.

111, 222, 333 are triplet digits.
Can you find more such numbers that follow the pattern?

Ans. *

444	555	666	777	888

Q.15 Here are more numbers that look the same, from left to right and right to left

353 868

Finding them is a fun game. Write other such numbers.

Ans. *

565	121	787	636	424

Q.16 Teji likes numbers with zeroes. She knows numbers like 210 404 and 800 .

Write more such numbers :

Ans. *

270	303	810	390	408

Let us Do (NCERT Pg 125)

Q.17 I have 6 blank paper slips. I can write 100, 10 or 1 on each of them. What numbers can I make with these 6 slips? Discuss.

Six slips with 100 written on them. Six hundred.

Four slips with 100 written on them and two slips with 10 on them. 420

100	100	100
100	100	100

100	100	10
100	100	10

(i) What will you write on these slips for making 231?

(ii) What will you write on these slips for making 123?

(iii) Make other numbers.

(a) Number is ....

(b) Number is ....

(iv) What is the largest number that can be made?

(v) Are there numbers which cannot be made using these slips? Find out.

(vi) What is the smallest number that can be made?

Ans. (i)

100	100	10
10	10	1

(ii)

100	10	10
1	1	1

(iii) *

(a) 141 = 100 10 10 10 10 1

(b) 312 = 100 100 100 10 1 1

(iv) 600 is the largest number that can be made.

(v) So many numbers cannot be made using only six slips.
e.g. 331, 340 etc.

(vi) 6 is the smallest number that can be made.

My numbers (NCERT Pg 126)

Q.18 Take the digits 3 and 8 and make as many 2 or 3 digit numbers as you can. You can repeat the digits.

Jojo, with 3 and 8, I can make 38.

I can make 338, 388

3	8		8	3

3	8

3	3	8

3	8	8

2 digit numbers	3 digit numbers

Arrange the numbers

Smaller to greater

....

....

Smallest number =

Largest number =

Ans.

2 digit numbers	3 digit numbers
33	333
88	888
38	388, 833, 383, 338, 883, 838
83	

- Smaller to greater
  33, 38, 83, 88, 333, 338, 383, 388, 833, 838, 883, 888
- Smallest number = 33
- Largest number = 888

Let us Think (NCERT Pg 126-127)

Q.19 (i) Teji is making numbers using words! She shows the Colur-1 cards and says it is 12. She shows the Colour-2 cards and says 14. Why?

Colour-1 cards   Colour-2 cards

Figure out what Teji is doing.

(ii) Write the numbers, for the following cards.

(a) (b)

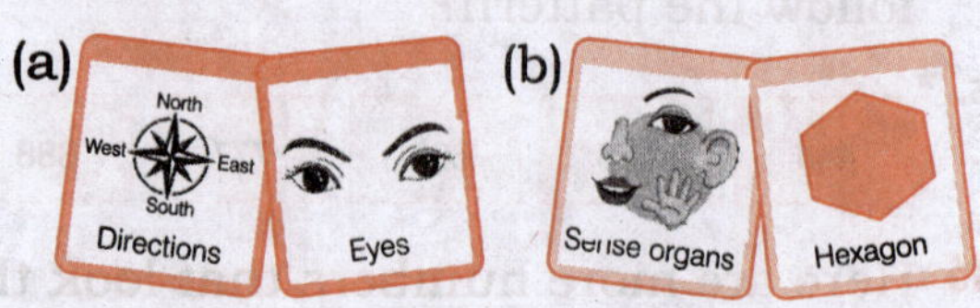

(iii) Think of other words for 0-9.

Make new cards for the numbers 15, 27 and 94.

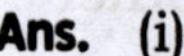

Ans. (i)

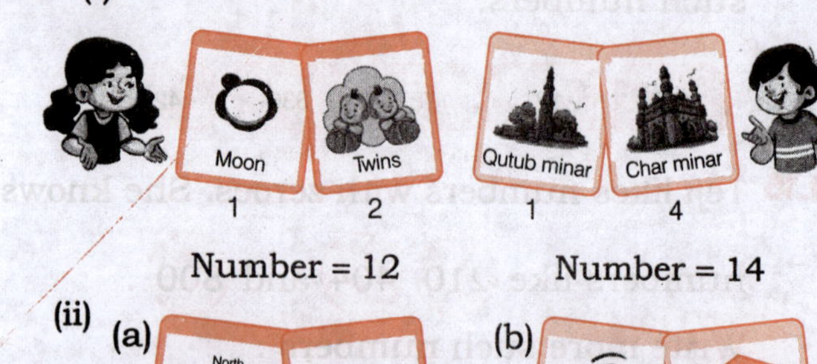

Number = 12   Number = 14

(ii) (a)

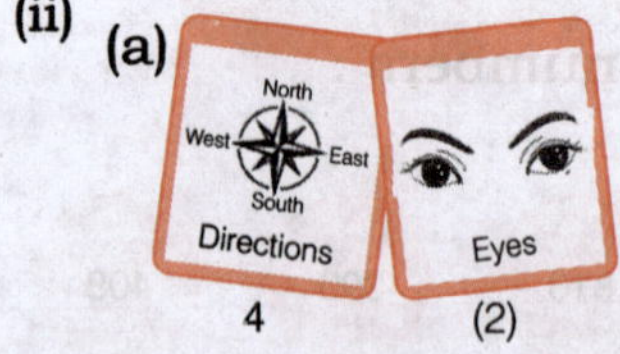

(b)

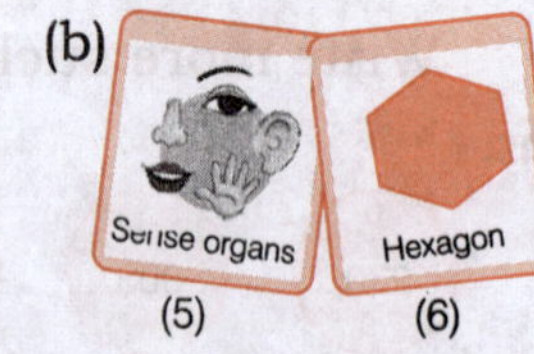

Number = 42   Number = 56

*(iii) For number 15,

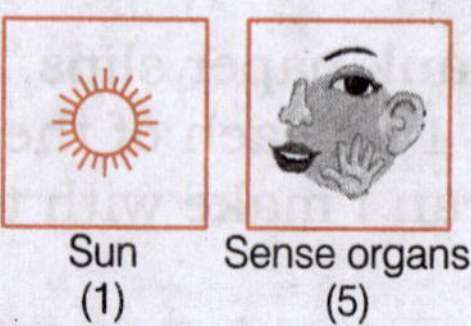

For number 27,

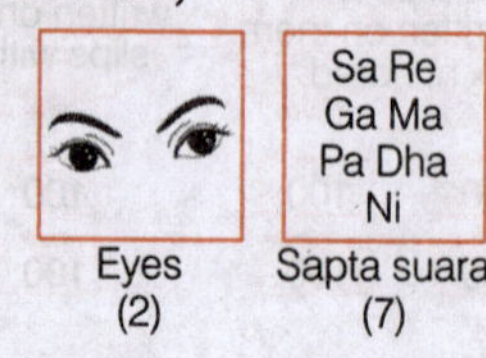

For number 54,

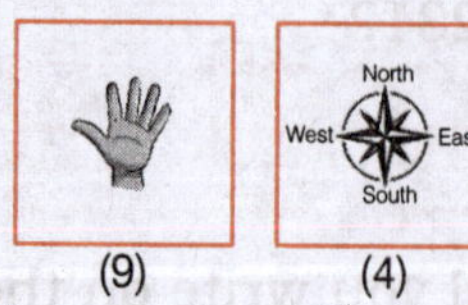

PRACTICE QUESTIONS

1. Fill in the blanks.

	Number	**Neighbouring tens**
(i)	978	_______ and _______
(ii)	423	_______ and _______
(iii)	897	_______ and _______
(iv)	550	_______ and _______

2. Multiple choice questions.

(i) Which number lies between 331 and 350?

(a) 358 (b) 379
(c) 348 (d) 329

(ii) 970 and 980 are the neighbouring tens of

(a) 953 (b) 967
(c) 989 (d) 979

(iii) 9 hundreds, 5 tens and 7 ones is

(a) 970 (b) 975
(c) 957 (d) 795

(iv) Complete the pattern

527, 627, 727 ____ ?

(a) 729 (b) 780 (c) 820 (d) 827

(v) Which of the following is nearest ten for 53?

(a) 70 (b) 20 (c) 50 (d) 60

3. Match the following.

(i)	558	(a)	3 hundreds + half century
(ii)	350	(b)	Number between 670 and 700 and its middle digit is 7.
(iii)	235	(c)	I have a number in which 5 hundreds, 5 tens and 8 ones.
(iv)	100	(d)	I have 5 as unit digit and I am less than 240.
(v)	678	(e)	I have zero tens and zero ones.

4. (i) Make largest three-digit number using 7 and 5. You can repeat the digits.

(ii) Make smallest three-digit number using digits 2 and 5. You can repeat the digits.

(iii) What is the greatest three digit whole number you can make using all the following digits? 3, 5, 1.

5. Fill the appropriate sign ‘ >’ more than and ‘ <’ less than.

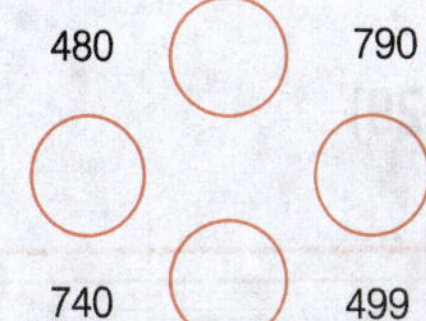

ANSWERS & SOLUTIONS

1. (i) 970, 980 (ii) 420, 430
(iii) 890, 900 (iv) 540, 560

2. (i) (c) (ii) (d) (iii) (c)
(iv) (d) (v) (c)

3. (i) (c) (ii) (a)
(iii) (d) (iv) (e)
(v) (b)

4. (i) 775 (ii) 225 (iii) 531

5.

CHAPTER 10 FUN AT CLASS PARTY

This chapter is all about understanding measurements in a fun and engaging way. We will learn how to measure various objects using different techniques and understand the importance of accurate measurements.

Measurement Measurement is a system to measure the height, weight, capacity or even amount of certain objects.

Height The measurement of the distance of an object from the base to the top is called height.

Length Length is a measure of how long something is. The standard unit of length is 'metre'.

NCERT FOLDER

Let us Do (NCERT Pg 128-129)

Q.1

Discuss and explain how you answer these questions based on the picture given above.

(i) What are the various activities shown in the picture?

(ii) How does Shelly find the height of the door?

(iii) Leena and Adi use their hand spans to measure the length of the same table. Will they both get the same measurement?

(iv) Circle the child with the longest ponytail.

(v) Tick (✓) paper strings in the classroom that are as long as the height of the window.

(vi) Find the distance between the two walls of the classroom. How did you find it? Can there be other ways of measuring it?

(vii) Identify all the ways that children are using to measure length in this picture. Which way do you think is better and why?

** Students can write alternate answer as per their choice.*

Ans. (i) Some children are decorating the board. A girl is measuring the height of the door. Two children are measuring the length of the table by hand span. A boy is measuring distance between the walls by foot step.

(ii) Shelly is finding the height of the door using ruler.

(iii) No, they will get different measurement because hand spans vary due to hand size. Therefore, both of them will get different hand spans but the length of the table will remain same.

(iv) Do yourself.

(v) Do yourself.

*(vi) I am using a ruler to find the distance between walls. Yes, there is another ways of measuring it. e.g. using hand span and foot span.

*(vii) The students are measuring the length using scale, hand span, foot span and stretching arms. I think Shelly's method of measurement is better as it will give accurate measurement.

Let us Do (NCERT Pg 129)

Q.2 Children of class 3 are decorating the board with paper string of different colours.

(i) In the picture above, colour the paper strings as instructed below.

(a) Colour the shortest paper string with red. Discuss how you identified the shortest string.

(b) Colour the longest paper string with green. Discuss how you identified the longest string.

(ii) How many of are needed to decorate the entire border of the board?

Ans. (i) (a) Do yourself.

(b) Do yourself.

(ii) 30 are needed to decorate the entire border of the board.

Let us Do (NCERT Pg 130-131)

Q.3 Cut and paste a wool or cotton thread as long as the line given below.

Ans. Do yourself.

Q.4 Draw a string longer than the string given below.

Ans. *

Q.5 Draw a string shorter than the decoration string Shelly and Adi are holding.

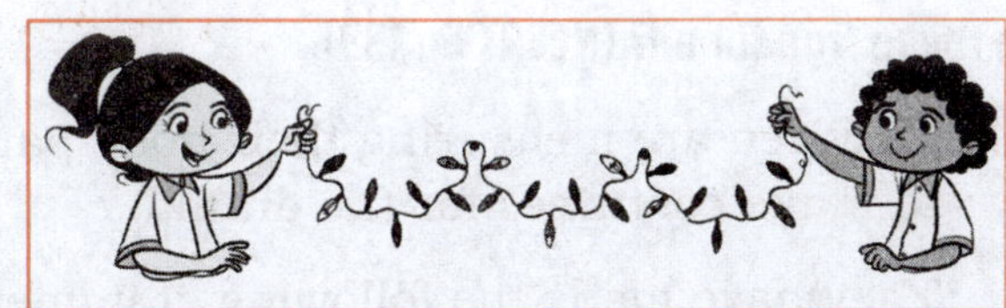

Ans. *

Q.6 Draw the other half of the moustache which is as long as the half of the moustache on the face shown in the picture.

Ans.

Q.7 Look at the strings and help Adi choose the longest one. How did you find out? Discuss.

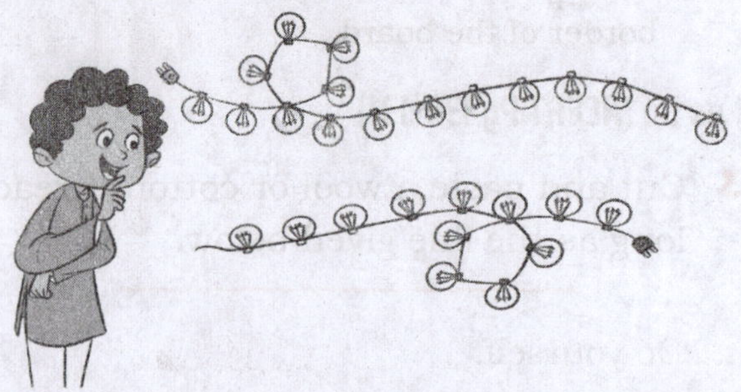

Ans. First, count the number of bulbs in both strings, then decide after compairing.

The upper string has more bulbs than that of lower string. So, upper string is longest.

Let us Play (NCERT Pg 132)

Q.8 Can you name some things that cannot pass through your school gate? Discuss.

Ans. * Truck, Excavator and other big vehicles. Vehicles exceeding the height of the school gate can not pass through the school gate.

Are these true for all? (NCERT Pg 133)

Q.9 Children are measuring their body parts to make costumes for the drama.

They have made the following statements. Do you think they are true for all children? Let us check. Take help from your friends to measure. Choose the correct answer.

(i) Your head is 3 handspans round. (True/False)

(ii) The length of your forearm is equal to the length of your feet. (True/False)

(iii) Your height is equal to the length of your arms wide open. (True/False)

Ans. *(i) False *(ii) False *(iii) True

NCERT Pg 135-136

Q.10 Write the names of your friends whose heights are more than one metre and whose heights are less than one metre.

Heights more than one metre		Heights less than one metre	

Ans. Do yourself.

Q.11 Tell the tallest among these children.

Who is the tallest among them? Discuss.

Ans. The first girl from the left side is tallest.

Q.12 Write the names of the objects around you, whose length is one metre, more than one metre, and less than one metre.

Objects of length more than one metre	Objects of length less than one metre	Objects of length equal to one metre

Ans. *

Objects of length more than one metre	Objects of length less than one metre	Objects of length equal to one metre
Almirah	Water bottle	Dressing mirror
Door	Corner table	Shoe rack
Bed	Flower vase	Window
Sofa	Book	Study-table
Cupboard	Broom	Water tank
Curtain	Bucket	Measuring rod

Let us Do (NCERT Pg 137)

Q.13 Find the lengths of different objects by using one metre, half meter, and quarter metre ropes. Write their names and tick (✓) in the appropriate boxes.

Objects	Less than a quarter metre	More than a quarter metre	Less than a half metre	More than a half metre	Less than one metre	More than one metre

Ans. *

Objects	Less than a quarter metre	More than a quarter metre	Less than a half metre	More than a half metre	Less than one metre	More than one metre
Desk						✓
Chair					✓	
Pen	✓					
Sofa						✓
Lamp	✓	✓				
Book	✓	✓				

Q.14 Mark a line on the floor as a start line and then mark another line one metre from the Start line. Stand on the Start line and jump. Write the names of children who jump more than a quarter of a metre, half of a metre and a metre.

Ans. Do yourself.

Q.15 Take a ball or disc and try to throw it as far as you can. Now measure how far the throw was.

Ans. Do yourself.

Let us Do (NCERT Pg 138)

Q.16 (i) Measure the height of your teacher or parent using a metre long rope or a strip.

(ii) Estimate and cut one-metre long wool or thread. Ask your friends to do the same. Now, verify with the help of the metre rope whose estimate is the closest.

(iii) Cut a one-metre long rope into 4 equal pieces. How many cuts did you make?

(iv) How many footsteps fit into a metre rope?

(v) Use a metre rope to find how long is a side of the class wall?

Ans. (i) Do yourself.

(ii) Do yourself.

(iii) I made 3 cuts to make 4 equal parts.

(iv) Do yourself.

(v) Do yourself.

PRACTICE QUESTIONS

1. Fill in the blanks.

(i) The length of the table is .... pencils.

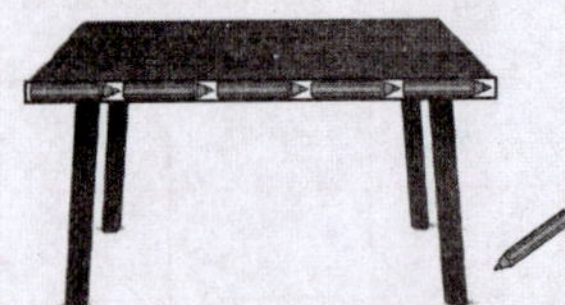

(ii) The length of your tooth brush is approximately .... a metre.

(iii) The length of the bed is .... bats.

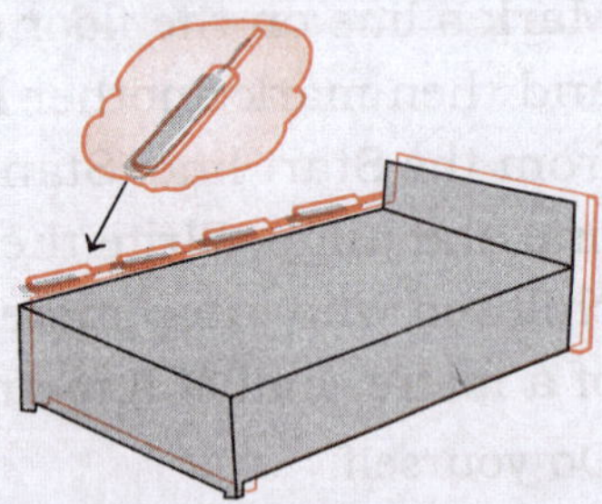

2. True or false.

(i) Length of your maths book is approximately less than a metre.

(ii) Length of mobile is approximately a metre.

(iii) Length of a table is approximately a centimetre.

3. Multiple choice questions.

(i) What is the difference between the length of the piece of ribbon and the pencil?

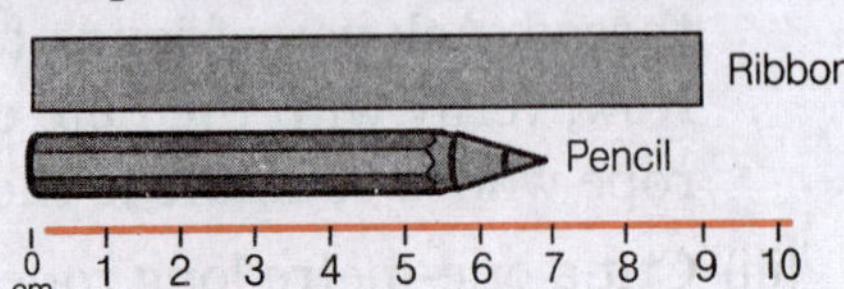

(a) 1 centimetre (b) 2 centimetre

(c) 4 centimetre (d) 3 centimetre

(ii) Which of these will be measured in metres (m)?

(a) Length of paper (b) Mobile screen

(c) Length of a curtain (d) Television screen

(iii) Which of the following ribbons is the longest?

(a) (b)

(c) (d)

4. Choose the unit you would like to measure the length.

(i) Length of a small window

(a) metre (b) centimetre (c) kilometre

(ii) Height of the mountain

(a) metre (b) centimetre (c) kilometre

(iii) Length of a shoe

(a) metre (b) centimetre (c) kilometre

5. Picture based question

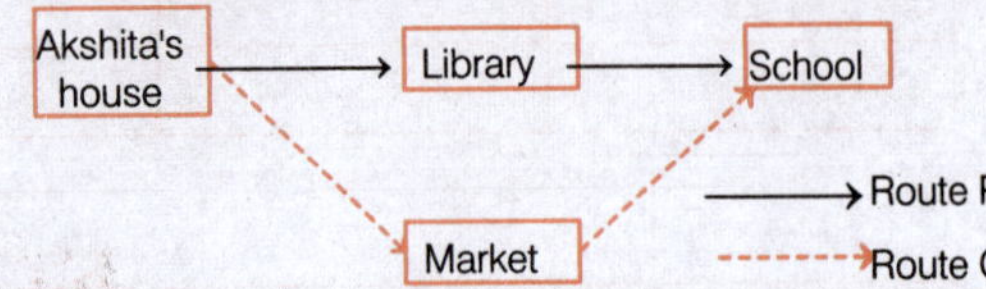

There are two possible routes that Akshita can take to reach her school from her house. Which route is shorter?

6. Some students and their heights are given in the following table.

Name of Students	Height of students
Ramesh	1 metre
Rohan	Less than 1 metre
Sanjay	1 metre
Manjeet	1 metre
Priya	Less than 1 metre

(i) How many students have the height less than 1 metre?

(ii) Who is the taller between Priya and Ramesh?

(iii) Is Sanjay is taller than Manjeet?

ANSWERS & SOLUTIONS

1. (i) 5 (ii) less than (iii) 4

2. (i) True (ii) False (iii) False

3. (i) (b) (ii) (c) (iii) (c)

4. (i) (b) (ii) (a) (iii) (b)

5. Route *P* is shorter.

6. (i) Rohan and Priya only two students have the height less than 1 metre.

(ii) It is clear from the given table, Priya's height is less than 1 metre and Ramesh's height is 1 metre.

Hence, Ramesh is taller than Priya.

(iii) No, Sanjay and Manjeet both have equal height.

FILLING AND LIFTING

Capacity

The maximum amount that a container or space can hold is called capacity.

Measuring weight

Weight is the measure of how heavy an object or a person. Unit of weight is kilogram.

NCERT FOLDER

How much can you drink? (NCERT Pg 139)

Q.1 Why do you think Chintu does not take the challenge?

Ans. Chintu is afraid of finishing 6 bigger glasses of juice.

Q.2 Do you think you can take the challenges?

Ans. * No, I cannot accept the challenge and drink 6 glasses of juice.

Whose glass holds more? (NCERT Pg 140-141)

Nita and Monu visit Ritu's house. Ritu's mother gives them milk in different glasses. Who do you think gets the most milk?

Ritu's elder sister finds out who drinks the most milk like this. She pours the content of the glasses in three same-sized glasses.

** Students can write alternate answer as per their choice.*

Q.3 Who drank the most milk?

Ans. Ritu drank the most milk.

Q.4 Who drank the least milk?

Ans. Nita drank the least milk.

Q.5 Fill in the blanks with 'more' or 'less'.

(a) Nita's glass holds .... milk than Monu's glass.

(b) Monu's glass holds .... milk than Nita's glass.

(c) Ritu's glass holds .... milk than Nita's glass.

Ans. (a) less (b) more (c) more

Q.6 Choose the right name.

(i) Nita/Monu/Ritu's glass holds the most milk.

(ii) Nita/Monu/Ritu's glass holds the least milk.

Ans. (i) Ritu's glass holds the most milk.

(ii) Nita's glass holds the least milk.

Let us Do (NCERT Pg 141)

Q.7 Get three vessels (like a small bowl, glass and bottle) of different sizes from your home.

Guess : how many small bowls will fill the glass? How many glasses will fill the bottle? First guess and then pour water from one vessel into another to check if your guess is correct.

Ans. *

Vessel	My guess for the number of small bowls	How many bowls
Glass	4	6
Bottle	12	18

Q.8 Fill in the blanks with 'the most' or 'the least'.

(i) The glass holds .... water.

(ii) The bottle holds .... water.

Ans. (i) the least (ii) the most

Q.9 Name the vessels that are used in your home that can store more water than your bottle.

Ans. * Buckets, water tanks, jugs, storage and bins etc.

Let us Do (NCERT Pg 142)

Q.10 (i) How many ladles fill the bowl?

(ii) How many glasses can be filled by the jug?

(iii) What will you use to fill half of the glass?

(iv) Which of these would you use for distributing the lemonade in glasses? Why?

(v) How many glasses can be filled with 3 jugs of lemonade?

(vi) How many ladles are needed to fill 4 glasses?

(vii) Can you use a ladle, bowl or a glass to find out how much lemonade a jug can hold?

Ans. (i) 2 ladles.

(ii) 4 glasses.

(iii) A bowl or two laddles.

(iv) We will use the jug for distributing the lemonade in glasses because it can hold more lemonade than glass.

(v) Since, 4 glasses can be filled with 1 jug. So, number of glasses that can be filled with 3 jugs = 4 × 3 = 12

(vi) Since, 2 ladles fill one bowl, then 4 ladles fill 2 bowls and 2 bowls fill 1 glass. Therefore, 4 laddles fill 1 glass. So, number of ladles needed to fill 4 glasses = 4 × 4 = 16

(vii) Yes, We can use a ladle, bowl or a glass to find out how much lemonade a jug can hold.

Let us Discuss (NCERT Pg 143-144)

Q.11 Choose the appropriate word in the sentences given below.

(i) The glass holds <u>more than/less than</u> 1 litre.

(ii) The bowl holds <u>more than/less than</u> 1 litre.

(iii) The jug holds <u>more than/less than/exactly</u> 1 litre.

Ans. (i) less than

(ii) less than

*(iii) exactly

Q.12 Find the vessels at home that are exactly 1 litre. Use your 1 litre bottle to check.

Ans. * Water bottle, cooking oil bottle, juice bottle etc.

Q.13 Identify vessels that are more than or less than 1 litre.

Ans. * **More than 1 litre** Large cooking pot, glass containers etc.

Less than 1 litre Mug, drinking glass, small bowl, coffee mug etc.

Let us Think (NCERT Pg 144)

Q.14 Look at the picture and find the appropriate word.

(i) The mug holds a litre/half litre of water.

(ii) The glass holds a litre/half litre/quarter litre of water.

Ans. (i) half litre (ii) quarter litre

Let us Explore (NCERT Pg 144)

Q.15 First guess and check with the 1 litre bottle

(i) How much water does a bucket hold at your home, more than/less than/equal to 1 litre.

(ii) How much water does a mug hold at your home, less than/more than/equal to half a litre.

(iii) How much water does a glass hold, less than/more than/equal to a quarter litre.

Ans. (i) more than 1 litre

*(ii) equal to 1 litre

*(iii) less than 1 litre

Heavy or Light (NCERT Pg 145)

Q.16 Do you and your friends agree on which is lighter and heavier?

Ans.

Things to compare	My observation	My friend's observation
Lunch box and Pencil box	Lunch box is heavier than Pencil box	Pencil box is heavier than Lunch box.
Your school bag and Lunch box	School bag is heavier than Lunch box	School bag is heavier than Lunch box
Apple and watermelon	Watermelon is heavier than apple.	Watermelon is heavier than apple
A balloon filled with air and a basketball	Basketball is heavier than balloon	Balloon is heavier than basketball

Let us Do (NCERT Pg 146)

Q.17 Write the names of the objects and their weights in the table given below.

Ans. *

	Object	How many coins or erasers balance the object?
(a)	Pencil	4 erasers
(b)	Ping Pong Ball	2 coins
(c)	Ball pen	3 erasers
(d)	Sharpener	3 coins
(e)	Compass	5 coins

Q.18 Let us make another weight to measure slightly heavier objects. Fill a matchbox with sand and use this to weigh the following objects. Guess the weight in terms of matchboxes and then verify.

Ans. *

Object	Your guess for the number of matchboxes needed to balance the object	Number of matchboxes used to balance the object
Pencil box	10	10
A spoon	5	4
4 marbles	8	6
10 erasers	8	9
20 sharpener	13	15

Q.19 Write the names of all things measured in the order of lightest to heaviest.

Ans. A spoon, 4 marbles, 10 erasers, pencil box, and 20 sharpeners.

Let us Do (NCERT Pg 147)

Q.20 **Weight hunt** Do this activity in groups. Among your group find a bag that is heavier than your bag. Find a bag that is lighter than your bag. Discuss.

(i) Why is your bag heavier or lighter?

(ii) Count the number of books to see if there is a difference in the number of books in the bag.

(iii) Can you make the two bags of about the same weight by moving a book? Discuss.

Ans. *(i) My bag is heavier because it has more notebooks and books.

*(ii) Yes, there is a difference between my bag and my friend's bag as my bag has 2 more notebooks.

*(iii) Yes, I can make two bags equal in weight by shifting maths book from my bag to my friend's bag.

Q.21 **How much is 1 Kilogram?**

With the help of your parents, find objects in your home on which 1 kilogram is written. Feel it with your hand and guess what other objects may be 1 kilogram. Verify by checking on the label of the object or by asking your parents.

Write the names of the objects that are 1 kilogram.

Ans. *A bag of sugar, a bag of flour, a bag of rice etc.

Q.22 Can you guess which of these things are likely to be lighter or heavier than 1 kilogram? Put a tick ✓ mark in the appropriate box.

Ans. *

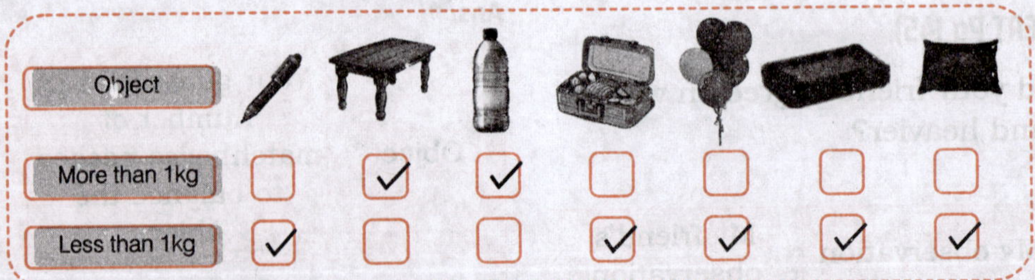

Q.23 Look at the balance and find the correct word.

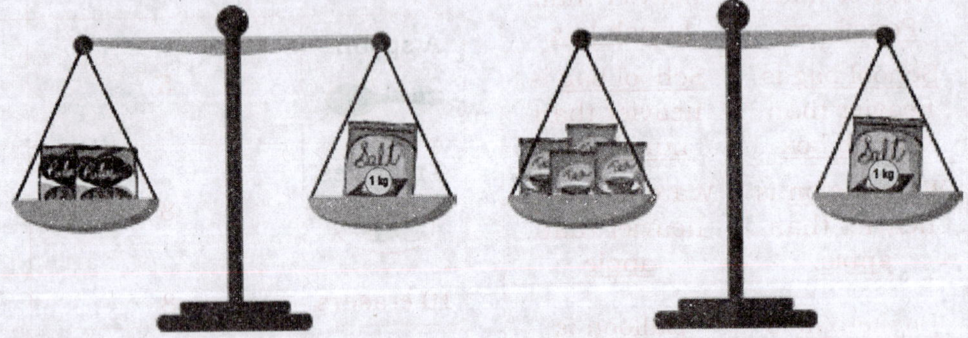

(a) Each daal packet weighs a <u>half kilogram/kilogram</u>.

(b) Each tea packet weighs a <u>half kilogram/quarter kilogram/kilogram</u>.

Ans. (a) Each daal packet weighs a half kilogram.

(b) Each tea packet weighs a quarter kilogram.

Let us Explore (NCERT Pg 148)

Q.24 Look around your house and identify objects that are about half a kilogram and quarter of a kilogram. Feel these things with your hand and guess what other things are a half or quarter kilogram. List the objects that are about a quarter kilogram and a half kilogram. Verify with the 1 kilogram salt packet.

Ans. Do yourself.

Tricky balls (NCERT Pg 149)

Q.25 Montu poses a puzzle to his friends, 3 balls look similar in size. One of them is heavier and 2 balls are equal in weight. You have only a pan-balance and no weights. Using the 3 balls and the pan-balance, can you identify which is the heavy ball?

(i) How many times will you have to weigh?

(ii) Use the balance only one time and tell which is the heavy ball.

Ans. (i) We need to weigh only once to identify the heavier ball.

(ii) Weigh any two balls against each other on the pan-balance.
If they do not balance, the heavier ball will be on the side that goes down.
If they balance out (equal weight), the third ball, which was not weighed, is the heavier one.

Q.26 There are three same-sized balls of different weights and colours:

Red, Orange and Green.

You can use the pan balance for it but cannot use weights.

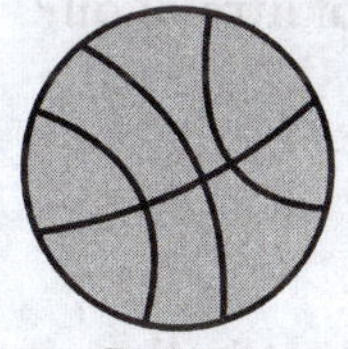
Red ball

Orange ball

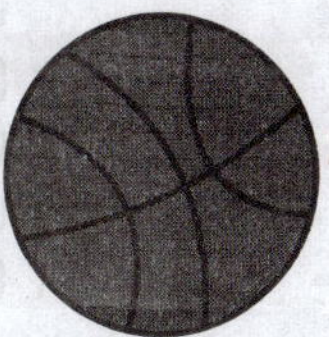
Green ball

How will you find which one is the heaviest and which one is the lightest?

Ans. **Step I** Weigh the red ball against the orange ball.

If one is heavier, set it aside as a potential heaviest. The other is lighter.

Step II Weigh the heavier ball (from step I) against green ball.

It the green ball is heavier, it's the heaviest and other is the middle-weight.

If green ball is lighter, then the other ball is heaviest.
Now, weigh the green ball and the lighter ball (from step I). If the green ball is heavier, then the other ball is the lightest. If the other ball is heavier, then the green ball is the lightest.

PRACTICE QUESTIONS

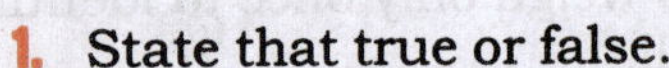

1. State that true or false.

(i) The basketball is heavier than feather.

(ii) Water bottle holds the less water than tea cup.

(iii) The small bowl holds the less water than glass.

(iv) The jug holds exactly 1 litre of water.

2. Multiple choice questions.

(i) Which one of the following can holds the more water?

(a) Bucket (b) Glass
(c) Cup (d) Bowl

(ii) Which one of the following can hold less than half quarter of litre of oil?

(a) Oil bottle
(b) Eye drops bottle
(c) Glass
(d) Cooker

(iii) Which ball is lightest in the given three figures?

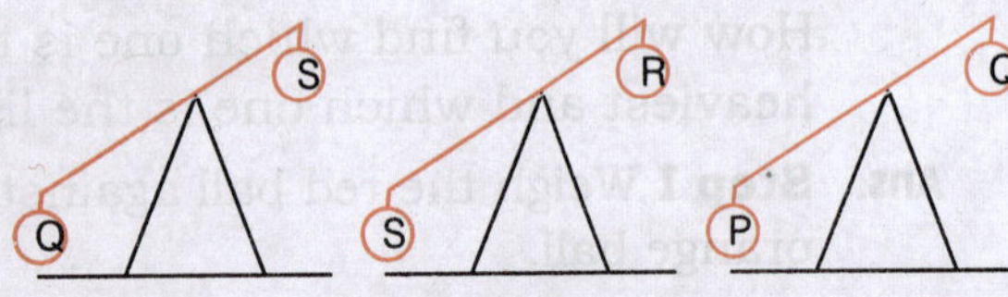

(a) P (b) Q
(c) R (d) S

(iv) Which of the following weighs can be more than 1 kg?

(a) Watermelon (b) Pea
(c) Apple (d) Banana

(v) The weight of an apple is best measured in

(a) Litre (b) Kilogram
(c) Kilometre (d) Metre

(vi) How many oranges ( ) can balance the weight of one cube ( )?

(a) 10 oranges (b) 2 oranges
(c) 4 oranges (d) 16 oranges

3. (i) Choose which object weights more than 1 kg.

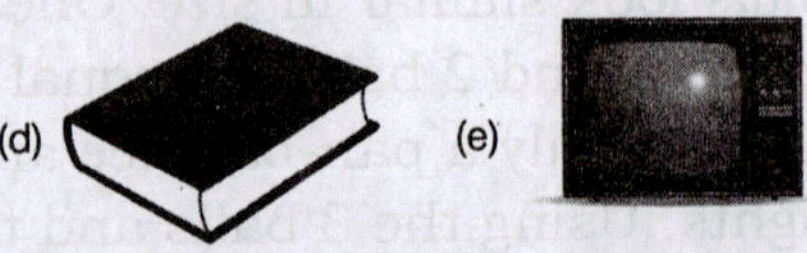

(ii) Choose which object weights less than 1 kg.

(a)
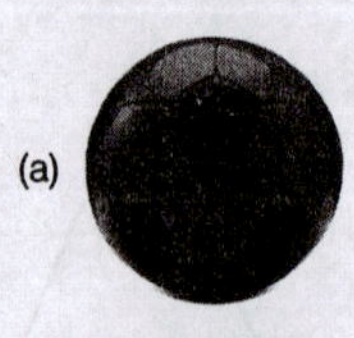

(b)
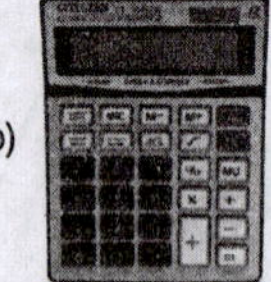

(a)

(b)

ANSWERS & SOLUTIONS

1. (i) True (ii) False (iii) True (iv) False

2. (i) (a) (ii) (b) (iii) (c) (iv) (a)
(v) (b) (vi) (b)

3. (i) (a), (c), (e) (ii) (b), (c)

GIVE AND TAKE

In this chapter, we will learn about the concept of addition and subtraction with different method through fun engaging activities.

Addition

It is the process of combining two or more numbers to get a new total.

e.g. $5 + 3 = 8$

Subtraction

It is a process of finding the difference between two numbers or quantities.

e.g. $5 - 3 = 2$

NCERT Pg 150

Q.1 Fill in the blanks.

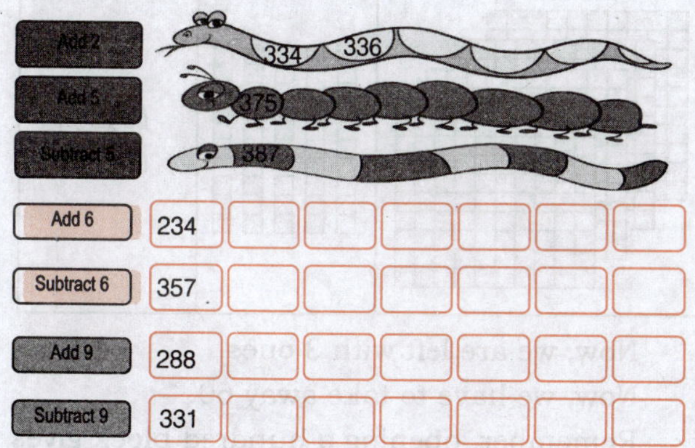

Ans.

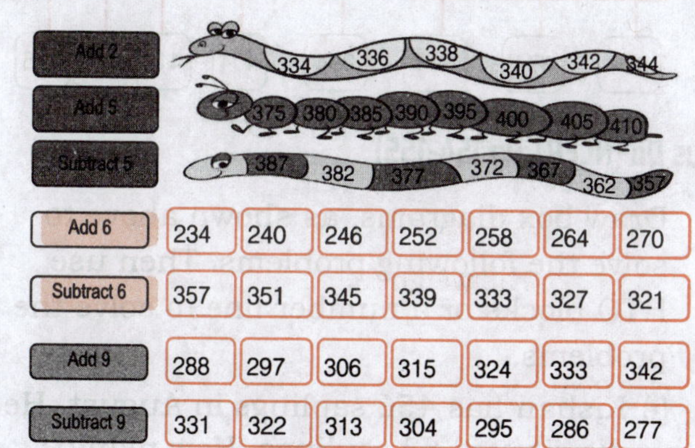

** Students can write alternate answer as per their choice.*

NCERT Pg 151

Q.2 Kishan had 364 saplings of different herbs and flowers. Then, he went to his friend's village and brought 52 saplings from there. How many saplings does he have now?

Let us draw a box diagram for the problem.

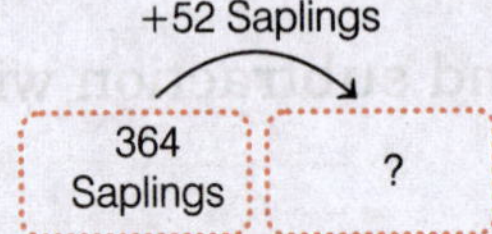

364 Saplings + 52 Saplings

= __________ Saplings

364 + 52 = __________

You can also use a number line to solve it.

Ans.

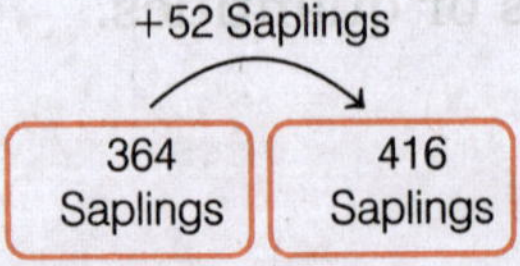

364 Saplings + 52 Saplings = 416 Saplings

$364 + 52 = 416$

Hence, he has 416 saplings now.

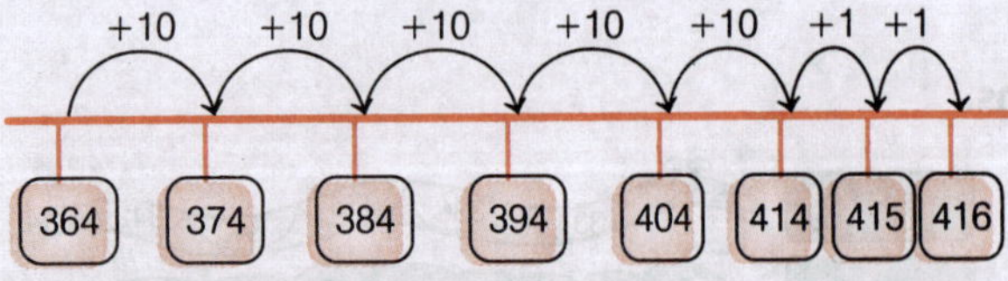

Let us Do (NCERT Pg 154-155)

Q.3 Draw box diagrams, as shown above to solve the following problems. Then use HTO blocks or a number line to solve the problems.

(i) Kishan has 456 saplings in August. He distributed 63 saplings. How many saplings are left with him?

(ii) Kishan has a collection of 309 saplings. He gets 80 more saplings of flowering plants. How many saplings does he have now?

(iii) Kishan has 270 saplings of herbs and his friend has 36 saplings of herbs.

How many more saplings does Kishan have than his friend?

Ans. (i) Box diagram for the problem

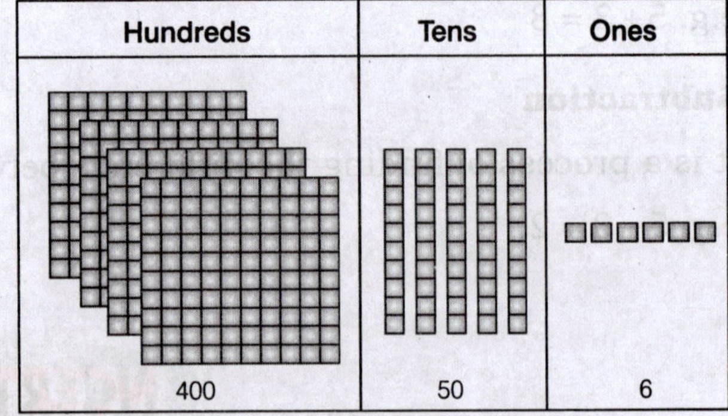

Let us represent 456 saplings using HTO blocks.

Hundreds	Tens	Ones
400	50	6

We have to subtract 63 from 456.

To take away 3 ones from 6 ones.

Hundreds	Tens	Ones

Now, we are left with 3 ones.

Now, we have to take away 60.

Remember, opening a hundred block gives us 10 blocks of Tens.

Then, take away 60.

Hundreds	Tens	Ones

We are left with 9 Tens.

Hundreds	Tens	Ones

Thus, 393 saplings are left with Kishan.

On number line.

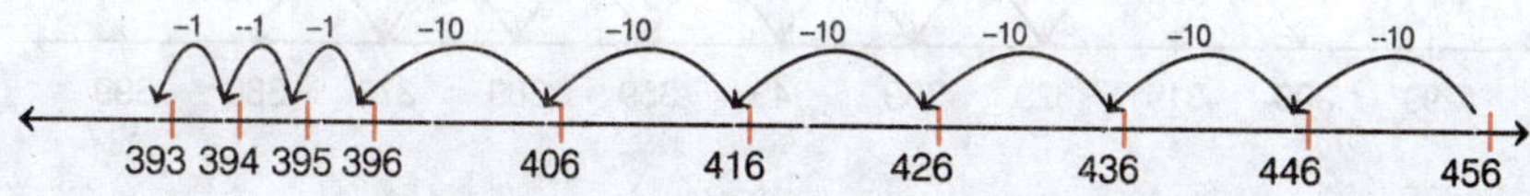

(ii) Box diagram

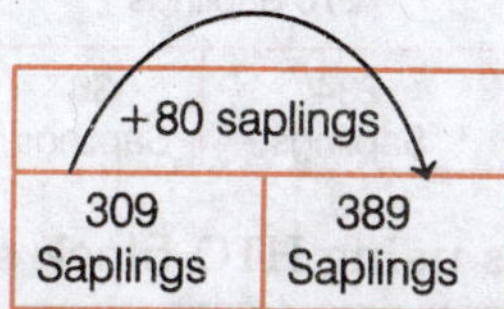

Let us represent 309 and 80 saplings using HTO block separately.

Hundreds	Tens	Ones

Hundreds	Tens	Ones

On adding 309 to 80. we get 3 hundreds, 8 tens and 9 ones.

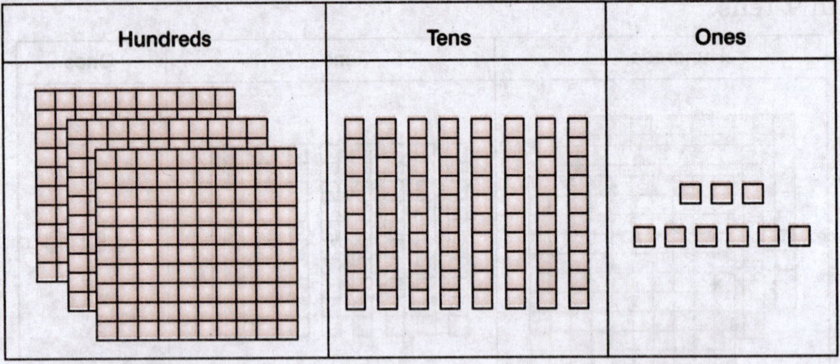

Thus, Kishan has 389 saplings.

On number line

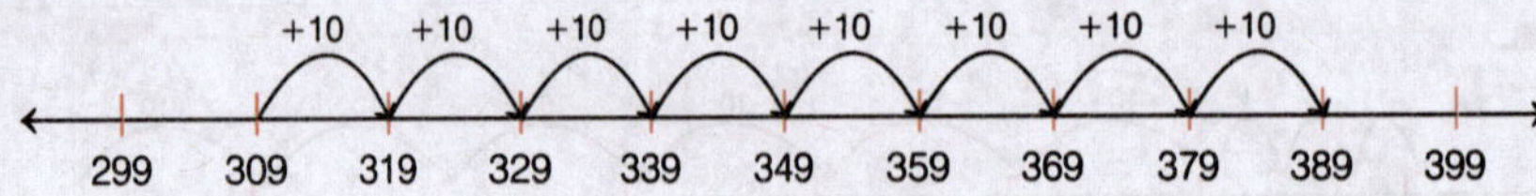

(iii) Box diagram

270 Saplings	
234 Saplings	36 Saplings

Let us represent 270 and 36 saplings using HTO block separately.

Hundreds	Tens	Ones

Hundreds	Tens	Ones

Converting 1 ten into ones and take out 6 ones from it.

Hundreds	Tens	Ones

Now, we have to take away 30.

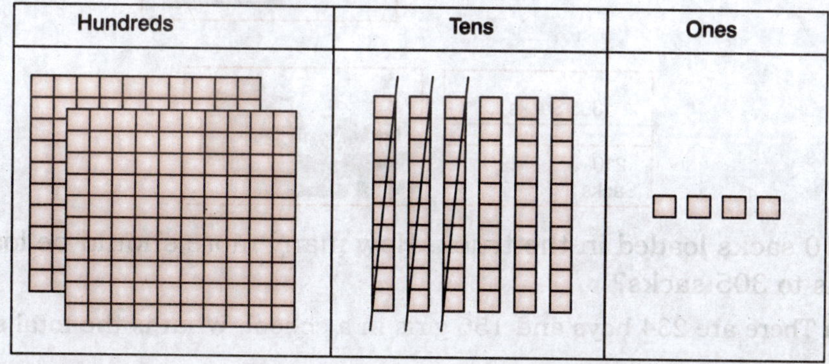

We are left with this.

Hundreds	Tens	Ones

Thus, Kishan has 234 more samplings than his friend.

Q.4 Write word problems using the numbers given in the box diagrams below and solve them. You can take help from the pictures for appropriate contexts.

(i)

+156 Girls

234 Boys | ?

(ii)

LIBRARY

−138 Books

356 Books | ?

(iii)

305 Sacks

210 Sacks | ?

There are 210 sacks loaded in the truck. How many more should be loaded to make the total of sacks to 305 sacks?

Ans. (i) **Word Problem** There are 234 boys and 156 girls in a school. What is the total strength of the school?

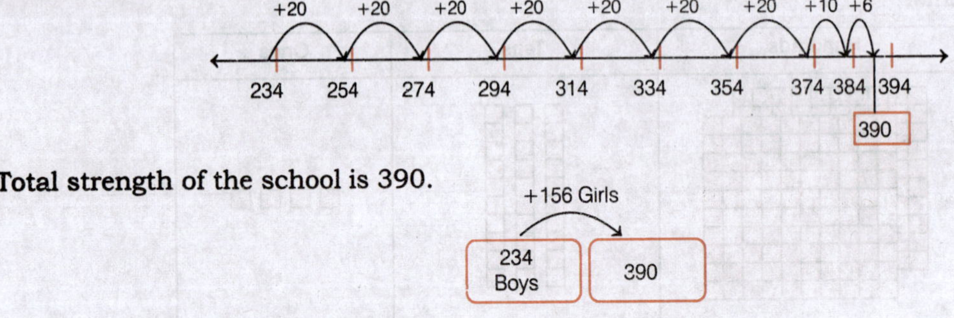

Total strength of the school is 390.

(ii) There are 356 books in a library.

Word Problem If 138 books are for children, then how many books are not for children?

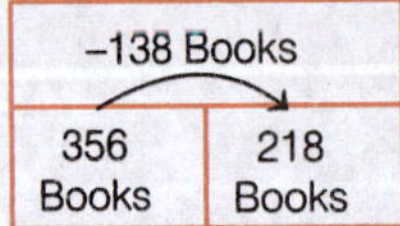

(iii) **Word Problem** There are 305 sacks have to be loaded in truck. 210 sacks are loaded. How many sacks are left to load in the truck?

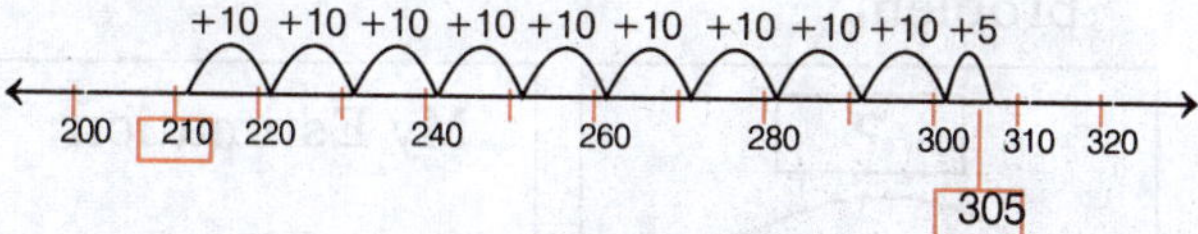

Hence, 95 more sacks should be loaded in the truck.

305 Sacks	
210 Sacks	95 Sacks

Q.5 Use the grid below to solve the following questions. Shade your answers in the grid.

Ans.

521	522	523	524	525	526	527	528	529	530
511	512	513	514	515	516	517	518	519	520
501	502	503	504	505	506	507	508	509	510
491	492	493	494	495	496	497	498	499	500
481	482	483	484	485	486	487	488	489	490
471	472	473	474	475	476	477	478	479	480
461	462	463	464	465	466	467	468	469	470
451	452	453	454	455	456	457	458	459	460

456 + 10 = 466   481 + 19 = 500   489 + 21 + 15 = 525

405 + 23 = 428   467 + 51 = 518   519 – 40 = 479

NCERT Pg 156

Q.6 Do as Directed

Ans.

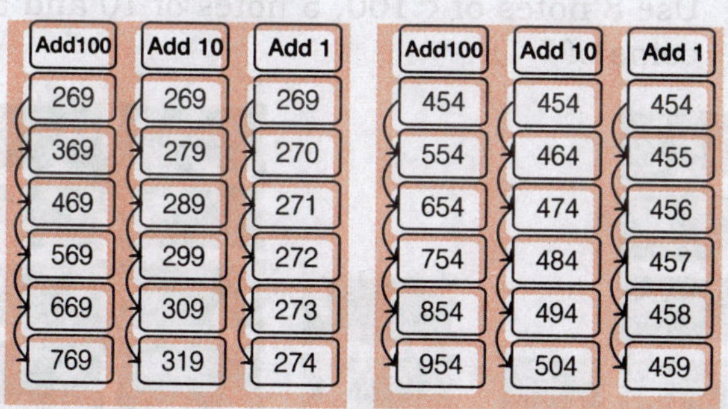

NCERT Pg 157-159

Q.7 Salma buys two bottles of milk for ₹ 100. Kiran buys a basket of pomegranates for ₹ 100. Choose the one that costs more : a milk bottle or a pomegranate?

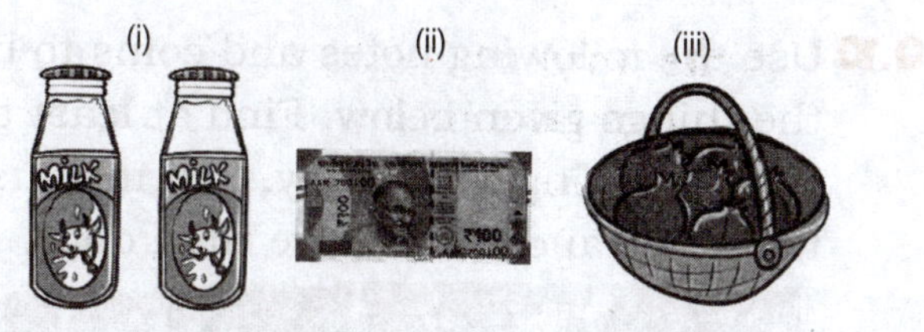

Ans. (ii) Note of hundred.

Q.8 Think of two things that we can buy using the same note.

Ans. *

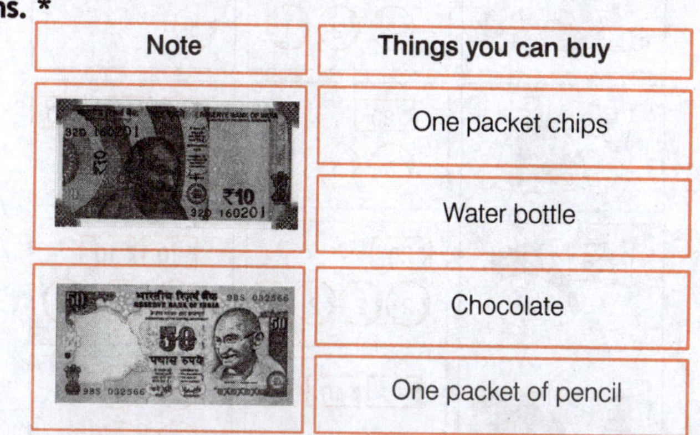

Note	Things you can buy
₹10 note	One packet chips
	Water bottle
₹50 note	Chocolate
	One packet of pencil

Q.9 Match the notes and coins in the two columns that have the same values.

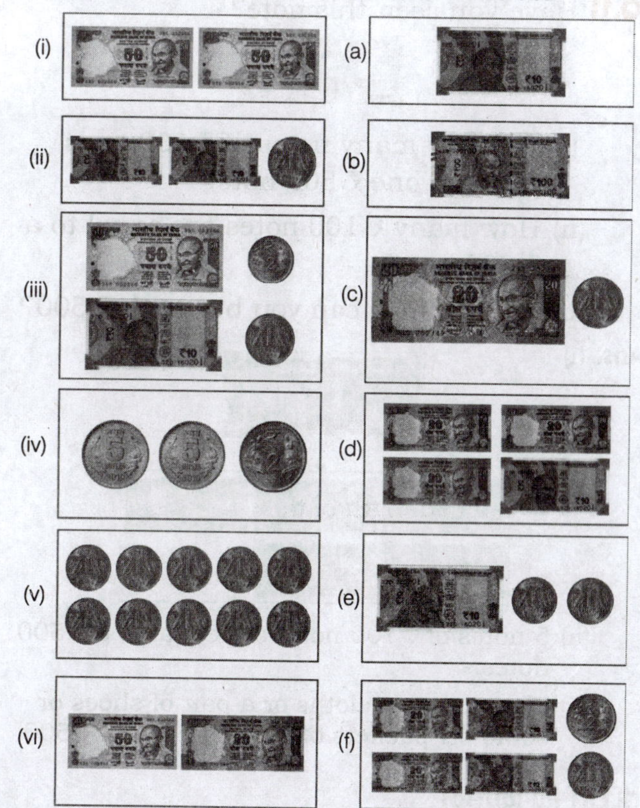

Ans. (i) → (b), (ii) → (c), (iii) → (f), (iv) → (e), (v) → (a), (vi) → (d)

Q.10 Use the following notes and coins to buy the things given below. Find at least two ways of giving the money. You may use the notes and coins more than once.

Ans. *

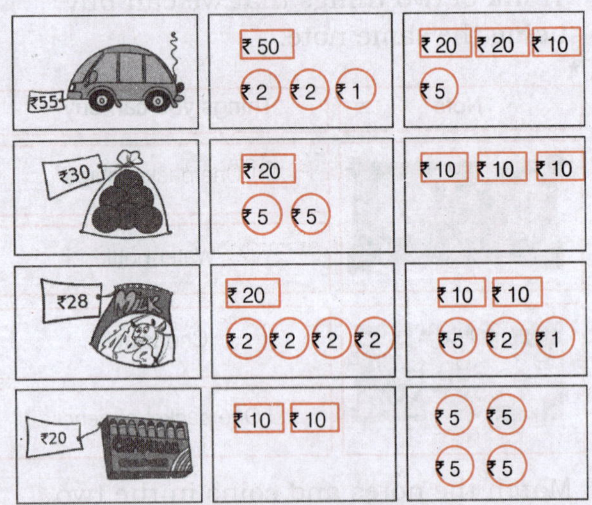

Q.11 Have you seen this note?

(i) Draw as many notes of ₹ 100 as is equal to one ₹ 500 note.

(ii) How many ₹ 100 notes are equal to a ₹ 500 note?

(iii) What things can you buy with ₹ 500?

Ans. (i)

(ii) 5 notes of ₹ 100 notes are equal to a ₹ 500 notes.

*(iii) We can buy a cloths or a pair of shoes or some big packets of chocolates with ₹ 500.

NCERT Pg 160-161

Q.12 In the morning, Peter uncle has ₹ 465 in his money box. By afternoon, he has ₹ 756. How much has he earned since morning?

Let us draw a box diagram for the problem.

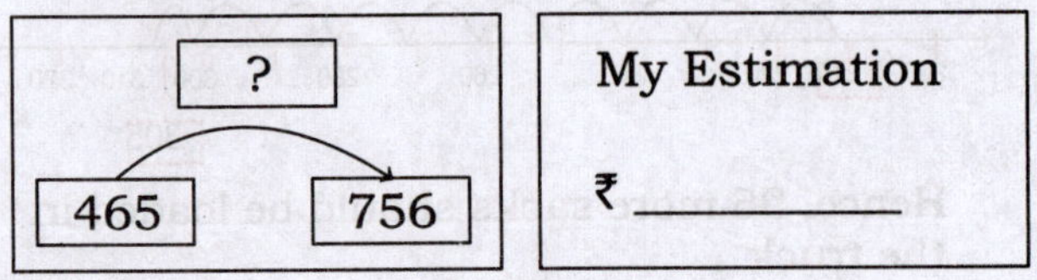

Ans.

My estimation = ₹ 291

So, he earned since morning = ₹ 291

Q.13 Today, Peter uncle sold rice for ₹ 640 and sugar for ₹ 215. How much money has he earned from this sale?

Draw a box diagram for the problem.

My estimate = ₹ ________

Use  or a number line to solve it.

Ans. Box diagram for the problem.

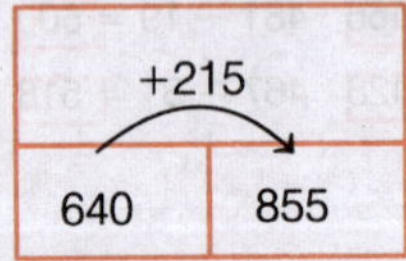

My estimate = ₹ 855.

Use 8 notes of ₹ 100, 5 notes of 10 and 5 coins of ₹ 1.

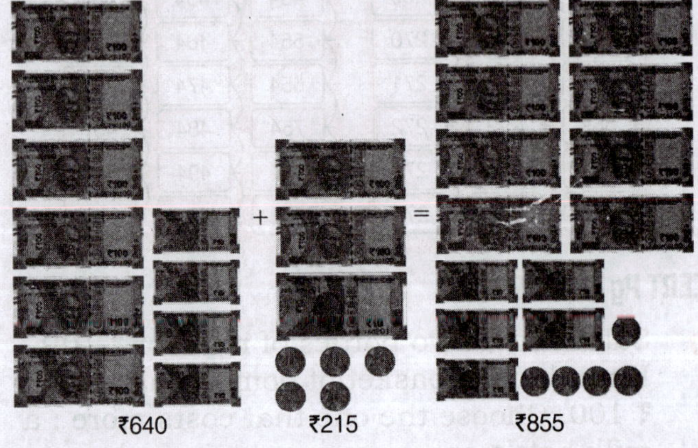

On number line

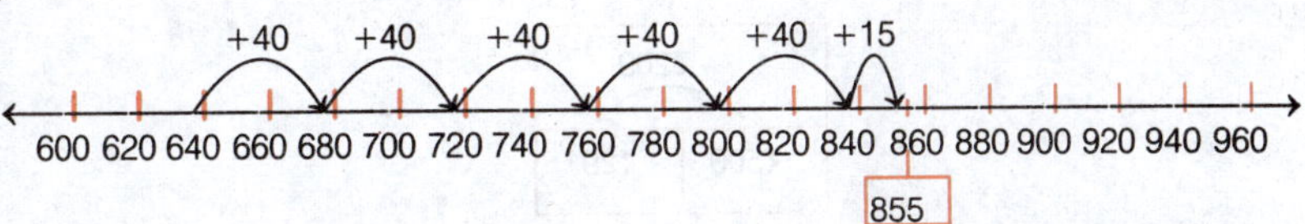

Thus, Peter uncle earned ₹ 855 from this sale.

Let us Do (NCERT Pg 161-164)

Q.14 Solve the following problems using box diagrams. Estimate the answers. Then, use notes of ₹ 100s, ₹ 10s and ₹ 1s or a number line to solve the problems.

(i) One day Peter uncle earned ₹ 650. The next day he earned ₹ 250 more. How much money had he earned by the second day?

(ii) Reena bought groceries for ₹ 209. She gave a ₹ 500 note to Peter uncle. How much money should Peter uncle return to Reena?

(iii) Shireen has ₹ 150 in her piggy bank. She puts ₹ 100 every week in her piggy bank. How much money does she have at the end of four weeks?

(iv) Peter uncle saved ₹ 250 in the first month, ₹ 125 in the second month and ₹ 350 in the third month. How much has he saved in these three months?

Ans. (i) Box diagram for the problem

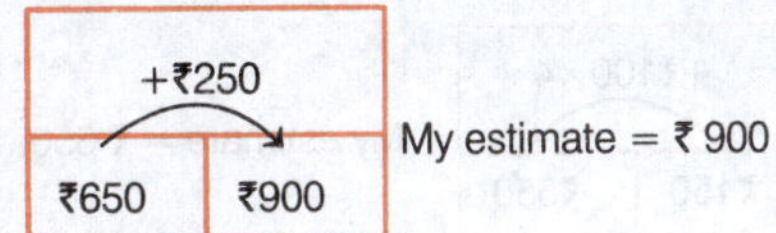

Thus, Use 8 notes of ₹ 100 and 10 notes of ₹ 10.

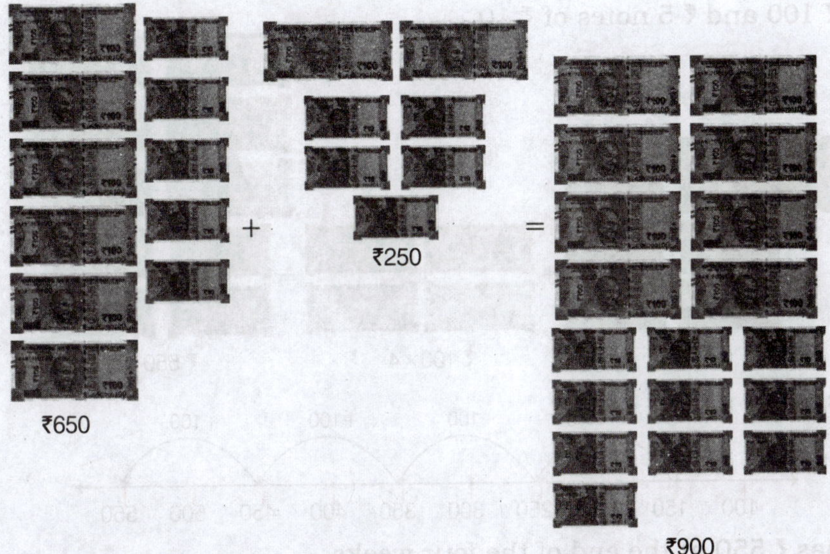

On number line

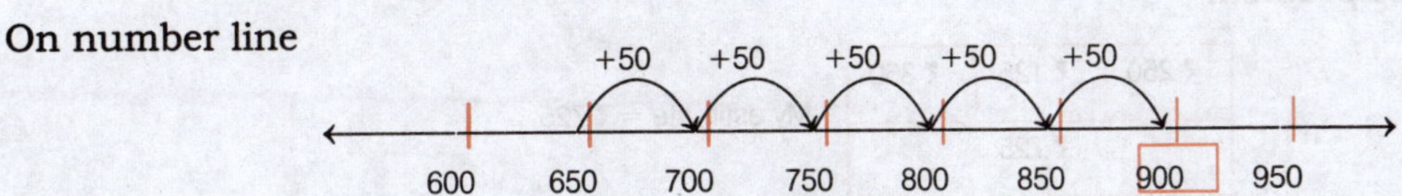

Thus, Peter uncle earned ₹ 900 by the second day.

(ii) Box diagram for the problem

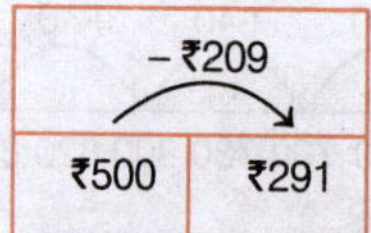

Use 6 notes of ₹ 100, 9 notes of ₹ 10 and 19 coins of ₹ 1.

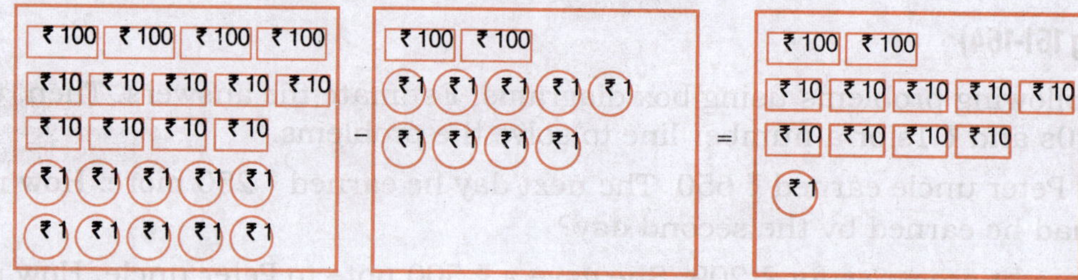

On number line

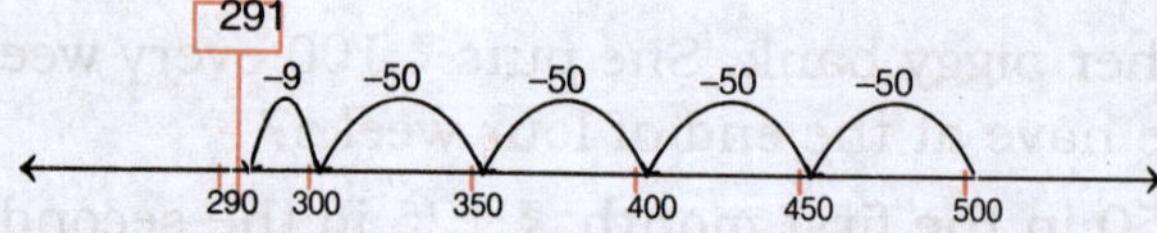

Thus, Peter uncle should return ₹ 291 to Reena.

(iii) Box diagram for the problem.

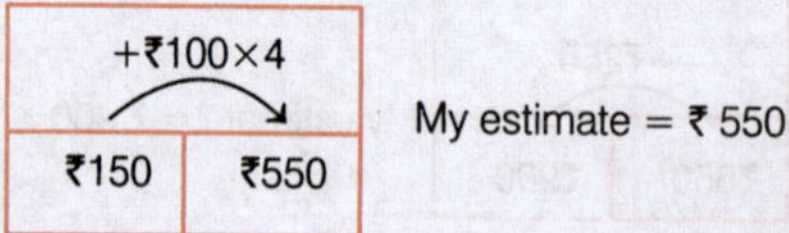

My estimate ₹ 550.

Use 5 notes of ₹ 100 and ₹ 5 notes of ₹ 10.

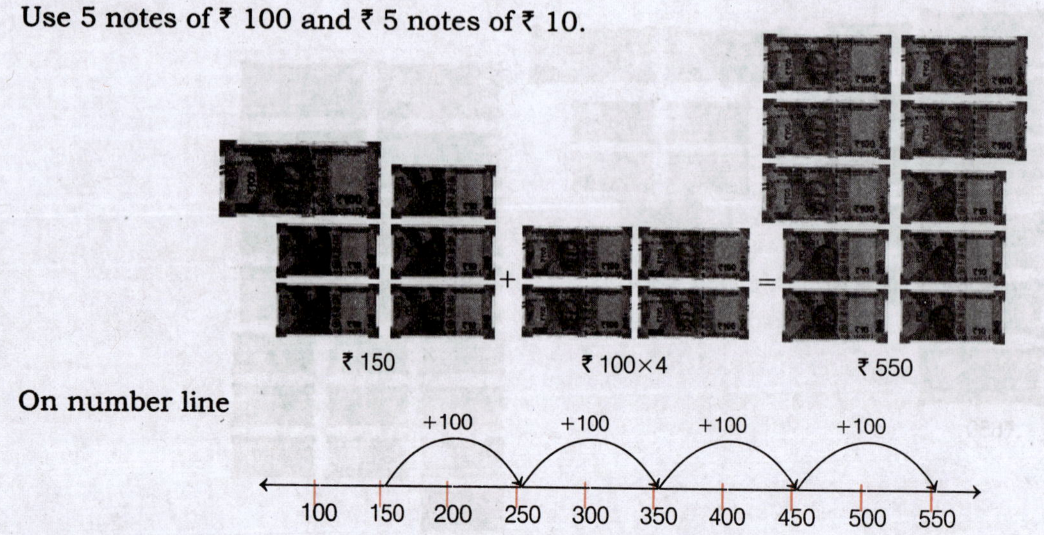

On number line

+100 +100 +100 +100

100 150 200 250 300 350 400 450 500 550

Thus, Shireen has ₹ 550 at the end of the four weeks.

(iv) Box diagram for the problem

₹ 250	₹ 125	₹ 350
₹ 725		

My estimate = ₹ 725

My estimate ₹ 725

Use 6 notes of ₹ 100, 12 notes of ₹ 10 and 5 coins of ₹ 1.

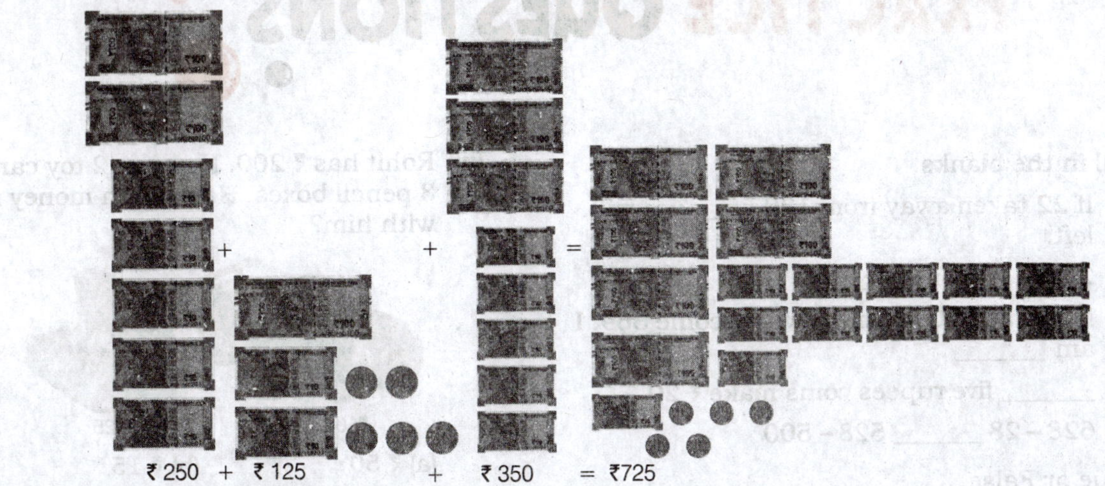

Thus, Peter uncle saved ₹ 725 in three months.

Q.15 Estimate the answers to the nearest hundred. Share your thinking in the class.

Ans.

Number Sentence	Nearest Hundred
156 + 34=190	200
125 – 15 = 110	100
105 + 195 = 300	300
205 + 215 = 420	400
500 – 395 = 105	100
765 – 567 = 198	200
505 + 405 = 910	900

Q.16 Compare the given problem statements in each row without calculating. Circle the one that is more. Share your thinking in class.

Ans.

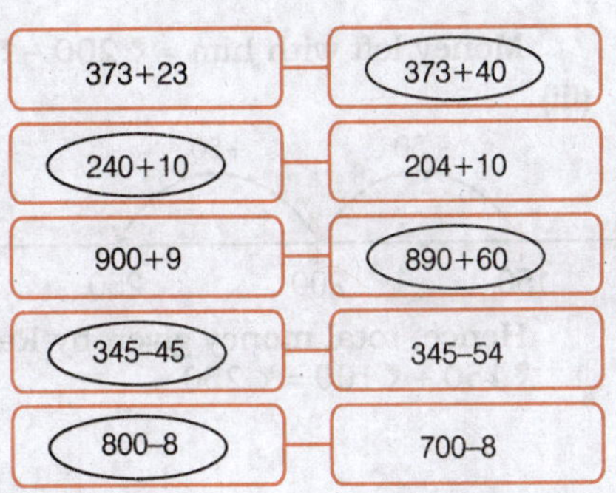

Q.17 Find the pairs that are equal. Share your thinking in class.

Ans.

516 + 100 | 615 – 200 | 350 + 50

400 + 15 | 450 – 50 | 816 – 200

Q.18 Fill in the boxes with appropriate numbers.

Ans.

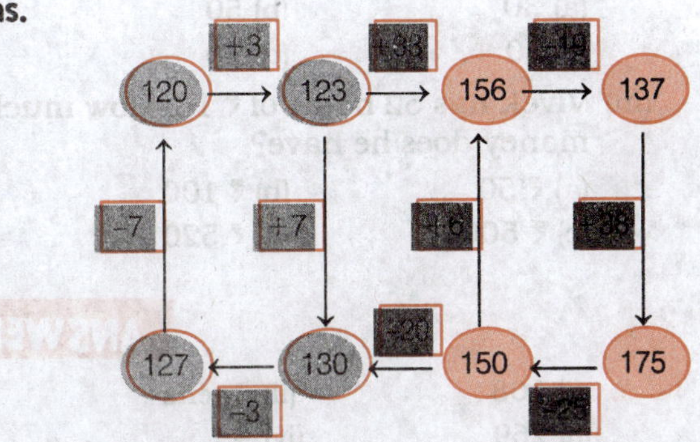

Let us Do (NCERT Pg 164)

Q.19 (i) 265+9

(ii) 405+56

(iii) 825+175

(iv) 600 – 82

(v) 568 – 5

(vi) 653 – 356

Ans. (i) 265 + 9 = 274 (ii) 405 + 56 = 461

(iii) 825 + 175 = 1000 (iv) 600 – 82 = 518

(v) 568 – 5 = 563 (vi) 653 – 356 = 297

PRACTICE QUESTIONS

1. Fill in the blanks.
   (i) If 22 taken away from 130, _______ will left.
   (ii) 2 tens + 4 tens _______ = 90.
   (iii) If you add 100 to me, I will become 369. I am _______ .
   (iv) _______ five rupees coins make ₹ 20.
   (v) 628 − 28 _______ 528 − 500.
2. True or False.
   (i) 256 + 54 is nearest to 400.
   (ii) 356 + 219 = 570
   (iii) 508 + 8 > 500 + 8
   (iv) 516 + 100 = 816 − 200
3. Multiple choice questions.
   (i) 570 + 430 = how many tens?
   (a) 100 (b) 43
   (c) 57 (d) 1000
   (ii) Subtract 3 tens from 9 tens is equal to
   (a) 30 (b) 50
   (c) 60 (d) 70
   (iii) Vivek has 52 notes of ₹ 10. How much money does he have?
   (a) ₹ 50 (b) ₹ 100
   (c) ₹ 500 (d) ₹ 520
   (iv) Rohit has ₹ 200. He buys 2 toy cars and 3 pencil boxes. How much money is left with him?

₹50 ₹25

   (a) ₹ 50 (b) ₹ 15
   (c) ₹ 25 (d) ₹ 100
   (v) Find the exact answer for 900 − 201?
   (a) 699 (b) 700
   (c) 710 (d) 799
   (vi) 481 + 231 =
   (a) 611 (b) 612
   (c) 732 (d) 712
4. Word Problems (Solve using number line)
   (i) A market sells 425 apples in one week and 342 apples in the next week. How many apples have been sold in total?
   (ii) Rakesh got ₹ 200 from his father. He bought a football for ₹ 175. How much money was left with him?
   (iii) Radha gave ₹ 150 to her daughter and ₹ 100 to her son. Find the total money given by Radha to her children.

ANSWERS & SOLUTIONS

1. (i) 108 (ii) 3 tens
   (iii) 269 (iv) 4
   (v) '>'
2. (i) False (ii) False
   (iii) True (iv) True
3. (i) (a) (ii) (c) (iii) (d) (iv) (c) (v) (a) (vi) (d)
4. (i)

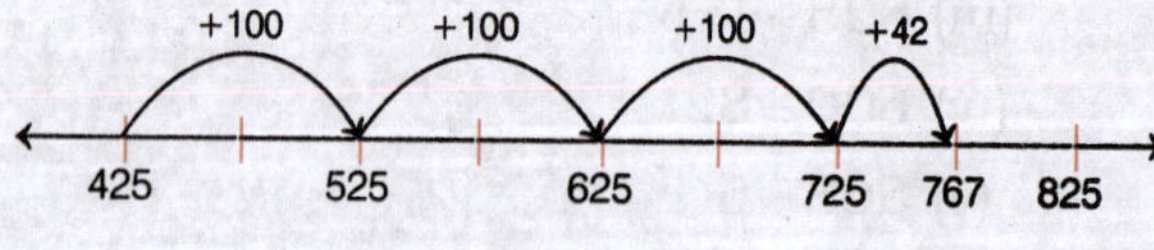

425 + 342 = 767 apples

(ii)

-5 -10 -20 -20 -20 -20 -20 -20 -20 -20
20 25 30 40 60 80 100 120 140 160 180 200

Money left with him = ₹ 200 − ₹ 175 = ₹ 25

(iii)

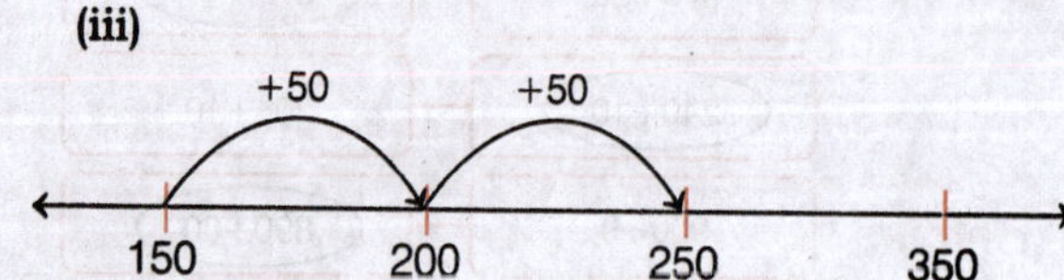

Hence, total money given by Radha is ₹ 150 + ₹ 100 = ₹ 250

TIMES GOES ON

Time

Time is something that says by what duration or period something happens. Time can be measured by using some devices called calendar or clock.

- In clocks, time is measured in terms of hours, minutes and seconds.
- In calendar, time is measured in terms of days, months and years.

Calendar

A method of placing the days in a series on paper is called calendar. We can have days, weeks and months in a calendar. A calendar is usually made for a year i.e. 365 days.

- In a week, we have 7 days.
- In a year, we have 12 months.

Clock

The clock is a device used to measure time.

- 1 hour = 60 minutes
- 1 minute = 60 seconds

There are two types of clock using in our daily life.

- **Digital Clock** A digital clock shows time using digits.

- **Analog Clock** A clock shows time with second, minute and hour hands, is called an analog clock.

Let us Do (NCERT Pg 166)

Q.1 Make the calendar for the month of July 2024.

Observe the July month and complete the following.

Ans.

Monday (सोमवार)	Tuesday (मंगलवार)	Wednesday (बुधवार)	Thursday (गुरुवार)	Friday (शुक्रवार)	Saturday (शनिवार)	Sunday (रविवार)
1	2	3	4	5	6	7
8	9	10	11	12	13	14
15	16	17	18	19	20	21
22	23	24	25	26	27	28
29	30	31				

(i) Number of Sundays is 4

(ii) The dates in this month that are Thursdays are 4, 11, 18 and 25

(iii) Three days after July 22 is July 25

The day on this date is Thursday

(iv) The date on which the school will open is 22 July

Let us Explore (NCERT Pg 167)

Collect calendars for the last two years. Observe the following in both the calendars.

Q.2 What is the same? What is changing in the years?

Choose the correct answer.

(i)	Names of the months	Same/ Changes
(ii)	Days in a month	Same/ Changes
(iii)	Days in a week	Same/ Changes
(iv)	Number of Sundays	Same/ Changes
(v)	Number of weeks in a year	Same/ Changes

Ans. (i) same (ii) changes (iii) same (iv) changes (v) same

** Students can write alternate answer as per their choice.*

Q.3 Circle the festivals that fall on the same date.

Ans. *

Festival	Date Month Year DD/MM/YY	Date Month Year DD/MM/YY
Deepawali	12/11/23	31/10/24
Ganesh Chaturthi	19/09/23	17/09/24
Eid-ul-fitr	22/04/23	11/04/24
Dussehra	24/10/23	12/10/24
Buddha Purnima	5/05/23	12/05/24
(Christmas)	25/12/23	25/12/24
(Makarsankranti)	15/01/23	15/01/24
Mahavirjayanti	4/04/23	21/04/24
(Independence Day)	15/08/23	15/08/24
Gurupurab	27/11/23	15/11/24
(Republic Day)	26/01/23	26/01/24
(Your Birthday)	21/06/23	21/06/24

Let us Do (NCERT Pg 167)

Q.4 (i) Write the names of the 12 months in a year.

(ii) Months that have less than 30 days ....

(iii) Number of days in a year ....

(iv) Hetal says there are 53 weeks in a year. Is she right? Yes/No.
If not, how many weeks did you find in a year?

Ans. (i) (a) January (b) February
(c) March (d) April
(e) May (f) June

(g) July (h) August

(i) September (j) October

(k) November (l) December

(ii) February (iii) 365

(iv) No, there are 52 weeks in a year.

Age Fun (NCERT Pg 168)

Q.5 Talk to your mother and find the following.

Age of my mother's mother when my mother was born:

My mother's age today:

Ans. *

Q.6 Hetal is twice as old as her brother. She is also 10 years older than her brother. Guess the age of Hetal and her brother.

Ans. Hetal's age is 20 years and her brother's age is 10 years.

Let us Do (NCERT Pg 169)

Q.7

Form Number 5

Government of Kerala

BIRTH CERTIFICATE

This is to certify that this information is taken from the original record of birth which is in the register for the year 2015 of Kottayam Panchayat.

Name:	Bincy Thomas Jacob
Sex:	Female
Date of Birth:	02/05/2015 (Second May Two Thousand Fifteen)
Place of Birth:	Kadampuzha Hospital
Name of Father:	Jacob Tharakan
Name of Mother:	Lara Thomas
Date of Registration:	02/05/2015
Registration Number:	815/15

Date 18.05.2015 Signature Authority

Look at the birth certificate of Bincy and answer the following question.

(i) 2/5/2015 shows that Bincy was born on 2 (April/May/ June/July) in the year 2015.

(ii) How old will Bincy be on 2 May 2025?

(iii) How old will she be in 2030?

(iv) Eighth Birthday of Bincy was on ......

(v) Bincy was .... months old on 2 August 2015.

(vi) After how many days of her birth was the certificate issued?

Ans. (i) Bincy was born on 2 May in the year 2015.

(ii) Bincy will be 10 years old on 2 May 2025.

(iii) She will be 15 years old in 2030.

(iv) Eighth Birthday of Bincy was on 2 May 2023.

(v) Bincy was 3 months old on 2 August 2015.

(vi) After 16 days of her birth certificate was issued.

Let us Do (NCERT Pg 170)

Q.8 Make your own birth certificate.

Form Number ________

Government of ________

BIRTH CERTIFICATE

This is to certify that this information is taken from the original record of birth which is in the register for the year __________ *and* ________.

Name: ____________

Sex: ____________

Date of Birth: ____________

Place of Birth: ____________

Name of Father: ____________

Name of Mother: ____________

Date of Making Cerificate: ____________

Age on the date of making the cerificate: ____________

Your Signature

Ans. Do yourself.

Q.9 Complete the following by writing the dates in the boxes given below.

Date of Birth	Date on which you were admitted in the school.	Date on which you were admitted in Class I.	Date on which you were admitted in Class III.

Ans. Do yourself.

Let us Do (NCERT Pg 171)

Q.10 Hetal started her breakfast at 7 o'clock in the morning. She finished her breakfast at 07:15 in the morning.

(a) 07 : 00

(b) 07 : 15

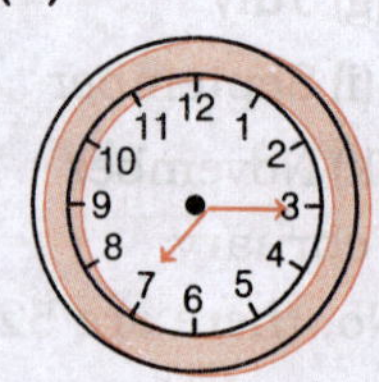

She took .... minutes to eat her breakfast. How do you know?

Ans. She took 15 minutes to eat her breakfast. Because we know that by subtracting 7 : 00 from 7 : 15, we get 0 : 15 that is 15 minutes.

Q.11 Draw the hour hand and minute hand on the clock to show the following.

(a) 8:15 or quarter past 8

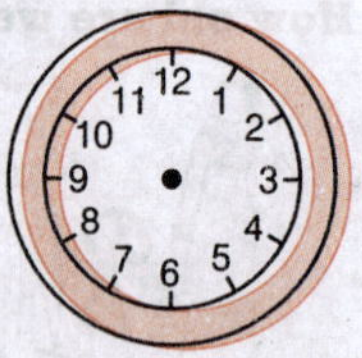

(b) 8:30 or half past 8

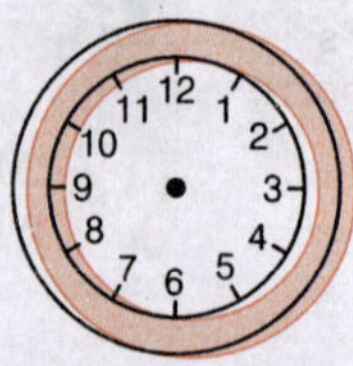

Ans. (a) 8 : 15 or quarter past 8

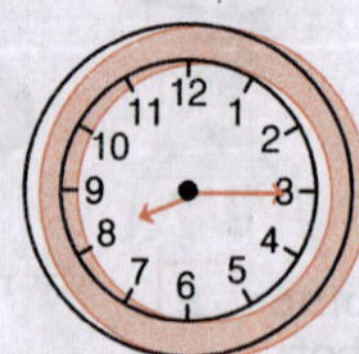

(b) 8 : 30 or half past 8

Let us Do (NCERT Pg 172)

Q.12 **A day in the life of Hetal**

Match the activity with the statement shown in the picture. Write the time and draw the minute hand and the hour hand wherever it is required.

Ans.

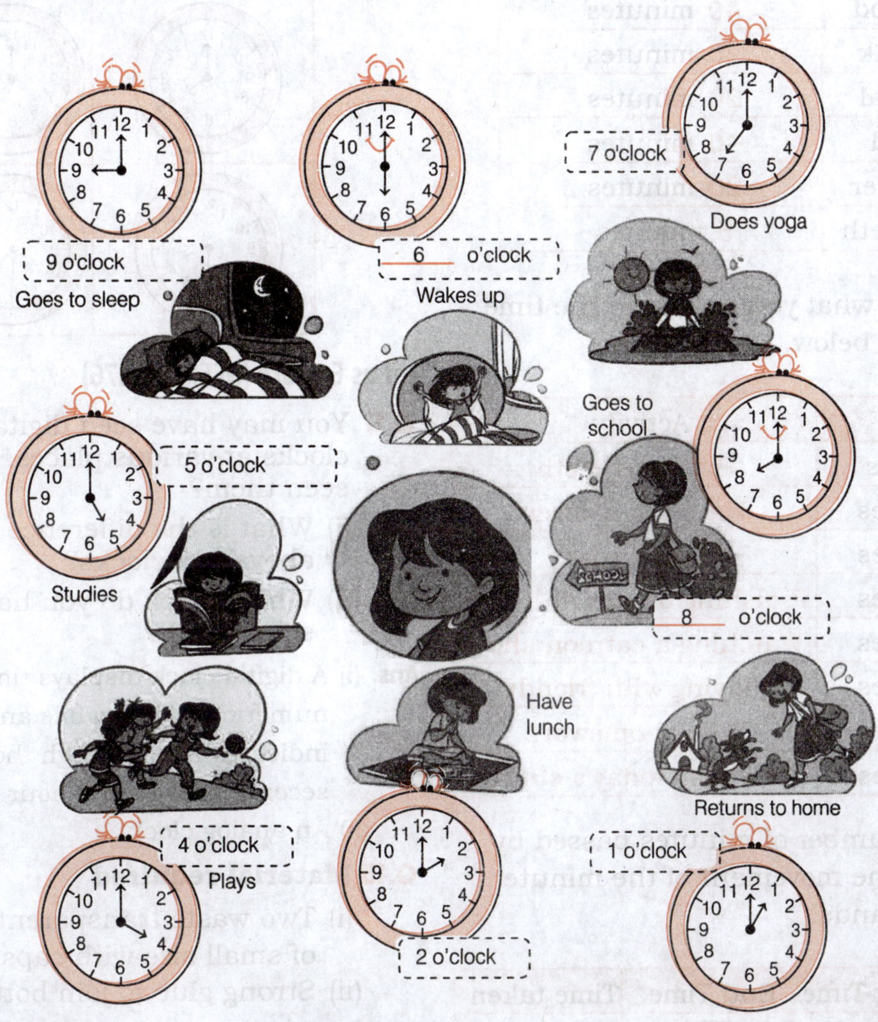

Let us Think (NCERT Pg 173-175)

Q.13 Fill the table by writing events or activities from your daily life that can take the following durations of time. One is written as an example in each column.

Ans.

Takes months	Takes weeks	Takes days	Takes hours	Takes minutes
Changing from summer to winter	Completing a chapter in class	Knitting a sweater	Stitching a shirt	Taking a shower
Constructing building	Revision before exam	Going to native by bus	Playing	Drinking water
Completing the full course	Recovering from injuries	Shifting home	Completing homework	Having lunch
Summer vacation	Completion of games	Going on a tour	Watching movie	Sending Message

Q.14 Write the number of minutes taken for the following activities.

Ans. *

Activity	Time taken
School Period	40 minutes
Lunch Break	30 minutes
Midday Meal	20 minutes
Play Period	40 minutes
Eating Dinner	20 minutes
Brushing Teeth	5 minutes

Q.15 Write down what you can do in the time frame given below.

Ans. *

Time	Activity
5 minutes	Brushing teeth
10 minutes	Having a shower
15 minutes	Doing yoga
20 minutes	Finishing dinner or lunch
25 minutes	Watching a catroon show
30 minutes	Playing with friends
45 minutes	Doing homework
60 minutes	Revising today's study

Q.16 Write the number of minutes passed by looking at the movement of the minute and hour hands.

Ans.

Beginning Time	End Time	Time taken
		5 minutes
		10 minutes
		135 minutes or 2 hours 15 minutes

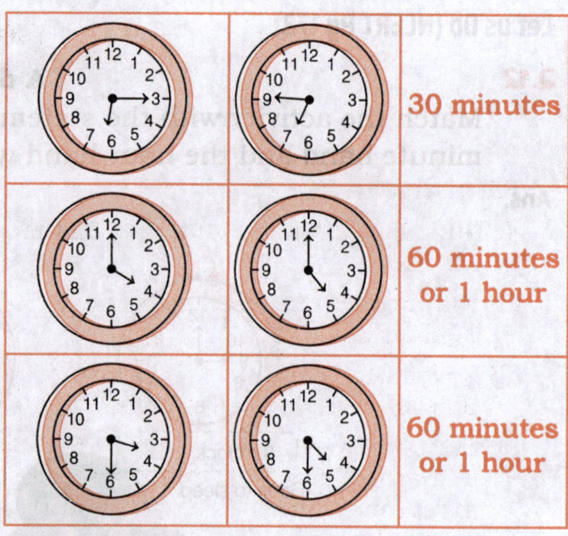

Let us Explore (NCERT Pg 176)

Q.17 You may have seen digital watches or clocks at various places. Where have you seen them?

(i) What is the difference between the above two clocks?

(ii) Which clock do you have on your school wall?

Ans. (i) A digital clock displays time using numerical digits, while an analog clock indicates time through the positions of its second, minute and hour hands.

(ii) An analog clock.

Q.18 **Material required**

(i) Two waste transparent or glass bottles of small size with caps.

(ii) Strong glue to join bottle caps.

Process

Join the tops of the bottle caps with each other using a strong glue. Make a small hole with a fine needle at the centre of the joined caps. Fill one of the bottles half way with fine sand and close the bottle with the joined caps. Attach the second bottle on the other side of the joined caps.

Find out how much time it takes to shift the sand from one bottle to the second one by looking at the clock. Your sand clock is ready for use. You may use it to time while playing different games.

Ans. Do yourself.

PRACTICE QUESTIONS

1. Fill in the blanks.
   (i) Number of days in February 2024 is ....
   (ii) Number of months in a year have 30 days, is ....
   (iii) Navya was born on 15 February 2024. She will complete 6 years on ....
   (iv) Sarita started her breakfast at 6 o' clock in morning and she finished it at 06:18 in morning. She took .... minutes to eat her breakfast.
   (v) A quarter of an hour is .... minutes.
2. True or False.
   (i) There are 30 days in a month of May 2024.
   (ii) There are 4 Saturdays in May 2024.
   (iii) There are 12 months in a year.
   (iv) 1 hour = 90 minutes
   (v) The hour hand completes 2 rounds in a day.
3. Multiple choice questions
   (i) How many months in a year have 31 days?
   (a) 8 (b) 7 (c) 6 (d) 5
   (ii) The month with neither 31 days nor 30 days is:
   (a) February (b) April
   (c) November (d) December
   (iii) Durga's birthday is on October 20. Madhavi's birthday is six days after that. When is Madhavi's birthday?
   (a) October 14 (b) October 26
   (c) October 25 (d) October 27
   (iv) If a month ends on Wednesday, then from which day will the next month start?
   (a) Thursday (b) Monday
   (c) Wednesday (d) Friday
   (v) How much time will quarter past 4 takes to be half past 4 ?
   (a) 6 hours (b) 74 minutes
   (c) 15 minutes (d) 60 minutes
4. Word Problem:
   (i) Priya started her homework at 7 : 30 pm. She finished it at 8 : 05 pm. How long did she take to do her homework?
   (ii) A chess game started at 10 : 30 am and ended at 12 : 30 pm. How long did the game last?
   (iii) John and Susan placed their order at 7 : 40 in morning and their food come out at 8 : 30 in morning. How long were they waiting for their food?

ANSWERS & SOLUTIONS

1. (i) 29 (ii) 4
   (iii) 15 February 2030 (iv) 18
   (v) 15
2. (i) False (ii) True
   (iii) True (iv) False
   (v) True
3. (i) (b) (ii) (a) (iii) (b) (iv) (a) (v) (c)
4. (i) We have,

   Priya started her homework at 7:30 pm. She finished it at 8:05 pm.

   To find the time taken to do it by her. We subtract starting time from the finishing time.

   That is 8:05 pm – 7: 30 pm = 35 minutes

   Hence, Priya take 35 minutes to do her homework.

   (ii) We have,

   The chess game started at 10:30 am that is at 10:30 in morning and game ended at 12:30 pm that means 12:30 in afternoon.

   To find the time taken the game last we subtract the starting time from the ending time.

   Therefore, 12:30 – 10:30 = 2 hours
   Hence, the game last till 2 hours.

   (iii) We have,

   John and Susan placed their order at 7:40 am. They got it at 8:30 am

   Therefore, time taken for wait
   = 8:30 am – 7:40 am

   That is 50 minutes.

   Hence, they were waiting 50 minutes for their food.

Symmetrical shape A shape that can be divided into two identical halves or where one half is a mirror image of other, is called symmetrical shape.

e.g.

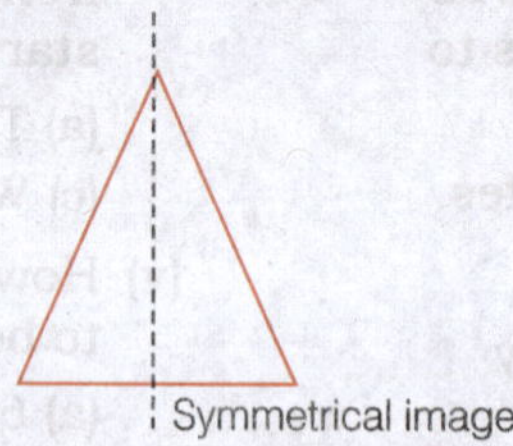

Symmetrical image

Mirror image A mirror image is a reflection of an object that appears in a mirror with the left and right sides reversed.

e.g.

Mirror image

Let us Discuss (NCERT Pg 177)

Q.1

***** *Students can write alternate answer as per their choice.*

(i) What do you see in the picture?

(ii) Spot things in the picture that look the same from the left and right side.

Ans. (i) We see people with their children, a big gate, decorated shops, balloon seller and many tiles patterns on the floor etc.

(ii) The entry gate, lamp, floor in front of gate look same.

Let us Do (NCERT Pg 178-179)

Q.2 (i) Colour the beads in the strings using two colours (⚫⚪) to show the malas that you have made.

(a) 

(b)

(c)

(d)

(e)

(f)

(g)

(h)

(ii) Choose the malas that are symmetrical.

Ans. *(i) (a)

(b)

(c)

(d)

(e)

(f)

(g)

(h)

*(ii) Malas (e) and (h) are symmetrical.

Q.3 How many such malas can be made? Discuss.

(i) Choose the malas that are symmetrical.

(ii) Use 6 beads of one colour and 2 beads of another colour to make symmetrical malas.

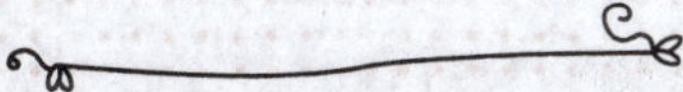

Ans. (i) Malas (a) and (d) are symmetrical.

*(ii)

Let us Think (NCERT Pg 180)

Q.4 Observe the rangolis given below. Are all rangolis symmetrical?

 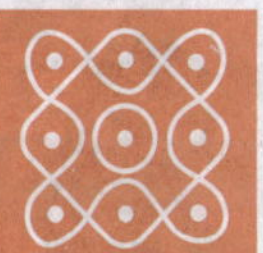 

Ans. Yes, as these can be divided into two equal halves. So, all the rangolis are symmetrical.

Q.5 Trace above rangolis on a paper. Fold the tracing paper in such a way that one half of the rangoli lies exactly on the other half.

Ans. Do yourself.

Q.6 Draw lines in the given rangolis that divide them into two identical halves.

Ans.

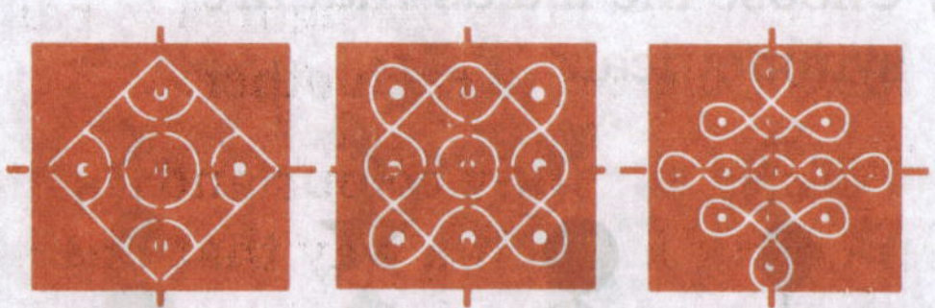

Q.7 Look for other symmetrical things around you. Discuss.

Ans. Do yourself.

Let us Do (NCERT Pg 181)

Q.8 Draw and complete the symmetrical rangolis given below.

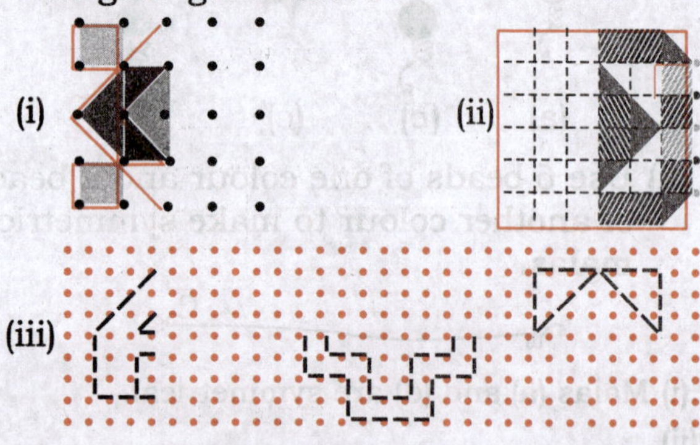

Ans.

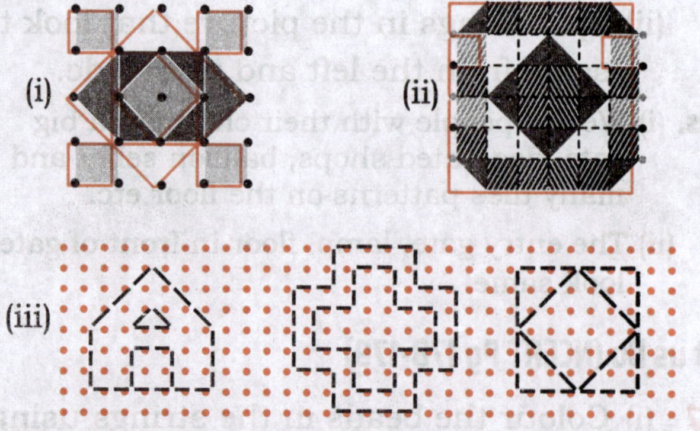

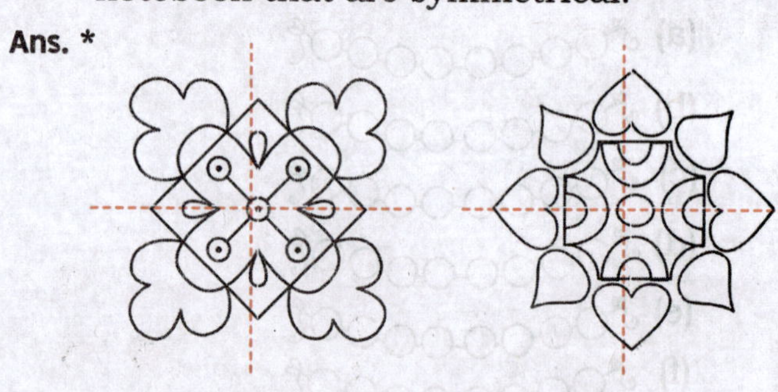

Q.9 Draw some more rangolis in your notebook that are symmetrical.

Ans. *

Let us Think (NCERT Pg 183)

Q.10 **Tit for Tat**

Soni gets her picture made by a painter.

What is the trick the painter is playing? Find things for the painter to draw so that he can no longer play the trick. Draw three such things here.

Ans. * Painter is playing the trick of making halves of symmetrical figures.
Three such things here.

Above all three figures are not symmetrical. so the painter can no longer play the trick to drawing them.

The Mirror Game (NCERT Pg 184)

Q.11 (i) Has Avi placed the counters at the right places? Check it by placing the mirror on the line drawn.

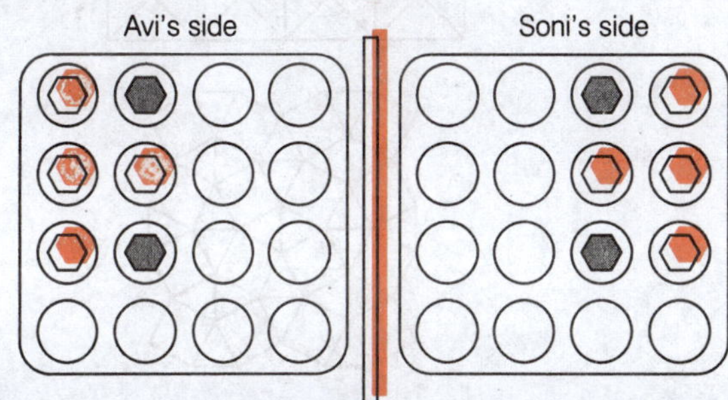

(ii) The counters placed by me are the mirror image of the counters placed by you. Do you agree? Check.

Ans. (i) Yes, Avi placed the counters at the right places.

(ii) Yes, the counters placed by Avi are the mirror image of the counters placed by Soni.

Let us Explore (NCERT Pg 185)

Q.12 Pick the odd one out and give reasons.

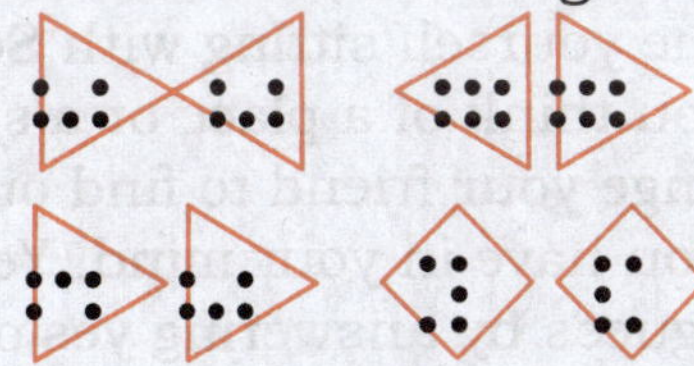

Ans.

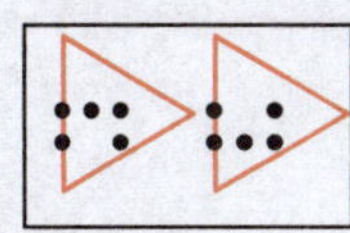

It is odd one because the figures of pair are not mirror images of each other.

Q.13 Fill 4 boxes with any colour and 3 with other colour in such a way that one side is the mirror image of the other.

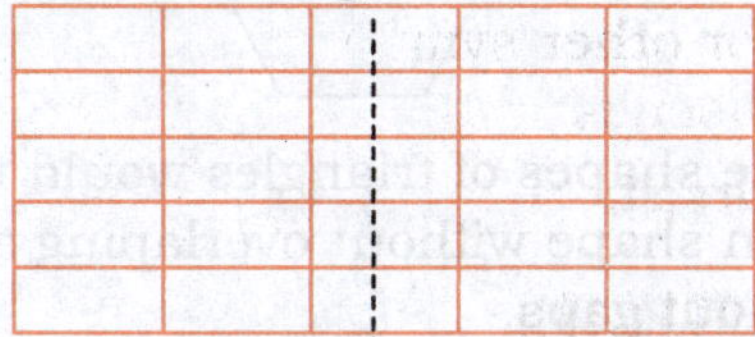

In how many ways can you fill it? Think, think!

Ans. * We can fill it with many ways. One of them as shown below.

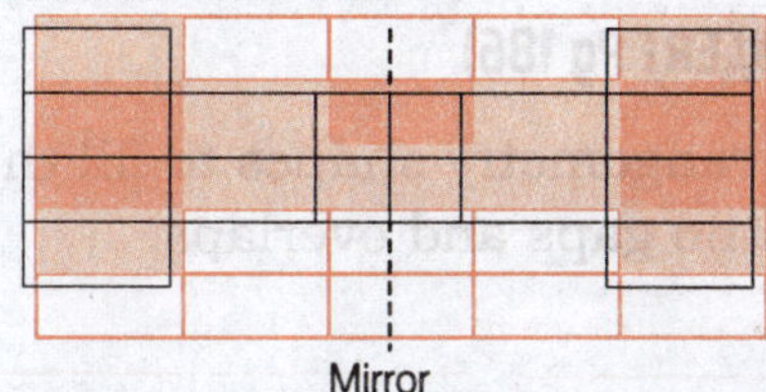

Q.14 Make Micy's side the same as that of Catty's side. You can rearrange only three balls in Micy's side.

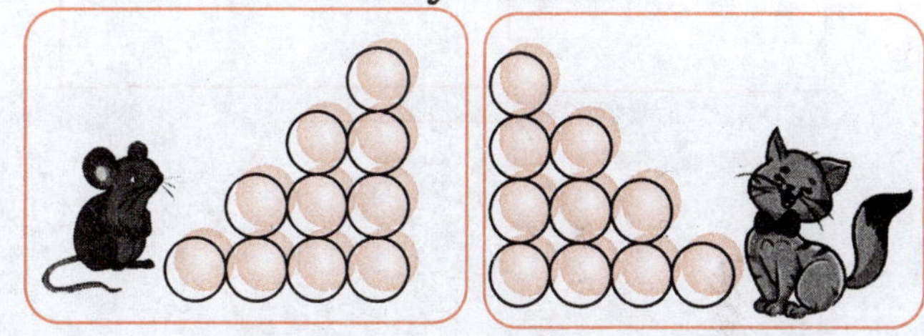

Ans. *

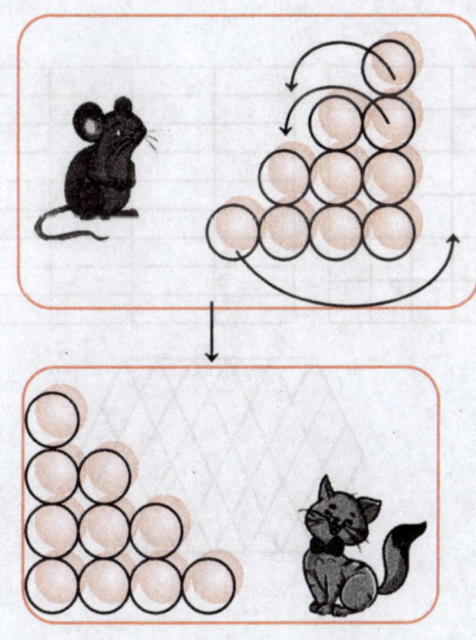

Q.15 Which shape cutouts would fit in the given shape without overlapping and without gaps.

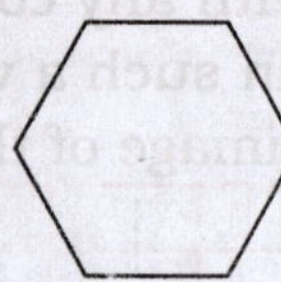

Ans. * The shapes of triangles would fit in the given shape without overlaping and without gaps.

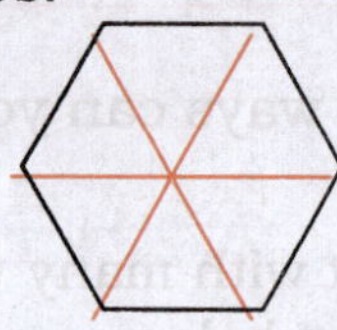

Let us Do (NCERT Pg 186)

Q.16 Use rangometry shapes to fill the shapes with no gaps and overlaps.

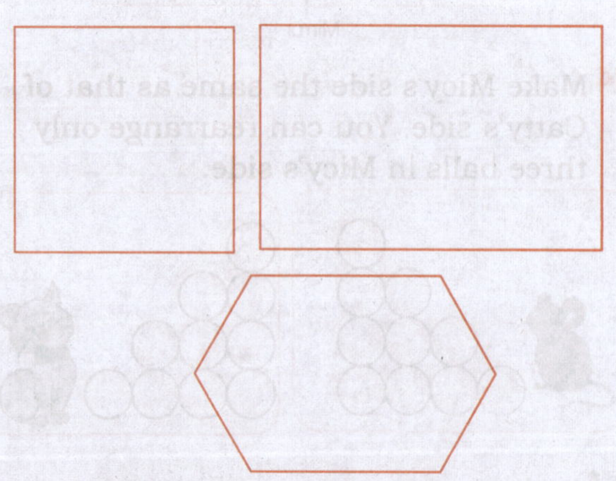

Ans. *

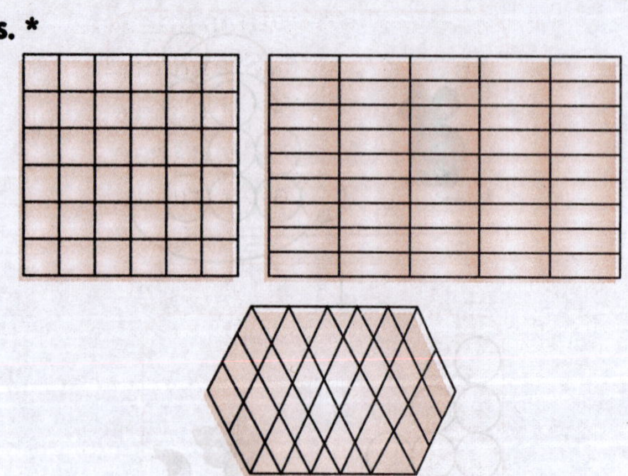

Let us Do (NCERT Pg 187)

Q.17 Use two or more rangometry shapes to create your tiles. Now, trace the tiles to create different paths.

Ans. Do yourself.

Q.18 Try making these paths.

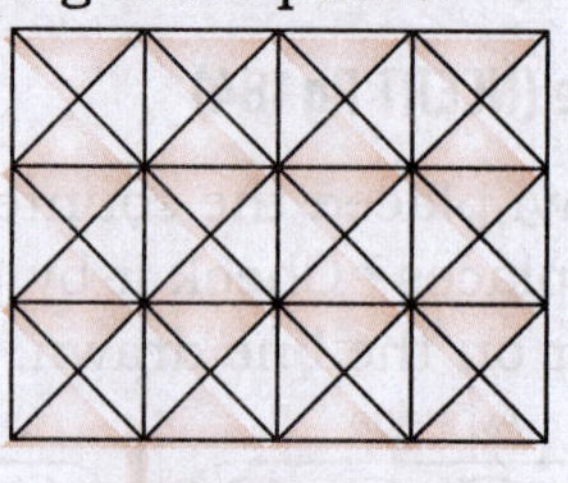

Ans. Do yourself.

Let us Play (NCERT Pg 188)

Q.19 Imagine yourself sitting with Soni and Avi. You think of a place or a stall and challenge your friend to find out which stall you have in your mind. You can help them guess by answering yes or no.

Ans. Do yourself.

Search for Dada and Dadi (NCERT Pg 189-190)

Q.20

Soni and Avi's Dada and Dadi were missing. They hear their announcement.

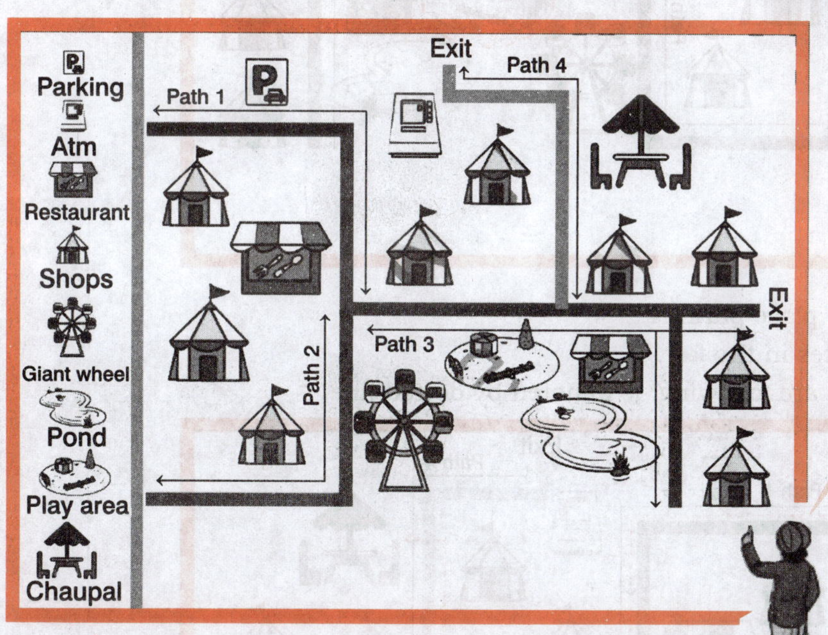

(i) Help Soni and Avi read the map and find the following.

(a) Which place does the [chaupal sign] sign show?

(b) Circle the picture in the map that shows the play area?

(c) Which place does the [P sign] sign show?

(d) How many exit routes are there in the fair?

(ii) Follow the path that Avi and Soni are following.

(a) Walk on the path-1.

(b) Turn right on the path-2.

(c) You will see a restaurant on your right. Don't sit there.

(d) Take a left towards the path-3.

(e) Take the first left turn towards the path-4. Stalls will be seen on the way.

(f) Pass the stalls to find the Chaupal and meet Dada Dadi.

(iii) An uncle asks Dada ji, the way to the ATM. Tell him the way to the ATM from the chaupal.

Ans. (i) (a) The sign [chaupal sign] shows the place chaupal.

(b)

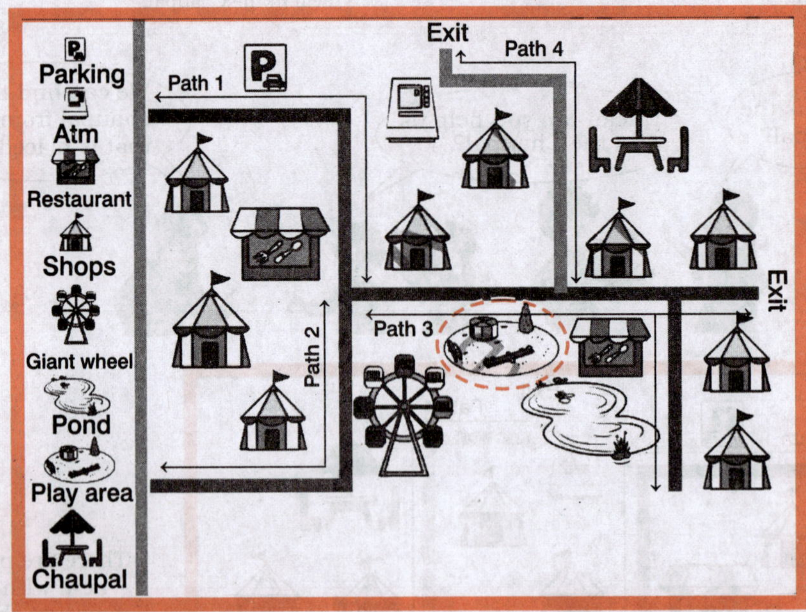

(c) The sign [parking sign] shows the place parking.

(d) There are two exit routes in the fair.

(ii) The path that Avi and Soni are following, is denoted by dotted line.

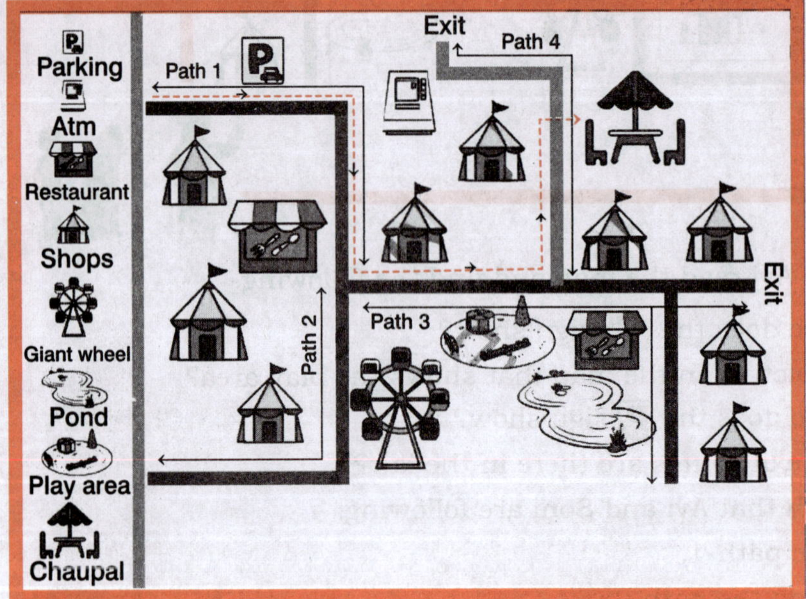

(iii) To way to the ATM from the chaupal follow the path following

(a) Walk on the Path 4. (b) Turn right on the Path 3. (c) Pass the stalls and see ATM.

Let us Do (NCERT Pg 191)

Q.21 (i) There are two ways to go out of the Surajkund fair. One seems to be a maze and the other goes straight there. Follow the maze with Soni and Avi to exit the fair.

(ii) Share the way you went through the maze. Write the things you found on the way.

Ans. (i)

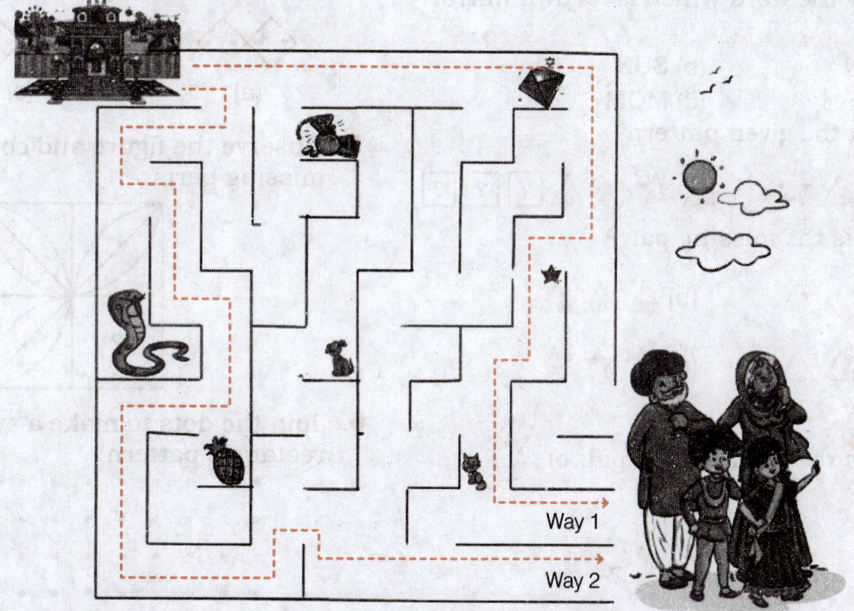

*(ii) I follow the way 1 (as shown in above figure) and found diamond, star and cat.

1. State that true or false for the following figures are symmetrical.

(i) 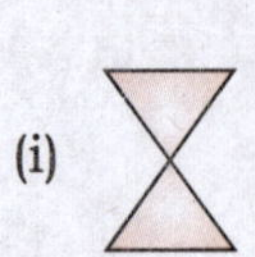

(ii) 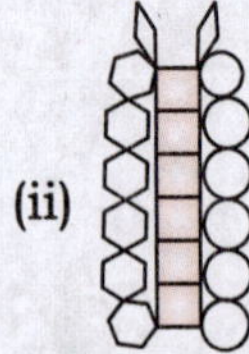

2. Multiple choice questions.

(i) What shape do you see in this tessellation?

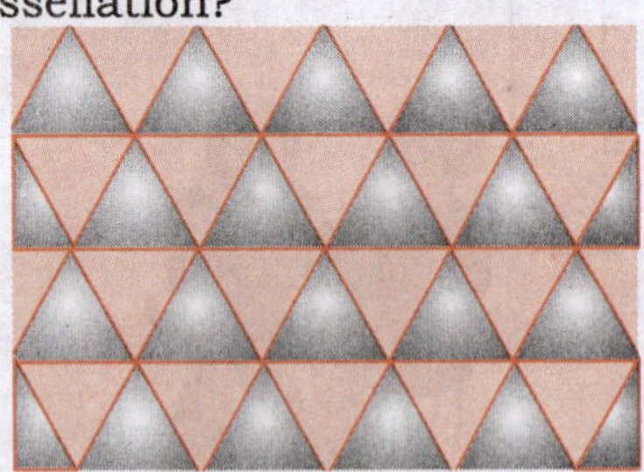

(a) Triangles
(b) Squares
(c) Hexagons
(d) Triangles and rectangles

(ii) Identify the word which is its own mirror image.

(a) WON (b) SUN
(c) DO (d) MOM

(iii) Look at the given pattern

Which is the missing part?

(a)  (b) 

(c)  (d) 

(iv) Identify the symmetrical pair of

(a) 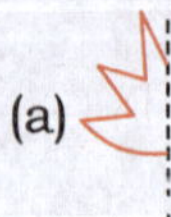 (b) 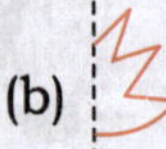

(c) 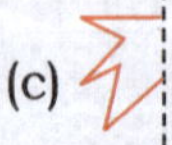 (d) 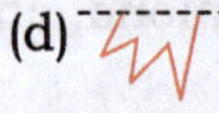

3. Match the following pictures which have similar halves along dotted lines.

	Column A		Column B
(i)		(a)	V
(ii)		(b)	A
(iii)		(c)	T
(iv)		(d)	M

4. Find odd one out.

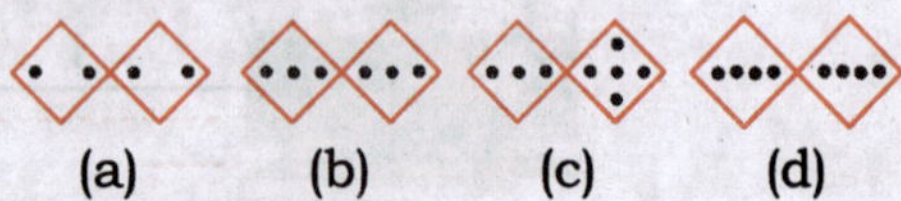

5. Observe the figure and complete the missing parts.

6. Join the dots to make a symmetrical rectangle pattern.

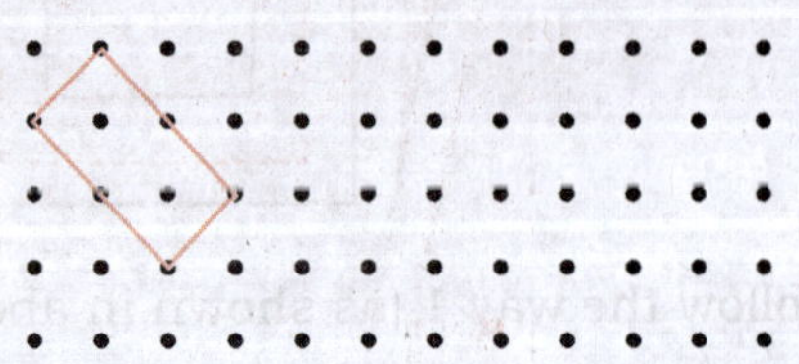

7. Draw the lines in the rangolis (as shown figure below) that divide them into two identical halves.

8. Complete the pictures by drawing the mirror image.

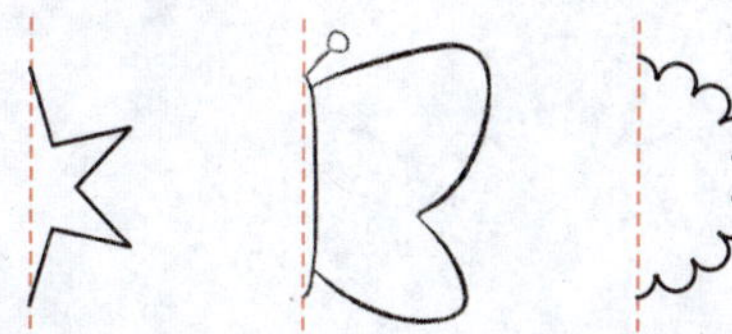

9. Draw the other half of each symmetrical shape.

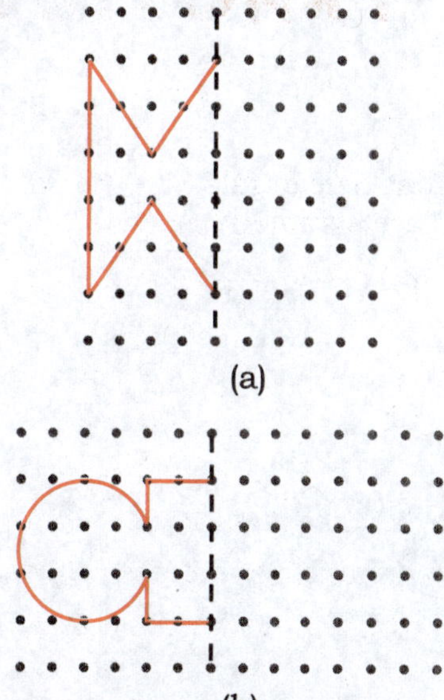

(a)

(b)

ANSWERS & SOLUTIONS

1. (i) True (ii) False
2. (i) (a) (ii) (d) (iii) (a) (iv) (b)
3. (i) → (c) (ii) → (d) (iii) → (a) (iv) → (b)
4. We have the following figures

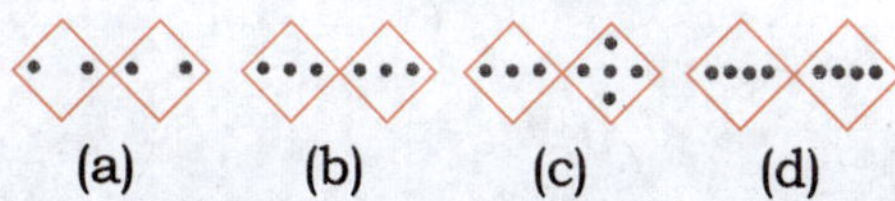

(a) (b) (c) (d)

Here, we see that figure (a), (b) and (d) can be divided into two identical halves. So, we can say that fig (a), (b) and (d) are symmetrical. Figure (c) can not be divide into two identical halves. Therefore, figure (c) is not symmetrical. Thus, figure (c) is odd one.

5. The given figure is symmetrical. So, the missing part is shown below.

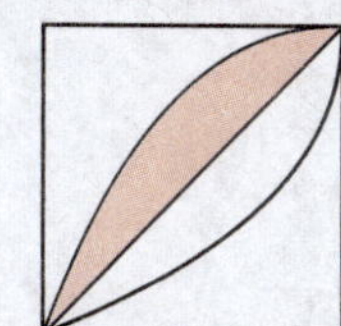

6.

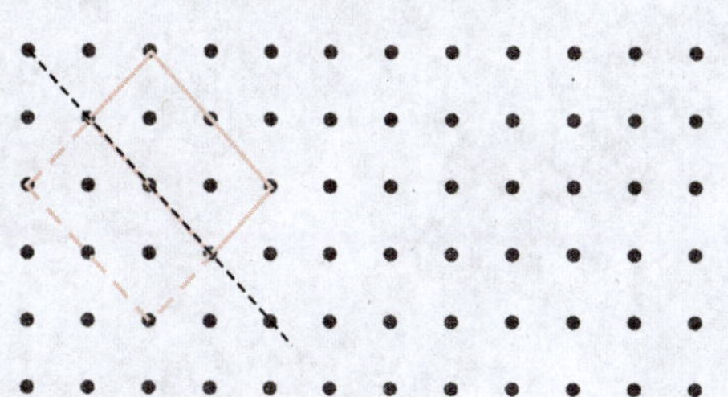

7.

Here, the dotted lines are dividing the given figures into two identical halves.

8. Complete pictures of the given halves images by drawing the mirror image is shown below.

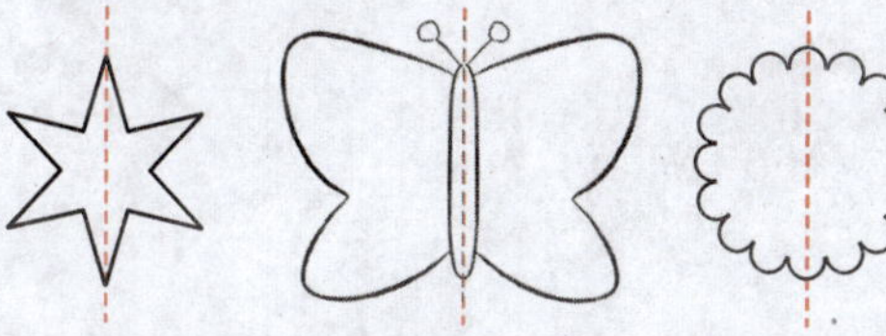

9. On drawing the other half of both given symmetrical shapes are shown below.

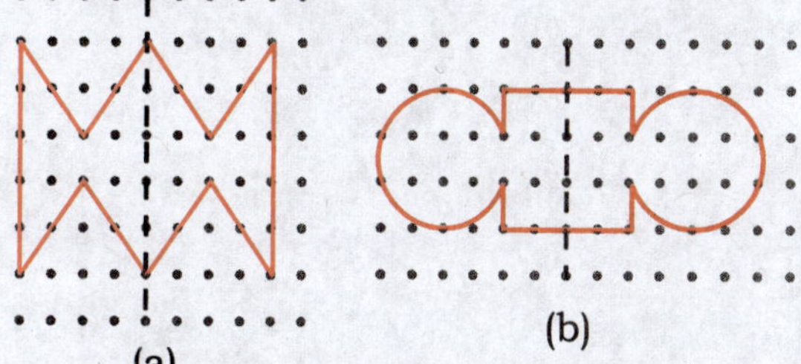

(a) (b)

Santoor
(English)

Unit 1

FUN WITH FRIENDS

Summary A duck and a hen are planning to take their children to the village fair. On the way, they come across a stream. The hen tells the duck that she doesn't know how to swim. The duck tells her that she has a plan. She asks the hen to get on her back and the chicks to get on the back of her ducklings. The duck and the ducklings swim and carry the hen and chicks across the stream on their backs.

Word-Meaning *Village fair - A festival in a village where people get together to enjoy, sell handicrafts, play games etc.*

Chicks - Children of a hen, or young bird.

Ducklings - Children of a duck or young duck.

Stream - A small river

Now discuss with your friends (Page 3)

Q.1 How many ducklings and chicks can you see in the picture given on page no. 2 and of the NCERT?

Ans. There are three chicks and three ducklings in the picture.

Q.2 The duck and the hen — are they friends? How do you know?

Ans. Yes, the duck and the hen are friends. We know this as duck and ducklings help the hen and the chicks to get across the stream.

Q.3 How did the hen and the chicks cross the stream?

Ans. The hen and the chicks crossed the stream by riding on the back of the duck and the ducklings.

Q.4 Have you ever helped your friend? How did you help?

Ans. Yes, I have helped my friend in class. Once, my best friend forgot to bring her pencil box and needed a pencil. I had an extra pencil so I gave it to my friend.

Q.5 Did you feel happy to help your friend?

Ans. Yes, I feel happy when I help my friend.

Q.6 Match the following animals with their young ones.

	Animals	Young Ones	
	Duck	Kitten	
	Hen	Calf	
	Cow	Puppy	
	Cat	Duckling	
	Dog	Chick	

Ans.

Duck – Duckling
Hen – Chick
Cow – Calf
Cat – Kitten
Dog – Puppy

COLOURS

Summary of the Poem The poem talks about different colours. It also shows how sharing things with our friends makes our life more fun! In the poem, there are two children. They are friends. One friend suggests sharing their crayons with the other. So that they both can have a full pack of crayons.

Stanza 1

You have a few crayons,
Red, yellow and blue.
Green, purple and black,
I have some too.

Exp. In these lines, one of the children explains that they have Green, Purple and Black crayons in their box of colours. While Their friend has Red, Yellow, Blue crayons.

Stanza 2

I need the red
and you need the black.
If we share our crayons,
we have a full pack!

Exp. In these lines, the child tells the friend that they need the red colour and the friend needs black colour crayon.

The child suggests that if they share their crayons, they both can have a full pack of crayons.

Let us Think! (Page 5-6)

A. Answer the questions.

Q.1 How many children are there in the poem?

Ans. There are two children in the poem.

Q.2 Why did the children want to share the crayons?

Ans. The children wanted to share the crayons so that they can both have a full pack of crayons.

Q.3 How can the children in the poem have a full pack?

Ans. The children can have a full pack of crayons if they share their crayons with each other.

B. Think and say

Q.1 The children in the poem shared their crayons. Do you share anything with your friends? What do you share?

Ans. Yes, I share my pencils, erasers, pens, chocolates, lunch and snacks with my friends.

Q.2 You have only green, blue and red crayons. Talk in pairs what you would want to draw.

Ans. You can make a scenery, a fish in a pond, fruit basket, etc with green, blue and red crayons.

Q.3 Now you have blue, green, red, yellow, brown and orange crayons. What can you draw?

Ans. We can draw a blue bird, green trees, red apple, yellow banana, brown ball, orange fruit, etc.

Q.4 Rearrange the letters to find the hidden colour.

(a) LEBU (b) LYLEWO (c) RENEG

(d) RUPPEL (e) NROBW

Ans. (a) BLUE, (b) YELLOW, (c) GREEN, (d) PURPLE (e) BROWN

Let us Speak! (Page 6-7)

A. Say aloud.

This is a green crayon.
The word green begins with 'gr'.
The word crayon begins with 'cr'.

Now say these words aloud:

gr	green	grey	grass	grapes	grandmother
cr	crayon	crab	crane	crow	cradle
dr	draw	drum	dress	drop	dragon
pr	prince	princess	prize	pray	present

Form a sentence using each of these words and say it aloud.

Ans.
- **Green** The tree has green leaves.
- **Grey** Jasmine was wearing a grey jacket.
- **Grass** My grandfather likes to walk on the grass in the morning.
- **Grapes** Grapes are my mother's favourite fruit.
- **Grandmother** My grandmother makes yummy food for me.
- **Crayon** Me and my best friend share the red crayon.
- **Crab** The crab has two big claws to grab things with.
- **Crane** The crane in the sky was white in colour.
- **Crow** A black crow flew into my room.
- **Cradle** The baby sleeps in the cradle.
- **Draw** I like to draw beautiful pictures.
- **Drum** The drum set is my favourite instrument.
- **Dress** Nancy was wearing a pretty blue dress.
- **Drop** Be careful not to drop the heavy books on your foot.

- **Dragon** The dragon was waiting for the knight outside the cave.
- **Prince** The prince bought flowers.
- **Princess** The princess was very tall.
- **Prize** Mohan won the first prize in the race.
- **Pray** We should pray to God every morning.
- **Present** I was present in the school yesterday.

B. *Have fun! (With colours) (on NCERT page no. 7)*

Ans. Do it yourself.

Let us Learn! (Page 7-13)

A. *Words used to show actions are called action words. Read the words given below. Circle the action words. (on NCERT page no. 7)*

carrot	laugh	dance	leg	eat
cry	swim	potato	sleep	play
sun	dig	jump	run	book
face	write	cat	smile	push

Ans. Following are the action words :
Laugh, dance, eat, cry, swim, sleep, play, dig, jump, run, write, smile, push

B. *Find the action words in the grid below. One is done for you.*

p	u	p	p	y	n	b	h	walk
t	y	o	k	a	r	q	p	yawn
x	v	u	j	w	a	l	k	pour
c	a	r	w	n	o	s	e	cough
o	t	g	s	r	p	o	q	give
u	y	i	e	y	e	g	g	see
g	i	v	e	t	n	d	a	open
h	v	e	q	h	e	l	p	help

Ans.

p	u	p	p	y	n	b	h
t	y	o	k	a	r	q	p
x	v	u	j	w	a	l	k
c	a	r	w	n	o	s	e
o	t	g	s	r	p	o	q
u	y	i	e	y	e	g	g
g	i	v	e	t	n	d	a
h	v	e	q	h	e	l	p

C. *There are 26 letters in the English Alphabet. (Refer to NCERT page no. 8-12 to learn more about them.)*

Let us arrange some words in alphabetical order. Write these colours in alphabetical order.

YELLOW BLUE PURPLE GREEN RED

Ans. BLUE GREEN PURPLE RED YELLOW

Let us Do! (Page 14)

A. *Look at these words. Match each word with its friend-word. Write the new word in the space given. The picture clue will help you. One has been done for you*

Word	Friend	New word	Clue
rain	paper	______	
blue	ball	______	
news	bow	rainbow	
basket	worm	______	
Earth	berry	______	

Ans. rainbow, blueberry, newspaper, basketball, earthworm

PRACTICE QUESTIONS

Multiple Choice Questions

1. What are the children sharing in the poem?
   (a) crayons (b) books
   (c) toys (d) pencils
2. The child wanted .... colour crayon.
   (a) red (b) green
   (c) blue (d) black
3. From this poem we learn the importance of ....
   (a) more crayons
   (b) having a friend
   (c) playing with a friend
   (d) sharing
4. Who has the blue crayon?
   (a) The child
   (b) The child's friend
   (c) Both of them
   (d) No one

Ans. 1. (a) 2. (a) 3. (d) 4. (b)

True or False

1. Both the children have crayons.
2. The child wanted a blue-coloured crayon.
3. The child's friend has green, purple and black crayons.
4. The child wants to share their crayons with their friend.

Ans. 1. True 2. False 3. False 4. True

Answer the Following Questions

1. What are the colours of the crayons the children have?

Ans. Children have red, yellow, blue, green, purple and black colours of the crayons.

2. What colour of crayon did the child's friend need?

Ans. The child's friend needed a black crayon.

3. What colour of crayons do the children need to have a full pack?

Ans. The children need red and black crayons to have a full pack.

4. Why do you think sharing is important?

Ans. Sharing is important because it is a kind act and it can make us and others feel happy.

Jumbled Letters

Rearrange the letters to find the hidden words:

1. GINSARH

Ans. SHARING

2. GLCDUKIN

Ans. DUCKLING

3. OURCLOS

Ans. COLOURS

Let's Write

Look at the picture carefully. Observe what is happening in the picture. Write five lines on what is happening in the picture and what youlearn from it.

Ans. 1. Two friends are sharing lunch with each other.
2. One of the friends is giving a sandwich to the other friend.
3. Sharing food with friends is a good habit.
4. It shows that we care for our friends and love them.
5. We should always share things with our friends and family.

CHAPTER 2 BADAL AND MOTI

Summary

A boy named Badal, lived in a village with his mother happily. One day Badal was returning back from school. He saw a puppy shivering in the cold. He brought the puppy home and asked his mother if he could keep him. His mother agreed but only if Badal promised to take care of the puppy. They named the puppy Moti. As Moti grew up, he and Badal became best friends.

On a rainy day, on his way back from school, Badal slipped on a muddy lane and fell into a deep pit. When he didn't return home, Badal's mother got worried. She gathered the villagers to search for Badal. Moti caught Badal's scent and found him in the pit. He barked loudly to alert everyone. The villagers were able to rescue Badal. Badal hugged and thanked Moti for saving his life.

WORD-MEANING

Shivering - Shaking slightly as a result of being cold, scared or happy, **Slipped** - To fall, **Muddy** - Covered in mud, dirty, **Pit** - A large hole in the ground, **Accompanied** - Go somewhere with a friend or companion, **Relieved** - Feeling happy or relaxed after a problem being solved.

NCERT FOLDER

Let us Think! (Page 18-19)

A. Answer the following.

Q.1 What did Badal come across by the side of the road?

Ans. Badal came across a puppy by the side of the road.

Q.2 What did Badal and his mother name the puppy?

Ans. Badal and his mother named the puppy Moti.

Q.3 What did Badal fall into?

Ans. Badal slipped on a muddy lane and fell into a deep pit.

Q.4 How did Moti find Badal?

Ans. Moti caught Badal's scent and followed it to find Badal.

Q.5 Write 'T' for True and 'F' for False.

(a) Badal lived with his grandmother.

(b) Moti grew up and loved Badal.

(c) Badal's mother was worried when he did not come home in time.

(d) Moti caught Badal's photo.

(e) Badal hugged his puppy Moti and thanked him.

Ans. (a) False, (b) True, (c) True, (d) False, (e) True

B. Think and Discuss in pairs.

Q.1 Do you remember when you fell down last time? How did you fall? Who picked you up? Share your experiences.

Ans. Yes, I remember when I fell down the last time. It was about a month ago, when I was running down the stairs of my home. It was a race between me and my sister. I was reaching the ground floor when I slipped because of some water that was spilled here. I rolled down a whole flight of stairs. I was hurt really bad and was not able to stand on my own. Luckily, my parents heard me scream. They came to help me and my father picked me up.

Q.2 Do you have a pet? Do you know someone who has a pet?

Ans. No, I don't have a pet. However, my aunt has two pet cats- Dory and Nemo. My aunt cares for them very much. The little cats are very friendly. They have soft white fur, green eyes and they love to play. They are very fluffy and I love to play with them the whole day.

Q.3 If you were allowed to keep any animal as a pet, which animal would you choose? Why?

Ans. If I am ever allowed to keep a pet, I would like to keep a dog. I would choose them because I love dogs very much. They are so loyal and lovable. If you love them, they love you ten times more.

Let us Learn! (Page 19-20)

A. Look at the following words from the lesson.

lived loved shared gathered thanked

Notice that all these words end with 'ed'. All these actions have already happened.

Add 'ed' and write

walk + ed = ____________

play ____________

talk ____________

ask ____________

touch ____________

Ans. walked, played, talked, asked, touched

B. Match the words to make pairs. Colour each pair with the same colour. Two have been done for you.

paper		ball
chair		thread
bat	and	key
needle		pencil
lock		sambar
idli		table

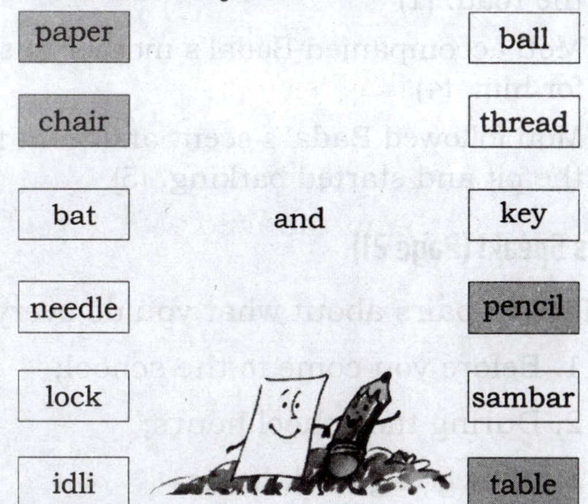

Ans. Paper and Pencil
Chair and Table
Bat and Ball
Needle and Thread
Lock and Key
Idli and Sambar

Let us Listen! (Page 20)

A. Your teacher will read out the story of Badal and Moti once again to you. Now read the following sentences and number them in the sequence of the story.

The first sentence has already been marked for you.

One rainy day, he slipped and fell into a deep pit. ( )

Badal and his mother named the puppy Moti. ( )

Badal hugged Moti. ( )

Badal came across a puppy by the side of the road. (1)

Moti accompanied Badal's mother to search for him. ( )

Moti followed Badal's scent and went near the pit and started barking. ( )

Ans. One rainy day, he slipped and fell into a deep pit. (3)

Badal and his mother named the puppy Moti. (2)

Badal hugged Moti. (6)

Badal came across a puppy by the side of the road. (1)

Moti accompanied Badal's mother to search for him. (4)

Moti followed Badal's scent and went near the pit and started barking. (5)

Let us Speak! (Page 21)

A. Talk in pairs about what you do every day

1. Before you come to the school;
2. During the school hours;
3. After going back home.

B. You may use the following clues.

1. Every day I ________ up at ________ in the morning. Then I ________ my teeth and go to the ________. After that, I take a ________ and dress up for school. I ________ breakfast and I ________ to school.
2. ____________________
3. ____________________

Ans. 1. Before you come to school.

Every day I <u>wake</u> up at <u>six</u> in the morning. Then I <u>brush</u> my teeth and go to the <u>toilet</u>. After that, I take a <u>shower</u> and dress up for school. I <u>have</u> breakfast and I <u>go</u> to school.

2. During the school hours.

In school, I study.

I learn how to read and write.

I also play with my friends during break time.

3. After going back home.

After school, I go home.

I rest for sometime, eat food and watch television.

In the evening, I play outside with my friends.

I also do my homework.

Then, I have my dinner and fall asleep.

Let us Write! (Page 21-23)

A. Look at the pictures. They show a story of two friends: a pigeon and an ant. But the pictures are jumbled up. Number them to get the correct order to make a story.

Ans. 3, 4, 5, 1, 2, 6

B. Now fill in the blanks using the words in the box to complete the story.

leaf flew branch climbed fell stream hunter

A dove was resting on a (i)______ of a tree near a (ii)______. An ant (iii)______ into the stream and cried for help. The dove dropped a (iv)______ into the stream. The ant (v)______ on the leaf and landed safely. Another day the ant saw a (vi)______ aiming at the dove. She quickly climbed up and bit the hunter's hand. The dove (vii)______ away unhurt.

Ans. (i) branch (ii) stream
(iii) fell (iv) leaf
(v) climbed (vi) hunter
(vii) flew

C. Look at these sentences from the lesson.
"Can this puppy stay with us, Maa?"
"Yes beta, but only if you promise to take care of the puppy."
Add a (?) or a (.) to the following:

1. The Sun rises in the East ______
2. What is your name ______
3. I like to eat mangoes ______
4. May I borrow your English textbook ______
5. Brinda and Namrata are good friends ______
6. Whose shoes are these ______

Ans. 1. The Sun rises in the East.
2. What is your name?
3. I like to eat mangoes.
4. May I borrow your English textbook?
5. Brinda and Namrata are good friends.
6. Whose shoes are these?

D. Complete the following conversation between two children

Hint : An example has been done for you below.

Ans.

Let us Do! (Page 24)

A. Look at the picture given below. It shows three children playing. Would you like to add anything to this picture? Use your crayons or colour pencils to add to the picture.

Ans. You can draw what you want to add in the picture. Some suggestions include

- Boy playing with a ball.
- Children playing Badminton.
- Some children enjoying a picnic with their parents or friends.

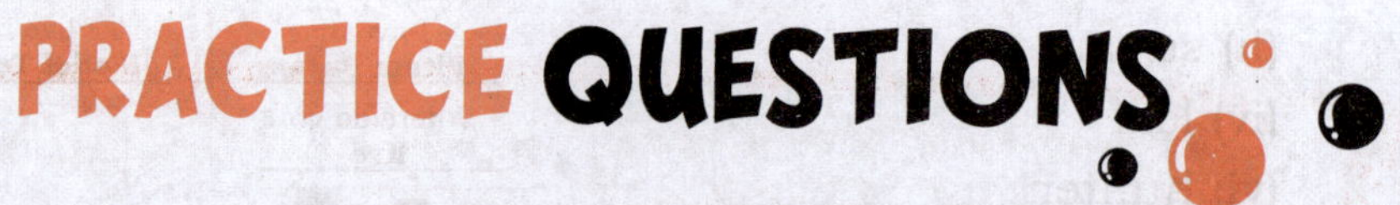

PRACTICE QUESTIONS

Multiple Choice Questions

1. Why was the puppy shivering when Badal found him?
   (a) Because he was scared.
   (b) Because of cold.
   (c) Because he was hungry.
   (d) Because he was sick.

2. Badal brought the puppy __________.
   (a) to school
   (b) to the park
   (c) home
   (d) to his friend's house

3. Badal's mother allowed him to keep the puppy if he promised to __________.
   (a) name it Moti
   (b) bathe the puppy
   (c) finish his homework
   (d) take care of the puppy

4. Badal and Moti were __________.
   (a) enemies
   (b) brothers
   (c) best friends
   (d) None of the above

5. Moti __________ Badal.
   (a) loved
   (b) hated
   (c) was scared of
   (d) All of the above

Ans. 1. (b), 2. (c), 3. (d)
4. (c), 5. (a)

Answer the Following Questions

1. What happened to Badal on his way home one rainy day?

Ans. On a rainy day, when Badal was on his way home, he slipped on the muddy lane and fell into a deep pit.

2. How did Moti alert everyone about Badal's location?

Ans. Moti alerted everyone about Badal's location by barking loudly while standing near the pit.

3. How did the villagers pull Badal out of the pit?

Ans. The villagers used a rope to pull Badal out of the pit.

Let's Write

1. All of use want a have a pet. Suppose, your parents gift you a dog. You are required to take care of your pet. Write 4 sentences on how you will care for your pet.

Ans. If I am ever given a dog as a pet I would do many things to take care of it.
1. I would make sure that he/she gets proper food on time.
2. I would make sure that he/she is clean and healthy at all time.
3. I would play with him/her.
4. I would take him/her on a walk in the nearby park.
5. I would not feed him/her sweets because I read somewhere that they are poisonous for dogs.

BEST FRIENDS

Summary

There were four friends - Circle, Square, Triangle and Rectangle. One day they fought about which shape was the best. They all gave reasons for why they are the best but still couldn't decide who was the best.

They decided to ask the first person they met to help them. After some time they met star. They asked her to choose the best shape.

The star was wise and said that they all are friends. They should not fight. She told them that together they can create the most beautiful pictures and patterns. The friends realised their mistake. They decided to never fight and be best friends forever!

WORD-MEANING

Edge - A line where an object begins or ends, **Decide** - To make a choice, **Pattern** - A design that is repeated multiple times to create something new, **Amazing** - Very good and surprising.

Let us Think! (Page 29)

A. Answer the following.

Q.1 Who were the four friends?

Ans. The four friends were Circle, Square, Rectangle and Triangle.

Q.2 Why were they fighting?

Ans. They were fighting to decide who was the best shape among them.

Q.3 Who helped them to end their fight?

Ans. The star helped them to end their fight.

Q.4 What lesson did the friends learn in the end?

Ans. The friends learned that they can create many beautiful things and patterns together. So they don't need to fight to decide which is the best shape.

Q.5 Write 'T' for True and 'F' for False.

(a) The circle does not have sharp edges.

(b) A square has four sides but not all of them are equal in size.

(c) The triangle has two sides.

(d) The friends could decide who was the best among them.

Ans. (a) True (b) False (c) False (d) False

Q.6 Who is your friend? What are the things you can do when your friend helps you?

Ans. Rashi is my dear friend. She always helps me whenever I need it. So, I also help her whenever she needs support. We help each other with homework, dance practice and many other things.

Q.7 Look around you. Talk about the shapes of what you see.

Ans. I can see many things around me made from the following shapes.

Circle Clock, Coin, Roti, etc.

Square Carrom board, Windows, Barfi, etc.

Triangle Samosa, Sandwich, Mountain, etc.

Rectangle Table, TV screen, Door, etc.

Let us Speak! (Page 30)

Divide into groups of 5.

Each of you will be one character in the story — circle, square, triangle, rectangle and the star. Take turns and read out the story.

Enjoy by adding actions to what you say.

Ans. You can perform this in the class with your friends or classmates as an exercise.

Let us Learn! (Page 30-31)

A. Fill in the blanks using 'a'.

1. _________ dog is barking at the postman.

Ans. A dog is barking at the postman.

2. My mother gives chapattis to _______ cow everyday.

Ans. My mother gives chapattis to a cow everyday.

3. In summers, ________ sparrow builds its nest on the mango tree near our house.

Ans. In summers, a sparrow builds its nest on the mango tree near our house.

B. Fill in the blanks using 'an'.

1. I saw ______ eagle yesterday.

Ans. I saw an eagle yesterday.

2. Maya bought _________ umbrella for the monsoon.

Ans. Maya bought an umbrella for the monsoon.

3. ________ ice-cream man brings his cart in the evenings.

Ans. An ice-cream man brings his cart in the evenings.

C. Fill in the blanks using 'a' or 'an'.

1. _________ brown hen laid _______ egg.

Ans. A brown hen laid an egg.

2. _______ eagle sat on _______ building.

Ans. An eagle sat on a building.

3. Mary ate _______ apricot, ________ chikoo and _______ orange.

Ans. Mary ate an apricot, a chikoo and an orange.

Let us Write! (Page 31-32)

A. Paste a picture of your friend.

Ans. Do it yourself.

B. Write a few lines about your friend by filling in the blanks.

My Friend

1. My friend's name is _______.
2. He/She is a boy/girl.

3. He/She is ________ years old.
4. His/Her favourite colour is _______ .
5. He/She likes to play ________.
6. He/She wants to becomes ________ .

I love my friend.

Ans. Do it yourself.

Let us do! (Page 32)

A. Use the space given below to draw the four friends you met in Chapter 3.

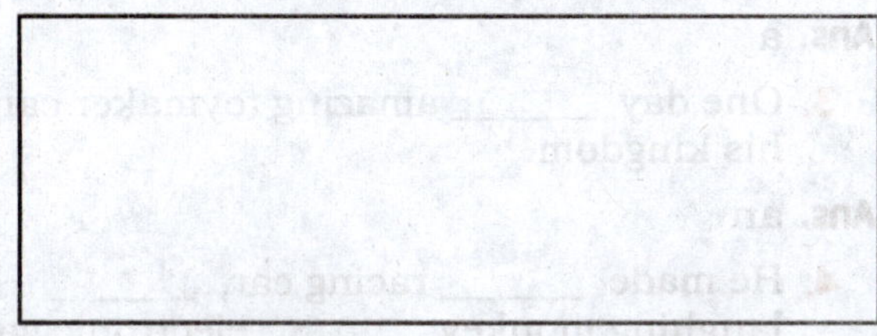

Ans.

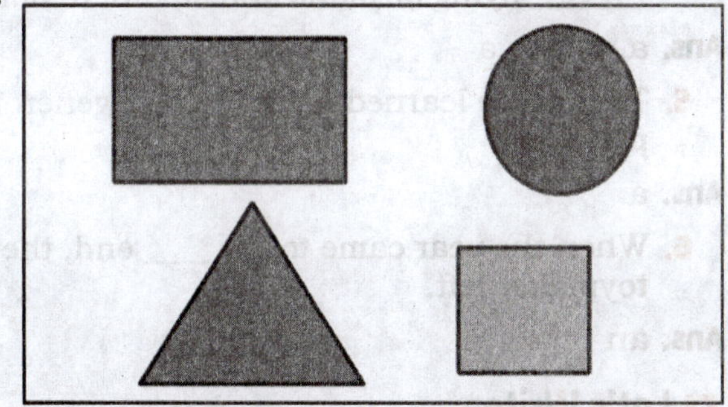

Let us Explore! (Page 33)

A. Draw pictures using the four friends mentioned in chapter 3. You can use the pictures given in your NCERT Textbook on page no. 33 for ideas.

Hint : Use the shapes square, circle, rectangle and triangle to make a scenery in the space given above.

Fun with Words (Page 34-35)

What do You do?

Who are you?
And what do you do?
We are birds.
We chirp and sing.
Who are you?
And what do you do?
We are monkeys.
We jump and swing.
Who are you?
And what do you do?
We are dogs.
We run and bark.
Who are you?
And what do you do?
We are cats.
We mew in the dark.
Who are you?
And what do you do?
We are elephants.
We raise our trunks.
Who are you?
And what do you do?
We are lions.
We roar and hunt.

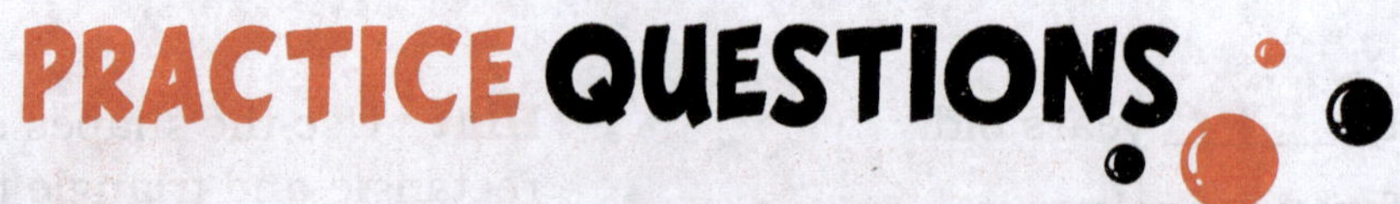

PRACTICE QUESTIONS

Multiple Choice Questions

1. Circle thought that it was the best shape as it was ______________.
   (a) round
   (b) beautiful
   (c) used to make a smiling face
   (d) All of the above
2. Children enjoy biscuits in the shape of ______________.
   (a) triangle (b) square
   (c) rectangle (d) circle
3. Which of the following food items is not in a triangle shape?
   (a) Ice cream cone
   (b) Pizza slice
   (c) Ladoo
   (d) Pastry
4. The star was in a __________ shape.
   (a) happy (b) wise
   (c) kind (d) rude
5. We should not __________ with our friends.
   (a) fight (b) dance
   (c) share (d) jump

Ans. 1. (d), 2. (c), 3. (c), 4. (b), 5. (a)

Answer the following Questions

1. Which shapes said that they are beautiful?

Ans. All of the shapes- circle, square, triangle, rectangle, said that they are beautiful.

2. Which shape has four equal sides?

Ans. Square has four equal sides.

3. Why did triangle think it was the best shape?

Ans. Triangle thinks that it was the best shape because it has three sides. Children used it to draw mountains. They enjoyed many yummy snacks in its shape.

4. What can the shapes create together?

Ans. All the shapes can create wonder together.

Fill in the blanks

Complete the following sentences by putting articles 'a' or 'an' in blanks below.

1. Once upon ______ time there was _____ little prince who was used to having everything.

Ans. a, a

2. He was _______ spoiled child and didn't like sharing his toys with anyone.

Ans. a

3. One day _______ amazing toymaker came to his kingdom.

Ans. an

4. He made _______ racing car, _______ laughing monkey, _______ electronic gadget, _______ flying airplane and so much more.

Ans. a, a, an, a

5. The prince learned to be _______ generous person.

Ans. a

6. When the year came to _______ end, the toymaker left.

Ans. an

Let's Write

1. Who according to you is a good friend? Write a paragraph on a good friend.

Ans. **A Good Friend**

Friends are a very valuable to our life. They will always be companion in happiness or sadness. A good friend contributes to our well-being. They provide joy and comfort.

A good friend loves you, cares for you, and is loyal. They will never talk behind your back. Also, a good friend will always listen and try to solve your problems. They'll be the ones with whom you have the most amazing memories. Nothing can come between you; you have been pillars in each other's lives. Life without a friend will be too dull. A good friend makes life easy for you.

Unit 2

TOYS AND GAMES

Picture Reading

Look at the picture and answer.

Q.1 Count how many there are and write in the blanks :

children ________, girls ________, boys ________, women ________ and animals ________

Ans.

Children	–	16
Girls	–	7
Boys	–	9
Women	–	3
Animals	–	0

Q.2 What games are the children playing?

Ans. The children are playing, ringa-ringa roses, hide and seek, hopscotch, and spinning tops. They are also playing with marbles.

Q.3 Children are playing in the open space in front of their houses. Where do you usually play?

Ans. I usually play in the park near my house.

Q.4 Some children are not playing games. What are they doing?

Ans. Some children are not playing games. One girl is reading a newspaper and a boy is listening to her. Another girl is talking to a woman and a boy is coming out of the house with a kite. A boy with crutches is looking at other children playing with marbles.

Q.5 There are some women in the picture. What are they doing?

Ans. One woman is making a garland using flowers. One woman is sorting and cleaning food grains. Another woman is talking to a little girl.

Q.6 Who is reading the newspaper?

Ans. A girl is reading the newspaper.

Q.7 What are the children playing with?

Ans. The children are playing with a kite, marbles, a blindfold and two spinning tops.

Q.8 What is the old man doing?

Ans. The old man is watching three boys playing with marbles.

Q.9 What is your favourite game?

Ans. I enjoy playing all ball games, but volleyball is my favourite of them all.

Q.10 If you were in the picture, which game would you play?

Ans. If I were in the picture, I would have been playing the marbles along with the boys. I would play the game because my father had told me about the game. It seemed fun and interesting to me.

A. Point out the following in the picture.

1. The boys are playing with marbles.
2. A girl is playing hopscotch.
3. A boy and a girl are spinning tops.
4. A boy is blindfolded.
5. A boy is holding a kite.

Ans. Do it yourself.

B. Identify the playthings used to play. Write their names below.

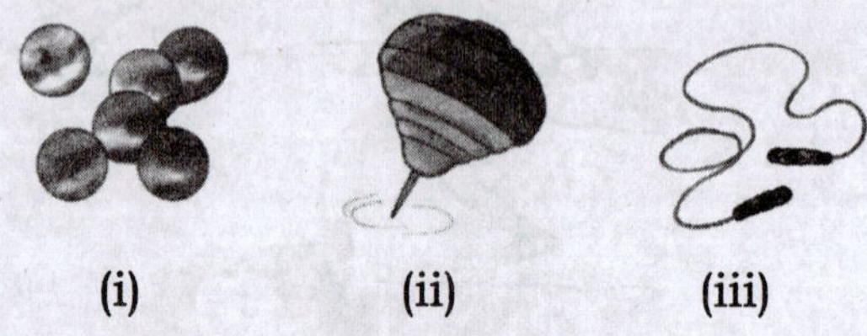

(i) (ii) (iii)

Ans. (i) Marbles (ii) Spinning Top (iii) Skipping Rope

CHAPTER 4 OUT IN THE GARDEN

Summary The poem talks about playing outside in the garden. The child says that he likes to play with his ball, a kite and his friends. He also tells us about many activities that he does like bouncing the ball, tugging the kite, running and playing with his friends and much more.

Stanza 1

Out in the garden,
Each fine day.
With my ball,
I like to play.
I bounce my ball,
I throw my ball.
I catch my ball,
On each fine day.

Word-Meaning *Bounce - To jump up and down repeatedly.*

Exp. In these lines, the child says that everyday he likes to play with his ball outside, in the garden.
He likes to bounce, throw and catch the ball.

Stanza 2

Out in the garden,
Each fine day.
With my kite,
I like to play.
I tug my kite,
I pull my kite.
I fly my kite,
On each fine day.

Word-Meaning *Tug - To pull something.*

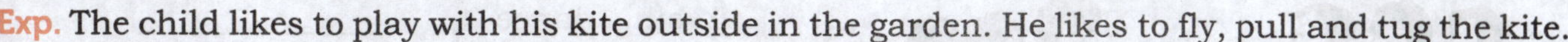

Exp. The child likes to play with his kite outside in the garden. He likes to fly, pull and tug the kite.

Stanza 3

Out in the garden,
Each fine day.
With my friends,
I like to play.
We run and skip,
We jump and sway.
We slide and swing,
On each fine day.

Word-Meaning *Skip - To jump from one foot to another. Sway - To move side to side. Slide - To move something easily over a surface. Swing - To move back and forth.*

Exp. The boy likes to play with his friends outside in the garden. He likes to run, skip, jump, sway, slide and swing with his friends.

NCERT FOLDER

Let us Think! (Page 41)

A. Answer the following.

Q.1 What are the children doing with the ball?

Ans. The children are playing outside with the ball. They are bouncing, throwing and catching the ball.

Q.2 How are children playing with the kite?

Ans. The children are playing with the kite by pulling, tugging and flying it.

Q.3 Where are the children playing?

Ans. The children are playing in the garden.

B. Think and answer.

Q.1 Where do you play?

Ans. Do it yourself.

Hint : In the park, inside the house, etc.

Q.2 What games do you play outside?

Ans. Do it yourself.

Hint : Kho-kho, tug of war, video games, etc.

Q.3 What happens if we are not careful while playing outside?

Ans. If we are not careful while playing outside, we might get hurt.

Let us Speak! (Page 41-42)

Look at some more games. Do you know them? Have you played them? What do you call them in your mother tongue?

Talk about what you know.

Ans. Following are the names of the games shown:

(i) Tug of war	(ii) Cup telephone
(iii) Thread spinner toy	(iv) Hopscotch
(v) London Bridge	(vi) Skipping rope
(vii) Spinning a tyre	(viii) Pitthu gram

Let us Learn! (Page 42-43)

In the poem, we find -

run **and** skip

jump **and** sway

slide **and** swing

Here we use '**and**' to link two words.

Combine these words using 'and' and write them in the blanks. One has been done for you.

1. give, take   <u>give and take</u>
2. sing, dance   ____________
3. eat, drink   ____________
4. catch, throw   ____________
5. run, catch   ____________

Ans. 2. Sing and dance   3. Eat and drink

4. Catch and throw   5. Run and catch

Can you think of two more word pairs? Write them here.

Ans. Read and Write, Tug and Pull, Up and Down, etc.

PRACTICE QUESTIONS

Multiple Choice Questions

1. How does the boy like to play with the ball?
   (a) Throwing the ball.
   (b) Playing cricket with the ball.
   (c) Spin the ball.
   (d) None of the above
2. The boy likes to __________ the kite.
   (a) bounce
   (b) pull
   (c) swing
   (d) tie
3. What does the boy mean when he says he likes to 'skip with his friends'?
   (a) He likes to miss school with his friends.
   (b) He likes to go out to eat with his friends.
   (c) He likes to play with a skipping rope with his friends.
   (d) He likes to jump from one foot to another with his friends.
4. What does the boy like to do with his friends?
   (a) Skip
   (b) Slide
   (c) Jump
   (d) All of the above
5. Pick the word that describes the boy's day?
   (a) Happy
   (b) Sad
   (c) Confused
   (d) None of the above

Ans. 1. (a), 2. (b), 3. (c), 4. (d), 5. (a)

Answer the following Questions

1. What does the child play with?

Ans. The child plays with a ball, a kite and a skipping rope. He also plays with his friends.

2. How does the child feel when he is playing?

Ans. The child feels happy when he is playing.

3. What does the child like to do each fine day?

Ans. The child likes to play, run, skip, jump and sway each fine day.

Let's Write

1. Have you ever been to a garden? It must have been beautiful with many flowers and plants. Think of what else can you find in a garden and write paragraph on 'A Visit to a Garden'.

   Start your paragraph like this

   I love gardens. There are many plants and flowers ....

Ans. I love gardens. There are many plants and flowers that makes the air fresh. Thus, I love visiting gardens. A visit to a garden is always very refreshing. The air is pure, cool, and fragrant. The green trees, the flowering bushes, and the grass give delight.

The moment you enter, you feel you are in another world. After the busy day, or early in the morning, a walk in the garden restores life and freshness to the tired body. To lie in the sun on a bright winter afternoon is a very good exercise which helps to keep the body healthy. Gardens are like lungs in the human body.

TALKING TOYS

Summary

It was a holiday so the local market was full of people. The toy shop opened at 9 am. It had a variety of toys like wooden toys, soft toys, board games, bats, balls, etc. The toys in a toy shop are waiting in the shop to see who buys them. Many children came to the shop. The toys got excited on seeing them. Every toy wished that the children would buy it. The children bought some of the toys and left the shop cheerfully.

WORD-MEANING

Local - A place that is near your home, Exclaimed - To say something suddenly, Displayed - To arrange things in a way that it can be seen by everyone, Sighed - Deep breathing, Excitement - Feeling of finding something interesting and full of joy, Eagerly - Waiting for something, Confidently - To be sure and strongly believe in something.

NCERT FOLDER

Let us Think! (Page 49)

A. *Answer the following.*

Q.1 Name the toys in the toy shop.

Ans. Toy kitten, board games like snakes and ladders, bat, ball, talking doll, toy elephant, Vande Bharat toy train, toy aeroplane, toy phone, spinning top, dancing dolls.

Q.2 What toy did the little boy request his mother to buy him?

Ans. The little boy requested his mother to buy him a Vande Bharat toy train.

B. *Think and answer.*

Q.1 Talk in pairs. How do you feel when someone buys or gives a toy to you?

Ans. Do it yourself.

Q.2 Have you seen the 'Jaadui Pitara'?

Ans. Do it yourself.

Let us Learn! (Page 49-51)

A. *Read these words.*

happy boy	pretty doll
blue frock	red cap

The words boy, doll, frock and cap are **naming words**.

The word happy tells us **more about the naming word** 'boy'.

The words red, talking and blue tell us more about the naming words beside them.

Add a word from the help box to the given naming words. You may use the same word more than once. One has been done for you as an example

brown, clean, cold, white, cotton, large

For example

yellow	**mango**
Clean	food
Cotton	kurta
Cold	water
White	paper
Large	tree

Now try writing more such words.

Ans. Do it yourself.

Hint : Green shirt, big apple, small box, pretty dress, bad boy, smart girl, angry mother, etc.

B. Look at these words.

toy	toys
boy	boys

You have learnt that we add 's' for more than one thing. These are called plural words.

Write the plural of the given word by adding 's'.

(i) Cat — Cats
(ii) Cup — Cups
(iii) Doll — Dolls
(iv) Shop — Shops
(v) Train — Trains

For some words we add -es to make a plural word.

Write the plural of the given word by adding 'es'. One has been done for you as an example

For example

Box	**boxes**
(i) Class	Classes
(ii) Bus	Buses
(iii) Pouch	Pounches
(iv) Brush	Brushes
(v) Mango	Mangoes

Let us Listen! (Page 51-52)

A. Listen to your teacher. Your teacher will recite a poem given in your NCERT Textbook about a top. Then, you repeat along with your teacher.

Ans. Do it yourself.

B. Look at the box given. Circle the names of colours used in the poem.

red	pink	green	blue
yellow	white	brown	purple

Ans. Red, Yellow, Green, Brown

Let us Write! (Page 52-54)

A. Look at the pictures.

These pictures tell us how a mother bird made a kite for her baby bird.

Use the following clues to complete the given sentences.

little chick – kite – onion peel – thread from spider web – gum from a tree – leaf blade from the palm tree

Making a Kite

A baby bird wanted to fly a kite.

The mother bird brought (i)...............from onions. Then, she (ii)............. . Next, the mother bird (iii)............ . Finally, (iv)......... .

Ans. (i) an onion peel

(ii) brought a thread from a spider web

(iii) brought some gum from a tree

(iv) she brought a leaf blade from the palm tree

B. Draw a bird using the letter 'B' as shown in the picture.

Ans. Follow the instructions and do it yourself.

Let us Do! (Page 55)

Let's make jute or cardboard puppets.

Ans. Do it yourself.

PRACTICE QUESTIONS

Multiple Choice Questions

1. At what time did the shop open?
   (a) 10 a.m. (b) 10 p.m.
   (c) 9 a.m. (d) 9 p.m.
2. Who bought the board game?
   (a) Two girls
   (b) A girl who came with her father and brother
   (c) A boy who came with his mother
   (d) No one bought the board game
3. The boy with the red cap bought ....
   (a) toy elephant (b) marbles
   (c) dolls (d) spinning top
4. How did the children feel after buying the toys?
   (a) Sad (b) Angry
   (c) Bored (d) Cheerful

Ans. 1. (c), 2. (b), 3. (d), 4. (d)

Answer the following Questions

1. What was the name of the board game that a little girl bought in the beginning?

Ans. The little girl bought the board game named 'Snakes and Ladders' in the beginning.

2. How did the little boy feel when his Aayi bought him the toy train?

Ans. The little boy felt happy when his Aayi bought him the toy train.

3. Who bought the toy aeroplane?

Ans. A girl bought the toy aeroplane.

Let's Write

1. We all have many toys. Which one is your favourite? Write a Description of your favourite toy in 10 lines.

Ans. I have many toys. My favourite toy is a collection of Hot Wheels cars set along with a small racecourse gifted to me by my parents. The cars are of many colours- red, blue, yellow, black, silver and golden.

The cars make racing sounds and I love pretending to race it with my friends.

I imagine I am a race car driver winning a big competition. Sometimes, I take my car on adventures around the house. I create obstacle courses using cushions and toys. My toy cars always zoom over the obstacles! I take good care of them.

PAPER BOATS

Summary

One day, a girl named Meena went to the stream in her village near the bamboo bridge.

She had made a paper boat. She put it in the water and it sailed smoothly down the stream. This made Meena happy. So she put more paper boats in the stream.

But then, she saw a naughty boy pushing the boats into the water.

Meena got angry and told the boy not to do so. The boy said he won't do it again. He also wants to play. He told Meena that he doesn't know how to make a paper boat. So Meena showed him how to fold the paper and make a paper boat. They both then put their boats in the stream and watched them sail away.

WORD-MEANING

Stream - A body of running water, **Bridge** - It connects two roads, across a river, **Delighted** - To be very happy, **Floated** - To stay on the surface of water and not sink, **Angrily** - To be annoyed, **Overturning** - To turn over or destroy, **Sailed** - To travel on water in a ship or boat, **Gently** - Being calm.

Let us Think! (Page 58-59)

A. *Answer the following.*

Q.1 What was Meena playing with?

Ans. Meena was playing with paper boats.

Q.2 Meena was angry. Why?

Ans. Meena was angry as she saw a naughty boy overturning her boats in the stream.

Q.3 How did Meena help the boy?

Ans. Meena helped the boy by teaching him how to fold the paper sheets and make paper boats.

B. *Think and answer.*

Q.1 Meena made paper boats. What else can you make with paper? Discuss in small groups.

Ans. We can make aeroplane, flower, heart and more. (You can write any other things you can think of).

Q.2 What games do you play with your friends? Which one do you like the most? Why?

Ans. Do it yourself.

C. *Say whether True or False.*

Q.1 The boy thought it was fun to overturn paper boats.

Q.2 Meena ran home to complain about the boy.

Q.3 The boy did not know how to make paper boats.

Q.4 Meena had only white paper.

Ans. 1. False 2. False
3. True 4. False

Let us Speak! (Page 60)

Look at the pictures.

Tell the story of 'Manish saves the ant' to the class.

Ans. One day, Manish was walking back from school. On his way, he saw a tiny ant drowning in the river. Manish quickly took out a piece of paper from his bag and made a paper boat. He kept the boat in the water and pushed it towards the ant. The ant quickly got on the boat. When the boat floated near the edge of the river, Manish pulled the boat out. The ant thanked Manish for his help.

Let us Learn! (Page 61-62)

Read the following sentences. Observe the underlined words.

Example 1

- Meena walked towards the stream near the bamboo bridge.
- She bent a little and launched a paper boat.

In the second sentence, **'she'** is used instead of Meena.

Example 2

- The boy jumped into the stream and pulled the boat out.
- He gave it to Meena

In the second sentence, **'he'** is used instead of the word 'boy'.

A. Fill in the blanks using 'he' or 'she'.

1. Rani likes playing outside. .... likes flying kites.
2. Sahil has a top. .... plays with it every day.
3. Durga is five years old. .... is going to school.
4. Ranjit goes to school, regularly. .... likes reading stories.

Ans. 1. She, 2. He, 3. She, 4. He

B. Look at the picture.

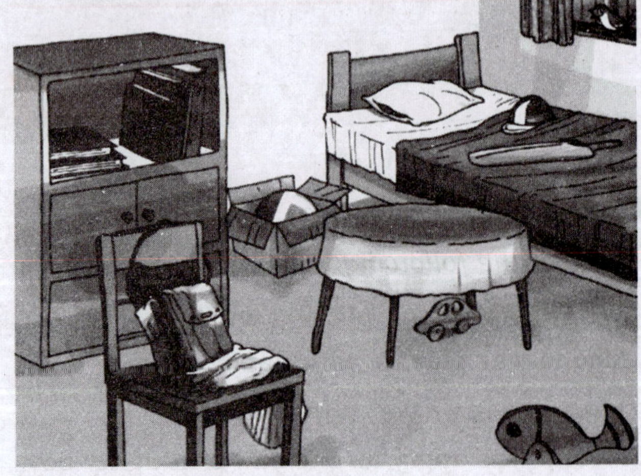

Write where each thing is. Choose the correct word from the brackets.

1. The bat is .... (on/under) the bed.
2. The bag is .... (in/on) the chair.
3. The ball is .... (in/under) the box.
4. The car is .... (in/under) the table.
5. The books are .... (in/on) the shelves.

Ans. 1. on 2. on 3. in 4. under 5. on

Let us Do! (Page 63)

A. Follow the steps to draw a rangoli.

Ans. Follow the instructions given on page 63 of your NCERT Textbook to make the rangoli.

Let us Write! (Page 64-65)

A. Write a few lines about the picture using the following clues.

park children playing see-saw swings slide enjoying happy

Ans. Make sentences on your own. Some examples are given below.

- The **children** are **playing** in the **park**.
- They are happy to ride on the **swings**.
- They are **enjoying** themselves.
- A little girl is going down the **slide**.

B. Solve the crossword puzzle.

Hint : All the answers are related to toys and games.

Across

2. A round object that spins on a needle
3. An object used to hit a ball
4. A round glass ball used for playing

Down

1. A game played using a ball and your foot
3. A round object used to play
5. A seat tied by ropes and which moves front and back

Ans.

Across	Down
2. Top	1. Football
3. Bat	3. Ball
4. Marbles	5. Swing

Let us Explore! (Page 66)

A. Talk to your elders at home. Find out what games they played when they were young. Learn a game from them and share with your friends preferably in small groups.

Ans. Discuss with the elders in your family.

PRACTICE QUESTIONS

Multiple Choice Questions

1. Meena went to the stream near the ____________________ .

   (a) toy shop (b) fields of rice
   (c) bamboo bridge (d) school

2. How many boats did Meena put in the stream?

   (a) One (b) Three
   (c) Twenty (d) Several

3. Why did the boy overturn the boats?

   (a) Because he thought it was fun
   (b) Because he was angry
   (c) Because he didn't like Meena
   (d) Because he was happy

Ans. 1. (c), 2. (d), 3. (a)

True or False

1. Meena put the paper boats on the bamboo bridge.
2. Meena didn't like that the boy destroyed her boats.
3. Meena and the boy made paper boats together.
4. Meena's sister taught the boy how to make paper boats.

Ans. 1. False, 2. True, 3. True, 4. False

Answer the following Questions

1. What happened to the paper boats after Meena put them in the stream?

Ans. After Meena put the paper boats in the stream, a small boys was pushing her boats into the water.

2. What kind of paper did Meena have to make paper boats?

Ans. Meena used many coloured paper of different sizes to make her paper boats.

3. The boy agreed to not overturn the boats. What did he want in return?

Ans. The boy agreed not to overturn the boats but he wanted to play with Meena.

Fill in the Blanks

A. *Fill in the blanks using 'he' or 'she'.*

1. Anita was taking a dance class.
   .... loved to dance.

Ans. She

2. Jackson went to Las Vegas recently.
   .... won a lottery there.

Ans. He

3. Megan is a sweet girl.
   .... always helps everyone around her.

Ans. She

4. Deepak went to the market.
   .... bought some toys.

Ans. He

5. Martin was sad yesterday.
   .... did not score well in th exam.

Ans. He

B. *Fill the blanks using the correct option.*

1. The slippers are .... (on/under) the bed.

Ans. under

2. The teddy bear is .... (on/in) the chest of drawers.

Ans. on

3. The painting is hanging .... (on/in) the wall.

Ans. on

4. The child will sleep .... (in/under) the bed.

Ans. in

C. *Make sentences using the following words.*

1. happy ____________________

Ans. Everyone was happy on his success.

2. spinning top ____________________

Ans. She is playing with spinning top.

3. snow ____________________

Ans. We will go to hill station to see the snow.

4. paper boats ____________________

Ans. Children are playing with paper boats in the rain.

5. stream ____________________

Ans. Water stream is near my house.

Let's Write

1. Origami is the art of folding paper into different beautiful shapes. You developed an interest in this art form. Write a story on how you saw origami for the first time and how you wanted to learn about it.

   You my start your story using the given prompt.

   I first came across origami in a cartoon.
   In the show, children were showing their origami to their teacher. At that time, I ____________

Ans. I first came across origami in a cartoon.
In the show, children were showing their origami to their teacher. At that time,
I thought it was just imagination and not real. I was in Class 1 at that time. In class 2, I got to know that origami is real and we can make this paper art. Our school had organised an arts and craft workshop for all of us. In that workshop, the teacher showed us some very beautiful designs using origami paper.

I saw a rose, a butterfly and even a rabbit. How wonderful! The entire show was amazing. Later, I talked to my art teacher about it. She told me that she could teach me how to make origami.
I agreed and the first thing I made was a paper boat. When I showed it to my parents, they praised me and encouraged to learn it. Now, I am learning how to make different things from origami and I enjoy every bit of it.

Unit-3

GOOD FOOD

Picture Reading (Page 68-69)

Look at the picture and answer.

Q.1 What can you see in Picture 1?

Ans. In Picture 1 we can see a farm. A lady is picking the grains from the fields. The collected grains are filled in sacks and loaded in a truck.

Q.2 Look at Picture 2. What is the man doing with the wheat?

Ans. The man is putting the grains in a machine. The machine is grinding the wheat grains to make flour.

Q.3 Look at Picture 4. Who are they? What are they doing?

Ans. Picture 4 shows a man and a woman. The man is kneading flour and the woman is making chapattis.

Q.4 What is the girl doing in the last picture?

Ans. The girl in the last picture is eating her food.

Q.5 What do you have along with chapatti?

Ans. I have vegetables, lentils and curry with chapatti.

Q.6 Have you seen a field? What was growing there? Speak about it.

Ans. Yes I have seen a field. Grains, fruits and vegetables were growing in the field.

THE BIG LADDOO

Summary of the Poem The poem talks about imagining big things like a giant laddoo, a huge child and a large sea. It also talks about what would happen if we combine small things to make a big thing. The poem encourages imagination and shows us how exciting it can be.

Stanza 1

If all the laddoos were one Laddoo
Oh! What a BIG Laddoo it would be!

Exp. The child wonders if we combine all the laddoos in the world, it would make a very big laddoo.

Stanza 2

If all the children were one child
Oh! What a BIG child that would be!
If all the seas were one sea
Oh! What a BIG sea it would be!

Exp. The child wonders if we combine all the children in the world, it would make a very big child. He also wonders if we combine all the seas in the world, it would make a very big sea.

Stanza 3

Then if the BIG child
picked the BIG Laddoo
And threw it into the BIG sea
Oh! What a BIG SPLISH-SPLASH it would be!

Word-Meaning *Splish-splash - Sudden disturbances in a liquid surface.*

Exp. The child wonders if the big child would throw the big laddoo in the big sea, it would make a big splash.

Let us Think! (Page 72)

Q.1 Have you seen a big laddoo? How big was it? Did you eat it all by yourself? Tell your friends about it.

Ans. Yes, I have seen a big laddoo. My grandmother made it at home for me. It was not as big as the one mentioned in the poem but it was as big as my cricket ball. It was so big that I couldn't eat it by myself. I had to share it with my brother and sister.

Q.2 Have you eaten anything that is very big? What was it? Talk about it.

Ans. Yes, I once ate a large piece of cake. It was very yummy!

Q.3 What different kinds of laddoos have you eaten?

Ans. I have eaten besan laddoo, boondi laddoo, motichoor laddoo, laddoo made out of wheat flour, etc.

Q.4 Name a few things that are round in shape. Can you eat all of them? Write them in the correct column.

Ans. The list below has some examples.

That can be eaten	That cannot be eaten
Laddoo	Coin
Chapatti	Bangle
Cake	Ball
Pizza	Plate
Watermelon	Wheel

Q.5 The child threw the big laddoo into the sea. What do you think happened to the Laddoo?

Ans. I think when the child threw the big laddoo into the sea there was a huge splash and a lot of water would have come out. I also think that the laddoo will sink in the water as it is very big and heavy.

Let us Speak! (Page 73)

Jithu and Meena are friends. Meena cannot see properly. It was her birthday. Jithu gifted her a box of mixed sweets. She felt the sweets and excitedly picked up the big laddoo. She said, "I love laddoos!" Jithu was surprised and asked her, "How did you know it was a laddoo?"

Think and say what Meena answered.

Ans. I think Meena answered that she felt the round shape of the laddoo and its texture which helped her guess it was a laddoo.

Let us Learn! (Page 73)

Laddoos are sweets, commonly eaten in every house. Write words that tell us about the laddoo.

Ans. Round in shape, sweet, yummy, delicious, homemade.

Let us Write! (Page 74)

A. *Frame a few sentences using the given words.*

Q.1 play ____________________

Ans. Yash and Daisy like to play badminton.

Q.2 plum ____________________

Ans. Mohan climbed the plum tree.

Q.3 cloud ____________________

Ans. The clouds in the sky are grey today.

Q.4 clock ____________________

Ans. I set my alarm clock for 5 a.m. in the morning.

Q.5 blue ____________________

Ans. Rahul is wearing a blue dress.

Q.6 blanket ____________________

Ans. We use blankets in the winter.

B. *Match the following.*

1.	Cock	lioness
2.	Lion	cow
3.	Peacock	hen
4.	Mare	duck
5.	Bull	peahen
6.	Drake	horse

Ans. 1. Cock - hen
2. Lion - lioness
3. Peacock - peahen
4. Mare - horse
5. Bull - cow
6. Drake - duck

Let us Explore! (Page 75)

A. Look at these objects shown here. Collect and put them one by one into a tub of water. See which one will float and which one will sink. Tick the objects that float and cross the objects that sink.

1. A piece of paper ✓

2. A small stone ✗

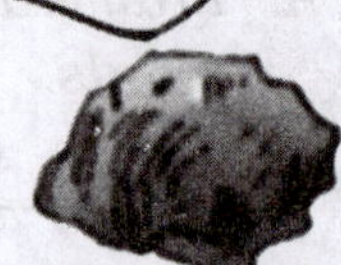

3. A green leaf ✓

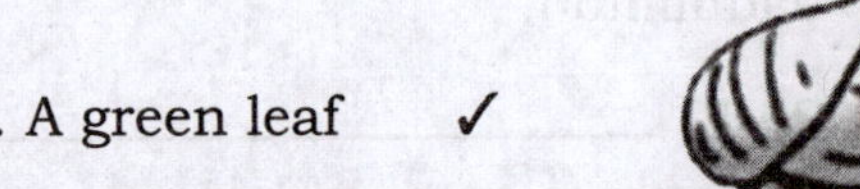

4. A pencil ✓

5. An eraser ✗

6. A feather ✓

7. A spoon ✗

Let us Write (Page 77)

A. Which is your favourite festival? Write the names of some sweets and dishes prepared on that day.

Ans. My favourite festival is Janmashtami On that day, sugar coated peanuts, gond ki barfi, coconut laddoos, sweetened white butter are prepared at home.

PRACTICE QUESTIONS

Multiple Choice Questions

1. What can make a big child?
   (a) All the laddoos (b) All the girls
   (c) All the boys (d) All the children
2. What happens when we throw a big laddoo in the big sea?
   (a) Water will splish-splash out.
   (b) The laddoo will sink in the sea
   (c) The laddoo with float on the sea
   (d) Nothing will happen
3. The poem encourages .... in a child.
   (a) imagination (b) wonder
   (c) sadness (d) None of these

Ans. 1. (d), 2. (a), 3. (a)

True or False

1. All the laddoos in the world will make a big laddoo.
2. All the seas in the world make an ocean.
3. The small child throws the big laddoo into the big sea.

Ans. 1. True, 2. False, 3. False

Answer the Following Questions

1. Who picks up the big laddoo?

Ans. The big child picked up the big laddoo.

2. What sound does the big sea make when the big laddoo is thrown into it?

Ans. When a big laddoo is thrown into a big sea, it makes a big splish-splash sound.

3. Are all the big things in the poem real?

Ans. No, the big things in the poem are not real.

Let's Write

1. We all know eating many laddoos or a big laddoo can be bad for our health. Then, what should we eat for a good health. Write a paragraph on 'Healthy Food Habits' talking about what you should eat and what you should avoid.

Ans. Our elders often say that 'Health is Wealth'. One of the most important factors in maintaining health is the food that we eat. Healthy food refers to food that contains the right amount of nutrients to keep our body fit. It includes fruits, vegetables, pulses, milk, dairy products and water. We should avoid fried food, junk food, cold drinks and sweets as much as we can. If we eat healthy food, we will avoid getting ill and be free from diseases. We will have a strong body and a healthy mind. Healthy food can uplift our mood and make us feel good.

CHAPTER 8 THANK GOD

Summary

Once there was a farmer who liked fruits. He decided to grow different fruits on his land, and took good care of them. Once the fruits were ripe, the farmer decided to give the best fruit to the king. That year his best fruits were grapes and watermelons.

The watermelons were too heavy to carry. So the farmer decided to take the grapes for the king. When the farmer reached the palace, the guard took him to the royal garden. The king was playing with his daughter, the princess, so he waited. When the king sat down to rest, the guard gave him the basket of grapes and pointed at the farmer.

Being in a playful mood, the king took some grapes. He popped one in his mouth and threw one at the farmer. When the grape hit the farmer's forehead, the farmer thanked god. The king was surprised and threw a grape again, but the farmer thanked god again. The king asked the farmer why he would thank god.

The farmer replied that this year his best fruits were grapes and watermelons, but decided to give the king the grapes. He was thankful to god that he didn't bring the watermelons as they could have caused him more harm if they were thrown at him.

WORD-MEANING

Ripe - To be ready and fully grown, **Plucked out** - To take and remove out, **Popped** - To put something suddenly, **Surprised** - To do or see something unexpected, **Blessed** - To bring luck and happiness, **Wise** - Being smart and full of knowledge, **Mighty** - To be strong and powerful.

Let us Think! (Page 82)

A. Answer the following.

Q.1 What did the farmer grow on his farm?

Ans. The farmer grew different types of fruits on his farm. He took special care of fruits like grapes and watermelons that he grew in a small corner of the farm.

Q.2 What did his wife say?

Ans. The farmer's wife said that this year the best fruits on their farms were grapes and watermelons.

Q.3 Why did the farmer decide to take the grapes?

Ans. The farmer decided to take the grapes because they were lighter in weight than watermelons and easier to carry.

Q.4 What did the King do playfully?

Ans. The King playfully threw some grapes at the farmer.

Q.5 Why did the farmer say, 'Thank God!' ?

Ans. The farmer said 'thank god' as he was thankful that he chose to bring grapes for the king instead of watermelons.

B. Think and Say.

Q.1 The farmer in the story grew fruits. What else can a farmer grow?

Ans. The farmer can grow vegetables like potatoes, cauliflower, onions and grains like wheat, rice, maize. They can also grow spices like pepper, coriander seeds and flowers like roses, jasmine, and many more.

Q.2 Are there women farmers? Do you know any?

Ans. Yes, there are women farmers. No, I do not know any.

Q.3 If you meet a farmer, what would you say to them?

Ans. If I meet a farmer, I would thank them for growing all the healthy and nutritious food for us. (You can write other variation of the answers)

Let us Learn! (Page 83-84)

A. The farmer knew that the watermelon was heavy and the grapes were light.

The words **heavy** and **light** are opposite in meaning.

Write the opposite of the underlined word.

1. thick book ______ book
2. long journey ______ journey 
3. soft cotton ______ rock 
4.  slow tortoise ______ rabbit 

Ans. 1. thin 2. short 3. hard 4. fast

B. Read the sentences.

The ball **is** round.

The tables **are** brown.

C. Fill in the blanks with 'is' or 'are'.

1. There ______ animals in the jungle.
2. The table ______ made of wood.
3. These mangoes ______ sweet.
4. Raghuram ______ a tall boy.
5. The toys ______ on the shelf.
6. The book ______ on the table.
7. The girls ______ at the shop.
8. The car ______ on the road.

Ans. 1. are 2. is 3. are 4. is 5. are 6. is 7. are 8. is

Let us Listen! (Page 85)

Aachoo!

The poem talks about an elephant who got sick. He goes out to buy a handkerchief. The sales girl tells him that he doesn't have a handkerchief as big as the elephant. The elephant sneezed loudly and asked her for a big sheet instead.

Let us Speak! (Page 86)

Q.1 Imagine you are visiting the Big Elephant. You know that the elephant has a cold.

What food items will you take with you? Say them aloud.

Ans. When someone has a cold, we give them a lot of hot things like tea, soup, khichdi. We also give them fruits like chikoo, mango, berries, etc.

Let us Write! (Page 86)

Chandu's Fruit Salad

Chandu has written the steps for preparing a salad on a few slips of paper. He mixed them up. Think of the proper order and write down in the space given below.

( ) Next, I put in papaya cubes.
( ) Mother cuts some fruits for me.
( ) First I take some banana slices.
( ) Finally, I squeeze a lemon on it, adding a pinch of salt.
( ) Then I add the apple slices.
( ) Then I mix them all.
( ) After that I add some grapes from a bunch.

Ans. (3) Next, I put in papaya cubes.
(1) Mother cuts some fruits for me.
(2) First I take some banana slices.
(7) Finally, I squeeze a lemon on it, adding a pinch of salt.
(5) Then I add the apple slices.
(6) Then I mix them all.
(4) After that I add some grapes from a bunch.

Let us Explore! (Page 87)

A. Find fruits in the grid given below.

S	M	F	X	C	U	D	M	MANGO
P	A	P	A	Y	A	H	G	PAPAYA
E	N	G	K	S	B	T	U	GRAPES
A	G	R	A	P	E	S	A	BANANA
R	O	Z	D	H	Y	L	V	GUAVA
A	X	B	A	N	A	N	A	PLUM
Z	P	E	A	C	H	O	G	PEACH
P	L	U	M	H	Q	P	W	PEAR

Ans.

S	M	F	X	C	U	D	M	MANGO
P	A	P	A	Y	A	H	G	PAPAYA
E	N	G	K	S	B	T	U	GRAPES
A	G	R	A	P	E	S	A	BANANA
R	O	Z	D	H	Y	L	V	GUAVA
A	X	B	A	N	A	N	A	PLUM
Z	P	E	A	C	H	O	G	PEACH
P	L	U	M	H	Q	P	W	PEAR

PRACTICE QUESTIONS

Multiple Choice Questions

1. Which fruits did the farmer take special care of ?
   (a) Grapes
   (b) Watermelons
   (c) Both (a) and (b)
   (d) None of these
2. Who took the farmer to the King?
   (a) The princess
   (b) The palace guard
   (c) The farmer's wife
   (d) None of these
3. How did the King react to the farmer saying 'Thank God'?
   (a) Surprised (b) Angry
   (c) Confused (d) Excited

Ans. 1. (c), 2. (b), 3. (a)

True or False

1. The King was having tea in the garden when the farmer arrived.
2. The King threw a grape at the farmer's arm.
3. The farmer was a wise man.

Ans. 1. False, 2. False, . True

Answer the Following Questions

1. Where did the farmer grow grapes and watermelons?

Ans. The farmer grew grapes and watermelons in a small corner of his farm.

2. What was the King doing when the farmer arrived?

Ans. When the farmer arrived, the king was playing with the princess.

3. What did the King ask the farmer?

Ans. The king asked the farmer why he was thanking god when he was throwing the grapes at him.

Fill in the Blanks

Fill in the blanks using 'is' or 'are'

1. There ____________ some people waiting to see you.
2. He __________ unfriendly.
3. The Taj Mahal ________________ beautiful.
4. The animals ______________ enjoying the rain.
5. The birds ____________ flying freely.
6. Shyam and Radha ____________ friends.
7. The woman ____________ behind a tree.
8. The newspaper ____________ on the bed.

Ans. 1. are, 2. is, 3. is, 4. are, 5. are, 6. are, 7. is, 8. is

Let's Write

1. Have you ever met a farmer? How they look and what do you think are their characteristics?
   Write a description of an Indian farmer in about 10 lines.

Ans. Farmers play an extremely important role in any country. They are the people who feed the whole nation. They grow crops and work very hard daily to earn a living. At first glance, a farmer seems to be simple village man who wears a shirt and a dhoti. He majorly talks in his regional language. He is someone who is dedicated and hard working.

He ploughs the land, sows the seeds, waters the plants, and do their best to protect the field and yield. They then wait patiently for the harvest time.

A farmer's life is plain and simple. He doesn't look forward to many luxuries. He expects a good harvest and getting a reasonable price for their crops.

MADHU'S WISH

Summary

The story is about a boy named Madhu. He loved to eat different kinds of food. One day, while having lunch under the banyan tree, he shares his food with an old man.

In return for Madhu's kindness, the old man asked Madhu to wish for anything he likes from the tree and it will be granted. Madhu felt happy and asked the tree for different kinds of food. The voice from the tree asked Madhu to think over his wish. But Madhu ignored the warning. The tree granted his wish and gave him different foods like laddoos, fruits and then savouries like matri and Kachoris. Madhu ate a lot but he got bored and finally, got hiccups.

He looked for water to stop them but could not find it. He asked for water but the voice from the tree said no.

So Madhu asked for *sharbat*, *kheer* and *badam* milk. He ate them but the hiccups didn't stop. Madhu realised his mistake and asked the tree to replace all the food with water. He said that he understood the importance of water now. The tree granted his wish and Madhu drank the water.

Appeared - To come in front of sight, Immediately - Without delay, Savouries - Food items that are salty or spicy, Huge - Very big, Louder - To make a lot of noise, Disappear - To not be seen, Instead - In place of, Replace - To take something and put something else in its place.

Let us Think! (Page 93)

A. *Answer the following.*

Q.1 What did Madhu enjoy?

Ans. Madhu enjoyed eating different types of food and snacks.

Q.2 Do you think the old man had magical powers? How do you know?

Ans. Yes I think the old man had magical powers. We know this because he granted Madhu's wishes with the tree in return for feeding him.

Q.3 Why did the tree ask Madhu to 'think over' his wish?

Ans. The tree asked Madhu to think over his wish as he wanted Madhu to be thoughtful and careful about what choice he makes before making it.

Q.4 Name some of the things that Madhu ate.

Ans. Some of the things Madhu ate are laddoos, fruits like grapes, mangoes, apples, bananas, jackfruit, melons, guavas, oranges, savoury snacks like *matri, samosa, kachori,* potato chips, vada and sweets like *sharbat, kheer, badam* milk etc.

B. *Think and say.*

Q.1 Have you experienced hiccups?

Ans. Yes, I have experienced hiccups.

Q.2 What do you do when you get hiccups?

Ans. When I get hiccups, I drink water slowly to make them go away.

Q.3 Do you think water is important? Why do you think so?

Ans. Yes, I think water is important. I think so as water helps us stay healthy and hydrated.

Q.4 If you were in Madhu's place, what would you wish for and why?

Ans. If I was in Madhu's place, I would have wished for a remote control aeroplane.

Let us Learn! (Page 94-97)

A. *Madhu enjoyed the following items. Write them in the correct basket.*

banana, *kheer*, melon, guava, *kachori*
potato chips, laddoo, vada, jackfruit, *samosa*

Ans. Fruits banana, melon, guava, jackfruit

Sweets *kheer*, laddoo

Salty snacks *kachori*, potato chips, vada, *samosa*

B. *Read the following sentences.*

Q.1 Madhu shared his food with the old man. He is kind.

Q.2 Madhu wanted to eat everything. He is greedy.

Q.3 The old man gave a special gift to Madhu. He is generous.

C. *Choose a word from the box to describe the people below.*

brave polite selfish lazy

1. Pramod doesn't share his toys with anyone. He is ________________.
2. The woman saved the boy from the robber. She is ________________.
3. Advait is always lying in bed and doing nothing. He is ________________.
4. Prerna always wishes everyone in the morning. She is ________________.

Ans. 1. selfish 2. brave 3. lazy 4. polite

D. Read the following sentences.

Q.1 Sam is watching television.

Q.2 Pratham is watching television.

Both Sam and Pratham are doing the same activity.

The two sentences can be combined in to a single sentence.

Sam and Pratham are watching television.

Now, look at the following sentences.

1. Aman has a pen.
2. Aman has a pencil.
3. Aman has an eraser.

The three sentences talk about Aman. The three sentences can be combined as one sentence using 'and'. The new sentence will be.

Aman has a pen, a pencil and an eraser.

Let us take one more example

1. Sam works in the afternoon.
2. Pratham works at night.

Both sentences talk about doing 'work' but by different people and at different times. The two sentences can be combined as:

Sam works in the afternoon but Pratham works at night.

Rewrite the following sentences using 'and' or 'but'.

1. I eat an apple. I eat an orange. I eat a peach. (and)
2. I like to watch cartoons. My sister likes to watch movies. (but)
3. Anita plays volleyball. Anju plays volleyball. (and)
4. Dolma wants a new comic book. She has spent all her pocket money on sweets. (but)
5. Rajesh wants to go to the park. He has not finished his homework. (but)

Ans. 1. I eat an apple, an orange and a peach.

2. I like to watch cartoons but my sister likes to watch movies.
3. Anita and Anju play volleyball.
4. Dolma wants a new comic book but she has spent all her pocket money on sweets.
5. Rajesh wants to go to the park but he has not finished his homework.

Let us Listen! (Page 97)

A. *Your teacher will read parts of the story. Listen carefully and tell the class what happened after that.*

1. Madhu said, "Oh tree, let me have different types of food. Nothing else."
2. As he was eating, he suddenly got hiccups. He wanted water.

Ans. 1. After Madhu told the tree that he wanted to eat different types of food, the tree asked him to think about it again. The tree wanted Madhu to think if he wanted only food and not water.

2. As Madhu got hiccups, he started to look for water around him. However, there was no water as he had asked for only food and not water from the tree.

Let us Write! (Page 98-99)

A. Complete the following story.

Vijaya is a young girl.

She lives with her father, mother, grandmother and grandfather in a small village.

Each day ______________________

Ans. Vijaya is a young girl. She lives with her father, mother, grandmother and grandfather in a small village. Each day she would go to school in the morning. In the afternoon, she helped her father by working on their farm. After helping her father, she would come home and do her homework. Her grandfather would help her with her English homework. In the evening she would play with her friends. At night, she helped her mom with household chores. Before she went to sleep, her grandmother would tell her a story which would help Vijaya fall asleep.

B. Notice that the first letter of each word has the same letter.

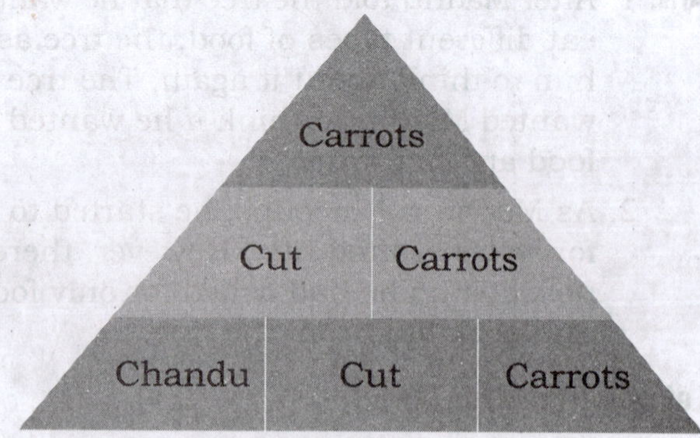

The first letter of each word is ______ .

Ans. The first letter of each word is 'C'.

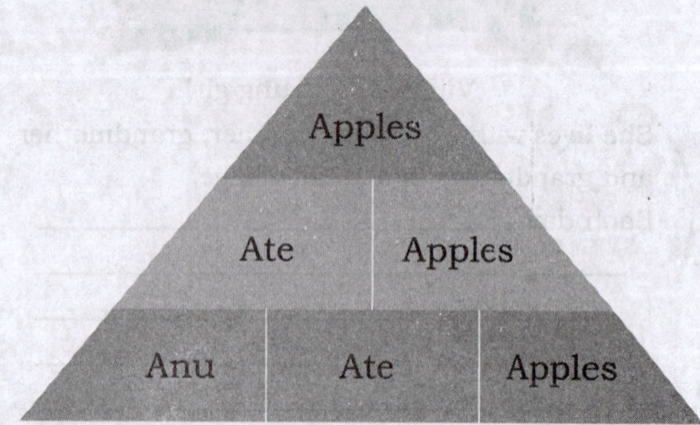

The first letter of each word is ______ .

Ans. The first letter of each word is 'A'.

C. Write down similar words as shown above using your name or any name of your choice.

Ans.

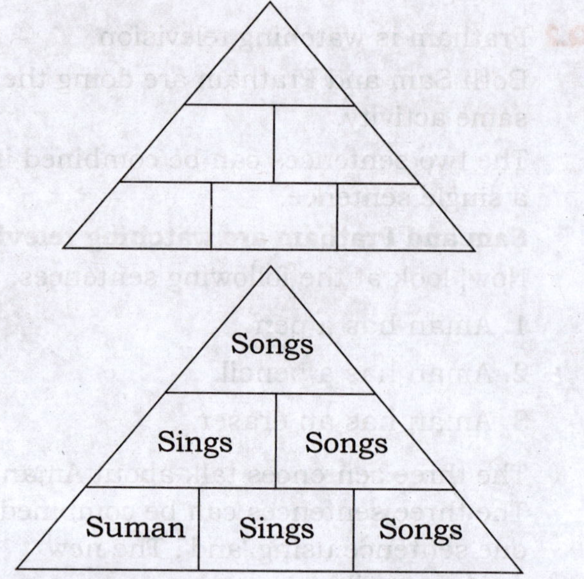

The first letter of the each word is ___S___ .

Let us Write! (Page 100)

A. *Read the incomplete sentences. Discuss with your friends and complete them.*

1. Madhu shared his food with the old man because ______ .
2. Madhu was happy because ______ .
3. After eating fruits, Madhu asked for savouries because ______ .
4. Madhu asked for water because ______ .

Ans. 1. the old man was hungry.
2. he could wish for different types of food from the tree.
3. he was bored of eating the fruits.
4. he got hiccups.

Let us Do! (Page 100-101)

Let us make a table mat by using the instructions given in NCERT textbook Page No. 100-101.

Ans. Follow the instructions to create your own table mat.

PRACTICE QUESTIONS

Multiple Choice Questions

1. Where would Madhu eat his lunch everyday?
   (a) At school
   (b) At home
   (c) Under the banyan tree
   (d) Near the water bridge
2. What did Madhu eat?
   (a) Fruits (b) *Matri*
   (c) *Kheer* (d) All of these
3. Madhu got ______________ after he ate a lot of food.
   (a) hiccups (b) vomits
   (c) headache (d) stomachache
4. What stopped the hiccups?
   (a) Drinking *sharbat*
   (b) Drinking tea
   (c) Drinking water
   (d) None of the above

Ans. 1. (c), 2. (d), 3. (a), 4. (c)

True or False

1. Madhu loved clothes.
2. Madhu asked the tree for different types of food.
3. In the end, Madhu asked for juice instead of food from the tree.
4. Madhu drank *sharbat* to stop the hiccups.

Ans. 1. False, 2. True, 3. False, 4. False

Answer the following Questions

1. What did the old man tell Madhu after sharing his lunch?

Ans. After Madhu shared his lunch with him, the old man told Madhu that he had been kind. So, in return Madhu could wish for anything from the tree and his wish will be fulfilled.

2. What was the first thing that appeared after the tree granted Madhu's wish?

Ans. The first thing that appeared after Madhu's wish was granted is laddoos.

3. What did Madhu realised in the end?

Ans. In the end, Madhu realised the importance of water.

Rewrite the following sentences using 'and' or 'but'.

1. Hritik likes laddoos. Simran likes noodles.

Ans. Hritik likes laddoos but Simran likes noodles.

2. Sunita likes tennis. Sunita likes swimming.

Ans. Sunita like tennis and swimming.

3. Neetu loves pasta. Neetu hates ice-cream.

Ans. Neetu loves pasta but hates ice-cream.

4. We go to the park on Saturdays. We go to the pool on Sundays.

Ans. We go to the park on Saturdays and the pool on Sundays.

5. I'd like to go to the movies. I don't have any money.

Ans. I'd like to go to the movies but I don't have any money.

Let's Write

1. Water is essential for life. However, today there is a scarcity of water. Write a paragraph on 'How to Save Water'.

Ans. **How to Save Water**

Water is the most important and valuable natural resource on Earth. It sustains all life. There is no life without water. Hence, we all must take steps to save water. First, we should make sure that no taps in our surrounding are leaking. We should not let the tap run while washing hands and face. Second, we must use water wisely so that no water is wasted.

Third, we should make provisions to store rainwater on rooftops and reuse the water for household purposes. Fourth, the industrial waste should be treated properly instead of dumping it into rivers. With these small and easy steps, we can save water for the future.

Unit 4

THE SKY

Picture Reading

NCERT FOLDER

Look at the picture given in NCERT textbook on page no 103 and answer.

Q.1 What can you see on both sides of the street?

Ans. I can see some shops and people going around on both sides of the street.

Q.2 Why are there two dustbins? Do you know why one is blue and the other is green in colour?

Ans. There are two dustbins for two types of waste. The green dustbin is for wet waste and the blue dustbin is dry waste.

Q.3 Why is the man in dark glasses holding a white stick?

Ans. The man in the dark glasses is most probably blind or visually impaired. He is holding the white stick to help him find his way.

Q.4 Do you know which toy the boys are playing with?

Ans. The boys are playing with spinning tops.

Q.5 How many bullock-carts are there in the picture?

Ans. There is one bullock-cart in the picture.

Q.6 Name the different animals in the picture.

Ans. The different animals in the picture are bull, dog, goats and cat.

NIGHT

Summary of the Poem The poem talks about the journey the sun takes from morning till night. The sun shines in the sky in the morning brightly and at night it goes behind the hills. The sky becomes dark. The child wonders where the sun goes at night. The child notices that at night when she goes to sleep, she wakes up to the sun shining again brightly in the sky.

Stanza 1

The sun that shines all day so bright,
I wonder where it goes at night.
It sinks behind a distant hill
And all the world grows dark and still.

Word-Meaning *Distant - Very far away, Still - To stay in one place or at rest.*

Exp. The child likes how the sun shines bright all day. She wonders where the sun goes at night after it goes behind the distant hills. When the sun goes away, she notices that the world becomes dark and quiet.

Stanza 2

And then I go to bed and sleep
Until the day begins to peep.
And when my eyes open,
I see the Sun is
shining down on me.

Word-Meaning *Peep - To look at something secretly.*

Exp. The child says that she goes to bed and sleep at night. But when the day begins, the sun comes back again. She notices that when she wakes up in the morning, the sun is in the sky shining brightly again.

Let us Think! (Page 106)

A. *Answer the following.*

Q.1 Where does the Sun go after the end of the day?

Ans. The sun goes down behind the distant hill at the end of the day.

Q.2 Which among the following needs the Sun? Why?

(a) sunflower (b) toys (c) plants (d) table (e) children

Ans. Among the options given, following need the Sun.

(a) sunflower (c) plants (e) children

Sunflower and the plants need the sun to grow healthy. Children need a little bit of sunlight to get natural vitamins.

Q.3 The poem talks about the Sun in the sky. What else do you see when you look up at the sky?

Ans. When I look at the sky, I can see the stars the moon, clouds, birds and sometimes aeroplanes, kites, etc.

B. *Think and answer.*

Q.1 What different colours do we get to see during sunrise and sunset?

Ans. During sunrise and sunset we get to see many different colours like orange, pink, yellow, purple, red, blue, etc.

Q.2 What do you see when you look at the sky at night?

Ans. When I look at the sky at night I see the moon and the stars. I once saw a shooting star too!

Q.3 How do you feel when you open your eyes in the morning?

Ans. I feel very energised and refreshed when I open my eyes in the morning.

Q.4 Imagine a day when the Sun doesn't come out. Talk about how the day would be.

Ans. If the sun doesn't come out one day, the day would be very dark and dim.

Let us Do! (Page 107)

Let's play a fun game called "I Spy"!

Ans. Play the game with your friends at school.

Let us Speak! (Page 107-108)

Read the following sentence: I spy a few stars in the sky.

The word **spy** begins with **sp**

The word **stars** begins with **st**

The word **sky** begins with **sk**

Now say these words aloud.

Star	Storm	Store	Stain
Stick	Stair	Spoon	Splash
Spin	Skin	Skate	Sky

Ans. Do it yourself.

Let us Learn! (Page 108)

A. Read the following words and circle the words that are found in the sky.

Stars	Storm	Store	Stain
Sun	Bicycle	Moon	Rain
Clouds	Flowers	Rainbow	Monkeys
Computer	Shoes		

Ans. Stars, sun, Clouds, Storm, Moon, Rainbow, Rain

B. Add 'Sun' to the following words to make new words. Write them in the space given. One has been done for you.

light flower rays set
rise glasses day

Sunlight ________ ________
________ ________ ________
____

Ans. Sunflower, Sunrays, Sunset, Sunrise, Sunglasses, Sunday

PRACTICE QUESTIONS

Multiple Choice Questions

1. How does the sun shine in the morning?
   (a) Brightly
   (b) Smoothly
   (c) Sharply
   (d) Softly
2. Which of the following don't you see in the sky?
   (a) Stars
   (b) Apples
   (c) Sun
   (d) Kite

Ans. 1. (a), 2. (b)

True or False

1. The sun sinks behind the distant buildings.
2. The world becomes still when the sun sinks.
3. The moon comes out when the child wakes up in the morning.

Ans. 1. False, 2. True, 3. False

Answer the following Questions

1. What happens when the sun sinks?

Ans. When the sun sinks, the world goes dark and still as it is night.

2. What happens when the child wakes up in the morning?

Ans. When the child wakes up, the sun is shining in the sky.

Let's Write

1. Look at the given image and write 5-10 lines on it.

Ans. The given image shows a night sky seen from the window of my room at Nainital. The night seems to be calm and peaceful. The soft moonlight falls on the beautiful mountain ranges making it a very beautiful scenery. The big white sphere is increasing the peace of the night. The only sounds that can be heard is cooing of the birds or the rustling of the leaves.

CHANDA MAMA COUNTS THE STARS

Summary

The story is about Chanda Mama (the moon) and how he tries to count the stars. Everytime he tries, he gets tired and falls asleep. Sometimes he would forget the counting. Sometimes he would forget where he had stopped.

One night he got very upset and began to cry. He asked the sun why he couldn't complete his counting. The sun smiled and told him to stop crying. He told him that the number of stars in the sky is equal to the number of lovely children in the world. Chanda Mama was happy to hear this.
Every night when he came out, he would look at the stars and then at the children in the world and he would smile happily.

WORD-MEANING

Count - To say numbers one after the other, **Yawn** - To open your mouth wide, **Asleep** - To sleep, **Peeped** - To look at something secretly, **Continued** - To do something without stopping, **Often** - To happen many times.

Let us Think! (Page 112)

A. Answer the following.

Q.1 Does the Moon look the same every night?
Ans. No, the moon does not look the same every night. It has varying size and shape every night.

Q.2 What did Chanda Mama try to count?
Ans. Chanda Mama was trying to count the number of stars in the sky.

Q.3 Why did Chanda Mama fall asleep?
Ans. Chanda Mama fell asleep as he would get tired while counting the stars.

Q.4 Who helped Chanda Mama?
Ans. The Sun helped Chanda Mama.

Q.5 Complete the sentence.
The number of stars in the sky is the same as ____________
Ans. the number of lovely children in the world.

B. *Think and say.*

Q.1 I call the Moon, Chanda Mama. What do you call him in your language?

Ans. Do it yourself.

Q.2 Chanda Mama was not able to count the stars. What things can you not count?

Ans. I cannot count the number of trees, ants, grains, bees, flowers, people, etc.

Q.3 The Moon is visible during the night. What can you see in the night sky?

Ans. I can see the stars in the night sky.

Let us Learn! (Page 113-114)

Here and There!

Look at the following sentences.

We are **here** on the Earth. The Moon is **there** in the sky.

I have a sharpener **here** in my pencil box.

The crayons are **there** in the big box.

The highlighted words in both sentences tell us about the location of 'sharpener' and 'crayons'. The distance of the objects from the speaker helps us in choosing between the words 'here' and 'there'.

We use **'here'** to tell the location of things that are near us. Similarly, **'there'** is used to tell the location of things that are far from us.

Fill in the blanks with 'here' or 'there'. One has been done for you.

(i) The students are playing *kabaddi* **there**.

(ii) ______ is your shirt.

(iii) ______ is my bicycle.

(iv) I went to Chandigarh last year. My brother lives ____.

(v) This is my bench. I sit ______ with my friends.

Ans. (ii) Here

(iii) There

(iv) there

(v) here

Let us Listen! (Page 115)

A. In the story, we read that the stars were too many to be counted.

Now, your teacher will read out a list of items for you. Put the items in the correct column in the given table.

1. Children in the classroom.
2. Flowers in a garden.
3. Books in the library.
4. Pencils in your pencil box.
5. Fingers on your right hand.
6. Children in your city or town.
7. Pages in your English notebook.
8. The hairs on your head.

Ans.

Can be counted easily	Too many to be counted
Children in the classroom	Children in your city or town
Pencils in your pencil box	Flowers in the garden
Fingers in your right hand	Books in the library
Pages in your english notebook	The hairs on your head

Let us Write! (Page 116)

A. It was a full moon night. Children had come out to see the Moon. Complete the conversation they had by picking the words from the help box.

a camera for the picture, so bright and big, says the full moon looks very beautiful, let's take a picture

Govind : Wow, look!

Safura : The moon looks so big and bright.

Sukanya : Isn't it?

Dhruv : My grandfather (i)........... .

Ramani : Let us take a picture.

Safura : My mother has (ii)........... .

Dhruv : Come. Stand here and

(iii)................ . Govind : The moon is
(iv)................ .

Ans. (i) says the full moon looks very beautiful
(ii) a camera for the picture
(iii) let's take a picture
(iv) so bright and big

Let us Do! (Page 117)

Project Work : Wind Chimes

Let us make 'Wind Chimes' with the shapes of the moon and the stars. Follow the instructions given in your NCERT textbook Page No. 117.

Ans. Do it yourself.

Multiple Choice Questions

1. What did Chanda Mama do every night?
   (a) Count the stars (b) Count the galaxies
   (c) Count the children (d) Count the clouds
2. Chanda Mama was __________ that he was unable to count the stars.
   (a) angry (b) happy
   (c) upset (d) scared
3. When did Chanda Mama wake up?
   (a) At night
   (b) In the evening
   (c) In the morning
   (d) In the afternoon

Ans. 1. (a), 2. (c), 3. (b)

True or False

1. Chanda Mama is round in shape all the time.
2. The sun peeps out from behind the clouds.
3. Chanda Mama would forget his count of the stars.

Ans. 1. False, 2. True, 3. True

Answer the following Questions

1. What was the sun's answer to Chanda Mama's problem?

Ans. The sun's answer to Chanda Mama's problem was that the number of stars in the sky is same as the number of children.

2. What did the sun ask Chanda Mama?

Ans. The sun asked Chanda Mama why he was crying.

3. How did Chanda Mama feel about the sun's answer to his question?

Ans. Chanda Mama felt very happy about the sun's answer to his questions.

Fill in the Blanks

Fill in the blanks with 'here' or 'there'

1. Do you want to stay __________ or go to another park?
2. Can you bring the dress from __________ to me?
3. Let's go to the mall. Jasmine will meet us __________.
4. I have lived __________ all my life.
5. Rohan can stay __________ with me.
6. Tamana's purse is __________, next to the magazines.

Ans. 1. here, 2. there, 3. there, 4. there, 5. here, 6. there

Let's Write

1. Write a letter to Chanda Mama to express wonder about what he must see from the sky.

Ans. Dear Chanda Mama

How are you up in the sky? I am doing well and hope that you are happy and healthy. Chanda Mama, how wonderful it would be up in the sky. Everything must look so small yet interesting. You must look at the big celebrities too. How amazing is that!

You must also look at all of us children and laugh at our naughtiness.

However, don't you get lonely? I hope not! But if you do, remember that all of us children love you, specially me.

Yours lovingly

Aayush

CHAPTER 12 CHANDRAYAAN

Summary

The story is about a girl named Rani who lived in a village. Rani was a very curious girl who asked a lot of questions. One evening, Rani's mother was singing the song 'Chanda mama door ke'.

Rani asked her how far is the moon. Her mother replied that it is very far away in the sky. Rani kept thinking about the moon at night and fell asleep.

The next morning, Rani's elder brother Pratik showed her that India's Chandrayaan has landed on the moon on the TV.

Rani was confused and asked her brother how Chandrayaan reached the moon. Pratik didn't know the answer, so he took Rani to meet his friend Vivaan's mother, Aunt Nandini who was a scientist.

Aunt Nandini told them that a rocket was used to reach the moon. She told them that 'Chandrayaan' means 'moon vehicle' and on 14th July, 2023 India became the first country to land on the far side of the moon. Rani was excited to hear this and asked if she could go to the moon one day. Aunt Nandini replied that maybe one day Rani can.

WORD-MEANING

Curious - An urge or want to know more, Pointing - To show the position of a thing or person by extending a finger at it and full of joy, Machines - Equipment with moving parts, Landing on - When a rocket or aeroplane reaches the ground, Confused - To not be able to think clearly, Chandrayaan - Moon vehicle, the name of the Indian rocket that was sent to space, Scientist - A person who studies science, Agreed - To have the same opinion as someone else, Rockets - A space vehicle.

Let us Think! (Page 122)

A. Answer the following.

Q.1 Rani was very curious. How do you know?

Ans. I know Rani is very curious as she likes to ask a lot of questions.

Q.2 What did Pratik say in excitement?

Ans. Pratik said that India has landed on the moon.

Q.3 Who was Nandini Aunty?

Ans. Nandini Aunty was the mother of Pratik's friend Vivaan. She was also a scientist.

Q.4 What do the words Chandra and Yaan mean?

Ans. The word 'Chandra' means 'moon' and 'Yaan' means 'vehicle'.

Q.5 Complete the sentence:

Chandrayaan-3 landed on the Moon on _____ .

Ans. 14th July, 2023

B. Think and say.

Imagine you are invited by the scientists to spend 10 days on the moon. Make a list of items that you would like to take with you.

1. ____________________
2. ____________________
3. ____________________
4. ____________________
5. ____________________
6. ____________________
7. ____________________
8. ____________________
9. ____________________
10. ____________________

Ans. 1. Food 2. Camera 3. Toys 4. Spacesuit 5. Water 6. Medicines 7. Bag 8. Binoculars 9. Watch 10. Books

Let us Speak! (Page 123)

Q.1 Chandrayaan travelled the distance between the Earth and the Moon. You may ask elders at home about their experiences of travelling to places that are far from home.

Ans. Do it yourself.

Q.2 Have you ever travelled to far-off places yourselves? If yes, share your experience with others.

Ans. Do it yourself. No, I have not been to any far-off place all by myself. However, I have visited some far-off states in India with my family.

Let us Learn! (Page 123-124)

Read the following lines.

There was **a** girl named Rani who lived in a village.

A hanky for **an** elephant.

Notice that we used **'a'** before girl, village and hanky, and **'an'** before elephant.

We use **'a'** before singular nouns that begin with consonants. **'An'** is used before singular nouns that begin with vowel sounds **(a, e, i, o, u)**.

A. Fill in the blanks using 'a'

1. _______ dog is barking at the postman.
2. My mother gives chapattis to _____ cow everyday.
3. In summers, _________ sparrow builds its nest on the mango tree near our house.

Ans. 1. A 2. a 3. a

B. Fill in the blanks using 'an'.

1. I saw ______ eagle yesterday.
2. Maya bought ______ umbrella for the monsoon.

3. ______ ice-cream man brings his cart in the evenings.

Ans. 1. an 2. an 3. An

C. *Fill in the blanks using 'a' or 'an'.*

1. ______ brown hen laid ______ egg.
2. ______ eagle sat on ______ building.
3. Mary ate ______ apricot, ______ chikoo and ______ orange.

Ans. 1. A, an 2. An, a 3. an, a, an

Let us Write! (Page 125)

A. *Fill in the blanks by forming words using 'sk', 'sw', 'sp', and 'st'.*

1. There are **sw**ings in the park.
2. The children throw ______ ones in the river.
3. I need a ______ oon and a bowl for soup.
4. Have you heard the ______ ory of the boy who cried wolf ?
5. The blue ______ irt matched with the pink shirt.

Ans. 2. stones 3. spoon 4. story 5. skirt

B. *Describing the Moon.*

Draw a picture of the Moon. With the help of your teacher, write a few lines about the Moon.

Ans. Do it yourself.

The Moon appears in the sky at night with the stars. It is earth's only natural satellite. It goes round the Earth everyday. It is big, made up of round rocks and has a lot of craters. But I think that it is beautiful.

Fun with Words (Page 126)

A. Read these sentences aloud with your teacher.

There are seven days in a week.

Sunday is the **first** day of the week.

Monday is the **second** day of the week.

Tuesday is the **third** day of the week.

Wednesday is the **fourth** day of the week.

Thursday is the **fifth** day of the week.

Friday is the **sixth** day of the week.

Saturday is the **seventh** day of the week.

B. Look at the words given below. Read them aloud. Find their position in a week using the text given above. One has been done for you.

Sunday	first
Monday	______
Tuesday	______
Wednesday	______
Thursday	______
Friday	______
Saturday	______

Ans.

Monday	**second**
Tuesday	**third**
Wednesday	**fourth**
Thursday	**fifth**
Friday	**sixth**
Saturday	**seventh**

Let us Do! (Page 127)

A. Divide yourselves into small groups. Each group shall collect newspaper or magazine clippings related to the Chandrayaan-3 mission. Paste it on a chart paper and display it in your class.

Ans. Do it yourself.

Let us Explore! (Page 127)

A. Do you know a song or a story about the moon in your mother tongue? If not, ask your family members and share it in the class.

Ans. Ask you parents and share it in your class.

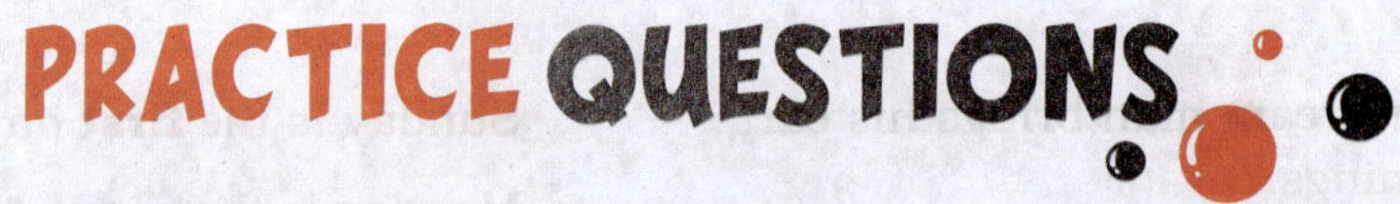

PRACTICE QUESTIONS

Multiple Choice Questions

1. What did Rani see on the TV?
   (a) Cartoon movie
   (b) News about sun and moon
   (c) Photos of some machines on moon
   (d) None of the above
2. Rani asked Pratik ....
   (a) why is the sky blue
   (b) how did Chandrayaan reach the Moon
   (c) where does the sun go at night
   (d) how far is the moon
3. What did Nandani aunty offer the children?
   (a) Chocolates (b) Snacks
   (c) Water (d) *Sharbat*
4. After learning more about the Chandrayaan mission, Rani felt ....
   (a) excited (b) confused
   (c) sad (d) scared

Ans. 1. (c), 2. (b), 3. (d), 4. (a)

Answer the following Questions

1. What did Rani ask her mother about Chanda Mama?

Ans. Rani asked her mother how far the Chanda Mama is.

2. Who did Pratik take Rani to answer her questions about the Chandrayaan?

Ans. Pratik took Rani to his friend Vivaan's mother, Aunt Nandini, to get answers to her questions about Chandrayaan.

3. What did Rani see inside Vivaan's house?

Ans. Rani saw many models and pictures of rockets in Vivaan's house.

True or False

1. Pratik showed Vivaan on the TV that India was on the moon.
2. Aunty Nandani welcomed Rani and Pratik into her home.
3. A rocket was used to reach the moon.
4. India became the second country to land on the far side of the moon.

Ans. 1. False, 2. True, 3. True, 4. False

Fill in the Blanks

Fill in the blanks using 'a' or 'an'.

1. Rhythm drives ____________ old car.
2. Do you have ____________ computer?
3. She drank ____________ cup of coffee in the morning.
4. I would like to buy ____________ pair of shoes I saw at ____________ shop today.
5. English is ____________ easy language.
6. Jeremy bought ____________ horse, ____________ ox and ____________ buffalo for the farm.

Ans. 1. an, 2. a, 3. a, 4. a, a, 5. an, 6. a, an, a

Let's Write

1. Aunt Nandini was a scientist. Imagine if you were an astronaut, what wonders you would see. Write a paragraph on 'If I were an Astronaut'.

Ans. Being an astronaut is a dream for many people. The thought of exploring the vast space and discovering new worlds is incredibly exciting. If I were an astronaut, I would have the opportunity to fulfill my lifelong ambition of exploring space. As an astronaut, I would be trained in various fields learning things that many people do not know.

Not to forget, I would see the space from the telescopes and later, see the moon and other planets such as Mars with my own eyes. Being an astronaut would be an unforgettable experience, one that I would cherish for the rest of my life.

वीणा
(हिंदी)

अध्याय 1

सीखो

कविता का सार

प्रस्तुत कविता 'सीखो' श्रीनाथ सिंह जी द्वारा लिखी गई है। इस कविता में कवि हमें अपने आस-पास के प्राकृतिक वातावरण से बहुत कुछ सीखने की शिक्षा देते हैं। कवि ने अनेक प्राकृतिक चीजों के माध्यम से यह समझाने की कोशिश की है कि हमें कभी भी निराश नहीं होना चाहिए। हमें सदैव मुस्कुराते हुए जीवन पथ पर आगे की ओर बढ़ते रहना चाहिए।

काव्यांशों की व्याख्या

काव्यांश 1

फूलों से नित हँसना सीखो, भौंरों से नित गाना।
तरु की झुकी डालियों से नित, सीखो शीश झुकाना।।
सीख हवा के झोंकों से लो, कोमल भाव बहाना।
दूध और पानी से सीखो, मिलना और मिलाना।।
सूरज की किरणों से सीखो, जगना और जगाना।
लता और पेड़ों से सीखो, सबको गले लगाना।।

शब्दार्थ नित-प्रतिदिन, तरु-पेड़, शीश-सिर, कोमल-मुलायम, लता-बेल।

संदर्भ/प्रसंग प्रस्तुत पंक्तियाँ हमारी पाठ्यपुस्तक 'वीणा भाग-1' में संकलित कविता 'सीखो' से ली गई हैं। इसके कवि श्रीनाथ सिंह हैं। इस अंश में कवि ने अनेक प्राकृतिक चीजों के माध्यम से मानव को कुछ-न-कुछ सीखने की बात कही है।

व्याख्या कवि कहता है कि हमें फूलों की तरह हमेशा खुश रहना चाहिए। भौंरों की तरह नित गाना अर्थात् अपने काम में मग्न रहना सीखना चाहिए। पेड़ों की फलों से भरी डाल की तरह झुकना सीखना चाहिए अर्थात् सबके साथ विनम्र रहना चाहिए। दूध और पानी से मिलना सीखना चाहिए; जैसे— दूध और पानी को मिलाने पर अलग करना मुश्किल है ठीक उसी प्रकार सभी के साथ प्रेम से मिलकर रहना चाहिए।

सूरज की किरणों से जगना और जगाना सीखना चाहिए; जैसे— सूरज खुद सबसे पहले उठकर सबको रोशनी देकर जगाता है। उसी प्रकार हमें भी जीवन में रोशन होकर दूसरों को रोशन करने में मदद करनी चाहिए। लता व पेड़ों की तरह हमें भी सबको अपनाना। अर्थात् गले लगाना सीखना चाहिए।

काव्यांश 2

दीपक से सीखो जितना, हो सके अंधेरा हरना।
पृथ्वी से सीखो प्राणी की, सच्ची सेवा करना।।
जलधारा से सीखो आगे, जीवन पथ में बढ़ना।
और धुएँ से सीखो हरदम, ऊँचे ही पर चढ़ना।।

शब्दार्थ *दीपक-दीया, हरना-दूर करना, प्राणी-जीव, पथ-रास्ता।*

प्रसंग पूर्ववत्

व्याख्या कवि कहते हैं कि जिस प्रकार दीपक के प्रकाश से सब कुछ प्रकाशमय होकर अज्ञानरूपी अंधकार मिट जाता है, उसी प्रकार हमें भी ज्ञान का प्रकाश फैलाना चाहिए। पृथ्वी जिस प्रकार वर्षा, धूप, गर्मी आदि अनेक कष्टों के बाद भी प्राणियों का पालन- पोषण करती है, उसी प्रकार हमें भी कठिनाइयों की चिंता न करते हुए मानवता के सच्चे सेवक बनना चाहिए।

अनेक कठिनाइयों का सामना करते हुए भी जलधारा निरंतर आगे की ओर बढ़ती जाती है। हमें भी अनेक बाधाओं का सामना करते हुए कर्त्तव्य पथ पर निरंतर बढ़ना चाहिए, जिस प्रकार धुआँ सदैव ऊपर ही उठता है।

NCERT फोल्डर

बातचीत के लिए

1. आपको इस चित्र में क्या-क्या दिखाई दे रहा है?

उत्तर सूरज, पेड़, पहाड़, पक्षी, आम, फूल, नदी, पत्थर, बादल।

2. इनमें से कौन-सी वस्तुएँ आप प्रतिदिन देखते हैं?

उत्तर सूरज, पक्षी, पत्थर, पेड़, फूल तथा बादल।

3. उगते हुए सूरज को देखकर आपके मन में किस प्रकार के भाव आते हैं?

उत्तर उगते हुए सूरज को देखकर मन में शांति के साथ नए दिन की शुरुआत के लिए सकारात्मक विचार आते हैं।

4. रंग-बिरंगे फूलों को देखकर आपको कैसा लगता है?

उत्तर रंग-बिरंगे फूलों को देखकर मेरा मन प्रसन्नता (खुशी) से भर जाता है व चेहरे पर मुस्कान आ जाती है।

कविता की बात

1. किससे क्या सीखें? मिलान कीजिए।

उत्तर

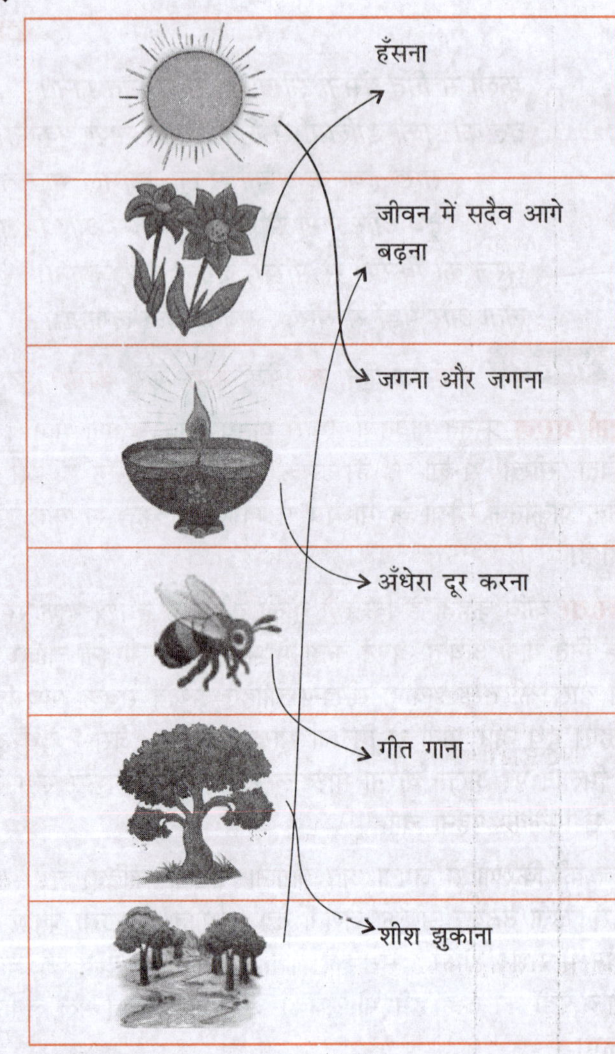

2. कविता में किससे सीखने की बात आपको अच्छी लगी? उसका चित्र बनाइए और नाम लिखिए।

उत्तर आपको सूरज, फूल, भँवरा, नदी, पेड़ जिसकी सीख सबसे अच्छी लगी, उसका चित्र बनाकर नाम लिखें।

3. पढ़िए और बताइए कि यह भाव कविता की किस पंक्ति में आया है?

(क) पेड़ों की झुकी डालियों से हमें यह सीखना है कि हमें हमेशा विनम्र रहना चाहिए।

(ख) हवा के झोंकों से हमें सीखना है कि हम हमेशा कुछ-न-कुछ काम करते रहें।

(ग) नदी-नहर से हमें सीखना है कि जीवन आगे बढ़ने का नाम है और हमें आगे बढ़ते रहना चाहिए।

उत्तर (क) **कविता की पंक्ति** तरु की झुकी डालियों से नित, सीखो शीश झुकाना।

(ख) **कविता की पंक्ति** सीख हवा के झोंकों से लो, कोमल भाव बहाना।

(ग) **कविता की पंक्ति** जलधारा से सीखो आगे, जीवन पथ में बढ़ना।

कविता से आगे

1. सूरज से जगना और जगाना सीखने की बात कही गई है। हम सूरज से और क्या-क्या सीख सकते हैं? कोई दो बातें लिखिए।

उत्तर (i) सूरज से हम बिना किसी स्वार्थ के लोगों के जीवन में प्रकाश देना सीख सकते हैं।

(ii) सूरज से हमें यह सीखना चाहिए कि जिस प्रकार सूरज बिना थके उदय एवं अस्त होता है ठीक उसी प्रकार हमें भी अपने कार्य नित्य करते रहना चाहिए।

2. लता और पेड़ों से एक-दूसरे के साथ प्रेम और सद्भाव की बात सीखने के लिए कहा गया है। इनसे हम और क्या-क्या सीख सकते हैं? कोई दो बातें लिखिए।

उत्तर (i) लता और पेड़ों से हमें सीख मिलती है कि सबसे मिलना और सबको मिलाना चाहिए।

(ii) लता एवं पेड़ से परोपकार की भावना की भी सीख मिलती है।

3. हम सभी में कोई-न-कोई विशेषता अवश्य होती है। आप अपने सहपाठी की कौन-सी बात सीखना चाहते हैं?

उत्तर मैं अपने सहपाठी से यह बात सीखना चाहता हूँ कि वह कक्षा में सभी की मदद करता है तथा मुश्किल समय में सबका साथ देता है।

भाषा की बात

शब्द	अर्थ
तरु	पेड़
शीश	सिर
पृथ्वी	धरती
हरना	दूर करना
पथ	रास्ता/मार्ग

1. ऊपर दी गई सूची को ध्यान से पढ़िए तथा इनमें से कोई दो शब्द लेकर वाक्य बनाइए।

उत्तर • **पथ**

वाक्य कभी-कभी **पथ** अत्यधिक कठिन होता है।

• **शीश**

वाक्य हम सब भगवान के चरणों में **शीश** झुकाते हैं।

2. दूध और पानी से सीखो मिलना और मिलाना। रेखांकित शब्दों के समान कुछ शब्द बनाए।

हँसना और हँसाना   **पीना और पिलाना**

....

....

उत्तर हँसना और हँसाना   पीना और पिलाना

रोना और रुलाना   खेलना और खिलाना

पढ़ना और पढ़ाना   जगना और जगाना

3. 'स' और 'प' वर्ण से प्रारंभ होने वाले शब्दों को कविता से खोजकर लिखिए।

उत्तर

स	प
सीखो	पानी
सूरज	पेड़ों
सबको	पृथ्वी
सके	पथ

4. तालिका 'अ' तथा 'ब' में दिए गए शब्दों का उच्चारण कीजिए और इनमें अंतर पहचानिए।

तालिका 'अ'	तालिका 'ब'
पड़ा	पढ़ा
बड़ा	बढ़ा
अड़ना	बढ़ना
उड़ना	पढ़ना
कड़ाई	कढ़ाई
लड़ाई	चढ़ाई

उत्तर छात्र स्वयं करें।

बूझो तो जानें

1. एक फूल एक फल भाई
दोनों मिलकर बने मिठाई

उत्तर गुलाब जामुन

2. बिना बाल की पूँछ लिए वह भाग रहा है।
सब सोते वह रात-रात भर जाग रहा है।
काट-काटकर कागज कपड़े खुश होता है
और धरातल के नीचे घर में सोता है।

उत्तर चूहा

अभ्यास प्रश्न

बहुविकल्पीय प्रश्न

1. हमें फूलों से नित क्या सीखना चाहिए?
(क) हँसना (ख) रोना (ग) पढ़ना (घ) गाना

2. हमें शीश को झुकाना किससे सीखना चाहिए?
(क) पेड़ और डालियों से (ख) भौंरों से
(ग) पेड़ों से (घ) नदियों से

3. दूध तथा पानी हमें क्या सिखाते हैं?
(क) मिलना और मिलाना (ख) चलना और चलाना
(ग) पढ़ना और पढ़ाना (घ) हँसना और हँसाना

4. जलधारा हमें क्या सिखाती है?
(क) जीवन पथ में बढ़ना (ख) रुकना
(ग) बैठना (घ) गिरना

5. हमेशा ऊँचाइयों पर चढ़ते जाना हम किससे सीखते हैं?
(क) पृथ्वी से
(ख) धुएँ से
(ग) पहाड़ से
(घ) जलधारा से

उत्तर

1. (क) हँसना
2. (क) पेड़ और डालियों से
3. (क) मिलना और मिलाना
4. (क) जीवन पथ में बढ़ना
5. (ख) धुएँ से

काव्यांश पर आधारित प्रश्न

निम्नलिखित काव्यांश को पढ़कर उस पर आधारित प्रश्नों के उत्तर दीजिए।

काव्यांश

दीपक से सीखो जितना हो सके अँधेरा हरना।
पृथ्वी से सीखो प्राणी की सच्ची सेवा करना।।
जलधारा से सीखो आगे, जीवन पथ में बढ़ना।
और धुएँ से सीखो हरदम, ऊँचे ही पर चढ़ना।।

1. जीवन पथ पर आगे बढ़ना कौन सिखा रहा है?
(क) जलधारा (ख) नदी
(ग) पृथ्वी (घ) दीपक

2. हमें किसकी तरह अँधेरा हरना चाहिए?
(क) सूरज की तरह (ख) चाँद की तरह
(ग) तारे की तरह (घ) दीपक की तरह

3. धुएँ की तरह हरदम कहाँ चढ़ना चाहिए?

4. प्राणियों की सच्ची सेवा करना किससे सीखना चाहिए?

उत्तर

1. (क) जलधारा
2. (घ) दीपक की तरह
3. धुएँ की तरह हरदम ऊँचे पर ही चढ़ना चाहिए।
4. प्राणियों की सच्ची सेवा करना हमें पृथ्वी से सीखना चाहिए।

निम्नलिखित प्रश्नों के उत्तर दीजिए

1. आपको प्रकृति की कौन-सी चीज़ या बात अच्छी लगती है?

उत्तर मुझे प्रकृति की सभी चीजें; जैसे—पेड़, फल, फूल, नदी, पशु आदि अच्छी लगती हैं।

2. प्रस्तुत कविता व कवि का नाम लिखिए।

उत्तर प्रस्तुत कविता का नाम 'सीखो' तथा इसके कवि श्रीनाथ सिंह हैं।

3. आप 'पर्वत' से क्या सीख सकते हैं?

उत्तर हम पर्वत से अडिग रहना सीख सकते हैं?

4. आपको इस कविता से क्या शिक्षा मिलती है?

उत्तर इस कविता से हमें यह शिक्षा मिलती है कि हमें प्रकृति की तरह विनम्र तथा दूसरों के प्रति सेवा की भावना रहनी चाहिए।

5. हमें किस पथ पर निरंतर बढ़ते रहना चाहिए?

उत्तर हमें कर्त्तव्य पथ पर निरंतर बढ़ते रहना चाहिए।

व्याकरण संबंधी प्रश्न

1. कविता में आए निम्न शब्दों के विलोम शब्द लिखिए
नित, हँसना, चढ़ना, आगे

2. कविता में आए किन्हीं पाँच संज्ञा शब्दों को छाँटकर लिखिए

उत्तर 1.

शब्द	विलोम
नित	कभी-कभी
हँसना	रोना
चढ़ना	उतरना
आगे	पीछे

2. (i) नदी (ii) फूल (iii) भौंरा
(iv) तरु (v) हवा

लेखन संबंधी प्रश्न

1. दिए गए चित्र का वर्णन कम-से-कम 30 शब्दों में करें।

उत्तर
- यह रात का चित्र है।
- इस चित्र में चाँद पूरा गोल है।
- वह बहुत सुंदर लग रहा है। साथ में टिमटिमाते तारे हीरे जैसे लग रहे हैं।
- चाँद के आस-पास काले बादल भी प्यारे लग रहे हैं।
- चित्र को देखकर मन बहुत ही खुश हो रहा है।

अध्याय 2 चींटी

कविता का सार

प्रस्तुत कविता 'चींटी' प्रकाश मनु द्वारा लिखी गई है, जिसमें कवि ने परिश्रमी चींटी के बारे में बताया है। वे कहते हैं कि चींटी हर मौसम में धूप, बारिश आदि की परवाह किए बिना निरंतर चलती जाती है। चींटी बहुत मेहनती होती है और वह किसी भी स्थिति में दाना चुनना नहीं छोड़ती। चींटी एक कलाकार की तरह होती है, जो अपने घर को अच्छे से सजाती है। चींटी छोटी होती है, परंतु इसके इरादे बहुत बड़े होते हैं। यह अपना कार्य धैर्य और साहस के साथ करती है। चींटी हमें यह सीख देती है कि हमें अपना कर्म (काम) करते रहना चाहिए, क्योंकि कर्म ही ईश्वर की पूजा है।

काव्यांशों की व्याख्या

काव्यांश 1

हर पल चलती जाती चींटी,
श्रम का राग सुनाती चींटी।
कड़ी धूप हो या हो वर्षा,
दाना चुनकर लाती चींटी।
सचमुच कैसी कलाकार है,
घर को खूब सजाती चींटी।

शब्दार्थ *पल–समय, श्रम–मेहनत, राग–धुन, कड़ी–बहुत/अत्यधिक।*

संदर्भ/प्रसंग प्रस्तुत पंक्तियाँ हमारी पाठ्यपुस्तक 'वीणा भाग-1' में संकलित कविता 'चींटी' से ली गई हैं। इसके कवि 'प्रकाश मनु' हैं। इस अंश में कवि ने चींटियों की मेहनत के बारे में बताया है कि वे किस प्रकार कठिनाइयों का सामना करते हुए दाना चुनकर लाती हैं।

व्याख्या कवि कहते हैं कि चींटी बहुत मेहनती होती है, जो खुद लगातार चलकर हमें मेहनत करना सिखाती है। कैसा भी मौसम हो बारिश अथवा धूप का वह मेहनत करके दाना चुनकर लाती है। इसके अतिरिक्त चींटी मेहनत से अपना घर बनाती है और उसको सजाती भी है, जिससे हमें यह पता चलता है कि चींटी एक अच्छी कलाकार भी है। चींटी हमें यह भी सिखाती है कि विपरीत परिस्थितियों में भी अपने कार्य में लगे रहना चाहिए, तभी हमें सफलता प्राप्त होगी।

काव्यांश 2

छोटा तन, पर बड़े इरादे, नहीं कभी घबराती चींटी।
नन्हें-नन्हें पैर बढ़ाकर, पर्वत पर चढ़ जाती चींटी।
काम बड़े करके दिखलाती, जहाँ कहीं अड़ जाती चींटी।
मेहनत ही पूजा है प्रभु की, हमको यही सिखाती चींटी।

शब्दार्थ *तन-शरीर, इरादे-हौसले, अड़ जाती-ठान लेती/जिद न छोड़ती।*

प्रसंग प्रस्तुत अंश में कवि ने बताया है कि चींटी है तो अत्यंत छोटी, पर काम उसके बड़े-बड़े हैं। मेहनत ही भगवान की पूजा है हमको चींटी यही सिखाती है।

व्याख्या चींटी का शरीर अत्यंत छोटा है, परंतु उसके इरादे बहुत बड़े-बड़े हैं। चींटी अपने से बड़ी वस्तु को भी उठाने से घबराती नहीं है। चींटी अपने छोटे-छोटे पैरों से चलकर पर्वत पर पहुँच जाती है। यदि चींटी कोई कार्य करने की ठान लेती है, तो वह बड़े-से-बड़े कार्य को भी कर लेती है। चींटी हमें यह सिखाती है कि हमें किसी भी परिस्थिति में घबराना नहीं चाहिए तथा अपने इरादों को मजबूत रखते हुए हमेशा सफलता पाने के लिए आगे बढ़ते रहना चाहिए अर्थात् जब तक लक्ष्य की प्राप्ति न हो जाए हार नहीं माननी चाहिए, क्योंकि हमारी मेहनत ही भगवान की पूजा है।

बातचीत के लिए

1. आपने अपने आस-पास घर और विद्यालय में कौन-कौन से जीव-जंतु देखे हैं?

उत्तर हमने अपने घर के आस-पास कुत्ता, बिल्ली, गिलहरी, चिड़िया और चींटी आदि देखे हैं।

2. आपने सबसे छोटा कौन-सा कीट देखा और कहाँ देखा है?

उत्तर मैंने सबसे छोटा कीट लकड़ी के अंदर एक दीमक को देखा है।

3. आपने चींटी के अतिरिक्त और कौन-कौन से श्रम करने वाले जीव देखे हैं?

उत्तर चींटी के अतिरिक्त हमने मकड़ी, मधुमक्खी और चिड़िया आदि को श्रम करने वाले जीव के रूप में देखा है।

4. नन्हीं चींटी के बारे में अपना कोई अनुभव बताओ।

उत्तर जब मैंने नन्हीं चींटी को अपने हाथ में उठाया तो मुझे उसकी निराशा तथा बेबसी का अहसास हुआ। वह बड़ी धीमी गति से चलती है और उसके नन्हें से पैरों को देखकर मैंने विचार किया कि कितनी मेहनत से वह अपना रास्ता तय करती है।

कविता से आगे

1. नीचे कुछ वस्तुओं के चित्र बने हैं। बताइए, चींटियाँ किसे खाना चाहेंगी? उस पर चिह्न बनाइए।

उत्तर लड्डू, गेहूँ के दाने, चीनी, शहद

2. निम्नलिखित पंक्तियों को पूरा कीजिए।

(क) घर को ....

(ख) पर्वत पर ....

(ग) दाना चुनकर ....

(घ) श्रम का राग ....

उत्तर (क) घर को – खूब सजाती चींटी।

(ख) पर्वत पर – चढ़ जाती चींटी।

(ग) दाना चुनकर – लाती चींटी।

(घ) श्रम का राग –सुनाती चींटी।

3. कविता के अनुसार चींटी हमको क्या-क्या करना सिखाती है? लिखकर बताइए।

उत्तर • मेहनत करना • लक्ष्य की ओर बढ़ते रहना
• कभी न घबराना • कभी न हारना

भाषा की बात

1. कविता में चींटी को क्या-क्या कहा गया है?

कलाकार ....

....

उत्तर • कलाकार • साहसी
• बड़े इरादों वाली • परिश्रमी

2. कितनी बार आई चींटी?

'चींटी' कविता में 'चींटी' शब्द कितनी बार आया है? इन्हें गिनिए और उतनी चींटियाँ बनाकर पंक्ति को पूरा कीजिए।

उत्तर कविता में चींटी शब्द 8 बार आया है।

3. आइए 'चींटी' कविता को आगे बढ़ाते हैं

चीनी का दाना दिख जाए,
उसको लेने जाती चींटी।

उत्तर चीनी का दाना दिख जाए, उसको लेने जाती चींटी।
राह में कई अड़चनें आएँ, फिर भी नहीं थकती चींटी।
बोझ उठाए बिना रुके, चलती जाती निरंतर चींटी।

4. शब्दों की तुकबंदी

दाना गाना धूप ....

कड़ी .... राग ....

उत्तर दाना — गाना
धूप — भूप
कड़ी — घड़ी
राग — आग

चींटी से भेंट

5. आपके घर में कई कोनों में चींटी आती-जाती है। एक दिन वह आपको रोककर आपसे कुछ कहती है। आपके और उसके बीच क्या-क्या बातें हुई होंगी? लिखिए।

आप नमस्ते चींटी! आज आप अकेली आई हैं?

चींटी ....

आप ....

चींटी ....

उत्तर **आप** नमस्ते चींटी! आज आप अकेली आई हैं?

चींटी नमस्ते! हाँ, आज मैं अकेली आई हूँ। आपसे कुछ जरूरी बात करनी थी।

आप बिल्कुल कहिए क्या बात है?

चींटी मैं आपसे यह कहना चाहती थी कि आप चलते समय थोड़ा हमारा ध्यान रखें।

आप ठीक है।

अभ्यास प्रश्न

बहुविकल्पीय प्रश्न

1. चींटी किस प्रकार का राग सुनाती है?

(क) भागने का (ख) सुख का
(ग) श्रम का (घ) दु:ख का

2. चींटी क्या चुनकर लाती है?

(क) फूल (ख) दाना
(ग) काँटे (घ) फल

3. चींटी के इरादे कैसे हैं?

(क) छोटे (ख) बड़े
(ग) टूटे (घ) अच्छे

4. चींटी नन्हें पैरों से कहाँ चढ़ जाती है?

(क) छत पर
(ख) पेड़ पर
(ग) पहाड़ पर
(घ) दीवार पर

5. कविता में चींटी को किसके समान बताया गया है?

(क) खतरनाक (ख) कलाकार
(ग) बदसूरत (घ) गुणवान

उत्तर

1. (ग) श्रम का 2. (ख) दाना
3. (ख) बड़े 4. (ग) पहाड़ पर
5. (ख) कलाकार

सत्य–असत्य

नीचे दिए गए वाक्यों में से सत्य या असत्य कथन की पहचान कीजिए।

1. चींटी अत्यंत ही मेहनती जीव है। (सत्य/असत्य)
2. चींटियाँ पहाड़ों पर चढ़ने में असमर्थ रहती हैं। (सत्य/असत्य)
3. चींटियाँ मेहनत करना नहीं जानतीं। (सत्य/असत्य)
4. चींटियाँ अपने घर को सजाती हैं। (सत्य/असत्य)

उत्तर

1. सत्य 2. असत्य
3. असत्य 4. सत्य

काव्यांश पर आधारित प्रश्न

निम्नलिखित काव्यांश को पढ़कर उस पर आधारित प्रश्नों के उत्तर दीजिए।

काव्यांश

छोटा तन, पर बड़े इरादे,
नहीं कभी घबराती चींटी।
काम बड़े करके दिखलाती,
जहाँ कहीं अड़ जाती चींटी।

1. कौन बड़े-बड़े काम करके दिखलाता है?

(क) गाय (ख) भौंरा
(ग) चींटी (घ) तितली

2. बड़े इरादे कौन रखता है?

(क) पेड़ (ख) चींटी (ग) मोर (घ) तितली

3. चींटी का शरीर कैसा होता है?
4. चींटी कब बड़े काम करके दिखाती है

उत्तर

1. (ग) चींटी 2. (ख) चींटी
3. चींटी का शरीर छोटा-सा होता है।
4. चींटी जब कहीं अड़ जाती है, तो बड़े काम करके दिखाती है।

निम्नलिखित प्रश्नों के उत्तर दीजिए

1. 'मेहनत ही पूजा है' यह हमें कौन बताता है?

उत्तर 'मेहनत ही पूजा है' यह हमें चींटी बताती है।

2. चींटी हर पल क्या करती है?

उत्तर चींटी हर पल मेहनत करती है।

3. कविता में चींटी को कलाकार क्यों कहा गया है?

उत्तर चींटी घर को सजाती है, इसलिए उसे कलाकार कहा गया है।

4. चींटी हमें क्या सीख दे रही है?

उत्तर चींटी हमें लगातार मेहनत करने की सीख दे रही है।

5. क्या दाना चुनने के लिए चींटी घबराती है?

उत्तर दाना चुनने के लिए चींटी किसी भी मौसम से नहीं घबराती है।

कितने पैर?

पाठ का सार

प्रस्तुत पाठ 'कितने पैर?' मंजुल भार्गव द्वारा रचित है। इस पाठ में लेखक ने अध्यापिका तथा बच्चों के मध्य बातचीत के माध्यम से जीव जगत के बारे में चर्चा की है। अध्यापिका बच्चों से कहती हैं कि आज हम जीवों के पैरों की संख्या की बात करेंगे। वे बताती हैं कि जीव अलग-अलग प्रकार के होते हैं तथा उनमें पैरों की संख्या भी अलग-अलग होती है। जीवों में पैरों की संख्या शून्य से लेकर कई सौ तक हो सकती है। इसके बाद वे बच्चों से प्रश्न करती हैं कि क्या कोई ऐसा जीव बता सकता है, जिसके पैर नहीं होते? एक विद्यार्थी बताता है कि उसने बरसात में केंचुओं को देखा है, जिनके पैर नहीं होते और वे पेट के बल सरकते हैं। फिर अध्यापिका बच्चों को बताती हैं कि दो पैर वाले जीवों को द्विपाद कहते हैं। मनुष्य के अतिरिक्त यदि आप किसी अन्य द्विपाद के विषय में जानते हैं, तो बताइए। तभी रमेश चिड़िया का उदाहरण देता है। अध्यापिका कहती हैं कि बिल्कुल सही उत्तर दिया। फिर वे दो पैरों वाले पशुओं की बात करती हैं।

अध्यापिका के पूछने पर सविता नाम की छात्रा बताती है कि उसकी माँ ने बताया था कि ऑस्ट्रेलिया में एक द्विपाद पशु रहता है, जो कूद-कूदकर चलता है, किंतु मैं उसका नाम भूल गई। तभी रजनी नाम की छात्रा कहती है कि उसका नाम कंगारू है। अध्यापिका बच्चों को कंगारू के विषय में बताती हैं और कहती हैं कि इसे चतुष्पाद भी कहते हैं, क्योंकि जब यह तेजी से चलता है, तो दो पैरों पर चलता है, लेकिन जब वह धीरे चलता है, तो झुककर चारों पैरों पर चलता है। यह कभी-कभी आगे बढ़ने के लिए अपनी पूँछ का भी प्रयोग करता है, इसलिए इसे पंचपाद भी कहते हैं। अध्यापिका कहती हैं कि अधिकतर जीव चार पैर वाले ही होते हैं; जैसे—गाय, भैंस आदि तभी समीर कुत्ता, बिल्ली, घोड़ा और वीणा बकरी, गधा, बंदर का नाम बताते हैं। रफिया मेंढक, ऊदबिलाव, घड़ियाल बताती है। रमेश शेर और चीता तथा विपिन जेबरा और जिराफ बताता है। अध्यापिका उन्हें शाबाशी देती हैं।

अध्यापिका बच्चों से आगे पूछती हैं कि चींटी या चींटे के कितने पैर होते हैं? मीना बताती है कि इनके छः पैर होते हैं। अध्यापिका बताती हैं कि इसी प्रकार मक्खी तथा भँवरे के भी छः पैर होते हैं। अध्यापिका कहती हैं कि अब हम ऐसे कीट के विषय में बात करेंगे, जिसके 30 से लेकर 382 तक पैर हो सकते हैं अर्थात् 15 जोड़ी से लेकर 191 जोड़ी तक पैर हो सकते हैं। इसका नाम कनखजूरा है। अध्यापिका बच्चों से पूछती हैं कि क्या किसी ने कभी इसे देखा है? सभी बच्चे नहीं में जवाब देते हैं, तब अध्यापिका बताती हैं कि यह अधिकतर गीले अथवा अँधेरे वाले स्थानों पर पाए जाते हैं। अध्यापिका कहती हैं कि इतने पैरों वाला कनखजूरा चलता कैसे होगा? यह अध्याय अध्यापिका के इसी प्रश्न के साथ समाप्त हो जाता है।

शब्दार्थ

धरती-पृथ्वी, सरकना-रेंगना, द्विपाद-दो पैर वाला, चतुष्पाद-चार पैरों वाला, पंचपाद-पाँच पैर वाला, भिन्न-भिन्न-अलग-अलग, कीट-कीड़ा, अतिरिक्त-अलावा।

बातचीत के लिए

1. कुछ अन्य जीवों के नाम बताइए, जिनका उल्लेख इस पाठ में नहीं है और साथ ही उन जीवों के पैरों की संख्या भी बताइए।

उत्तर **मछली** इनके पैरों की संख्या 0 होती है।
मच्छर इनके पैरों की संख्या 6 होती है।
भालू इनके पैरों की संख्या 4 होती है।
हिरन इनके पैरों की संख्या 4 होती है।

2. शरीर के कौन-से अंग इधर-उधर आने-जाने में सहायता करते हैं?

उत्तर पैर हमें इधर से उधर आने-जाने में सहायता करते हैं।

3. क्या पशु-पक्षियों और छोटे-छोटे कीटों को भी इधर-उधर जाने में पैर सहायता करते हैं?

उत्तर हाँ, पशु-पक्षियों और छोटे-छोटे कीटों को भी इधर-उधर जाने में पैर सहायता करते हैं।

4. केंचुए के अतिरिक्त आप कोई जीव बता सकते हैं, जिसके पैर नहीं होते हैं?

उत्तर केंचुए के अतिरिक्त साँपों व मछलियों के भी पैर नहीं होते हैं।

5. पैरों के अतिरिक्त हमारे शरीर में और कौन-कौन से अंग दो की संख्या में होते हैं?

उत्तर पैरों के अतिरिक्त आँख, कान, हाथ हमारे शरीर में दो की संख्या में होते हैं।

आपका पैर

अपने पैर और हाथ की बनावट को ध्यान से देखिए। आपके पैर और हाथ की बनावट में क्या समान है और क्या भिन्न है? पहचानिए और लिखिए।

	पैर	हाथ
1.	अँगूठे हैं	अँगूठे हैं
2.		
3.		
4.		
5.		

उत्तर

	पैर	हाथ
1.	अँगूठे हैं	अँगूठे हैं
2.	अँगुलियाँ हैं	अँगुलियाँ हैं
3.	नाखून हैं	नाखून हैं
4.	तलवे हैं	तलवे नहीं हैं, हथेली है
5.	एड़ी है	एड़ी नहीं है, कलाई है

पाठ के भीतर

1. सही कथन के आगे (✓) का चिह्न लगाइए।

(क) सभी जीवों के केवल दो ही पैर होते हैं। ( )
(ख) केंचुएँ अपने पेट के बल सरकते हैं, क्योंकि उनके पैर नहीं होते। ( )
(ग) दो पैरों वाले जीव को द्विपाद कहते हैं। ( )
(घ) गाय, भैंस, बकरी आदि चतुष्पाद हैं। ( )
(ङ) जीवों के पैरों की संख्या शून्य से लेकर कई सौ तक हो सकती है। ( )

उत्तर (क) (✗) (ख) (✓) (ग) (✓)
(घ) (✓) (ङ) (✓)

2. नीचे दी गई तालिका में पैरों की संख्या के अनुसार जीवों के नाम लिखिए।

शून्य पैर वाले	दो पैर वाले	चार पैर वाले	छः पैर वाले	आठ पैर वाले

आठ से अधिक पैर वाले ....

उत्तर

शून्य पैर वाले	दो पैर वाले	चार पैर वाले	छः पैर वाले	आठ पैर वाले
केंचुआ	पक्षी	भैंस	चींटी	मकड़ी
साँप	कंगारू	हाथी	मच्छर	ऑक्टोपस
मछली	मुर्गी	घोड़ा	मक्खी	बिच्छू

आठ से अधिक पैर वाला—कनखजूरा

3. कैसे रखें पैरों का ध्यान?

अपने सहपाठियों से चर्चा करें कि हम अपने पैरों का ध्यान कैसे रख सकते हैं?

उत्तर (क) नाखूनों को नियमित रूप से काटना चाहिए।

(ख) बाहर जाते समय पैरों में जूते या चप्पल पहनना चाहिए।

(ग) बाहर से आने के बाद पैरों को अच्छे से धोना चाहिए।

(घ) अपने पैरों को रात को धोकर कोई भी अच्छी-सी क्रीम या तेल लगाना चाहिए, ताकि पैर मुलायम रहे।

भाषा की बात

चार पैर वाले जीवों को चतुष्पाद कहते हैं। चतुष्पाद का प्रचलित शब्द चौपाया होता है, जिसका अर्थ है–चार पैर वाला।

1. इसी प्रकार चार की संख्या बताने वाले कुछ और शब्द खोजकर लिखिए।

उत्तर चतुर्भुज — चौराहा

चारपाई — चौकोर

चारमीनार — चौपाई

2. नीचे दिए गए उदाहण के अनुसार तालिका पूरी कीजिए।

उत्तर

एक	1	१
दो	2	२
तीन	3	३
चार	4	४
पाँच	5	५
छः	6	६
सात	7	७
आठ	8	८
नौ	9	९
दस	10	१०

सोचिए और लिखिए

कल्पना कीजिए कि एक दिन किसी स्थान पर कनखजूरा, केंचुआ, चिड़िया और आप एकसाथ मिलते हैं। कनखजूरा अपने पैरों की बात शुरू करता है, सोचकर लिखिए कि आप सबके बीच क्या-क्या बातें होंगी?

उत्तर
- **कनखजूरा** तुम लोगों में से सबसे ज्यादा पैर मेरे हैं। मैं तुम लोगों से श्रेष्ठ हूँ।
- **केंचुआ** पैर ज्यादा होने से कोई श्रेष्ठ नहीं हो जाता है।
- **चिड़िया** भले ही मेरे दो पैर हैं, लेकिन मैं तो उड़ सकती हूँ, इसलिए मैं श्रेष्ठ हूँ।
- **लड़का** सबकी अपनी-अपनी विशेषताएँ हैं।
- **लड़की** हाँ, हाँ क्यों नहीं! आप सभी श्रेष्ठ हैं।

पहेली से पहले

1. आपने देखा कि एक खेत में कुछ भैंसें चर रही हैं। आपने गिना तो उनके कुल मिलाकर 32 पैर निकले। बताइए कितनी भैंसें हैं?

उत्तर आपने कुल 32 पैर देखे और आप जानते हैं कि एक भैंस के 4 पैर होते हैं। अब आप 32 को 4 से भाग दे देंगे, तो आप जान जाएँगे कि कुल 8 भैंसें हैं।

2. आपने देखा कि एक स्थान पर कई मकड़ियाँ चल रही हैं। आपने गिनकर देखा, तो फिर से कुल 32 पैर निकले। बताइए कितनी मकड़ियाँ हैं?

उत्तर आपको पता है कि एक मकड़ी के 8 पैर होते हैं। आप 32 को 8 से भाग दे देंगे, तो आप जान जाएँगे कि कुल 4 मकड़ियाँ हैं।

3. अब एक और स्थान पर आपने देखा कि कई चींटियाँ और मकड़ियाँ चल रही हैं। आपने गिनकर देखा कि उनके कुल मिलाकर 34 पैर हैं। बताइए कितनी चींटियाँ और कितनी मकड़ियाँ हैं?

उत्तर एक चींटी के कुल 6 पैर होते हैं। हमने 6 को 3 से गुणा किया तो 18 आया। अब 18 को हम 34 में से घटा देंगे तो 16 बचेगा। अब हमें पता है कि एक मकड़ी के कुल 8 पैर होते हैं, तो हमने 8 को दो से गुणा किया और उत्तर आया 16। इस प्रकार कुल 3 चींटियाँ तथा 2 मकड़ियाँ हैं।

बूझो तो जानें

1. लालटेन के पंखों में उड़े अँधेरी रात में।
जलती बाती बिना तेल के, ठंड और बरसात में।।

उत्तर जुगनू

2. तीतर के दो आगे तीतर, तीतर के दो पीछे तीतर।
आगे तीतर, पीछे तीतर, बोलो कितने तीतर।।

उत्तर तीन

अभ्यास प्रश्न

बहुविकल्पीय प्रश्न

1. केंचुए के कितने पैर होते हैं?
   (क) एक भी नहीं (ख) दो
   (ग) तीन (घ) चार
2. इनमें से द्विपाद जीव कौन-सा है?
   (क) चिड़िया (ख) घोड़ा (ग) गाय (घ) बकरी
3. मानव के कितने पैर होते हैं?
   (क) द्विपाद (ख) पंचपाद
   (ग) एकपाद (घ) चतुष्पाद
4. कँगारू कहाँ पाया जाता है?
   (क) भारत में (ख) ऑस्ट्रेलिया में
   (ग) नेपाल में (घ) चीन में

उत्तर

1. (क) एक भी नहीं 2. (क) चिड़िया
3. (क) द्विपाद 4. (ख) ऑस्ट्रेलिया

रिक्त स्थान

नीचे दिए गए वाक्यों में रिक्त स्थान की पूर्ति उचित शब्द से कीजिए।

(चौपाया, बरसात, साँप, झींगुर)

1. .... के छः से अधिक पैर होते हैं।
2. मैंने केंचुए को .... में देखा है।
3. .... पेट के बल चलता है।
4. कुत्ता .... जानवर है।

उत्तर

1. झींगुर 2. बरसात
3. साँप 4. चौपाया

गद्यांश पर आधारित प्रश्न

निम्नलिखित गद्यांश को पढ़कर उस पर आधारित प्रश्नों के उत्तर दीजिए।

गद्यांश

अध्यापिका-वाह! वाह! आप सब बच्चे बड़े बुद्धिमान हैं। आपके पास मेरे सभी प्रश्नों के उत्तर हैं। जब वह तेजी से चलता है, तो दो पैरों पर कूदकर चलता है, लेकिन जब वह धीरे चलता है, तो झुककर चार पैरों पर चलने लगता है, इसलिए उसे चतुष्पाद भी कहते हैं और कभी-कभी आगे बढ़ने में वह अपनी पूँछ का भी उपयोग करता है, इसलिए उसे पंचपाद भी कहते हैं। वैसे अधिकतर पशुओं के तो चार पैर ही होते हैं; जैसे– गाय, भैंस और···?

समीर-कुत्ता, बिल्ली, घोड़ा····

वीणा-बकरी, गधा, बंदर···

रफिया-मेंढक, ऊदबिलाव, घड़ियाल·····

रमेश-शेर, चीता·········

विपिन-जेबरा, जिराफ······

1. बिल्ली कितने पैर वाली जीव है?
   (क) एक (ख) तीन (ग) दो (घ) चार
2. आगे बढ़ने के लिए अपनी पूँछ का प्रयोग कौन करता है?
   (क) कँगारू (ख) मेंढक (ग) चीता (घ) जेबरा
3. गद्यांश में आए चार चतुष्पाद जानवरों के नाम लिखिए।
4. रमेश ने कौन-से तथा कितने पैर वाले जानवरों के नाम बताए?

उत्तर

1. (घ) चार 2. (क) कँगारू
3. गद्यांश में आए चार चतुष्पाद जानवरों के नाम शेर, चीता, बकरी और गधा हैं।
4. रमेश ने चार पैर वाले जानवरों शेर तथा चीता का नाम बताया।

निम्नलिखित प्रश्नों के उत्तर दीजिए

1. चार पैर वाले दो जानवरों के नाम लिखिए।

उत्तर चार पैर वाले दो जानवर गाय व हिरन हैं।

2. दो पैर वाले जीवों को क्या कहते हैं?

उत्तर दो पैर वाले जीवों के नाम मानव व पक्षी हैं।

3. केंचुआ किस प्रकार का जीव है? यह कब दिखता है?

उत्तर केंचुआ बिन पैर वाला जीव है। यह बरसात में दिखाई देता है।

लेखन संबंधी प्रश्न

1. 'पाठशाला' पर लगभग 40 शब्दों में अनुच्छेद लिखिए।

उत्तर मेरी पाठशाला का नाम 'आदर्श पाठशाला' है। यह मेरे घर के पास ही है। मेरी पाठशाला दसवीं कक्षा तक है। इसकी इमारत बहुत सुंदर व मजबूत है। पाठशाला में विभिन्न प्रकार के कमरे हैं, जिनमें प्रधानाचार्य का कमरा, अध्यापकों का कमरा, योग कक्ष, हॉल आदि शामिल हैं। पाठशाला में बड़ा व सुंदर खेल का मैदान भी है। मुझे मेरी पाठशाला बहुत पसंद है।

अध्याय 4 बया हमारी चिड़िया रानी!

कविता का सार

प्रस्तुत कविता 'बया हमारी चिड़िया रानी' महादेवी वर्मा द्वारा रचित है, जिसमें उन्होंने 'बया' नाम के एक पक्षी के बारे में बताया है। कवयित्री कहती हैं कि बया अपना महलरूपी घोंसला बनाने के लिए दूर-दूर से तिनके चुनकर लाती है तथा उन तिनकों से पेड़ की सबसे ऊँची डाली पर लटकाते हुए अपना घोंसला बनाती है। कवयित्री कहती हैं कि हम बया को कभी भी अपने से दूर नहीं करेंगे। जब बया अंडे देगी तो उनमें से छोटे-छोटे बच्चे निकलने पर हम सब मिलकर बारी-बारी से बच्चों का ध्यान रखेंगे। कुछ समय बाद जब बच्चों के पर निकल आएँगे और वे सब उड़ जाएँगे, तब भी हम बया को कभी अकेला नहीं छोड़ेंगे। इसलिए बया तुम कभी उदास मत होना हम हमेशा तुम्हारे पास ही रहेंगे।

काव्यांशों की व्याख्या

काव्यांश 1

बया हमारी चिड़िया रानी!
तिनके लाकर महल बनाती,
ऊँची डाली पर लटकाती
खेतों से फिर दाना लाती
नदियों से भर लाती पानी।

तुझको दूर न जाने देंगे,
दानों से आँगन भर देंगे
और हौज में भर देंगे हम,
मीठा-मीठा ठंडा पानी।

शब्दार्थ *तिनके-घास के टुकड़े, महल-घर, हौज - कुंड, मटका (पानी का पात्र), आँगन- घर के आगे खुली जगह।*

संदर्भ/प्रसंग प्रस्तुत पंक्तियाँ हमारी पाठ्यपुस्तक 'वीणा भाग-1' में संकलित कविता 'बया हमारी चिड़िया रानी' से ली गई हैं। इसकी लेखिका महादेवी वर्मा जी हैं। इस कविता में उन्होंने बया के सुंदर घोंसले, उसके खाने-पीने तथा उसके प्रति अपने प्रेम का वर्णन किया है।

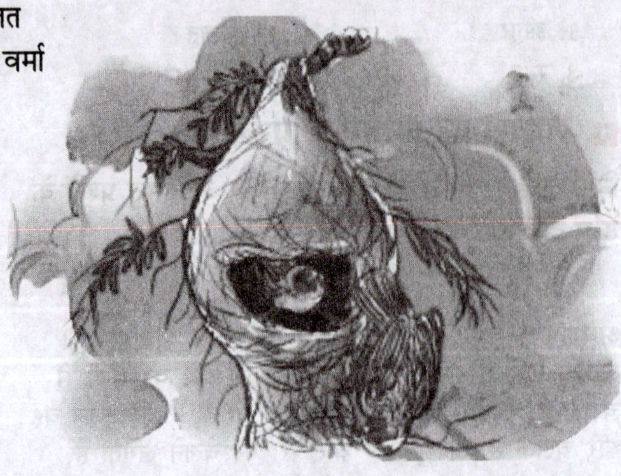

व्याख्या महादेवी जी कहती हैं कि बया छोटे-छोटे घास-फूस के तिनके लाकर अपना घर अर्थात् घोंसला बनाती है। वह अपने घोंसले को पेड़ की सबसे ऊँची डाली पर लटकाती है, जिससे उसके घोंसले को कोई नुकसान न पहुँचे। वह खेतों से दाना तथा नदियों से पीने के लिए पानी भी भरकर लाती है। इसलिए कवयित्री कहती हैं कि बया दानों और पानी के लिए दूर-दूर तक जाती है, लेकिन अब हम बया को दूर नहीं जाने देंगे। हम उसके घर के आँगन को ही दानों से भर देंगे और उसके पीने के लिए मटके में मीठा और ठंडा पानी भर देंगे।

काव्यांश 2

फिर अंडे सेयेगी तू जब
निकलेंगे नन्हें बच्चे तब,
हम आकर बारी-बारी से,
कर लेंगे उनकी निगरानी।

फिर जब उनके पर निकलेंगे,
उड़ जाएँगे बया बनेंगे,
हम सब तेरे पास रहेंगे,
तू मत रोना चिड़िया रानी।

शब्दार्थ *सेयेगी-अंडे से बच्चे बनने की प्रक्रिया, बारी-बारी से-क्रम से, निगरानी - देखभाल, पर-पंख।*

प्रसंग प्रस्तुत पंक्ति में महादेवी जी ने बया के अंडों और उसमें से निकलने वाले उसके बच्चों के बारे में बात की है।

व्याख्या कवयित्री कहती हैं कि बया जब अंडे सेयेगी और उसमें से नन्हें-नन्हें बच्चे निकलेंगे, तो हम बारी-बारी से उसके बच्चों की रक्षा करेंगे। कुछ समय बाद जब तुम्हारे बच्चों के पंख निकल आएँगे और वे तुम्हे छोड़कर उड़ जाएँगे, तब भी हम तुम्हारे पास ही रहेंगे, तुम्हें अकेला नहीं छोड़ेंगे, तुम बिल्कुल भी मत रोना।

बातचीत के लिए

1. चित्र में क्या-क्या दिखाई दे रहा है?

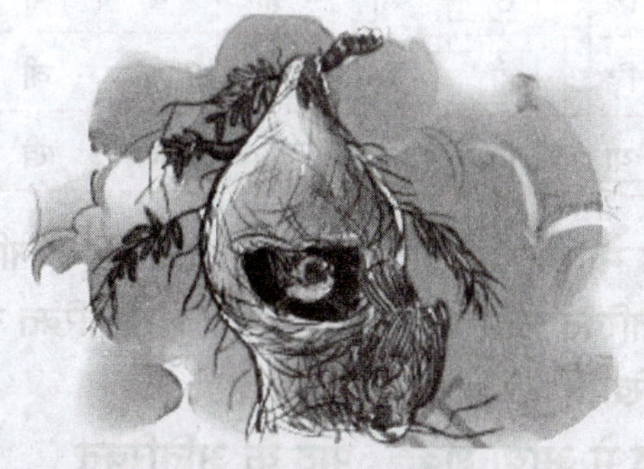

उत्तर चित्र में घोंसला, डाली, पत्तियाँ, चिड़िया और घोंसले के अंदर एक नन्हीं बया दिखाई दे रही है।

2. यह किस पक्षी का घोंसला है?

उत्तर यह बया पक्षी का घोंसला है।

3. आपके अनुसार घोंसले में बैठी बया क्या सोच रही होगी?

उत्तर घोंसले में बैठी बया सोच रही होगी कि वह भी जल्दी से बड़ी हो जाए और अपना घोंसला स्वयं बनाए।

4. चिड़िया अपना घर बनाने के लिए तिनके कहाँ से लाती होगी?

उत्तर चिड़िया अपना घर बनाने के लिए तिनके खेतों, मैदानों, झाड़ियों या पेड़ों के आस-पास से लाती होगी।

5. आपने किन-किन पक्षियों के घोंसले देखे हैं?

उत्तर मैंने चिड़िया, गौरैया और कबूतर का घोंसला देखा है।

सोचिए और लिखिए

1. बया रानी अपना घर तिनकों से बनाती है। हम अपना घर बनाते समय किन-किन वस्तुओं का उपयोग करते हैं? सोचकर लिखिए।

उत्तर हम अपना घर बनाते समय कई प्रकार की वस्तुओं का उपयोग करते हैं; जैसे—ईंट, सीमेंट, बालू, सरिया, लकड़ी, पत्थर, आदि।

2. पढ़िए समझिए और रिक्त स्थान की पूर्ति कीजिए।

बया के काम	आपके काम
दाना लाना	स्कूल के लिए तैयार होना
....	....
....	....
....	....

उत्तर

बया के काम	आपके काम
दाना लाना	स्कूल के लिए तैयार होना
घोंसला बनाना	नहाना, खाना
तिनके लाना	पढ़ाई करना
पानी लाना	खेलना

शब्दों का खेल

1. नीचे दिए गए शब्दों को उलटकर लिखिए और नए शब्दों का आनंद लीजिए।

नदी	दीन	खीरा	....
बस	....	नीरा	....
दबा	....	रीना	....

उत्तर नदी - दीन खीरा - राखी
बस - सब नीरा - रानी
दबा - बाद रीना - नारी

2. नीचे लिखे विपरीत अर्थ वाले शब्दों का मिलान कीजिए।

दूर	नीची
ऊँची	निकट
रोना	गर्म
ठंडा	हँसना

उत्तर दूर - निकट
ऊँची - नीची
रोना - हँसना
ठंडा - गर्म

3. नीचे दिए गए शब्दों में से तुक मिलने वाले शब्दों को ढूँढकर लिखिए।

> रानी, लाती, आकर, कहेंगे, जब, तिनके,
> तब, बनाती, रहेंगे, लाकर, पानी, जिनके

उत्तर (क) रानी - पानी
(ख) आकर - लाकर
(ग) जब - तब
(घ) लाती - बनाती
(ङ) कहेंगे - रहेंगे
(च) तिनके - जिनके

4. कविता को पढ़कर पंक्तियाँ पूरी कीजिए।

(क) तिनके लाकर .... लटकाती
(ख) तुझको दूर .... भर देंगे।

उत्तर (क) तिनके लाकर महल बनाती,
ऊँची डाली पर लटकाती।
(ख) तुझको दूर न जाने देंगे,
दानों से आँगन भर देंगे।

5. जब एक हो तो वह 'तिनका' कहलाता है और अनेक हों तो 'तिनके'। नीचे दिए गए एकवचन शब्दों के बहुवचन रूप लिखिए।

उत्तर

एकवचन	बहुवचन
तिनका	तिनके
दाना	दाने
अंडा	अंडे
बच्चा	बच्चे

खेल खेल में

1. कविता में आए शब्दों को खोजकर उन पर घेरा लगाइए।

उत्तर

दा	ना	सी	डा	ली	था	नि
पी	जी	खा	भू	ही	पे	ग
व	घी	ती	मैं	ऊँ	शा	रा
चि	ठं	डा	क्षी	ची	पा	नी
ड़ि	हौ	ज	धों	थे	वी	अं
या	ति	न	का	जा	खे	डा

2. पाठ में बया रानी नदियों से पानी लाती है। वह नदियों के अतिरिक्त कहाँ-कहाँ से पानी लाती होगी? रिक्त स्थान में लिखिए।

पाठ में आया शब्द	पाठ के अतिरिक्त
नदी	....

उत्तर

पाठ में आया शब्द	पाठ के अतिरिक्त
नदी	तालाब, नहर, झील, झरना, वर्षा का पानी, कुआँ।

3. अपनी मन पसंद चिड़िया का चित्र बनाइए उसमें रंग भरिए

उत्तर छात्र स्वयं करें।

4. आओ बया के लिए घर बनाएँ
केतकी बया के लिए घर बना रही है, उसे पहले क्या चाहिए क्या बाद में?

(क) केतकी ने बया के लिए बनाए घर पर रंग लीपा।

(ख) नन्हीं चिड़िया केतकी के बनाए घर में चली गई।

(ग) केतकी ने चिड़िया के घर को अपने दादाजी की मदद से पेड़ की डाली पर टाँग दिया।

(घ) केतकी ने सोचा उसे बया के लिए एक घर बनाना चाहिए।

(ङ) केतकी ने माँ से गत्ते, कील, कुछ कतरनें और कैंची माँगी।

(च) केतकी ने माँ की मदद से एक सुंदर घर बनाया।

उत्तर (घ) केतकी ने सोचा उसे बया के लिए एक घर बनाना चाहिए।

(ङ) केतकी ने माँ से गत्ते, कील कुछ कतरनें और कैंची माँगी।

(च) केतकी ने माँ की मदद से एक सुंदर घर बनाया।

(क) केतकी ने बया के लिए बनाए घर पर रंग लीपा।

(ग) केतकी ने चिड़िया के घर को अपने दादाजी की मदद से पेड़ की डाली पर टाँग दिया।

(ख) नन्हीं चिड़िया केतकी के बनाए घर में चली गई।

5. भूलभुलैया

चित्र में दी गई 'पक्षियों की भूलभुलैया' में घर ढूँढने में चिडिया के बच्चों की सहायता कीजिए।

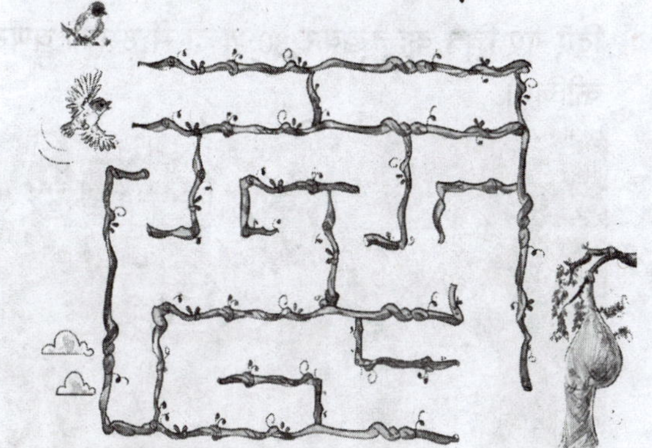

उत्तर छात्र स्वयं करें।

6. नीचे दिए गए चित्र को देखकर बताइए कि बया और इस बच्ची के बीच क्या बातचीत हो रही होगी?

उत्तर **बच्ची** नमस्ते! मैं रीना हूँ। आपसे जानना चाहती हूँ कि आप अपना घोंसला कैसे बनाती हो?

बया नमस्ते रीना! मैं अपना घोंसला दूर-दूर से तिनकों को चुनकर बनाती हूँ।

बूझो तो जानें

1. हरे वस्त्र और लाल चोंच है,
रटना जिसका काम।
कुतर-कुतरकर फल खाता है,
लेता हरि का नाम।

उत्तर तोता

2. कंठ सुरीला रंग से काली,
सबके मन को भाती।
बैठ पेड़ की डाल पर,
जो सबको गीत सुनाती।

उत्तर कोयल

3. बड़े सवेरे घर की छत पर,
मिलता गाँव-गाँव।
काले रंग का पक्षी होता,
करता काँव काँव।

उत्तर कौआ

अभ्यास प्रश्न

बहुविकल्पीय प्रश्न

1. बया तिनके लाकर क्या बनाती है?
(क) दीवार (ख) मंदिर
(ग) पुल (घ) घर

2. बया रानी दाना चुगने कहाँ जाती थी?
(क) खेतों में (ख) पहाड़ों पर
(ग) पेड़ों पर (घ) छत पर

3. बया घोंसले कहाँ लटकाती थी?
(क) ऊँची डाली पर (ख) दरवाजे पर
(ग) तार पर (घ) दीवार पर

4. बया पानी कहाँ से लाती थी?
(क) नदियों से (ख) घरों से
(ग) नलों से (घ) इनमें से कोई नहीं

5. अंडे कौन सेयेगा?
(क) बया (ख) कौवा (ग) गौरैया (घ) तोता

उत्तर

1. (घ) घर 2. (क) खेतों में
3. (क) ऊँची डाली पर 4. (क) नदियों से
5. (क) बया

काव्यांश पर आधारित प्रश्न

निम्नलिखित काव्यांश को पढ़कर उस पर आधारित प्रश्नों के उत्तर दीजिए।

काव्यांश

फिर अंडे सेयेगी तू जब
निकलेंगे नन्हें बच्चे तब,
हम आकर बारी-बारी से,
कर लेंगे उनकी निगरानी।
फिर जब उनके पर निकलेंगे,
उड़ जाएँगे बया बनेंगे,

1. प्रस्तुत काव्यांश में अंडे कौन देगी?
(क) बया (ख) बत्तख (ग) कोयल (घ) ये सभी

2. कुछ समय बाद किसके पंख निकल आएँगे?
(क) कोयल के बच्चों के (ख) मुर्गी के बच्चों के
(ग) बत्तख के बच्चों के (घ) बया के बच्चों के

3. काव्यांश में सेयेगी का क्या अर्थ है?

4. पर निकलने पर कौन उड़ जाएगा?

उत्तर

1. (क) बया 2. (घ) बया के बच्चों के
3. काव्यांश में सेयेगी का अर्थ अंडे से बच्चे बनने की प्रक्रिया है।
4. पर निकलने पर चिड़िया के बच्चे उड़ जाएँगे।

निम्नलिखित प्रश्नों के उत्तर दीजिए

1. बच्चे कब उड़ने के लिए तैयार हो जाएँगे?

उत्तर जब बच्चों के पर निकल आएँगे, तब वे उड़ने के लिए तैयार हो जाएँगे।

2. बया के अंडों से क्या निकलेंगे?

उत्तर बया के अंडों से बच्चे निकलेंगे।

3. मीठा-मीठा ठंडा पानी किसमें भरने की बात कही गई है?

उत्तर मीठा-मीठा ठंडा पानी हौज में भरने की बात कही गई है।

4. लेखिका किसको दूर नहीं जाने देना चाहती?

उत्तर लेखिका बया को दूर नहीं जाने देना चाहती।

लेखन संबंधी प्रश्न

1. दिए गए चित्र को देखकर 30 शब्दों में उसका वर्णन कीजिए।

उत्तर
- यह चित्र एक पाठशाला का है।
- इसमें चार बच्चे पाठशाला की सफाई कर रहे हैं। साथ में अध्यापक भी खड़े हैं, जो उन्हें काम करने के बारे में समझा रहे हैं।
- दो बच्चों ने सर पर पत्तों से भरी टोकरी रखी हुई है।
- एक लड़की झाड़ू से पत्ते इकट्ठे कर रही है।

आम का पेड़

पाठ का सार

गर्मियों के दिनों में सौरभ के चाचा जी ने सौरभ को अपने बगीचे के आमों की एक टोकरी भेजी। आम बहुत मीठे थे, जो सौरभ को बहुत पसंद आए। उसने अपने बगीचे में ऐसे ही मीठे आम का पेड़ लगाने की सोची। उसने अपने बगीचे में एक जगह मिट्टी खोदकर वहाँ आम की गुठली डाल दी और उसमें प्रतिदिन पानी डालने लगा। कुछ दिन बीत जाने के बाद भी जब आम का पौधा नहीं निकला तो सौरभ ने उदास होकर गड्ढे में पानी डालना बंद कर दिया।

एक दिन हल्की-हल्की बारिश हो रही थी। वह टहलते-टहलते अपने बगीचे में जा पहुँचा और उसने उसी जगह पर लाल-लाल कोंपलों वाला एक पौधा उगा देखा। यह देखकर सौरभ बहुत खुश हुआ और अपनी बहन प्रिया को वहाँ बुला लाया। पौधा देखकर प्रिया भी बहुत खुश हो गई।

वे दोनों खुशी से भागते हुए पिताजी के पास गए। पिताजी ने खुश होने का कारण पूछा तो प्रिया ने बताया कि पिताजी बगीचे में आम का पौधा निकल आया है। अगले वर्ष हम इसी पेड़ के आम खाएँगे। पिताजी हँसे और बच्चों को बताया कि एक पेड़ तैयार होने में चार से पाँच वर्ष का समय लगता है।

पिताजी की बात सुनकर प्रिया उदास हो जाती है, लेकिन सौरभ तुरंत बोल पड़ता है कि हम पौधे की देखभाल करेंगे और एक दिन जब यह फल देगा, तब हम जरूर खाएँगे। इसी के साथ पाठ का अंत हो जाता है।

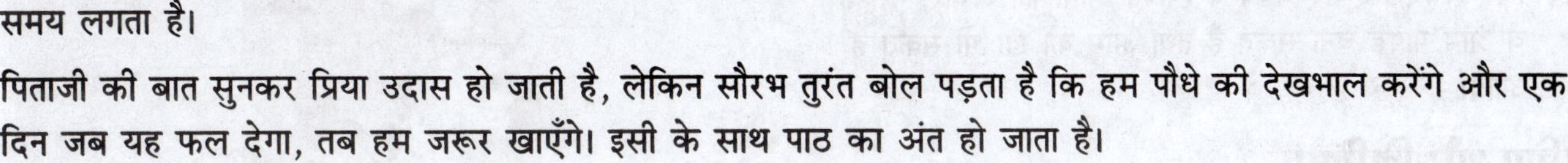

शब्दार्थ

गुठली-फल के अंदर का भाग, कोंपल-वृक्ष की नई एवं कोमल पत्ती, प्रसन्न-खुशी, शाखाएँ-टहनियाँ, उदास-दु:खी।

NCERT फोल्डर

बातचीत के लिए

1. आपको कौन-सा फल बहुत अच्छा लगता है? वह फल आपको क्यों पसंद है?

उत्तर मुझे लीची सबसे ज्यादा अच्छी लगती है, क्योंकि इसका रंग बहुत सुंदर होता है और यह स्वाद में भी सबसे अच्छी होती है।

2. आपके घर या विद्यालय में कौन-से पेड़-पौधे लगे हैं? उनकी देखभाल कौन करता है?

उत्तर हमारे घर में आम और जामुन का पेड़ लगा है और उनकी देखभाल मेरे पिताजी करते हैं। हमारे विद्यालय में पपीते का पेड़ है, जिसकी देखभाल माली काका करते हैं।

3. चित्र में कुछ आम धरती पर गिरे पड़े हैं। आम पेड़ के नीचे क्यों गिर गए होंगे?

उत्तर आम अधिक पक जाने के कारण अथवा तेज हवा चलने के कारण गिर गए होंगे।

4. चित्र में दिखाए गए बच्चे और व्यक्ति आमों का क्या करेंगे?

उत्तर चित्र में दिखाए गए बच्चे व व्यक्ति आमों का अचार, मुरब्बा व आम पापड़ बना सकते हैं तथा आम को खा भी सकते हैं आदि।

सोचिए और लिखिए

1. सौरभ के चाचा जी ने सौरभ को किस मौसम में आम भेजे?

उत्तर सौरभ के चाचा ने सौरभ को गर्मियों में आम भेजे थे।

2. आम खाकर सौरभ के मन में क्या विचार आया?

उत्तर आम खाकर सौरभ के मन में विचार आया कि वह भी मीठे आम का पेड़ अपने बगीचे में लगाएगा।

3. सौरभ ने पानी डालना क्यों बंद कर दिया? क्या उसे ऐसा करना चाहिए था?

उत्तर प्रतिदिन पानी डालने पर जब आम का पौधा नहीं निकला तो सौरभ ने पानी डालना बंद कर दिया। नहीं, सौरभ को ऐसा नहीं करना चाहिए था।

4. सौरभ और उसकी बहन क्यों प्रसन्न थे?

उत्तर सौरभ और उसकी बहन इसलिए प्रसन्न थे, क्योंकि आम का पौधा निकल आया था।

5. पिताजी ने आम के पौधे के बारे में सौरभ और उसकी बहन को कौन-सी बात बताई?

उत्तर पिताजी ने बताया कि आम के पौधे को वृक्ष बनने में चार से पाँच वर्ष लगते हैं।

आपका अनुमान, किसने क्या कहा?

1. नीचे कहानी से जुड़े कुछ चित्र दिए गए हैं। चित्र में दिख रहे पात्र आपस में क्या बात कर रहे होंगे? अनुमान लगाकर लिखिए।

उत्तर **प्रिया** देखो पौधा निकल आया

सौरभ यह पौधा मैंने लगाया है। इसमें खूब आम लगेंगे।

सौरभ चाचा जी आपके आम बहुत मीठे और स्वादिष्ट थे।

चाचाजी मुझे पता है कि तुम्हें आम बहुत पसंद हैं, इसलिए मैंने अपने बगीचे के आम भिजवाए थे।

प्रिया आपका धन्यवाद चाचा जी! हम सबने मीठे आम खाए।

आइए पौधा लगाएँ

1. यहाँ बहुत-सी वस्तुओं के चित्र बने हैं। उन वस्तुओं पर घेरा बनाइए, जो पौधा लगाने के काम आती हैं।

उत्तर

गुठली की बुआई का क्रम

2. सौरभ आम की गुठली बो रहा है। क्रम से बताइए कि उसने पहले क्या किया होगा?

(क) धरती पर पानी डाला।
(ख) खुरपी से धरती में गड्ढा खोदा।
(ग) गुठली बोने के लिए अपनी माँ से सही स्थान का सुझाव माँगा।
(घ) माता-पिता से गुठली बोने की इच्छा बताई।
(ङ) बाल्टी में पानी लेकर आया।
(च) माताजी से गुठली बोने की जानकारी ली।
(छ) गड्ढे में गुठली डालकर उस पर मिट्टी डाली
(ज) गड्ढे में खाद डाली।

उत्तर (घ) माता-पिता से गुठली बोने की इच्छा बताई।
(च) माताजी से गुठली बोने की जानकारी ली।
(ग) गुठली बोने के लिए अपनी माँ से सही स्थान का सुझाव माँगा।
(ख) खुरपी से धरती में गड्ढा खोदा।
(ज) गड्ढे में खाद डाली।
(छ) गड्ढे में गुठली डालकर उस पर मिट्टी डाली।
(ङ) बाल्टी में पानी लेकर आया।
(क) धरती पर पानी डाला

सौरभ और प्रिया के बगीचे की सैर

3. आइए, सौरभ और प्रिया के बगीचे की सैर करते हैं। पता लगाते हैं कि वहाँ क्या-क्या है? चित्र देखकर पेड़ों को पहचानिए और उनके नाम लिखिए।

उत्तर नीम केला जामुन अमरूद कटहल

4. सौरभ और प्रिया ने फल, साग और अनाज के नाम की सूची बनाई है। आइए सही टोकरी में सही वस्तु रखते हैं।

आम, करेला, गेहूँ, सेब, ककड़ी, आलू, बाजरा, मूली, पपीता, लौकी, चावल, लीची, केला, बैंगन, गाजर, अनार, मकई, पालक

उत्तर

फल	अनाज	सब्जी
आम	गेहूँ	करेला
सेब	बाजरा	ककड़ी
पपीता	चावल	आलू
लीची	मकई	मूली
केला		लौकी
अनार		बैंगन
		गाजर
		पालक

फल की टोकरी अनाज की टोकरी सब्जी की टोकरी

5. **मेरे विद्यालय में पेड़-पौधे**

(क) आपके विद्यालय में कौन-कौन से पेड़-पौधे लगे हैं? पता लगाइए और उनकी सूची बनाइए।

उत्तर हमारे विद्यालय में आम, नीम, बरगद, गुलाब के पौधे, गेंदे के पौधे, जामुन आदि हैं।

(ख) विद्यालय के पेड़-पौधों की देखभाल के लिए आप और आपके सहपाठी क्या योगदान देते हैं? लिखिए।

उत्तर विद्यालय के पेड़-पौधे की देखभाल के लिए मैं और मेरे सहपाठी पूरा ध्यान देते हैं कि कोई शरारती बच्चा पेड़-पौधे को बिना किसी कारण के तोड़े नहीं तथा समय मिलने पर हम उन्हें पानी भी देते हैं।

भाषा की बात

1. कहानी के अनुसार विशेषता लिखिए।

उत्तर

मीठे – आम

नन्हा – पौधा

छोटी – बहन

बड़ी-बड़ी – शाखाएँ

मोटा – तना

लाल-लाल – कोंपलें

2. कौन-सा पौधा लगाएँगे?

आप अपने बगीचे या गमले में कौन-सा पौधा लगाना चाहेंगे?

मैं अपने बगीचे या गमले में ·········· का पौधा लगाना चाहूँगी/चाहूँगा, क्योंकि ····························

उत्तर मैं अपने बगीचे या गमले में चम्पा का पौधा लगाना चाहूँगी/चाहूँगा, क्योंकि चम्पा से बहुत अच्छी खुशबू आती है और वह मेरी मम्मी का मनपसंद फूल है।

3. सौरभ ने आम की गुठली बोई। नीचे दी गई तालिका को पूरा कीजिए।

उत्तर

गुठली वाले फल	बिना गुठली वाले फल
आम	केला
लीची	अंगूर
जामुन	अनार
बेर	संतरा
खजूर	सेब
आड़ू	पपीता

4. काम और नाम वाले शब्द

कहानी में से काम और नाम वाले शब्द छाँटकर लिखिए।

उत्तर

काम वाले शब्द	नाम वाले शब्द
खोदना	चाचाजी
भेजना	सौरभ
लगाना	प्रिया
डालना	आम
बोलना	पिताजी

5. चाचा जी के प्रति सौरभ का आभार

सौरभ के चाचा जी ने उसके लिए मीठे-मीठे आम भेजे हैं। सौरभ उन्हें धन्यवाद कहना चाहता है। सौरभ को उन्हें क्या संदेश लिखना चाहिए?

उत्तर आदरणीय चाचा जी,

सादर प्रणाम।

मुझे आपके द्वारा भेजे गए आम मिले। आम बहुत ही मीठे और स्वादिष्ट थे। हम सबने मिलकर आम खाए। मैंने एक गुठली अपने बगीचे में भी लगा दी। कुछ सालों बाद मेरे बगीचे में भी मीठे आम का पेड़ होगा। जब आप आएँगे तो हम सब मिलकर आम का मजा लेंगे। आम भेजने के लिए आपका बहुत-बहुत धन्यवाद।

खेल-खेल में

नीचे दिए गए भूलभुलैया के खेल में एक फल को दूसरे फल से मिलाते हुए भूलभुलैया से बाहर निकलने में प्रिया की सहायता कीजिए।

सेब	भिंडी	केला	तोरी	नींबू
तरबूज	आम	पपीता	खरबूजा	आलू
पेठा	करेला	घीया	अनार	कद्दू
शिमला मिर्च	अरबी	बैंगन	आलूबुखारा	अनानास
कटहल	हरी मिर्च	लहसुन	अदरक	अंगूर

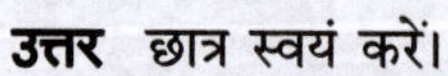

उत्तर छात्र स्वयं करें।

कला की कलाकारियाँ

1. नीचे दिया गया पेड़ का चित्र हाथ की छाप और उँगलियों की सहायता से बनाया गया है। आप भी अपने हाथ की छाप और उँगलियों की सहायता से ऐसा एक पेड़ बनाने का प्रयास कीजिए।

उत्तर छात्र स्वयं करें।

खोजें–जानें

1. **आम के प्रकार**

   आपने आम के विभिन्न प्रकार के नाम सुने होंगे–दशहरी, सिंदूरी, चौसा आदि। घर के बड़ों से पूछकर कुछ और नाम पता करके लिखिए।

उत्तर हाफूस, तोतापरी, मलीहाबादी, केसर आदि।

बूझो तो जानें

1. लाल-लाल डिबिया के अंदर,
   छोटे-छोटे पीले खाने।
   इन खानों के भीतर है,
   सफेद लाल मोती के दाने।

उत्तर अनार

2. ऊपर से तो है हरा,
   अंदर से है लाल।
   उतना मीठा रस भरा।
   जितनी मीठी खाल।

उत्तर तरबूज

अभ्यास प्रश्न

बहुविकल्पीय प्रश्न

1. चाचा जी ने सौरभ के लिए क्या भेजे?
   (क) आम (ख) केला
   (ग) पपीता (घ) अनार
2. आम का स्वाद कैसा था?
   (क) खट्टा (ख) कच्चा (ग) मीठा (घ) कड़वा
3. सौरभ की बहन का क्या नाम था?
   (क) रजनी (ख) प्रिया
   (ग) अंकिता (घ) दिव्या
4. सौरभ प्रतिदिन क्या करता था?
   (क) धूप देता था (ख) हवा देता था
   (ग) भोजन देता था (घ) पानी देता था
5. आम का पौधा बगीचे में किसने लगाया था?
   (क) सौरभ ने (ख) प्रिया ने
   (ग) पिताजी ने (घ) चाचा जी ने

उत्तर 1. (क) आम 2. (ग) मीठा 3. (ख) प्रिया 4. (घ) पानी देता था 5. (क) सौरभ ने

सत्य–असत्य

नीचे दिए गए वाक्यों में से सत्य या असत्य कथन की पहचान कीजिए।

1. सौरभ को आम दादाजी ने भेजे थे। (सत्य/असत्य)
2. आम का पेड़ सौरभ की बहन प्रिया ने लगाया था। (सत्य/असत्य)
3. सौरभ ने अपने बगीचे में गुठली बोई थी। (सत्य/असत्य)
4. सौरभ ने पौधे को पानी डालना बंद कर दिया था। (सत्य/असत्य)

उत्तर 1. असत्य 2. असत्य 3. सत्य 4. सत्य

रिक्त स्थान

नीचे दिए गए वाक्यों में रिक्त स्थान की पूर्ति उचित शब्द से कीजिए।

(प्रसन्न, गुठली, सौरभ, गर्मियों)

1. पौधा देखते ही सौरभ ········ हो उठा।
2. ········ के दिन थे।
3. ········ को आम बहुत अच्छे लगे।
4. वहाँ आम की एक ········ डाल दी।

उत्तर 1. प्रसन्न 2. गर्मियों 3. सौरभ 4. गुठली

गद्यांश पर आधारित प्रश्न

निम्नलिखित गद्यांश को पढ़कर उस पर आधारित प्रश्नों के उत्तर दीजिए।

गद्यांश

यह देखकर सौरभ बहुत खुश हुआ और अपनी बहन प्रिया को वहाँ बुला लाया। पौधा देखकर प्रिया भी बहुत खुश हो गई।

वे दोनों खुशी से भागते हुए पिताजी के पास गए। पिताजी ने खुश होने का कारण पूछा तो प्रिया ने बताया कि पिताजी बगीचे में आम का पौधा निकल आया है। अगले वर्ष हम इसी पेड़ के आम खाएँगे।

पिताजी हँसे और बच्चों को बताया कि एक पेड़ तैयार होने में चार से पाँच वर्ष का समय लगता है। पिताजी की बात सुनकर प्रिया उदास हो जाती है, लेकिन सौरभ तुरंत बोल पड़ता है कि हम पौधे की देखभाल करेंगे और एक दिन जब यह फल देगा, तब हम जरूर खाएँगे।

1. प्रिया किसे देखकर खुश हो गई थी?
   (क) पौधा (ख) पेड़
   (ग) फल (घ) शेर
2. सौरभ और प्रिया भागकर किसके पास गए थे?
   (क) पिताजी (ख) माताजी
   (ग) चाचाजी (घ) दादाजी
3. प्रिया के खुश होने का क्या कारण था?
4. पौधे की देखभाल की बात कौन कहता है?

उत्तर

1. (क) पौधा
2. (क) पिताजी
3. प्रिया के खुश होने का कारण बगीचे में आम का पौधा निकलना था।
4. पौधे की देखभाल की बात सौरभ कहता है।

निम्नलिखित प्रश्नों के उत्तर दीजिए

1. **सौरभ बगीचे में किसे देखकर प्रसन्न हो गया?**

उत्तर सौरभ बगीचे में लाल-लाल कोंपलों वाला नन्हा-सा पौधा देखकर प्रसन्न हो गया।

2. **सौरभ अपनी बहन का हाथ पकड़कर कहाँ ले गया?**

उत्तर सौरभ अपनी बहन का हाथ पकड़कर बगीचे में ले गया।

3. **एक पौधा कितने वर्षों में पेड़ बनकर तैयार होता है?**

उत्तर एक पौधा चार से पाँच वर्षों में पेड़ बनकर तैयार होता है।

4. **पिताजी ने बच्चों को पौधे के बारे में क्या बताया?**

उत्तर पिताजी ने बच्चों को बताया कि छोटे से पौधे को बड़ा होने में चार-पाँच वर्ष लगते हैं। बड़े होने पर इनका तना मोटा होगा एवं बड़ी-बड़ी शाखाएँ होंगी।

5. **दो मीठे फल व दो खट्टे फलों के नाम लिखिए।**

उत्तर आम और केला मीठे फल होते हैं। संतरा व आँवला खट्ठे फल होते हैं।

लेखन संबंधी प्रश्न

1. **'माँ' पर 5 वाक्य बनाकर लिखिए।**

उत्तर
- मेरी माताजी का नाम राजरानी है।
- मेरी माताजी मुझे बहुत प्यार करती हैं।
- मैं अपनी माँ के साथ रोज पार्क में घूमने जाता हूँ।
- मेरी माताजी बहुत अच्छा खाना बनाती हैं।
- मैं भी माताजी को बहुत प्यार करता हूँ।

बीरबल की खिचड़ी

पाठ का सार

अकबर के दरबार में अनेक विद्वान थे। बीरबल उनके दरबार में अपनी चतुराई के लिए बहुत प्रसिद्ध थे। कभी-कभी चतुराई में वे अकबर को भी हरा देते थे। एक बार अकबर सर्दी के दिनों में किसी गाँव से जा रहे थे। उन्होंने देखा कि गाँव के कुछ लोग आग जलाकर उसके चारों तरफ बैठकर बातें कर रहे थे। बादशाह अपने साथियों के साथ वहाँ पहुँचे, उनमें से एक व्यक्ति कह रहा था कि मैं यमुना के पानी में रात भर खड़ा रह सकता हूँ।

अकबर ने उसकी बातें सुनीं और कहा कि यदि तुम ऐसा करोगे तो मैं तुम्हें थैली भर मोहरें इनाम में दूँगा। अगली रात वह व्यक्ति सारी रात यमुना के ठंडे पानी में खड़ा रहा। सुबह वह दरबार में आया तो अकबर ने आश्चर्य से पूछा कि तुम इतनी देर पानी में कैसे खड़े रहे? उस व्यक्ति ने कहा, ''महाराज आपके राजमहल से दीपक का प्रकाश आ रहा था। मैं उसे देखकर सारी रात पानी में खड़ा रहा।'' अकबर ने कहा तुम्हें कोई इनाम नहीं दिया जाएगा, क्योंकि तुम मेरे दीपक की गरमी के कारण सर्दी से बच सके। वह व्यक्ति उदास होकर चला गया। बीरबल को लगा कि उस व्यक्ति की मदद करनी चाहिए।

दूसरे दिन बीरबल दरबार नहीं आए। अकबर को चिंता हुई कि कहीं बीरबल बीमार तो नहीं हो गए। अकबर के बुलावा भेजने पर बीरबल ने कहा कि बादशाह से कह दो मैं अभी खिचड़ी पका रहा हूँ। खिचड़ी पकने के बाद दरबार में उपस्थित हो जाऊँगा। बीरबल को दूसरे दिन भी दरबार में न देखकर अकबर स्वयं यह पता करने गए कि बीरबल कैसी खिचड़ी बना रहे हैं। जब अकबर बीरबल के यहाँ पहुँचे तो देखा कि एक लंबे बाँस पर काठ की हाँडी लटकी थी और हाँडी से बहुत नीचे जमीन पर आग जल रही थी। अकबर ने हैरान होकर पूछा कि ''बीरबल आखिर यह खिचड़ी कैसे पकेगी? हाँडी तो आग से बहुत दूर है।'' बीरबल ने कहा, ''जब वह व्यक्ति राजमहल के दीपक की गरमी के सहारे सारी रात ठंडे पानी में खड़ा रह सकता है, तो इस आग से मेरी खिचड़ी क्यों नहीं पक सकती?'' अकबर को सब बात समझ आ गई। फिर अगले दिन अकबर ने उस व्यक्ति को दरबार में बुलाकर उसे मोहरों की थैली भेंट की। इसी के साथ पाठ का अंत हो जाता है।

शब्दार्थ

आश्चर्य–हैरानी, सम्मान–इज्जत, प्रसिद्ध–मशहूर, भेंट–उपहार, हाँडी–मिट्टी का बर्तन, मोहरें–सिक्के, चाव–रुचि।

बातचीत के लिए

1. **आप सर्दी को कम करने के लिए क्या-क्या उपाय करते हैं?**

उत्तर हम सर्दी से बचने के लिए गर्म कपड़े पहनते हैं, आग व हीटर जलाते हैं, कंबल व रजाई ओढ़ते हैं और धूप लेते हैं।

2. **अपने द्वारा किए गए सबसे कठिन कार्य का अनुभव बताइए।**

उत्तर जब मैं एक बार दादीजी के घर गई थी, तो वहाँ मैं लकड़ी की सीढ़ियों से छत पर चढ़ी थी। लकड़ी की सीढ़ियों के सहारे छत पर चढ़ना एक कठिन कार्य है।

3. **आपके अनुसार पकाने के लिए बर्तन से आग कितनी दूर होनी चाहिए?**

उत्तर किसी भी सामान को पकाने के लिए बर्तन और आग एक-दूसरे को स्पर्श (छूना) करते हुए होने चाहिए।

4. **क्या आपने कभी खिचड़ी खाई है? क्या आपको पता है कि इसे कैसे बनाया जाता है?**

उत्तर हाँ, मैंने खिचड़ी खाई है। खिचड़ी बनाने के लिए सबसे पहले गैस जलाएँगे, फिर उस पर एक गहरा बर्तन रखेंगे। उसमें पानी डालेंगे, फिर उसमें चावल, दाल, हल्दी, नमक आदि डालेंगे तथा उसे तब तक उबालेंगे जब तक सब कुछ अच्छे से मिल न जाए, इस प्रकार खिचड़ी तैयार हो जाती है।

सोचिए और लिखिए

1. **बीरबल किसलिए प्रसिद्ध थे?**

उत्तर बीरबल अपनी चतुराई के लिए प्रसिद्ध थे।

2. **वह व्यक्ति पानी में पूरी रात कैसे खड़ा रहा?**

उत्तर वह व्यक्ति राजमहल के दीपक के प्रकाश को देखता हुआ पानी में पूरी रात खड़ा रहा।

3. **बादशाह को उस व्यक्ति की बात पर क्यों आश्चर्य हुआ?**

उत्तर बादशाह को लगा कि इतनी ठंड में उसका सारी रात पानी में खड़े रहना असंभव था, इसलिए बादशाह को आश्चर्य हुआ।

4. **बादशाह ने अगले दिन उस व्यक्ति को इनाम क्यों नहीं दिया?**

उत्तर बादशाह को लगा कि वह व्यक्ति पूरी रात राजमहल में जल रहे दीपक की गर्मी के सहारे ठंडे पानी में खड़ा रहा, इसलिए बादशाह ने उसे इनाम नहीं दिया।

5. **बीरबल ने उस व्यक्ति की सहायता कैसे की?**

उत्तर बीरबल ने आग और बर्तन दोनों को दूर-दूर रखकर खिचड़ी पकाने की प्रक्रिया द्वारा बादशाह को उनकी गलती का अहसास दिलाकर उस व्यक्ति की सहायता की।

भाषा की बात

1. **पढ़िए, समझिए और चिह्नित शब्दों के विपरीत शब्द लिखिए।**

जब बादशाह बीरबल के यहाँ पहुँचे तो उन्होंने देखा कि एक लंबे बाँस के ऊपरी सिरे पर एक हाँडी लटकी हुई है। हाँडी से बहुत नीचे भूमि पर बहुत थोड़ी-सी आग जल रही है। बादशाह ने हैरानी से पूछा, "बीरबल! भला यह खिचड़ी कैसे पक सकती है? हाँडी तो आग से बहुत दूर है।"

उदाहरण लंबे-छोटे

उत्तर

एक	अनेक
नीचे	ऊपर
बहुत	कम
दूर	पास

2. **वाक्य को सही करके लिखिए**

उदाहरण अकबर के दरबार अनेक विद्वान थे।

अकबर के दरबार में अनेक विद्वान थे।

(क) अकबर और बीरबल के बारे अनेक कहानियाँ प्रसिद्ध हैं।

उत्तर अकबर और बीरबल के बारे में अनेक कहानियाँ प्रसिद्ध हैं।

(ख) गाँव लोग आग जलाकर उसके चारों ओर बैठे बातें कर रहे थे।

उत्तर गाँव के लोग आग जलाकर उसके चारों ओर बैठे बातें कर रहे थे।

(ग) उन्होंने सोचा इस दुःखी व्यक्ति सहायता करनी चाहिए।

उत्तर उन्होंने सोचा इस दुःखी व्यक्ति की सहायता करनी चाहिए।

(घ) बीरबल कहलवाया कि मैं खिचड़ी पका रहा हूँ, पक जाने पर दरबार में उपस्थित हो जाऊँगा।

उत्तर बीरबल ने कहलवाया कि मैं खिचड़ी पका रहा हूँ, पक जाने पर दरबार में उपस्थित हो जाऊँगा।

3. वर्ग पहेली में खाने की वस्तुएँ ढूँढकर उन पर घेरा लगाइए।

उत्तर

व	ड़ा	इ	छा	छ	सां
दो	सा	ड	ढा	बा	भ
खा	ना	ली	छो	ले	र
रा	ज	मा	चा	व	ल
दा	ल	बा	टी	क	ढ़ी
पा	य	स	चू	र	मा

कहानी की बात

(क) "तुम इतनी सर्दी में सारी रात पानी में कैसे खड़े रहे?"

किसने कहा ....

किससे कहा ....

(ख) "चलो स्वयं ही चलकर देखें कि बीरबल कैसी खिचड़ी पका रहे हैं?"

किसने कहा ....

किससे कहा ....

उत्तर (क) अकबर ने, व्यक्ति से   (ख) अकबर ने, मंत्री से

जीवों एवं वस्तुओं की विशेषताएँ

ध्यानपूर्वक पढ़िए व समझिए

(क) लंगूर की पूँछ लंबी है।.......

(ख) वह लाल गुलाब है।.........

(ग) चिड़िया छोटी है।..........

(घ) बस का आकार बड़ा है..........

1. ऊपर दिए गए वाक्यों को आपने भली प्रकार समझ लिया। अब दिए गए वाक्यों में विशेषता बताने वाले शब्द भरिए।

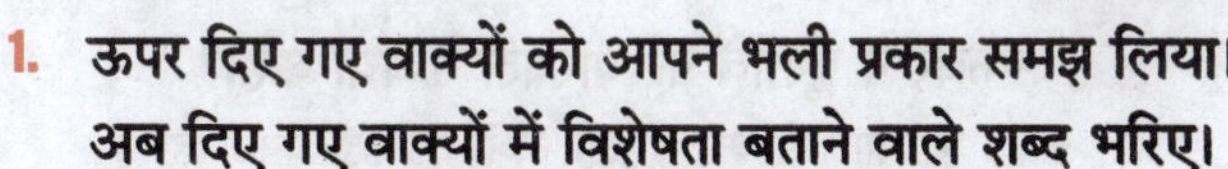

मीठा, साहसी, अच्छा, हरी, लंबा

(क) पीहू एक .... लड़की है।

(ख) गौरव अपने साथियों में सबसे .... है।

(ग) पेड़ की पत्तियाँ .... हैं।

(घ) अदम्य एक .... लड़का है।

(ङ) आम बहुत .... है।

उत्तर (क) साहसी   (ख) लंबा   (ग) हरी

(घ) अच्छा   (ङ) मीठा

2. नीचे लिखे शब्दों में से जो सही शब्द हैं, उनमें रंग भरिए।

(क) सूबह   सुबह

(ख) वर्षा   वरसा

(ग) सवेरा   सुवेरा

(घ) सुझ-भूझ   सूझ-बूझ

उत्तर (क) सुबह   (ख) वर्षा

(ग) सवेरा   (घ) सूझ-बूझ

• छात्र गोले में रंग अपनी पसंद के अनुसार भरें।

आइए कुछ बनाएँ

1. आइए आज एक स्वादिष्ट व्यंजन बनाते हैं, जिसका नाम है– चटपटी भेलपुरी। इसके लिए आपको जो सामग्री चाहिए वह है

- मुरमुरे (एक कटोरी)
- बारीक कटा प्याज (एक)
- बारीक कटा टमाटर (एक छोटा)
- बारीक कटा खीरा (एक छोटा टुकड़ा)
- बारीक कटी हरी मिर्च (एक)
- नींबू का रस (आधा)
- नमक (स्वाद के अनुसार)
- चाट मसाला (छोटा चम्मच)
- अमचूर (एक चुटकी)
- धनिया पत्ती (सजावट के लिए)

इसको मिलाइए और चटपटी भेलपुरी बाँटकर आनंद से खाएँ।

उत्तर छात्र स्वयं करें।

पता कीजिए

1. इस कहानी में यमुना नदी का जिक्र किया गया है। भारत की कुछ और नदियों के बारे में पता कीजिए तथा उनका नाम लिखिए।

यमुना   गंगा

....

....

....

उत्तर यमुना   गंगा

सरस्वती   कावेरी

कोसी   भागीरथी

गंडक   ताप्ती

झटपट कहिए

चार छाते छाते चार
चारों चक्कर खाएँ
चार-चार के आठ
आठ के चार चक्कर
खाएँ चारम चार

(छात्र झटपट कहने का प्रयास स्वयं करें)

आइए सुनें कहानी

बीरबल की तरह एक और विद्वान तेनालीराम भी अपनी चतुराई के लिए बहुत प्रसिद्ध थे। उनके बारे में पता कीजिए और उनके किस्से पढ़कर कक्षा में अपने साथियों को सुनाइए।

उत्तर छात्र स्वयं करें।

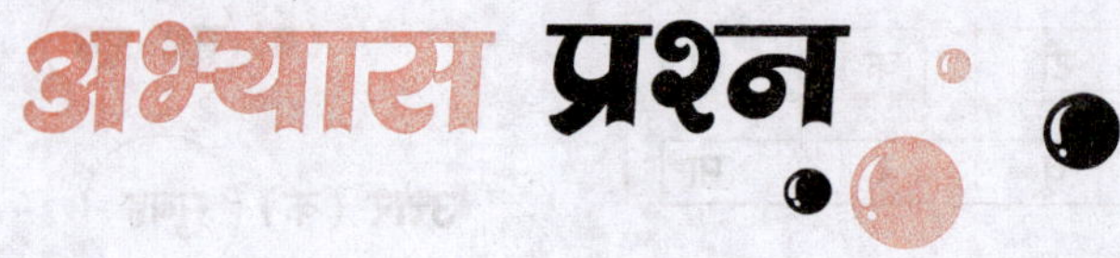

अभ्यास प्रश्न

बहुविकल्पीय प्रश्न

1. बीरबल किसके दरबार के विद्वान थे?

(क) अकबर के (ख) अबुल के
(ग) तानसेन के (घ) फजल के

2. बीरबल अपनी किस आदत के लिए प्रसिद्ध थे?

(क) चतुराई (ख) दुष्टता
(ग) कामचोर (घ) चालाक

3. गाँव के लोग क्या जलाकर बैठे थे?

(क) आग (ख) दीपक
(ग) लालटेन (घ) लाइट

4. व्यक्ति क्या देखकर सारी रात यमुना के ठंडे पानी में खड़ा रहा?

(क) लालटेन (ख) चाँद
(ग) तारे (घ) राजमहल का दीपक

5. अकबर को किसकी चिंता हुई?

(क) उस व्यक्ति की (ख) मोहरों की
(ग) बीरबल के न आने की (घ) दरबार की

उत्तर

1. (क) अकबर के 2. (क) चतुराई
3. (क) आग 4. (घ) राजमहल का दीपक
5. (ग) बीरबल के न आने की

गद्यांश पर आधारित प्रश्न

निम्नलिखित गद्यांश को पढ़कर उस पर आधारित प्रश्नों के उत्तर दीजिए।

गद्यांश

दूसरे दिन बीरबल दरबार नहीं आए। अकबर को चिंता हुई कि कहीं बीरबल बीमार तो नहीं हो गए। अकबर के बुलावा भेजने पर बीरबल ने कहा कि बादशाह से कह दो मैं अभी खिचड़ी पका रहा हूँ। खिचड़ी पकने के बाद दरबार में उपस्थित हो जाऊँगा। बीरबल को दूसरे दिन भी दरबार में न देखकर अकबर स्वयं यह पता करने गए कि बीरबल कैसी खिचड़ी बना रहे हैं। जब अकबर बीरबल के यहाँ पहुँचे तो देखा कि एक लंबे बाँस पर काठ की हाँडी लटकी थी और हाँडी से बहुत नीचे जमीन पर आग जल रही थी।

अकबर ने हैरान होकर पूछा कि "बीरबल आखिर यह खिचड़ी कैसे पकेगी? हाँडी तो आग से बहुत दूर है।" बीरबल ने कहा, "जब वह व्यक्ति राजमहल के दीपक की गरमी के सहारे सारी रात ठंडे पानी में खड़ा रह सकता है, तो इस आग से मेरी खिचड़ी क्यों नहीं पक सकती?"

अकबर को सब बात समझ आ गई। फिर अगले दिन अकबर ने उस व्यक्ति को दरबार में बुलाकर उसे मोहरों की थैली भेंट की।

1. बीरबल के न आने पर अकबर को क्या चिंता हुई?

(क) कहीं बीरबल सो तो नहीं रहे
(ख) कहीं बीरबल बीमार तो नहीं हो गए
(ग) कहीं बीरबल खो तो नहीं गए
(घ) कहीं बीरबल मर तो नहीं गए

2. अकबर ने बुलावे पर बीरबल ने क्या कहा?

(क) बादशाह से कह दो, मैं अभी खिचड़ी पका रहा हूँ
(ख) बादशाह से कह दो, मैं नहीं आ रहा हूँ
(ग) बादशाह से कह दो, मैं सो रहा हूँ
(घ) उपरोक्त में से कोई नहीं

3. दूसरे दिन भी बीरबल को दरबार में न देखकर अकबर ने क्या किया?

4. जब अकबर बीरबल के यहाँ पहुँचे तो उन्होंने क्या देखा?

उत्तर

1. (ख) कहीं बीरबल बीमार तो नहीं हो गए
2. (क) बादशाह से कह दो, मैं अभी खिचड़ी पका रहा हूँ
3. दूसरे दिन भी बीरबल को दरबार में न देखकर अकबर स्वयं बीरबल का पता लगाने चल दिए।
4. अकबर ने देखा कि एक लंबे बाँस पर काठ की हांडी लटकी थी। हाँडी से बहुत नीचे आग जल रही थी।

निम्नलिखित प्रश्नों के उत्तर दीजिए

1. बीरबल अपनी चतुराई से किसे हरा देते थे?

उत्तर बीरबल अपनी चतुराई से बादशाह को भी हरा देते थे।

2. बादशाह जब गाँव से गुजर रहे थे, तो एक व्यक्ति क्या कह रहा था?

उत्तर बादशाह जब गाँव से गुजर रहे थे, तो एक आदमी कह रहा था कि मैं यमुना के पानी में रातभर खड़ा रह सकता हूँ।

3. बीरबल खिचड़ी किसमें पका रहे थे?

उत्तर बीरबल खिचड़ी हाँडी में पका रहे थे।

4. अकबर को किस बात का विश्वास नहीं हुआ?

उत्तर अकबर को विश्वास नहीं हुआ कि वह व्यक्ति सर्दी में पूरी रात पानी में खड़ा रहा।

5. गाँव के लोग क्या कर रहे थे?

उत्तर गाँव के लोग आग जलाकर उसके चारों ओर बैठे बातें कर रहे थे।

व्याकरण संबंधी प्रश्न

1. नीचे लिखे वाक्यों में संज्ञा शब्दों पर गोला लगाइए।

- मैं दिल्ली जा रही हूँ।
- गाय कहाँ है?
- राम जा रहा है।
- आम मीठा है।

2. विराम चिह्नों को देखकर उनका नाम लिखिए।

- । ....
- ? ....
- , ...
- ! ....

3. चार क्रिया शब्द लिखिए।

उत्तर

1. • दिल्ली • गाय
   • राम • आम
2. • पूर्ण विराम • प्रश्नवाचक चिन्ह
   • अल्प विराम • विस्मयादिबोधक चिन्ह
3. • लिखना • पढ़ना
   • चलना • खेलना

लेखन संबंधी प्रश्न

1. मित्र को अपने जन्मदिन पर बुलाने हेतु पत्र लिखिए।

उत्तर बी 662,
विकासपुरी,
नई दिल्ली-1100XX
दिनांक 20 नवम्बर, 20XX

प्रिय मित्र अमोल,
सप्रेम नमस्ते!

तुम्हें यह जानकर खुशी होगी कि दिनांक 25 नवम्बर को मेरा जन्मदिन है। इस खुशी पर मेरे माता-पिता ने एक समारोह का आयोजन किया है। कार्यक्रम सायं 6 बजे प्रारंभ होगा, केक 7 बजे काटा जाएगा एवं 8 बजे प्रतिभोज आरंभ हो जाएगा। मैं तुम्हें सादर आमंत्रित करता हूँ।

धन्यवाद
तुम्हारा मित्र
आरव

मित्र को पत्र

पाठ का सार

'मित्र को पत्र' पाठ में रूपम नाम के बालक ने अपने मित्र अभिषेक को पत्र लिखा है। पत्र में रूपम ने लिखा है कि वह गरमी की छुट्टियाँ मनाने अपने नाना-नानी के घर गुवाहाटी आया है। गुवाहाटी भारत के पूर्वोत्तर प्रदेशों का प्रवेशद्वार है। यह एक महानगर है, जो ब्रह्मपुत्र नदी के तट पर स्थित है।

ब्रह्मपुत्र नदी में भारत का सबसे बड़ा द्वीप 'माजुली' द्वीप है।

माजुली में असम के विश्वप्रसिद्ध वैष्णव मठ 'सत्र' में हमने सत्रिया नृत्य देखा। सत्रिया नृत्य भारत के शास्त्रीय नृत्यों में से एक है। गुवाहाटी नगर के समीप नीलांचल पर्वत पर कामाख्या देवी का मंदिर है।

हम लोग पिछले गुरुवार को यहाँ दर्शन करने गए थे। हम उमानंद मंदिर भी गए थे। यहाँ पहुँचने के लिए नाव से तथा थोड़ी दूर पैदल भी चलना पड़ता है।

पैदल चलते हुए नानी ने बताया कि स्वस्थ रहने के लिए पैदल चलना व खेलना बहुत आवश्यक है। उन्होंने बताया कि स्वस्थ तन में स्वस्थ मन का वास होता है।

मैंने नानी को बताया कि मैं अपने मित्रों के साथ बहुत खेल खेलता हूँ। हम लोग खो-खो, पिट्ठू, क्रिकेट एवं फुटबॉल खेलते हैं। खेल की बात सोचते हुए मुझे तुम्हारी याद आने लगी। मैं तुम्हें यहाँ के बहुत अनुभव सुनाना चाहता हूँ।

शब्दार्थ

तट-किनारा, तन-शरीर, द्वीप-स्थल का वह भाग, जिसके चारों ओर पानी हो, श्रद्धालु-भक्तगण, समीप-निकट, विशाल-बड़ा।

बातचीत के लिए

1. **रूपम ने किसे पत्र लिखा और उसमें क्या लिखा है?**

उत्तर रूपम ने अपने मित्र अभिषेक को पत्र लिखा है। पत्र में गुवाहाटी व उसके आस-पास के स्थानों का सुंदर वर्णन किया गया है।

2. **पत्र के अनुसार रूपम अपनी गरमी की छुट्टियाँ बिताने कहाँ गया हुआ है?**

उत्तर पत्र के अनुसार रूपम अपनी गरमी की छुट्टियाँ बिताने अपने नाना-नानी के घर गुवाहाटी गया हुआ है।

3. **आप अपनी गरमी की छुट्टियाँ बिताने कहाँ गए थे? बताइए।**

उत्तर मैं अपनी गरमी की छुट्टियाँ बिताने अपने मामा के घर गया था। मेरे मामा आगरा शहर में रहते हैं। वहाँ मैंने ताजमहल, फतेहपुर सीकरी और आगरा किला देखा।

4. **शारीरिक श्रम के बारे में रूपम की नानी ने उसे क्या सलाह दी?**

उत्तर शारीरिक श्रम के बारे में रूपम की नानी ने उसे सलाह दी कि स्वस्थ रहने के लिए खेलना बहुत आवश्यक है। उन्होंने यह भी बताया कि स्वस्थ तन में स्वस्थ मन का वास होता है। इसलिए पढ़ाई के साथ-साथ खेलकूद भी अति आवश्यक है।

सोचिए और लिखिए

1. **इस पत्र से गुवाहाटी नगर के बारे में आपको क्या-क्या जानकारी मिली?**

उत्तर गुवाहाटी भारत के पूर्वोत्तर प्रदेशों का प्रवेशद्वार है। यह एक सुंदर और विशाल महानगर है। यह नगर ब्रह्मपुत्र नदी के तट पर स्थित है। गुवाहाटी के पास नीलांचल पर्वत पर कामाख्या देवी का मंदिर है। उमानंद मंदिर भी गुवाहाटी के पास है, जहाँ नाव से जाना पड़ता है।

2. **शारीरिक श्रम करना क्यों आवश्यक है? क्या आप प्रतिदिन कोई शारीरिक श्रम करते हैं?**

उत्तर शारीरिक श्रम करने से व्यक्ति शरीर और मन से स्वस्थ व ऊर्जावान रहता है। कहा गया है कि "स्वस्थ तन में स्वस्थ मन का वास होता है।" शारीरिक श्रम से हम तंदुरूस्त और मजबूत बनते हैं। पाचन क्रिया ठीक रहती है।

जी हाँ, मैं प्रतिदिन विभिन्न तरह के खेल खेलता हूँ; जैसे—खो-खो, फुटबॉल, क्रिकेट आदि खेलना भी एक शारीरिक श्रम है।

3. **पत्र के अनुसार रूपम और अभिषेक कौन-कौन से खेल खेलते हैं?**

उत्तर पत्र के अनुसार, रूपम और अभिषेक खो-खो, पिट्ठू, क्रिकेट और फुटबॉल खेलते हैं।

4. **आपको कौन-कौन से खेल खेलना पसंद है? सूची बनाइए और लिखिए।**

उत्तर

कबड्डी	खो-खो
लूडो	बैडमिंटन
शतरंज	रस्साकशी
फुटबॉल	क्रिकेट

भाषा की बात

1. **आपने जो पत्र पढ़ा, उसमें कुछ खेलों के नाम आए हैं। आप और भी अन्य खेलों के नाम जानते और उन्हें खेलते होंगे। नीचे दी गई वर्ग पहेली में कुछ खेलों के नाम ढूँढिए और लिखिए।**

का	क्रि	वॉ	रा	पि	जा
गु	के	ली	नी	ट्	कि
फु	ट	बॉ	ल	ठू	ब
डा	हु	ल	खो	हॉ	की
बु	या	य	खो	न	त
ओ	गि	ल्	ली	डं	डा

उत्तर फुटबॉल, पिट्ठू, गिल्ली डंडा, वॉलीबॉल, खो-खो, हॉकी।

2. **क्या आपके घर अथवा विद्यालय में कोई अन्य खेल भी खेले जाते हैं? उनके नाम नीचे लिखिए।**

उत्तर हाँ! मेरे घर अथवा विद्यालय में अन्य खेल भी खेले जाते हैं। ये हैं—लूडो, साँप सीढ़ी, कुश्ती, ताश का खेल, ऊँची कूद, लंबी कूद, लुका-छिपी, साइकिल रेस।

3. **पत्र में 'त्र' तथा 'श्र' संयुक्त अक्षरों का प्रयोग हुआ है?**

(क) 'त्र' संयुक्त अक्षर त् और र के मेल से बनता है।

(ख) 'श्र' संयुक्त अक्षर श और र के मेल से बनता है।

अब आप पाठ में आए 'त्र' और 'श्र' संयुक्त अक्षरों के प्रयोग से बने शब्दों को ढूँढकर नीचे लिखिए। आप अपनी

सोच से भी 'त्र' तथा 'श्र' संयुक्त अक्षरों के प्रयोग से बने नए शब्द लिख सकते हैं।

'त्र' वाले शब्द	'श्र' वाले शब्द
....	....
....	....
....	....
....	....
....	....

उत्तर

'त्र' वाले शब्द	'श्र' वाले शब्द
त्रेता	श्रमिक
त्रिलोक	श्रवण
त्रिनेत्र	श्रद्धा
त्रिशूल	श्रीनगर
पत्र	श्रम

4. शब्द लड़ी बनाइए – जैसे 'घर' में अंतिम वर्ण 'र' है, तो अगली कड़ी में 'र' से 'रस्सी' लिखा है। अब आप इस शब्द लड़ी को पूरा कीजिए।

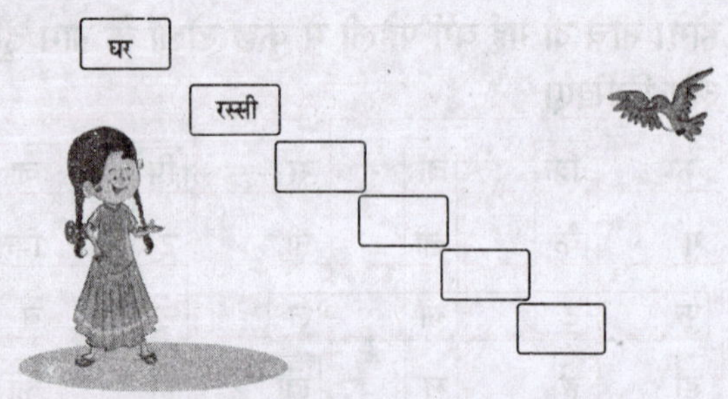

उत्तर सीख, खजूर, रथ, थरमस

5. पत्र में आए निम्नलिखित शब्दों में से नाम वाले शब्द (संज्ञा) ढूँढकर उनमें अपनी पसंद का रंग भरिए। उदाहरण नगर, पर्वत, रूपम आदि।

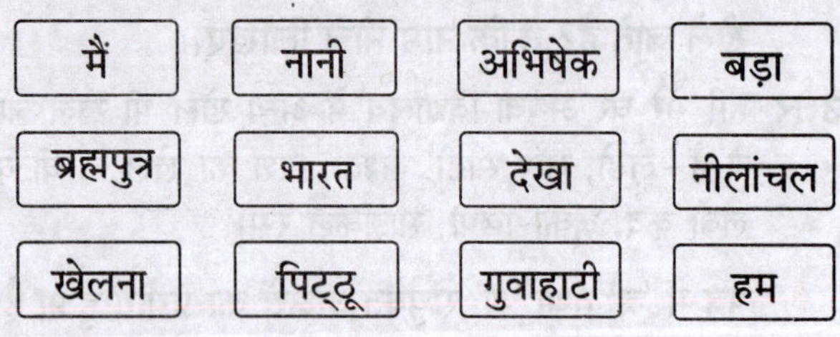

उत्तर नाम वाले शब्द

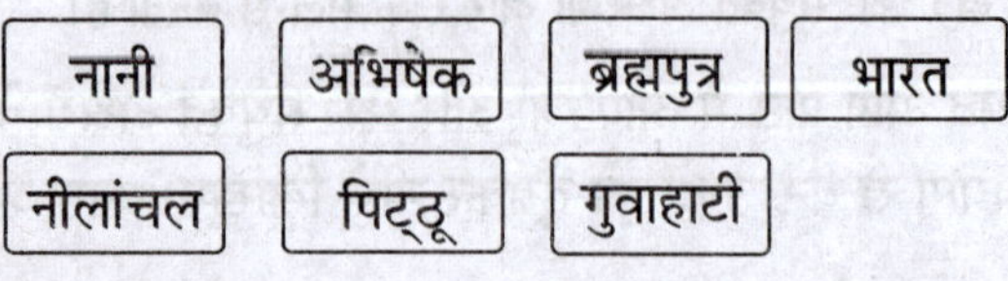

- छात्र रंग स्वयं भरें।

थोड़ा और जानिए

1. भारत के पूर्वोत्तर क्षेत्र में आठ प्रदेश हैं। ये अपनी प्राकृतिक सुंदरता और विविध परंपराओं हेतु प्रसिद्ध हैं। ये आठ प्रदेश हैं–

> असम, मणिपुर, मेघालय, सिक्किम
> मिजोरम, नागालैंड, अरुणाचल प्रदेश, त्रिपुरा

कक्षा में अपने सहपाठियों और शिक्षक के साथ पूर्वोत्तर प्रदेशों पर चर्चा कीजिए।

उत्तर भारत में पूर्वोत्तर क्षेत्र में आठ प्रदेश हैं। ये अपनी प्राकृतिक सुंदरता और विविध परंपराओं हेतु प्रसिद्ध हैं।

प्रदेश	राजधानी	देखने योग्य स्थान
असम	दिसपुर	काजीरंगा राष्ट्रीय उद्यान, कामाख्या मंदिर, शिव सागर
मणिपुर	इंफाल	लोकटक झील, इमा बाजार, केइबुल लामजाओं
मेघालय	शिलांग	बालपक्रम, चेरापूँजी, लिविंग रूट ब्रिज
सिक्किम	गंगटोक	पेलिंग, चांगु झील, रूमटेक
मिजोरम	आइजोल	थेनजोल, वतारंग झरना
नागालैंड	कोहिमा	नतांगकी राष्ट्रीय उद्यान, खो नोमा, मोकोक चुंग
अरुणाचल प्रदेश	ईटानगर	नामदफा राष्ट्रीय उद्यान, तवांग मठ, जीरो
त्रिपुरा	अगरतला	उज्ज्यंता पैलेस, त्रिपुरा सुंदरी मंदिर, रूद्र सागर झील

2. इस पत्र में आपने गुवाहाटी स्थित दो मंदिरों के बारे में पढ़ा है।

आपके राज्य में भी कुछ धार्मिक स्थल होंगे। ऐसे स्थानों के बारे में अपने घर के सदस्यों से जानकारी प्राप्त कीजिए और कक्षा में सबको बताइए।

उत्तर छात्र स्वयं करें।

खेल गीत

1. समूह में खेले जाने वाले बहुत-से खेलों के साथ सामूहिक रूप से गीत या तुक बंदियाँ गाई जाती हैं, जैसे कि हरा समंदर गोपी चंदर। ऐसे ही कोई दो गीत लिखिए।

उत्तर छू-छू मंतर बोले सिकंदर
गोटी पकड़े हो जाए बंदर।
पोसंपा भई पोसंपा
देखो सज गए पोसंपा।

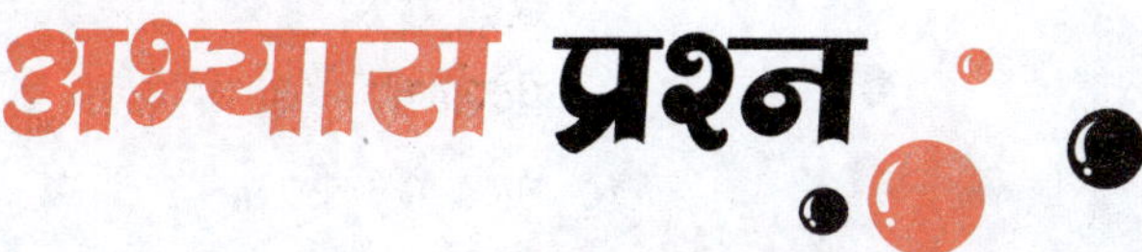

अभ्यास प्रश्न

बहुविकल्पीय प्रश्न

1. पत्र किसने लिखा था?
(क) अभिषेक ने (ख) राहुल ने (ग) रूबी ने (घ) रूपम ने
2. रूपम के नाना-नानी का घर कहाँ है?
(क) गुवाहाटी में (ख) नागालैंड में
(ग) असम में (घ) सिक्किम में
3. गुवाहाटी किस नदी के तट पर स्थित है?
(क) गंगा (ख) यमुना (ग) नर्मदा (घ) ब्रह्मपुत्र
4. रूपम ने किसको पत्र लिखा था?
(क) अभिषेक को (ख) नाना को
(ग) नानी को (घ) पिताजी को

उत्तर
1. (घ) रूपम ने 2. (क) गुवाहाटी में
3. (घ) ब्रह्मपुत्र 4. (क) अभिषेक को

गद्यांश पर आधारित प्रश्न

निम्नलिखित गद्यांश को पढ़कर उस पर आधारित प्रश्नों के उत्तर दीजिए।

गद्यांश

तुम्हें यह जानकर आश्चर्य होगा कि ब्रह्मपुत्र इतनी विशाल नदी है कि इसमें 'माजुली' नाम का एक बहुत बड़ा द्वीप भी है। यह नदी में स्थित भारत का सबसे बड़ा द्वीप है। माजुली में असम के विश्वप्रसिद्ध वैष्णव मठ 'सत्र' में हमने सत्रिया नृत्य देखा। यह भारत के शास्त्रीय नृत्यों में से एक है।

1. माजुली नाम का द्वीप किस नदी में है?
(क) गंगा में (ख) गोदावरी में
(ग) यमुना में (घ) ब्रह्मपुत्र में
2. विश्वप्रसिद्ध वैष्णव मठ कहाँ स्थित है?
(क) असम में (ख) नेपाल में
(ग) भारत में (घ) चीन में
3. सत्रिया नृत्य कहाँ का है?
4. गद्यांश के अनुसार शास्त्रीय नृत्य कौन-सा है?

उत्तर
1. (घ) ब्रह्मपुत्र में 2. (क) असम में
3. सत्रिया नृत्य असम का है।
3. गद्यांश के अनुसार सत्रिया शास्त्रीय नृत्य है।

निम्नलिखित प्रश्नों के उत्तर दीजिए

1. रूपम ने पत्र में कौन-कौन से खेल की बात की है?

उत्तर रूपम ने पत्र में खो-खो, क्रिकेट एवं फुटबॉल खेलों की बात की है?

2. नानी ने स्वस्थ रहने के लिए क्या आवश्यक बताया?

उत्तर नानी ने स्वस्थ रहने के लिए खेलना अति आवश्यक बताया।

3. कौन-से मंदिर जाने के लिए थोड़ा पैदल चलना पड़ता है?

उत्तर उनानंद मंदिर पहुँचने के लिए थोड़ा पैदल चलना पड़ता है।

4. नीलांचल पर्वत कहाँ स्थित है?

उत्तर नीलांचल पर्वत गुवाहाटी नगर के समीप स्थित है।

लेखन संबंधी प्रश्न

1. 'रक्षाबंधन' पर कम-से-कम 40 शब्दों में अनुच्छेद लिखिए।

उत्तर रक्षाबंधन भाई-बहन का पवित्र त्योहार है। यह त्योहार प्रत्येक वर्ष सावन माह की पूर्णिमा को मनाया जाता है। इस दिन बहन भाई को राखी बाँधती है व उसकी कुशलता की कामना करती है। भाई बहन की रक्षा करने का वचन देता है। इस दिन घर में विभिन्न प्रकार की मिठाई व पकवान बनते हैं।

अध्याय ४ चतुर गीदड़

पाठ का सार

प्रस्तुत कहानी मगरमच्छ, कछुआ तथा चतुर गीदड़ की है, जिसमें मगरमच्छ तालाब के किनारे बैठे-बैठे यह सोच रहा था कि तालाब की सारी मछलियाँ तो उसने चट कर ली हैं, अब वह क्या खाएगा?

भूख के मारे तो उसके प्राण ही निकल जाएँगे। उसे बड़े जोर की भूख लगी थी, तभी उसका मित्र कछुआ वहाँ आता है। कछुए को मगरमच्छ अपनी सारी परेशानी बताता है। मगरमच्छ कछुए से गीदड़ को खाने की बात करता है और कछुए से सहायता भी माँगता है। मगरमच्छ ने कहा कि मित्र कुछ उपाय करो कि वह मेरी पकड़ में आ जाए। मैं तुम्हारा उपकार मानूँगा। कछुआ मगरमच्छ की बात मान लेता है। कछुआ मगरमच्छ के कान में कुछ कहता है। मगरमच्छ उसकी बात सुन लेता है और एक तरफ मगरमच्छ साँस रोककर लेट जाता है। गीदड़ को वहाँ आते देख कछुआ जोर-जोर से रोने लगता है। मेरे प्यारे मित्र को न जाने क्या हो गया। अचानक उसके प्राण निकल गए। गीदड़ ने कछुए से रोने की वजह पूछी तो कछुए ने बताया कि मेरा प्यारा मित्र मगरमच्छ स्वर्ग सिधार गया।

गीदड़ पूछता है कि क्या सच में मगरमच्छ मर गया? गीदड़ अंदर-ही-अंदर खुश होता है कि वह अब बिना किसी डर के तालाब का पानी पी सकेगा। गीदड़ कछुए से कहता है कि यह तो बड़े दु:ख की बात है, मैं तुम्हारी क्या सहायता करूं? कछुआ कहता है कि आओ, उस पर कुछ सूखे पत्ते डालकर उसे ढक दें। गीदड़ डरते-डरते मगरमच्छ के पास जाता है, तो मगरमच्छ धीरे-धीरे साँस लेता रहता है। तभी गीदड़ समझ जाता है कि मगरमच्छ अभी जिंदा है। गीदड़ ने अपनी चतुराई दिखाते हुए कहा कि भाई मैंने तो सुना है कि मर जाने पर मगरमच्छ की पूँछ हिलती रहती है, तभी मगरमच्छ धीरे-धीरे अपनी पूँछ हिलाने लगता है। ऐसा करने से गीदड़ समझ जाता है कि मगरमच्छ अभी जिंदा है। इस प्रकार चतुराई से गीदड़ अपनी जान बचाता है। कछुआ और मगरमच्छ स्वयं मूर्ख बन जाते हैं।

शब्दार्थ

मित्र-दोस्त, स्वर्ग सिधारना-मर जाना, ढाँप-ढँकना, चट करना-खा जाना, प्रयत्न-कोशिश, चतुर-चालाक।

NCERT फोल्डर

बातचीत के लिए

1. आपको भूख लगती है, तो आपको कैसा लगता है?

उत्तर जब मुझे भूख लगती है, तो कुछ भी अच्छा नहीं लगता। ऐसा लगता है कि भूख से मैं मर ही जाऊँगा। उस समय जो कुछ भी भोजन मेरे सामने होता है, वह सब अच्छा लगने लगता है। ऐसी फल-सब्जियाँ, जिसे हम खाना पसंद नहीं करते हैं, भूख लगने पर वह भी मैं खा लेता हूँ।

2. अपने मित्र की सहायता आप किस-किस प्रकार से करते हैं?

उत्तर जब मेरा मित्र कभी स्कूल में पेन, पेंसिल, कॉपी या पुस्तक लाना भूल जाता है, तब मैं उसे अपना सामान दे देता हूँ।

जब मेरे मित्र को अकेले सामान लेने बाजार जाना पड़ता है, तब मैं उसके साथ चला जाता हूँ।

जब मेरे दोस्त की तबीयत खराब होती है, तो मैं उसके पास बैठता हूँ। उसे पानी और फल लाकर देता हूँ।

सुख-दु:ख में मैं अपने मित्र का हमेशा साथ देता हूँ।

3. कहानी का शीर्षक 'चतुर गीदड़' क्यों है?

उत्तर कहानी का शीर्षक 'चतुर गीदड़' इसलिए है, क्योंकि गीदड़ ने सूझ-बूझ और चतुराई से अपनी जान बचाई।

4. आप इस कहानी को और क्या नाम देना चाहेंगे?

उत्तर मैं इस कहानी को निम्न नाम देना चाहूँगा

- होशियार गीदड़
- मूर्ख मगरमच्छ
- कछुए की मित्रता
- मगरमच्छ और गीदड़
- बुद्धिमान गीदड़ इत्यादि।

5. अपनी सूझ-बूझ का कोई अनुभव बताइए।

उत्तर छात्र स्वयं करें।

सोचिए और लिखिए

1. तालाब में मछलियाँ क्यों नहीं थीं?

उत्तर तालाब में मछलियाँ इसलिए नहीं थीं, क्योंकि तालाब की सारी मछलियों को मगरमच्छ ने खा लिया था।

2. कछुए ने क्या उपाय सोचा?

उत्तर कछुए ने सोच-विचारकर एक उपाय खोजा कि तालाब के किनारे मगरमच्छ चुपचाप अपनी साँस रोके मरा हुआ-सा पड़ा रहेगा। जैसे ही गीदड़ आएगा मैं जोर-जोर से रो-रोकर मित्र के मर जाने का दु:ख व्यक्त करूँगा। इस तरह सुखे पत्ते डालकर ढकने का बहाना बनाकर कछुआ उसे पास बुलाएगा और मगरमच्छ तुरंत गीदड़ को पकड़ लेगा।

3. गीदड़ ने समझदारी कैसे दिखाई?

उत्तर गीदड़ ने समझदारी दिखाते हुए कछुए से कहा, "भाई मैंने तो सुना है कि मर जाने पर मगरमच्छ की पूँछ हिलती रहती है। लगता है, अभी यह पूरी तरह नहीं मरा।" यह कहकर गीदड़, मगरमच्छ के पूँछ हिलाने का इंतजार करने लगा।

4. गीदड़ को मगरमच्छ की सच्चाई कैसे पता चली?

उत्तर गीदड़ ने जब कहा कि मरने पर मगरमच्छ की पूँछ हिलती रहती है, तो इतना सुनते ही मूर्ख मगरमच्छ अपने को मरा हुआ साबित करने के लिए अपनी पूँछ जोर-जोर से हिलाने लगा। यह देखकर गीदड़ को मगरमच्छ की सच्चाई का पता चल गया कि वह मरा नहीं जिंदा है।

कहानी से

1. नीचे कहानी से जुड़े चित्र और बातें हैं। उनका आपस में मिलान कीजिए।

भूख के मारे प्राण निकलना

गीदड़ को लाने का प्रयत्न

डर के मारे प्यासा रह जाना

पूँछ हिलाना

उत्तर

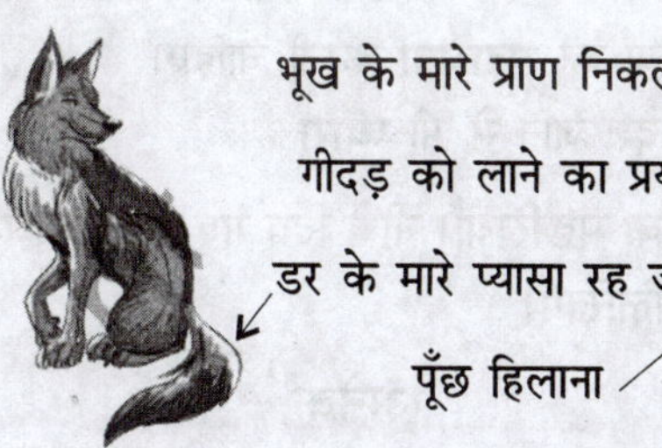

भाषा की बात

1. कहानी में पशुओं के लिए तालाब ही पानी का स्रोत है। नीचे दी गई वर्ग पहेली से पानी के अन्य स्रोतों को ढूँढकर लिखिए।

ता	ल	ष	झ	थे	बा
ला	पा	न	र	मू	रि
ब	न	ह	ना	क	श
ते	दी	र	पो	ख	र
रि	ब	पी	ये	कु	आँ
बो	र	वे	ल	गा	था

उत्तर पोखर, नदी, नहर, कुआँ, झरना बारिश, बोरवेल, तालाब

2. सही वाक्य बनाइए

'दो मित्र कहीं जा रहे हैं'
इस वाक्य में 'द'को 'क', 'म' को 'ग' और 'ह' को 'प' से बदल दिया गया है।
इस तरह नया वाक्य बना– 'को गित्र कपीं जा रपे पैं'
अब दिए गए वाक्य में 'ल' को 'ह' और 'स' को 'भ' से बदलकर नया वाक्य बनाइए। मैं बलुत सूखा/सूखी हूँ।
सही वाक्य ....

उत्तर मैं बहुत भूखी/भूखा हूँ

3. कहानी में आए शब्दों का प्रयोग करते हुए नए वाक्य बनाकर लिखिए

कठिन ....
प्रयत्न ....
सहायता ....
प्यारा ....

उत्तर **कठिन** मजदूर **कठिन** परिश्रम करके अपना पेट भरते हैं।
प्रयत्न मैंने अपने **प्रयत्न** से इस जंगल को हरा-भरा कर दिया।
सहायता हमें गरीबों की **सहायता** करनी चाहिए।
प्यारा मुझे भारत देश जान से भी **प्यारा** है।

4. एक मछली, अनेक मछलियाँ। नीचे दिए गए शब्दों के एक और अनेक रूप लिखिए।

एक	अनेक
मछली	मछलियाँ
चूड़ी	....
....	मक्खियाँ
लड़की	....
....	टोपियाँ
ककड़ी	....

उत्तर

एक	अनेक
मछली	मछलियाँ
चूड़ी	चूड़ियाँ
मक्खी	मक्खियाँ
लड़की	लड़कियाँ
टोपी	टोपियाँ
ककड़ी	ककड़ियाँ

पता कीजिए और लिखिए

1. इस कहानी में मगरमच्छ, गीदड़ और कछुए जैसे पात्र आपने देखे हैं। मगरमच्छ जल और थल दोनों पर ही रहता है, जबकि गीदड़ केवल थल पर ही रहता है। आप इस तरह के और प्राणियों के नाम पता करके नीचे दी गई तालिका में लिखिए

उत्तर

जल व थल पर रहने वाला जीव	थल पर रहने वाला जीव
साँप	गिलहरी
मेंढक	कुत्ता
कछुआ	शेर
घड़ियाल	घोड़ा

मेरी सोच

1. यदि हम गीदड़ के स्थान पर होते तो क्या करते?

उत्तर यदि हम गीदड़ के स्थान पर होते, तो
- हम कछुए से कभी बात नहीं करते।
- हम उस तालाब के किनारे कभी नहीं आते।

आगे छात्र स्वयं उत्तर दें

आप क्या सोचते हैं?

1. अगर मगरमच्छ पूँछ न हिलाता तो अनुमान लगाइए कि कहानी का क्या अंत होता?

उत्तर अगर मगरमच्छ पूँछ न हिलाता तो गीदड़ उसके पास खड़ा रहता और पलक झपकते ही मगरमच्छ गीदड़ को खा जाता।

अभ्यास प्रश्न

बहुविकल्पीय प्रश्न

1. तालाब की सारी मछलियाँ कौन चट कर गया?
(क) मगरमच्छ (ख) गीदड़ (ग) कछुआ (घ) बंदर
2. भूख के मारे किसके प्राण निकल रहे थे?
(क) कछुए के (ख) गीदड़ के
(ग) मछलियों के (घ) मगरमच्छ के
3. मगरमच्छ की पकड़ में कौन नहीं आता था?
(क) गीदड़ (ख) कछुआ (ग) मछली (घ) साँप
4. चतुर कौन था?
(क) मछली (ख) मगरमच्छ (ग) गीदड़ (घ) कछुआ
5. कछुआ किसका दोस्त था?
(क) मछलियों का (ख) मगरमच्छ का
(ग) साँप का (घ) गीदड़ का

उत्तर
1. (क) मगरमच्छ 2. (घ) मगरमच्छ के
3. (क) गीदड़ 4. (ग) गीदड़
5. (ख) मगरमच्छ का

गद्यांश पर आधारित प्रश्न

निम्नलिखित गद्यांश को पढ़कर उस पर आधारित प्रश्नों के उत्तर दीजिए।

गद्यांश

गीदड़ क्या कहा? मगरमच्छ मर गया? (अपने आप से) अब तो मैं निश्चिंत होकर तालाब का पानी पी सकता हूँ। उसके डर से मैं कई बार प्यासा ही रह जाता था?

कछुआ क्या कहा, क्या कहा?

गीदड़ नहीं, कुछ नहीं, कुछ नहीं यह तो बड़े दुःख की बात है। मैं तुम्हारी क्या सहायता कर सकता हूँ।

1. गीदड़ से किसने सहायता माँगी?
(क) कछुए ने (ख) मगरमच्छ ने
(ग) मछली ने (घ) शेर ने
2. मगरमच्छ के मरने पर कौन खुश हो गया?
(क) कछुआ (ख) गीदड़ (ग) बिल्ली (घ) बंदर
3. गीदड़ मन-ही-मन क्या सोच रहा था?
4. मगरमच्छ के डर से तालाब का पानी कौन नहीं पी पाता था?

उत्तर
1. (क) कछुए ने 2. (ख) गीदड़
3. गीदड़ मन-ही-मन सोच रहा था कि अब मैं बिना डरे तालाब का पानी पी सकूँगा।
4. मगरमच्छ के डर से गीदड़ तालाब का पानी नहीं पी पाता था।

निम्नलिखित प्रश्नों के उत्तर दीजिए

1. कई दिन से कौन भूखा था?

उत्तर कई दिनों से मगरमच्छ भूखा था।

2. तालाब में पानी पीने कौन नहीं गया था?

उत्तर गीदड़ तालाब का पानी पीने नहीं गया था।

3. गीदड़ को खाने की योजना मगरमच्छ किसके साथ बना रहा था?

उत्तर गीदड़ को खाने की योजना मगरमच्छ और कछुआ साथ में बना रहे थे।

4. मगरमच्छ किसे खाकर अपनी भूख मिटाना चाहता था?

उत्तर मगरमच्छ गीदड़ को खाकर अपनी भूख मिटाना चाहता था।

लेखन संबंधी प्रश्न

1. कक्षा की खिड़की का काँच टूट जाने पर क्षमा माँगते हुए प्रधानाचार्य को पत्र लिखिए।

उत्तर सेवा में,

प्रधानाचार्य

सर्वोत्तम विद्यालय

नई दिल्ली 1100XX

विषय कक्षा की खिड़की का काँच टूट जाने के विषय में।

महोदय,

मैं आपके विद्यालय की कक्षा III का छात्र हूँ। मैं गेंद से कक्षा में खेल रहा था, जो खिड़की पर जा लगी तथा काँच टूट गया। आपसे निवेदन है कि मुझे क्षमा कीजिए। आगे से ऐसी गलती न हो, इसका मैं पूरा ध्यान रखूँगा।

धन्यवाद

भवदीय

नीरज

कक्षा-III (B)

अध्याय ९ प्रकृति पर्व–फूलदेई

पाठ का सार

'फूलदेई' उत्तराखंड का प्रसिद्ध त्योहार है, जो उत्तराखंड के अलग-अलग क्षेत्रों में आठ दिन से लेकर एक माह तक मनाया जाता है। इस त्योहार को बच्चों द्वारा मनाए जाने के कारण 'बाल-पर्व' भी कहते हैं। यह चैत्र मास की संक्रांति के दिन मनाया जाता है। चैत्र मास हिंदू नववर्ष का पहला महीना होता है। फूलदेई बसंत ऋतु के आगमन का प्रतीक है। यह ऋतु आते ही ऊँची-ऊँची पहाड़ियों से बर्फ पिघलने लगती है और उत्तराखंड के पहाड़ फूलों से लद जाते हैं। जानकी भी अपने दोस्तों के साथ कई प्रकार के फूल डलिया में इकट्ठे कर लेती है।

अब यह टोली, जिसे 'फुलारी' कहा जाता है, हर घर की देहली (मुख्य द्वार) पर अक्षत के साथ फूल रखती है तथा गीत गाती है। बच्चे गीत गाकर भगवान से प्रार्थना करते हैं कि आपकी देहली फूलों से भरी रहे, ईश्वर सबकी रक्षा करें, सबको क्षमा करें, सबका मंगल करें, सबके घर में सुख-समृद्धि हो और सबके घर में अन्न के भंडार भरे रहें। सभी घरों में फुलारी के आने की तैयारी की जाती है।

घरों की देहली को गोबर-मिट्टी से लीपा जाता है। फुलारी द्वारा जब गाकर अपना आशीर्वाद दिया जाता है, तो उन्हें भेंट के रूप में चावल, गुड़ तथा कुछ पैसे दिए जाते हैं। बच्चों द्वारा एकत्रित किए गए चावल व गुड़ से हलवा, छोई या साई व पापड़ी जैसे स्थानीय व्यंजन बनाए जाते हैं तथा पैसों से घी या तेल खरीदा जाता है।

फूलदेई बच्चों को प्रकृति प्रेम और सामाजिक सद्भाव की सीख देता है।
यह त्योहार लोकगीत, मान्यताओं तथा परंपराओं से जुड़ने का अवसर प्रदान करता है। यह त्योहार प्रकृति तथा संस्कृति से जुड़े रहने की प्रेरणा भी देता है।

शब्दार्थ

पकवान-भोजन सामग्री, टोली-समूह, मास-महीना, समृद्धि-धन, सुख, देहली-चौखट/घर का मुख्य द्वार, अक्षत-साबुत चावल/पूजा में प्रयोग होने वाले चावल।

बातचीत के लिए

1. **त्योहार क्यों मनाए जाते हैं?**

उत्तर त्योहार संस्कृति व प्रकृति के साथ जुड़े रहने की प्रेरणा देने के साथ मानव जीवन में आनंद, उत्साह व मेल मिलाप रखने की शिक्षा देते हैं। त्योहारों के माध्यम से यह शिक्षा सबको मिले, इसलिए त्योहार मनाए जाते हैं।

2. **आपका प्रिय त्योहार कौन-सा है?**

उत्तर होली का त्योहार मेरा प्रिय त्योहार है।

3. **आप अपना प्रिय त्योहार कैसे मनाते हैं?**

उत्तर होली के दूसरे दिन हम सब मिलकर एक-दूसरे को रंग-गुलाल लगाते है। घर-घर जाकर मिठाइयाँ एवं गुँजिया खाते हैं और हम सब प्रेम से आपस में गले मिलते हैं। इस तरह मैं होली का त्योहार मनाता हूँ।

4. **वसंत ऋतु के आगमन पर भारत में मनाए जाने वाले त्योहार कौन-कौन से हैं?**

उत्तर वसंत पंचमी, मकर संक्रांति, बिहू, होली, लोहड़ी, बुद्ध पूर्णिमा, बैसाखी, गुड़ी-पड़वा, शिवरात्रि आदि वसंत ऋतु के आगमन पर भारत में मनाए जाने वाले त्योहार हैं।

5. **उत्तराखंड के कुमाऊँ क्षेत्र में माँ को इजा कहकर पुकारते हैं। आप अपनी माँ को क्या कहकर पुकारते हैं?**

उत्तर मम्मी, अम्मी, आई, माई, मम्मा।

सोचिए और लिखिए

1. **फुलारी किसे कहते हैं?**

उत्तर उत्तराखंड के पहाड़ी इलाकों में बच्चों की टोली कई प्रकार के फूल अपनी छोटी-छोटी डलियों में एकत्रित करती है और घर के मुख्य द्वार पर चावल व फूल डालती है। इस टोली को ही फुलारी कहा जाता है।

2. **फुलारी को मिले चावल और गुड़ से क्या-क्या बनाया जाता है?**

उत्तर फुलारी को मिले चावल और गुड़ से हलवा, छोई या साई व पापड़ी जैसे अन्य स्थानीय पकवान बनाए जाते हैं।

3. **फूलदेई को बाल-पर्व क्यों कहा जाता है?**

उत्तर फूलदेई का त्योहार बच्चों द्वारा मनाया जाता है, इसलिए इसे 'बाल-पर्व' कहा जाता है।

4. **फूलदेई पर्व बच्चों को प्रकृति से कैसे जोड़ता है?**

उत्तर फूलदेई पर्व को मनाने के लिए बच्चे सुंदर पहाड़ों में फूल खिलने का इंतजार करते हैं। ऊँची-ऊँची पहाड़ियों से जब बर्फ पिघलने लगती है, तब इस संकेत से बच्चे खुश होते हैं कि वसंत ऋतु का आगमन हो चुका है। विभिन्न फूलों को एकत्रित कर जब बच्चों की टोली देहली पर गाती हुई फूल डालती है, तब बच्चे प्रकृति से जुड़ाव महसूस करते हैं। इस तरह यह पर्व बच्चों को प्रकृति से जोड़ता है।

भाषा की बात

ऊपर दिए गए चित्र में शिक्षक पूजा से प्रश्न पूछ रहे हैं। पूजा उत्तर देते हुए अपने और अपने मित्रों के बारे में बता रही है। इन दोनों उदाहरणों में पूर्ण विराम (।) अल्प विराम (,) और प्रश्नवाचक चिह्न (?) का प्रयोग किया गया है।

नीचे दिए गए वाक्यों में इन विराम चिह्नों का उपयोग कर वाक्य ठीक कीजिए।

गरिमा को फल खाना बहुत पसंद है वह अपने मित्र गौरव दीपक ममता और नवजोत को भी फल खाने की सलाह देती है क्या आपको भी फल खाना पसंद है

उत्तर गरिमा को फल खाना बहुत पसंद है। वह अपने मित्र गौरव, दीपक, ममता और नवजोत को भी फल खाने की सलाह देती है। क्या आपको भी फल खाना पसंद है?

पता कीजिए

1. **फूलदेई वसंत ऋतु (मार्च-अप्रैल) में मनाया जाने वाला त्योहार है। ऐसे ही शरद ऋतु (सितंबर-अक्टूबर) और हेमंत ऋतु (नवंबर-दिसंबर) में मनाए जाने वाले त्योहारों की जानकारी खोजिए और लिखिए।**

उत्तर

शरद ऋतु में मनाए जाने वाले त्योहार	हेमंत ऋतु में मनाए जाने वाले त्योहार
नवरात्रि	दीपावली
दशहरा	छठपूजा
करवाचौथ	भाईदूज

2. आपके विद्यालय में मिलने वाले अवकाशों की जानकारी प्राप्त कीजिए और ऋतुओं के आधार पर नीचे दी गई तालिका में लिखिए।

उत्तर

अवकाश	कब से कब तक	कितने दिनों तक
ग्रीष्मकालीन अवकाश	1 मई से 25 जून तक	56 दिन
शरदकालीन अवकाश	9 अक्टूबर से 14 अक्टूबर तक दशहरा की छुट्टियाँ	6 दिन
शीतकालीन अवकाश	25 दिसंबर से 31 दिसंबर तक	7 दिन

3. आइए अपना घर सजाएँ
फूलदेई के दिन घरों को स्वच्छ करके मुख्य द्वार की देहली को गोबर-मिट्टी से लीपकर तैयार किया जाता है। आप अपने घर को त्योहारों के लिए सजाने हेतु किन-किन वस्तुओं का प्रयोग करते हैं?

उत्तर रंगोली, तोरण, दीया, फूल।

मेरी कलाकारी

1. फूल, आम और अशोक के पत्तों से या अन्य किसी भी वस्तु के उपयोग से सुंदर तोरण बनाइए।

उत्तर छात्र स्वयं करें।

कल्पना कीजिए

1. मधुरानी एक दिन उद्यान में गई। वह बहुत प्रसन्न थी। वहाँ उसे मिली सूरजमुखी बहन और सूरज मामा। सोचकर लिखिए, वे तीनों आपस में क्या बातचीतकर रहे होंगे?

उत्तर **मधुरानी** सूरजमुखी बहन! तुम सुबह जल्दी उठ जाती हो?

सूरजमुखी हाँ मधुरानी! देखो सूरज मामा भी जागकर रोशनी फैला रहे हैं।

मधुरानी सूरज मामा आप रोज सवेरे सबसे पहले क्यों जाग जाते हो?

सूरज मामा मैंने यदि देर कर दी मधुरानी! तो सारा जग सोता ही रह जाएगा।

अभ्यास प्रश्न

बहुविकल्पीय प्रश्न

1. जानकी किस पर्व के लिए प्रसन्न थी?
(क) होली के (ख) फूलदेई के
(ग) करवाचौथ के (घ) दीपावली के

2. जंगल की ओर सब क्या लेकर गए?
(क) डलिया (ख) थैली (ग) झोला (घ) टोपी

3. हिंदू नववर्ष का पहला महीना कौन-सा होता है?
(क) कार्तिक (ख) माघ (ग) चैत्र (घ) आश्विन

4. फूलदेई किस ऋतु के आने का प्रतीक है?
(क) ग्रीष्म (ख) शीत (ग) शरद (घ) वसंत

उत्तर
1. (ख) फूलदेई के 2. (क) डलिया
3. (ग) चैत्र 4. (घ) वसंत

सत्य-असत्य

नीचे दिए गए वाक्यों में से सत्य या असत्य कथन की पहचान कीजिए।

1. देहली को पेंट से लीपकर तैयार किया जाता है। (सत्य/असत्य)

2. फूलदेई त्योहार झारखंड में मनाया जाता है। (सत्य/असत्य)

3. व्यंजन को सब एकत्रित होकर और मिलकर खाते हैं। (सत्य/असत्य)

4. उत्तराखंड के सुंदर पहाड़ फूलों से लद जाते हैं। (सत्य/असत्य)

उत्तर
1.असत्य 2. असत्य 3. सत्य 4. सत्य

रिक्त स्थान

नीचे दिए गए वाक्यों में रिक्त स्थान की पूर्ति उचित शब्द से कीजिए।

(बाल-पर्व, बच्चों, फूलदेई, फुलारी)

1. .... उत्तराखंड का एक प्रसिद्ध त्योहार है।
2. इसे .... भी कहा जाता है।
3. सभी घरों में .... के आने की तैयारी की जाती है।
4. यह त्योहार .... द्वारा मनाया जाता है।

उत्तर

1. फूलदेई 2. बाल-पर्व 3. फुलारी 4. बच्चों

गद्यांश पर आधारित प्रश्न

निम्नलिखित गद्यांश को पढ़कर उस पर आधारित प्रश्नों के उत्तर दीजिए।

गद्यांश

सभी घरों में फुलारी के आने की तैयारी की जाती है। घरों को पूर्णत: स्वच्छ करके देहली को गोबर-मिट्टी से लीपकर तैयार किया जाता है। फुलारी द्वारा जब गाकर अपना आशीर्वाद दिया जाता है, तो भेंट के रूप में उन्हें चावल, गुड़ और कुछ पैसे दिए जाते हैं। जानकी और सभी मित्र दिनभर देहली पूजकर बहुत थक गए थे, पर वे बहुत प्रसन्न थे।

1. घर की देहली को किससे लीपा जाता है?
   (क) मिट्टी से (ख) पेंट से
   (ग) गोबर-मिट्टी से (घ) फूल से
2. फुलारी को भेंट के रूप में क्या दिया जाता है?
   (क) डलिया (ख) पैसे
   (ग) पेड़ (घ) फूल
3. भेंट के रूप में फुलारी को पैसों के अतिरिक्त और क्या दिया जाता है?
4. जानकी और उसके मित्र क्या पूजकर थक गए थे?

उत्तर

1. (ग) गोबर-मिट्टी से
2. (ख) पैसे
3. भेंट के रूप में फुलारी को पैसों के अतिरिक्त चावल और गुड़ दिया जाता है।
4. जानकी और उसके मित्र देहली पूजकर थक गए थे।

निम्नलिखित प्रश्नों के उत्तर दीजिए

1. चैत्र ऋतु आते ही क्या होता है?

उत्तर चैत्र ऋतु आते ही पहाड़ियों से बर्फ पिघलने लगती है एवं ठंडे दिन बीत जाते हैं।

2. जानकी और उसके मित्रों ने कौन-कौन से फूल इकट्ठे किए?

उत्तर जानकी और उसके मित्रों ने बुरांस, फ्योंली और कई प्रकार के फूल इकट्ठे किए।

3. फुलारी के आने की तैयारी कैसे की जाती है?

उत्तर फुलारी के आने पर घरों को साफ करके देहली को गोबर-मिट्टी से लीपकर तैयार किया जाता है।

4. क्या आपको प्रकृति से प्रेम है?

उत्तर हाँ, मुझे प्रकृति से बहुत प्रेम है।

व्याकरण संबंधी प्रश्न

1. दिए गए शब्दों के विलोम लिखिए।
   - दिन
   - छोटी
   - सुबह
   - आगमन
2. पाठ में आए चार संज्ञा शब्दों को लिखिए।

उत्तर

1. दिन-रात, छोटी-बड़ी, सुबह-शाम, आगमन-गमन
2. (i) जानकी (ii) फुलारी (iii) फूलदेई (iv) वसंत

लेखन संबंधी प्रश्न

1. 'प्रिय मित्र' पर कम-से-कम 40 शब्दों में अनुच्छेद लिखिए।

उत्तर मेरे प्रिय मित्र का नाम रवि है। मैं और रवि पक्के मित्र हैं। हम दोनों एक ही कक्षा में पढ़ते हैं। रवि और मैं एकसाथ लंच करते हैं तथा एकसाथ ही पार्क में खेलने जाते हैं। हम रविवार को एकसाथ मिलकर देर तक खेलते हैं। मैं और रवि दो साल से एकसाथ हैं। रवि समझदार है और काम पड़ने पर वह मेरी मदद भी करता है।

रस्साकशी

कविता का सार

'रस्साकशी' नामक कविता 'कन्हैयालाल मत्त' द्वारा लिखी गई है। यह एक खेल गीत है। रस्साकशी खेल खेलने के लिए दो समूहों व एक रस्सी की आवश्यकता होती है। दोनों समूह अपने पैरों को जमीन में गड़ाते हैं व पीठ को अकड़कर खड़े होते हैं। दोनों समूह रस्सी को अपनी ओर खींचने के लिए जोर लगाते हैं। एक-दूसरे का जोश बढ़ाने के लिए बच्चे एक सुर में गाना भी गाते हैं— जोर लगाओ हेई सा। सभी बच्चे पसीने से तरबतर होकर खेल का आनंद लेते हैं। यह कविता हमें सिखाती है कि एकजुट होकर रहने में कितनी शक्ति होती है।

काव्यांशों की व्याख्या

काव्यांश 1

जोर लगाओ हेई सा! हेई सा! भई, हेई सा!
सीना ताने रहो अकड़कर
रस्सा दोनों ओर पकड़ कर,
तिरछे पड़कर कमर जकड़ कर,
जोर लगाओ, हेई सा! हेई सा! भई हेई सा!

शब्दार्थ सीना-छाती, जकड़कर-कसकर।

संदर्भ/प्रसंग प्रस्तुत पंक्तियाँ हमारी पाठयपुस्तक 'वीणा भाग-1' में संकलित कविता 'रस्साकशी' से ली गई हैं। इसके रचयिता कन्हैयालाल मत्त जी हैं। इस कविता में कवि ने रस्साकशी खेल और इस खेल को खेलकर बच्चे कैसे आनंदित होते हैं, का वर्णन किया है।

व्याख्या कवि दोनों समूहों के बच्चों से कहते हैं कि रस्सी पकड़कर जोर लगाओ। जोर लगाओ और जोर लगा के हेई सा! कहो। सब रस्सी को अच्छे से पकड़ो और जोर लगाकर सीना ताने रहो।

दोनों समूह रस्सी को पकड़ो और ताकत के साथ अपनी-अपनी ओर खींचो। कभी तिरछे होकर जोर से खींचो, कभी कमर जकड़कर जोर से खींचो। बस किसी भी तरीके से रस्सी अपनी-अपनी ओर खींचो। जोर से हेई सा! कहकर रस्सी खींचो।

काव्यांश 2

खींचो-खींचो जोर लगाओ,
पैर गड़ा कर पीठ अड़ाओ,
आड़ी तिरछी चाल भिड़ाओ
जोर लगाओ, हेई सा! हेई सा!, भई, हेई सा!

शब्दार्थ *पैर गड़ाकर-जमीन पर जमाकर पैर रखना।*

प्रसंग पूर्ववत्।

व्याख्या कवि कहते हैं कि रस्सी को अपनी-अपनी ओर जोर लगाकर खींचो। कभी पैरों को जमीन में गड़ाकर और पीठ को सामने से अड़ाकर जोर लगाओ। रस्सी को अपनी तरफ लाने के लिए कभी आड़े होकर खींचो, तो कभी तिरछे होकर खींचो। जोर लगाओ और जोर लगाकर कहो हेई सा, भई हेई सा!

काव्यांश 3

रस्सा नहीं फिसलने पाए,
साथ नहीं बिचलने पाए,
जोश खरोश न ढलने पाए,
जोर लगाओ, हेई सा!
हेई सा! भई, हेई सा!

शब्दार्थ *बिचलने-इधर-उधर होना, जोश-खरोश-जोर-शोर।*

प्रसंग पूर्ववत्।

व्याख्या कवि कहते हैं कि रस्सी को अपनी-अपनी तरफ खींचते हुए रस्सी को जोर से पकड़िए, जिससे वह आपके हाथ से फिसल न पाए। इस बात का भी ध्यान रखिए कि कोई भी साथी यहाँ-वहाँ न बिखर जाए। रस्सी को इस तरह पकड़ो कि साथियों का जोश बना रहे और वे कमजोर न पड़ें।

काव्यांश 4

हुए पसीने से तर सारे
सफल हुए सब दाव करारे
इधर हमारे, उधर तुम्हारे, कड़ा
जोर लगाओ, हेई सा!
हेई सा! भई, हेई सा!

शब्दार्थ *दाव-मौका, करारे-कड़ा।*

प्रसंग पूर्ववत्।

व्याख्या कवि कहते हैं कि दोनों समूहों के बच्चे रस्सी खींचकर पसीने से तरबतर हो गए हैं तथा इस खेल में लगाए गए सभी तरीके सफल रहे। जिस समूह में जो-जो थे, वे सब उधर ही रह गए। इधर हमारे समूह के बच्चे थे और उधर तुम्हारे समूह के बच्चे थे, फिर भी जोर लगाते जाओ और कहो जोर लगाओ हेई सा!

NCERT फोल्डर

बातचीत के लिए

1. **आप कौन-कौन से खेल खेलते हैं?**

उत्तर मैं खो-खो, लूडो, कैरम, आँख मिचौली, रस्सीकूद, साँप सीढ़ी, फुटबॉल इत्यादि खेल खेलता हूँ।

2. **आपका सबसे प्रिय खेल कौन-सा है?**

उत्तर मेरा सबसे प्रिय खेल आँख-मिचौली है।

3. **ऐसे खेलों के नाम बताइए, जिनमें दो टीमें आमने-सामने होती हैं?**

उत्तर कबड्डी, फुटबॉल, हॉकी, क्रिकेट, खो-खो इत्यादि ऐसे खेल हैं, जिनमें दो टीमें आमने-सामने होती हैं।

4. **आपने रस्सी का प्रयोग करते हुए कौन-कौन से खेल खेले हैं?**

उत्तर हमने रस्सी का प्रयोग करते हुए रस्सीकूद, रस्साकशी, ऊँची कूद, छलाँग आदि खेल खेले हैं।

5. **वे कौन-से खेल हैं, जिन्हें खेलने के लिए हमें अधिक साथियों की आवश्यकता पड़ती है?**

उत्तर खो-खो, कबड्डी, आँख-मिचौली, पोसंपा इत्यादि खेल के लिए अधिक साथियों की आवश्यकता पड़ती है।

सोचिए और लिखिए

1. **कविता में "जोर लगाओ, हेई सा! हेई सा! भई, हेई सा!" क्यों कहा गया है?**

उत्तर कविता में 'रस्साकशी' खेल के बारे में बताया गया है। इस खेल में बच्चों का उत्साह व आत्मविश्वास को बढ़ाया जाता

है। जीतने के लिए उत्साहवर्धक शब्द 'जोर लगाओ हेई सा!' ही सार्थक वाक्य है। इस वाक्य को सुनते ही बच्चे जोश से भर उठते हैं और खूब जोर लगाते हैं। इसलिए कविता में "जोर लगाओ, हेई सा, हेई सा भई, हेई सा" कहा गया है।

2. कविता में शरीर से जुड़े किन-किन अंगों का वर्णन हुआ है? ढूँढकर लिखिए।

उत्तर कविता में शरीर से जुड़े अंग सीना, कमर, पैर एवं पीठ का वर्णन हुआ है।

3. रस्साकशी खेल में जीतने के लिए क्या-क्या करना पड़ता है?

उत्तर रस्साकशी खेल में जीतने के लिए रस्सी को जोर से पकड़ना पड़ता है। सीना तानकर, अकड़कर खड़े रहना पड़ता है। थोड़ा-सा तिरछे होकर, कमर से जोर लगाना पड़ता है, ताकि रस्सी तनकर अपनी तरफ आ जाए।

यह ध्यान रखना पड़ता है कि रस्सी हाथ से न फिसले। साथी इधर-उधर न गिरे दाँव-पेंच लगाकर पूरे जोश को बरकरार रखना पड़ता है।

4. चित्र में दिखाया गया खेल रस्साकशी कैसे खेला जाता है? लिखिए।

उत्तर
- रस्साकशी के खेल में दो समूह दोनों ओर से एक रस्सी को मजबूती से पकड़ते हैं।
- दोनों समूह की कोशिश होती है कि रस्सी पूरी ताकत से अपनी ओर खींच लो। इसके लिए वे जोर लगाते हैं।
- कभी तिरछे खड़े होकर, कभी कमर से जकड़कर रस्सी को अपनी ओर खींचने का प्रयास करते हैं।
- ध्यान रखते है कि कहीं हाथ से रस्सी न फिसल जाए, जोश में कोई कमी या कसर नहीं होनी चाहिए।
- सारे दाँव-पेंच लगाकर रस्सी अपनी ओर खींचनी होती है।
- रस्सी खींचते समय जोर लगाओ हेई सा! कहें और अपनी ओर रस्सी खींचकर जीत जाते हैं।

5. आपने बहुत-से खेल खेले होंगे। आइए, चित्र देखकर खेल पहचानिए।

उत्तर
- कबड्डी
- स्टापू
- पोसंपा
- गिल्ली डंडा

भाषा की बात

1. कविता में अकड़-पकड़ जैसे तुक मिलने वाले शब्दों का प्रयोग किया गया है। आप भी तुक मिलने वाले शब्द सोचकर लिखिए।

उत्तर

अकड़	पकड़
अड़ाओ	लड़ाओ
बजाएँ	सजाएँ
बस्ता	सस्ता
पानी	नानी

2. आइए खेलें 'मात्रा हटाओ, दूसरा शब्द बनाओ, जादू दिखाओ' का खेल

उदाहरण— भार-भर

इसी प्रकार नीचे दिए गए शब्दों की मात्रा हटाइए और उसके सामने नया शब्द लिखते हुए अपना जादू दिखाइए।

(क) काम .... (ख) बीस ....

(ग) मेला .... (घ) यही ....

उत्तर (क) काम-कम (ख) बीस-बस
(ग) मेला-मल (घ) यही-यह

कविता से आगे

1. **नीचे कुछ खेलों के नाम दिए गए हैं। इनमें से कुछ खेल घर से बाहर मैदान में खेले जाते हैं और कुछ घर के भीतर खेले जाते हैं। घर से बाहर तथा घर के भीतर खेले जाने वाले खेलों को छाँटते हुए उन्हें अलग-अलग लिखिए।**

फुटबॉल, लूडो, साँप-सीढ़ी, हॉकी, शतरंज, चिड़िया उड़, रस्साकशी, क्रिकेट, कैरमबोर्ड, खो-खो, टेबल टेनिस, गिट्टे

उत्तर घर के भीतर खेले जाने वाले खेल

- लूडो
- साँप सीढ़ी
- शतरंज
- चिड़िया उड़
- कैरमबोर्ड
- गिट्टे

घर के बाहर खेले जाने वाले खेल

- फुटबॉल
- हॉकी
- रस्साकशी
- क्रिकेट
- खो-खो
- टेबल टेनिस

2. **आपका सबसे प्रिय खेल कौन-सा है? उसके बारे में चार पंक्तियाँ लिखिए।**

उत्तर
- मेरा प्रिय खेल छुपन-छुपाई है।
- मैं यह खेल अपने दोस्तों के साथ मिलकर बगीचे में खेलता हूँ।
- एक बच्चा आँख मूँदकर 10 तक गिनती गिनता है।
- हम सब छिप जाते हैं और वह हम सबको ढूँढता है।

3. **आओ बताएँ**

1. मेरा नाम सलोनी है। तुम्हारा नाम क्या है?
2. मैं प्रतिदिन शाम को मित्रों के साथ खेलती हूँ। तुम कब और किसके साथ खेलते हो?
3. मुझे छिपा-छिपी खेलना बहुत अच्छा लगता है और तुम्हें?
4. खेलने से मैं शरीर में ऊर्जा और फुर्ती अनुभव करती हूँ।

उत्तर
1. मेरा नाम राजीव है।
2. मैं प्रतिदिन शाम को अपने मित्र राकेश, राहुल, मोहन, रोशन और अन्य साथियों के साथ खेलता हूँ।
3. मुझे खो-खो खेलना बहुत अच्छा लगता है। साथ ही सभी मित्रों को लेकर मैं क्रिकेट भी खेलता हूँ।
4. मैं भी खेलने से शरीर में ऊर्जा और फुर्ती का अनुभव करता हूँ। खेलने से मेरा व्यायाम भी हो जाता है।

बनाइए

1. **खेल-खेलते समय प्राय: छोटी-छोटी चोट लग जाती है। जब आपको चोट लगती है, तब आप क्या-क्या करते हैं? अपने लिए एक छोटा-सा डिब्बा बनाइए और बताइए कि आप उसमें रूई और पट्टी के अतिरिक्त क्या-क्या रखेंगे?**

उत्तर खेल खेलते समय जब चोट लग जाती है, तो बच्चे उस पर मिट्टी लगा लेते हैं, चोट वाले स्थान पर कागज लगा लेते हैं आदि।

मैं, डिब्बे में डेटॉल, आयोडेक्स, रूई, बीटाडीन, थर्मामीटर, स्प्रिट-मूव, लोशन, पट्टी टेप, बैंडेज़, दर्द निवारक गोली, कैंची रखूँगा।

कुछ नया करें

1. **नीचे कुछ खेलों के चित्र दिए गए हैं। आप इनमें से अपने मनभावन खेल को पहचानिए और उस खेल में रुचि होने का कारण भी लिखिए।**

उत्तर मुझे कंचे खेलना बहुत पसंद है। रंग-बिरंगे त्र छोटे-बड़े कंचों को देखकर मेरा मन प्रफुल्लित हो उठता है। कंचे काँच की छोटी-छोटी गोलियों को कहते हैं। अलग-अलग रंगों के कंचों को निशाना लगाकर मारा जाता है, जिसके लिए हाथों की अँगुलियों का इस्तेमाल किया जाता है, जो साथी जितना सटीक निशाना लगाता है, वह कंचा उसका हो जाता है। खुशी देने वाली बात यह होती है कि कंचों को जीतकर हासिल किया जाता है।

2. **चित्रों में अपनी रुचि के अनुसार रंग भरिए। चित्रों में दर्शाए गए किसी एक खेल के बारे में अपने विचार लिखिए।**

उत्तर छात्र स्वयं करें।

अभ्यास प्रश्न

बहुविकल्पीय प्रश्न

1. रस्साकशी में कितने समूह होते हैं?

(क) तीन (ख) दो
(ग) एक (घ) चार

2. बच्चे किस खेल में पसीने से तरबतर हो गए?

(क) क्रिकेट में (ख) फुटबॉल में
(ग) रस्साकशी में (घ) वॉलीबाल में

3. रस्साकशी खेल में क्या नहीं फिसलना चाहिए?

(क) गेंद (ख) बैट
(ग) रस्सी (घ) कपड़ा

4. रस्साकशी खेल में कैसी चाल भिड़ानी चाहिए?

(क) आड़ी-तिरछी (ख) आड़ी
(ग) सीधी (घ) तिरछी

उत्तर

1. (ख) दो
2. (ग) रस्साकशी में
3. (ग) रस्सी
4. (क) आड़ी-तिरछा

काव्यांश पर आधारित प्रश्न

निम्नलिखित काव्यांश को पढ़कर उस पर आधारित प्रश्नों के उत्तर दीजिए।

काव्यांश

सीना ताने रहो अकड़ कर,
रस्सा दोनों और पकड़ कर
तिरछे पड़कर, कमर जकड़ कर
जोर लगाओ हेई सा!
हेई सा! भई हेई सा।।

1. क्या तानकर अकड़ कर रहना है?

(क) सीना (ख) पैर
(ग) हाथ (घ) आँख

2. .... ओर पकड़ कर। रिक्त स्थानों की पूति करें।

(क) तिरछे (ख) आड़े
(ग) रस्सा दोनों (घ) अकड़

3. बच्चे अपने अंदर जोश लाने के लिए क्या बोलते हैं?

4. रस्सी को कितनी ओर से पकड़ना पड़ता है?

उत्तर

1. (क) सीना
2. रस्सा दोनों
3. बच्चे अपने अंदर जोश लाने के लिए 'जोर लगाओ, हेई सा!' बोलते हैं।
4. रस्सी को दो ओर से पकड़ना पड़ता है।

निम्नलिखित प्रश्नों के उत्तर दीजिए

1. रस्साकशी खेल में चाल को कैसे भिड़ाना चाहिए?

उत्तर रस्साकशी खेल में चाल को आड़ी-तिरछी भिड़ाना चाहिए।

2. क्या गड़ाकर रस्सी को खींचना है?

उत्तर पैर गड़ाकर रस्सी को खींचना है।

3. कविता में साथियों का साथ न छूटने पाए, ऐसा क्यों कहा गया है?

उत्तर कविता में साथियों का साथ न छूटने पाए, ऐसा इसलिए कहा गया है कि साथ छूटने से वह टीम हार जाएगी।

4. रस्साकशी खेल खेलते समय जोश को कम क्यों नहीं होने देना है?

उत्तर रस्साकशी खेल खेलते समय जोश को कम नहीं होने देना चाहिए। ऐसा करने से जीतने की संभावना अधिक रहती है।

लेखन संबंधी प्रश्न

1. 'कबूतर' के बारे में लगभग 40 शब्दों में अनुच्छेद लिखिए।

उत्तर कबूतर आमतौर पर घरों के आस-पास दिखाई देता है। कबूतर देखने में भोला-भाला पक्षी है। यह राख के रंग या सफेद रंग या चितकबरे रंग का भी होता है। पुराने समय में कबूतर संदेश पहुँचाने का काम करते थे। कबूतरों को लोग घरों में भी पालते हैं। कबूतर शाकाहारी होते हैं।

अध्याय 11 एक जादुई पिटारा

कविता का सार

प्रस्तुत कविता 'एक जादुई पिटारा' में एक जादुई पिटारे के बारे में बताया गया है। जादुई पिटारा एक ऐसा डिब्बा है, जिसमें से बहुत सारी जादुई और मजेदार चीजें निकलती हैं।

काव्यांशों की व्याख्या

काव्यांश 1

एक पिटारा हमने खोला,
उसमें से निकला गप्पू गोला।
गोले पर जब बाँधी सुतली,
लगा नाचने बन कठपुतली।

शब्दार्थ *पिटारा-डब्बा, सुतली-धागा।*

संदर्भ/प्रसंग प्रस्तुत पंक्तियाँ हमारी पाठ्य पुस्तक 'वीणा भाग-1' में संकलित हैं, जो कविता 'एक जादुई पिटारा' से ली गई हैं। इस कविता में एक ऐसे जादुई पिटारे के बारे में बताया गया है, जिसे खोलते ही अलग-अलग चौकाने वाली वस्तुएँ निकलती हैं।

व्याख्या कवि कहते हैं कि जब बच्चों ने जादुई पिटारा खोला, तो उसमें से गप्पू गोला निकला। गोले पर जब सुतली बाँधी, तो वह कठपुतली बन गया और नाचने लग। यह देखकर बच्चे प्रसन्न हो गए।

काव्यांश 2

कठपुतली ने गाड़े खूँट, उसमें निकले नौ सौ ऊँट।
उन ऊँटों पर हुई सवारी, मिली राह में एक सुपारी।

शब्दार्थ *खूँट-जमीन में गाड़ा गया लकड़ी का एक छोटा टुकड़ा, राह-रास्ता।*

प्रसंग पूर्ववत्।

व्याख्या कवि कहते हैं कि कठपुतली ने जमीन में खूँटा गाड़ा, तो उसमें से नौ सौ ऊँट निकले, जब वे ऊँटों पर सवार होकर चले, तो रास्ते में उन्हें एक सुपारी मिली।

काव्यांश 3

उस सुपारी को जब काटा, उसमें निकला नौ मन आटा।
उस आटे पर नारियल फोड़ा, उसमें निकल पड़ा इक घोड़ा।

शब्दार्थ *मन-40 किग्रा, इक-एक।*

प्रसंग पूर्ववत्।

व्याख्या कवि कहते हैं कि जब उस सुपारी को काटा, तो उसमें से नौ मन आटा निकला, फिर जब उस आटे पर नारियल फोड़ा गया, तो उसमें से एक घोड़ा निकला।

काव्यांश 4

घोड़े को जब ऐड़ लगाई, आसमान ले पहुँचा भाई।
पाया वहाँ एक गुब्बारा, जिस पर छेद हुए थे बारा।

शब्दार्थ *ऐड़ लगाई - मारना, बारा-बारह।*

प्रसंग पूर्ववत्।

व्याख्या कवि कहते हैं कि जैसे ही घोड़े को ऐड़ लगाई (मारा), तो वह सीधे आसमान में लेकर पहुँच गया। वहाँ उसे एक गुब्बारा मिला, जिसमें बारह छेद थे।

काव्यांश 5

एक छेद पर था इस्टेशन, जिस पर खड़ा हुआ था इंजन।
उस इंजन को धोया ऐसे, उसमें निकल पड़े दो भैंसे।

शब्दार्थ *इस्टेशन-स्टेशन।*

प्रसंग पूर्ववत्।

व्याख्या कवि कहते हैं कि उन बारह छेदों में से एक पर स्टेशन था, जहाँ एक इंजन खड़ा हुआ था। उस इंजन को धोया गया, तो उसमें से दो भैंसे निकल आए।

काव्यांश 6

भैंसे लाकर जोता खेत, नाज हुआ बारह सौ सेर।
खा-खा नाज हुए दीवाने, चले चाल, बेहद मस्ताने।

शब्दार्थ *जोता-जुताई करना, नाज-अनाज।*

प्रसंग पूर्ववत्।

व्याख्या कवि कहते हैं कि किसानों ने भैंसों को लाकर खेत जोता, जिससे बारह सौ सेर अनाज उगा। किसान उस अनाज को खाकर दीवाने से हो गए और मस्त होकर चलने लगे।

सोचिए और लिखिए

1. कविता के अनुसार जब पिटारा खोला गया, तो उसमें से क्या-क्या निकला?

उत्तर कविता के अनुसार जब पिटारा खोला गया, तो उसमें से गप्पू गोला, कठपुतली, नौ सौ ऊँट, एक सुपारी, नौ मन आटा, नारियल, एक घोड़ा, एक गुब्बारा, स्टेशन, एक इंजन, दो भैंसे, बारह सौ सेर अनाज आदि निकले।

2. कविता में गिनती के कौन-कौन से अंक आए हैं? ढूँढकर लिखिए।

उत्तर

एक - 1	नौ-सौ - 900	बारह - 12
दो - 2	नौ - 9	बारह सौ-1200

3. नौ मन आटा किसमें निकला?

उत्तर एक सुपारी को काटने पर उसमें से नौ मन आटा निकला।

4. किसान खेतों को जोतने के लिए किसका सहारा लेते हैं?

उत्तर किसान खेतों को जोतने के लिए भैंसों का सहारा लेते हैं।

खोजिए और लिखिए

1. नीचे लिखे शब्दों से तुक मिलने वाले शब्द कविता से ढूँढकर लिखिए।

उत्तर
- खोला - गोला
- खूँट - ऊँट
- सवारी - सुपारी
- सुतली - कठपुतली

2. जब एक हो तो 'गोला' कहलाता है अनेक हो तो 'गोले'। नीचे दिए शब्दों को भी एक से अधिक मानकर उनके लिए शब्द लिखिए।

पिटारा .... घोड़ा ....
भैंस .... गुब्बारा ....

उत्तर

एकवचन	बहुवचन
पिटारा	— पिटारे
घोड़ा	— घोड़े
भैंस	— भैंसे
गुब्बारा	— गुब्बारे

3. नीचे दिए चित्रों को पहचानते हुए खेलों के नामों के साथ उनका मिलान कीजिए।

उत्तर

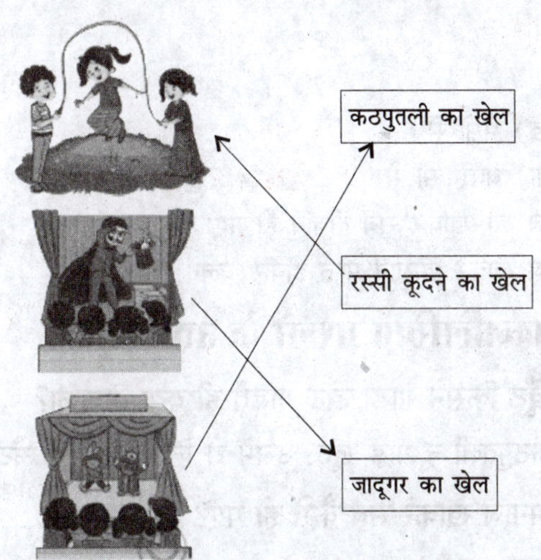

4. कविता के आधार पर पंक्तियों का मिलान कीजिए।

(क) गोले पर जब बाँधी सुतली – आसमान ले पहुँचा भाई।

(ख) एक पिटारा हमने खोला – लगा नाचने बन कठपुतली।

(ग) उन ऊँटों पर हुई सवारी – उसमें से निकला गप्पू गोला।

(घ) घोड़े के जब ऐड़ लगाई – मिली राह में एक सुपारी।

उत्तर

(क) गोले पर जब बाँधी सुतली — लगा नाचने बन कठपुतली।

(ख) एक पिटारा हमने खोला — उसमें से निकला गप्पू गोला।

(ग) उन ऊँटों पर हुई सवारी — मिली राह में एक सुपारी।

(घ) घोड़े के जब ऐड़ लगाई — आसमान ले पहुँचा भाई।

5. नीचे लिखे अक्षरों के क्रम को व्यवस्थित करके सही शब्द लिखिए। उदाहरण ड़ा/घो- घोड़ा

उत्तर (क) चा/ना — नाचा

(ख) रा/टा/पि — पिटारा

(ग) ला/क/नि — निकला

(घ) ला/गो — गोला

(ङ) श/का/आ — आकाश

6. नीचे दिए गए चित्रों में रंग भरिए। यदि आपको इनमें से किसी की सवारी करने का अवसर मिले तो आप किसकी सवारी करना चाहेंगे? उसके बारे में 4–5 पंक्तियों में अपने विचार लिखिए।

उत्तर चित्र में रंग छात्र स्वयं भरें।

यदि मुझे इनमें से किसी की सवारी करने का अवसर मिले, तो मैं घोड़े की सवारी करना चाहूँगा।

- घोड़ा एक पालतू पशु है।
- घोड़ा बहुत तेज दौड़ता है।
- घोड़े काले, भूरे, सफेद रंगों के होते हैं।
- घोड़े की गर्दन पर लंबे बाल होते हैं।
- घोड़ा हरी घास खाता है।

7. नीचे जादुई पिटारे का एक चित्र दिया गया है, उसमें अपनी पसंद के रंग भरिए। आप भी अपना एक जादुई पिटारा बनाइए और बताइए कि आप उसमें क्या-क्या रखना चाहेंगे?

उत्तर मैं अपने जादुई पिटारे में निम्नलिखित वस्तुएँ रखूँगा

1. छोटी-छोटी दो कार
2. बोलने वाली फुँटबाल
3. आइसक्रीम
4. फोन
5. मीठी टॉफी
6. बोलने वाली गुड़िया

मेरी कलाकारी

1. नीचे दिए गए चित्रों में तीलियों वाले पुतले दिखाए गए हैं। आप भी अपनी पसंद के फल, फूल, साग, पशु-पक्षियों व जानवरों के पुतले तैयार कीजिए। कठपुतलियों का एक पिटारा तैयार करने में अपने शिक्षक को सहयोग दीजिए।

नोट विद्यार्थी चित्र NCERT पाठ्यपुस्तक के पृष्ठ 98 पर देखें।

उत्तर विद्यार्थी स्वयं करें।

अभ्यास प्रश्न

बहुविकल्पीय प्रश्न

1. गोले पर क्या बँधी थी?

(क) डोरा (ख) रस्सी
(ग) धागा (घ) सुतली

2. ऊँटों पर सवारी करते हुए रास्ते में क्या मिला?

(क) आटा (ख) ऊँट
(ग) घोड़ा (घ) सुपारी

3. नारियल किस पर फोड़ा गया?

(क) ईंट पर (ख) आटे पर
(ग) घोड़े पर (घ) चाँद पर

4. गुब्बारे में कितने छेद हुए थे?

(क) बारह (ख) नौ
(ग) दो (घ) एक

उत्तर

1. (घ) सुतली 2. (घ) सुपारी
3. (ख) आटे पर 4. (क) बारह

काव्यांश पर आधारित प्रश्न

निम्नलिखित काव्यांश को पढ़कर उस पर आधारित प्रश्नों के उत्तर दीजिए।

काव्यांश

भैंसे लाकर जोता खेत,
नाज हुआ बारह सौ सेर।
खा-खा नाज हुए दीवाने,
चले चाल बेहद मस्ताने।

1. खेत किससे जोता गया?

(क) घोड़ों (ख) भैंसों से (ग) ऊँट से (घ) गायों से

2. नाज कितने सेर हुआ था?

(क) बारह सौ सेर (ख) नौ सेर
(ग) दो सौ सेर (घ) दो सेर

3. नाज खा-खाकर सब कैसे हो गए?

4. नाज खाकर किसान कैसे चलने लगे?

उत्तर

1. (ख) भैंसों से
2. (क) बारह सौ सेर
3. नाज खा-खाकर सब दीवाने हो गए।
4. नाज खाकर किसान मस्त होकर चलने लगे।

निम्नलिखित प्रश्नों के उत्तर दीजिए

1. खूँट किसने गाड़ा खूँट गाड़ते ही क्या निकला?

उत्तर कठपुतली ने गाड़े खूँट, उसमें से निकले नौ सौ ऊँट।

2. अनाज खाकर सब कैसें हो गए?

उत्तर अनाज खाकर सब दीवाने हो गए।

3. जादुई पिटारे से क्या निकला?

उत्तर जादुई पिटारे से गप्पू गोला निकला।

4. नारियल फोड़ने के बाद क्या हुआ?

उत्तर नारियल फोड़ने के बाद उसमें से घोड़ा निकला।

लेखन संबंधी प्रश्न

1. चित्र को देखकर उसका वर्णन 30 शब्दों में कीजिए।

उत्तर उपरोक्त चित्र में दो बच्चे बारिश में खेल रहे हैं। लड़की के हाथ में कागज की एक नाव है। उसे वह पानी में बहा रही है। दोनों बच्चे बहुत खुश है। उनकी नाव अपने सफर पर निकल पड़ी है। यह चित्र बड़ा ही मनभावन लग रहा है।

अपना-अपना काम

पाठ का सार

एक दिन सिमरन बाग में बैठी स्कूल का काम कर रही थी। जब वह काम करते करते थक गई, तो उसके मन में एक ख्याल आया कि कितना अच्छा होता यदि मुझे पढ़ना न पड़ता। सिमरन की नजर बाग में उड़ती मधुमक्खी पर जाती है, जो एक फूल से दूसरे फूल पर उड़ रही थी। सिमरन ने सोचा कि मैं भी मधुमक्खी बन जाऊँ, तभी एक मधुमक्खी रुकी और बोली, ''सारा दिन उड़कर रस इकट्ठा करते करते हमारे पंख थक जाते हैं।'' सिमरन ने सोचा कि सारा दिन पंख फैलाकर उड़ना पड़े तो मैं तो बहुत थक जाऊँगी।

फिर सिमरन की नज़र फलों से लदे हुए एक पेड़ पर जाती है। वह सोचने लगी कि यदि वह पेड़ होती, तो कितना अच्छा होता। पेड़ को तो आराम से एक ही जगह खड़े-खड़े सब कुछ मिल जाता है। पेड़ कहता है, ''मेरे शरीर का तो हर अंग दिन-रात काम करता है। जड़ें मिट्टी से पानी खींचती हैं और पत्ते दिनभर खाना बनाते हैं। इतने परिश्रम के पश्चात् फल उगते हैं।'' यह सुनकर सिमरन को पेड़ के लिए बहुत दु:ख हुआ। सिमरन ने सोचा पेड़ तो बहुत परिश्रम करते हैं और इनके फल हम खा लेते हैं।

फिर सिमरन की नजर उड़ती हुई चिड़िया पर पड़ती है। सिमरन ने सोचा मैं भी चिड़िया बन जाती तो ठीक था। तभी चिड़िया बोली, ''मैं एक-एक दाना चुगने के लिए सारा दिन उड़ती हूँ और घोंसला बनाने के लिए भी बहुत परिश्रम करती हूँ।''

सभी बातें सुनकर सिमरन बोली मैं समझ गई परिश्रम से ही सब जीते हैं। मुझे भी परिश्रम करना चाहिए और मन लगाकर पढ़ना चाहिए। सिमरन उत्साह के साथ अपना काम करने बैठ जाती है।

शब्दार्थ

बाग-बगीचा, आनंदपूर्वक-खुशी से, परिश्रम-मेहनत, अचंभित-आश्चर्य, भाग-हिस्सा, पश्चात्-बाद।

NCERT फोल्डर

बातचीत के लिए

1. आप क्या-क्या काम करते हैं?

उत्तर मैं सुबह उठकर मुँह धोता हूँ, फिर नाश्ता करता हूँ। स्कूल जाता हूँ और पढ़ाई करता हूँ घर आकर अपना होमवर्क करता हूँ। शाम को पौधों को पानी देता हूँ और दोस्तों के साथ खेलता हूँ। रात में खाना खाकर सो जाता हूँ।

2. आपको कौन-कौन से काम बहुत अच्छे लगते हैं?

उत्तर मुझे स्कूल जाना और नई-नई चीजें सीखना बहुत अच्छा लगता है। कहानी की किताबें पढ़ना भी मुझे बहुत पसंद है। मुझे पौधों में पानी देना भी अच्छा लगता है।

3. इस कहानी में आपको किसका काम अच्छा लगा और क्यों?

उत्तर इस कहानी में मुझे सबसे अच्छा काम पेड़ का लगा, क्योंकि पेड़ के सभी अंग अलग-अलग काम करते हैं। पेड़ का सबसे अच्छा काम यह लगा कि पेड़ अपने लिए फल न उगाकर दूसरों के लिए उगाते हैं। वह दूसरों की सेवा कर हम सबको प्रेरणा देता है।

सोचिए और लिखिए

1. सिमरन क्यों थक गई थी?

उत्तर सिमरन अपना स्कूल का काम करते-करते थक गई थी।

2. सिमरन मधुमक्खी क्यों बनना चाहती थी?

उत्तर सिमरन मधुमक्खी इसलिए बनना चाहती थी, क्योंकि उसे लगा कि मधुमक्खियाँ बस उड़ती रहती हैं और उनका काम आसान है।

3. पेड़ क्या-क्या काम करते हैं?

उत्तर पेड़ अनेक काम करते हैं; जैसे— पेड़ की जड़ें पानी खींचती हैं, पत्तियाँ भोजन बनाती हैं तथा वे हमें फल और छाया के साथ औषधि भी देते हैं।

4. सिमरन को चिड़िया का काम सरल क्यों लगा?

उत्तर सिमरन को चिड़िया का काम सरल इसलिए लगा, क्योंकि चिड़िया बस इधर से उधर घूमती रहती है और दाना खाती रहती है।

5. आपके अनुसार सिमरन अंत में पुस्तकें उठाकर काम क्यों करने लगी?

उत्तर सिमरन ने अंत में समझा कि हर काम में मेहनत होती है, इसलिए उसने सोचा कि उसे भी मेहनत से पढ़ाई करनी चाहिए और वह मन लगाकर काम करने लगी।

कहानी से

1. आप पूरे दिन में क्या-क्या काम करते हैं? सूची बनाइए।

उत्तर
- अपना बिस्तर खुद साफ करता हूँ।
- स्कूल बैग में प्रतिदिन पुस्तक रखता हूँ।
- पूजा के लिए फूल तोड़कर लाता हूँ।
- दादी को दवाई और पानी देता हूँ।
- अपने जूते सही जगह पर रखता हूँ।
- प्रतिदिन पढ़ाई-लिखाई करता हूँ।

2. आपके घरों में कौन-कौन से काम किसके द्वारा किए जाते हैं? रिक्त स्थानों में लिखिए।

काम		करने वाला
1. पेड़ पौधों को पानी देना	—	माँ
2.		....
3.		....
4.		....
5.		....

उत्तर

काम		करने वाला
1. पेड़ पौधों को पानी देना	—	माँ
2. खाना बनाना	—	माँ
3. कपड़े धोना	—	माँ
4. बाजार से सामान लाना	—	पिताजी
5. घर की सफाई	—	सब मिलकर

3. सिमरन और मधुमक्खी की बात को आगे बढ़ाइए।

सिमरन ओह! पढ़ने-लिखने का मुझे बहुत काम करना पड़ता है। तुम्हारा काम सरल है इस फूल से उस फूल बस घूमते रहो ....।

मधुमक्खी

उत्तर तुम तो इतनी सुखी हो, तुम क्यों हम जैसा नन्हा कीड़ा बनना चाहती हो? सारे दिन उड़-उडकर रस इकट्ठा करते-करते हमारे पंख थक जाते हैं।

4. **दिए गए वाक्यों को कहानी से पूरा कीजिए।**

उसने देखा कि मधुमक्खियाँ आनंदपूर्वक ....।

मेरे शरीर का तो हर अंग दिन-रात ....

.... वे भी हम तुम्हें दे देते हैं।

उसने अपनी पुस्तकें ....।

उत्तर उसने देखा कि मक्खियाँ आनंदपूर्वक एक फूल से दूसरे फूल तक उड़ रही थीं।

मेरे शरीर का तो हर अंग दिन-रात काम करता है। जड़ें मिट्टी से पानी खींचती हैं। पत्ते दिनभर खाना बनाते हैं और इतने परिश्रम के पश्चात् जो फल उगते हैं, वे भी हम तुम्हें दे देते हैं।

उसने अपनी पुस्तकें उठाईं और उत्साह से स्कूल का काम करने बैठ गई।

5. **मधुमक्खी एक फूल से दूसरे फूल पर जाकर शहद बनाती है। क्या आप बता सकते हैं कि शहद हमारे किस-किस काम आता है?**

उदाहरण दूध को मीठा करने के लिए।

उत्तर शहद हमारे निम्न प्रकार काम आता है

- मिठाई बनाने के लिए
- वजन कम करने के लिए
- पाचन ठीक रखने के लिए
- खाँसी और कफ ठीक करने के लिए

भाषा की बात

1. **कहानी में कुछ संज्ञाओं (नाम वाले शब्दों) का प्रयोग किया गया है। उन्हें ढूँढकर रिक्त स्थानों में लिखिए।**

चिड़िया ..... सिमरन ....

.... (संज्ञा) ....

....

उत्तर चिड़िया, पुस्तक, सिमरन, मधुमक्खी, फल, पेड़।

कल्पना कीजिए

1. **यदि आप अपनी इच्छा से एक दिन के लिए कुछ भी बन सकते तो आप क्या बनते? कल्पना कीजिए और लिखिए।**

उत्तर एक दिन के लिए मैं बारिश की बूँद बनती और ऊपर से गिरते हुए पूरी पृथ्वी को देखती। मुझे इसमें बड़ा ही मजा आता।

चित्रकारी

1. **सिमरन को पेड़ ने बताया कि वे हमें फल देने के लिए बहुत सारे काम करते हैं। आप एक फलदार पेड़ का सुंदर चित्र बनाइए और उसमें रंग भरिए।**

उत्तर छात्र स्वयं करें।

बहुविकल्पीय प्रश्न

1. **सिमरन कहाँ बैठकर स्कूल का काम कर रही थी?**
(क) घर पर (ख) कुर्सी पर
(ग) बालकनी में (घ) बाग में

2. **एक फूल से दूसरे फूल पर कौन उड़ रहा था?**
(क) भौरा (ख) चिड़िया
(ग) तितली (घ) मधुमक्खी

3. **सिमरन क्या बनना चाहती थी?**
(क) चिड़िया (ख) मधुमक्खी (ग) पेड़ (घ) ये सभी

4. **किसके शरीर का हर अंग दिन-रात काम करता है?**
(क) पेड़ (ख) मधुमक्खी
(ग) सिमरन (घ) चिड़िया

5. **दाना चुनने के लिए सारा दिन कौन उड़ता है?**
(क) चिड़िया (ख) सिमरन (ग) मधुमक्खी (घ) पेड़

उत्तर

1. (घ) बाग में 2. (घ) मधुमक्खी
3. (घ) ये सभी 4. (क) पेड़
5. (क) चिड़िया

◘ सत्य–असत्य

नीचे दिए गए वाक्यों में से सत्य या असत्य कथन की पहचान कीजिए।

1. सिमरन पेड़ नहीं बनना चाहती थी। (सत्य/असत्य)
2. सिमरन सोचती थी, कि कितना अच्छा होता यदि मुझे पढ़ना न पड़ता। (सत्य/असत्य)
3. पेड़ की जड़ें मिट्टी से पानी खींचती हैं। (सत्य/असत्य)
4. सिमरन सबकी बातें सुनकर पढ़ने बैठ जाती है। (सत्य/असत्य)

उत्तर

1. असत्य 2. सत्य
3. सत्य 4. सत्य

◘ रिक्त स्थान

नीचे दिए गए वाक्यों में रिक्त स्थान की पूर्ति उचित शब्द से कीजिए।

(मधमक्खियाँ, फल, परिश्रम, पुस्तक)

1. .... रख सिमरन चारों ओर देखने लगी।
2. भिनभिन करती .... रुक गईं।
3. .... तो हम ही खा लेते हैं।
4. मुझे भी .... करना चाहिए और मन लगाकर पढ़ना चाहिए।

उत्तर

1. पुस्तक 2. मधुमक्खियाँ 3. फल 4. परिश्रम

◘ गद्यांश पर आधारित प्रश्न

निम्नलिखित गद्यांश को पढ़कर उस पर आधारित प्रश्नों के उत्तर दीजिए।

गद्यांश

फिर उसने ऊपर देखा फलों से लदा पेड़। "हाँ, अगर मैं पेड़ होती तो अच्छा था। आराम से एक जगह खड़े-खड़े सब कुछ मिल जाता।" पेड़ हँसने लगा, "मैं समझ गया। तुम सोचती हो कि मैं आराम से खड़ा रहता हूँ, बस!"

1. पेड़ किससे लदा था?
   (क) पत्तियों से (ख) टहनियों से
   (ग) डालियों से (घ) फलों से
2. कौन सोच रहा था कि "पेड़ होती तो अच्छा था"?
   (क) मधुमक्खी (ख) चिड़िया
   (ग) पेड़ (घ) सिमरन
3. पेड़ क्यों हँसने लगा?
4. सिमरन क्या सोचती थी?

उत्तर

1. (घ) फलों से 2. (घ) सिमरन
3. "आराम से एक जगह खड़े-खड़े सब कुछ मिल जाता।" सिमरन की यह बात सुनकर पेड़ हँसने लगा।
4. सिमरन सोचती थी कि पेड़ एक जगह आराम से खड़े रहते हैं।

◘ निम्नलिखित प्रश्नों के उत्तर दीजिए

1. सिमरन क्या-क्या बनना चाहती थी?

उत्तर सिमरन मधुमक्खी, पेड़ व चिड़िया बनना चाहती थी।

2. सिमरन चिड़िया को देखकर क्या सोचती थी?

उत्तर सिमरन सोचती कि चिड़ियों की तो मौज है।

3. पेड़ किस प्रकार मेहनत करते हैं?

उत्तर पेड़ के सभी भाग अलग-अलग कार्य करके मेहनत करते हैं; जैसे— जड़ें मिट्टी से पानी सोखती हैं, पत्ते खाना बनाते हैं आदि।

4. सबके जवाब सुनने के बाद सिमरन ने क्या किया?

उत्तर सबके जवाब सुनने के बाद सिमरन अपना काम करने बैठ गई।

◘ लेखन संबंधी प्रश्न

1. अवकाश हेतु प्रार्थना-पत्र लिखिए।

उत्तर सेवा में,

श्रीमान प्रधानाचार्य,
आदर्श विद्यालय,
नई दिल्ली– 1100 XX

विषय अवकाश हेतु प्रार्थना-पत्र।

महोदय,

विनम्र निवेदन है कि मुझे कल रात से तेज बुखार है, जिसके कारण मैं विद्यालय नहीं आ सकता। कृपा करके मुझे दो दिन का अवकाश प्रदान करें। आपकी अति कृपा होगी।

धन्यवाद

आपका आज्ञाकारी शिष्य
मनोज भाटी
कक्षा– III B
अनुक्रमांक-12

पेड़ों की अम्मा 'थिमक्का'

पाठ का सार

प्रस्तुत पाठ 'पेड़ों की अम्मा-थिमक्का' एक महान पर्यावरणविद् पर आधारित है, जो एक सामाजिक कार्यकर्ता भी हैं। उन्हें 'अम्मा' और 'वृक्षमाता' के नाम से भी जाना जाता है। उनका जन्म कर्नाटक के तुमकुरु जिले में हुआ था। वे पिछले 80 वर्षों से सड़कों के किनारे पौधे लगा रही हैं। वृक्षारोपण के अपने अच्छे काम के लिए उन्हें अनेक पुरस्कार भी मिल चुके हैं। अम्मा को भारत सरकार द्वारा वर्ष 2019 में पद्मश्री पुरस्कार भी प्राप्त हुआ है। उन्होंने हुलिकल और कुदुर के बीच स्थित 45 किमी लंबे राजमार्ग पर 385 बरगद के पेड़ लगाए हैं। उन्होंने अलग-अलग स्थानों पर 8000 से भी अधिक पेड़ लगाए हैं। अपने कार्यों के बल पर लोगों की प्रेरणा बनकर वे 107 वर्ष की उम्र में आज भी अपने इस कार्य में जुटी हुई हैं।

शब्दार्थ

विख्यात–प्रसिद्ध, रमणीय–सुंदर, उत्कृष्ट–उत्तम, खान–खदान, वनीकरण–वनों को बढ़ाना, अभाव–कमी।

1. पेड़ हमारे किस-किस काम आते हैं?

उत्तर पेड़ों से हमें फल, फूल मिलते हैं। पेड़ों की लकड़ी फर्नीचर बनाने और ईंधन के काम आती है। पेड़ों से हमें ऑक्सीजन भी मिलती है।

2. क्या आपने कभी किसी पौधे की देखभाल की है? कैसे?

उत्तर हाँ, मैंने इमली के पेड़ को उगाया है। मैंने एक गड्ढा खोदकर इमली का बीज उसमें डाल दिया और समय-समय पर उसमें खाद और पानी डालता रहा। कुछ महीनों बाद पौधा मिट्टी से बाहर आकर बढ़ने लगा।

3. यदि आपको समाज के लिए उपयोगी काम करने का अवसर मिले, तो आप कौन-सा काम करेंगे?

उत्तर यदि मुझे समाज के लिए उपयोगी काम करने का अवसर मिले, तो मैं वातावरण को स्वच्छ बनाने में अपना योगदान दूँगा।

सोचिए और लिखिए

1. थिमक्का अपने किस काम के कारण प्रसिद्ध हुईं?

उत्तर थिमक्का हुलिकल और कुदुर के बीच स्थित 45 किमी लंबे राजमार्ग पर लगभग 385 बरगद के पेड़ लगाने के लिए प्रसिद्ध हुईं।

2. थिमक्का को और किस-किस नाम से जाना जाता है?

उत्तर थिमक्का को अम्मा, वृक्षमाता, सालूमरदा थिमक्का के नाम से भी जाना जाता है।

3. अम्मा ने बरगद के पौधे लगाने क्यों शुरू किए थे?

उत्तर पर्यावरण को बनाए रखने के लिए अम्मा ने बरगद के पौधे लगाने शुरू किए थे।

4. इतने सारे पेड़ लगाने के लिए अम्मा को किन-किन चुनौतियों का सामना करना पड़ा होगा?

उत्तर इतने सारे पेड़-पौधे लगाने के लिए अम्मा को पौधे, बीज आदि खरीदने के लिए धन की समस्या आई होगी, क्योंकि थिमक्का आर्थिक रूप से इतनी सक्षम नहीं थीं। 45 किमी के मार्ग में पौधे लगाने के लिए इतनी दूरी तय करना, इतनी दूर तक पौधे लाना, ले जाना, पानी देना, मौसम आदि चुनौतियों का सामना करना पड़ा होगा।

पाठ के आगे

1. यदि आपको थिमक्का अम्मा का परिचय देना हो तो आप कैसे देंगे?

उत्तर थिमक्का अम्मा 107 वर्ष की हैं। कर्नाटक में रहने वाली थिमक्का 80 वर्षों से सड़कों के किनारे पौधे लगा रही हैं। इन्होंने हुलिकल और कुदुर के बीच स्थित 45 किमी लंबे राजमार्ग पर लगभग 385 बरगद के पौधे लगाए। इस कार्य के लिए भारत सरकार से उन्हें पद्मश्री सम्मान भी प्राप्त हुआ है। आज भी थिमक्का वनों के विकास से जुड़े कार्यों में संलग्न रहकर समाज सेवा कर रही हैं।

2. यदि आपको अम्मा के काम में उनकी सहायता करने का अवसर मिले तो आप कैसे करेंगे?

उत्तर यदि मुझे अम्मा के काम में सहायता करने का अवसर मिले तो मैं अपने द्वारा खाए जाने वाले फलों के बीज इकट्ठा करके अम्मा को दे दूँगा।

भाषा की बात

1. थिमक्का में 'क्का' आया है। ऐसे व्यंजनों को द्वित्व व्यंजन कहते हैं। ऐसे और शब्द सोचकर दिए गए स्थान पर लिखिए।

उदाहरण रस्सी

उत्तर दिल्ली, बिल्ली, बच्चा,
अम्मा, कुत्ता, मुन्ना, मक्का

2. पेड़ को वृक्ष भी कहा जाता है। क्या आप बता सकते हैं कि अलग-अलग भाषाओं में पेड़ को क्या-क्या कहा जाता है?

उत्तर अंग्रेजी - ट्री   संस्कृत - तरु   फ्रेंच - आबरि

3. कई बार हम एक वर्ण और एक अक्षर को मिलाकर एक नया 'संयुक्त अक्षर' बनाते हैं; जैसे-

संयुक्ताक्षर	उदाहरण
क् + ष = क्ष	क्षमा, दक्ष, पक्ष
ज् + ञ = ज्ञ	प्रतिज्ञा, ज्ञानी, विज्ञान
त् + र = त्र	त्रिशूल, त्रिभुज, त्रिनेत्र
श् + र = श्र	श्रमिक, आश्रित, आश्रय

उपरोक्त उदाहरणों के आधार पर नीचे दिए गए चित्रों को देखकर शब्द पूरे कीजिए।

उत्तर वृक्ष, नेत्र, त्रिभुज, कक्षा, श्रमिक

कुछ नया करें

1. आपने थिमक्का के बारे में पढ़ा और उनके काम से प्रेरित हुए। थिमक्का को एक पत्र लिखकर उन्हें अपने मन की बात बताइए।

उत्तर छात्र स्वयं करें।

2. चित्र देखकर उन वस्तुओं पर गोला बनाएँ, जो हमें पेड़ों से मिलती हैं।

उत्तर

अभ्यास प्रश्न

बहुविकल्पीय प्रश्न

1. थिमक्का कितने वर्षों से पौधे लगा रही हैं?
(क) 70 वर्षों से (ख) 80 वर्षों से
(ग) 50 वर्षों से (घ) 20 वर्षों से

2. थिमक्का पहले कहाँ काम करती थीं?
(क) बाग में (ग) संस्था में
(ख) घर में (घ) खान में

3. 'सालूमरदा' शब्द का क्या अर्थ है?
(क) वृक्षारोपण (ख) पेड़ों से लाभ
(ग) पेड़ों की पंक्ति (घ) पेड़ों के प्रकार

4. थिमक्का कितने वर्ष की हैं?
(क) 103 वर्ष
(ख) 105 वर्ष
(ग) 108 वर्ष
(घ) 107 वर्ष

उत्तर
1. (ख) 80 वर्षों से 2. (घ) खान में
3. (ग) पेड़ों की पंक्ति 4. (घ) 107 वर्ष

गद्यांश पर आधारित प्रश्न

निम्नलिखित गद्यांश को पढ़कर उस पर आधारित प्रश्नों के उत्तर दीजिए।

गद्यांश

थिमक्का हुलिकल और कुदुर के बीच स्थित 45 किमी लंबे राजमार्ग पर लगभग 385 बरगद के पेड़ लगाने के लिए विख्यात हैं। इन पेड़ों के कारण राजमार्ग अत्यंत रमणीय और सुसज्जित लगने लगा। इसके अतिरिक्त उन्होंने अनेक स्थानों पर पेड़ लगाए, जिनकी संख्या 8000 से अधिक है। इनसे पर्यावरण को बहुत लाभ हुआ। इस कार्य में उन्हें उनके पति ने भी पूरा सहयोग दिया।

1. थिमक्का का सहयोग किसने किया?
(क) सरकार (ख) घरवाले (ग) बच्चे (घ) पति

2. 385 बरगद के पेड़ लगाने के लिए कौन विख्यात हैं?
(क) सरकार (ख) राजमाता
(ग) थिमक्का (घ) नंदिनी

3. थिमक्का ने पेड़ लगाने का कार्य कहाँ किया?

4. पेड़ लगाने से राजमार्ग कैसा हो गया?

उत्तर
1. (घ) पति 2. (ग) थिमक्का
3. थिमक्का ने हुलिकल और कुदुर के बीच लंबे राजमार्ग पर पेड़ लगाने का कार्य किया।
4. पेड़ लगाने से राजमार्ग अत्यंत रमणीय और सुसज्जित लगने लगा।

निम्नलिखित प्रश्नों के उत्तर दीजिए

1. थिमक्का को किन कार्यक्रमों के लिए आमंत्रित किया गया?

उत्तर थिमक्का को कई वनीकरण कार्यक्रमों में आमंत्रित किया गया।

2. थिमक्का को किन नामों से जाना जाता है?

उत्तर थिमक्का को 'वृक्षमाता' और 'अम्मा' के नाम से जाना जाता है।

3. थिमक्का को किससे सम्मानित किया गया?

उत्तर थिमक्का को पद्मश्री से सम्मानित किया गया।

4. वर्तमान समय में थिमक्का की आयु कितनी है?

उत्तर वर्तमान समय में थिमक्का की आयु 107 वर्ष है।

लेखन संबंधी प्रश्न

1. 'बगीचा' पर कम-से-कम 40 शब्दों में अनुच्छेद लिखिए।

उत्तर मेरे घर के पास एक बड़ा बगीचा है। वहाँ पर मैं रोज शाम को माताजी के साथ घूमने जाती हूँ। वह बगीचा बहुत सुंदर है। उसमें आम, जामुन, नीम, पीपल, अशोक के बड़े-बड़े पेड़ हैं। वह हरी घास से घिरा हुआ मैदान है, जिसमें हम सभी बच्चे देर तक खेलते हैं।

अध्याय 14 किसान की होशियारी

पाठ का सार

एक किसान अपना खेत जोत रहा था, तभी अचानक कहीं से एक भालू आ गया। भालू किसान को मारने के लिए झपटा तो किसान ने कहा, ''मुझे क्यों मारते हो! फसल होने दो, जो कहोगे, वही खिलाऊँगा।''

भालू मान गया और उसने कहा, ''भूमि के ऊपर की फसल मेरी और नीचे की तुम्हारी।'' किसान ने आलू बो दिए, जिससे भालू को केवल पत्ते खाने को मिले। अगली बार भालू ने कहा ''देखो इस बार जमीन के नीचे की फसल मेरी और ऊपर की तुम्हारी।'' इस बार किसान ने गेहूँ बो दिए, जिससे किसान को तो गेहूँ मिले और भालू को केवल जड़ें मिलीं।

भालू ने किसान को पाठ पढ़ाने की सोची और उसने किसान से कहा, ''भूमि के सबसे ऊपर और सबसे नीचे की फसल मेरी।'' किसान मान गया और इस बार उसने गन्ने की फसल उगाई, जिससे भालू को केवल पत्ते और जड़ें ही मिले। इस प्रकार किसान ने भालू को अपनी होशियारी दिखाई।

शब्दार्थ

जोत–जमीन को चीरना, झपटा – हमला करना, अचानक–एकदम से, उपज–फसल, जड़ें–मिट्टी के नीचे का भाग, खीझकर–चिढ़कर, सिर चकराना–कुछ भी समझ न आना।

बातचीत

1. आपको अपनी कौन-कौन सी वस्तुएँ प्रिय हैं?

उत्तर मुझे मेरी किताबें, खिलौने, रंगों वाला डिब्बा तथा फ्रॉक वाली गुड़िया प्रिय हैं।

2. यदि आप भालू के स्थान पर होते तो किसान से क्या कहते?

उत्तर यदि मैं भालू के स्थान पर होता तो किसान से कहता कि मुझे भूमि के नीचे या ऊपर की फसल नहीं, बल्कि तैयार फसल का आधा हिस्सा चाहिए।

3. आप किसान की चतुराई के विषय में क्या सोचते हैं?

उत्तर किसान चतुर था, इसलिए उसने हर बार भालू की बात भी रखी और अपनी फसल भी बचा ली तथा अपनी जान भी बचा ली।

सोचिए और लिखिए

1. किसान ने भालू से बचने के लिए उससे क्या कहा?

उत्तर किसान ने भालू से बचने के लिए उससे कहा कि, "मुझे क्यों मारते हो? उपज होने दो जो कहोगे, वही खिलाऊँगा।"

2. भालू ने दूसरी बार नीचे की उपज क्यों माँगी?

उत्तर भालू ने दूसरी बार नीचे की उपज इसलिए माँगी, क्योंकि पहली बार ऊपर की उपज माँगने पर उसे केवल पत्ते ही खाने को मिले थे। किसान ने चतुराई से आलू की फसल बो दी थी, जिसमें आलू जमीन के नीचे होते हैं।

3. अंत में किसान ने बुद्धिमत्ता कैसे दिखाई?

उत्तर भालू ने किसान से भूमि के सबसे ऊपर और भूमि के नीचे की उपज माँगी थी। अत: किसान ने बुद्धिमानी दिखाते हुए गन्ना बो दिया, जिसमें नीचे जड़ें और सबसे ऊपर पत्ते होते हैं।

4. आप किसान के स्थान पर होते तो क्या करते?

उत्तर यदि मैं किसान की जगह होता तो मैं भी किसान की तरह चालाकी से काम करता।

भाषा की बात

1. उचित विराम चिह्न दिए गए खानों में लिखिए।

(क) भालू किसान पर झपटा ☐
(ख) मुझे क्यों मारते हो ☐
(ग) उपज आई तो भालू को पत्ते खाने को मिले ☐
(घ) हम यह काम कैसे करेंगे ☐
(ङ) किसान को मिले चमकीले गेहूँ ☐

उत्तर (क) भालू किसान पर झपटा [।]
(ख) मुझे क्यों मारते हो [?]
(ग) उपज आई, तो भालू को पत्ते खाने को मिले [,]
(घ) हम यह काम कैसे करेंगे [?]
(ङ) किसान को मिले चमकीले गेहूँ [।]

2. दिए गए मुहावरों के अर्थ लिखकर उनका वाक्यों में प्रयोग कीजिए।

पाठ पढ़ाना, सिर चकराना

उत्तर **पाठ पढ़ाना** सबक सिखाना

वाक्य प्रयोग किसान ने अपनी चालाकी से भालू को पाठ पढ़ाया।

सिर चकराना कुछ समझ न आना

वाक्य प्रयोग पेपर देखकर मेरा सिर चकरा गया।

कहानी से आगे

1. यदि भालू आगे भी हार न मानता तो किसान क्या करता? कल्पना करके बताइए।

उत्तर यदि भालू आगे भी हार न मानता तो किसान हर फसल का आधा-आधा बँटवारा करता या खेती करना छोड़ देता।

2. आपके अनुसार उपज पर अधिकार किसान का होना चाहिए था या भालू का?

उत्तर उपज पर अधिकार किसान का होना चाहिए था, क्योंकि हर बार मेहनत किसान करता था।

वर्ग पहेली

1. चित्रों को पहचानिए और उनके नाम वर्ग पहेली में से ढूँढकर नीचे लिखिए।

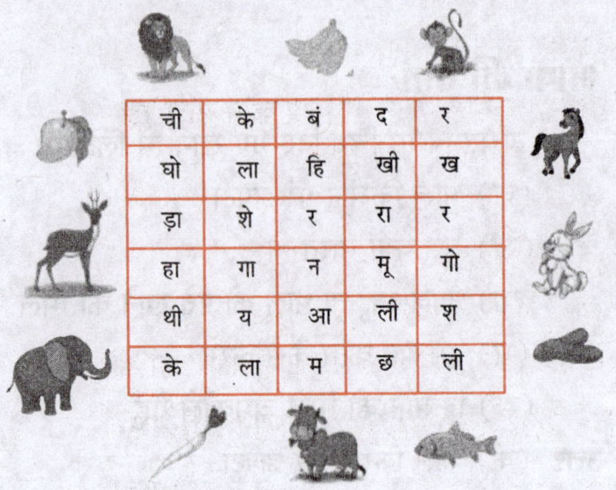

चि	के	बं	द	र
घो	ला	हि	खी	ख
ड़ा	शे	र	रा	र
हा	गा	न	मू	गो
थी	य	आ	ली	श
के	ला	म	छ	ली

उत्तर घोड़ा, हाथी, केला, मछली, गाय, शेर, बंदर, हिरन, खरगोश, खीरा, मूली, आम

आनंद के लिए

1. किसको क्या खाना अच्छा लगता है? पहचानिए।

उत्तर

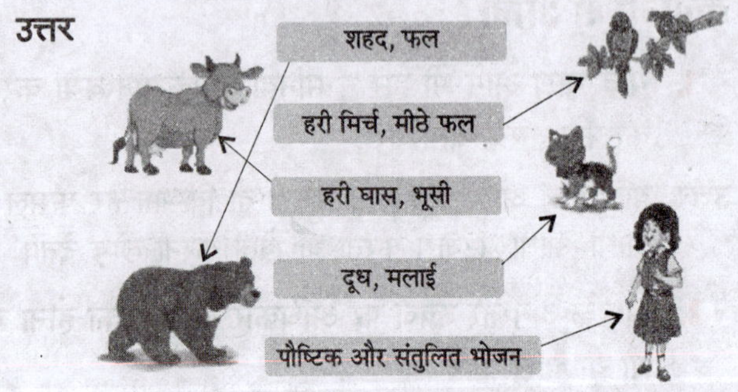

2. आपके घर में जितने भी साग आते हैं, उन्हें वर्गीकृत कीजिए।

उत्तर

साग वर्गीकरण का आधार	साग
भूमि के नीचे पैदा होने वाले	— आलू, गाजर, मूली, शलजम
पत्ते के रूप में खाए जाने वाले	— पालक, सरसों, बथुआ, धनिया
फल के रूप में उगने वाले	— केला, आम, पपीता
फली के रूप में खाए जाने वाले	— सेम, बींस, मटर

कुछ नया करें

1. कल्पना कीजिए कि कहानी वाला भालू आपके स्कूल में आया है। आप भालू से क्या बातचीत करेंगे?

उत्तर
- **आप** अरे भालू भाई! आज हमारे स्कूल में कैसे आए?
- **भालू** बच्चों, मैं खाने की तलाश में जंगल से बाहर आ गया।
- **आप** तो आओ, हम तुम्हें शहद खिलाते हैं।
- **भालू** मेरा खेलने का भी मन है।
- **आप** पहले अपनी भूख मिटाओ, फिर हम सब मिलकर खेलेंगे।

मेरी चित्रकारी

1. भालू का एक सुंदर चित्र बनाकर उसमें मनचाहे रंग भरिए।

उत्तर छात्र स्वयं करें।

झटपट कहिए

ऊँचा ऊँचा, ऊँचा ऊँट
ऊँची ऊँट की पीठ।
पीठ ऊँची, पूँछ भी ऊँची,
ऊँची पूँछ, ऊँचा ऊँट।

उत्तर छात्र स्वयं करें।

अभ्यास प्रश्न

बहुविकल्पीय प्रश्न

1. किसान के खेत में कौन आ गया?
(क) गधा (ख) शेर (ग) घोड़ा (घ) भालू

2. किसान ने सबसे पहले क्या बोया?
(क) टमाटर (ख) आलू (ग) गेहूँ (घ) गन्ना

3. गेहूँ की उपज में भालू को क्या खाने को मिला?
(क) चावल (ख) चमकीले गेहूँ
(ग) जड़ें (घ) पत्ते

4. भालू ने किसान को क्या पढ़ाने की सोची?
(क) कहानी (ख) उपाय
(ग) पाठ (घ) तरकीब

उत्तर

1. (घ) भालू 2. (ख) आलू
3. (ग) जड़ें 4. (ग) पाठ

गद्यांश पर आधारित प्रश्न

निम्नलिखित गद्यांश को पढ़कर उस पर आधारित प्रश्नों के उत्तर दीजिए।

गद्यांश

इस बार किसान ने गेहूँ बो दिया। जब उपज हुई तो किसान को मिले चमकीले गेहूँ। भालू को मिली केवल जड़ें, भालू खीझकर रह गया। इस बार भालू ने किसान को पाठ पढ़ाने की सोची। उसने किसान से कहा, ''भूमि के सबसे ऊपर और भूमि के नीचे की उपज मेरी'' किसान मान गया।

1. किसान ने क्या बोया था?
(क) चावल (ख) दाल
(ग) गेहूँ (घ) सब्जी

2. चमकीले गेहूँ किसको मिले?
(क) गधे को
(ख) किसान को
(ग) भालू को
(घ) शेर को

3. खीझकर कौन रह गया?

4. किसान को पाठ पढ़ाने के लिए कौन सोच रहा था?

उत्तर

1. (ग) गेहूँ
2. (ख) किसान को
3. खीझकर भालू रह गया।
4. किसान को पाठ पढ़ाने के लिए भालू सोच रहा था।

निम्नलिखित प्रश्नों के उत्तर दीजिए

1. भालू के झपट्टा मारने पर किसान ने क्या कहा?

उत्तर भालू के झपट्टा मारने पर किसान ने कहा, ''मुझे क्यों मारते हो? उपज होने दो, जो कहोगे, वही खिलाऊँगा।''

2. दूसरी बार की उपज तैयार होने के समय भालू और किसान की क्या बात हुई?

उत्तर दूसरी बार की उपज तैयार होने के समय भालू ने किसान से कहा कि अगली बार उसे भूमि के ऊपर व नीचे दोनों की उपज चाहिए।

3. गन्ने की उपज में भालू को क्या मिला?

उत्तर गन्ने की उपज में भालू को जड़ें और पत्ते मिले।

4. क्या भालू के साथ सही हुआ?

उत्तर हाँ, भालू के साथ सही हुआ।

लेखन संबंधी प्रश्न

1. 'तिरंगा' विषय पर कम-से-कम 40 शब्दों में अनुच्छेद लिखिए।

उत्तर तिरंगा भारत का राष्ट्रीय ध्वज है। हमारे राष्ट्रीय ध्वज में चार रंगों का प्रयोग हुआ है। इसमें पहले केसरिया फिर सफेद (सफेद पर नीला चक्र) व उसके बाद हरे रंग का उपयोग हुआ है सफेद रंग पर जो नीले रंग का चक्र बना हुआ है उसे 'अशोक चक्र' कहते हैं। हमें हमेशा राष्ट्रीय ध्वज का सम्मान करना चाहिए।

अध्याय 15 भारत

कविता का सार

प्रस्तुत कविता 'भारत' सोहनलाल द्विवेदी जी द्वारा लिखी गई है। इस कविता में कवि ने भारत की महिमा का वर्णन किया है और इसे सभी देशों में सबसे प्यारा और अनोखा बताया है। कवि ने हिमालय को इसका मुकुट और समुद्र को इसके चरण धोने वाला बताया है। यहाँ गंगा-यमुना की पवित्र धाराओं का उल्लेख है, जो पूरे संसार को पवित्र करती हैं। यहाँ के अन्न, फूल-फल और जल की महिमा का वर्णन किया गया है और इन्हें रत्नों और जवाहरातों से भरपूर बताया गया है।

कवि द्वारा भारत को राम और कृष्ण जैसी महान आत्माओं की भूमि होने का गौरव भी बताया गया है।

अंत में कवि संकल्प करते हैं कि वे हमेशा भारत की प्रशंसा करेंगे और इसके गौरव को बढ़ाने के लिए हर संभव प्रयास करेंगे।

काव्यांशों की व्याख्या

काव्यांश 1

भारत तू है हमको प्यारा,
तू है सब देशों से न्यारा।
मुकुट हिमालय तेरा सुंदर,
धोता तेरे चरण समुंदर।
गंगा-यमुना की है धारा,
जिनसे है पवित्र जग सारा।

शब्दार्थ *न्यारा-अलग, विशेष, मुकुट-सिर पर पहना जाने वाला राजसी आभूषण, जग-संसार।*

संदर्भ/प्रसंग प्रस्तुत पंक्तियाँ हमारी पाठ्यपुस्तक वीणा भाग-1 में संकलित कविता 'भारत' से ली गई हैं। इसके कवि सोहनलाल द्विवेदी हैं। इस कविता में भारत देश की महिमा का वर्णन किया गया है।

व्याख्या कवि कहते हैं कि भारत देश तू हमें बहुत प्यारा है, क्योंकि तू सब देशों से अनोखा है। उत्तर दिशा में स्थित हिमालय तेरे सिर पर सुंदर मुकुट की तरह विराजमान है और दक्षिण दिशा में स्थित समुद्र ऐसा लगता है, जैसे तेरे पैर धो रहा हो। यहाँ गंगा-यमुना जैसी नदियाँ बहती हैं, जो सारे जग (संसार) को पवित्र करती हैं।

काव्यांश 2

अन्न, फूल, फल, जल हैं प्यारे,
तुझमें रत्न जवाहर न्यारे!
राम, कृष्ण से अंतर्यामी,
तेरे सभी पुत्र हैं नामी।
हम सदैव तेरा गुण गाएँ,
सब विधि तेरा सुयश बढ़ाएँ।

शब्दार्थ *रत्न जवाहर*–हीरे मोती, *अंतर्यामी*–सब कुछ जानने वाला, *सदैव*–हर समय।

प्रसंग पूर्ववत्।

व्याख्या कवि कहते हैं कि मेरे देश में अन्न, फूल, फल, जल सब कुछ प्यारे हैं। यहाँ की धरती में अनोखे रत्न जवाहरात छिपे हुए हैं।

मन की बात जान लेने वाले राम, कृष्ण जैसे तेरे पुत्रों को विश्व में कौन नहीं जानता। हे! भारत भूमि, यही कामना है कि हम हमेशा तेरे गुण गाएँ और हर प्रकार से तेरा यश बढ़ाएँ।

NCERT फोल्डर

बातचीत के लिए

1. अपने देश के विषय में आप क्या जानते हैं? बताइए।

उत्तर मेरा देश भारत है। यह बहुत बड़ा और सुंदर है। यहाँ विभिन्न धर्म, भाषा और संस्कृति के लोग रहते हैं। भारत में अनेक पर्वत, नदियाँ और समुद्र तट हैं। हमारे देश की राजधानी नई दिल्ली है।

2. अपने देश की प्रसिद्ध नदियों और पर्वतों के नाम बताइए।

उत्तर भारत की प्रमुख नदियाँ गंगा, यमुना, नर्मदा, गोदावरी और ब्रह्मपुत्र हैं। भारत के प्रमुख पर्वतों में हिमालय, अरावली, कैलाश, विंध्याचल और सतपुड़ा शामिल हैं।

3. राम और कृष्ण के विषय में आप क्या जानते हैं? बताइए।

उत्तर भगवान राम का जन्म अयोध्या में हुआ था और उन्होंने रावण का वध करके धर्म की स्थापना की। भगवान कृष्ण का जन्म मथुरा में हुआ था। उन्होंने अपने मामा कंस का वध किया था। उन्होंने महाभारत में महत्त्वपूर्ण भूमिका निभाई थी तथा गीता का उपदेश भी दिया था।

सोचिए और लिखिए

1. भारत हमें क्यों प्यारा है?

उत्तर भारत हमें इसलिए प्यारा है, क्योंकि यह हमारी जन्मभूमि है। यहाँ की विविधता, संस्कृतियाँ, परंपराएँ और त्योहार हमें एक विशेष पहचान देते हैं। भारत की प्राकृतिक सुंदरता, ऐतिहासिक धरोहर और देशभक्ति की भावना हमें गर्व का अनुभव कराती है।

2. हिमालय को सुंदर मुकुट क्यों कहा गया है?

उत्तर हिमालय को सुंदर मुकुट इसलिए कहा गया है, क्योंकि यह पर्वत श्रृंखला भारत के उत्तर में स्थित है और इसकी बर्फ से ढकी चोटियाँ बहुत ही सुंदर और आकर्षक दिखती हैं। यह पर्वत हमारे देश की रक्षा भी करता है।

3. आप अपने देश का यश कैसे बढ़ाएँगे?

उत्तर मैं अपने देश का यश बढ़ाने के लिए अच्छा नागरिक बनूँगा, नियमों का पालन करूँगा, अपने काम में मेहनत करूँगा और दूसरों की मदद करूँगा। मैं अपने देश की सांस्कृतिक धरोहर और परंपराओं का सम्मान करूँगा और उन्हें आगे बढ़ाऊँगा।

4. हमारे देश के समान हमारे गाँव और नगर भी न्यारे-न्यारे हैं। आप अपने गाँव या नगर के बारे में सोचकर लिखिए।

उत्तर मेरा गाँव बहुत अच्छा है। गाँव में हरे-भरे खेत, बाग-बगीचे एवं साफ-सुथरी गलियाँ हैं। गाँव के लोग मेहनती और मिलनसार हैं। हमारे गाँव में मंदिर, डाकघर, अस्पताल, विद्यालय, बैंक जैसी सुविधाएँ भी हैं।

कविता से

1. कविता के आधार पर पंक्तियाँ पूरी कीजिए।

भारत तू है हमको प्यारा, ...।
.........................., धोता तेरे चरण समुंदर,
गंगा-यमुना की है धारा, ...।
.........................., तुझमें रत्न जवाहर न्यारे!
.........................., तेरे सभी पुत्र हैं नामी।
हम सदैव तेरा गुण गाएँ, ...।

उत्तर भारत तू है हमको प्यारा, तू है सब देशों से न्यारा
मुकुट हिमालय तेरा सुंदर, धोता तेरे चरण समुंदर।
गंगा–यमुना की है, धारा, जिनसे है पवित्र जग सारा।
अन्न, फूल, फल, जल हैं प्यारे, तुझमें रत्न–ज्वाहर न्यारे!
राम, कृष्ण से अंतर्यामी, तेरे सभी पुत्र हैं नामी।
हम सदैव तेरे गुण गाएँ, सब विधि तेरा सुयश बढ़ाएँ।

शब्दों का खेल

1. **कविता में आए समान ध्वनि वाले शब्दों की जोड़ी बनाइए**

उत्तर	
प्यारा	न्यारा
सुंदर	समुंदर
न्यारे	प्यारे
बढ़ाएँ	गाएँ
धारा	सारा
अंतर्यामी	नामी

2. **दिए गए समान ध्वनि वाले शब्दों की सहायता से कविता पूरी कीजिए।**

महान, मान, फूल, अभिमान

उत्तर

देश की माटी, देश की धूल,
खिलते रंग-बिरंगे ...फूल...
अपने देश का है विशेष ...अभिमान...
मिलकर इसका रखें ...मान...
जिसके हम गाएँ गुणगान
वह मेरा भारत देश ...महान...

खेल–खेल में खोजें

1. **कविता में आए शब्दों पर घेरा लगाकर लिखिए।**

सुं	द	र	व	भा
आ	ज	वा	ह	र
मु	कु	ट	फू	त
ह	सा	फ	ल	गं
ह	सा	फ	ल	गं
धा	रा	म	गं	गा

समझिए और लिखिए

कुछ शब्दों के एक से अधिक अर्थ भी होते हैं। नीचे दिए गए शब्दों के दो सही अर्थ ढूँढकर लिखिए।

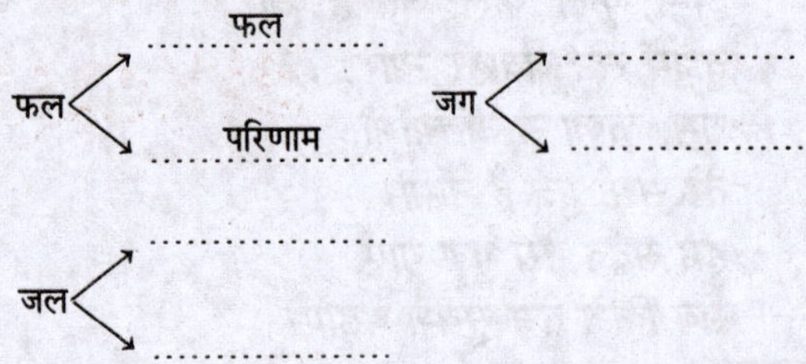

उत्तर जग-संसार, जगना; जल-पानी, जलना

2. **इन वाक्यों के अर्थ वाली पंक्तियाँ कविता से ढूँढकर लिखिए**

(क) भारत सब देशों से भिन्न है।
(ख) गंगा-यमुना से सारा संसार पवित्र है।
(ग) हम सदैव तेरी प्रशंसा करें।
(घ) हम देश का नाम ऊँचा करें।

उत्तर (क) भारत तू है हमको प्यारा, तू है सब देशों से न्यारा।
(ख) गंगा-यमुना की है धारा, जिनसे है पवित्र जग सारा।
(ग) हम सदैव तेरा गुण गाएँ।
(घ) सब विधि तेरा सुयश बढ़ाएँ।

3. **कविता में भारत के प्रसिद्ध व्यक्तियों के बारे में बताया गया है – 'तेरे सभी पुत्र हैं नामी' भारत के प्रसिद्ध पुत्र और पुत्रियों के नाम लिखिए।**

उत्तर

पुत्रियाँ	**पुत्र**
लक्ष्मीबाई	महात्मा गाँधी
इंदिरा गाँधी	भगतसिंह
लता मंगेशकर	डॉ. अब्दुल कलाम
सावित्री बाई फुले	लालबहादुर शास्त्री

कला की कलाकारियाँ

1. **रंग-बिरंगे कागज और कैंची की सहायता से अपने लिए एक मुकुट बनाइए।**

उत्तर छात्र स्वयं करें।

2. **भारत का राष्ट्रीय ध्वज (तिरंगा) बनाकर उसमें रंग भरिए**

उत्तर छात्र स्वयं करें।

बूझो तो जानें

1. **उत्तर में रखवाली करता खड़ा रहता है सदा ही मौन। बोलो भैया बोलो बहना, भारत का वह रक्षक कौन?**

उत्तर हिमालय

2. **दो आँखों के ऊपर आँखें, आँखों में से आँखें झाँकें।**

उत्तर चश्मा

अभ्यास प्रश्न

बहुविकल्पीय प्रश्न

1. कौन-सा देश हम सबको प्यारा है?
   (क) भारत (ख) रूस
   (ग) नेपाल (घ) चीन

2. समुंदर किसके चरण धोता है?
   (क) नेपाल के
   (ख) अमेरिका के
   (ग) भारत के
   (घ) जर्मनी के

3. गंगा-यमुना की धारा कहाँ बहती है?
   (क) भारत में (ख) रूस में
   (ग) नेपाल में (घ) चीन में

4. किसकी धारा से सारा जग पवित्र है ?
   (क) नल की (ख) गंगा-यमुना की
   (ग) नहर की (घ) नलकूप की

उत्तर

1. (क) भारत 2. (ग) भारत के
3. (क) भारत में 4. (ख) गंगा-यमुना की

काव्यांश पर आधारित प्रश्न

निम्नलिखित काव्यांश को पढ़कर उस पर आधारित प्रश्नों के उत्तर दीजिए।

काव्यांश

गंगा-यमुना की है धारा,
जिनसे है पवित्र जग सारा।
अन्न, फूल, फल, जल हैं प्यारे
तुझमें रत्न जवाहर न्यारे।

1. गंगा-यमुना की धारा कहाँ बहती है?
   (क) उत्तर प्रदेश में
   (ख) विदेश में
   (ग) भारत में
   (घ) हिमाचल प्रदेश में

2. सारा जग किससे पवित्र है?
   (क) गंगा-यमुना से (ख) नहर से
   (ग) पानी से (घ) कुओं से

3. अन्न, फूल, फल, जल किसके प्यारे हैं?

4. जवाहर, रत्न कहाँ पाए जाते हैं?

उत्तर

1. (ग) भारत में
2. (क) गंगा-यमुना से
3. अन्न, फूल, फल, जल सब भारत के प्यारे हैं।
4. जवाहर, रत्न भारत में पाए जाते हैं?

निम्नलिखित प्रश्नों के उत्तर दीजिए

1. भारत की क्या-क्या विशेषताएँ हैं?

उत्तर भारत की सुंदरता, विशेष व्यक्ति, नदियाँ पहाड़, अन्न, फल, फूल, कीमती रत्न भारत की विशेषताएँ हैं।

2. भारत में कौन-सी नदियों की धारा बहती है?

उत्तर भारत में गंगा-यमुना की धारा बहती है।

3. हिमालय किसका मुकुट है?

उत्तर हिमालय भारत का मुकुट है।

4. भारत के नामी पुत्र कौन है?

उत्तर भारत के नामी पुत्र राम और कृष्ण हैं।

5. भारत देश क्यों प्यारा है? बताइए।

उत्तर भारत देश बहुत न्यारा है इसलिए बहुत प्यारा है।

लेखन संबंधी प्रश्न

1. 'मेरा परिचय' विषय पर कम-से-कम 40 शब्दों में अनुच्छेद लिखिए।

उत्तर मेरा नाम मोहित है। मैं आठ वर्ष का हूँ। मैं तीसरी कक्षा में पढ़ता हूँ। मेरे विद्यालय का नाम 'आदर्श विद्यालय' है। मुझे दोस्तों के साथ खेलना बहुत पसंद है। मेरा जन्मदिन दस अगस्त को आता है। मेरा एक भाई व एक बहन है। मेरे भाई-बहन मुझसे बड़े हैं।

अध्याय 16 चंद्रयान (संवाद)

पाठ का सार

इस अध्याय में चाँद और चंद्रयान मिशन के बारे में एक रोचक बातचीत का वर्णन किया गया है। इसमें अध्यापिका और विद्यार्थियों के बीच चाँद, चंद्रयान और भारत के वैज्ञानिकों की उपलब्धियों पर चर्चा की गई है। अध्यापिका जब कक्षा में आती हैं, तो बच्चों से चाँद के बारे में बातचीत शुरू करती हैं। बच्चे बताते हैं कि उन्होंने चाँद देखा है, लेकिन वे यह नहीं समझ पाते कि चाँद कभी दिखाई देता है और कभी नहीं। एक बच्चा कहता है कि चाँद का मन है, वह कभी दिखता है और कभी नहीं।

इसके बाद चंद्रयान मिशन के बारे में बातचीत कर बच्चे बताते हैं कि वे चंद्रयान-I, II और III के बारे में जानते हैं। अध्यापिका उन्हें समझाती हैं कि चंद्रयान-III के माध्यम से भारत ने चाँद के दक्षिणी ध्रुव पर सफलतापूर्वक लैंडिंग की है और यह हमारे देश के लिए गर्व की बात है। बच्चों में यह जानने की उत्सुकता बढ़ती है कि चाँद पर क्या है? अध्यापिका उन्हें बताती हैं कि चाँद पर विक्रम लैंडर और प्रज्ञान नामक मशीनें भेजी गई हैं, जो चाँद पर मिट्टी, पानी से संबंधित अन्य जानकारियाँ इकट्ठा कर रही हैं। यह जानकर बच्चे और भी उत्साहित हो जाते हैं। वे कल्पना करते हैं कि वे चंद्रयान से चाँद की सैर करेंगे। अध्यापिका बताती हैं कि एक रहस्य जानने के बाद वैज्ञानिकों की जिज्ञासा बढ़ती है। वैज्ञानिकों ने चंद्रयान-I भेजा, जो चाँद पर पानी का पता लगाता है। फिर चंद्रयान-II भेजा, पर यह कुछ खराबी के कारण चाँद पर नहीं उतर पाया। उसके बाद उन्होंने चंद्रयान-III भेजा, जो सफलतापूर्वक चाँद के दक्षिणी ध्रुव पर उतरा। अध्याय में बच्चों की चाँद के प्रति जिज्ञासा और विज्ञान के प्रति उनके बढ़ते आकर्षण को बड़े ही सरल और रोचक तरीके से प्रस्तुत किया गया है।

शब्दार्थ

आगमन-प्रवेश, अभिवादन-श्रद्धापूर्वक किया जाने वाला नमस्कार, रॉकेट-एक प्रकार का अंतरिक्ष में भेजा जाने वाला यान, ध्रुव-पृथ्वी के सबसे उत्तरी-दक्षिणी बिंदु, यान-यात्रा करने का साधन, सैर-घूमना, जुटना-किसी काम में लगना।

NCERT फोल्डर

बातचीत के लिए

1. आप आकाश में सूरज, चाँद, तारे एवं और भी बहुत कुछ देखते हैं। चाँद से जुड़ा अपना कोई अनुभव, कोई रोचक बात या कोई कविता सुनाइए।

उत्तर एक बार गर्मियों की रात में जब मैं अपने परिवार के साथ छत पर बैठा था, तब हमने चाँद को बहुत करीब से देखा। वह बहुत सुंदर और चमकदार लग रहा था। उस समय मेरी दादी ने हमें एक कविता सुनाई

चाँद की चाँदनी रात,
ले आती है सपनों की बात।
चंदा मामा दूर हैं,
पर जगते हैं पूरी रात।

2. आपने कक्षा दो की अपनी पाठ्यपुस्तक 'सारंगी भाग-2' में चाँद के बारे में पढ़ा है न! कुछ याद करके सुनाइए कि क्या पढ़ा था?

उत्तर गिरे ताल में चंदा मामा, सबने देखा सबने देखा,
फँसे जाल में चंदा मामा, सबने देखा सबने देखा,
सबने देखा एक अचंभा, मछुआरे ने जाल समेटा
कहीं नहीं थे चंदा मामा, कहाँ गए जी चंदा मामा।

3. आपको कुछ ऐसे त्योहारों के बारे में अवश्य पता होगा, जिनका चाँद के दिखने से बहुत गहरा संबंध है। याद करके बताइए वे कौन-कौन से त्योहार हैं?

उत्तर हाँ! मुझे ऐसे त्योहारों के बारे में पता है, जिनका चाँद से गहरा संबंध है— ईद, करवाचौथ, चतुर्थी व्रत आदि।

4. आपने चंद्रयान के बारे में जो कुछ सुना, पढ़ा या देखा है, बताइए।

उत्तर चंद्रयान भारत का एक अद्भुत अंतरिक्ष यान है, जो चाँद के बारे में जानने में मदद कर रहा है। चंद्रयान-I ने चाँद पर पानी और बर्फ की खोज की थी। चंद्रयान-II चंद्रमा पर उतरने में असफल रहा।

चंद्रयान-III वर्ष 2023 में लॉन्च किया गया था और चाँद के दक्षिणी ध्रुव पर सफलतापूर्वक उतरा। यह चाँद पर खनिजों का अध्ययन करेगा।

सोचिए और लिखिए

1. यह पाठ अध्यापिका और विद्यार्थियों के बीच एक संवाद है। यह संवाद किस विषय पर है?

उत्तर यह संवाद चंद्रयान और उसके मिशन के बारे में है। इसमें चंद्रयान के विभिन्न पहलुओं, उसकी महत्त्वपूर्ण खोजों और उसके मिशन के उद्देश्यों के बारे में जानकारी मिलती है।

2. दिए गए प्रश्नों के उचित विकल्प का चयन कर सही (✔) का चिह्न लगाएँ।

(i) चाँद पर जाने के लिए किस वाहन का प्रयोग किया जाता है?
(क) रॉकेट ☐ (ख) बस ☐ (ग) हवाईजहाज ☐

(ii) अभी हाल ही में चाँद पर सफलतापूर्वक उतरने वाले यान का क्या नाम है?
(क) चंद्रयान-I ☐ (ख) चंद्रयान-II ☐
(ग) चंद्रयान-III ☐

(iii) वैज्ञानिक चाँद पर क्यों जाना चाहते हैं?
(क) वैज्ञानिक समूची धरती घूम चुके हैं। ☐
(ख) वैज्ञानिक चाँद के बारे में जानना चाहते हैं। ☐
(ग) वैज्ञानिक चाँद पर कविता लिखना चाहते हैं। ☐

(iv) चंद्रयान-II के विषय में कौन-सी बात सही है?
(क) चंद्रयान-II चाँद की सतह पर नहीं उतर पाया। ☐
(ख) चंद्रयान-II चाँद के चारों तरफ चक्कर नहीं लगा पाया। ☐
(ग) चंद्रयान-II चाँद पर जाने के लिए नहीं बनाया गया था। ☐

उत्तर (i) (क) रॉकेट (ii) (ख) चंद्रयान-III
(iii) (ख) वैज्ञानिक चाँद के बारे में जानना चाहते हैं।
(iv) (क) चंद्रयान-II चाँद की सतह पर नहीं उतर पाया।

3. कल्पना कीजिए कि आपको चाँद पर भेजा जा रहा है, आप
(क) अपने साथ किसे ले जाना चाहेंगे और क्यों?

उत्तर मैं एक अनुभवी वैज्ञानिक को साथ ले जाना चाहूँगा, क्योंकि वे मुझे चाँद और उसकी विशेषताओं के बारे में बता सकते हैं।

(ख) चाँद पर जाने से पहले किस प्रकार की व्यवस्था करेंगे?

उत्तर चाँद पर जाने से पहले हमें कुछ विशेष वस्तुओं को पैक करना होगा; जैसे— अंतरिक्ष सूट, ऑक्सीजन, चिकित्सा उपकरण, खाना, पानी और वैज्ञानिक उपकरण।

4. यान जोड़कर शब्द बनाइए।
चंद्र ....
जल ....
वायु ....

उत्तर
- चंद्र — चंद्रयान
- जल — जलयान
- वायु — वायुयान

5. आपका अवलोकन और चाँद का आकार

(i) रात्रि को लगभग 10 मिनट के लिए अपने घर के किसी बड़े सदस्य के साथ पंद्रह दिनों तक आकाश में चाँद को देखिए। अपनी दैनिकी में चाँद के आकार को लेकर अपना अवलोकन लिखिए। अपने अवलोकन के आधार पर चाँद के बढ़ते-घटते आकार का चित्र बनाइए।

उत्तर छात्र स्वयं करें।

(ii) आपने अपने घर के बड़ों या फिर सहपाठियों से 'अमावस्या और पूर्णिमा' के बारे में सुना होगा। ईद के त्योहार को भी चाँद दिखने पर मनाया जाता है। पता लगाइए कि इन दिनों में चाँद का आकार कैसा होता है?

उत्तर छात्र स्वयं करें।

6. यदि आपके विद्यालय में चंद्रयान-III से जुड़े वैज्ञानिक आते हैं, तो आप उनसे कौन-कौन से प्रश्न पूछना चाहोगे? कोई तीन प्रश्न लिखिए।

उत्तर

(i) चंद्रयान-III से चंद्रमा के बारे में क्या-क्या जानकारी मिली?

(ii) चंद्रयान-III से भारत देश को क्या लाभ होने वाला है?

(iii) चंद्रयान-III कैसे काम करेगा?

7. चाँद तुम्हारे कितने नाम? चाँद को बहुत-से बच्चे चंदा मामा कहकर बुलाते हैं। कुछ लोग चंद्रमा भी कहते हैं। चाँद के कुछ और नामों का पता लगाइए और दिए गए स्थान पर लिखिए।

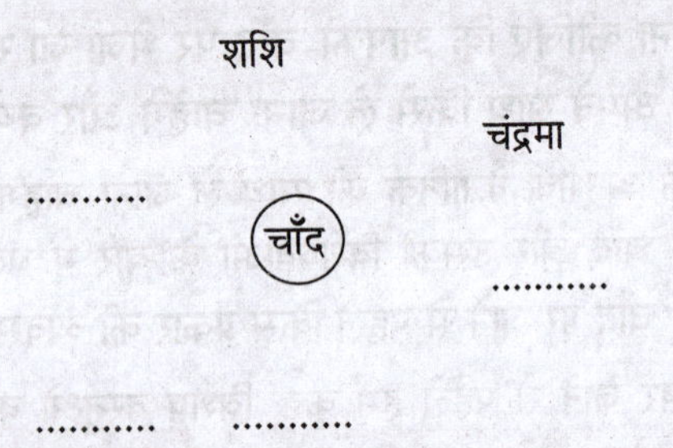

उत्तर

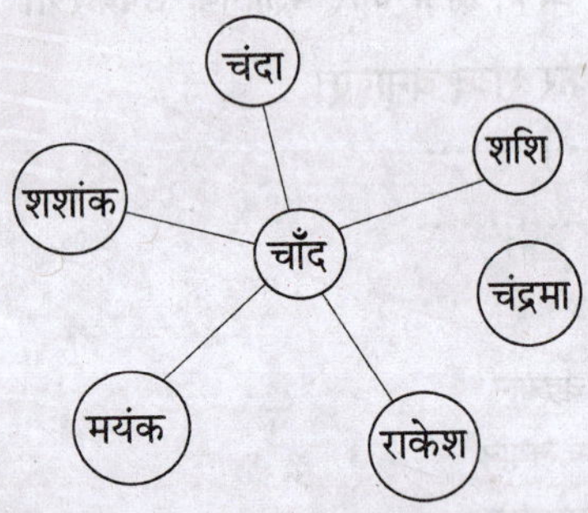

भाषा की बात

1. "अब चंद्रयान-III चाँद पर घूम-घूमकर पता लगा रहा है....."

ऊपर लिखे वाक्य में घूम-घूमकर शब्द पर ध्यान दें। हम अपनी बातचीत में कभी-कभी एक शब्द को दो बार कहते हैं। इस तरह के कुछ और शब्द बनाइए और दिए गए स्थान पर लिखिए।

उत्तर
- खेल-खेलकर
- चल-चलकर
- पढ़-पढ़कर
- देख-देखकर
- बोल-बोलकर
- चढ़-चढ़कर

2. नीचे दिए गए वाक्यों के लिए सही शब्द छाँटकर लिखिए

कृषक, सैनिक, शिक्षक, चिकित्सक, वैज्ञानिक

(क) विज्ञान की नई खोज करने वाले ....

(ख) देश की रक्षा करने वाले ....

(ग) शिक्षा देने वाले ....

(घ) रोग की चिकित्सा करने वाले ....

(ङ) खेतों में अन्न उगाने वाले ....

उत्तर

(क) विज्ञान की नई खोज करने वाले—वैज्ञानिक

(ख) देश की रक्षा करने वाले—सैनिक

(ग) शिक्षा देने वाले—शिक्षक

(घ) रोग की चिकित्सा करने वाले—चिकित्सक

(ङ) खेतों में अन्न उगाने वाले—कृषक

समझिए और लिखिए

1. सही शब्द लिखकर वाक्य पूरा कीजिए

(क) लगातार परिश्रम करने से कठिन काम भी .... हो जाता

(ख) चंद्रयान-II की असफलता पर वैज्ञानिक निराश थे, लेकिन चंद्रयान-III की .... पर सभी प्रसन्न हुए।

(ग) आप तो बहुत कुछ जानते हैं, लेकिन मैं .... नहीं जानता।

(घ) चाँद बादलों के साथ छुपन-छुपाई खेलता होगा। कभी बादलों से झाँककर दिखाई देता तो कभी .... जाता।

उत्तर

(क) लगातार परिश्रम करने से कठिन काम भी **आसान** हो जाता है।

(ख) चंद्रयान-II की असफलता पर वैज्ञानिक निराश थे, लेकिन चंद्रयान-III की **सफलता** पर सभी प्रसन्न हुए।

(ग) आप तो बहुत कुछ जानते हैं, लेकिन मैं **थोड़ा भी** नहीं जानता।

(घ) चाँद बादलों के साथ छुपन-छुपाई खेलता होगा। कभी बादलों से झाँककर दिखाई देता तो कभी **गायब** हो जाता।

कुछ बनाइए

1. पुराने समाचार-पत्रों से चंद्रयान मिशन से जुड़े समाचार और चित्र काटकर पुस्तिका में चिपकाएँ। इस तरह से एक चित्र पुस्तिका तैयार करें।

उत्तर छात्र स्वयं करें।

अभ्यास प्रश्न

बहुविकल्पीय प्रश्न

1. रॉकेट के माध्यम से कहाँ जाया जाता है?

(क) ग्रह पर (ख) सूर्य पर
(ग) चंद्रमा पर (घ) तारों पर

2. चाँद पर अब तक भारत के कितने रॉकेट गए हैं?

(क) 1 (ख) 2
(ग) 3 (घ) 4

3. दक्षिणी ध्रुव पर कौन-से चंद्रयान को उतारा गया?

(क) चंद्रयान-I (ख) चंद्रयान-II
(ग) चंद्रयान-III (घ) चंद्रयान-V

4. कौन-सा रॉकेट खराबी के कारण चंद्रमा पर नहीं उतर पाया?

(क) पहला (ख) तीसरा
(ग) दूसरा (घ) चौथा

उत्तर

1. (ग) चंद्रमा पर 2. (ग) 3
3. (ग) चंद्रयान-III 4. (ग) दूसरा

गद्यांश पर आधारित प्रश्न

निम्नलिखित गद्यांश को पढ़कर उस पर आधारित प्रश्नों के उत्तर दीजिए।

गद्यांश

अध्यापिका एकदम, सही! आप तो बहुत कुछ जानते हैं। आपको तो पता है कि चाँद धरती से बहुत दूर है। इसलिए वैज्ञानिकों ने चाँद पर एक रॉकेट भेजा और जानने का प्रयास किया कि वहाँ क्या-क्या है? उन्होंने इसे 'चंद्रयान मिशन' नाम दिया। 'चंद्रयान' ने चाँद के चारों ओर चक्कर लगाया और यह पता लगता कि चाँद पर पानी है।

1. धरती से बहुत दूर कौन है?

(क) चंद्रमा (ख) वैज्ञानिक (ग) मिशन (घ) रॉकेट

2. वैज्ञानिकों ने चाँद पर क्या भेजा?

(क) जहाज
(ख) रॉकेट
(ग) हवावई जहाज
(घ) पतंग

3. वैज्ञानिकों ने इस मिशन को क्या नाम दिया?

4. 'चंद्रमा पर पानी है' यह किसने पता लगाया?

उत्तर

1. (क) चंद्रमा 2. (ख) रॉकेट
3. वैज्ञानिकों ने इस मिशन को 'चंद्रयान मिशन' नाम दिया।
4. चंद्रमा पर पानी का पता चंद्रयान-I ने लगाया।

निम्नलिखित प्रश्नों के उत्तर दीजिए

1. विक्रम लैंडर अपने साथ कौन-सी मशीन ले गया है?

उत्तर विक्रम लैंडर अपने साथ 'प्रज्ञान' नाम की मशीनें ले गया है।

2. किसका परिश्रम रंग लाया?

उत्तर वैज्ञानिकों का परिश्रम रंग लाया।

3. कौन-सा चंद्रयान चंद्रमा पर सफलतापूर्वक नहीं उतर पाया?

उत्तर चंद्रयान-II चंद्रमा पर सफलतापूर्वक नहीं उतर पाया।

4. अब तक चंद्रमा पर कितने चंद्रयान भेजे गए?

उत्तर अब तक चंद्रमा पर तीन चंद्रयान भेजे गए हैं।

लेखन संबंधी प्रश्न

1. आपके जन्मदिन पर उपहार भेजने के लिए मौसी जी को धन्यवाद पत्र लिखिए।

उत्तर बी 311, राम पार्क
नई दिल्ली 1100XX

दिनांक

विषय उपहार के धन्यवाद करने हेतु।

प्रिय मौसी जी,

सादर प्रणाम,

आपने मेरे जन्मदिन पर प्रेमपूर्वक जो उपहार भेजा है, उसे पाकर मैं बहुत खुश हूँ। आपके द्वारा भेजा गया रंगों का डिब्बा भी मुझे प्रिय है। मैंने तो इनसे चित्रकारी करना भी शुरू कर दिया है।

आपका बहुत-बहुत धन्यवाद।

मौसी जी को मेरा प्रेम भरा प्रणाम

आपकी प्रिय

अनुपमा

बोलने वाली माँद

पाठ का सार

एक दिन जंगल में एक शेर, जिसका नाम खरनखर था, बहुत भूखा था। वह दिनभर आहार की खोज में इधर-उधर भटकता रहा, लेकिन उसे कुछ खाने को नहीं मिला। शाम होने पर उसे एक माँद दिखी और वह उसमें रात बिताने के लिए घुस गया। शेर ने सोचा जब माँद का निवासी लौटेगा, तब उसे मारकर खा जाऊँगा।

उस माँद में एक सियार रहता था, जिसका नाम दधिपुच्छ था। जब सियार वापस आया तो उसने देखा कि शेर के पैर के निशान माँद में जा रहे हैं, लेकिन बाहर नहीं आ रहे हैं। उसे समझ आ गया कि शेर माँद के अंदर है। सियार ने अपनी जान बचाने की योजना बनाई।

सियार ने माँद के बाहर खड़े होकर माँद को पुकारा और कहा ''ऐ मेरी माँद, आज तू क्यों नहीं बोल रही? पहले तो तू मुझे बुलाने पर हमेशा जवाब देती थी। यदि आज तूने जवाब नहीं दिया तो मैं किसी और माँद में चला जाऊँगा।'' शेर ने सोचा कि सचमुच माँद जवाब देती है, इसलिए उसने सियार को खुद जवाब दिया। शेर की दहाड़ सुनते ही सियार समझ गया कि उसकी योजना काम कर गई और वह वहाँ से भाग गया।

शब्दार्थ

आहार-खाने का सामान, माँद-गुफा या खोह, दबोच-कसकर पकड़ लेना, सूझ-समाधान की जानकारी होना, चौकन्ना-सतर्क, सावधान, चंपत-भाग जाना, फरार होना।

बातचीत के लिए

1. आपको भूख लगती है, तो आप क्या-क्या खाने की कामना करते हैं?

त्तर जब मुझे भूख लगती है, तो मैं चपाती और सब्जी, चावल और दाल, फल, बिस्किट और चॉकलेट खाने की कामना करता/करती हूँ।

...या आपने किसी पशु के पैर के चिह्न देखे हैं? किस-किस पशु के देखे हैं?

...ओं के पैर के चिह्न देखे हैं। मैंने कुत्ते, बिल्ली, गाय और बकरी के पैर के चिह्न देखे हैं।

3. सिंह माँद यानी गुफा में रहता है। माँद में कौन-कौन से जानवर रहते हैं?

उत्तर सिंह के अतिरिक्त भालू, तेंदुआ और भेड़िया माँद यानी गुफा में रहते हैं।

4. कठिन समय में बुद्धि अधिक काम आती है या शक्ति?

उत्तर कठिन समय में बुद्धि अधिक काम आती है, क्योंकि बुद्धि से हम सही रास्ता ढूंढ सकते हैं और समस्याओं का समाधान कर सकते हैं।

सोचिए और लिखिए

1. दधिपुच्छ ने कैसे जाना कि माँद में खरनखर बैठा है?

उत्तर दधिपुच्छ ने माँद की ओर सिंह के पैरों के जाने के निशान देखे, लेकिन वापस लौटने के नहीं। इससे उसे पता चला कि शेर माँद के अंदर ही बैठा है।

2. इस कहानी में सिंह का नाम खरनखर है और सियार का नाम दधिपुच्छ, आप इनके क्या नाम रखेंगे?

उत्तर मैं सिंह का नाम 'शेरू' और सियार का नाम 'चतुर' रखूँगा।

3. यदि आप सिंह के स्थान पर होते तो क्या करते?

उत्तर यदि मैं सिंह के स्थान पर होता, तो सियार की बातों पर विश्वास नहीं करता और पहले खुद से अच्छी तरह सोचता कि क्या माँद बोल सकती है? मैं अपने आस-पास के वातावरण को ध्यान से देखता और समझने की कोशिश करता।

4. जब सियार ने पुकारा 'ऐ मेरी माँद', तब सिंह ने उत्तर दिया। सिंह ने उत्तर में क्या कहा होगा?

उत्तर सिंह ने दहाड़ते हुए सियार को अंदर आने के लिए कहा होगा।

शब्दों का खेल

1. कहानी में 'माँद' शब्द कितनी बार आया है?

उत्तर कहानी में माँद शब्द 17 बार आया है।

2. कहानी में आए चंद्रबिंदु (ँ) वाले शब्द छाँटकर लिखिए।

उत्तर अँधेरा, माँद, लूँगा, आऊँगा, पुकारूँगा, जाऊँगा, मुँह, गूँज।

3. समान अर्थ वाले शब्दों की जोड़ी बनाकर लिखिए

शेर, गुफा, जंगल, द्वार, माँद, दरवाजा, सिंह, वन

उत्तर शेर - सिंह

गुफा - माँद

द्वार - दरवाजा

जंगल - वन

4. नीचे लिखे शब्दों की सहायता से वाक्य पूरा कीजिए

नदी, पहाड़, झरना, पेड़, गुफा, माँद, तितली, हवा, बादल, जाल

उत्तर

भूल गई	भूल गया
माँद! क्या तू भूल गई?	जाल! क्या तू भूल गया?
तितली! क्या तू भूल गई?	पेड़! क्या तू भूल गया?
नदी! क्या तू भूल गई?	बादल! क्या तू भूल गया?
हवा! क्या तू भूल गई?	पहाड़! क्या तू भूल गया?
गुफा! क्या तू भूल गई?	झरना! क्या तू भूल गया?

5. सही शब्द चुनकर रिक्त स्थान भरिए

बाहर, चुप, जवान, सचमुच, उजाला

उदाहरण अँधेरा हो रहा था, उजाला हो रहा था।

(क) सिंह इस समय भी माँद के भीतर है या ········ निकल गया।

(ख) आज बोलती क्यों नहीं? ········ क्यों है?

(ग) मैं बूढ़ा हो गया हूँ। पहले तो मैं ········ था।

(घ) यह माँद झूठ-मूठ ही जवाब देती है या फिर ········ बोलती है।

उत्तर

(क) सिंह इस समय भी माँद के भीतर है या **बाहर** निकल गया।

(ख) आज बोलती क्यों नहीं? **चुप** क्यों है?

(ग) मैं बूढ़ा हो गया हूँ। पहले तो मैं **जवान** था।

(घ) यह माँद झूठ-मूठ ही जवाब देती है या फिर **सचमुच** बोलती है।

6. सही अर्थ की जोड़ी बनाइए

(क) एक चूहा तक हाथ नहीं लगा बड़े संकट में फँस गया।

(ख) मेरी जान पर ही आ जाती भाग गया।

(ग) सियार वहाँ से चंपत हो गया कोई शिकार नहीं मिला।

उत्तर

(क) एक चूहा तक हाथ नहीं लगा कोई शिकार नहीं मिला।

(ख) मेरी जान पर ही आ जाती भाग गया।

(ग) सियार वहाँ से चंपत हो गया बड़े संकट में फँस गया।

7. अपने मन से वाक्य बनाइए

उदाहरण यदि चुप रहा तो हाथ आया शिकार भी चला जाएगा।

उत्तर (क) यदि बोला तो झगड़ा हो जाएगा।

(ख) यदि अधिक वर्षा हुई तो हर जगह पानी भर जाएगा।

(ग) यदि कड़ी धूप हुई तो पौधे मुरझा जाएँगे।

(घ) यदि अँधेरा हुआ तो हम रास्ता नहीं देख पाएँगे।

कला की कलाकारियाँ

1. यहाँ सिंह या सियार का मुखौटा (NCERT पृष्ठ 144) दिया गया है। आप दोनों में से अपनी रुचि के अनुसार मुखौटा बनाइए।

उत्तर छात्र स्वयं करें।

2. क्या आपने किसी पशु के पदचिह्न देखे हैं? अपने आसपास किसी पशु के पदचिह्न खोजिए और यहाँ उसका नाम लिखिए। दिए गए स्थान पर उसका चित्र बनाइए

उत्तर छात्र स्वयं करें।

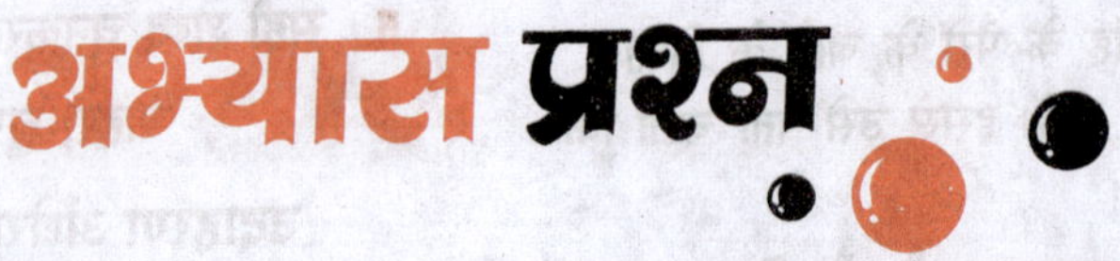

अभ्यास प्रश्न

बहुविकल्पीय प्रश्न

1. खरनखर किसका नाम था?
(क) सियार का (ख) सिंह का
(ग) लोमड़ी का (घ) बिल्ली का

2. शेर को अचानक क्या दिखाई दिया?
(क) कुआँ (ख) गड्ढा (ग) बिल (घ) माँद

3. माँद में कौन रहता था?
(क) सियार (ख) चूहा (ग) नेवला (घ) लोमड़ी

4. दधिपुच्छ किसका नाम था?
(क) सिंह का (ख) चूहे का (ग) सियार का (घ) बिल्ली का

उत्तर
1. (ख) सिंह का 2. (घ) माँद
3. (क) सियार 4. (ग) सियार का

गद्यांश पर आधारित प्रश्न

निम्नलिखित गद्यांश को पढ़कर उस पर आधारित प्रश्नों के उत्तर दीजिए।

गद्यांश

उस माँद में दधिपुच्छ नाम का एक सियार रहा करता था। वह माँद की ओर आ रहा था। माँद के द्वार पर उसने देखा तो उसे सिंह के पैरों के चिह्न दिखाई दिए। चिह्न माँद की ओर जाने के तो थे, पर लौटने के नहीं। उसने सोचा हे भगवान! आज तो मेरी जान पर ही आ बनी। इसके भीतर अवश्य कोई सिंह घुसा बैठा है। उसे समझ में नहीं आ रहा था कि वह क्या करे? वह पता करना चाहता था कि सिंह इस समय भी माँद के भीतर है या बाहर निकल गया है।

1. माँद के अंदर कौन बैठा था?
(क) सिंह (ख) चूहा (ग) सियार (घ) बिल्ली

2. किसकी जान पर आ बनी थी?
(क) सियार की (ख) चूहे की (ग) शेर की (घ) कुत्ते की

3. माँद के द्वार पर दधिपुच्छ ने क्या देखा?

4. दधिपुच्छ क्या पता करना चाहता था?

उत्तर
1. (क) सिंह 2. (क) सियार की
3. माँद के द्वार पर दधिपुच्छ ने सिंह के पैर के निशान देखे।
4. दधिपुच्छ पता करना चाहता था कि सिंह इस समय भी माँद के भीतर है या बाहर निकल गया।

निम्नलिखित प्रश्नों के उत्तर दीजिए

1. सिंह क्या सोचकर माँद में जाकर बैठ गया?

उत्तर सिंह यह सोचकर माँद में बैठ गया कि इसका निवासी जब आएगा तो उसे खाऊँगा।

2. वह माँद किसकी थी?

उत्तर वह माँद सियार की थी।

3. दधिपुच्छ ने माँद से क्या कहा?

उत्तर दधिपुच्छ ने माँद से कहा, अरे! तुझे आज क्या हुआ है? बोलती क्यों नहीं?

4. दधिपुच्छ को कैसे पता चला कि सिंह अंदर है?

उत्तर दधिपुच्छ ने माँद की ओर जाते सिंह के पैरों के निशान देखे, जिससे उसे पता चला कि सिंह माँद के अंदर है।

हम अनेक किंतु एक

कविता का सार

यह कविता 'हम अनेक किंतु एक' कवि द्वारिका प्रसाद माहेश्वरी द्वारा लिखी गई है। इस कविता में भारत की विविधता तथा एकता का वर्णन किया गया है। कवि कहता है कि भले हम विभिन्न प्रदेशों से आते हैं और हमारे रंग-रूप में भिन्नता है, फिर भी हम सभी भारत के अंग हैं।

शब्दार्थ *प्रदेश-राज्य या क्षेत्र, विविध-विभिन्न, टोलियाँ-छोटे-छोटे समूह, कंठ-गला या स्वर, मातृभूमि-जन्मभूमि, पितृभूमि-पूर्वजों की भूमि।*

काव्यांशों की व्याख्या

काव्यांश 1

हैं कई प्रदेश के, किंतु एक देश के,
विविध रूप-रंग हैं, भारत के अंग हैं,
भारतीय वेश एक, हम अनेक किंतु एक।

संदर्भ/प्रसंग प्रस्तुत पंक्तियाँ हमारी पाठ्यपुस्तक 'वीणा भाग-1' में संकलित कविता 'हम अनेक, किंतु एक' से ली गई हैं। इस कविता में भारतवासियों की अनेकता में एकता की भावना को दर्शाया गया है।

व्याख्या भारतवासियों के मन की बात बताते हुए कवि कहते हैं कि हम अलग-अलग राज्यों के होते हुए भी एक देश के ही हैं। हम अलग-अलग रंग-रूप के होते हुए भी भारत का ही हिस्सा हैं। हमारा पहनावा अलग-अलग होने पर भी भारतीय ही है, क्योंकि हम अनेक होते हुए भी एक हैं अर्थात् हम सब भारतीय ही हैं।

काव्यांश 2

बोलियाँ हजार हैं, टोलियाँ हजार हैं,
कंठ भी अनेक हैं, राग भी अनेक हैं,
किंतु गीत-बोल एक, हम अनेक किंतु एक।

प्रसंग पूर्ववत।

व्याख्या हम चाहे कई तरह की बोलियाँ बोलें, धर्म-जाति के अनुसार चाहे हमारे समूह भी कई हों, हमारे कंठ और राग भी प्रदेशों की विशेषता के अनुसार कई तरह के हों, लेकिन इसके बाद भी हमारे गीत और उनके बोलों में भारतीयता समाई हुई है, क्योंकि हम अनेक होते हुए भी एक हैं।

काव्यांश 3

एक मातृभूमि है, एक पितृभूमि है,
एक भारतीय हम, चल रहे मिला कदम,
लक्ष्य के समक्ष एक,
हम अनेक किंतु एक।

प्रसंग पूर्ववत्।

व्याख्या हमारी मातृभूमि (जन्मभूमि) और पितृभूमि (कर्मभूमि) भारत ही है। हम सब भारतीयों का एक ही लक्ष्य है—अपने देश के मान-सम्मान और गौरव को बनाए रखना तथा अपनी विजय पताका को पूरे विश्व में फहराना। इसके लिए हम कदम-से-कदम मिलाकर चल रहे हैं अर्थात् एकसाथ प्रयास कर रहे हैं। हम अनेक होते हुए भी एक हैं।

बातचीत के लिए

1. **आप किस देश में रहते हैं? आपका प्रदेश कौन-सा है?**

उत्तर मैं भारत देश में रहता हूँ। मेरे प्रदेश का नाम उत्तर प्रदेश है।

2. **आपके घर में कौन-सी भाषा बोली जाती है?**

उत्तर मेरे घर में हिंदी भाषा बोली जाती है।

3. **आपके घर के आस-पास के लोग कौन-सी भाषा बोलते हैं?**

उत्तर हमारे घर के आस-पास के लोग हिंदी भाषा बोलते हैं।

4. **सभी प्रदेश अलग हैं, लेकिन सबका देश एक है। आपकी मित्रों की टोली में कौन-कौन है?**

उत्तर मेरे मित्रों की टोली में अलग-अलग प्रदेश के बच्चे हैं; जैसे—दिल्ली, उत्तर प्रदेश, लखनऊ, राजस्थान, हरियाणा।

सोचिए और लिखिए

1. **'हम अनेक हैं, किंतु एक हैं' उदाहरण देकर इस बात को समझाइए।**

उत्तर 'हम अनेक हैं, किंतु एक हैं' का अर्थ है कि हम सभी भारतीय विभिन्न धर्मों, भाषाओं, संस्कृतियों और परंपराओं से आते हैं, लेकिन हम सब एक देश (भारत) के नागरिक हैं।

2. **कविता में भारत के विविध रंग-रूप के बारे में बताया गया है। विविध रूप-रंग का क्या अर्थ है?**

उत्तर विविध रूप-रंग का अर्थ है— भारत की विभिन्नताएँ; जैसे—अलग-अलग भाषाएँ, पहनावे, खान-पान, त्योहार और संस्कृतियाँ।

3. **'चल रहे मिला कदम' इस पंक्ति में किनके कदम मिलाकर चलने की बात कही गई है?**

उत्तर 'चल रहे मिला कदम' इस पंक्ति में सभी भारतीयों के कदम मिलाकर चलने की बात कही गई है।

शब्दों का खेल

1. **कविता के समान ध्वनि वाले शब्द छाँटकर लिखिए।**

प्रदेश .... हम ....
रंग .... बोलियाँ ....

उत्तर
- प्रदेश—वेश/देश
- हम—कदम
- रंग—अंग
- बोलियाँ—टोलियाँ

2. **समान ध्वनि वाले कुछ शब्द अपने मन से लिखिए।**

बोली .... , ... , ... , ...,
एक .... , ... , ... , ...,
राग .... , ... , ... , ...,

उत्तर
- बोली—होली, गोली, टोली, डोली।
- एक—अनेक, नेक, शेख, टेक।
- राग—भाग, नाग, आग, बाग।

3. **भूमि शब्द जोड़कर नए शब्द बनाइए**

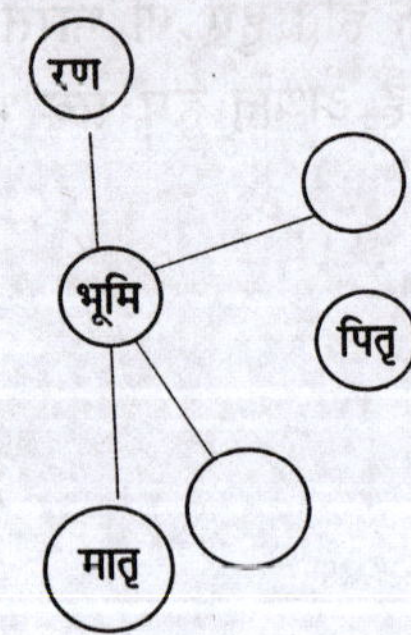

उत्तर
- रणभूमि
- कर्मभूमि
- पितृभूमि
- जन्मभूमि
- मातृभूमि

समझिए और लिखिए

1. कविता की पंक्तियाँ पूरी कीजिए।

हैं कई प्रदेश के, बोलियाँ हजार हैं, एक मातृभूमि है,
................, ..., ...
विविध रूप-रंग हैं, ... , ...
.... , राग भी अनेक हैं। चल रहे मिला कदम,
.... , ..., लक्ष्य के समक्ष एक,
हम अनेक किंतु एक। हम अनेक किंतु एक। .... ।

उत्तर

हैं कई प्रदेश के, बोलियाँ हजार हैं, एक मातृभूमि है,
किंतु एक देश के, टोलियाँ हजार हैं, एक पितृभूमि है,
विविध रूप-रंग हैं, कंठ भी अनेक हैं, एक भारतीय हम,
भारत के अंग हैं, राग भी अनेक हैं। चल रहे मिला कदम,
भारतीय वेश एक, किंतु गीत-बोल एक, लक्ष्य के समक्ष एक,
हम अनेक किंतु एक। हम अनेक किंतु एक। हम अनेक किंतु एक।

2. सही अर्थ को जोड़ी बनाकर लिखिए।

कंठ – वेशभूषा
पहनावा – सामने
विविध – गला
समक्ष – कई प्रकार के

उत्तर
कंठ — गला
पहनावा — वेशभूषा
विविध — कई प्रकार के
समक्ष — सामने

3. सही अर्थ वाले वाक्य पर सही ✔ का निशान लगाइए।

(क) 'भारतीय वेश एक' का अर्थ है

- सभी भारतीयों का एक पहनावा है। ☐
- भारत में अनेक प्रकार की वेशभूषा है, लेकिन सभी भारतीय एक हैं। ☐

(ख) 'बोलियाँ हजार हैं' में हजार का अर्थ है

- बहुत सारी बोलियाँ हैं। ☐
- हजार बोलियाँ हैं। ☐

उत्तर

(क) भारत में अनेक प्रकार की वेशभूषा है, लेकिन सभी भारतीय एक हैं।
(ख) बहुत सारी बोलियाँ हैं।

पता कीजिए

1. आप अपने प्रदेश के आस-पास के तीन-चार प्रदेशों की भाषा, खान-पान, वेशभूषा, तीज-त्योहारों के बारे में पता कीजिए और साथियों के साथ चर्चा कीजिए।

उत्तर छात्र स्वयं करें।

अभ्यास प्रश्न

बहुविकल्पीय प्रश्न

1. विविध रंग-रूप कहाँ हैं?
(क) भारत में (ख) देश में (ग) प्रदेश में (घ) उत्तर प्रदेश में

2. हजार बोलियाँ कहाँ पाई जाती हैं?
(क) प्रदेश में (ख) देशभर में
(ग) भारत देश में (घ) उत्तर प्रदेश में

3. एक मातृभूमि कहाँ है?
(क) भारत में (ख) दिल्ली में
(ग) आगरा में (घ) कानपुर में

4. कदम मिलाकर कौन चल रहा है?
(क) भारतीय (ख) यूरोपीय
(ग) बच्चे (घ) आदमी

उत्तर

1. (क) भारत में
2. (ग) भारत देश में
3. (क) भारत में
4. (क) भारतीय

सत्य-असत्य

नीचे दिए गए वाक्यों में से सत्य या असत्य कथन की पहचान कीजिए।

1. भारतीयों की वेशभूषा अलग अलग होती है। (सत्य/असत्य)
2. भारत में एक भी राज्य नहीं है। (सत्य/असत्य)
3. भारत में अलग-अलग बोलियाँ हैं। (सत्य/असत्य)

4. सभी भारतीय अलग-अलग चलते हैं। (सत्य/असत्य)

उत्तर

1. असत्य 2. असत्य 3. सत्य 4. असत्य

रिक्त स्थान

नीचे दिए गए वाक्यों में रिक्त स्थान की पूर्ति उचित शब्द से कीजिए।

लक्ष्य, गीत, पितृभूमि, बोलियाँ

1. .... हजार हैं टोलियाँ हजार हैं।
2. किंतु .... बोल एक हम अनेक किंतु एक।
3. एक .... है एक मातृभूमि है।
4. .... के समक्ष एक हम अनेक किंतु एक।

उत्तर

1. बोलियाँ 2. गीत 3. पितृभूमि 4. लक्ष्य

काव्यांश पर आधारित प्रश्न

निम्नलिखित काव्यांश को पढ़कर उस पर आधारित प्रश्नों के उत्तर दीजिए।

काव्यांश

बोलियाँ हजार हैं
टोलियाँ हजार हैं,
कंठ भी अनेक हैं,
राग भी अनेक हैं,
किंतु गीत बोल एक
हम अनेक किंतु एक।

1. भारत में कितनी बोलियाँ हैं?
   (क) सौ (ख) हजार (ग) एक (घ) पचास
2. हजार कंठ किस देश में हैं?
   (क) भारत में (ख) रूस में (ग) चीन में (घ) नेपाल में
3. भारत में बोल कैसे हैं?
4. भारत में राग कैसे हैं?

उत्तर

1. (ख) हजार
2. (क) भारत में
3. भारत में एक ही प्रकार के बोल हैं।
4. भारत में राग अनेक प्रकार के हैं।

निम्नलिखित प्रश्नों के उत्तर दीजिए

1. भारत की बोलियों की क्या विशेषता है?

उत्तर भारत की बोली की विशेषता यह है कि यहाँ हर राज्य की बोली अलग-अलग है।

2. भारत की एकता कैसी है?

उत्तर भारत में अनेकता में एकता है।

3. भारत के बोल के बारे में लिखिए।

उत्तर भारत के बोल निराले हैं। यहाँ विभिन्न प्रकार की भाषा, पहनावा, खान-पान है, लेकिन सबमें एक जैसा मिलन है।

4. भारत देश कैसा है? लिखिए।

उत्तर भारत देश बहुत सुंदर है। यहाँ पर्वत, नदियाँ, झरने, पवन आदि की सुंदरता मनभावन है। यहाँ का खान-पान, लोक परंपरा निराली है।

व्याकरण संबंधी प्रश्न

1. पाठ में आए चार तुकांत शब्दों को लिखिए
2. पाठ में आए चार संज्ञा शब्दों को लिखिए।

उत्तर

1. बोलियाँ टोलियाँ
   हम कदम
   अनेक एक
   देश प्रदेश
2. रंग, भारत, प्रदेश, कंठ

लेखन संबंधी प्रश्न

1. 'पिकनिक' विषय पर कम-से-कम 40 शब्दों में अनुच्छेद लिखिए।

उत्तर पिकनिक का नाम सुनते ही मन में उत्साह भर आता है। कुछ समय पहले मैं अपने परिवार के साथ पिकनिक मनाने एक बड़े मैदान में गया था। वह जगह बहुत सुंदर थी। वहाँ पर एक बड़ा तालाब था, जिसमें सुंदर-सुंदर मछलियाँ व बत्तख तैर रही थी। हमने तालाब के पास चटाई बिछाकर खाना खाया। खूब खेले व शाम को वापस घर आ गए।

Our Wondrous World
(EVS)

FAMILY AND FRIENDS

About the Chapter

This chapter shows various members of the family and their relationship with one another. It highlights how families live together happily by helping and caring for each other. In this chapter, we meet a little girl, Bela and her family. Her family has Dadaji, Dadiji, her parents, her two brothers- one younger and one older and her pet dog Shiru. All of them play together, enjoy their time in the garden and help each other in all household work. Their neighbours Kusum Mausi and her daughter, Munni share a special bond with Bela's family. They join them during festivals and take part in various activities like making rangoli and cooking delicious dishes.

Folk Song A song that belong to the language of any place like Marwari songs in Rajasthan, Marathi songs in Maharashtra.

Pitthoo A game in which two teams play, one team places stones over other stones and another team has to throw a ball on the stones.

Rangoli A beautiful art drawn on the floors with colourful patterns.

Braids Tying hairs after taking two or three layers of hairs at a time.

Puddles A small pit or hole at the roads which is filled with rainwater during the rainy days.

Discuss (Page 6)

Q.1 Who are the members in Bela's family?

Ans. Dadaji, Dadiji, Mother, Father, one elder brother, one little brother and a pet Shiru are the members in Bela's family.

Q.2 What do you and your family members do when it rains?

Ans. I and my family members sit under the shed in our garden, enjoy the rain, sing songs and have good food like pakoras and tea.

Q.3 Can you think of a rain song and sing it with your friends in the class?

Ans. Do it yourself

Write (Page 6)

Q.1 Write the names of your family members in the table below.

Name	Relationship with you	You call them (You address them as)
Urmila	Mother's sister	Mausi

Ans. Do it yourself

Find Out (Page 7)

Q.1 Do you know what games your grandparents used to play when they were young?

Ans. My grandparents used to play games like gillidanda, kho-kho and kanche in their childhood.

Page 8

Q.1 Would you call Bela's family a big or a small family?

Ans. We will call Bela's family a big family.

Discuss (Page 8)

Q.1 What games do you play with elders and other members of your family?

Ans. I play games like ludo, chess, snakes and ladders with my elders.

Q.2 Which animals, come to your home or your neighbourhood?

Ans. Cats, dogs and some cows come to my home and neighbourhood.

Q.3 Have you ever shared food with the animals who come to your home? Share your experience.

Ans. Yes, I have shared food with animals who come to my home.

I feed roti to cows and bread and milk to the street dogs who come to my home.

I go to a place near my home everyday with my grandfather to feed the birds.

Q.4 Why do you think we should not hurt or tease animals?

Ans. We should not hurt or tease animals because they are also living creatures. Animals also feel bad and painful but they cannot speak like us when we tease them.

Activity 1 (Page 9)

Q.1 Tick and colour the activities that you seen in your family.

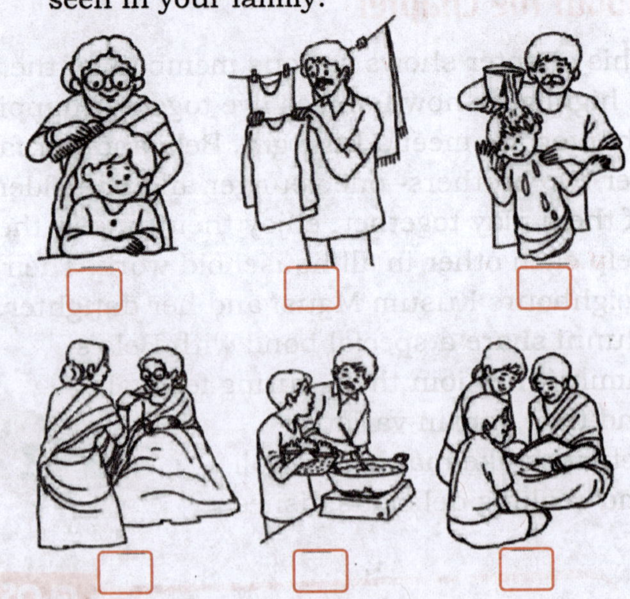

Ans. Do it yourself

Draw (Page 11)

Q.1 You can draw some more pictures to show how your family members help each other.

Ans. Do it yourself

Page 12

Q.1 What all have you learnt from your family and from whom?

Ans. I have learnt good manners and good values from my grandmother. I have learnt yoga and discipline from my grandfather. My mother has taught me how to care for others and my father teaches me various games. He also taught me how to help your family and live together with everyone.

Q.2 Has anyone learnt anything from you?

Ans. Yes, my younger brother has learnt riding a bike from me.

Activity 2 (Page 12)

Q.1 Collect some leaves and flowers that have fallen on the ground and create a rangoli.

Ans. Do it yourself

Discuss (Page 12)

Q.1 How do you help your family?

Ans. I help my family in many ways. I help my mother with small tasks like making my bed, arranging my books, cleaning my room, laying out the dining table and preparing food. I help my father with gardening. I help my grandparents by giving them the things they often forget. I make sure they take their medicine on time. I help my younger brother/sister with their homework.

Q.2 Some people in the family need special care and support like grandparents, small children, or someone who is sick. How do you help them?

Ans. I help my grandparents, any sick member of the family by helping them with things that they need. It can be medicines, spectacles, etc. I take good care of them and take them wherever they want to go by holding their hands. I make sure that they are never alone and do not carry any heavy bags. I do their tasks for them.

I help my younger brother/sister by playing with them, helping them with their homework. I take his/her care when no elder is around and make sure to give them food. I always keep a watch on him/her.

Write (Page 12)

Q.1 Who is the oldest person in your family?

Ans. My grandfather is the oldest person in my family.

Hint : You can write the name of the oldest member in the family.

Q.2 Who is the youngest person in your family?

Ans. My younger sister/brother is the youngest person in the family or I am the youngest person in the family.

Q.3 Who is the tallest person in your family?

Ans. My dad is the tallest person in my family.

Q.4 Do you have any members in your family who do not live with you? Who are they and where do they live? How often do you meet them?

Ans. My uncle does not live with us. He lives in Bangalore. He visits us once a month.

Q.5 What are the names of your friends who play with you at home or in your neighbourhood?

Ans. Pooja, Amit and Dev are my friends. Every evening, we all play in the park in our neighbourhood.

Activity 3 (Page 13)

Q.1 Look at the pictures below and write down Bela's relationship with all the members of her family.

Ans. The Bela's relationship with all the members of her family are

1. Dadiji
2. Dadaji
3. Little brother
4. Pet dog
5. Mausi
6. Mother
7. Father
8. Bhaiya

Activity 4 (Page 14)

Q.1 Draw a picture of the members of your family and write your relationships with them. You can look at the example given on page number 13.

Ans. Do it yourself

Write (Page 15)

Q.1 Write down the names of relatives who visit your family. How are they related to you?

Name of the relative	How are you related	What do you call them?

Ans. Do it yourself

Find Out (Page 15)

Q.1 In Bela's family everyone does some work. Who does what work in your family? Find and fill in the table.

Work	Who does it?
Cooking food	
Watering plants	
Mending things, repairing household items, sewing buttons, etc.	
Cleaning the house	
Buying things from the market	

You may add to the list other work that your family members do in your home.

Ans.

Work	Who does it?
Cooking food	My mother or grandmother
Watering plants	Me or my younger brother
Mending things, repairing household items, sewing buttons, etc	My grandparents or parents
Cleaning the house	Everyone in the family
Buying things from the market	My father or mother

Let us Reflect (Page 17 & 18)

Write

Q.1 How do family members show their love and care for each other?

Ans. Family members show their love through sitting together,talking to each other, cooking together and laughing with each other. They can show care by supporting each other, taking care of each other's need and playing with each other.

Q.2 What games do you play with your friends?

Ans. Hide and seek, rock-paper-scissor, chess, football, etc.

B. Draw (Page 17)

Q.1 Draw some of the happy moments you enjoy together with your family.

Ans. Do it yourself

C. Discuss

Q.1 What do you learn from elders in your family?

Ans. We learn moral values like love, care, respect and honesty from our elders.We also learn old games from our elders that they used to play at their age.

Q.2 How do we show our love and care for people in our family?

Ans. We show our love and care for people in our family by helping each other, playing with each other and doing fun activities together. Everyone takes care of each other's needs in the family.

Q.3 We care for many others who are not in our family. Who are they? How do we care for them?

Ans. We care for many others like dogs, cats, cows and buffaloes who are not in our family. We can care for them by feeding, not hurting them and taking them to the doctors if they are injured or having any disease.

D. Activity

Q.8 Find and Circle

Circle five words related to games in the grid below. One example is done for you.

P	A	D	C	F	R	Z
K	L	M	J	T	O	P
B	A	L	L	R	C	C
Q	L	U	D	O	H	T
N	H	B	A	T	E	O
E	N	N	M	C	S	Y
T	E	F	L	F	S	S

Ans. Ball, Ludo, Net, Bat, Chess.

GOING TO THE MELA

About the Chapter

This chapter is about family, friends and neighbours. We learn about fun activities together and also about how they take care of their elders. Nita and Radha's family are going to the mela with their neighbours, Sneha and Rohit's family. Their relatives, Mohan Chacha's family, are also going with them. They go by bus and reach the mela. They see a lot of stalls and buy a lot of things there. They also enjoy good food together and learn many interesting things about melas.

Reserved A fixed seat in a bus or train for some people like older people or disabled people.
Puppets Small dolls that can be moved by thin ropes or hands.
Volunteer One who takes the responsibility of completing any work like helping people, organising event, etc.
Spinning tops A toy which has a needle in its centre. Top is rotated through the needle.
Trinkets A piece of jewellery or small object for decoration.

Discuss Page 21

Q.1 What do you think was in the special bag that Nita and Radha's family carried?

Ans. There can be many items in the special bag that Nita and Radha's family carried like;

- Water bottles
- Fruits
- Snacks
- Candies
- Chocolates
- Napkins
- Mirrors
- Money bag
- Mobile phone

Q.2 How do you prepare yourself for a trip?

Ans. I prepare myself for the trip by doing the following things

- Making a list of things that I need to pack.
- Packing things into a suitcase properly.
- Booking transportation and hotels in advance.

Discuss (Page 24)

Q.1 What transport do you take to travel within your city /town/ village?

Ans. I usually take the bus to travel within my city.

Q.2 Why should safety measures be followed when travelling by bus, car or while riding a bicycle?

Ans. We should follow the safety measures while travelling by bus, car or while riding a bicycle to protect us and other people from any accident.

Write (Page 24)

Q.1 Describe briefly any trip that you have taken with your friends, neighbours or family.

Ans. You can describe any trip that you went on recently with your family. You can include the following pointers to do so

- Name of the place
- Why did you go?
- What did you see?
- Name of the hotel.
- What did you eat?
- What activities you did?

Write (Page 29)

Q.1 What is the purpose of 'Lost and Found' booth?

Ans. The purpose of 'Lost and Found' booth is to find the missing child or person. It also helps to find any missing objects like watch, bag, bottle,etc. and to help these items reach to its right owner.

Q.2 What is the role of the police dog?

Ans. Police dogs are trained dogs who help in searching and tracking any missing person or any missing items. They can smell doubtful objects like bombs.

Q.3 Have you ever been to a mela? What are the things you liked most in the mela?

Ans. Yes, I have been to a mela many times. I like games, rides and food stalls at the mela. I also purchased some hand-made craft items.

Discuss (Sharing experience) (Page 29)

Q.1 Imagine yourself in place of Nita, Radha, Sneha and Rohit. Share with the class the interesting things you do in the mela.

Ans. In the mela, I would like to take fun rides like giant wheel. I would try delicious food items like matka kulfi, chaat, jalebi, chole bhature, aloo tikki, etc. I would also like to watch the magic show.

Find Out (Page 29)

Q.1 Talk to the elders in the family and find out how melas were different when they were young.

Ans. You can talk to your grandparents and write about their experience in the melas.

Q.2 Why are fire engines and ambulances present in a mela?

Ans. Fire engines are present in a mela because they can fight the fire (if any fire breaks out at the mela) using long water pipes.

Ambulances are present in the mela because they can help carry any person who gets injured or sick, to the hospital.

Activity 1 Reading a sketch (Page 30)

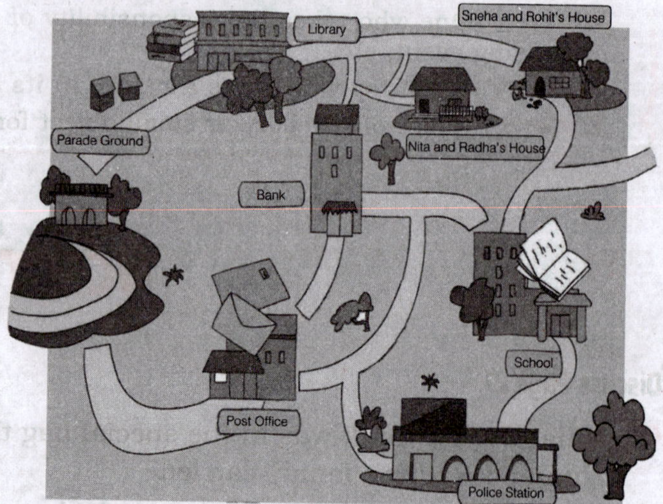

Study the sketch and answer

(i) Find and circle Rohit and Sneha's house on the map.

Ans. Do it yourself

(ii) Find and circle Nita and Radha's house on the map.

Ans. Do it yourself

(iii) Whose house is closer to the parade ground?

Ans. Nita and Radha's house is closer to the parade ground.

(iv) If you have to go from the police station to the parade ground, places would you pass through?

Ans. The places I would pass through are school, Sneha and Rohit's house and library.

Draw (Page 31)

Q.1 Sketch the route from home to school that you follow every day.

Ans. Do it yourself.

Let us Reflect (Page 32 & 33)

A. Discuss in the Class.

Q.1 How can we care for our elders?

Ans. We can care for our elders in many ways such as

- At home, we can spend the time with our elders by playing games with them, eating with them and sharing jokes with them.
- We can take care of the things that they need like, medicines.
- While going out, we can hold their hands. We can help them sit on the seat of bus, car or rickshaw.

Q.2 What kinds of vehicles do we see around us?

Ans. We see following types of vehicles around us

- Four-wheelers like car, taxi.
- Three-wheelers like Autorickshaw, e-rickshaw .
- Two-wheelers like bicycle, scooters.
- Large vehicles like buses, trains.

Q.3 How can we ensure safety during travel?

Ans. We can ensure safety during travel in the following ways

- Keeping our hands or head inside the window.
- Wearing helmets while riding on a two-wheeler.
- Driving according to the speed limit.
- Crossing the road after looking both sides of the road.

B. Match the pictures with the words.

Pick a suitable word from the list, match it with a picture, and write the word below the picture. One has been done for you.

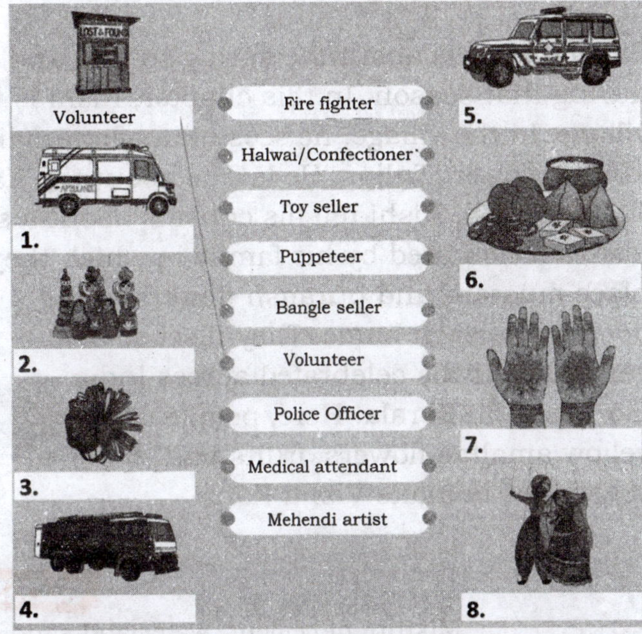

Ans. 1. Medical attendant 2. Toy seller
3. Bangle seller 4. Fire fighter
5. Police officer 6. Halwai/Confectioner
7. Mehendi artist 8. Puppeteer

C. Draw in your notebook

Draw and label different vehicles that you see around your school and home.

Ans. Do it yourself.

D. Role play: Organise a mock *mela*

With the help of your teacher, organise a mock mela in your classroom. Discuss and plan the different roles, stalls, and games that are part of a mela. Use learning-teaching materials available locally, e.g., toys, puppets, play money, miniatures and clay models to set up your stalls and role-play buyers and sellers.

Ans. Do it yourself with your friends.

CELEBRATING FESTIVALS

Chapter at Glance

This chapter is about the spring season and different festivals celebrated in the country during that season. In this chapter, Rishi is travelling from Jammu to his mama and mami's village. In the village, he sees many flowers like roses, marigolds and hibiscus and a new kind of flower, Tulips. He learns about the Kashmir Tulip festival. Rishi tell his cousins about a spring festival celebrated by his family in which they place mustard and buransh flowers at the doorstep of each home. They discuss about various festivals celebrated across India like Vishu in Kerala. Here, people use yellow amaltas flowers, fruits and vegetables to make Vishu Kani.

Concrete Mixture of cement, water and sand to make roads.

Auspicious Something that brings good luck.

Ritual A religious ceremony

Procession A group of people walking together for a ceremony.

Germinated Seed which has started to be developing into the plant

Peak The topmost point of the mountain.

Discuss (Page 35)

Q.1 Have you ever travelled in a bus? If yes, share the experience with your classmates.

Ans. Yes, I have travelled in a bus. I went to Jaipur with my classmates. We ate so many snacks and shared our tiffin with our teachers. There were so many flowers, green plants and tall trees on the way. We saw Aravalli mountains in our journey.We stopped at a Dhaba for the lunch. It was a wonderful journey as we all played *Antakshari* in the bus.

Q.2 What types of trees and flowers did you see during your trip?

Ans. I saw green plants and colourful flowers like yellow, pink, orange and red. There were some small plants with spines. There was grass also which was being eaten by the herd of cows.

Q.3 What safety measures should you take while travelling?

Ans. We should take the following safety measures while travelling,

- Not keeping our head, hands, and arms outside the window.
- Driving slowly and according to speed limit, specially in the mountain region.
- Wearing helmets while riding two wheelers.
- Do not stand or jump around in the moving bus.

Q.4 What safety measures should you take while riding a bicycle and while walking on the road?

Ans. We should take the following safety measures while riding a bicycle,

- Wear a helmet, and pads on knees and elbows.
- Always ride bicycle on the left side of the road.
- Always check the brakes and cycle chains before riding a bicycle.
- Do not paddle the bicycle while standing over the seat.

While walking we should follow following safety measures,

- We should always walk on the footpath.
- We should not run on the road .
- Use zebra crossing for crossing the road.
- Cross the road only after looking both sides of the road.

Activity 1 (Page 36)

Match the signboards Column A with their meanings in Column B.

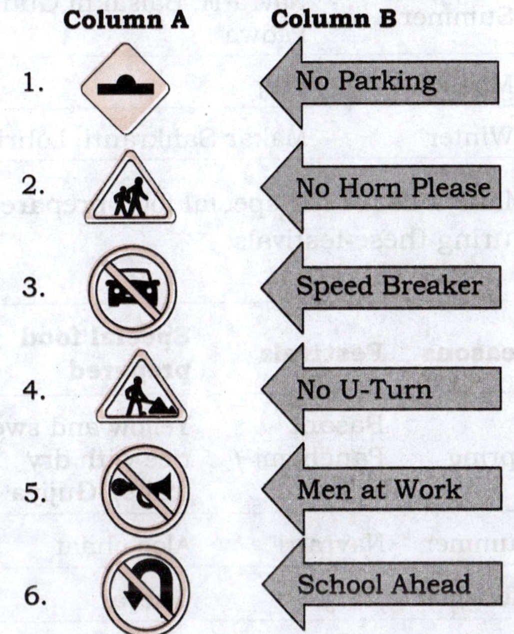

Ans. 1. Speed Breaker 2. School Ahead 3. No Parking 4. Men at work 5. No Horn Please 6. No U-Turn

Draw (Page 36)

Q.1 You would have observed many signboards on the road. Draw and label any three road signboards that are not listed above.

Ans. You can draw U-turn ahead, divergence ahead, speed limit, no entry, etc.

Write (Page 40)

Q.1 Ask your elders about the names of festivals celebrated in your locality for each of the seasons given below.

Spring, Summer, Monsoon, Winter

Ans.

Seasons	Festivals
Spring	Basant Panchami, Holi
Summer	Navratri, Baisakhi,Gudi Padwa
Monsoon	Teej
Winter	Makar Sankranti, Lohri

Q.2 Make a list of the special food prepared during these festivals.

Ans.

Seasons	Festivals	Special food prepared
Spring	Basant Panchami / Holi	Yellow and sweet rice with dry fruits/ Gujiya
Summer	Navratri	Aloo chaat
Monsoon	Teej	Ghevar
Winter	Makar Sankranti	Khichdi

Q.3 What special dresses do you wear during festivals?

Ans. There are so many festivals celebrated and every festival has unique traditional dress, which is given in the table below

Festivals	Men	Women
Diwali	Kurta pyjama	Saree/ Lehenga
Eid	White kurta pyjama, skull cap	Sharara suits
Navratri	Kurta pyjama, traditional dhoti and salwar	Ghaghra choli

Activity 3 (Page 41)

Q.1 Match the name of the food with the festival from the list given below.

Bihu, Chhath Puja ,Christmas, Eid-ul-Fitr, Holi, Onam, Ugadi

Ans.

Food prepared during festivals		Name of the Festivals
	Thekua	Chhath Puja
	Pitha	Bihu
	Plum Cake	Christmas
	Gujiya	Holi
	Sadya	Onam
	Holige	Ugadi
	Seviyan	Eid- ul- fitr

Find Out (Page 42)

Q.1 Do you think everyone celebrates festivals with a variety of special food and new clothes?

Ans. Yes, everyone celebrate festivals with a variety of special food and new clothes. For example, on the day of Christmas, people wear the Santa Claus dress and distribute gifts to the children.

On the day of Durga Puja, Bengali people wear white and red traditional saree.

Q.2 Are there any mountains, rivers or streams close to where you live? Have you ever visited relatives in a far away place? How does it feel there?

Ans. Do it yourself.

Let us Reflect (Page 42 & 43)

A. Discuss

Q.1 What are the different modes of transport used during travel?

Ans. The different modes of transport used during travel depend upon the distance that people want to cover or the money that they can spend. These include

- For very short distance like 15-30 kms, we can use land transport like two wheelers, autorickshaw and even cars.
- For short distance like 50 km we can use transport like car or bus.
- For long distance like 100 km we can use land or rail transport like car, bus or trains.
- For very long distance more than 400 km we can use rail network or air transport like aeroplane.

Q.2 How can one be saved during travels?

Ans. One can be saved in many ways during travels,

- Never take the head and arms out of the window.
- Always follow the speed limit and blow horn on turns.
- Always follow the safety signboards on the road.
- Do not stand on the gates of moving bus and train.
- Do not eat anything given by strangers.
- Always remember your phone numbers of your parents in case of any emergency.

Q.3 What special foods are prepared during the festivals?

Ans. Every festival has special food like,

- On Holi, we eat *gujiya*, *dahi bhalle* and *gol gappas*.
- On Lohri, we eat revri, moongfali and jaggery (*ladoo*).
- On Gudi Padwa, we eat puran poli, kothimbir vadi.
- On Pongal, people eat *Pongal khichdi* made up of rice, *moong dal*, curry leaves, etc.
- On Eid, people eat *seviyan* and *sheer khurma*.

Q.4 How do festivals and celebrations bring us together?

Ans. Festivals and celebrations bring us together because we all celebrate the festivals together, share sweets and gifts with our neighbours and friends. People meet each other, wear new clothes, laugh together, sing and dance and pray to the God. This brings joy and happiness to everyone.

Q.5 Do you feel happy spending time in nature? What about nature makes you feel happy?

Ans. Do it yourself.

B. Write

Q.1 Name any two relatives you have visited recently.

Ans. Do it yourself.

Q.2 How do you spend time with your cousins and relatives?

Ans. Do it yourself.

Fill in the blanks

1. Chiya and Nonikaa live in a small village near the__________.
2. The bus went along the _______ roads where the hills were covered with the colourful flowers.
3. Rishi and his family walked to his Mama's house through a narrow ______ road.
4. The red flowers that bloom in spring are called _______ .
5. ________ is a kind of leafy vegetable eaten with hot rice.

Ans. 1. mountains 2. curved 3. mud 4. buransh 5. Haakh

C. Draw

Q.1 Take a chart paper and draw signboards for the following. You can use any image and colour of your choice for creating the sign boards. Explain what you have created.

- School library
- Toilet
- Assembly
- Drinking water point
- Playground
- My classroom
- Stairs

Ans. Do it yourself.

CHAPTER 4 GETTING TO KNOW PLANTS

About the Chapter

This chapter introduces us to the different types of plants in our surroundings. We learn about their physical features and importance. There are various types of plants like trees, shrubs, herbs, grasses, climbers and creepers. Leaves of different plants smell different from each other. We can identify some fruits and leaves by their smell. All the plants have various parts like root, shoot, leaves, flower and fruits with each part having a particular role.

GLOSSARY

Bark The brown outer, hard covering of a tree trunk.

NCERT FOLDER

Write (Page 49)

Q.1 Write the names of trees that you can recognise. Try to remember where you have seen these trees. Which of these trees have you seen near your home or on your way to school?

Ans. Name of some trees that I can recognise are as follows

- Peepal – Near my home
- Banyan – On the way to school
- Mango – On the way to school
- Neem- Near my home

Write (Page 50)

Q.1 Write the names of some shrubs. Have you seen any of the shrubs shown in the pictures below?

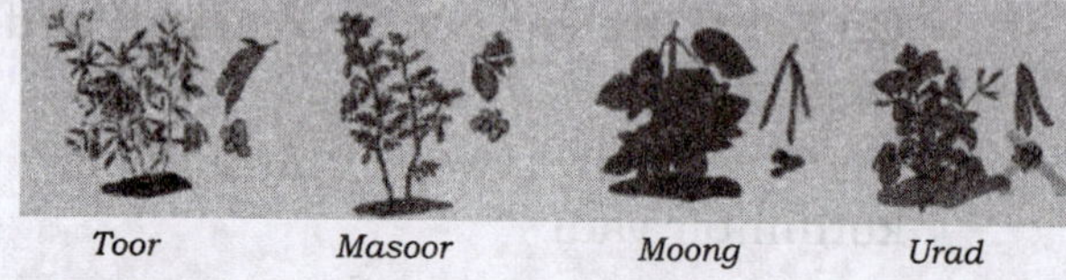

Toor *Masoor* *Moong* *Urad*

Ans. Curry leaf , Rose, Hibiscus, Touch-me-not plant are some shrubs. No, I have not seen the shrubs shown in the pictures.

Q.2 Do you know what they are called in your mother tongue?

Ans. Yes, the Basil is called as *Tulsi*, curry leaves as *curry patta* and touch -me-not as *chhui-mui* in our mother tongue.

Write (Page 52)

Q.1 Write the names of some herbs that you have seen and where you have seen them.

Ans. The name of some herbs that I have seen are as follows

- Coriander (*Dhaniya*) – At home
- Mint (*Pudina*)- At home
- Mustard (*Sarso*) – While travelling.

Guess Page 54

Q.1 Is this a creeper or a climber? What do you call it in your language?

Snake gourd

Ans. Yes, it is a climber.We call it *Chichinda* or *Saanpa Lauki* in our language.

Write (Page 54)

Q.1 Write the names of some climbers or creepers that you have seen and where you have seen them. Are any of them in the pictures given on page 53? What are they called in your language?

Ans. I have seen money plant(home), bottle gourd (farm) and ridge gourd (home).They all are climbers.Yes money plant and bottle gourd are given on the Page 53.

Bottle gourd is called *lauki* and *ridge* gourd is called *torai* in our language.

Q.2 Name these plants in your language.Say if they are a tree, shrub, climber or creeper.

Marigold	Neem	Jujube or Ber
Banthi in (Telugu)	*Bevugida* in (Kannada)	*Boroi in* (Manipure)

Ans.

Mar'gold	Neem	Jujube or Ber
Genda (Hindi)	*Neem* (Hindi)	*Ber* (Hindi)
It is a shrub	It is a tree	It is a tree

Activity 1 Page 54

Q.1 Stand in groups of two to four, next to any tree or shrub that is in or near your school.

- Now look around, as far as you can see. Remember to look down near your feet as well!
- How many kinds of trees, shrubs, herbs, grasses, climbers or creepers can you spot?

Ans. Do it yourself

Make Friends with a Plant! Page 55

Q.1 Choose one plant, preferably a shrub with a thick stem or a tree that you want to make friends with. You can do this by yourself or with a group of your classmates.

Name your plant, just like you might name a pet. Take care of the plant by watering it each day. Also protect it as your friend.

Now observe your plant friend closely. Here are a few things to observe — its leaves, flowers and fruits. Are there many, a few or no leaves, flowers and fruits? Record your observations in the table.

Time and date of observation: __________

Month: ______________

Weather on the day you are recording this information: ____________

Plants parts	**Many, a few or none**	**Colour**	**Shape (describe or draw)**	**Any other observ-ations**
Leaves				
Flowers				
Fruits				

Ans. Name of the plant : Lemon Tree

Time and date of observation : 20.09.2024, 5:00 p.m. Month : September

Weather on the day you are recording this information : Cloudy (no rain)

Plants parts	**Many, a few or none**	**Colour**	**Shape** (describe or draw)	**Any other observation**
Leaves	Many	Dark green	Medium and broad with sharp edges where it joins the stem.	Centre stem is highlighted easily
Flowers	Many	White	Small and waxy petals	Soft, lemon fragrance
Fruits	Many	Yellow	Round	Sour fragrance

Activity 3 Page 56

Q.1 Do you find new leaves growing on the plant? Do the colour of the leaves change as they grow larger?

Ans. Yes, I have noticed new leaves growing on the plant.

Yes, the leaves become darker when they grow large in size.

Q.2 Do the old brown leaves fall to the ground?

Ans. Yes, old brown leaves fall to the ground because they get dry.

Q.3 Do you find flowers appearing or notice any fruit?

Ans. Yes, I saw many small waxy petals and yellow-green round fruit on the tree.

Q.4 What are other observations you have?

Ans. Many flowers were dried. The butterflies were flying around the flowers.

Write (Page 56)

Write about a plant in your notebook.

Ans. A rose plant is a type of shrub. It has green leaves and flowers in red colour. Sometimes, there can be flowers of different colours like pink, white, yellow, etc.

It has a stiff stem and the flowers of this plant are very fragrant.

Activity 4 (Page 57)

Q.1 Observe the leaves in your surroundings.

Ans. You can take a mango, neem, peepal , banyan, etc. tree leaf and observe them.

Q.2 Draw, colour and label them in your notebook.

Ans. Do it yourself

Q.3 Describe their colour, shape, size, texture and smell to your friend in the class.

Ans. Mango leaves are heart-shaped, long and taper-ended. They are medium sized with smooth texture. They have a pleasant fruity smell.

Q.4 What statements can we make about leaves after doing this activity?

Ans. Every plant has a unique shape, size, smell and texture of the leaf. Thus, one can identify the leaves even after touch or smell.

Page 58

Q.1 What are the parts of a plant?

Ans. Roots,stem, leaves, fruits and flowers are the parts of a plant.

Q.2 Mark different parts of the plant and label them.

Ans.

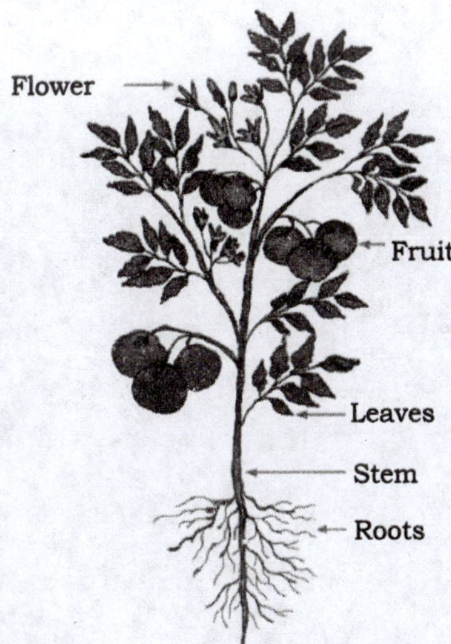

Page 59

Q.1 Did you notice any other animals, birds and insects on the plant?

Ans. Yes, I noticed ants, bees, squirrels,spiders, and many more animals, birds and insects on the plants.

Q.2 What were they doing?

Ans. Every animal was doing different activity like

- Ants were moving and carrying something
- Squirrels were playing near the tree.

Let us Reflect (Page 60 & 61)

A. Discuss

Q.1 What would happen if there were no plants?

Ans. If there were no plants, then the life on the Earth would not be possible because plants gives us many things like

- Oxygen to breathe
- Shade to protect from heat
- Cool air
- Food like cereals, fruits and vegetables to eat.
- Medicines to free from disease
- Shelter to the birds, animals and insects.

Q.2 How does the root help a plant to grow?

Ans. Roots absorb the essential nutrients and water from the soil which is very important for the growth of a plant.It also holds the soil tightly with its hairs and strong branches which supports the plant to stand even in fast winds.

Q.3 What is the role of the stem?

Ans. The role of the stem is as follows

- It transports essential nutrients from the roots to the other parts of the plants.
- It also transports water from the roots to the other parts of the plant.
- It supports the growth of the branches and leaves.
- Stem also stores food inside it.

B. Write

Q.1 List the names of plants that you have seen in your school, park or near your home. Identify what types of plants they are — tree, shrub, herb, grass, climber or creeper.

Ans.

Name of the Plant	**Type of Plant**	**Place where seen**
Neem	Tree	Near home
Banyan	Tree	School
Mint	Herb	At home
Giloy	Climber	At home
Curry leaves	Shrub	At home

Q.2 Which particular part of the plant helped you to identify the type of the plant?

Ans. The height of the stem helped us to identify the type of the plant. For example, we can identify the tree with its thick trunk.

Q.3 Describe your favourite plant. Why is it your favourite?

Ans. You can write about your favourite plant and its special feature like

- Money plant (spreads with beautiful shape leaves)
- Rose (beautiful flowers)
- Neem(looks soothing in monsoon with green leaves, gives medicines)
- Curry leaves (pleasant fragrance; adds good taste to food); etc. or other plants.

C. Draw

Q.1 Draw different types of leaves you have seen around you.

Ans. Do it yourself

D. Make a Rangoli

Q.1 Collect leaves and flowers fallen on the ground. Arrange them in patterns to make a *Rangoli*. You may also create different animal shapes using the collected leaves.

Ans. Do it yourself

CHAPTER 5 PLANTS AND ANIMALS LIVE TOGETHER

About the Chapter

This chapter is about the relationship between plants and animals. Many animals live near plants and use them for various things like food, shelter and a place to rest. Animals use plants in many different ways. Some animals, like squirrels, use tree hollows to hide and rest, while others, like caterpillars eat leaves for food. Some animals also live in the soil, for example, insects like ants, termites and earthworms. These small creatures help to keep the soil healthy, which helps the plants grow.

GLOSSARY

Shelter A covered place to protect from heat, cold, rain and dangers.

Hollow Something which is empty from inside.

Termites Group of insects that feed on decaying plants.

Perch To sit on something narrow like a branch.

Creatures A living thing such as animal, a bird or an insect.

NCERT FOLDER

Discuss (Page 64)

Q.1 Which of the animals shown on page 63 of the NCERT, have you seen before?

Ans. I have seen elephants, earthworms, tailorbird, ants, bugs, frog, butterflies, squirrels.

Find Out (Page 64)

Q.1 Why do these animals choose to live near plants?

Ans. Animals choose to live near plants because of the following reasons

- Plants provide shelter to the animals. For example, squirrels live in tree hollow.
- Plants provide food to animals. For example, elephants eat grass, caterpillars eat leaves, etc.
- Plants protect the animals from their enemies. For example, chameleon can hide in green leaves and change its colour.

Page 64

Q.1 What colour is the soil under your feet?

Ans. Brown

Activity 1 (Page 64)

Q1. Pick up a little soil near your plant friend with your hands.

- How does it look and feel?
- Is it dry, damp, rough, smooth, hard or grainy?
- Did you find any leaves or insects in the soil?
- Now smell this soil and remember it.

My soil felt	Rough ☐	Smooth ☐	Hard ☐	Grainy ☐
My soil had	Nothing ☐	Leaves ☐	Small stones ☐	Insects ☐

Ans. My soil felt grainy as it had small stones. It was dry.

No there were no insects but there were some dried leaves.

Page 65

Q.1 Examine the soil more carefully. What small things do you notice in it?

Ans. There are some small things in the soil like

- Pieces of stones
- Small creatures like snails, earthworms, etc.
- Dried leaves, twigs

Discuss (Page 66)

Q.1 In the monsoons, you may find many more plants and animals around. Where did these new plants and animals come from? Why could you not see them earlier?

Ans. We find many more plants in the monsoon season because during monsoon, rains brings nutrients and moisture. Thus, seeds start growing into new plants.

We find many animals like snails, earthworms and snakes during the monsoon season because these animals live deep inside the soil and when the soil gets wet, they come out.

Activity 2 (Page 66)

Q.1 Stand near your plant friend and look around. How many different animals can you spot? Describe them in words and fill in the table.

I saw ..... (Describe)	**It was on....**	**What was it doing?**
A small hoping insect	The grass	Jumping around
A thin plant that curls	Another plant nearby	Nothing
A black bird		

Ans.

I saw ..... (Describe)	**It was on....**	**What was it doing?**
A small hoping insect	The grass	Jumping around
A thin plant that curls	Another plant nearby	Nothing
A black bird	branches	Sitting and singing cuckoo-cuckoo
A big animal with its baby animal	Near a tree	Playing with its baby animal
A beautiful bird	In the fields	Dancing spreading its feathers

Page 68

Q.1 How many of these animals have you seen? Watch out for them!

Ans. I have seen camels, owls, crows, monkeys, squirrels and butterflies.

Activity 3 (Page 68)

Sound of Birds

Q.1 Close your eyes and try to listen to the sounds of birds.

Do you hear any bird sounds?

Can you see which birds are making these sounds?

Ans. Yes, I can hear some bird sounds.

I can see some of the birds making these sounds.

Different birds, different sounds

Q.1 Recall the bird sounds you have listened to. Try to produce the sounds that different birds make.

Now try to write down in the following table the sound of any birds you have heard.

Name of the Bird	Sound Made
Pigeon	Gutru gu

Ans.

Name of the Bird	Sound Made
Pigeon	Gutru gu
Cuckoo	Koo-koo
Sparrow	Tweet-tweet
Owl	Hoo-hoo
Crow	Caw-caw
Parrot	Squawk-squawk

If you do not hear any sounds of birds, what do you think is the reason?

Ans. If we do not hear any sounds of birds, there may be many reasons like

- In winters, sometimes birds migrate to hotter places.
- Loss of plants and trees leads to the loss of birds.

Q.2 Do you hear more bird sounds

In the early morning?

In the afternoon?

In the evening?

Ans. More bird sounds are heard in early morning and in the evening because in morning, they begin the day for food search and in the evening, they return back to their nests.

Let us Reflect Page 70 & 71

A. Discuss

Q.1 What was the colour and texture of the two soil specimens that you collected during the previous activity? In which month did you pick them up? Did they smell different and can you describe the smells?

Ans. (Hint: make a table for two specimens of the soil and then compare)

Observation of different features	Soil type 1	Soil type 2
Colour	Dark brown(coffee)	Very dull brown
Texture	Moist and soft	Grainy
Smell	Wet and pleasant (rain)	Dusty
Month of collection	September	December

Q.2 During which month did fresh new leaves appear on the plant that you were observing?

Ans. During the month of July and August (monsoon season) and February and March (spring season), new leaves appear on the plant.

Q.3 Which animals, birds and insects did you notice around plants?

Ans. Hints : We may notice

many animals like monkeys, cows, etc.

Birds like cranes, sparrow, peacock, etc.

Insects like bees, earthworms, butterflies, etc around plants.

Q.4 Recall and write about how animals, birds and insects rely on plants. Which one was your favourite example?

Ans. Animals, birds and insects rely on plants for shelter, food and other activities like restings. My favourite example was elephants eating the grass.

Q.5 What is soil made up of?

Ans. Soil is made up from rocks that are broken into small pieces. It also includes old leaves, roots, stems and dead animals like insects.

B. Write

(i) Names of two animals that you observed near or on plants.

(ii) Describe the shape, size and colours of these animals.

(iii) Guess why these animals were staying near these plants?

(iv) What other interesting things did you notice about these animals

Ans. (i) Monkey and Squirrels

(ii) Monkey is a medium sized animal. His shape is almost like a human. The colour of monkey is golden brown.

Squirrels are small in size shaped like a rat. They are grey or brown colour with black stripes on the back.

(iii) Monkeys love to eat leaves, fruits from the plants and trees. Monkeys enjoy jumping from one branch to another.

Squirrels eat nuts and seeds taken from plants. They drink water from the fruits like berries from the tree.They use the twigs, leaves and small branches to make their nest.

(iv) Monkeys use their tail to hang on the branches. They jump from one branch to another. They use their hands to pluck the fruit from the tree and store it in their mouth for long time.

Squirrels move very fast. They can jump very high, store their seeds and build their nests at their own

C. Draw

Q.1 Remember you wrote about your plant friend. Now try and draw your plant friend. Use different coloured small dots in your drawing to show the places where you spotted animals, birds or insects.

Ans. Do it yourself

D. Put in order

Q.1 One day Suma found a caterpillar on a *tagar* plant. She found it interesting. She observed it for about 10 minutes. It was eating tender leaves continuously. Her mother came close to her. She guided her to observe the caterpillar each day. Suma became more curious. Consult an elder person and organise the following changes in order.

- ☐ Now it was a butterfly.
- ☐ The caterpillar formed a cocoon.
- ☐ It flew away gently.
- ☐ One day it stopped eating.
- ☐ It came out of cocoon.

Ans. 4, 2, 5, 1, 3

LIVING IN HARMONY

About the Chapter

In this chapter, we will learn how plants and animals help each other. All the elements of nature like plants, animals and human beings need each other. Plants and trees are home to many animals and birds. When animals eat the fruits of the trees, they throw seeds which help in growing new plants. We also get fruits, vegetables and other things from plants like medicines, fibre for clothes and wood for houses. Animals provide us with many things like milk. Plants and animals help in making the soil fertile. They also need our support and care.

Harmony Living happily without any fight.
Fibre A thin thread that comes out of plant or animals to make cloth.
Dispersing Spreading out things on the ground.
Fertile Making the soil healthy so that plants can grow in it.
Companion A friend or partner who stays with you always.

Discuss (Page 73)

Q.1 Do any of the animals, birds, insects and plants live with you in your house?

Ans. Yes, there is a hibiscus and rose plant in my garden. There is a cat who doesn't live with me but it visits my house and I feed it milk.

Q.2 Do you and your family take care of them?

Ans. Yes, my grandmother always waters the plants regularly. We also feed wheat grains and bajra to the birds and feed milk and bread to the cat.

Find Out (Page 73)

Q.1 Are there any animals, birds and insects that you have spotted that are not in the picture given on NCERT page 72?

Ans. Yes, I have spotted animals like peacock, lizards, cockroaches, crows that are not in the picture.

Q.2 Try to find out their names and write them in the table given below. One example has been done for you.

Name of the animal	Place where you have seen them
Monkey	Tree

Ans.

Name of the animal	Place where you have seen them
Monkey	Tree
Squirrels	Tree
Dog	On the street
Beetles	School ground
Pigeon	In the garden

Page 73

Q.1 Discuss with elders in your family which animals and plants they kept at home when they were young.

Ans. Hint : My grandmother kept cows and dogs, when she was young. She used to wash the cows and feed them with straw. She also fed the dog and played with it. She had so many plants like tulsi, shami, marigold, etc.

Discuss (Page 74)

Q.1 Which are the uninvited animals, birds and insects that visit your home?

Ans. Uninvited animals like monkeys, squirrels, lizards, pigeon, etc. visit our homes.

Q.2 Why do you think they come to your homes?

Ans. They come for food, water, shelter and some love to our homes.

Q.3 How do you feel about their presence in your home?

Ans. I feel very happy and relaxing after feeding the animals. However, there are some animals like lizards that make me feel scared.

Q.4 Which of them do you like?

Ans. I like cows, dogs, cats, pigeons and sparrow.

Q.5 What do you do when you do not like them?

Ans. There are some insects and animals that I don't like, such as lizards, spiders and rats. I ask my grandmother to get these out of the house.

Discuss (Page 77)

Q.1 How are we dependent on plants and animals?

Ans. We are dependent upon the plants for many things like

- Oxygen and fresh air
- Food, medicines and fibre for clothes
- Wood for our houses and shade
- We are dependent upon the animals for food, milk, meat.

Q.2 How do plants help animals?

Ans. Plants help animals in many ways like

- Plants provide oxygen and food.
- They provide shelter and resting place to the animals. For example, birds make nests on the trees.

Q.3 How do animals help plants?

Ans. Animals help plants by dispersing the seeds and making the soil fertile through their waste.

Q.4 How do you look after plants and animals in your surroundings?

Ans. We can look after our plants and animals in the following ways

- Giving them water regularly.
- Keeping the grains, seeds for birds on our roof.

- Keeping the plants in proper sunlight.
- Giving milk and food to the animals.
- Showing love, care and kindness to the plants and animals.

Q.5 How do animals and plants depend on us?

Ans. Plants and animals are dependent on us for our love , care and protection.

Activity 1 (Page 78)

Observe the animals around you.

Choose any animal that you see often, such as a goat, cow, dog, cat or bird like a crow, pigeon, sparrow, parrot or duck.

Observe it closely whenever you get a chance. You can also keep a bowl of water and some grains for it.

Ans. Do it yourself

Write (Page 78)

Write a short description of the animal or bird—

Q.1 Name and describe the animal or bird that you have chosen.

Ans. Dog

Q.2 When and where did you first see it?

Ans. I have seen it on the street near my home.

Q.3 Was it there alone or with its friends?

Ans. It was with its friends.

Q.4 Describe its movement.

Ans. It was running here and there with its friends.

Q.5 What sounds did it make?

Ans. It was making the **bhaw-bhaw** (bark) sound.

Q.6 Did you see it eating, sleeping, talking to its friends or maybe fighting sometimes?

Ans. Yes, the dog sleeps at noon. It talks to its friends and plays with them sometimes. It fights with its friends sometimes.

Q.7 Did it do anything that surprised you or made you laugh?

Ans. Yes, when the dog gets injured, it heals it's wound by licking it with its tongue. That surprised me a lot.

Activity 2 (Page 79)

You may do this activity near your plant friend, in your classroom or at home. Bring small amounts of three types of food from your kitchen

- Sweet like sugar or jaggery;
- Fried like a *papad* or *murukku*;
- Boiled or cooked like bread, *chapati*, *idli*, rice or ragi.

Keep these three types of food on the floor in a straight line with one foot distance between them.

Make a Guess

Q.1 Who will come for the food?

Ans. Ants will come for sweet food.

Rats would come for papads.

Birds would come for rice.

Monkey would come for *chapati*.

Q.2 Which will be their favourite food?

Ans. Ants would love sweet food like sugar or jaggery; Monkeys may love chapati; Birds may love rice; Rats like munching things like murukku.

Q.3 Will any ants come to your food?

Ans. Yes

Q.4 Where would they come from?

Ans. Ants come from outside the windows, holes in our walls, garden, etc.

Q.5 Will all the ants look the same?

Ans. No, all the ants do not look same. Some ants are black and some are red in colour.

Q.6 What food item will they go to first?

Ans. Ants will go to the sweet food first.

Q.7 How many ants will come to the food?

Ans. Many ants will come to the food.

Q.8 What will they do with the food?

Ans. They will stick to the food and start carrying the food back to their hole.

Activity 3 (Page 80)

Guess Who I Am ?

Sit in pairs. One of you will think of the name of an animal, bird, insect or tree and whisper it in the ear of your partner. Make sure you don't say it too loud! Your partner will have to act and move like the animal, bird or insect and the class will have to guess it! You can switch roles after this. For example

Q.1 Gopa's friend Ali whispered 'Frog' into his ear. What do you think Gopa did?

Ans. I think that Gopa would have jumped like a frog.

Q.2 Sukhiya's friend Surya whispered 'Peepal tree' into her ear. What do you think Sukhiya did?

Ans. Sukhiya may have acted like scaring someone or doing the tree pose.

Let us Reflect (Page 81 & 82)

A. Discuss

Q.1 How are we dependent on plants and animals?

Ans. For answer, refer to NCERT Folder, Discuss (Page 77), Q.1

Q.2 How should we care for plants and animals in our environment?

Ans. For answer, refer NCERT Folder, Discuss (Page 77), Q. 4

Q.3 How do plants and animals depend on us?

Ans. For answer, refer NCERT Folder, Discuss (Page 77), Q. 5

B. Write

Q.1 Complete these sentences with the names of plants, birds, animals or insects.

(a) I like looking at ________ because________ ________________________

(b) _______ make me laugh because ________________________

(c) My friend ________likes________ because ________________________

(d) I would like to take care of __________ because ________________

Ans. (a) rose plants; they have pretty red coloured roses with beautiful fragrance.

(b) Dogs ; they look very cute when they play with their friends and take out their tongue.

(c) (Name of your friend); elephants because they are big and move their trunk upwards.

(d) dogs and cows ; they are very innocent.

Q.2 (a) Which is your favourite animal, bird, insect or plant among those you have named above?

Ans. Dogs and elephants are my favourite animals.

(b) Why do you like it?

Ans. Dogs are very friendly. They take care of our house also.

Elephants move their trunks and they throw water from their nose.

(c) Write down the names of all the animals, birds, insects that you have seen or learned about from the smallest to the largest.

Ans. Ants < Flies < Grasshoppers < Butterflies < Squirrels < Rabbits < Deer < Cow < Lion < Elephant

C. Draw

Q.1 Name and draw animals, birds and insects that have

(a) Two legs (b) Four legs

(c) Six legs (d) Eight legs

Ans. Two legs – Ostrich and Penguin

Four legs – Dog, Frogs and lion

Six legs – Ant

Eight legs – Spiders

Do You Know Page 83

This is a story of a small town called Valparai in Tamil Nadu. Throughout the school year, the children and teachers in different schools in Valparai look for and record birds that come to their town.

Just after the rains and in the winter months they plan a special welcome for these birds, Grey Wagtails! These birds commonly known as *Vaalatti kuruvi* in Tamil. During the cold winter months the Grey Wagtails arrive all the way from the mountains to the warmer parts of India and stay there for a few months.

When the first Grey Wagtails arrive in Valparai, the children and teachers celebrate their arrival by putting up welcome posters for the birds and they distribute sweets to everyone!

Q.1 Do you know why these birds are called Wagtails? Find out!

Ans. These birds are called wagtails because they move (wag) their tail in different directions like up and down.

Q.2 Do you want to give a title to the story?

Ans. "Wagtail-A Special Guest" or "Welcoming Wagtails"

WATER–A PRECIOUS GIFT

About the Chapter

This chapter is about water, a precious gift of nature. We learn about rainwater, different sources of water, storage of water and reducing the wastage of water. We get water from many sources like wells, tubewells, borewells, taps, tankers, etc. We can get this water using hand pumps or electric motors. Water can be stored in various vessels and bottles. We cannot live without drinking the water. It helps us in activities like cooking and cleaning. We can take steps to reduce the wastage of water. We should offer clean drinking water to whoever comes to our house, especially in the summer season.

GLOSSARY

Puddles Small holes in the roads which gets filled with rainwater.
Pulley A wheel which is fixed with a rope to pull something.
Borewell A large pit or hole in the ground to insert the water pumps.
Exhibition A large display of art or any precious things for the people.

Write (Page 87)

Q.1 I think it will rain today because ... (write at least 2 clues)

Ans. The clues can be
(a) there are dark clouds in the sky.
(b) there is a thunderstorm.
(c) strong winds are blowing.

Q.2 I think it will not rain today because ... (write at least 2 clues)

Ans. The clues can be
(a) the sky is clear
(b) the Sun is shining bright
(c) there is no wind

Activity 1 (Page 88)

Ask yourself as many questions as you can about the rain.

Q.1 Is it a heavy rain or a light one?

Ans. It is a very heavy rain.

Q.2 Are the raindrops big or small?

Ans. Raindrops are very big in size.

Q.3 Do they come down fast or slow?

Ans. The raindrops come down very fast.

Q.4 Is the rain so heavy that you do not see the water drops, but only lines or sheets of water?

Ans. Yes, the rain is so heavy that I cannot see the raindrops, but only the lines of water falling on the ground.

Q.5 Is the rain falling straight down? Is it slanting or changing its direction? Guess why.

Ans. The rain is falling slanting. This is so because the wind moves the water in a slanting direction.

Q.6 Collect the rainwater in a vessel. Does it look clean or dirty?

Ans. The rainwater in the vessel looks clean.

Draw (Page 88)

Q.1 Draw a picture of the rain that you observed.

Ans. Do it yourself.

Find Out (Page 89)

Q.1 Do you think it will rain again today or tomorrow? Why do you think so?

Ans. Yes, it will rain again today and even tomorrow because there are many dark clouds in the sky.

Q.2 Did it rain only in your area or in other nearby places as well? Make a guess, then ask and find out.

Ans. It rained only in my area. My friend who lives near my place told me that there was no rain in her area.

Q.3 Find some songs about the rain or make up one, in your language or any other. Sing some songs about the rain.

Ans. You can write or sing bollywood songs like *Barso re Megha Megha, Ghanan-Ghanan*, etc.

Q.4 Did the rain make you happy? Did it make everyone happy?

Ans. Yes, the rain made me happy because our school declared a holiday due to heavy rain.

The rain does not make my parents happy because my mother faces problem in drying the clothes and my father gets wet while going to work.

Find Out (Page 90)

Q.1 Is there a stream, river, pond or lake near your village or city?

Ans. Yes, there is a river near my city.

Q.2 Find out its name and some information about it. Visit it and draw its picture. Draw any trees, birds or animals that you see around it.

Ans. The name of the river is Ganga.

Q.3 Find a poem about a river and sing it in the class.

Ans. Do it yourself.

Discuss (Page 91)

Q.1 Where do you get water from?

Ans. We get water from many sources like

- Rain
- Groundwater from the wells, hand pumps, borewells
- Tankers
- Rivers and streams

Find Out (Page 91)

Q.1 Do you get water delivered in a tanker? If yes, find out where the tankers bring water from. Does your water come from a well, river or lake near your village or city?

Ans. Yes, one day a tanker delivered us the water. It brought water from a big tank in our area. Water in our city comes from a well.

Q.2 Do you know anyone who faces difficulty in getting water every day?

Ans. Yes, my aunt who lives in Rajasthan faces difficulty in getting water. There is a fixed time in the morning to get water. They have to store water in containers.

Write (Page 92)

Q.1 List all the activities you can think of for which we need water.

Ans. The activities for which we need water are as follows

- Bathing
- Brushing and cleaning
- Cooking
- Washing clothes and utensils
- Watering the plants

Q.2 How many mugs of water do you need to brush your teeth? How much water do you use to take a shower?

Ans. I need less than a mug of water for brushing my teeth. To take a shower, I use 7-9 mugs of water.

Find Out (Page 93)

Ask your grandparents or any elder:

Q.1 How did they get water? Did they use water in the same way as you do?

Ans. My grandparents got water from hand pumps and wells in their house.

Yes, they also used water in the same way as I do in activities like cleaning , washing and bathing.

Q.2 How did they store water?

Ans. My grandparents store water in large steel and brass buckets called *pawalis*. They also stored the water in big steel tubs.

Q.3 Write a short story about what you found out.

Ans. Imagine a day when a little child goes to a far away well to fetch water with his/her grandfather. The journey to well or water source is very difficult. Describe how you went, what you observed, and how you carried water back home.

Activity 3 (Page 94)

Q.1 Identify different vessels used to keep water in your home.

Ans. There are vessels like bucket, *pateela*, jug, etc. to keep water in my home.

Q.2 Ask the elders in your family what types of vessels they stored water in.

Ans. My elders use buckets, pots, big bowls to store the water in it.

Q.3 Were they different from what we use now?

Ans. Yes, they were different from the vessels we use now.Today we use plastic vessels but my elders mostly used the steel and brass vessels.

Q.4 Did the vessels have different names?

Ans. Yes, all the vessels had different names like surahi, pawali, pateela, etc.

Q.5 On a separate sheet of paper draw a picture of any vessel that you find interesting and write its name in your language.

Ans. Draw any vessel like clay pot or steel vessel, etc.

Q.6 Put up an exhibition of these pictures in your classroom with the help of your teacher.

Ans. Do it yourself with the help of your teachers.

Q.7 Walk around and observe the drawings by your classmates.

Ans. Hint : Walk around and see the drawings. Make a list of different vessels they draw.

Q.8 How many different kinds of vessels have been drawn?

Ans. There are many vessels like lota, buckets, pateela, etc. have been drawn.

Q.9 Did you find any patterns on the vessels?

Ans. Yes , there are many patterns on the vessels like horizontal lines, triangular patterns, floral patterns and many more.

Page 96

Q.1 Don't you think everyone must get clean drinking water anywhere, anytime?

Ans. Yes, everyone should get clean drinking water anywhere , anytime because water is the most precious thing for our life.

Activity 4 (Page 97)

Q.2 Prepare a birdbath — offer water to birds in the hot summer months.

Ans. Do it yourself.

Let Us Reflect (Page 98-99)

A. Write

Q.1 You waited for rain and watched how raindrops fell to the ground. You collected rainwater and observed if it was clean or dirty. You saw what happened to the rainwater that fell in different places. Now write a few lines on your observations of the rain.

Ans. There were different raindrops. Some drops were big and falling fast on the ground while some were very small and falling very slow.

You may collect the rainwater in a glass and then observe the rain water. The rainwater would be clean because it has fallen directly from the clouds.

The rainwater is absorbed by the soil. Then it slowly flows under the soil and joins a stream and a river which finally goes into seas and oceans.

Q.2 You found out the name and some information about a stream, river, well, pond or lake near your place. Write it in a few lines: Is this water used for drinking? If yes, how is this water carried to your home? If it is not used, why not? Was it used in the past?

Ans. There is Ganga river near my place.

Yes, this river water is used in drinking. Water flows from these rivers into the broad pipes and then it is cleaned in the big factories. The clean water is carried out through the small pipes to our houses.

Yes, it was also used in the past by big factories. People also took bath in the river.

B. Draw

Q.1 Draw a picture of your birdbath. Write the names of the birds and insects that come to drink water from your birdbath.

Ans. Do it yourself

C. Discuss

Q.1 Water is very precious. We should be cautious about how we use it. We should not waste even a drop of water. Discuss among yourselves and list the activities in your house or outside, due to which water gets polluted or wasted. How can we avoid wastage of water? Think of three solutions with your group and write them in your notebook.

Ans. The activities that may pollute the water are as follows

Inside the House

- Using more water for bathing.
- Keeping the tap open while brushing teeth.
- Washing the car with water pipe.

Outside the House

- Washing clothes in the rivers.
- Letting animals like buffaloes take bath in the river
- Adding chemicals to the water

Solutions for avoiding wastage of water are given below

- Reuse water, for example use the waste water for flushing the toilets.
- Keeping the tap closed while brushing teeth.
- Using the bucket instead of shower for bathing.

FOOD WE EAT

About the Chapter

This chapter discusses about healthy food and the importance of a balanced diet. A girl named Shirin learns about the importance of diet from a running champion. We learn about different foods like fruits, vegetables, grains, etc. which are a part of a balanced diet. Home cooked food and a balanced diet are important for staying healthy. We eat a variety of foods according to different seasons. For example, in the summer we eat and drink cold things and in winters, we eat and drink warm things like soups. Drinking water is important for our body, especially when we sweat during a physical activity.

GLOSSARY

Balanced Diet A mixture of necessary nutrients like protein, carbohydrates, fats , vitamins and minerals.

Ingredients The materials that are used to make any dish.

NCERT FOLDER

Draw (Page 100)

Q.1 Draw pictures of your favourite homemade food dishes and name them.

Ans. You may draw the pictures of dishes like *rice, gujiya, rajma*, etc. of their own choice.

Activity 1 (Page 101)

Q.1 Share your reasons for why you like the food items you have drawn.

Ans. I like rice because they are very soft and easy to chew.

I like *gujiya* because it is very sweet and filled with many dry fruits. I like *rajma* because it has lots of tomatoes and tastes good.

Q.2 We all like to eat and drink different things. Some of these food items are sweet, some are sour, some are spicy and some are bitter. We eat fruits, we eat vegetables and we eat rice, dal or roti. We drink milk, lassi or juice. Have you wondered why we eat and drink?

Ans. We eat to get essential nutrients. For example, vitamins from fruits and energy from foods like rice and chapati.

We need to drink water because our body needs a lot of water. We sweat a lot and lose water from our body. That is why, we need to drink things like *nimbu paani, aam panna*, buttermilk, sugarcane juice or coconut water.

Find Out (Page 101)

Q.1 Talk to the elders in your family and discuss in the class: Why do we need to eat and drink?

Ans. For answer, refer NCERT Folder, Activity 1 Page 101, Q.2.

Discuss (Page 103)

Q.1 Why do we need to eat healthy food?

Ans. We need to eat healthy food because of the following reasons

- To get essential nutrients like proteins, vitamins and minerals.
- To stay away from the diseases.
- To remain energetic so that we can play and study a lot.

Activity 2 (Page 103)

Q.1 Tick the food items you eat regularly from the pictures given below.

Ans. I eat vegetables, salads, fruits, rice, dal, roti, milk, juice and paneer.

Q.2 Which food above do you think should be part of a balanced diet?

Ans. Vegetable, salad, fruits, rice, dal, roti , milk, lassi, Juice and paneer should be the part of a balanced diet.

Find Out (Page 104)

Q.1 Make a list of fruits and vegetables available and special food items that are prepared in the summer and in the winter.

Summer	Winter

Ans.

Food Items	Summer	Winter
Fruits	Watermelons, Litchis, Cucumber	Apples, Grapes
Vegetables	Bottle Gourd, Lady finger, Ridge Gourd	Fenugreek, Spinach, Carrots,
Special Foods	Coconut Water, Aam Panna	Soup, Til ke Laddoo, Gajar ka Halwa

Page 104

Q.1 Name these drinks in your language.

Tender Coconut Water | Mango Juice | Aam Panna

Orange Juice

Lime Water

Ans. Tender Coconut Water-*Nariyal Pani*; Mango Juice-*Aam Ras*; Lime Water-*Nimbu Paani*; Aam Panna-*Aam Panna*; Orange Juice-*Santre Ka Ras*

Page 105

Q.1 How often do you drink water?

Ans. I drink around 8-10 times water in a day.

Q.2 Where does food come from?

Ans. Food comes from both the plants and animals.

The food we get from the different parts of plants are given below

- We get food like cabbage and coriander from the plant leaves.
- We get food like carrots and radish from plant roots.
- We get fruits mango and apple from the plant.
- We get food like milk, cheese, ghee, eggs and meat from the animals like cow, buffalo, hen and goat.

Find Out (Page 105)

Q.1 Do you know which foods are grown in the fields? Write a few names of such crops.

Ans. Yes, I know that foods like paddy(rice), wheat, bajra, cabbage, ragi, spinach, etc., are grown in the fields.

Q.2 Discuss and write down in what form some of these foods are cooked.

Ans. These foods can be cooked in various forms like

- Rice is used to make *kheer*, *biryani* and it is served with rajma beans, *dal*, *kadhi*, etc.
- Wheat is used to make chapati, puri , *kachori*, etc.
- Bajra is used to make khichri.
- Cabbage is used to make manchurian.
- Ragi is used to make chapati, baked biscuits, etc.

Page 106

Q.1 We eat different parts of plants. Some examples are given below. Put a tick (✓) against the items that you eat.

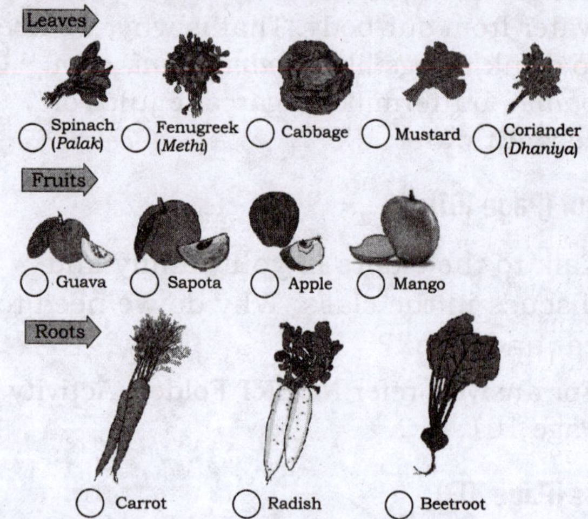

Ans. Put a tick in the circle of the given food items.

Puzzle Time (Page 107)

Q.1 Two of our most commonly used ingredients are neither obtained from plants nor from animals. Name at least one of these ingredients.

Ans. The two most commonly used ingredients are water and salt.Water is obtained from ground after the rain falls on it.Salt is obtained from seawater.

Page 107

Q.2 Would you share your food with your friend if your friend does not bring lunch?

Ans. Yes, I always share my lunch with my friend if his/her mother gets ill. My friend also shares his/her lunch with me whenever I do not bring the lunch.

Let us Reflect Page 108

A. Discuss

Q.1 Why do we need different kinds of food?

Ans. We need different kinds of food because every food has different nutritional value like

- Pulses have protein which helps in our body building.
- Milk, rice and wheat give us carbohydrates that makes us energetic.
- Fruits and vegetables have vitamins which protects us from diseases.

Q.2 Why do we eat seasonal foods?

Ans. We eat seasonal foods for many reasons like;

- These foods protect us from diseases due to any changes in the seasons.
- These foods are freshly grown and that is why these food contains essential nutrients.
- These foods give us lots of energy.

Q.3 How can you tell if a food is healthy or unhealthy?

Ans. Healthy food has nutrients like vitamins and minerals. We feel energetic after eating them. Unhealthy food has too much sugar, oil, fat and salt. It can make us sick.

Q.4 Why is it important to avoid wasting food? Can you think of some ways to reduce food waste at home?

Ans. It is important to avoid wasting food to protect the environment.Wasting food means wasting money and useful resources of nature. Certain germs and mosquitoes start growing on waste foods, which is unhealthy.

There are many ways to reduce food waste at home, like

- We can ask our elders to cook the less amount of food.
- Taking as much food as we can eat.
- Sharing the food with street dogs , cows in our area.
- Storing the food in air tight containers to keep it fresh .

B. Write

Q.1 List the fruits and vegetables eaten in your family.

Ans. In our family we eat different fruits and vegetables in different seasons which are mentioned in the table below.

Seasons	Fruits	Vegetables
Winter	Apples, oranges, grapes, kiwi, guava	Peas, fenugreek (*methi*) , mustard *sarso*), *bathua* leaves, water chestnuts (*singhara*)
Summers	Melons, mango, litchi, jamun	Bottle gourd, bitter gourd , parwal, cucumber

Q.2 Write the recipe of your favourite dish.

Ans. You may ask your elder for your favourite dish recipe like rajma rice, pav bhaji, dosa or fried idlis.

Q.3 Write a name of a food item that includes both plant and animal based ingredients. For example, *lassi* includes yogurt/curd which is prepared from milk (animal based ingredient) and sugar which is prepared from sugar (a plant based ingredient).

Ans. Sarso ka Saag contains both plant and animal based ingredients because mustard leaves are obtained from plants. Lots of Ghee in it is obtained from cow milk which is an animal product.

C. Draw

Q.1 Draw three plates or *thalis* with various food items in your notebook.

Ans. Do it yourself

Q.2 In these plates draw and label food items that you eat in the morning, afternoon and at night.

Ans. Do it yourself

D. Eating Together

Q.1 Bring any fruit to the class. Prepare a fruit chaat or salad with the help of your teacher. Share it with your friends.

Ans. Do it yourself

E. Think

Q.1 Imagine, you suddenly have a guest visiting your home. What kind of food would you serve them and why?

Ans. If the guests suddenly visit our house, we can serve them healthy foods like fruit salad and lime water for starters and biryani with vegetable salad and buttermilk in the main course meal.

CHAPTER 9 STAYING HEALTHY AND HAPPY

About the Chapter

This chapter is about good habits that we should follow to keep ourselves healthy. To keep ourselves healthy, we can follow some simple habits which keep us clean and free from diseases. A girl named Moyna uses a toothbrush to brush her teeth but her grandfather uses datun of neem or babool twigs. Animals also like to keep themselves clean. For example, monkeys groom each other and birds use their beaks to clean. We can keep our body fit by exercising. It makes our heart work better. Our body and mind can also be kept fit by playing indoor games like chess. We should stay safe while playing outside.

GLOSSARY

Twig Small and thin branches of shrub or trees.
Particles Very small pieces of dust, food or any leaf.
Groom To clean the fur or skin of an animal.
Surroundings Places or things around us.

NCERT FOLDER

Clean and Bright (Page 110)

Ask yourself these questions.

Q.1 Did I brush my teeth today?

Ans. Yes, I brushed my teeth today.

Q.2 Did I take a shower?

Ans. Yes, I took a shower.

Q.3 Did I comb my hair?

Ans. Yes, I combed my hairs.

Q.4 Did I wash my hands with soap?

Ans. Yes, I washed my hands with soap.

Q.5 Are my nails trimmed and clean?

Ans. Yes, my nails are clean and trimmed.

Find Out (Page 111)

Q.1 Ask your grandparents or any elderly person in your neighbourhood - What did they use to wash their hair, body and clothes and clean their teeth when they were young? Can these things be found now?

Ans. My grandparents use the following things when they were young

Body parts	Things used to clean by my grandparents
Hairs	Amla, shikakai, dahi, methi
Body	Besan, multani mitti, rosewater
Clothes	Wooden bat, herbs for soap
Teeth	Neem and babool twigs, mustard oil with salt

Yes, we can find all these things in the market even today.

Activity 2 (Page 114)

Hop, skip, jump!

Try the following moves:

The following moves:

Walk like a duck.

Jump like a frog.

Run like a cat.

Q.1 Which moves did you enjoy the most?

Ans. I enjoyed jumping like a frog at the most.

Q.2 Which other games do you play with a skipping rope?

Ans. We play games like partner skipping, skipping relay race and cross jump with a skipping rope.

Name the Game! (Page 115)

Q.1 What types of games do you like to play outside your home?

Ans. I like to play the games like *kho-kho, kabaddi, cricket and pakdam-pakdai* outside my home.

Q.2 Can you identify the games shown here? Have you played them before?

Ans. Yes, I can identify these games shown here. Yes, I have played all of them before.

Find Out (Page 115)

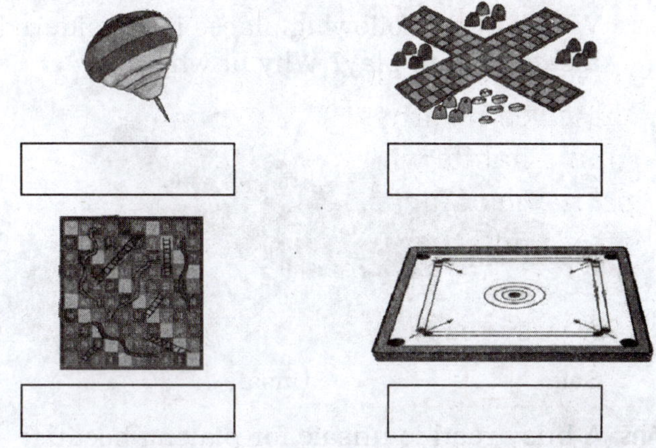

Ans. Spinning top (*lattoo*), Snakes and ladders, Ludo, Carrom

I Spy! (Page 116)

Can you find the names of all the games hidden here? Are any of these your favourites? One has been done for you.

B	I	U	A	F	Y	L	S	T	B	S	L
J	A	T	U	E	R	G	X	E	A	C	L
K	A	D	K	E	G	N	M	N	S	I	A
V	H	C	M	Z	X	O	I	N	K	T	B
S	O	O	Y	I	C	I	C	I	E	S	Y
H	G	J	K	L	N	R	D	S	T	A	E
W	R	N	Q	H	I	T	V	I	B	N	L
C	V	G	N	C	O	F	O	Z	A	M	L
Y	W	Z	K	X	V	P	A	N	L	Y	O
H	V	E	D	S	I	H	W	Q	L	G	V
D	T	R	T	L	L	A	B	T	O	O	F
L	X	K	A	B	A	D	D	I	P	H	P

Ans. Yes, I can find the hidden names of the games. These are Badminton, Kho Kho, Hockey, Cricket, Tennis, Basketball, Gymnastics, Volleyball, Football.

My favourite game is volleyball and badminton.

On Page 117

Playing Safely

Q.1 It is important to be safe while having fun. Which of the following places is considered a safe area to play? Why or why not?

A busy road

Safe ☐ Unsafe ☐

Ans. A busy road is unsafe for playing because there are so many moving vehicles that may cause accident while we play.

A park

Safe ☐ Unsafe ☐

Ans. A park is safe for playing because it is specially made for the children so that they can play with their friends.

A school ground

Safe ☐ Unsafe ☐

Ans. A school ground is safe for playing because in schools playground are made for the children to play different games like kho-kho, basketball, etc. and enjoy after studying.

A roof without railings

Safe ☐ Unsafe ☐

Ans. A roof without railing is completely unsafe because our leg may slip, and we may fall down, which may cause serious injuries.

A construction site

Safe ☐ Unsafe ☐

Ans. A construction site is unsafe because there are so many big machines. There are also bricks, iron rods which may hurt us while jumping or running.

Let us Reflect (Page 119 & 120)

A. Write Make Your Weekly Health Table.

Q.1 What makes you feel sleepy, hungry or tired? Feelings are the body's way of telling us that something is amiss. We all have different needs. We should each know what is good for our body and mind. For this, track your activities for a week and observe how you feel.

Day	Did I brush my teeth twice?	Did I use the toilet in the morning?	Did I take shower?	How much time did I sleep?	What did I have for breakfast?	How long did I watch TV or play on the phone?	How long did I play outdoors?	How did it make me feel? (Good, okay, not so good, bad)
Mon								
Tue								
Wed								
Thu								
Fri								
Sat								
Sun								

Ans. Do it yourself

B. Draw

Draw a big circle in your notbook and divide it into 24 slices. Imagine that each slice is one hour of the day. Now colour these slices differently based on the number of hours you spend doing different activities in one entire day of 24 hours.

For example, Moyna spends 8 hours sleeping, 2 hours eating, 6 hours in school or studying at home, 2 hours playing outside, 2 hours helping her parents at home, 1 hours watching TV or playing on the phone, 1 hour in the toilet and 2 hours on other activities. This is what Moyna's circle looked like.

Ans.

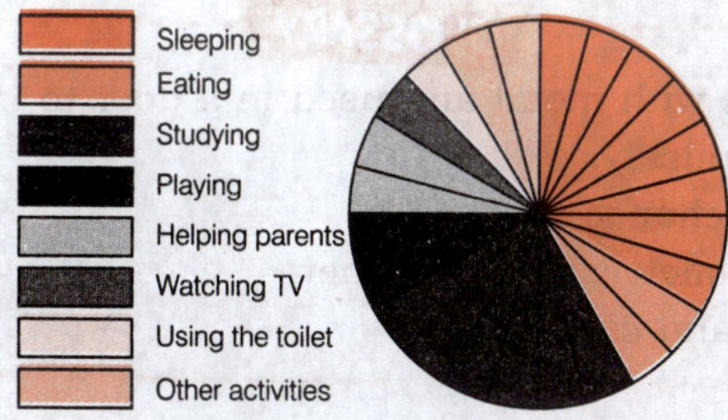

Ans. Do it yourself

C. Discuss

Q.1 Think of one activity you would like to do at least twice a week to improve your stamina. It could be running, jumping, climbing stairs or anything else. Discuss it with your friends and try doing such activities together.

Ans. I do jumping and running with my friends every evening in the playground near my house.

THIS WORLD OF THINGS

About the Chapter

This chapter discusses about different objects and the various materials used to make them. It also makes us aware about the properties of different objects. Some things are made of wood, some are made of metal. Different objects have different features. We can see clearly through some objects but we cannot see clearly through others. Some objects are soft, flexible and can bend easily while other objects are hard and rigid. There are some objects which do not change shape but other objects change their shape and flow easily. Natural things are those which exist in nature. Things made by people are called man-made things.

GLOSSARY

Hinges A movable joint made with metal and used in a door to make the door open or close.
Flexibility Ability to change quickly.
Rigid Something that do not change its shape.
Pour To put any liquid from one vessel to another.
Alive Things which have life and can breathe.

Page 123

Q.1 Can you name the things that Khushi has drawn? Write in the boxes given.

Ans. Yes, I can name the things that Khushi has drawn.I have written the names in the boxes.

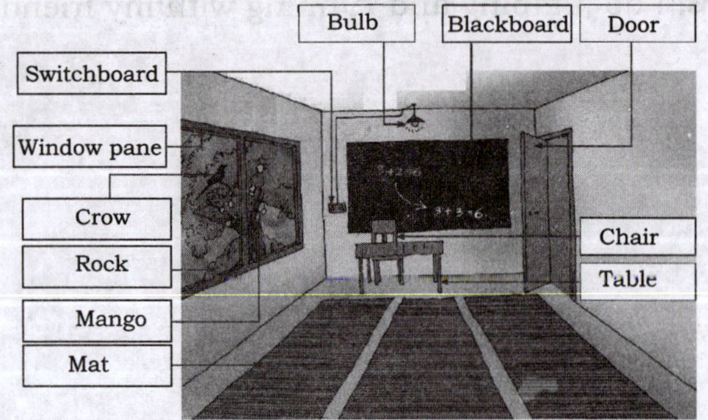

Q.2 Do you see the window glass? Why or why not?

Ans. No, I cannot see the window glass, but I can see the outside of it. I cannot see the window glass because it is a transparent object.

Activity 1 (Page 124)

Understand your Classroom

Q.1 Draw a picture of your classroom in your notebook. Label the things that you have drawn.

Ans. Do it yourself

Activity 2 (Page 125)

Spot the Metals

Q.1 Find as many things or parts of things, that are made of metals. Which metals do you recognise around you? If you do not know the name of the metal, ask your friends or an elder. Make a list of these metals in your notebook.

Ans. I found the following things made of metals.

Things	Metals
Door handle	Iron
Spoon	Steel/Copper
Ear rings	Gold
Hawan Kund	Copper

Find Out (Page 125)

Q.1 What are other things in the classroom, such as mats, bulbs and electric switches, made of ?

Ans. In the classrooms, things like mats are made up of fabric like cotton or jute.

Bulbs are made up of glass and tungsten.

Electric switches are made up of plastic and copper.

Page 125

Q.1 Does your window have a glass pane?

Ans. Yes, my window has a glass pane.

Q.2 Can you see through it?

Ans. Yes, I can see through it.

Q.3 What do you see?

Ans. I can see many things like the Sun, the rain, plants and children playing outside my window.

Activity 3 (Page 126)

Seeing through things

Q.1 Collect a few small objects of different materials from your surroundings like bottles, papers, cloth and utensils, etc. Look at a light bulb or a candle flame through them. You can see through some objects very clearly, you can partially see through some others, while you cannot see through some objects at all. Order these objects from those you can see through very clearly, to those you cannot see through at all.

See through clearly	See through partially	Cannot see through at all

Ans. The observations are given below

See through clearly	See through partially	Cannot see through at all
Glass	Bottles	Paper
Magnifying Glass	Butter paper	Cloth
Spectacles	Balloon	Utensils
Transparent plastic sheet	Ice cube	Wooden Door
Empty glass jar	Oil paper	Book

Activity 4 (Page 127)

Let us colour the world!

Collect two or three see through bags, bottles or thin cloth of different colours. Look at a sheet of white paper through them.

Q.1 Does the colour of the paper appear to change?

Ans. Yes, the colour of the paper appears to change.

Q.2 Does white paper appear different when you look at it through thin blue plastic or glass? Or, thin yellow plastic or glass?

Ans. Yes, the white paper appears blue when we look it through a blue plastic or glass.

Similarly, it will appear yellow if we look at it through the yellow plastic or glass.

Q.3 Do the colours of different objects appear to change? How did a blue object look through thin yellow plastic?

Ans. Yes, the colours of different objects appear to change when they are looked through another colour object.

The blue object will appear black if we look it through yellow plastic.

Q.4 Have you earlier experienced looking through coloured transparent objects? Try to recall such experiences.

Ans. Yes, I have experienced looking through coloured transparent objects earlier also. When we play Holi, we look each other through water filled balloons.

Write (Page 128)

Chain game

- In the table below, Khushi has grouped objects according to the materials that they are made of. Her list of objects is in the first column of the table. The names of the materials are in the second column.
- The third column of the table is for you to complete. Here write the names of some objects you have seen that are made from that material. Some objects around you may be made from materials not in this list, e.g., clay and rubber are missing in Khushi's list. Use one of these to add an additional row in the table.

Khushi's list	Name of the material	Objects made of this material which are in your classroom or home
Table, chair, door	Wood	For example, Pencil
Door, hinges, nails	Metal	
Window panes, light bulb	Glass	
Electric switches	Plastic	

Ans. The complete list for Khushi's classroom materials is given below in the table.

Khushi's list	Name of the material	Objects made of this material which are in your classroom or home
Table, chair, door	Wood	Pencil
Door, hinges, nails	Metal	Knife
Window panes, light bulb	Glass	Magnifying glass, spectacles
Electric switches	Plastic	Geometry box, water bottle
Eraser	Rubber	Water bottle covers

Page 128

Q.1 Where do all these materials come from? Can you locate their source?

For example, Wood - Tree

Metals ______________

Cloth ______________

Ans. The source of the given materials is given below

Metals - Ores , Rocks

Cloth- Plant , Animal and Chemical

Find Out (Page 129)

Talk to your Grandparents

Q.1 In their childhood, were these things made of the same materials?

Ans. Yes, in my grandparents's childhood, many things were made up of the same materials like chairs were made up of wood.

But there are some other things like spoons and bowls were made up of brass. Today are made up of steel and plastic.

Q.2 Are there new materials now that they might not have seen before?

Ans. Yes, there are some new materials like ceramic, melamine, glass, etc.

Q.3 Are there any materials that they saw in their childhood that are not in use now? Why?

Ans. No, there is no such material.

Find Out (Page 129)

Q.1 What material is your spoon made of?

Ans. My spoon is made up of steel.

Q.2 Is it made of metal, wood, or some other material? Can you guess?

Ans. Yes, I can guess, it is a mixture of metals.

Q.3 Which of these words or phrases describe the spoon ?

Smooth	Rough	Dull	Shiny
	Feels cold to touch		

Ans. The word or phrase that describe the spoon are smooth, shiny and feels cold to touch.

Write Odd Pairs

Q.1 List five objects and pair them with a material that is not suitable for it! Explain why these materials will not work to make these objects. One example is done for you.

Objects	Materials	Reasons
Umbrella	Paper	Paper will tear if it gets wet in the rain.

Ans.

Objects	Materials	Reasons
Umbrella	Paper	Paper will tear if it gets wet in the rain.
Bedsheets	Aluminium	It will tear if we sit on it.
Balloon	Glass	Air cannot be blown inside it.
Table	Fabric	It will fall if we keep any object on it.
Bottle Opener	Rubber	Rubber opener will not be able to open a bottle.

Activity 6 (Page 130)

Let's group them another way!

Here are the names of some objects: ink, a stone, smoke, ice, steam, a spoon, honey, a bottle, a bag, water.

If it is a solid, write its name on the tray; if it is a liquid, write its name in the bottle; if it is a gas, write its name in the balloon.

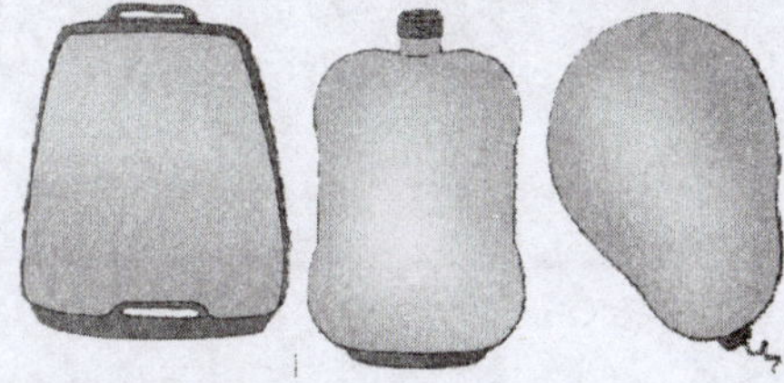

Add some of your own objects in the tray, bottle and balloon.

Some objects could be confusing, such as sand or a sponge or clay. Identify more such objects and write names of at least three of them.

Ans. Objects in the tray are - stone, ice, bottle, bag, chair, blackboard, flower pot.

Objects in the bottle are- ink, honey, water, juice, oil, milkshake.

Objects in the balloon are- smoke, steam, air, fog, oxygen.

Page 133

Things that are made by people are called 'artificial' like clothes, shoes, tables, etc.

List out five things in each group.

Natural: ______________________

Artificial: ______________________

Ans. Natural- Flowers, carrots, river, mountains, and seeds.

Artificial- Chocolate, buildings, mobile phones, chapati, and school bag.

Find Out (Page 133)

Q.1 Have you seen trees around you that bear flowers and fruits at special times of the year? If you have ever eaten a ripe mango or seen mangoes in the market or watched a mango tree through the year, try to guess- at what time of the year did Khushi draw her picture? Could it be around January or around June?

Ans. Khushi would have drawn this picture around June because mangoes grow in the summer season from April to July.

Let us Reflect (Page 134)

A. Write

Q.1 Things around us are made of different types of materials. Write down the names of three materials we commonly see around us.

Ans. The three most common materials around us are wood, glass, and plastic.

B. Discuss

Q.1 Suppose you find a shining spoon. You don't know if it is made of metal or whether it is made of some other material and then painted with shiny paint. How would you find out?

Ans. We can find the material used in spoon in the following manner

- Rigid and hard- Metals are very hard because they cannot change its shape.
- Shine -Metals have a shiny surface.
- Sound -Whenever we hit the metal to any surface, it creates a sound.
- Spoon has all the three features given above, thus, we can say that spoon is made up of metal.

C. Draw

Q.1 Draw three natural and three artificial things.

Ans. Do it yourself

Q.2 Match the pairs

A.	Transparent	1.	A lamp shade made of paper
B.	Translucent	2.	A plate
C.	Opaque	3.	A glass used in spectacles

Ans. A-3, B-1, C-2

MAKING THINGS

About the Chapter

In this chapter, we learn about the art of making different things from clay. We learn about pottery, brick making, and making houses. Mini is a little girl whose grandfather is a potter. A potter makes clay pots on the potter wheel using wet clay. The pots are baked in a special oven called a kiln. Some patterns are drawn on pots to make them beautiful. We can also see patterns on plants and animals. Bricks are also made of mud. They are prepared in moulds to give them shape and then baked in a kiln. Bricks are used in construction of houses. Houses are also built with other materials like mud, grass, wood, cow dung, cement, etc. It is important to follow safety rules while making the buildings.

GLOSSARY

Consistency To maintain the continuity in any work every time.

Kiln A kiln is a potter's oven which is used to bake the clay items.

Mould A hollow container used to give shapes to the hot liquid materials when it cools and hardens.

Sturdy Something which is built strongly and will not break or slide easily.

You must have seen or used a pot for storing water. You have also seen a *gullak* (piggy bank), birdbath, cup (*kulhad*) and so many such things at home and around you. Have you ever wondered?

Q.1 What are these things made of?

Ans. Things like *kulhad*, *gullak* are made of clay.

Q.2 Who has made them and how?

Ans. Potters (*Kumhars*) had made them using the potter's wheel.

Discuss (Page 137)

Q.1 What are pots used for?

Ans. Pots are used for storing water, grains and decorative flowers, etc.

Q.2 What other kinds of things do potters make?

Ans. The other kinds of things that potters make are earthen lamps, piggy banks, clay toys, etc.

Q.3 Why is the pot baked in a kiln?

Ans. The pot is baked in a kiln because the kiln has fire inside it. This fire bakes the pot and make it strong to use.

Activity 1 (Page 138)

Q.1 In what ways do you help your parents and grandparents?

Ans. I help my parents in cooking, washing clothes and cleaning the room.

I help my grandparents in gardening, massaging their legs and giving them medicines on time.

Activity 3 (Page 139)

Q.1 Arrange the images in the correct order by numbering them from 1 to 5.

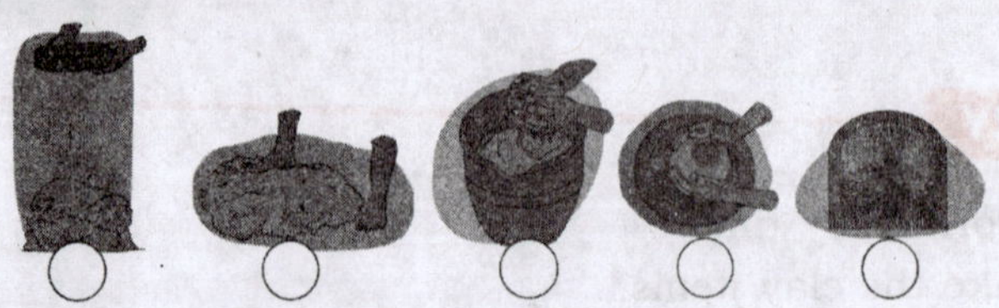

Ans. 1, 3, 2, 4, 5

Activity 4 Page 140 & 141

Q.1 The following are some patterns with repeating shapes and lines.

Look around for patterns on plants.

Draw any pattern of a leaf in the given box. Give an example of your own.

Look around for patterns on animals.

Draw an animal which has patterns in the given box.

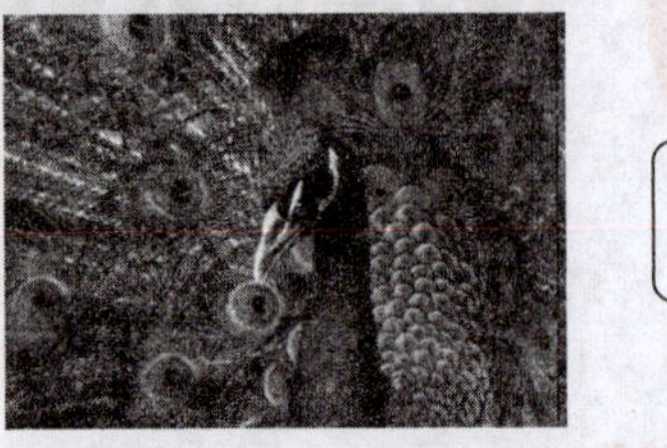

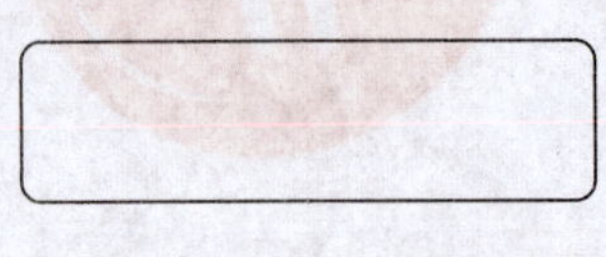

Look around for patterns on things.

Draw a pattern in the box.

Decorate the given objects with patterns.

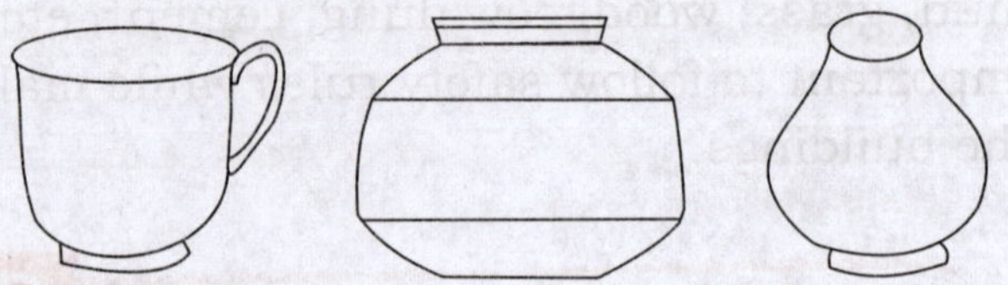

Ans. Do it yourself

Q.2 These are some beautiful forms of pottery from different parts of India. Tick the ones that have patterns on them.

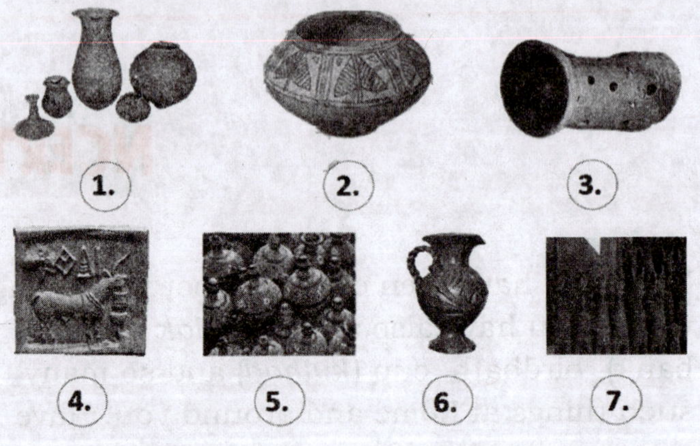

Ans. 1, 2, 3, 5, 6

Page 142

Q.1 Where have you seen bricks?

Ans. I have seen bricks in the under construction buildings of my school, neighbourhood and in brick kilns while travelling.

Q.2 Have you ever seen how bricks are made?

Ans. Yes, I have seen that bricks are made with clay. This clay is put into a mould which is placed inside the kiln. Finally it gets baked and dried.

Discuss (Page 144)

Q.1 Are all houses made of bricks?

Ans. No, all houses are not made of bricks.

Q.2 What do you think are other materials used to build houses?

Ans. Some houses are built with mud, straw and cow dung.

Write (Page 144)

Q.1 Why do you think mud houses are better for the environment?

Ans. Mud houses are better for the environment because of the following reasons

(a) They are made of the natural materials like mud, straw and cow dung. These materials are not harmful for the environment.

(b) These houses give natural cooling effect in summers.

Q.2 Look around at the houses in your neighbourhood. What are the houses made of?

Ans. The houses in my neighbourhood are made of the bricks, cement and iron.

Activity 5 (Page 145)

Look at the pictures below. Guess the name of each types of house. Fill it in the given table below.

Ans.

Picture of houses	What is this type of a houses called?	What are these houses made of?
	Tent	Clothes
	Sky Scraper/ Flats	Bricks, glasses, iron, wood
	Cottage	Stones
	Houseboat	Wood

Activity 6 (Page 146)

Make a Wall

Make some bricks using a matchbox mould, small paper boxes, clay or *atta* (*dough*). Stack them in these two arrangements shown in the drawing.

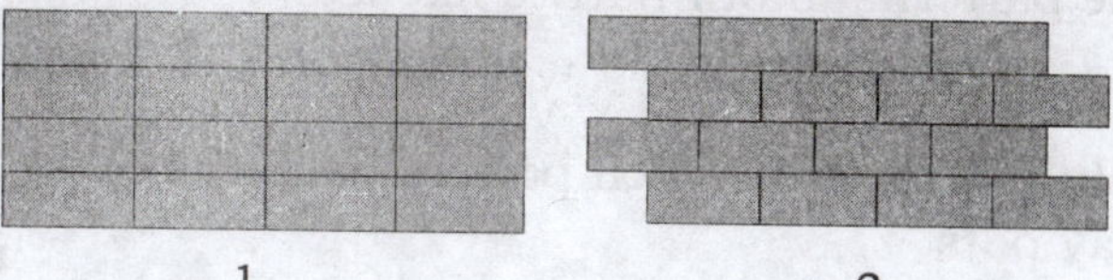

1. 2.

Q.1 Which one is sturdier ?

Ans. The second image (below) will be sturdier.

Q.2 Which one falls more easily when pushed?

Ans. The first image (above) will fall easily when pushed.

Discuss (Page 146)

Q.1 Are there any safety rules at home?

Ans. Yes, there many safety rules at home like

- Do not play with fire.
- Do not play with the sharp objects like knife.
- Never run on wet floor.
- Always avoid swinging on the railings.

Q.2 Do you have any safety rules at school?

Ans. There are following safety rules at the school

- Not run fast at the stairs.
- Always walk in the queue.
- Do not jump or climb upon the walls, or desks in the classroom.

Let us Reflect (Page 147)

A. Write

Q.1 What is the process of pot making?

Ans. The process of making pot is as follows

- Step 1 Taking the clay.
- Step 2 Adding water to make it wet.
- Step 3 Kneading a dough.
- Step 4 Shaping of clay on a stone wheel.
- Step 5 Drying those pots in the kiln.

Q.2 How do artists get ideas for their arts?

Ans. Artists get the ideas for their arts through the patterns in our nature like leaf.

Q.3 What is a kiln?

Ans. Kiln is a oven in which potters bake the clay pots.

Q.4 What are houses made of?

Ans. Houses are made of different materials like cement, bricks and iron.Some houses are also built of mud and straw.

Q.5 You may also try to find videos on YouTube that show the process of things being made. Write down the steps in as much detail as possible.

Ans. Do it yourself.

B. Draw and colour any three different kinds of houses.

Ans. Do it yourself

C. Discuss

Q.1 Why do we have different kinds of houses?

Ans. We have different kinds of houses according to the climate needs of the place. For example,

- In summers people make mud houses to give cooling effect inside.
- In hilly areas people slanting roof so that snow may slide off easily.

Q.2 Why do people wear helmets at construction sites?

Ans. People wear helmets at construction sites because there are many iron objects like rods and pillars. Helmets protect their heads in case any hard object falls.

Q3. What would happen if there were no patterns in nature?

Ans. If there were no patterns in nature, will not be able to differentiate the objects. For example, tigers and leopards would look same without patterns.

D. Interview

Q.1 Interview someone who makes crafts or toys in your locality. Share the information in the class.

Ans. Do it yourself with the help of your parents.

Q.2 Find out how some commonly used objects like pencils, erasers, pens and notebooks are made.Ask your elders.

Ans. Prepare a list of questions to ask your elders.

Do You Know? (Page 148)

Q.1 Have you seen any statues in your town or city?

Ans. Yes, I have seen many statues in my town.

Q.2 Do you know if these statues are also made of the same clay that is used to make pots and bricks?

Ans. Sometimes, these statues are made of the same clay that is used to make pots but majorly, sculpting clay is used to make statues. It is easy to mould.

TAKING CHARGE OF WASTE

About the Chapter

In this chapter, we learn about different types of waste, the ways to manage waste and how to keep our surroundings clean. We produce different types of waste through our daily activities like peels of fruits and vegetables, pencil shavings, bottles, paper, etc. It is important to manage the waste correctly to solve issues like collection of garbage piles.

We can use three methods to manage waste : **reduce**, **reuse** and **recycle**. We can also manage waste by separating the waste and throwing the dry waste in green dustbin and wet waste in blue dustbin. National Cleanliness Day is celebrated on 30th January every year. Many villages like Silluk in Arunachal Pradesh, Chota Narena and cities like Mysuru are waste-free.

Pencil Shavings Waste created after sharpening the pencil.

Pile A huge collection of something.

Cleanliness Drive A program organised for cleaning the surroundings like street, park or any garden.

Eco-Friendly Any object or activity that is not harmful to the environment.

Personalised Any object that has been designed by a person with love.

Zero-Waste Reducing our waste as much as possible.

Pledge A promise which we take for our whole life.

Rot It means somethings that has gone bad.

Discuss (Page 150)

Q.1 What are the children and the teacher doing in the picture?

Ans. The children and the teacher are cleaning the garden.

Q.2 Why are they cleaning the park?

Ans. They are cleaning the park as they are celebrating National Cleanliness Day.

Q.3 Have you ever seen piles of waste lying around your home or school?

Ans. Yes, I have seen the piles of waste lying around my house and school.

Q.4 Have you ever thought about how this waste is created?

Ans. This waste is created by the people. The waste comes from our houses. For example, bottles, vegetable peels and wrappers.

Activity 1 (Page 150)

Q.1 Recall different activities that you and your elders do during the day. How do these activities create waste? Finally, what do we do with the waste?

Ans. The activities that create waste are described in the table below.

Activities	How Waste is created?	What do we do with the waste?
Eating biscuits	Wrappers of biscuit packet	Throw in the dustbin
Peeling fruits and vegetables	Peels of fruits and vegetables	Use as a manure in plants
Drinking soft drinks	Plastic bottles and Cans	Reuse bottles as water bottle and flower pot
Sharpening of pencils	Pencil shavings	Throw in the dustbin

Q.2 Share your findings with your classmates.

Ans. Do it yourself.

Page 151

Q.3 How do you feel about it?

Ans. It feels very dirty to see these piles of waste.

Q.4 Do you think we can do something about it?

Ans. We can do the following things about it

(a) We can talk to our neighbours to clean it once a week.

(b) We can inform the Municipal Corporation

(c) We can start a reuse and recycle program.

Discuss (Page 152)

Q.1 How clean are the surroundings of your school?

Ans. The surroundings of our school are very clean. But, sometimes there is a pile of garbage in our school ground.

Q.2 Do you find waste lying in or outside your classrooms or on the school grounds?

Ans. No, there is no waste lying outside in our classrooms because they get cleaned every day.

Yes, there are waste leaves in the ground.

Draw (Page 153)

Q.1 Draw or paste a picture of a locality. Identify the places where there is garbage or wastewater or smoke by circling them in red. Try to find out how the waste gets there.

Ans. Do it yourself.

Activity 3 (Page 153)

Q.2 How can you help in reducing waste?

Ans. We can help In reducing waste in many ways such as

- Using cloth bags instead of plastic to carry fruits and vegetables.
- Re using plastic containers.
- Using the peels to make compost for plants.
- Donating old things like clothes, books, papers to the needy people.

Activity 4 (Page 155)

Q.1 How can you reuse things to reduce waste?

Ans. We can reuse things to reduce waste in the following ways

- Using the waste items like matchbox, bottles, egg tray to make crafts like showpieces.
- Making carpets, cushion covers with the old clothes.

Activity 5 (Page 157)

Q.1 Create an item using waste material that you can give as a gift to someone.

Ans. Do it yourself

Find Out (Page 157)

Q.1 Ask your elders, if there is any village, town or city that they know about, which is known for its cleanliness. You can share the information you learn from your elders in your class.

Ans. Mawlynnlong village in Meghalaya is known as the cleanest village in India.

Q.2 Find out from your parents or teachers about the *Swachh Bharat Mission.*

Ans. *Swachh Bharat Mission* was launched by our Prime Minister Narendra Modi on 2nd October, 2014. It was launched to make toilets. It was inspired by the Mahatma Gandhi's idea of cleanliness.

Activity 6 (Page 159)

Separate Your Waste

Q.1 Two dustbins are drawn below. Write the names of the waste material which will go into each of them.

Plastic bottles, leaves, onion peels,light bulbs, rotten fruit, paper, eggshells, used plastic milk packets, cloth

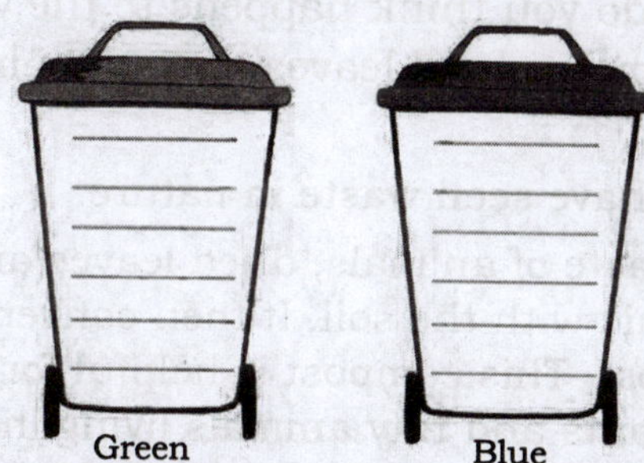

Ans. Green Dustbin Leaves, onion peels, rotten fruit, eggshells

Blue Dustbin Plastic bottles, light bulbs, paper, used plastic milk packets, cloth

Write (Page 160)

Q.1 List the things that you can do to keep your home and classroom clean?

Ans. Things I can do to clean my home are

- Keeping my room tidy.
- Keeping my books properly.
- Keeping my clothes at the proper place.
- After eating any toffee, throwing the wrappers in the dustbin.

Things I can do to clean my classroom are

- Throwing the foil paper in the dustbin during my lunch break.
- Throwing the pencil shavings into the dustbin.

Q.2 Make a list of tools you have seen being used in your school or neighbourhood for cleaning.

Ans. Things that we use for cleaning in schools or neighbourhood are broom, mop, wiper, dustbin, water pipes, etc.

Q.3 Have you ever observed the tools that are used in your home for cleaning? Make a list of these tools.

Ans. The tools used for cleaning are broom, water mugs, buckets,brush, old clothes, foam pads, bathroom cleaners, etc.

Let us Reflect (Page 161 & 162)

A. Discuss

Q.1 How is waste created?

Ans. Waste is created by throwing many things such as old clothes, pencil shavings, tea leaves, old batteries, plastic bottles, etc.

Q.2 How can we manage waste?

Ans. We can manage waste by following ways

- By reducing our waste like using cloth bag.
- By reusing our old clothes to make bags or quilts.
- By separating the dry and wet waste into the two dustbins.

B. Write

Q.1 To avoid use of plastic bags and bottles, look at your home and school closely. List all the items of plastic material and write how these could be replaced by other safe materials.

Ans. The plastic materials at our home and their safer alternatives are given below

Plastic Materials	Safe Materials
Plastic Bottles	Steel bottle or pots
Disposable spoons plates	Paper plates
Plastic casserole	Steel

Q2. Name three things in your school and home that you would put in the green dustbin and three things that you would put in the blue dustbin.

Ans. The things that we put in the green dustbin are egg shells, vegetable waste and dried leaves.

The things that we put in the blue dustbin are metal, glass and paper waste.

C. Draw in your notebook

Q.1 Make a poster to show a village or town that is managing its waste well. Give your poster a suitable title.

Ans. You can cover the following points in your conversation. Clean Town

- People keep me clean.
- There is no garbagee on the roadsides
- Dustbins are kept at every 2 km.
- All roads are clean.
- No drain in overflowing
- Dirty Town
- People throw garbage here and there
- Trash is lying on my roadsides
- Drains are overflowing with dirty water
- There are very few dustbins

D. Enact in pairs

Q.1 You can be a clean town and your partner a dirty town. Engage in a short conversation talking about how you feel about being the way you are.

Ans. Do it yourself

E. Think, Reflect and Share

Q.1 Imagine you are having a birthday party at your home. What are some of the ways in which you can try to have a zero-waste birthday party? For this, first think about what kind of waste may be created in the birthday party and how you can avoid or reduce it.

Ans. We can organise a zero waste birthday party in many ways

- For decoration, use natural things like flowers rather than any plastic material.
- Serve home made drinks instead of any packaged drinks which come in plastic bottles.
- Serve the food and drinks in steel utensils.

Q.2 Have you seen waste in nature? What do you think happens to the waste of animals, dried leaves and so on in a forest?

Ans. Yes, I have seen waste in nature.

The waste of animals, dried leaves and other gets mix with the soil. It then converts into compost. This compost is helpful for both the plants and tiny animals living in the soil.